ASP.NET Solutions—
23 Case Studies

ASP.NET Solutions— 23 Case Studies

Best Practices for Developers

Rick Leinecker

✦▾Addison-Wesley

Boston • San Francisco • New York • Toronto • Montreal
London • Munich • Paris • Madrid
Capetown • Sydney • Tokyo • Singapore • Mexico City

Many of the designations used by manufacturers and sellers to distinguish their products are claimed as trademarks. Where those designations appear in this book, and Addison-Wesley was aware of a trademark claim, the designations have been printed with initial capital letters or in all capitals.

The author and publisher have taken care in the preparation of this book, but make no expressed or implied warranty of any kind and assume no responsibility for errors or omissions. No liability is assumed for incidental or consequential damages in connection with or arising out of the use of the information or programs contained herein.

The publisher offers discounts on this book when ordered in quantity for bulk purchases and special sales. For more information, please contact:

U.S. Corporate and Government Sales
(800) 382-3419
corpsales@pearsontechgroup.com

For sales outside of the U.S., please contact:

International Sales
(317) 581-3793
international@pearsontechgroup.com

Visit Addison-Wesley on the Web: www.awprofessional.com

Library of Congress Cataloging-in-Publication Data
Leinecker, Richard C.
   ASP.Net solutions : 23 case studies : best practices for developers /
Rick Leinecker.
       p. cm.
Includes bibliographical references and index.
   ISBN 0-321-15965-9 (Paperback : alk. paper)
   1. Active server pages.   2. Web site development.   3. Web
sites—Design—Case studies.   I. Title.
   TK5105.8885.A26L43 2003
   005.2'76—dc21

                                  2003012533

ISBN 0-321-15965-9
Text printed on recycled paper
1 2 3 4 5 6 7 8 9 10—CRS—0706050403
First printing, September 2003

This book is dedicated to my counselors in the spirit:
Lisa Griffin and Ted Hopkins.

Contents

Chapter 9 Using XML: Creating a Guest Book Application . . . 329

Chapter 10 Dynamic Charts and Graphs 361

Chapter 11 Animated Banners 399

Chapter 12 Using NT Services: An Ad Banner Management Application 423

Preface

I've been teaching ASP.NET for more than two years and things have changed. It's not just the course material that's changed, but more importantly it's the ability of my students to be extremely productive. They can create enterprise applications in a fraction of the time it used to take. Many of my students are seasoned Web developers who work for Fortune 1000 companies. They have taken what they've learned back to the workplace, and saved their employers thousands of dollars. And the savings have been possible because the cost of developing enterprise applications with ASP.NET is so much lower. That's because ASP.NET gives developers so much of the plumbing that they used to have to write themselves, such as Web services, XML rendering, and remoting.

This book should not be the first book on ASP.NET development that you read. While there is a fair amount of teaching throughout, it assumes that you know the basics of Web development using ASP.NET. This book is full of solutions that can be easily added to your Web site. The solutions also show you lots of recommended practices. Learning these recommended practices is the next step past learning the basics of ASP.NET that you need. It's kind of like once you've learned to spell and write sentences, you can correctly learn to craft coherent prose. This book teaches you how to tie all of the ASP.NET pieces together. It teaches you how to get the most out of the ASP.NET platform.

Many of the applications in this book would cost you significant dollars if you purchased them. Examples of this are the Forum application, the Classifieds application, and the Graphing class. As a developer, I often look for applications and classes that I can use. Finding these cuts my cost of development significantly since I don't have to write them myself. And even if you do have to modify these applications to suit your needs, they give you a starting point that'll still save you lots of time.

I have a Web site so that you can see the applications. The Web site is at www.ASPNET-Solutions.com. Besides giving you the opportunity to see the applications in action, this Web site offers updates. If for some reason I find bugs or make modifications, I'll post them on the Web site. There's a forum on the Web site, too, where you can ask questions and make comments.

You can also contact me directly via e-mail at Rick@JSVentures.com. I can usually answer your questions within several days. There are times, though, when I'm in the final stages of a project when it might take me as long as a week to answer your e-mail. Be patient and I'll respond as soon as possible. I also welcome questions that go beyond the material in the book—if you have a related question in your own development, please ask and I'll try to get you an answer.

Acknowledgments

I have to thank Sondra Scott from the bottom of my heart. She is a great editor, and I appreciate her deeply. Addison-Wesley is lucky to have her, and I have been lucky to work with her over the past year.

Scott Seely is the best technical editor I've ever had. He identified problem areas and made a number of suggestions for material that should be added, to provide greater value for readers. Of course, any good technical editor is hard on an author, but in this case I am grateful because it made such a positive difference in the quality of this book.

Vincent Minden provided material for Chapters 5, 15, and 19. I appreciate his help more than I can say. Ian Hadgraft helped out a great deal with the Regular Expressions material.

Clifton Griffin was a huge help. He helped create some of the support material for subjects such as writing NT Services and using WMI. He also did some of the grunt work in testing and fixing parts of the Web site. I really appreciate his help over the past year.

About the Author

Rick Leinecker is a seasoned developer with 21 years of experience. Included in his list of jobs are director of technology for IntraCorp, senior software engineer for MCI's Digital Imaging Division, senior software engineer for Landmark Communications, and professor at Rockingham Community College.

Rick has written more than a dozen books on the subject of programming and hundreds of magazine articles. He's written more than 12 front-line entertainment programs such as *Trump Castle* and *The Cardinal of the Kremlin*. He also provides ASP.NET training around the country for shows such as *VSLive*.

Besides the technical side, Rick does a lot of music. He plays the French horn, trumpet, guitar, and bass; he sings in a number of groups; and he can even be seen on stage acting in musicals such as *Bye Bye Birdie*.

About the Technical Reviewer

Scott Seely works for Microsoft as a part of the XML Enterprise Services team. Scott has been a speaker at several industry conferences and has authored numerous articles for MSDN. Scott is also the author of *SOAP: Cross Platform Web Service Development Using XML* (Prentice Hall PTR), *Windows Shell Programming* (Prentice Hall PTR), and co-author of *Creating and Consuming Web Services in Visual Basic* (Addison-Wesley).

CHAPTER 1

Getting Started with .NET

In This Chapter:

- Common Language Runtime
- Base Class Libraries (BCL)
- Assemblies
- .NET Languages
- ASP.NET
- ADO.NET

This book teaches you how to use the .NET Framework and the C# and VB languages to build great applications. Before we dive in and start building, though, we need to lay down the fundamentals so that you'll have a better understanding of what you're doing as you develop applications. If you're new to .NET programming, this overview chapter is important; but if you're familiar with .NET programming, you can skip it.

In this chapter, you'll learn about the .NET architecture, including the common language runtime, the Base Class Libraries (BCL), and assemblies. A general discussion of .NET languages, which will help you understand the C# language better, follows. Most applications in this book are built using ASP.NET, so we'll introduce the basics of ASP.NET. Web Forms and WinForms provide a unified user interface mechanism, so we'll spend a short time discussing the basics of WinForms. WinForms are used to create desktop applications with a standard Windows user interface, while Web Forms are used to create Web applications. And finally, we'll introduce Microsoft's newest database-access technology, ADO.NET, an extremely important .NET technology because so many applications access databases.

In general, most examples will be created and built with Visual Studio .NET. You can, however, create the applications and examples in the book without Visual Studio .NET if you are willing to use a text editor and the .NET command-line utilities such as the CSC (for C#) and VBC (for VB) compilers.

Common Language Runtime

The common language runtime, similar to the Java runtime, is the substrate of the .NET Framework. The common language runtime resides just above the operating system and provides functionality such as memory management and garbage collection to the .NET Framework. The common language runtime implements and uses a type system that is baked into every aspect of the Framework. These types are accessible by all programming languages, thus facilitating cross-language interoperability.

The common language runtime is a complete execution engine. Programming languages that target the .NET Framework translate source code into special instructions that the common language runtime can understand (more about this shortly). Code that targets the common language runtime is known as **managed code.** Managed code takes advantage of cross-language integration, cross-language exception handling, enhanced security, versioning and deployment support, a simplified model for component interaction, and debugging and profiling services.

.NET language compilers output Microsoft intermediate language (MSIL). MSIL is data that contains information that provide descriptions about code. This self-describing data contains information about the data types used; the classes, methods, and properties used; security and context; and any other information the common language runtime requires to execute an application. A methodology known as **reflection** exists whereby a .NET assembly can be interrogated for such information.

Metadata contains

- Identity information
- Version, culture, publisher
- Type definitions for both internal and exported types; classes, interfaces, structures, enumerations; methods, properties, fields, and events

- Type references to dependent types defined elsewhere, and versions of dependent types
- The `SoapExtension` class
- Custom attributes that developers use

An important element that the common language runtime offers is automatic memory management. With automatic memory management, managed applications never need to worry about releasing memory after it has been allocated and used, because their memory is automatically reclaimed when it is no longer needed. This means there are no more memory leaks (memory that never gets freed). Because C++ applications have been notorious for their memory leaks, this one common language runtime feature alone will lure many C++ programmers to the .NET world.

The common language runtime's memory management system is advanced. It not only eliminates memory leaks; it also provides high-performance memory allocation, which can make applications perform much faster overall. This improved performance means that the cost of allocating memory is reduced compared to traditional memory allocation strategies.

Compilers that target the .NET Framework expose the runtime's functionality in ways intended to be useful and intuitive to their developers. This means that some runtime features might be more noticeable in one environment than in another. For example, how you as a developer experience runtime depends on which language compilers or tools you use. If you are a Visual Basic developer, you might notice that, with the common language runtime, the Visual Basic language has more object-oriented features than before. The following benefits of the runtime might be particularly interesting to you:

- Improved performance
- Improved exception handling
- An implementation inheritance model
- The capability to easily use components developed in other languages
- Extensible types provided by a class library
- A broad set of language features

When a .NET language is compiled, it isn't output as native x86 code (the binary machine codes that 80x86 family CPUs execute). The binary image that's saved contains a small amount of bootstrap x86 code (which kicks off the common language runtime's execution engine—MSCOREE.DLL), the metadata (the self-describing data), and the MSIL body of data.

MSIL cannot be executed by x86 CPUs. MSIL is intermediate language, similar to what is known as pseudo code. MSIL is somewhere between the language source code and the machine code. It has been compiled into a form in which it can be turned into machine code—many compiler operations have already been performed, and the step from MSIL into machine code is relatively easy.

At execution time, the common language runtime takes the MSIL and compiles it into machine code that can be executed by the CPU. This process is known as just-in-time (JIT) compilation. The common language runtime doesn't, however, compile the entire application image, but compiles each discreet piece of code as it is needed. The compiled machine code stays in memory in its compiled form until the application is terminated.

You might be asking why the compilers output MSIL instead of machine code. At first glance, to simply output machine code would seem more practical—after all, that's what the CPU needs to correctly execute the intentions of the programmer. Microsoft, however, has made MSIL an open specification, in the hope and with the plan that non-Microsoft platforms such as UNIX will eventually implement a common language runtime and thus be able to use the same MSIL that a Windows-based operating system uses.

BCL

A rich set of base classes reside directly above the common language runtime in the .NET hierarchy. They are known as the Base Class Libraries (BCL), or sometimes the Framework class libraries (FCL). The BCL include classes, interfaces, and value types that expedite and optimize the development process and provide access to system functionality. To facilitate interoperability among languages, the .NET Base types are Common Language Specification (CLS) compliant, and can therefore be used from any programming language whose compiler conforms to the CLS.

The .NET Framework types are the foundation upon which .NET applications, components, and controls are built. The .NET Framework includes types that perform the following functions:

- Build on the base data types and exceptions
- Perform I/O
- Access information about loaded types
- Invoke .NET Framework security checks
- Provide data access; rich, client-side GUI; and server-controlled, client-side GUI

The BCL provide a rich set of interfaces, as well as abstract and concrete (non-abstract) classes. You can use the concrete classes as is, or, in many cases, derive your own classes from them. To use the functionality of an interface, you can either create a class that implements the interface or derive from one of the .NET Framework classes a class that implements the interface.

The System namespace is the root namespace for fundamental types in the .NET Framework. This namespace includes classes that represent the base data types used by all applications: `Object` (the root of the inheritance hierarchy), `Byte`, `Char`, `Array`, `Int32`, `String`, and so on. Many of these types correspond to the primitive data types that your programming language uses. When you write code using .NET Framework types, you can use your language's corresponding keyword when a .NET Framework base data type is expected.

Table 1.1 lists some of the value types the .NET Framework supplies, briefly describes each type, and indicates the corresponding type in Visual Basic, C#, and the Managed Extensions for C++. The table also includes entries for the `Object` and `String` classes, for which many languages have corresponding keywords.

In addition to the base data types, the System namespace contains almost 100 classes, ranging from classes that handle exceptions to classes that deal with core runtime concepts, such as application domains and the garbage collector.

The System namespace also contains many second-level namespaces. Table 1.2 shows the categories of functionality the System namespace covers, the second-level namespaces in each category, and a brief description of each namespace. Although many of the second-level namespaces contain other namespaces, only a few of the third-level namespaces are included in this table.

Table 1.1 The .NET Framework Types

Category	Class Name	Description	Visual Basic Data Type	C# Data Type	Managed Extensions for C++ Data Type	JScript Data Type
Integer	Byte	An 8-bit unsigned integer	Byte	byte	char	byte
	SByte	An 8-bit signed integer; not CLS compliant	Sbyte - No built-in type.	sbyte	signed char	SByte
	Int16	A 16-bit signed integer	Short	short	short	short
	Int32	A 32-bit signed integer	Integer	int -or- long	int	int
	Int64	A 64-bit signed integer	Long	long -or- __int64	long	
	UInt16	A 16-bit unsigned integer; not CLS compliant	UInt16 - No built-in type.	ushort	unsigned short	UInt16
	UInt32	A 32-bit unsigned integer; not CLS compliant	UInt32 - No built-in type.	uint	unsigned int -or- unsigned long	UInt32
	UInt64	A 64-bit unsigned integer; not CLS compliant	UInt64 - No built-in type.	ulong	unsigned __int64	UInt64

Category	Type	Description				
Floating point	Single	A single-precision (32-bit) floating-point number	Single	float	float	float
	Double	A double-precision (64-bit) floating-point number	Double	double	double	double
Logical	Boolean	A Boolean value (true or false)	Boolean	bool	bool	bool
Other	Char	A Unicode (16-bit) character	Char	char	wchar_t	char
	Decimal	A 96-bit decimal value	Decimal	decimal	Decimal	Decimal
	IntPtr	A signed integer whose size depends on the underlying platform (a 32-bit value on a 32-bit platform and a 64-bit value on a 64-bit platform)	IntPtr - No built-in type.	IntPtr - No built-in type.	IntPtr - No built-in type.	IntPtr

(continued)

Table 1.1 The .NET Framework Types (*cont.*)

Category	Class Name	Description	Visual Basic Data Type	C# Data Type	Managed Extensions for C++ Data Type	JScript Data Type
	UintPtr	An unsigned integer whose size depends on the underlying platform (a 32-bit value on a 32-bit platform and a 64-bit value on a 64-bit platform); not CLS compliant	UintPtr – No built-in type.	UintPtr – No built-in type.	UintPtr – No built-in type.	UintPtr
Class objects	Object	The root of the object hierarchy	Object	object	Object*	Object
	String	An immutable, fixed-length string of Unicode characters	String	string	String*	string

Table 1.2 Functionality Provided by the System Namespace

Category	Namespace	Functionality
Component model	System.CodeDom	Representation of the elements and structure of a source code document, and compilation and handling of such code
	System.ComponentModel	Implementation of components, including licensing and design-time adaptation
	Configuration System.Configuration	Retrieval of application configuration data
	Data System.Data	Access and management of data and data sources
	System.Xml	Standards-based support for processing XML
	System.Xml.Serialization	Bidirectional object-to-XML mapping
Framework services	System.Diagnostics	Application instrumentation and diagnostics
	System.DirectoryServices	Access to the Active Directory of an Active Directory service provider, such as a Windows domain
	System.Management	Services and application management tools that work with the Web-Based Enterprise Management (WBEM) standards
	System.Messaging	Microsoft Message Queue (MSMQ) access and management, and the sending and receiving of messages
	System.ServiceProcess	Installation and execution of Windows-based service applications; does not access specific services, such as Active Directory or XML Web Services
	System.Timers	Event raising on an interval or more complex schedule

(continued)

Table 1.2 Functionality Provided by the System Namespace (*cont.*)

Category	Namespace	Functionality
Globalization and localization	System.Globalization	Support for internationalization and globalization of code and resources
	System.Resources	Resource management and access, including support for localization
Net System.Net		Support for sending and receiving data over a network, including simple programming interfaces for common network protocols such as HTTP and SMTP
Common tasks	System.Collections	Collections of objects, such as lists, queues, arrays, hash tables, and dictionaries
	System.IO	Basic data stream access and management, including file I/O, memory I/O, and isolated storage
	System.Text	Character encoding, character conversion, and string manipulation
	System.Text. RegularExpressions	Full regular expression support
	System.Threading	Multithreaded programming support, including locking and synchronization
Reflection	System.Reflection	Access to type metadata and dynamic creation and invocation of types
Rich, client-side GUI	System.Windows.Forms	Rich user interface features for Windows-based applications
Runtime infrastructure services	System.Runtime. CompilerServices	Support for compilers that target the runtime

Table 1.2 Functionality Provided by the System Namespace (*cont.*)

Category	Namespace	Functionality
	System.Runtime.InteropServices	Support for interoperability with COM and other unmanaged code
	System.Runtime.Remoting	Support for creating tightly or loosely coupled distributed applications
	System.Runtime.Serialization	Object serialization and deserialization, including binary and SOAP encoding support
.NET Framework security	System.Security	Access to the underlying mechanisms of the .NET Framework security system, including policy resolution, stack walks, and permissions
	System.Security.Cryptography	Cryptographic services, including encoding and decoding of data, hashing, random number generation, message authentication, and formation of digital signatures
Web Services	System.Web	Support for Web server and client management, communication, and design. Provides core infrastructure for ASP.NET, including Web Forms support
	System.Web.Services	Client- and server-side support for SOAP-based Web services

Assemblies

A requirement of the common language runtime is that .NET-compiled code must belong to an assembly. Assemblies give a scope context to code: The code might be global to the server, or local to an application. And assemblies provide the names for types that are used in common language runtime applications.

In general, the types in an assembly are deployed as an indivisible unit. The assumption is that all types within an assembly were compiled at the same time. To this end, version management is done on an assembly-wide basis. Additionally, types within an assembly can be given more access privileges to one another than types that are outside of the assembly.

Assemblies and Modules

An **assembly** is a logical collection of type definitions. Within that logical collection, the type definitions may be spread across multiple physical files, or modules. A **module** is an executable file that contains common language runtime metadata and executable code. All code for a given type exists in exactly one module.

An assembly contains a **manifest** that is the top-level directory to the adjunct files that contain the actual code. In general, the references to external modules appear as relative paths and are evaluated relative to the locations of the file that contains the assembly manifest. The manifest also contains a list of references to external assemblies that this assembly is dependent upon. When loading an assembly, the common language runtime loader makes sure that all subordinate assemblies can be loaded prior to executing the first line of code.

Manifests

Each module begins with a module manifest. Note that a module manifest consists primarily of a list of references to external assemblies that the module's types depend on. For example, if a contained type T had a field of type E, and E was defined in an external assembly, the module manifest for T's module would contain a reference to E's assembly.

Exactly one module in an assembly is distinguished by also containing the assembly manifest. The **assembly manifest** is a superset of a **module manifest,** because it also contains a list of subordinate files/modules that may contain type definitions. All types defined in subordinate modules are scoped by the name of the containing assembly. Also interesting to note is that the assembly references or manifests contained in its subordinate modules are in addition to those references needed for types defined in the assembly modules themselves.

Private Assemblies

Private assemblies are assumed to be for the exclusive use of a small number of applications and are not generally visible to all applications. Private assemblies must be co-located with the application(s) that use(s) them. A private assembly must be located in the directory that is a descendant of the loading application's root directory. The probe path for private assemblies is always at least ApplicationBase and ApplicationBase\AssemblyName, in which ApplicationBase is the base directory (or URL) of the loading application, and AssemblyName is the name of the assembly.

The probe path can be augmented using an XML configuration file. The common language runtime looks for an XML configuration file with the same name as the loading application, but with a .cfg extension rather than an .exe extension.

Global Assemblies

Global assemblies reside in the Global Assembly Cache (GAC) and are strongly named (or globally unique for an enterprise). They are intended for wide-spread use across applications created by multiple organizations. In general, a global assembly differs from a private assembly only in how it is named. Private assemblies are named using a simple name that matches the file containing the manifest. Global assembly names have three additional components: an originator, a version, and a culture identifier. The **originator** identifies the organization that developed the component. The version is a four-part version number that identifies the major, minor, build, and revision numbers of the component. The **culture identifier** indicates what language and region the component is intended for.

When building a global assembly, one must explicitly specify the originator and version, and may optionally specify the culture using compiler attributes. The following code shows the attributes that set the originator to the public key stored in the file jsventures.snk, the version number to 9.8.7.6, and the culture to U.S. English:

```
using System.Runtime.CompilerServices;
[assembly: AssemblyKeyFile("jsventures.snk")]
[assembly: AssemblyVersion("9.8.7.6")]
[assembly: AssemblyCultre("en-US")]
namespace JSVentures.IceCream
{
    public class Flavor
```

```
    {
        // Ice Cream flavor stuff goes here
    }
}
```

Global assemblies must be installed into a machine-wide (global) assembly cache known as the GAC. The GAC is located under the %SystemRoot%\Assembly directive. A custom Explorer shell extension allows administrators and users to examine entries in the GAC. Additionally, one can run the gacutil.exe utility to install, uninstall, or list the assemblies in the GAC.

.NET Languages

The common language runtime defines a common runtime for all .NET languages. Although C# and VB.NET are the two flagship languages of .NET, any language that targets the common language runtime is on equal footing with any other language. In this section we'll talk about the features that the .NET languages offer.

Classes and Objects

The common language runtime deals in managed types. The runtime can load types, execute methods of a type, and instantiate objects of a type. Although the common language runtime supports several forms of types, such as classes, interfaces, structures, enumerations, and delegates, all of these forms ultimately are represented as classes at the lowest levels of the runtime. And although the common language runtime does support exporting entry points that are not enclosed in a type, at least two languages (VB.NET and C#) do not support entry points outside of a type definition.

Although in OOP it is possible to invoke some class methods without objects, the most common use of classes is to produce objects. In the common language runtime, an object is an instance of exactly one class. The operations that may be performed on an object are determined by the object's class. The amount and type of storage used by the object is determined by the object's class. In essence, the class acts as a factory or template for objects that belong to that class.

The common language runtime supports instantiating objects based on a class. Each programming language exposes this functionality somewhat differently. In C# and VB.NET, for example, the new keyword is used to create a new object of a given class, as shown in the following two code snippets:

C#
```
IceCream ic = new IceCream();
ic.MakeACone();
```

VB
```
Dim ic as new IceCream();
ic.MakeACone ()
```

Classes are defined in C# and in VB.NET using the class keyword. The following code shows sample classes in each:

C# Class
```
public class IceCream
{
    string strFlavor = "Chocolate";
    public void MakeACone()
    {
        System.Console.Write( "I have made a cone. My flavor is "
);
        System.Console.WriteLine( strFlavor + "." );
    }
}
```

VB.NET Class
```
Public Class IceCream
    Dim strFlavor as string = "Chocolate"

    Public Sub MakeACone()
        System.Console.Write("I have made a cone. My flavor is ")
        System.Console.WriteLine(strFlavor & ".")
    End Sub
End Class
```

Protection

By default, all class members are implicitly private and can be accessed only by methods of that class. This access can be made explicit using the `private access` modifier. Class members can be made accessible to all parties using the `public access` modifier, which informs the runtime that any party that can access the class can access this particular member.

Table 1.3 The Protection Keywords

	C#	VB.NET	Description
Type	public	Public	Type is visible everywhere
	internal	Private	Type is only visible inside of assembly
Member	public	Public	Member is visible everywhere
	internal	Friend	Member is visible only inside of assembly
	private	Private	Member is visible only inside of declaring type
	protected	Protected	Member is visible to type and deriving type only

Class members can also be made accessible only when the assembly that contains the class is accessible. This is accomplished using the `internal access` modifier. Members marked `internal` can be accessed only by code that is compiled into the same assembly as the containing class. Table 1.3 shows the various protection keywords.

Constructors

Unless the programmer takes special steps, the fields of the class will be set to a well-known initial value when an object is created. Numeric types are set to zero, and objects are set to `null` (C#) or `Nothing` (VB). You can change the values that are used by writing a constructor. A **constructor** is a special method that is called automatically to set the class's fields to a programmer-determined state prior to the first use of the object (or class).

Constructors are called when a new object is created, before the new operator returns the reference to the new object. Constructors may accept parameters, and they may be overloaded based on parameter count or type. The following code shows typical constructors:

C#
```
public class IceCream
{
    private int i = 5;
    public IceCream()
    {
        System.Console.WriteLine( "This is delicious!" );
    }
}
```

```
VB.NET
Public Class IceCream
    Sub New()
        System.Console.WriteLine( "This is delicious!" )
    End Sub
End Class
```

Namespaces

Namespaces in the .NET runtime are used to organize classes and types into separate spaces. You define namespaces using the namespace keyword, as shown in the following code:

```
namespace Rick
{
    public class MyClass
    {
        public static void DoSomething()
        {
        }
    }
}
```

The using keyword in C# promotes elements in other namespaces into the global namespace. The following code shows an example of referencing two separate namespaces with the using keyword:

```
using Rick;
using System;

MyClass.DoSomething();
Console.WriteLine( "Just called DoSomething()" );
```

Interface Basics

An **interface** is a special kind of type in the common language runtime. Interfaces are used to partition the space of all possible objects into subcategories based on shared semantics. When two objects support the same interface, one can assume that the two objects share the functionality or behavior implied by the shared interface. A given object might support multiple interfaces, which implies that it belongs to multiple categories of objects.

Interface-based design was first popularized in component-based software engineering (such as COM and CORBA). Interface-based designs tend to express application constraints in a less implementation-specific manner than traditional class-based, object-oriented software engineering. In general, interface-based software is more extensible, maintainable, and easier to evolve than traditional class-based designs.

Part of a class definition is the list of supported interfaces. A given class may support as many interfaces as it wishes. Each language provides a syntax for expressing the list of supported interfaces. In C#, a class definition must list the interfaces it supports between the class name and the opening curly brace, as show in the following code:

```
public interface IIceCream
{
    void TakeABite();
    void AddSyrup();
}

public class Sundae : IIceCream
{
    public void TakeABite()
    {
        // code goes here...
    }

    public void AddSyrup()
    {
        // Code goes here...
    }
}
```

When a class supports an interface, instances of that class are acceptable anywhere a reference of the supported interfaces is allowed. This means that variables of a given class type may be passed where a supported interface type is expected.

Interfaces typically have one or more method declarations. When an interface contains a **method declaration,** all that is specified in the interface definition is the signature of the method; no actual executable code is provided in the interface definition. Rather, each class that supports the interface must provide its own implementation of that method signature that complies with the method's semantics as documented.

The method declarations that appear inside an interface definition are sometimes called abstract methods. **Abstract methods** are method declarations that must be supported in a derived class. If a given class does not provide an implementation of every method defined in every interface it claims to support, that class is itself abstract and cannot be used to instantiate objects.

Interfaces that have methods typically have several methods that work together in concert to define a protocol for interacting with objects of that type. The order of method invocation and acceptable parameter values often are documented as part of this protocol. To this end, interfaces act as useful fools for partitioning a software project into largely independent components.

Interfaces themselves can be marked as either `public` for inter-assembly use or `internal` for intra-assembly use. All methods of an interface must be public. In support of this requirement, it is illegal to use the `public` keyword inside of an interface definition.

Virtual Methods

The common language runtime supports two **method-invocation mechanisms: virtual** and **non-virtual.** With both mechanisms, the actual method invoked is based on type. In the case of non-virtual methods, the choice of implementation is based on the compile-time type of the variable expression used to invoke the method. In the case of virtual methods, the choice of implementation is based on the run-time type of the most-derived class of the object, independent of the compile-time type of the object reference used to invoke the method.

All abstract methods are also virtual. This means that all methods invoked via interface-based references are virtual. For example, because they are abstract, all methods declared in an interface are virtual.

Each language provides its own syntax for indicating that a method is virtual. In C#, methods declared in a class are virtual if they use either the abstract or virtual method modifiers. In VB.NET, methods declared in a class are virtual if they use either the `MustOverride` (wherein there is no default implementation) or `Overridable` (wherein there is a default implementation) method modifiers. A method declared as virtual/overridable must have a method implementation. However, a derived type is permitted to override the base class's implementation with one of its own.

When a derived class declares a method whose name and signature matches a method declared in a base class or interfaces, there is room for confusion. To keep the confusion to a minimum, the common language runtime requires the derived type to indicate its relationship to the base type's method declaration. The rules work differently depending on whether the base method declaration was virtual or non-virtual.

When a derived class declares a method whose name and signature matches a method declared as virtual or abstract in its base class, the derived class must indicate whether it is overriding the virtual method of the base or trying to introduce a new method. In C#, the derived method declaration must use the `override` method modifier. In VB.NET, the derived method declaration must use the `override` method modifier. The following code shows a C# class with a virtual method, and a derived class overriding the method:

```
public class BaseClass {
    public virtual void DoIt() {
        Console.WriteLine( "In BaseClass.DoIt()" );
    }
}

public class DerivedClass : BaseClass {
    public override void DoIt() {
        Console.WriteLine( "In DerivedClass.DoIt()" );
    }
}
BaseClass bc = new DerivedClass();
bc.DoIt(); // Writes "In DerivedClass.DoIt()"
```

Properties

Each programming language provides its own constructs for defining properties. A property definition in C# looks like a hybrid of a field declaration with scoped method definitions. The following code shows a class with a property definition:

```
public class IceCreamCone
{
    int m_nScoops;
    public int Scoops
    {
        get { return m_nScoops; }
        set { m_nAge = p.nScoops; }
    }
}
```

```
// Using the property
using System;
IceCreamCone p = new IceCreamCone();
p.Scoops = 4;
Console.WriteLine( p.Scoops );
```

Attributes

Every language has its own way of allowing attributes to be applied. The following code shows how to apply attributes to a C# class:

```
[ ShowInToolbox(true) ]
public class ThisControl : WebControl
{
    private string text;

    [ Bindable(true), DefaultValue("") ]
    [ Category("Appearance") ]
    public string Text
    {
        get { return text; }
        set { text = Value; }
    }
}
```

Exceptions

Exceptions are instances of classes that extend the System.Exception type either directly or indirectly. The common language runtime provides built-in exception types that extend System.Exception, System.ApplicationException, and System.SystemException. The following code shows how to catch an exception in C#:

```
using System;
using System.IO;
public Class MyClass
{
    public static void Main()
    {
        try
        {
            File f( "C:\\SomeData.txt" );
            f.Delete();
```

```
        }
        catch( DirectoryNotFoundException ex )
        {
            // This is a common exception for I/O.
            Console.WriteLine( ex.Message );
        }
        catch( Exception ex )
        {
            // Here we catch all other exceptions.
        }
    }
}
```

ASP.NET

ASP.NET is a platform that excels in the realm of Web application development. It also can be used in stand-alone applications. ASP.NET produces HTML content—some static and unchanging, some dynamic and changeable.

The static HTML content that's output using ASP.NET is similar to what you can create with Notepad or FrontPage. When you use an authoring tool such as FrontPage, you typically use the WYSIWYG editor and save the file somewhere—usually to a Web server. The HTML content is then served up when a client machine makes a request to the Web server.

Many times, though, the content needs to adapt itself to the situation. A particular user might need additional menu choices in the Web application. Or if your business offers specials each Tuesday, you might need special images to appear next to those items in you product catalog each Tuesday. As a technology for dynamically creating HTML, ASP.NET works in instances such as these.

Many of you have developed ASP applications in which the files all have .asp extensions. ASP.NET application files have an .aspx extension to differentiate them from ASP files. Because their extensions are different, both classic ASP and ASP.NET can function side-by-side in the same Web site.

ASP.NET files have a major performance advantage over ASP files. The first time they are requested, they are compiled into native code, which makes them execute much faster than the interpreted ASP files.

In classic ASP, you didn't have many language choices. Anything you could do in HTML, such as JScript and JavaScript, were available. For server-side programming, VBScript was one choice, and for ISAPI programming, VB and C++. Now, with ASP.NET, you get VB, C#, and JScript out of the box. And other languages—Cobol, RPG, Pascal, and many others—are under development by third-party vendors. ASP.NET was developed from the ground up to be language agnostic—in other words, any language should give you similar final results.

In terms of extra effort required, this multiple-language support and runtime compilation to native code doesn't come at any price to developers. To save an ASP.NET file, all you have to do is save it to disk—no compile button and no other steps.

ASP.NET has a new control-based, event-driven execution model. You can hook a `Page_Load()` method, an event that a server-side control fires off such as an `OnItemCommand()` method, or any other event that is available. The naming of `Page_Load()` in C# is the default behavior. The event handler could be named iRool and not affect whether the event was called. By comparison, in VB.NET, similar methods end with `handles Page.Load`.

In all, the new model that ASP.NET follows offers these benefits: It requires that you write less code, it encapsulates functionality into easy-to-use classes, and it reduces the amount of spaghetti code you'll be inclined to write.

Many of the applications we'll write in this book use Visual Studio .Net as the development tool, with ASP.NET as the deployment and runtime environment. We chose this combination because of the heavy emphasis that Microsoft is placing on distributed applications, and the rising need for you to develop enterprise and distributed applications.

ADO.NET

With many new features and improvements, ADO.NET puts a new face on the old ADO model. The most notable of these advances are the elimination of the ADO recordset and that the internal data structures of ADO.NET are now XML based. Having gained support for XML, it should be no surprise that ADO.NET incorporates as much of XML as possible. XML was selected for the core data representation for several reasons: XML offers a wider array of supported data types, data can easily pass through firewalls and internal networks, XML does not care about databases or query languages, and it allows binding to any user-defined interface. ADO.NET replaces the eliminated recordset with a new and more complete object called the DataSet. This object represents a disconnected, cached copy of data that behaves much like a database by storing a collection of hierarchical data tables, rows, columns, relationships, and constraints.

Before you use ADO.NET components, the appropriate namespaces must be included. The System.Data namespace will always need to be included because it contains the core database components. Next, depending on the source of your data, one of two namespaces will need to be included. For best performance for a direct Microsoft SQL Server 2000 connection, the System.Data.SqlClient namespace should be used for best performance. For all other connection types, such as Access and Oracle, the System.Data.OleDb namespace is required.

Summary

Now is an exciting time. Microsoft has recently released the .NET Framework and all of its pieces. This release opens the door to development of more sophisticated, robust, and rich applications in a fraction of the time it used to take. And this book will lead you through a learning process that will quickly get you up to speed.

In the next chapter, we dive into WebForms, ADO.NET, and building a Resumé application using these technologies.

CHAPTER 2

Effective Web Forms: Creating a Resumé Application

In This Chapter:

- Web Form Controls
- Web User Controls
- Page Execution Sequence
- Data Validation
- The Resumé Application
- Extending and Modifying the Resumé Application
- Deploying the Resumé Application

ASP.NET has a collection of objects that make creating user interfaces easy for developers. These objects are server controls that you can place into .aspx pages. Then, when a page is served up by the server to a client machine, the pages are rendered as HTML. The pages execute on the server and generate HTML code that's inserted into the outgoing HTML stream. The browser sees the pages as HTML, whereas the ASP.NET page and developer see them as controls.

Visual Basic developers are used to working with a form onto which they place controls. The addition of the Web Forms paradigm into the ASP.NET realm offers a unified programming model. Even Visual C++ now offers this approach to programming. Having these options means that a developer can more easily switch between developing desktop applications in Visual Basic, C#, or Visual C++ and developing enterprise applications in ASP.NET.

This chapter focuses on the ASP.NET server controls. Various aspects of the controls that are used in Web Forms will be discussed throughout. And to tie all of this together, a Resumé application will be used to demonstrate the topics.

The Resumé application performs database access via the ADO.NET namespace. Because I want to focus on Web Forms, the explanations in this area will be limited to explanations of the resumé code itself and will not include in-depth ADO.NET explanations. A more complete explanation of ADO.NET can be found in Chapter 3.

Note: This book is intended for VB and C# programmers. The Web site (described later in this chapter) contains both VB and C# code. I will also alternate the language used in each chapter between VB and C#. The featured applications for the even-numbered chapters are in C#, and the featured applications for the odd-numbered chapters are in VB. For example, this chapter's application is written in C#, the next is in VB, and so forth.

Code snippets that illustrate a topic and that are not part of the application will be shown in both VB and C#.

Web Form Controls

Most Web development involves interacting with user data in one way or another. Much of this data is contained in forms that users have filled out. Other items that fall into the user data category are passed as parameters or contained in session variables (see Chapter 7 for in-depth coverage of session-state and application-state topics). Web development in the past has always dealt with these kinds of user data. The ASP.NET Web Form controls provide a new way to interact with this data.

ASP programming can be used to create ASP pages that contain both HTML and server-side VBScript code. The HTML is static—it doesn't change—whereas the server-side VBScript code dynamically generates HTML that is sent to the client machine. When this type of ASP programming was first introduced, it offered a powerful way to quickly and easily develop Web applications. The problem with this approach, of course, is that alternating between HTML and ASP code is confusing, and the code is difficult to follow and decipher. Classic ASP is much like the fabled spaghetti code that was so common in early BASIC programs.

Classic ASP development also offers some challenges that are not so obvious. For instance, what if you have a list of items in a <select> object? You might have 10 or 15 objects, perhaps that describe merchandise colors. Depending on the situation, such as a previously chosen user selection, or some item that may be on sale, you might want different items in the list to be selected. For instance, if red sweaters are on sale this week, you might want to default the color selector to red. Maybe your company has an abundance of red sweaters, and by making red the default, you feel you can sell more red sweaters. So you have to decide which of the items in the selection list is designated when the page first appears to the user. In classic HTML, you do this by adding the selected attribute to one of the option items. And if you are creating static HTML, this is easy to do. But when you need to make a dynamic decision on which item to add this attribute to, things become more complicated. What you end up doing is including a conditional test in the code, and then outputting the selected attribute to the appropriate item. Although developers have used this "tried and true" method over the past five years, it tends to lead to unreadable and possibly even unmanageable code.

The following classic ASP code in Listing 2.1 shows the exact situation I just described. For your benefit, I have included the resulting HTML code in Listing 2.2.

Listing 2.1 Classic ASP Code That Dynamically Selects a Color

```
<select size="1" name="Colors">
  <option value=Red>Red</option>
  <option value=Green>Green</option>
  <option value=Blue>Blue</option>
<%
  If SESSION( "User" ) = "JOHN" Then
    Response.Write( "<option selected value=Magenta>Magenta</option>" )
    Response.Write( "<option value=Orange>Orange</option>" )
    Response.Write( "<option value=Teal>Teal</option>" )
  ElseIf SESSION( "User" ) = "GEORGE" Then
    Response.Write( "<option value=Magenta>Magenta</option>" )
    Response.Write( "<option selected value=Orange>Orange</option>" )
    Response.Write( "<option value=Teal>Teal</option>" )
  Else
    Response.Write( "<option value=Magenta>Magenta</option>" )
    Response.Write( "<option value=Orange>Orange</option>" )
    Response.Write( "<option selected value=Teal>Teal</option>" )
  End If
%>
</select>
```

Listing 2.2 The Result of Listing 2.1 When the User Is GEORGE

```
<select size="1" name="Colors">
  <option value=Red>Red</option>
  <option value=Green>Green</option>
```

```
  <option value=Blue>Blue</option>
  <option value=Magenta>Magenta</option>
  <option selected value=Orange>Orange</option>
  <option value=Teal>Teal</option>
</select>
```

With ASP.NET, the preceding ASP code can be replaced with much simpler code that is easier to organize. First, a DropDownList Web Form control is added to the Web Form (more about doing this in the section entitled "Placing Controls" later in the chapter). The option values must be added, and the resulting .aspx code is shown in Listing 2.3.

Listing 2.3 A DropDownList Control Alternative to an HTML Select

```
<asp:DropDownList id="DropDownList1" runat="server">
  <asp:ListItem Value="Red">Red</asp:ListItem>
  <asp:ListItem Value="Green">Green</asp:ListItem>
  <asp:ListItem Value="Blue">Blue</asp:ListItem>
  <asp:ListItem Value="Magenta">Magenta</asp:ListItem>
  <asp:ListItem Value="Teal">Teal</asp:ListItem>
</asp:DropDownList>
```

Now, to simply select one of the items, you can use the code shown in Listing 2.4.

Listing 2.4 The Code to Select an Item when Using DropDownList Control Code

```
C#
if( Session["User"] == "JOHN" )
{
  DropDownList1.SelectedIndex = 0;
}
else if( Session["User"] == "GEORGE" )
{
  DropDownList1.SelectedIndex = 1;
}
else
{
  DropDownList1.SelectedIndex = 2;
}
```

OR
```
switch (Session["User"] ) {
    case "JOHN":
      DropDownList1.SelectedIndex = 0;
        break;
    case "George":
      DropDownList1.SelectedIndex = 1;
        break;
    default:
      DropDownList1.SelectedIndex = 2;
        break;
}
```

VB
```
If Session("User") = "JOHN" Then
  DropDownList1.SelectedIndex = 0
ElseIf Session("User") = "GEORGE" Then
  DropDownList1.SelectedIndex = 1
Else
  DropDownList1.SelectedIndex = 2
End If
```

OR
```
Select Case Session("Test")
 Case "John"
  DropDownList1.SelectedIndex = 0
 Case "George"
  DropDownList1.SelectedIndex = 1
 Case Else
  DropDownList1.SelectedIndex = 2
End Select
```

Web User Controls

Server-side controls all derive from System.Web.UI.WebControls. ASP.NET offers another group of controls, though, which fall into the category of HTML controls. HTML controls are simply server-side representations of standard or normal HTML elements. Any HTML element that is contained in an .aspx page and is marked with a **runat="server"** attribute becomes an HTML control on the server. These controls all derive from the `System.Web.UI.HtmlControl` class. If you use an HTML element that has functionality that can't be represented with anything that has server-side functionality, such as `<div>` or `<span>` has, it is represented as an HTML generic control instance.

These HTML controls are designed to have direct equivalences from normal HTML instances. This pairing means you can more easily transfer your classic ASP applications to ASP.NET applications by changing their HTML elements and adding a **`runat="server"`** attribute. Then you can simply change the file extension from .asp to .aspx. This combination gives you an ASP.NET page with a complete set of server-side controls.

NOTE: I mention the HtmlControls only for completeness. We won't be using them in the Resumé application.

Placing Controls

When you first create an ASP.NET application in Visual Studio, you'll see a blank form onto which you can place controls. You can find the controls we'll be using in the Toolbox under the Web Forms category, as shown in Figure 2.1. If for some reason the Toolbox can't be seen somewhere on the screen (by default, it's on the left side of Visual Studio), go to the View menu and select Toolbox, which will cause it to appear.

To place Web Form controls, simply grab the one you want and drag it onto the form. Once the controls have been placed on the form, they can be moved around, aligned, and edited.

TIP: The Label control simply displays HTML text in the browser. This control is a server-side control that executes and then renders by outputting HTML code.

If you don't need to programmatically alter or access the label or its contents, you should use simple HTML text instead of a Label control. That's because simple HTML text doesn't have to execute as a server-side control but is simply sent to the client without any processing.

Using HTML text instead of Label controls when you don't need the flexibility that Label controls offer can improve the performance of your Web Form application.

When I develop the interface for ASP.NET applications, I find FlowLayout easier to use for the page than GridLayout. GridLayout gives

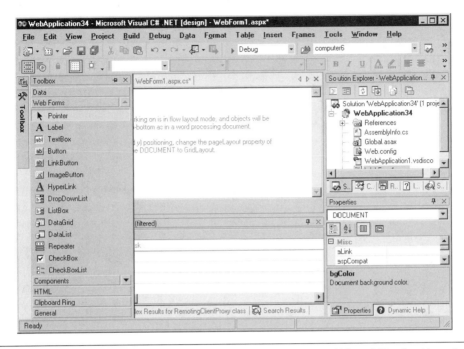

Figure 2.1 By Default, the Toolbox Is Seen at the Left Side of Visual Studio. Hovering Your Cursor over the Toolbox Reveals the Controls.

you the capability to place controls using absolute coordinates. But I have found that GridLayout actually makes creating clean and well-organized screens more difficult. By default, ASP.NET pages are set to GridLayout. You can change the settings with the DOCUMENT Properties window, as shown in Figure 2.2.

Control Properties

Once a control has been placed on the form, its properties can easily be edited. To do so, simply single-click on the control with the left mouse button, which will select the control and reflect the control's properties in the property window.

What kinds of properties can you set for controls? That depends on the control and what is appropriate. Label controls let you set properties having to do with the display of text, such as color, font, size, and the text content. TextBox controls let you set other properties that relate to text editing,

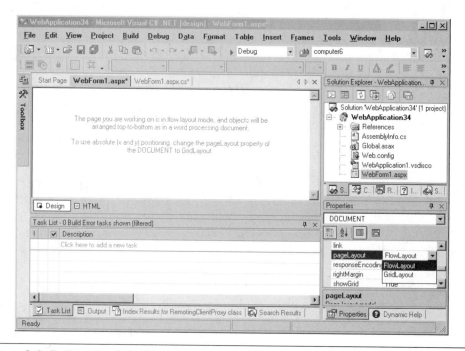

Figure 2.2 To Develop ASP.NET Application Interfaces, FlowLayout Might Be Easier to Use than GridLayout.

such as columns, rows, type (single line, multi-line, or password), and other similar characteristics.

Many controls, such as the DropDownList control, let you enter the data items using the Properties window. Alternatively, you can just type in the data items with HTML View selected. As a matter of fact, you can edit a control's properties while in HTML view simply by typing in the property and its value. The following example shows a Label control that is set to render as yellow text, with the text content being "Some Text Here".

```
<asp:Label id="Label1" runat="server" ForeColor="Yellow">Some
Text Here</asp:Label>
```

NOTE: You might have noticed that the Visual Studio edit window has two tabs—Design and HTML. The Design tab opens by default and lets you graphically edit your page. The HTML tab lets you access the raw HTML, which gives you more control.

The Web Form controls, however, are included with the raw HTML. You won't see the rendered HTML when these controls are present, but you'll see the server control that eventually will render the HTML.

Control Events

Most Web Form controls have events that can fire in response to user interaction. Buttons, for instance, can fire off an event handler, to which you can add code and perform some tasks.

All the controls that have events have a default event. This default is the event that developers will use 99 percent of the time in conjunction with a control. For example, a Button control has as its default event a Click event. The default event fires in response to users clicking the button. But the Button control also can respond to other events, including a Command event. I have used the Button's Command event only once since I've been developing ASP.NET applications, but it is there for those rare cases when it's needed. Command events give developers an opportunity to specify events other than the default event.

Default events are so important because handler methods are easily created for them by simply double-clicking on the control in the Design window. This means you can quickly create an application that responds to a button click.

I've created a simple application named SimpleWebFormDemo by doing the following:

- Create a C# ASP.NET application named SimpleWebFormDemo.
- Add a TextField into which users can type text.
- Add a Label into which the TextField contents will be placed.
- Add a button.
- Double click on the button to create an event handler.
- Add the following code using the event-handler method:

```
Label1.Text = TextBox1.Text;
TextBox1.Text = "";
```

You can see this simple application in Figure 2.3.

The Web Site

The Web site that supports this book can be found at www.ASPNetSolutions.com. For demonstration, you can find all programs in

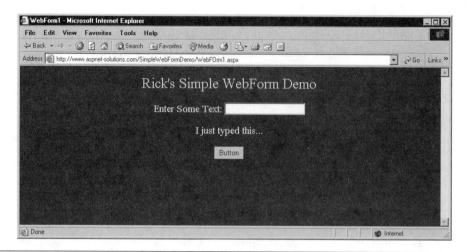

Figure 2.3 The `Button Event()` Method Puts the TextField Data into the Label. The TextField Is Then Cleared.

the book at this site. You can also download the code for the substantive programs, such as the Resumé application. (Short programs such as SimpleWebFormDemo are not made available for download simply because they are so short.)

To find the SimpleWebFormDemo program, go to the Chapter Examples link from the Web site's main page. Then select the Chapter 2 link. This will bring you to a page from which you can launch the SimpleWebFormDemo program.

AutoPostBack

Not all events automatically fire an event. A good example of this is the CheckBox control. By default, this control simply allows its state to benignly toggle on and off. Even if you double-click a CheckBox control and create an event handler, the event handler will never get called.

The trick to calling the event is to set the control's `AutoPostBack` property to `true`. This setting will cause the page to **post back** (more on post backs in the next section, "Page Execution Sequence") to the server; then, if you created an event handler, the event will be invoked.

I created a simple program named CheckBoxEvent. You can find this program from the Chapter 2 page on the ASPNetSolutions.com Web site. This program shows how you can use the `AutoPostBack` property to cause CheckBox controls to immediately respond to user interaction with a post back.

Radio buttons are also prime candidates to use for setting AutoPostBack to `true` when the application needs to respond immediately to a selection.

Page Execution Sequence

Knowing the order in which ASP.NET page methods are executed is important. I'm not going to go into great detail here because there are a number of methods that most ASP.NET developers never see. I'll just talk about several that you'll commonly encounter.

When you create an ASP.NET Web application, Visual Studio creates boilerplate code for the Web Forms. Of these methods, the `OnInit()` method is the first executed when a page is loaded. From this method, the `InitializeComponent()` and the `base.OnInit()` methods are called. The `InitializeComponent()` method sets the event-handler delegates for each component that has event-handler methods. The `base.OnInit()` method allows the base class to perform initialization of its own.

We need to talk about an important notion now. That is the concept of **post backs**. ASP.NET performs a lot of its magic by posting itself (including its form data) to the server for processing. The server processes information and then serves up the same page to the client. So, in other words, when you click a button, the system first sends an `HTTP POST` command to the server. The server receives this command and then simply resends the page after having performed any addition processing.

The page controls, such as TextFields and Labels, are preserved in a hidden HTML field called VIEWSTATE. When the page is POSTed to the server, the server picks up this hidden field and is able populate the controls from the data the field contains. Then, when the page is served back to the client, the controls contain the persisted data.

If the page is being received in response to a post back, you can find this out. A page property called `IsPostBack` is `true` when the invocation is in response to a post back; when the invocation is not in response to a post back, the property is `false`. The following code shows how to determine whether the page is being posted back from inside the Page.Load event handler:

C#

```
private void Page_Load(object sender, System.EventArgs.e)
{
```

```
if( IsPostBack )
{
   // You only get here for post backs.
}
}
```

VB

```
Private Sub Page_Load(ByVal sender as object, _
  ByVal e as System.EventArgs.e) Handles MyBase.Load
  If IsPostBack Then
     ' You only get here for post backs.
  End If
End Sub
```

After the `OnInit()` method, the `Page_Load()` method is called. In many cases, user-interface objects are populated in the `Page_Load()` method. These objects will persist their data between post backs. For this reason, you don't need to repopulate them for each page invocation because they might already be populated. Populating controls unnecessarily will create a load on the server that it doesn't need to bear.

The last thing that happens is that event handlers for any controls for which an event was fired will be invoked. This means that, contrary to what you might guess, your event handlers invoke the events after OnInit() and Page_Load(). We often have an intuitive sense that button events will happen before the post back, but that is the opposite of what really happens.

Data Validation

In this section, I talk about data validation in ASP.NET. ASP.NET provides a group of validation controls that will make your job as a Web Forms developer much easier. These controls easily handle the task of data validation in form elements, and provide a consistent programming model for developers.

When do you need data validation in an HTML form? Any time you need to ensure that the user data is either present or in a specific format. For instance, if you are asking the user to enter an e-mail address, and he types **XYZ**, that is not a valid e-mail address. The user might have purposely entered an invalid e-mail address, or he might have inadvertently entered it. If the e-mail address is not valid, your database will contain an invalid e-mail address. If, for example, you have to notify users via e-mail of upcoming events, this invalid address will cause a problem.

The problem becomes even worse when users enter invalid data, that data is put in your database, and some sort of ODBC error or ADO error is generated. Then you have to handle the database error, which adds a lot of extra code. Of course, many applications don't even handle the database errors correctly. If you surf the Internet, you can see that they don't, by the SQL errors that are displayed on many Web pages.

Data validation has two types. The first type is client-side data validation, and the second is server-side data validation. Both are valuable techniques, and they both have their place.

Client-side validation happens inside the browser. Before a form is submitted back to the server, a piece of client-side script looks at the data and decides whether it is valid. Before the release of ASP.NET, the developer would write the JavaScript, which had to evaluate the data to ensure it was correctly evaluated. For years, developers have been writing such script as they create robust Web applications. Unfortunately, though, they end up writing the same code over and over and over again, which is a very inefficient way to go about developing Web applications. Now you might say, "Well, they can simply reuse the same code as they create new forms that need data to be validated." Yes, that is true, but many times the code must be altered for a slightly different situation. To be able to do this without having to drop down and write some JavaScript code that validates data would be much nicer.

And as a matter of fact, the ASP.NET validation controls automatically generate the client-side JavaScript code that does data validation. Developers don't even have to think about JavaScript; all they have to do is set the ASP.NET data-validation-control properties to validate the data in the way that they want.

The other type of data validation is **server-side validation**. With server-side validation, data validation code is executed on the server. For server-side data validation to be accomplished, the form must be submitted to the server first. Then the code is executed on the server side for validation. Server-side validation is not a new thing—it is being done every day in most Web applications. Forms are submitted; some code looks at the data; and then a decision is made about whether or not the data is valid. If the data is valid, the form continues to be processed. But for each Web application, a developer must decide how invalid data is to be handled and how to notify the user that the data has some sort of error. As in the client-side validation, a lot of duplicated work goes on here. Developers tend to reinvent the wheel over and over and over again. Even though they might be able to copy code they have used in the past into their new projects, they still end up doing work they could avoid if there were some easy and unified way to take care of server-side data validation.

It is important to note that a good application needs both client-side and server-side data validation. On the client side, you want to make sure that data is valid before the form is submitted to the server—that the client-side code catches the error in the data before the form is submitted. This insurance cuts down on the amount of traffic to and from the server. But a client-side-only approach has some inherent problems. One problem might be that users could figure out how to get around the problem. They might even create their own form code and submit code to your server side that defeats your entire data-validation scheme. So you should use both client-side and server-side data validation, to ensure that the data you get is valid. Any client-side validation should be duplicated on the server. The only reason to do client-side validation is to save round trips (to cover the 99.9 percent of the cases). For the other 0.1 percent, those who have malicious intent, server-side validation is also required

RequiredFieldValidator

What if I just want to make sure that users have typed something in the editable text field? To evaluate whether their names are actually valid names is going to be difficult. But I do want to make sure they have at least typed something in. For these situations, ASP.NET provides the Required-FieldValidator control. To use this control for my application, all I do is drag it from the Toolbox onto the form, then edit its properties so that the `ControlToValidate` property is set to the Web Forms control that must be validated.

If I run my application now, and I submit with nothing in the editable field, I get a message in red text saying `RequiredFieldValidator`. If I type something in the editable field, then I do not get that message. Actually, for this message to come up with the text `RequiredFieldValidator` to alert the user of some sort of an error is not very user friendly. Instead, I should edit the ErrorMessage field so the user gets something a lot more meaningful. If I take a look at the RequiredFieldValidator's properties, I will see an `ErrorMessage` property. To change the ErrorMessage, I simply edit this to something that is more suitable to my application. Now, when I run my application and don't have anything in the editable field, I see a more user-friendly message.

You should pay attention to one other very important property for these validation controls. That property is the `Display` property, which indicates whether the ErrorMessage of the control should occupy space when it is not visible. ASP.NET also gives you further control so that you can determine from anywhere in your ASP code whether the fields in your page are valid. The `Page` class maintains a list of all the validation controls. Each validation control implements its own interface that does the validation. But the most important of these interfaces is the `IsValid` property. The `IsValid` property determines the validity of any given validator control on the page. When you look at the page's `IsValid` property, it returns `True` if all fields on the page are valid and `False` if any are invalid. This property gives you a great way to programmatically determine whether any of the fields are invalid. Doing this might be important so that you can catch data-validation errors even before the validation controls take over and display warnings or error messages to the user. The following code shows how easy it is to determine whether the validation controls in a page are valid:

C#
```
if( IsValid )
{
    Label2.Text = "Page fields are all valid.";
}
else
{
    Label2.Text = "Page fields are not all valid.";
}
```

VB
```
If IsValid Then
    Label2.Text = "Page fields are all valid."
Else
    Label2.Text = "Page fields are not all valid."
End If
```

Server-side data validation occurs during a post-back sequence. The validation is done immediately before the page load event is fired. But client-side validation is normally used because it is always implemented on up-level browsers. That is, if a Web Form validation control detects that a browser is capable of handling the JavaScript code necessary for client-side validation, the HTML that is emitted will contain the client-side validation.

Other Validation Controls

ASP.NET offers more validation controls than the one we have already talked about, the RequiredFieldValidator. It offers in addition the ValidationSummary, the CompareValidator, the RangeValidator, the RegularExpressionValidator, and the CustomValidator controls. The ValidationSummary control is used to display a summary of all the ErrorMessages on a given form. So if you want to somehow summarize for the user the data-validation errors that have occurred in a form, you could use the ValidationSummary control. The CompareValidator control is used to compare the value of one field to another field. The RangeValidator control is used to verify that the field value falls within a given range. For instance, if you are asking a user for some sort of number that falls between the values of 5 and 25, the RangeValidator control verifies that the value the user typed is truly in this range. The RegularExpressionValidator might be the most powerful of all validation controls. This control can use regular expressions to verify the contents of a field. And last, the CustomValidator control is used to build your own validation algorithm on the client side, in case even regular expressions are not enough.

The Resumé Application

It's time to turn our attention to the Resumé application. Its purpose is to illustrate how to effectively use Web Forms to create applications. I have used this program in my classes for this very purpose, and it never fails that students want to go on and add lots of nice features and extras. If I allowed this to happen for my presentation in this chapter, the Resumé application would suddenly be complicated, and it wouldn't illustrate the use of Web Forms as well because of the added complexities the cool extras would create.

Suffice it to say that you can easily extend the Resumé application for your own purposes. A section at the end of the chapter offers suggestions for making useful modifications. But in our examples, we'll keep things manageable in the name of learning.

Database Schema

Before we get too far, the database schema must be revealed. It's pretty simple—there are five tables. A description of the tables follows.

The Login Table

The Login table contains the user's login name, password, and user ID. The schema for the Resumé Login table can be seen in Figure 2.4:

The PersonalInfo Table

The PersonalInfo table contains personal information, such as mailing address and phone number. The schema for this table can be seen in Figure 2.5.

The EducationInfo Table

The EducationInfo table contains information relating to an individual's education. The schema for this table can be seen in Figure 2.6.

The SkillsInfo Table

The SkillsInfo table contains information relating to an individual's skillset. The SkillsInfo table schema can be seen in Figure 2.7.

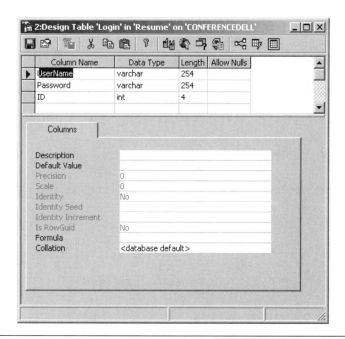

Figure 2.4 The Resumé.Login Table

Figure 2.5 The Resumé.PersonalInfo Table

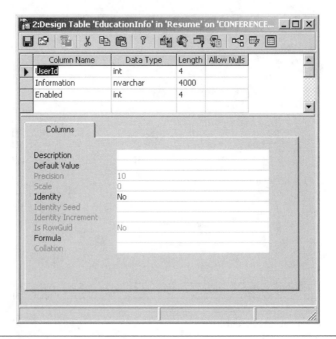

Figure 2.6 The Resumé.EducationInfo Table

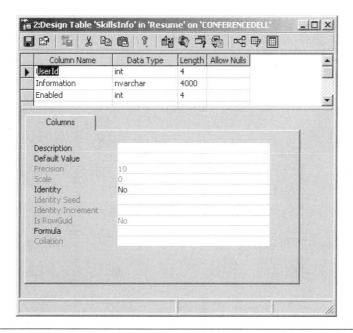

Figure 2.7 The Resumé.SkillsInfo Table

The WorkInfo Table

The WorkInfo table contains information relating to an individual's work history. The schema for this table can be seen in Figure 2.8.

The Program in Action

The Resumé program has several distinct screens in which it performs various tasks. In this section, I introduce the major screens and talk about what they do.

The Main Screen

The main screen lets users search for a resumé, or log in and edit their resumés. If they don't have a login name or user ID, they can select the "I am a new user" checkbox, and a new record will be created. You can see the main screen in Figure 2.9. The file name for this screen is default.aspx.

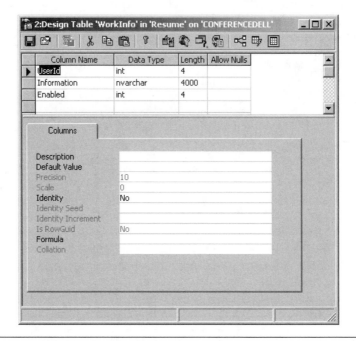

Figure 2.8 The Resumé.WorkInfo Table

The Editing Screen

Resumés can be edited from the screen that the Edit.aspx file contains. Users can enter information into any of four sections: Personal, Education, Work, and Skills. A CheckBox exists for each of these sections, and if the box is not selected for any given section, that section's information won't appear in the displayed resumé. You can see the editing screen in Figure 2.10.

The Viewing Screen

The screen that actually displays resumés (as opposed to allowing them to be edited) is contained in View.aspx. This screen takes resumé information from the database and renders it to the screen for viewing. A rendered resumé can be seen in Figure 2.11.

The Search Results Screen

A simple screen contained in Search.aspx displays any results for a user's search. The results can be displayed via hyperlinks that are displayed in this page.

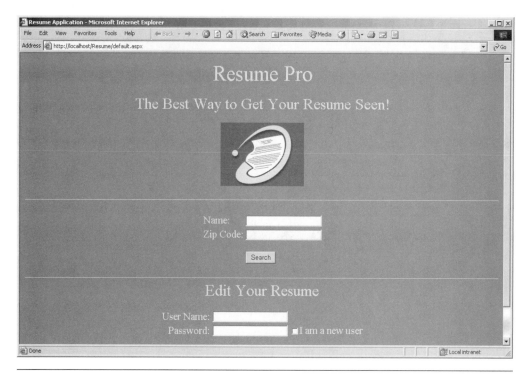

Figure 2.9 The Main Screen Lets You Search, or Log In to Edit a Resumé.

Code Listings and Explanations

This section contains the code listings for the Resumé application. Each code listing is explained so that you can fully understand how it works.

The default.aspx.cs Code

Users can do three things from the main application screen: search, create a new user login and then edit a resumé, or enter a valid name and password and then edit a resumé. The code you see in Listing 2.5 is called when users with existing credentials want to edit their resumé.

The DoLogin() method shown in Listing 2.5 first creates a connection to the database by creating a SqlConnection object. The connection string isn't shown because it is contained in the Global.asax file. Keeping the connection string in a central location means that when it's changed, only one place must be edited. Having to search through all your code to change

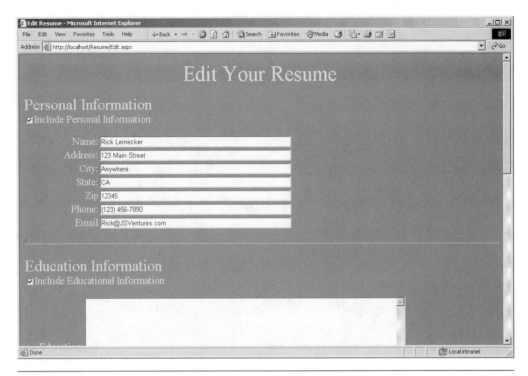

Figure 2.10 The Resumé Is Edited from Edit.aspx.

a connection string is a lot of extra work and could cause bugs if any occurrences are missed. The following line shows the connection string that's being used in the Resumé application:

```
Application["DBConnectString"] =
    "server=localhost;uid=sa;pwd=;database=Resume";
```

A try/catch construct will manage any errors that happen as a result of the database access. All of the database-related classes throw exceptions when something goes wrong.

Inside of the try, the connection is opened, a SQL string is formed, and the SQL is executed with the `ExecuteReader()` method. This method returns a recordset in the form of a `SqlDataReader` class.

If a record was found as a result of the query, then the `reader.Read()` method will return the value `true`. The `bFound` flag will be set to `true` so that the code knows that a match for the specified user name

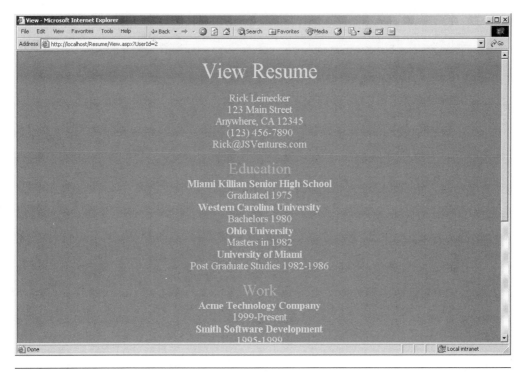

Figure 2.11 The Resumé Is Shown from View.aspx.

was found. The password that was typed in is then compared with what is in the recordset, and if they match, the resumé can be edited.

If the user name wasn't found or the password was incorrect, the user will be notified of the error. This is done by a string assigned to the Login-Message Label object. Putting text in a Label object couldn't be easier. All you must do is set the `Text` property to the text that you want contained in the Label.

Listing 2.5 This Code Logs In an Existing User.

```
private void DoLogin()
{

    SqlConnection myConnection =
        new SqlConnection(
            Convert.ToString( Application["DBConnectString"] ) );
```

```
try
{
    myConnection.Open();
    SqlCommand myCommand;

    string strSql = "select * from Login where UserName='" +
        UserName.Text.Trim() + "'";
    myCommand  = new SqlCommand( strSql, myConnection );
    SqlDataReader reader = myCommand.ExecuteReader();

    bool bFound = false;
    string strPassword = "";
    int nID = 0;

    if( reader.Read() )
    {
        bFound = true;
        strPassword =
          Convert.ToString( reader["Password"]).ToUpper();

        nID = reader.GetInt32( 2 );
    }

    reader.Close();
    if( !bFound )
    {
        LoginMessage.Text = "User name not found.";
    }
    else if( strPassword != Password.Text.ToUpper() )
    {
        LoginMessage.Text = "The password is incorrect.";
    }
    else
    {
        Session["UserID"] = nID;
        Response.Redirect( "Edit.aspx" );
    }
}
catch( Exception ex )
{
    LoginMessage.Text = ex.Message.ToString();
}
finally
```

```
    {
        if( myConnection.State == ConnectionState.Open )
        {
            myConnection.Close();
        }
    }
}
```

The code in Listing 2.6 (which follows) that creates a new user record has some similarities to the code that finds a match for a user and password, which you just looked at in Listing 2.5. You'll notice the same SqlConnection object that's created, and the same call to the Open() method. The code includes a query to see whether the user name is in the database, to void duplicate user names. All of this is similar to what you've already seen.

The code in Listing 2.6 differs significantly in that once it has been established that the user name in the UserName TextField object is unique, the remainder of the code is intended to create new records in the database tables.

This code is a little more complicated than I had intended. That's because I'm using a SqlTransaction object in case an error occurs along the way. The SqlTransaction object either commits all the database operations in a transaction, or it rolls them all back. The action is all or nothing, and if something goes wrong, none of the operations are committed.

You see, if one of the records isn't created in the one of the tables, such as in the SkillsInfo table, then when a user goes to edit or view the table, a database error will occur because part of the data will not be available. And it's better to catch the problem here than later on.

I originally didn't have this code in place, but one of my students was getting errors and asked that we add transactions. Because I couldn't give him a good reason to avoid using a transaction object (how would it sound to say I just didn't want to go to the effort?), I added the transactional support. The student works for a Fortune 500 bank, and I guess not having transactional support goes against his very nature. We'll talk more about ADO.NET in Chapter 3, so you'll get this transaction code for now without much explanation.

Most of the database tables have default values. For this reason, the code to add records to the tables is simple—it simply inserts the user ID and lets the default values be used for the other fields. For the Login table, though, the user name and password are inserted so that the user can log in later on.

There is one more interesting thing regarding the creation of the Login table record. The ID field in this table is an Identity field. That means the database will automatically create a unique value for this field. This value is then used by the program to uniquely identify a resumé and all its related data. For this reason, getting the ID value immediately after the record is created is important.

It is common to perform a query immediately after the initial record creation, to retrieve the value of an identity column. But this approach requires extra code and one more trip to the database. A mechanism exists by which you can get an identity value back, and that mechanism can be seen in this code (which is extracted from Listing 2.6 below):

```
myTransaction = myConnection.BeginTransaction(
IsolationLevel.ReadCommitted, "NewUser" );
strSql = "insert into Login (UserName,Password) VALUES ('" +
UserName.Text.Trim() + "','" +
    Password.Text.Trim() + "') select @ID = @@IDENTITY";
myCommand  = new SqlCommand( strSql, myConnection, myTransaction );
myCommand.Parameters.Add( "@ID", SqlDbType.Int );
myCommand.Parameters["@ID"].Direction = ParameterDirection.Output;
myCommand.ExecuteNonQuery();
```

We will go into more detail about command parameters in Chapter 3.

You can also see in Listing 2.6 where the transaction is committed. This event occurs only if no exceptions are thrown. You can also see where a session variable is set to contain the ID value. We cover application and session variables in more detail in Chapter 7.

Listing 2.6 This Code Creates New User Records.

```
private void CreateNewUserAndDoLogin()
{

    SqlConnection myConnection =
        new SqlConnection(
            Convert.ToString( Application["DBConnectString"] ) );
    SqlCommand myCommand;
    SqlTransaction myTransaction = null;

    try
    {
```

```
myConnection.Open();

string strSql = "select * from Login where UserName='" +
    UserName.Text.Trim() + "'";
myCommand  = new SqlCommand( strSql, myConnection );
SqlDataReader reader = myCommand.ExecuteReader();

bool bFound = false;

if( reader.Read() )
{
    bFound = true;
}

reader.Close();

if( bFound )
{
    LoginMessage.Text =
        "The user name you chose already exists.";
    myConnection.Close();
    return;
}

myTransaction =
    myConnection.BeginTransaction( IsolationLevel.ReadCommitted,
        "NewUser" );
strSql = "insert into Login (UserName,Password) VALUES ('" +
    UserName.Text.Trim() + "','" +
    Password.Text.Trim() + "') select @ID = @@IDENTITY";
myCommand  =
    new SqlCommand( strSql, myConnection, myTransaction );
myCommand.Parameters.Add( "@ID", SqlDbType.Int );
myCommand.Parameters["@ID"].Direction =
    ParameterDirection.Output;
myCommand.ExecuteNonQuery();

int nID = Convert.ToInt32( myCommand.Parameters["@ID"].Value );

myCommand =
  new SqlCommand( "insert into PersonalInfo (UserID) VALUES (" +
  Convert.ToString( nID ) +
      ")", myConnection, myTransaction );
```

```
            myCommand.ExecuteNonQuery();
            myCommand =
             new SqlCommand( "insert into EducationInfo (UserID) VALUES (" +
                 Convert.ToString( nID ) +
                 ")", myConnection, myTransaction );
            myCommand.ExecuteNonQuery();
            myCommand =
               new SqlCommand( "insert into WorkInfo (UserID) VALUES (" +
                 Convert.ToString( nID ) +
                 ")", myConnection, myTransaction );
            myCommand.ExecuteNonQuery();
            myCommand =
               new SqlCommand( "insert into SkillsInfo (UserID) VALUES (" +
                 Convert.ToString( nID ) +
                 ")", myConnection, myTransaction );
            myCommand.ExecuteNonQuery();

            myTransaction.Commit();

            Session["UserID"] = nID;
            Response.Redirect( "Edit.aspx" );
        }
        catch( Exception ex )
        {
            LoginMessage.Text = ex.Message.ToString();

            if( myTransaction != null )
            {
                myTransaction.Rollback();
            }
        }
        finally
        {
            if( myConnection.State == ConnectionState.Open )
            {
                myConnection.Close();
            }
        }
    }
```

When a user clicks the Edit button from the main screen, a button handler is fired. The handler takes a look at the NewUser CheckBox object. If the box is checked, the `CreateNewUserAndDoLogin()` method is called; otherwise, the `DoLogin()` method is called, as shown in Listing 2.7.

Listing 2.7 This Code Is for the Button Event-Handler Method Called from default.aspx When the User Clicks the Edit Button.

```
private void LoginButton_Click(object sender, System.EventArgs e)
{

    if( NewUser.Checked )
    {
        CreateNewUserAndDoLogin();
    }
    else
    {
        DoLogin();
    }
}
```

The Edit.aspx.cs Code

The Resumé editing page is fairly straightforward. The process begins by loading the data for a user's resumé and putting that data into TextField objects with which the user can edit the resumé. After the user is done editing, she clicks on the OK button to save to edited information. The data is then saved back to the database.

Listing 2.8 shows the method that loads a user's personal information and places it into the correct TextField objects.

Listing 2.8 This Method Loads Personal Information to Be Edited for a User.

```
private void LoadPersonalInfo( SqlConnection myConnection )
{
    string strSql = "select * from PersonalInfo where UserID=" +
        Convert.ToString( Session["UserID"] );
    SqlCommand myCommand = new SqlCommand( strSql, myConnection );
    SqlDataReader reader = myCommand.ExecuteReader();
```

```
if( reader.Read() )
{
    Name.Text = reader.GetString("Name" );
    Address.Text = reader.GetString("Address" );
    City.Text = reader.GetString("City" );
    State.Text = reader.GetString("State" );
    Zip.Text = reader.GetString( "Zip" );
    Phone.Text = reader.GetString("Phone" );
    Email.Text = reader.GetString("Email" );
    if( reader.GetInt32( 9 ) == 0 )
    {
        IncludePersonal.Checked = false;
    }
}


reader.Close();
}
```

Listing 2.9 shows three methods, each of which loads a different category of information: education, work, and skills. If the database flag that indicates whether the category is enabled is set to a value of 1, the data is placed into the TextField object with which the user can edit the data.

Listing 2.9 These Methods Load Education, Work, and Skills Information for a User so That Information Can Be Edited.

```
private void LoadEducationInfo( SqlConnection myConnection )
{
    string strSql = "select * from EducationInfo where UserID='" +
        Convert.ToString( Session["UserID"] )  + "'";
    SqlCommand myCommand = new SqlCommand( strSql, myConnection );
    SqlDataReader reader = myCommand.ExecuteReader();

    if( reader.Read() )
    {
        Education.Text = reader.GetString( 1 );
        if( reader.GetInt32( 2 ) == 0 )
        {
            IncludeEducation.Checked = false;
        }
    }
```

```
        reader.Close();
}


private void LoadWorkInfo( SqlConnection myConnection )
{
    string strSql = "select * from WorkInfo where UserID='" +
        Convert.ToString( Session["UserID"] )  + "'";
    SqlCommand myCommand = new SqlCommand( strSql, myConnection );
    SqlDataReader reader = myCommand.ExecuteReader();

    if( reader.Read() )
    {
        Work.Text = reader.GetString( 1 );
        if( reader.GetInt32( 2 ) == 0 )
        {
            IncludeWork.Checked = false;
        }
    }

    reader.Close();
}


private void LoadSkillsInfo( SqlConnection myConnection )
{
    string strSql = "select * from SkillsInfo where UserID='" +
        Convert.ToString( Session["UserID"] )  + "'";
    SqlCommand myCommand = new SqlCommand( strSql, myConnection );
    SqlDataReader reader = myCommand.ExecuteReader();

    if( reader.Read() )
    {
        Skills.Text = reader.GetString( 1 );
        if( reader.GetInt32( 2 ) == 0 )
        {
            IncludeSkills.Checked = false;
        }
    }

    reader.Close();
}
```

When the Edit.aspx page is first loaded, the `Page.Load` event is fired and calls each of the methods that load resumé data and populate the Web Forms objects. This code can be seen in Listing 2.10. The code shows creating and opening a connection, calling the four methods to retrieve data, and closing the connection. All exceptions are caught in the `Page_Load()` method, not in the separate data-retrieval methods.

Listing 2.10 This Method Responds to the `Page.Load` Event.

```
private void Page_Load(object sender, System.EventArgs e)
{
    if( !IsPostBack )
    {
        try
        {
            SqlConnection myConnection =
                new SqlConnection(
                    Convert.ToString( Application["DBConnectString"] ) );
            myConnection.Open();
            LoadPersonalInfo( myConnection );
            LoadEducationInfo( myConnection );
            LoadSkillsInfo( myConnection );
            LoadWorkInfo( myConnection );
            myConnection.Close();
        }
        catch( Exception ex )
        {
            ErrorLabel.Text = ex.Message.ToString();
        }
    }

}
```

Personal information is saved with a single SQL update statement, as shown in Listing 2.11. You create the SQL statement is created by concatenating the data that's in the TextField objects.

Listing 2.11 This Method Saves Personal Information for a User after It Has Been Edited.

```
private void SavePersonalInfo( SqlConnection myConnection )
{
    int nUseIt = 1;
```

```
if( !IncludePersonal.Checked )
{
    nUseIt = 0;
}

string strSql = "update PersonalInfo set Name='" + Name.Text +
    "',Address='" + Address.Text +
    "',City='" + City.Text +
    "',State='" + State.Text +
    "',Zip='" + Zip.Text +
    "',Phone='" + Phone.Text +
    "',Email='" + Email.Text +
    "',Enabled=" + Convert.ToString( nUseIt ) +
    " where UserId=" + Convert.ToString( Session["UserID"] );

SqlCommand myCommand = new SqlCommand( strSql, myConnection );
myCommand.ExecuteNonQuery();
}
```

Listing 2.12 shows the three methods that save the education, work, and skills data to the database. None of these methods is catching exceptions; rather, the code that calls the method is doing so.

Listing 2.12 These Methods Save Education, Work, and Skills Information After It Has Been Edited.

```
private void SaveEducationInfo( SqlConnection myConnection )
{
    int nUseIt = 1;
    if( !IncludeEducation.Checked )
    {
        nUseIt = 0;
    }

    string strSql = "update EducationInfo set Information='" +
        Education.Text +
        "',Enabled=" + Convert.ToString( nUseIt ) +
        " where UserId=" + Convert.ToString( Session["UserID"] );

    SqlCommand myCommand = new SqlCommand( strSql, myConnection );
    myCommand.ExecuteNonQuery();
}
```

```
private void SaveWorkInfo( SqlConnection myConnection )
{
    int nUseIt = 1;
    if( !IncludeWork.Checked )
    {
        nUseIt = 0;
    }

    string strSql = "update WorkInfo set Information='" + Work.Text +
        "',Enabled=" + Convert.ToString( nUseIt ) +
        " where UserId=" + Convert.ToString( Session["UserID"] );

    SqlCommand myCommand = new SqlCommand( strSql, myConnection );
    myCommand.ExecuteNonQuery();
}

private void SaveSkillsInfo( SqlConnection myConnection )
{
    int nUseIt = 1;
    if( !IncludeSkills.Checked )
    {
        nUseIt = 0;
    }

    string strSql = "update SkillsInfo set Information='" +
        Skills.Text +
        "',Enabled=" + Convert.ToString( nUseIt ) +
        " where UserId=" + Convert.ToString( Session["UserID"] );

    SqlCommand myCommand = new SqlCommand( strSql, myConnection );
    myCommand.ExecuteNonQuery();
}
```

When a user clicks the OK button, an event handler is fired, as shown in Listing 2.13. This event method creates and opens a database connection, and then calls the four methods that save the resumé data.

Exceptions are caught in this method rather than in the individual data-saving methods. The Cancel button simply redirects the user back to the main page.

Listing 2.13 This Code Is for the OK Button Event Handler.

```
private void OKButton_Click(object sender, System.EventArgs e)
{
    try
    {
        SqlConnection myConnection =
            new SqlConnection(
                Convert.ToString( Application["DBConnectString"] ) );
        myConnection.Open();
        SavePersonalInfo( myConnection );
        SaveEducationInfo( myConnection );
        SaveSkillsInfo( myConnection );
        SaveWorkInfo( myConnection );
        myConnection.Close();

        Response.Redirect( "default.aspx" );
    }
    catch( Exception ex )
    {
        ErrorLabel.Text = ex.Message.ToString();
    }

}

private void CancelButton_Click(object sender, System.EventArgs e)
{
    Response.Redirect( "default.aspx" );
}
```

The Search.aspx.cs Code

The search page calls into a method named SearchResumes(), as shown in Listing 2.14. This method takes two parameters that contain the search criteria (these criteria were passed from default.aspx), forms a SQL query, executes the query, and then renders any results as selectable hyperlinks.

The parameters are retrieved with the QueryString() method. For instance, a parameter named Info can be retrieved as follows:

```
string strInfo = Convert.ToString( Request.QueryString["Info"] );
```

The SQL query can contain either one or two pieces of information—Name or Zip. Because this is true, some relatively simple code constructs the query, based on whether one or two parameters have been specified.

Once the query string has been constructed, the `ExecuteReader()` method is called. If there are any results, then the `reader.Read()` method will return `true` for each record found. Each of the records is then output to the HTML stream with a call to the `Response.Write()` method.

Listing 2.14 This Method Searches for Resumés Based on the Search Criteria.

```
public void SearchResumes()
{
    try
    {
        SqlConnection myConnection =
            new SqlConnection(
                Convert.ToString( Application["DBConnectString"] ) );

        string strName = Convert.ToString( Request.QueryString["Name"]);
        string strZip = Convert.ToString( Request.QueryString["Zip"] );

        string strSql = "select Name,UserId from PersonalInfo where ";

        bool bNeedAnd = false;
        if( strName.Length > 0 )
        {
            strSql += "Name like '%" +  strName + "%'";
            bNeedAnd = true;
        }
        if( strZip.Length > 0 )
        {
            if( bNeedAnd )
            {
                strSql += " and ";
                strSql += "Zip like '%" +  strZip + "%'";
            }
        }

        myConnection.Open();
        SqlCommand myCommand = new SqlCommand( strSql, myConnection );
        SqlDataReader reader = myCommand.ExecuteReader();
```

```
    while( reader.Read() )
    {
        Response.Write(
            "<p align=\"center\"><font color=\"yellow\">" +
            reader.GetString( 0 ) +
            "</font> <a href=\"View.aspx?UserId=" +
            Convert.ToString( reader.GetInt32( 1 ) ) +
            "\">View</a></p>" );
    }
    reader.Close();
}
catch( Exception ex )
{
    Response.Write( ex.Message.ToString() );
}
finally
{
    if( myConnection.State == ConnectionState.Open )
    {
        myConnection.Close();
    }
}
}
```

The View.aspx.cs Code

The code to view resumé information is fairly simple. A database connection is created and opened in the `Page_Load()` method, as you see in Listing 2.15. The `LoadPersonalInfo()` method (as shown in Listing 2.16) is then called, and the personal information is placed into Label objects (named Name, Address, City, State, Zip, Phone, and Email). If, however, the Enabled column in the database is set to a value of 0, this information will not be rendered.

Listing 2.17 shows the three other information retrieval methods, which retrieve the education, work, and skills data from the database for the resumé.

Listing 2.15 This Code Is Fired When the Page First Loads. The Code Then Calls the Methods That Load the Information with Which the Resumé Will Be Rendered.

```
private void Page_Load(object sender, System.EventArgs e)
{
    if( !IsPostBack )
```

```
    {
        try
        {
            SqlConnection myConnection =
                new SqlConnection(
                    Convert.ToString( Application["DBConnectString"] ) );
            myConnection.Open();
            LoadPersonalInfo( myConnection );
            LoadEducationInfo( myConnection );
            LoadSkillsInfo( myConnection );
            LoadWorkInfo( myConnection );
            myConnection.Close();
        }
        catch( Exception ex )
        {
            ErrorLabel.Text = ex.Message.ToString();
        }
    }
}
```

Listing 2.16 This Method Loads Personal Information for a User so That It Can Be Viewed.

```
private void LoadPersonalInfo( SqlConnection myConnection )
{
    string strSql = "select * from PersonalInfo where UserID=" +
        Convert.ToString( Request.QueryString["UserID"] );
    SqlCommand myCommand = new SqlCommand( strSql, myConnection );
    SqlDataReader reader = myCommand.ExecuteReader();

    if( reader.Read() )
    {
        if( reader.GetInt32( 9 ) != 0 )
        {
            Name.Text = reader.GetString( 2 ) + "<br>\r\n";
            Address.Text = reader.GetString( 3 ) + "<br>\r\n";
            City.Text = reader.GetString( 4 ) + ", ";
            State.Text = reader.GetString( 5 ) + " ";
            Zip.Text = reader.GetString( 6 ) + "<br>\r\n";
            Phone.Text = reader.GetString( 7 ) + "<br>\r\n";
            Email.Text = reader.GetString( 8 );
            EmailLabel.Text = "Send Email: <a href=\"mailto:" + _
                Email.Text +
                    "\">" + Email.Text +
```

```
            "</a>";
        }
    }
    reader.Close();
}
```

Listing 2.17 These Methods Load Education, Work, and Skills Information for a User so That Information Can Be Viewed.

```
private void LoadEducationInfo( SqlConnection myConnection )
{
    string strSql = "select * from EducationInfo where UserID='" +
        Convert.ToString( Request.QueryString["UserID"] )  + "'";
    SqlCommand myCommand = new SqlCommand( strSql, myConnection );
    SqlDataReader reader = myCommand.ExecuteReader();

    if( reader.Read() )
    {
        if( reader.GetInt32( 2 ) != 0 &&
            reader.GetString( 1 ).Length > 0 )
        {
            Education.Text =
                "<font color=\"cyan\" size=\"5\">Education</font><br>" +
                reader.GetString( 1 ).Replace( "\r\n", "<br>\r\n" );
        }
    }

    reader.Close();
}

private void LoadWorkInfo( SqlConnection myConnection )
{
    string strSql = "select * from WorkInfo where UserID='" +
        Convert.ToString( Request.QueryString["UserID"] )  + "'";
    SqlCommand myCommand = new SqlCommand( strSql, myConnection );
    SqlDataReader reader = myCommand.ExecuteReader();

    if( reader.Read() )
    {
        if( reader.GetInt32( 2 ) != 0 &&
            reader.GetString( 1 ).Length > 0 )
        {
            Work.Text =
                "<font color=\"cyan\" size=\"5\">Work</font><br>" +
```

```
                    reader.GetString( 1 ).Replace( "\r\n", "<br>\r\n" );
        }
    }

    reader.Close();
}


private void LoadSkillsInfo( SqlConnection myConnection )
{
    string strSql = "select * from SkillsInfo where UserID='" +
        Convert.ToString( Request.QueryString["UserID"] )  + "'";
    SqlCommand myCommand = new SqlCommand( strSql, myConnection );
    SqlDataReader reader = myCommand.ExecuteReader();

    if( reader.Read() )
    {
        if( reader.GetInt32( 2 ) != 0 &&
            reader.GetString( 1 ).Length > 0 )
        {
            Skills.Text =
                "<font color=\"cyan\" size=\"5\">Skills</font><br>" +
                reader.GetString( 1 ).Replace( "\r\n", "<br>\r\n" );
        }
    }

    reader.Close();
}
```

Extending and Modifying the Resumé Application

The Resumé application begs to be extended. My students always make
suggestions for ways to improve the application and make it better. Here
are some suggestions that you might want to try:

- Let users select background colors for resumé rendering.
- Let users select background images for resumé rendering.
- Add additional information categories, such as memberships and
  publications.
- Offer formatting options such as bold and italic for the content.
- Offer more advanced searches, especially in the skills category.

Deploying the Resumé Application

You must follow a few steps to deploy the Resumé application on your server.

1. Start by creating a database named `Resume`.
2. Then restore the database, which you can obtain from the ASP-NetSolutions.com Web site. (The Web page with a link to this download is www.ASPNET-Solutions.com/Chapter_2.htm.)
3. Next, run Visual Studio .NET. Create a project on the server named Resume for a C# project, or ResumeVB for a VB project. You'll have to make sure you select the appropriate (C# or VB) type of ASP.NET project.
4. Compile the application once you have created it.
5. Close the project in Visual Studio .NET. Not doing so will create a sharing violation for the next steps.
6. Make sure you have downloaded the zipped projects from the Web site.
7. Unzip the projects (the Resume/ResumeVB applications) into the default Web site directory (usually c:\inetpub\wwwroot). You will be asked if you want to overwrite existing directories—answer Yes.
8. Open the application project.
9. Check the Global.asax file to make sure that the database connection string matches the connection string for your situation.
10. Compile the Global.asax file.

Your Resumé application should now be ready to use, and ready to modify as you see fit.

Summary

The Resumé application is a good example of how you can create useful applications with Web Forms. The application is not overly complex, so it should be easy to understand. Its simplicity also provides opportunity for expansion.

Web Forms offer a unifying programming model for any developer using Visual Studio and the .NET platform. Using this model will reduce future software development costs.

CHAPTER 3

Effective Use of ADO.NET: Creating a Survey Application

In This Chapter:

- ADO.NET Overview
- The Survey Application
- Extending and Modifying the Survey Application
- Deploying the Survey Application

This chapter talks about effectively using ADO.NET. I'll spend the first part of the chapter introducing ADO.NET, mostly how it relates to the SQL Server managed provider. In the second half of the chapter, I'll walk you through a Survey application that was built using ADO.NET, and which focuses on a number of best practices along with some recommended design patterns.

Because this is an odd-numbered chapter, the featured program's (the Survey application's) source code is shown in VB.NET (VB). For the full C#.NET (C#) source code, just go to www.ASPNET-Solutions.com, follow the links to the examples for Chapter 3, and download the C# source code. (You can also download the VB.NET source code from a link on the same page.)

I have included a section toward the end of the chapter named "Extending and Modifying the Survey Application." In this section, I talk about ways to enhance the application so that it's even more useful. I'll post any changes I make to the Survey application (including these suggestions) on the Web site. Check for them on the Chapter 3 page. The site also includes a forum for discussion about the Survey application. And if you want to send me your modifications, I'll gladly post them for other users.

ADO.NET Overview

Before you can use ADO.NET components, the appropriate namespaces must be included. The System.Data namespace always needs to be included because it contains the core database components. Next, depending on the source of your data, one of two namespaces needs to be included. For a direct SQL Server connection, the System.Data.SqlClient namespace should be used for best performance. For all other connection types, such as Access and Oracle, the System.Data.OleDb namespace is required. (An Oracle provider is now available at http://msdn.microsoft.com/downloads/default.asp?url=/downloads/sample.asp?url=/msdn-files/027/001/940/msdncompositedoc.xml.)

The SqlClient data provider is fast. It's faster than the Oracle provider, and faster than accessing a database via the OleDb layer. It's faster because it accesses the native library (which automatically gives you better performance), and it was written with lots of help from the SQL Server team (who helped with the optimizations).

Managed Providers

Managed providers are a central part of the ADO.NET framework. Managed providers enable you to write language-independent components that can be called from C# and VB. Currently, managed providers come in two types: one for direct access to Microsoft SQL Server 7.0 and higher, and one for accessing data via an OLE DB layer. Both types use similar naming conventions, with the only difference being their prefixes.

The managed provider classes include `Connection` (`SqlConnection` class), `Command` (`SqlCommand` class), `DataReader` (`SqlDataReader` class), and `DataAdapter` (`SqlDataAdapter` class). The first two classes provide the same functionality that was found in ADO: creating a connection to a data source and then executing a command. A data reader has a close resemblance to a read-only, forward-only recordset that is very optimized. Last, the DataAdapter allows for the retrieval and saving of data between a DataSet and the data source. The DataSet is covered in Chapter 4.

Connection

To create a database connection, you need to include the appropriate namespaces in your application. This requires the data provider to be known, so either a SqlClient or OleDb namespace connection can be included for the best performance. The following code samples (Listings 3.1 and 3.2) show how both SqlClient and OleDb connections are made in C# and VB.

Listing 3.1 Using the SqlConnection Object

C#
```
SqlConnection myConnection   =
      new SqlConnection( "server=localhost;uid=sa;pwd=;database=pubs" );
myConnection.Open();
// Do Something with myConnection.
myConnection.Close();
```

VB
```
Dim myConnection As New
SqlConnection("server=localhost;uid=sa;pwd=;database=pubs")
myConnection.Open()
' Do something with myConnection.
myConnection.Close()
```

Listing 3.2 Using the OleDbConnection Object

C#
```
OleDbConnection myConnection =
  new OleDbConnection("Provider=SQLOLEDB.1;" +
    "Data Source=localhost;uid=sa;pwd=;Initial Catalog=pubs" );
myConnection.Open();
// Do something the myConnection.
myConnection.Close();
```

VB
```
Dim myConnection As New _
    OleDbConnection("Provider=SQLOLEDB.1;Data " + _
    "Source=localhost;uid=sa;pwd=;Initial Catalog=pubs")
myConnection.Open()
' Do something the myConnection.
myConnection.Close()
```

RECOMMENDED PRACTICE: The above connection strings are hard-coded into the source code. If at any time you need to change the connect strings (such as when the database server changes), you'll need to change the connection strings. If the connection strings are scattered all over the code, changing them will be difficult, and there's a chance you'll miss one.

The usual recommended practice is to store the connection string in the Web.config file that I discuss in detail in Chapter 7 in the section entitled "Retrieving the `Database Connection` String from Web.config." For this application, though, I use an application variable and initialize it in the Global. asax file. I chose to do it this way to give you an example of another way to store a connection string. The following code shows how to initialize an application variable in a Global.asax file:

C#
```
protected void Application_Start(Object sender,
    EventArgs e)
{
    Application["DBConnectionString"] =
      "server=localhost;uid=sa;pwd=;database=Survey";
}
```

VB
```
Sub Application_Start(ByVal sender As Object, _
    ByVal e As EventArgs)
    Application("DBConnectionString") = _
      "server=localhost;uid=sa;pwd=;database=Survey"
End Sub
```

Both managed provider connection strings look similar. In fact, the OleDb connection string is exactly the same as its predecessor in ADO, which should be obvious if you are familiar with programming in ADO. Now look at the differences. The SQL Server managed provider uses the private protocol called **tabular data stream** that is designed to work with SQL Server 7.0 and later. It does not use OLE DB, ADO, or ODBC. You can use an OleDb connection to SQL Server, but if you do, you will see performance degradation. The SQL Server connection also supports a variety of connection string keywords. Table 3.1 shows the OLE DB providers that are available in ADO.NET.

Command

The Command object allows direct interaction with the data through the database connection. The example shown in Listing 3.3 returns all rows from the Publishers table in Microsoft's Pubs database and loads them into a SqlDataReader using the Command object's ExecuteReader() method. The SqlDataReader enables the information to be accessed and processed accordingly.

Table 3.1 OLE DB Providers

Driver	Provider
SQLOLEDB	SQL OLE DB Provider (for SQL Server 6.5 and earlier)
MSDAORA	Oracle OLE DB Provider
JOLT	Jet OLE DB Provider

Listing 3.3 Using the Command Object

C#

```csharp
SqlConnection myConnection  =
new SqlConnection( "server=localhost;uid=sa;pwd=;database=pubs" );
SqlCommand myCommand = new SqlCommand( "SELECT * FROM Publishers",
myConnection );

myConnection.Open();
myReader = myCommand.ExecuteReader();

while( myReader.Read() )
{
  // Do something with the data.
}

myReader.Close();
myConnection.Close();
```

VB

```vb
Dim myConnection as new
SqlConnection("server=localhost;uid=sa;pwd=;database=pubs")
Dim myCommand as new _
  SqlCommand("SELECT * FROM Publishers", myConnection)

myConnection.Open()
myReader = myCommand.ExecuteReader()

While myReader.Read()
  // Do something with the data.
End While

myReader.Close()
myConnection.Close()
```

In the example, the System.Data and System.Data.SqlClient namespaces must be included to get the correct SQL methods. Next, a SqlConnection is created to the Pubs database. A SQL SELECT statement and the reference to the Connection object are passed as SqlCommand parameters. The last declaration is a SqlDataReader that allows processing of the data fetched from the database. Finally, the connection and SqlDataReader are closed.

The example shown uses the SQL managed provider. However, if a connection to another database is required and the connection is using the OLE DB provider, then simply change the SQL command references to OleDb commands, and the remaining code will be the same.

RECOMMENDED PRACTICE: Garbage collection is non-deterministic. For this reason, you should always close ADO.NET objects, such as the SqlDataReader.

The best way to do that is in the `finally` block of a `try/catch/finally` construct, as follows:

```
// Declare objects here.
try
{
  // Open objects and use them here.
}
catch
{
}
finally
{
  // If objects are open here, close them.
}
```

DataReader

The DataReader object provides an easy and efficient way to parse a series of records, or even one record. The DataReader object behaves as a read-only, forward-only stream returned from the database, and only one record at a time is ever in memory. However, the DataReader object is not intended to handle large, complex relationships between tables and records, nor does it have the capability to pass data back to a database—a responsibility best left to the DataSet and DataRelation objects. In the previous example, the SqlDataReader was used to contain the data returned from the server.

In this example, shown in Listing 3.4, I've expanded the code to display all the data from the Authors table.

Listing 3.4 Displaying Data from the Authors Table

C#

```
SqlConnectiion myConnection = new SqlConnection("server=localhost;
uid=sa;pwd=;database=pubs" );
SqlCommand myCommand = null;
SqlDataReader myReader = null;
SqlDataReader myReader = null;

try
{
  myConnection.Open();
  myReader = myCommand.ExecuteReader();
  myCommand =  new SqlCommand( "SELECT * FROM Authors ",
    myConnection );

  Response.Write( "<table border=1>" );
  while( myReader.Read() )
  {
    Response.Write("<tr>");
    for( int i=0; i<myReader.FieldCount; i++ )
    {
      Response.Write( "<td>" + myReader[i].ToString() + "</td>" );
      Response.Write( "</tr>" );
    }
  }
  Response.Write( "</table>" );
}
catch
{
}
finally
{

  if ( myReader != null )
  {
    myReader.Close();
  }
  if( myConnection.State == ConnectionState.Open )
```

```
    {
      myConnection.Close();
    }
    }
}
```

VB

```
Dim myConnection as new _
  SqlConnection("server=localhost;uid=sa;pwd=;database=pubs" )
Dim myCommand as new _
  SqlCommand( "SELECT * FROM Authors ", myConnection )
Dim myReader As SqlDataReader = nothing

Try
  myConnection.Open()
  MyReader = myCommand.ExecuteReader()

  Response.Write( "<table border=1>" )
  While myReader.Read()
    Response.Write("<tr>")
    Dim i as Integer
    For i=0 To MyReader.FieldCount-1
      Response.Write( "<td>" + myReader(i).ToString() + "</td>" )
      Response.Write( "</tr>" )
    Next
  End While
  Response.Write( "</table>" )
Catch
Finally
  If myReader <> nothing Then     myReader.Close()
  End If
  If myConnection.State = ConnectionState.Open Then
    myConnection.Close()
  End If
End Try
```

The output of this example can be seen in Figure 3.1, which creates an HTML table for displaying the data. From the code, you will first notice the MoveNext () method is not part of the while loop for the SqlDataReader. The SqlDataReader's Read() method automatically advances the cursor and initially sets the cursor to the beginning of the data. To create the table dynamically, we use the FieldCount property of the DataReader to deter-

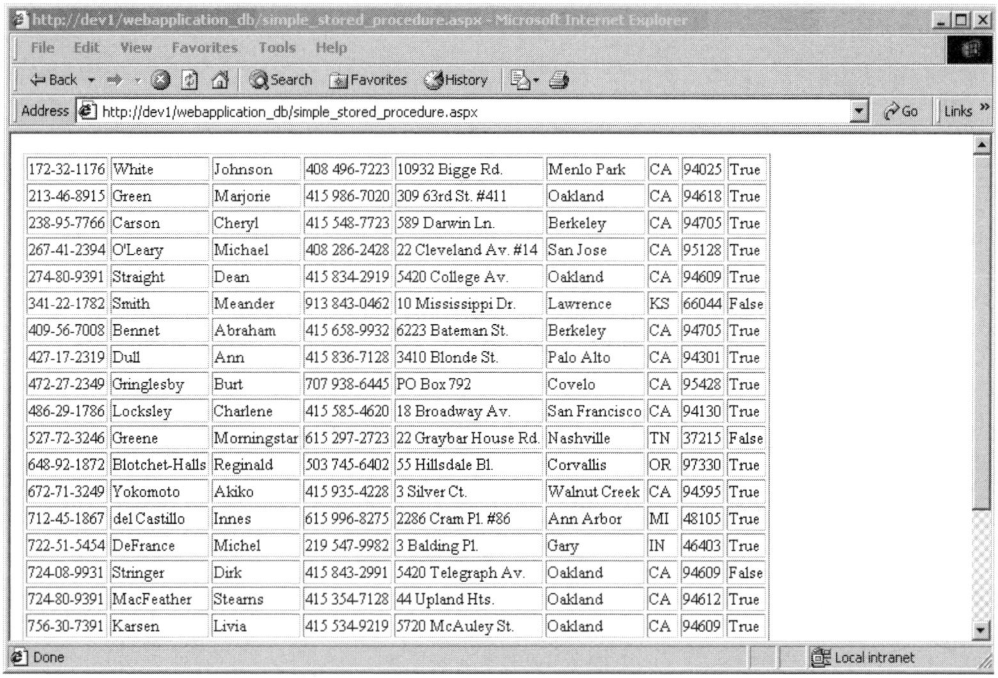

172-32-1176	White	Johnson	408 496-7223	10932 Bigge Rd.	Menlo Park	CA	94025	True
213-46-8915	Green	Marjorie	415 986-7020	309 63rd St. #411	Oakland	CA	94618	True
238-95-7766	Carson	Cheryl	415 548-7723	589 Darwin Ln.	Berkeley	CA	94705	True
267-41-2394	O'Leary	Michael	408 286-2428	22 Cleveland Av. #14	San Jose	CA	95128	True
274-80-9391	Straight	Dean	415 834-2919	5420 College Av.	Oakland	CA	94609	True
341-22-1782	Smith	Meander	913 843-0462	10 Mississippi Dr.	Lawrence	KS	66044	False
409-56-7008	Bennet	Abraham	415 658-9932	6223 Bateman St.	Berkeley	CA	94705	True
427-17-2319	Dull	Ann	415 836-7128	3410 Blonde St.	Palo Alto	CA	94301	True
472-27-2349	Gringlesby	Burt	707 938-6445	PO Box 792	Covelo	CA	95428	True
486-29-1786	Locksley	Charlene	415 585-4620	18 Broadway Av.	San Francisco	CA	94130	True
527-72-3246	Greene	Morningstar	615 297-2723	22 Graybar House Rd.	Nashville	TN	37215	False
648-92-1872	Blotchet-Halls	Reginald	503 745-6402	55 Hillsdale Bl.	Corvallis	OR	97330	True
672-71-3249	Yokomoto	Akiko	415 935-4228	3 Silver Ct.	Walnut Creek	CA	94595	True
712-45-1867	del Castillo	Innes	615 996-8275	2286 Cram Pl. #86	Ann Arbor	MI	48105	True
722-51-5454	DeFrance	Michel	219 547-9982	3 Balding Pl.	Gary	IN	46403	True
724-08-9931	Stringer	Dirk	415 843-2991	5420 Telegraph Av.	Oakland	CA	94609	False
724-80-9391	MacFeather	Stearns	415 354-7128	44 Upland Hts.	Oakland	CA	94612	True
756-30-7391	Karsen	Livia	415 534-9219	5720 McAuley St.	Oakland	CA	94609	True

Figure 3.1 An HTML Representation of the Authors Table

mine the number of columns, which allows sequencing through each column to get its value. Once all the data has been parsed, the `Read()` method will return a `null`. An alternate method to use to check for more data is the `HasMoreResults` property. This method is useful if you need to check for more records within a `loop` condition without advancing the record pointer.

CAUTION: One of the most common errors my students make is using a data reader when they're looking only for a single record. They almost always try to retrieve data from the DataReader before they call the `Read()` method. Remember: You must call the `Read()` method before you get any data from a DataReader.

The DataReader also contains a variety of `Get` methods that enable you to access field values, such as `GetInt()`, `GetDouble()`, `GetInt32()`, and `GetString()`, in native formats. To determine which one to use, the `GetFieldType` property can be called to get the appropriate column type. Then the correct `Get` method can be called to fetch the column data in its native format. To see the property type of each column, I could add the following code to my write statement:

```
myReader[i].GetFieldType.ToString();
```

Figure 3.2 shows the column-type name added to the output of the previous example by using the added statement.

The DataReader (unlike classic ADO) does not use the `MoveFirst()`, `MoveNext()`, and `MoveLast()` commands, or the `EOF` property. The initial call to the DataReader object's `Read()` command positions the record cursor at the beginning of the data and advances it after each subsequent call until all the data is processed. After all the data is processed, the `Read()` method returns a Boolean value. Moving the cursor back to the beginning is not permitted—remember, the DataReader is forward only. The DataSet object now provides bi-directional movement through the data.

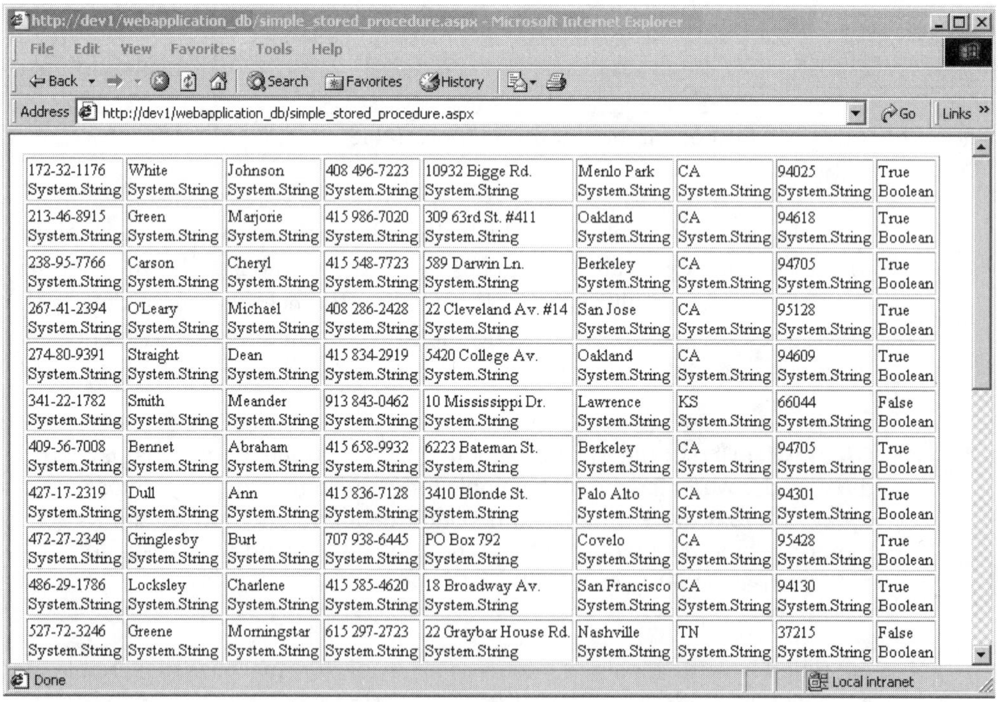

172-32-1176 System.String	White System.String	Johnson System.String	408 496-7223 System.String	10932 Bigge Rd. System.String	Menlo Park System.String	CA System.String	94025 System.String	True Boolean
213-46-8915 System.String	Green System.String	Marjorie System.String	415 986-7020 System.String	309 63rd St. #411 System.String	Oakland System.String	CA System.String	94618 System.String	True Boolean
238-95-7766 System.String	Carson System.String	Cheryl System.String	415 548-7723 System.String	589 Darwin Ln. System.String	Berkeley System.String	CA System.String	94705 System.String	True Boolean
267-41-2394 System.String	O'Leary System.String	Michael System.String	408 286-2428 System.String	22 Cleveland Av. #14 System.String	San Jose System.String	CA System.String	95128 System.String	True Boolean
274-80-9391 System.String	Straight System.String	Dean System.String	415 834-2919 System.String	5420 College Av. System.String	Oakland System.String	CA System.String	94609 System.String	True Boolean
341-22-1782 System.String	Smith System.String	Meander System.String	913 843-0462 System.String	10 Mississippi Dr. System.String	Lawrence System.String	KS System.String	66044 System.String	False Boolean
409-56-7008 System.String	Bennet System.String	Abraham System.String	415 658-9932 System.String	6223 Bateman St. System.String	Berkeley System.String	CA System.String	94705 System.String	True Boolean
427-17-2319 System.String	Dull System.String	Ann System.String	415 836-7128 System.String	3410 Blonde St. System.String	Palo Alto System.String	CA System.String	94301 System.String	True Boolean
472-27-2349 System.String	Gringlesby System.String	Burt System.String	707 938-6445 System.String	PO Box 792 System.String	Covelo System.String	CA System.String	95428 System.String	True Boolean
486-29-1786 System.String	Locksley System.String	Charlene System.String	415 585-4620 System.String	18 Broadway Av. System.String	San Francisco System.String	CA System.String	94130 System.String	True Boolean
527-72-3246 System.String	Greene System.String	Morningstar System.String	615 297-2723 System.String	22 Graybar House Rd. System.String	Nashville System.String	TN System.String	37215 System.String	False Boolean

Figure 3.2 An HTML Representation of the Authors Table with Column Data Types Shown

Parameter Binding with SQL Commands

Another feature of the SqlCommand object is its ability to easily bind parameter data for SQL statements and stored procedures. Each parameter has four key pieces of information: the name, the type, its data size, and the direction of the parameter.

For the SQL Server Managed provider, the parameter construction uses actual names of the parameters, just like regular T-SQL syntax uses. For example, the following code contains a single ID parameter that is passed to the SELECT command:

```
SELECT * FROM Authors WHERE au_id=@ID
```

To return values, I need to add parameters to the SELECT statement:

```
SELECT @Fname=au_fname, @Lname=au_lname FROM Authors WHERE au_id=@ID
```

Now I have one input and two output parameters. The code to bind the parameters to the SELECT command starts with a standard SQL connection, followed by the SQL SELECT statement, and finally a set of parameter bindings. The following code illustrates how the binding process works:

C#
```
SqlConnection myConnection =
new SqlConnection( "server=localhost;uid=sa;pwd=;database=pubs" );
SqlCommand myCommand =
  new SqlCommand(
    "SELECT @Fname=au_fname, @Lname=au_lname_FROM " +
    "Authors WHERE au_id=@ID", myConnection );

myCommand.Parameters.Add( "@ID", SqlDbType.VarChar, 11 );
myCommand.Parameters["@ID"].Direction = ParameterDirection.Input;
myCommand.Parameters["@ID"].Value = "172-32-1176";

myCommand.Parameters.Add( "@Fname", SqlDbType.VarChar, 20 );
myCommand.Parameters["@Fname"].Direction = ParameterDirection.Output;

myCommand.Parameters.Add( "@Lname", SqlDbType.VarChar, 40 );
myCommand.Parameters["@Lname"].Direction = ParameterDirection.Output;

myConnection.Open();
myCommand.Execute();
```

```
Response.Write( "First Name " + myCommand.Parameters["@Fname"].Value.
ToString() + "<br>" );
Response.Write( "Last Name " + myCommand.Parameters["@Lname"].Value.
ToString() );
myConnection.Close();
```

VB

```
Dim myConnection as new _
   SqlConnection( "server=localhost;uid=sa;pwd=;database=pubs" )
Dim myCommand as New _
   SqlCommand( "SELECT @Fname=au_fname, @Lname=au_lname FROM " + _
      "Authors WHERE au_id=@ID", myConnection )

myCommand.Parameters.Add( "@ID", SqlDbType.VarChar, 11 )
myCommand.Parameters("@ID").Direction = ParameterDirection.Input
myCommand.Parameters("@ID").Value = "172-32-1176"

myCommand.Parameters.Add( "@Fname", SqlDbType.VarChar, 20 )
myCommand.Parameters("@Fname").Direction = ParameterDirection.Output

myCommand.Parameters.Add( "@Lname", SqlDbType.VarChar, 40 )
myCommand.Parameters("@Lname").Direction = ParameterDirection.Output

myConnection.Open()
myCommand.Execute()
Response.Write( "First Name " + _
   myCommand.Parameters("@Fname").Value.ToString() + "<br>" )
Response.Write( "Last Name " + _
   myCommand.Parameters("@Lname").Value.ToString() )
myConnection.Close()
```

Notice in the example that the names of the parameters must match the names declared in the SQL SELECT statement. Otherwise, the parameters do not match up correctly. The data types are standard SQL types.

RECOMMENDED PRACTICE: If your query will return only a single record (rowset), then using a SqlDataReader object into which the data will be retrieved is unnecessary overhead. Using bound parameters instead will cause your code to execute faster.

NOTE: In the examples I use in this book in which parameters are added to a SqlCommand, I access the parameters by name. For instance, I might call a parameter `@ID` or `@Name`. You can alternatively use ordinals, which are zero-based numbers that identify a particular parameter from the collection. Using ordinals as opposed to names will give you a performance boost because a name lookup isn't performed during parameter access. I have been down this road, though, too many times to advise you to use ordinals. I have seen my students get into too many situations in which the ordinals got mixed up, and they ended up using the wrong ones. Consider this choice carefully. If performance is important, use ordinals; otherwise, keep with names.

The size value is necessary only for fields that contain an actual size. For values such as numeric, this value can be omitted. Finally, the direction value indicates how the parameter will be used. Table 3.2 shows the four different direction values.

Stored Procedures and Parameter Binding

Calling stored procedures and binding parameter data work much like the SQL `EXEC` statement. This section shows how to call stored procedures, pass parameters in and out, and return the exit value of the stored procedure. I will create a stored procedure, pass values in and out of the procedure, and access the stored procedure's return value.

First, I have to create a stored procedure that does all this. For this example I'll take the `SELECT` statement used in the "Parameter Binding with SQL Commands" section and create a stored procedure in the Microsoft SQL Server `Pubs` database, as shown below.

```
Create Procedure sp_GetAuthor
    @ID varchar(11),
    @Fname varchar(20) output,
    @Lname varchar(40) output
```

Table 3.2 Direction Values for Parameterized Queries

Direction	Description
Input	The parameter is an input parameter.
InputOutput	The parameter is capable of both input and output.
Output	The parameter is an output parameter.
ReturnValue	The parameter represents a return value.

```
AS
    SELECT @Fname = NULL
    SELECT @LName = NULL
    SELECT @Fname=au_fname, @Lname=au_lname FROM authors WHERE au_id=@ID
    if(@Fname IS NULL)
      return -100
    else
      return 0
```

To illustrate the return value parameter, I have included an `error` condition in the stored procedure. When the `SELECT` statement fails, a −100 is returned after the procedure checks the `@Fname` value for `null`. The initialization of the two output parameters is a precaution in the event a value is passed.

RECOMMENDED PRACTICE: Use `nVarChar` whenever possible. It looks like this may not make sense for the `Pubs` database, but `nVarChar` is better in most cases. Essentially, using `NVarChar` makes internationalization much easier and is inexpensive to do up front.

If you don't use `nVarChar` whenever you can, then you must have custom installations of SQL Server that use a different alphabet for each language you need to support. I've seen successful sales or company growth turn this simple mistake into something very expensive.

The SQL Server parameter binding works exactly the same as the SQL command statement. The only parameter addition is the binding to reference the stored procedure's return value.

C#
```csharp
SqlConnection myConnection =
      new SqlConnection( "server=localhost;uid=sa;pwd=;database=pubs" );
SqlCommand myCommand =
  new SqlCommand("sp_GetAuthor", myConnection );
myCommand.CommandType = CommandType.StoredProcedure;

myCommand.Parameters.Add( "@ID", SqlDbType.VarChar, 11 );
myCommand.Parameters["@ID"].Direction = ParameterDirection.Input;
myCommand.Parameters["@ID"].Value = List1.SelectedItem.Text;
```

```
myCommand.Parameters.Add( "@Fname", SqlDbType.VarChar, 20 );
myCommand.Parameters["@Fname"].Direction = ParameterDirection.Output;

myCommand.Parameters.Add( "@Lname", SqlDataType.VarChar, 40 );
myCommand.Parameters["@Lname"].Direction = ParameterDirection.Output;

myCommand.Parameters.Add( "RETURN_VALUE", SqlDbType.Int );
myCommand.Parameters["RETURN_VALUE"].Direction =
ParameterDirection.ReturnValue;

myConnection.Open();
myCommand.ExecuteNonQuery();

string strFirstName = myCommand.Parameters["@Fname"].Value.ToString();
string strLastName = myCommand.Parameters["@Lname"].Value.ToString();
strError = myCommand.Parameters["RETURN_VALUE"].Value.ToString();

myConnection.Close();
```

VB
```
Dim myConnection as _
 new SqlConnection( "server=localhost;uid=sa;pwd=;database=pubs" )
Dim myCommand as new SqlCommand("sp_GetAuthor", myConnection )
myCommand.CommandType = CommandType.StoredProcedure

myCommand.Parameters.Add( "@ID", SqlDbType.VarChar, 11 )
myCommand.Parameters("@ID").Direction = ParameterDirection.Input
myCommand.Parameters("@ID").Value = List1.SelectedItem.Text

myCommand.Parameters.Add( "@Fname", SqlDbType.VarChar, 20 )
myCommand.Parameters("@Fname").Direction = ParameterDirection.Output

myCommand.Parameters.Add( "@Lname", SqlDataType.VarChar, 40 )
myCommand.Parameters("@Lname").Direction = _
  ParameterDirection.Output

myCommand.Parameters.Add( "RETURN_VALUE", SqlDbType.Int )
myCommand.Parameters("RETURN_VALUE").Direction = ParameterDirection.
ReturnValue

myConnection.Open()
myCommand.ExecuteNonQuery()
```

```
string strFirstName = myCommand.Parameters("@Fname").Value.ToString()
string strLastName = myCommand.Parameters("@Lname").Value.ToString()
strError = myCommand.Parameters("RETURN_VALUE").Value.ToString()

myConnection.Close()
```

RECOMMENDED PRACTICE: Stored procedures are almost always preferred over ad hoc queries in your code. The following list summarizes the reasons:

- Stored procedures execute faster than ad hoc SQL because SQL Server has already compiled the procedures and created a plan.
- Stored procedures give you a single place to make changes or fix bugs when queries need changes.
- Stored procedures offer an abstraction to the application code under circumstances in which data access is separated from code.

The Survey Application

The application that's featured in this chapter is a Survey application, and it demonstrates the use of ADO.NET. The program in Chapter 2 used ADO.NET to perform database access, but in this chapter and with this application, we'll take time to explain the ADO.NET functionality in greater detail.

The Survey application contains three distinct parts. One is the administrative part, in which questions can be edited, added, and deleted. Another part consists of the code that generates the survey questions and answers based on some parameters. And the third part of the demo application is the main screen on which the actual survey data is shown, and user interaction mechanisms are provided.

NOTE: The Survey application can be viewed from the www.ASPNet-Solutions. com Web site. From the main page of the site, go to the Chapter Examples page. Then click on the Chapter 3 link. This page offers the capability to run the Survey application.

You can go directly to the www.ASPNet-Solutions.com/Chapter_3.htm page for the Survey application link.

The C# and VB source code and the backed-up database can be downloaded from the Chapter 3 page.

The Administrative Code

If you download the code from the Web site, you'll find all of the administrative functionality in administer.aspx.cs or administer.aspx.vb (depending on whether you are using the C# or VB version). This source code module contains all the methods that perform the administrative functions for the application. Table 3.3 shows what the methods are and describes the purpose of each.

When the program runs, you'll see a way to log in to the administrative section, and you'll see a survey appear in the right side of the screen, as shown in Figure 3.3.

PopulateQuestionList() and Page_Load()

The `PopulateQuestionList()` method is called from the `Page_Load()` method (which executes during the initial page-loading sequence). This method needs to be called only the first time that the page is loaded. When a page load is a post back, the QuestionList ListBox object is already populated because its state persists in the `VIEWSTATE` hidden field. In many situations, not calling `PopulateQuestionList()` in response to post backs will save the server some processor time.

In some situations, though, the `PopulateQuestionList()` method is called in response to a user-generated event. Examples of this are when a user adds or deletes a question. In these cases, the QuestionList object needs to be repopulated.

RECOMMENDED PRACTICE: Make sure your applications don't repopulate user interface objects for post backs unless it's absolutely necessary. For objects that query a database for their contents but never change throughout the life cycle of the application page requests, repopulating would represent an unnecessary burden on the server.

Check the `IsPostback` property to see whether the current request is a post back. The property will be `true` if it is.

We talked earlier in the chapter about SqlConnection objects. These objects will be used throughout the entire Survey application to connect to the database. The first thing that's done in Listing 3.5 (on page 87) is to create a SqlConnection object. Its one and only parameter is the connection string, which is contained in the Global.asax. Making any changes to this code is an easy matter because only one place must be edited for

Table 3.3 The Administrative Methods Found in administer.aspx.cs and administer.aspx.vb

Method	Listing	Description
PopulateQuestionList	3.5	This method populates the QuestionList ListBox object with all questions that are found in the database. It can optionally populate the CategoryList DropDownList object if the bPopulateCategoryList-Also flag is true.
UpdateButton_Click	3.6	This is the event handler that is fired when the Update This Question button is clicked. This method updates the database with the information that's in the user interface, such as the Question Text and the Answers.
DeleteButton_Click	3.7	This is the event handler that is fired when the Delete button is clicked. This method uses the QuestionID Session— Session["QuestionID"] for C# and Session("QuestionID") for VB—variable so that it knows which question number to delete from the database.
AddCategory_Click	3.8	This is the event handler that is fired when the Add It button is clicked. It takes the value that is in the NewCategory TextField object and adds it to the database.
AddButton_Click	3.9	This is the event handler that is fired when the Add New Question button is clicked. It essentially clears the editable text fields and sets other values to -1, which indicates there is no currently selected question.
MainButton_Click	3.9	This is the event handler that is fired when the Main Survey Page button is clicked. It simply redirects to the main Survey page.
QuestionList_Selected IndexChanged	3.10	This is the event handler that is fired when the QuestionList ListBox object detects a change in the selection index. This method populates the editable items on the page with the question information.

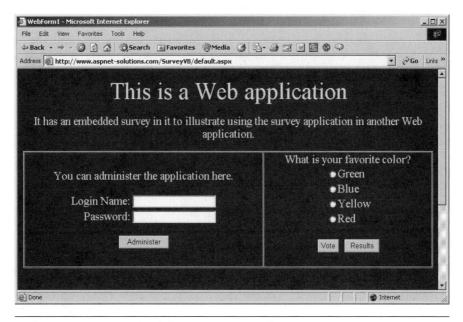

Figure 3.3 The Survey Application Lets Users Log In to the Administrative Functionality and Offers Them a Survey Item.

changes to take effect (this was mentioned as a recommended practice earlier in the chapter).

RECOMMENDED PRACTICE: It is always a bad idea to leave database connections open longer than necessary. I once had a student who opened a connection in the Global.asax. The connection stayed open until the application shut down. Several problems are inherent with doing this. The first is that a connection can have only one open DataReader, and if more than one user requests a page that causes simultaneous readers to be open, at least one exception will be thrown.

In addition, open connections consume resources. This means that if you leave a connection open for a long time, and you have a large number of users accessing the database, the server will have a large portion of its resources allocated to database connections.

Another issue is deploying the Web application in a Web farm. In these cases, you might really slow down SQL Server, connection pooling is the best bet. You can set the connection pool size in the database connection string as follows:

```
server=localhost;uid=sa;pwd=;database=pubs;Pooling=true;Max
Pool Size=500
```

After the database connection has been opened with the `Open()` method, a SqlCommand object is created that will call the `sp_QuestionList` stored procedure. This stored procedure returns a recordset containing all the questions in the database (whether or not they are enabled). The `sp_QuestionList` stored procedure follows.

```
CREATE PROCEDURE sp_QuestionList
AS
    SELECT Text FROM Questions ORDER BY Text
GO
```

Once a recordset has been obtained from the `sp_QuestionList` stored procedure by calling the SqlCommand object's `Execute-Reader()` method, the recordset will be bound to the QuestionList ListBox object. The QuestionList `DataTextField` and `DataValueField` property values are set so that the data-binding process knows to bind using the Text field that's in the recordset. The last two things to be done are to set the `DataSource` property to the SqlDataReader object, and to call the `DataBind()` method.

A flag named bPopulateCategoryListAlso indicates whether the CategoryList DropDownList object should be populated. Population will need to happen only once at initial page load (not for post backs).

To retrieve the list of categories, the `sp_CategoryList` stored procedure is called. To do this, we almost literally repeat the process used to retrieve the question list. The only difference is that we set the SqlCommand object to access the `sp_CategoryList` stored procedure. This stored procedure is shown below.

```
CREATE PROCEDURE sp_CategoryList
AS
    SELECT Text FROM Categories ORDER BY ID
GO
```

The `DataTextField` and `DataValueField` properties are set, the `DataSource` property is set, and the `DataBind()` method is called. This completes the process of populating the CategoryList object.

NOTE: SqlDataReader objects must always be closed before you retrieve another SqlDataReader object because you can't open more than one reader per connection. Not closing the SqlDataReader objects has two negative results: Resources won't be released, and an exception will be thrown. The SqlConnection object won't allow more than one simultaneous open SqlDataReader.

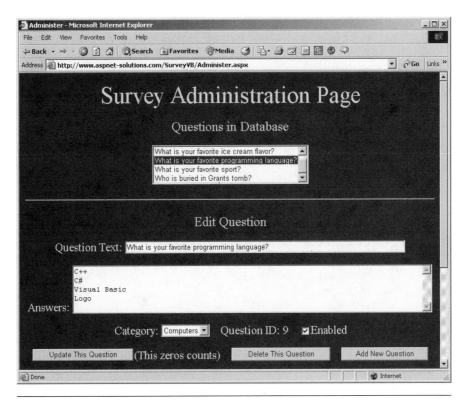

Figure 3.4 Selecting Questions in the QuestionList Object Populates the Fields.

The last thing to note, in Listing 3.5, is that code to close the database connection is in the `catch` block. This location is in case the database connection opens successfully, but, at some point after it has been opened, an exception is thrown. Figure 3.4 shows the application during execution.

Listing 3.5 The `PopulateQuestionList()` Method

```
Private Sub PopulateQuestionList(ByVal bPopulateCategoryListAlso As
Boolean)
    ' Create the connection object
    Dim myConnection As New _
        SqlConnection(Convert.ToString(Application("DBConnectionString")))

    Try
        myConnection.Open()
```

```vbnet
        ' Create the command object specifying the sp_QuestionList
        '   stored procedure, and set the CommandType property to
        '   CommandType.StoredProcedure.
        Dim myCommand As New SqlCommand("sp_QuestionList", _
          myConnection)
        myCommand.CommandType = CommandType.StoredProcedure

        ' Retrieve a SqlDataReader by calling the ExecuteReader()
        '   method. Then, databind the recordset with the
        '   QuestionList object. It's important to specify the
        '   column name for the
        '   DataTextField and DataValueField properties.
        Dim reader As SqlDataReader = myCommand.ExecuteReader()
        QuestionList.DataTextField = "Text"
        QuestionList.DataValueField = "Text"
        QuestionList.DataSource = reader
        QuestionList.DataBind()
        reader.Close()

        ' If the Boolean variable is true, we'll need to populate
        '   the CategoryList object.
        If bPopulateCategoryListAlso Then
            myCommand = New SqlCommand("sp_CategoryList", _
              myConnection)
            myCommand.CommandType = CommandType.StoredProcedure
            reader = myCommand.ExecuteReader()
            CategoryList.DataTextField = "Text"
            CategoryList.DataValueField = "Text"
            CategoryList.DataSource = reader
            CategoryList.DataBind()
            reader.Close()
        End If
    Catch ex As Exception
        Message.Text = ex.Message.ToString()
    Finally
        If myConnection.State = ConnetionState.Open Then
          myConnection.Close()
        End If
    End Try

End Sub

Private Sub Page_Load(ByVal sender As System.Object, ByVal e As _
  System.EventArgs) Handles MyBase.Load
```

```
If Not IsPostBack Then
    If Session("CurrentQuestionID") = Nothing Then
        Session("CurrentQuestionID") = -1
    End If
    PopulateQuestionList(True)
End If
End Sub
```

The *UpdateButton_Click()* Method

Users click the `UpdateButton_Click()` method on the update of a question's information. The items that are saved are the question text, the answers, the category, and whether the question is enabled.

The method starts by making sure the Question and Answers TextField objects contain data. Updating the question would be pointless without data in these fields. If either field is empty, a message is shown to the user (by being placed in the Message Label object). After the error message is set, the method then ends when a Return statement is encountered.

After the method checks for data in the Question and Answers objects, a SqlConnection object is created. This connection is used for all database access in this method.

The question ID (which is a unique key for the Question table in the database) is stored in a session variable. You will see that an integer variable named `nID` is assigned with the integer value in the `Session("CurrentQuestionID")` variable.

The database connection is opened with a call to the `Open()` method. A SqlCommand object named `myCommand` is created, and the `sp_UpdateQuestionInfo` stored procedure is specified as the command that will be performed. This `CommandType` property of the Sql-Command object is set to `StoredProcedure`. You can see the `sp_UpdateQuestionInfo` stored procedure below.

```
CREATE PROCEDURE sp_UpdateQuestionInfo
    @Text varchar(254),
    @CategoryID int,
    @Enabled int,
    @ID as int output
AS

    if( @ID <> -1 )
      begin
```

```
      DELETE Answers WHERE QuestionID=@ID
      UPDATE Questions SET
        Text=@Text,CategoryID=@CategoryID,Enabled=@Enabled
        WHERE ID=@ID
    end
  else
    begin
      INSERT INTO Questions (Text,CategoryID,Enabled)
        VALUES (@Text,@CategoryID,@Enabled)
          SELECT @ID=@@IDENTITY
    end
GO
```

The stored procedure expects four parameters: the question text (variable named @Text), the category ID (variable named @CategoryID), an indicator of whether the question is enabled (variable @Enabled), and the question ID (variable @ID). The question ID can be a valid question ID or −1, which indicates that this is a new question and should be added rather than updated.

The database provides unique question IDs because the ID field in the Questions table is an identity column. This arrangement means that the database will enforce uniqueness, and as a matter of fact will assign the ID value at the time a record is created. SQL Server makes available a mechanism whereby it is easy to get an identity column after a record has been created. The following code shows how T-SQL or a stored procedure can get an identity column into a parameter named @ID:

```
INSERT INTO SomeTable (FieldName1,FieldName2) VALUES ('Data1',
  'Data2')  SELECT @ID=@@IDENTITY
```

Once the four parameters have been set up, a call to the Execute-NonQuery() method is made. This updates or inserts the record, and for new records returns a unique question ID. This unique ID is retrieved with the following code:

```
If nID = -1 Then
    nID = Convert.ToInt32(myCommand.Parameters("@ID").Value)
End If
```

With the question added, we'll need to add the answers (or survey choices). The Answers TextField object contains answers that are all separated by carriage return/line feed (CR/LF) pairs. This is the perfect opportunity to use the String object's `Split()` method. The `Split()` method can easily find separator characters and split a string into an array of strings.

The only difficulty here is that our separator is a pair of characters, not the single character that the `Split()` method needs. For this reason, we'll use a newly created string that replaces the CR/LF pairs with ' | ' characters. This only works when there is no ' | ' symbol in the answer string, so make sure that your survey administrators understand this limitation. We can then easily use the `Split()` method and specify the ' | ' as the separator character. The following code shows how a single string of four answers (separated by three CR/LF pairs) is split into four substrings:

```
' Here's our initial string.
Dim strData as string = "Red"+ vbCrLf + "Green" + vbCrLf + "Blue" + _
vbCrLf + "Yellow"
' Here's the new string with '|' replacing the CR/LF pairs.
Dim strNewData as string = strData.Replace( vbCrLf, "|" )
' Here we perform the split.
Dim strAnswers as string() = _
  strNewData.Split( New Char {Chr(124)}, 100 )

' Now we'll loop through and use each substring.
Dim i as Integer
For i=0 to strAnswers.Length - 1
  ' Now do something with strAnswers(i)
Next
```

A stored procedure named `sp_AddAnswer` takes a question ID, the order of the answer (such as 0, 1, or 2), and the answer text and creates an answer in the database that can be used later when the question data is retrieved. The stored procedure can be seen below.

```
CREATE PROCEDURE sp_AddAnswer
    @QuestionID int,
    @Text varchar(254),
    @Ord int
AS
    INSERT INTO Answers (Text,QuestionID,Ord) VALUES
        (@Text,@QuestionID,@Ord)
GO
```

After the parameters (@Text, @QuestionID, and @Ord) are added to the SqlCommand object, a loop is used to treat each substring separately. Each substring is set into the @Text parameter, along with the @Ord parameter. A call to the stored procedure is made, thus storing the data in the database. Finally, the database connection is closed and a call to the PopulateQuestionList() method is made.

Listing 3.6 The UpdateButton_Click() Method

```
Private Sub UpdateButton_Click(ByVal sender As System.Object, _
  ByVal e As System.EventArgs) Handles UpdateButton.Click
    If Question.Text.Length = 0 Or Answers.Text.Length = 0 Then
        Message.Text = "You need text in the answers field."
        Return
    End If

    Dim myConnection As New _
SqlConnection(Convert.ToString(Application("DBConnectionString")))

    Try
        Dim nID As Integer = _
           Convert.ToInt32(Session("CurrentQuestionID"))

        myConnection.Open()
        Dim myCommand As New SqlCommand("sp_UpdateQuestionInfo", _
           myConnection)
        myCommand.CommandType = CommandType.StoredProcedure

        myCommand.Parameters.Add(New SqlParameter("@Text", _
           SqlDbType.VarChar, 254))
        myCommand.Parameters("@Text").Direction = _
           ParameterDirection.Input
        myCommand.Parameters("@Text").Value = Question.Text

        myCommand.Parameters.Add(New SqlParameter("@CategoryID", _
           SqlDbType.Int))
        myCommand.Parameters("@CategoryID").Direction = _
           ParameterDirection.Input
        myCommand.Parameters("@CategoryID").Value = _
           CategoryList.SelectedIndex

        myCommand.Parameters.Add(New SqlParameter("@Enabled", _
           SqlDbType.Int))
```

```
myCommand.Parameters("@Enabled").Direction = _
   ParameterDirection.Input
myCommand.Parameters("@Enabled").Value = 0

If Enabled.Checked Then
    myCommand.Parameters("@Enabled").Value = 1
End If

myCommand.Parameters.Add(New SqlParameter("@ID", _
   SqlDbType.Int))
myCommand.Parameters("@ID").Direction = _
   ParameterDirection.InputOutput
myCommand.Parameters("@ID").Value = nID

myCommand.ExecuteNonQuery()

If nID = -1 Then
    nID =
     Convert.ToInt32(myCommand.Parameters("@ID").Value)
    QuestionID.Text = Convert.ToString(nID)
End If

Dim strWork As String = Answers.Text.Replace(vbCrLf, "|")
Dim strAnswers As String() = _
   strWork.Split(New Char() {Chr(124)}, 100)
myCommand = New SqlCommand("sp_AddAnswer", myConnection)
myCommand.CommandType = CommandType.StoredProcedure
myCommand.Parameters.Add(New SqlParameter("@Text", _
   SqlDbType.VarChar, 254))
myCommand.Parameters("@Text").Direction = _
   ParameterDirection.Input

myCommand.Parameters.Add(New SqlParameter("@QuestionID", _
   SqlDbType.Int))
myCommand.Parameters("@QuestionID").Direction = _
   ParameterDirection.Input

myCommand.Parameters.Add(New SqlParameter("@Ord", _
   SqlDbType.Int))
myCommand.Parameters("@Ord").Direction = _
   ParameterDirection.Input

Dim i As Integer
For i = 0 To strAnswers.Length - 1
```

```
        If strAnswers(i).Length > 0 Then
            myCommand.Parameters("@Text").Value = _
                strAnswers(i)
            myCommand.Parameters("@QuestionID").Value = nID
            myCommand.Parameters("@Ord").Value = i
            myCommand.ExecuteNonQuery()
        End If
    Next

    myConnection.Close()

    PopulateQuestionList(False)

Catch ex As Exception
    If myConnection.State = ConnectionState.Open Then
        myConnection.Close()
    End If
    Message.Text = ex.Message.ToString()
End Try
End Sub
```

The DeleteButton_Click() Method

Questions can be deleted by clicking the Delete button. When users click the Delete button, the code in Listing 3.7 is called. The question ID is retrieved from the `Session("CurrentSessionID")` variable and stored in a local integer variable named `nID`. If the question ID is negative, this means no question is currently selected and therefore the user can't delete the question. A message is placed in the Message Label object indicating this condition, and the method is ended with a `Return` command.

If, however, the current question has a valid ID (greater than or equal to zero), the process moves forward to delete the question. First, a connection to the database is created and opened.

A SqlCommand object is then created that specifies that `sp_DeleteQuestion` stored procedure. This stored procedure takes a single parameter that represents the question ID, and deletes the question and all of its related answers. This stored procedure can be seen below.

```
CREATE PROCEDURE sp_DeleteQuestion
    @ID as int
AS
```

```
DELETE Answers WHERE QuestionID=@ID
DELETE Questions WHERE ID=@ID
GO
```

A call is made to the ExecuteNonQuery() method that performs the question-delete operation. The connection is closed, and several of the application variables, such as Session("CurrentQuestionID"), are set to indicate that there is no currently selected question.

Listing 3.7 The DeleteButton_Click() Method

```
Private Sub DeleteButton_Click(ByVal sender As System.Object, _
  ByVal e As System.EventArgs) Handles Button2.Click
    Dim nID As Integer = _
      Convert.ToInt32(Session("CurrentQuestionID"))
    If nID < 0 Then
       Message.Text = _
    "There is not a valid question that is currently being edited."
       Return
    End If

    Dim myConnection As New _
SqlConnection(Convert.ToString(Application("DBConnectionString")))

    Try
        myConnection.Open()
        Dim myCommand As New SqlCommand("sp_DeleteQuestion", _
          myConnection)
        myCommand.CommandType = CommandType.StoredProcedure

        myCommand.Parameters.Add(New SqlParameter("@ID", _
          SqlDbType.Int))
        myCommand.Parameters("@ID").Direction = _
          ParameterDirection.Input
        myCommand.Parameters("@ID").Value = nID

        myCommand.ExecuteNonQuery()
        myConnection.Close()

        QuestionList.SelectedIndex = -1
        Session("CurrentQuestionID") = -1
        Enabled.Checked = True
        QuestionID.Text = ""
```

```
            PopulateQuestionList(False)

    Catch ex As Exception
        If myConnection.State = ConnectionState.Open Then
            myConnection.Close()
        End If
        Message.Text = ex.Message.ToString()
    End Try
End Sub
```

The `AddCategoryButton_Click()` Method

Users can add to the list of categories if they don't find what they want. To do this, they simply enter a category into the New Category editable text field (which is type EditBox named NewCategory), and click the Add It button. This action invokes the `AddCategoryButton_Click()` method shown in Listing 3.8. This code takes the text in the NewCategory object and sends it to a stored procedure named `sp_AddCategory`, which is shown below.

```
CREATE PROCEDURE sp_AddCategory
    @Text varchar(254)
AS
    INSERT INTO Categories (Text) VALUES (@Text)
GO
```

This code follows the pattern that we've seen thus far: Create a database connection and open it (using a SqlConnection object), create a Command object (using a SqlCommand object), set up the parameters that the stored procedure expects (by using the SqlCommand object's Parameters collection), and execute the stored procedure (with the `ExecuteNonQuery()` method).

The only thing added to the basic pattern is that the newly created category's text is added to the CategoryList DropDownList object so that it is available to the user for selection.

Listing 3.8 The `AddCategoryButton_Click()` Method

```
Private Sub AddCategoryButton_Click(ByVal sender As System.Object, ByVal
e As System.EventArgs) _
        Handles Button5.Click
```

```
     If NewCategory.Text.Length > 0 Then
       Dim myConnection As New _
SqlConnection(Convert.ToString(Application("DBConnectionString")))

          Try
              myConnection.Open()
              Dim myCommand As New SqlCommand("sp_AddCategory", _
                myConnection)
              myCommand.CommandType = CommandType.StoredProcedure

              myCommand.Parameters.Add(New SqlParameter("@Text", _
                SqlDbType.VarChar, 254))
              myCommand.Parameters("@Text").Direction = _
                ParameterDirection.Input
              myCommand.Parameters("@Text").Value = NewCategory.Text

              myCommand.ExecuteNonQuery()

              Message.Text = "New category: '" + _
                NewCategory.Text + _
                "' was added."
              Dim item As New ListItem(NewCategory.Text)
              CategoryList.Items.Add(item)
          Catch ex As Exception
              Message.Text = ex.Message.ToString()
          Finally
              If myConnection.State = ConnectionState.Open Then
                  myConnection.Close()
              End If
          End Try
      End If
      NewCategory.Text = ""
End Sub
```

The *AddButton_Click()* and *MainButton_Click()* Methods

Two short and simple methods named AddButton_Click() and MainButton_Click() can be seen in Listing 3.9. The AddButton_Click() method is triggered in response to the user clicking on the Add New Question button. The AddButton_Click() method sets the Session("CurrentQuestionID") variable to −1 to indicate no currently selected question, clears the TextBox objects, deselects any question in the

QuestionList object by setting its `SelectedIndex` property to −1, and then sets the `Enabled` check so that it is on.

The `MainButton_Click()` method just redirects users to the Survey application's main page.

Listing 3.9 The `AddButton_Click()` and `MainButton_Click()` Methods

```
Private Sub AddButton_Click(ByVal sender As System.Object, _
  ByVal e As _
  System.EventArgs) Handles Button3.Click
    Session("CurrentQuestionID") = -1
    Question.Text = ""
    Answers.Text = ""
    QuestionList.SelectedIndex = -1
    Enabled.Checked = True
End Sub

Private Sub MainButton_Click(ByVal sender As System.Object, _\
  ByVal e As _
  System.EventArgs) Handles Button1.Click
    Response.Redirect("default.aspx")
End Sub
```

The `QuestionList_SelectedIndexChanged()` Method

A good bit of code executes when the user selects a question in the QuestionList object, as you can see in Listing 3.10. The purpose of this code is to find all the related data and populate all the fields on the page so that questions can be edited.

An interesting thing happens at the top of the `QuestionList_SelectedIndexChanged()` method. It declares a ListBox object named `lb` because that is the object type for which this event handler was created. The `lb` variable is then set to reference the Sender object that was passed into this method.

In C#, the declared object must be cast as a ListBox object, as follows:

```
ListBox lb = (ListBox) sender;
```

With a reference to the ListBox object, the text for the selected question can be retrieved. We'll eventually use this text as one of the stored procedure parameters.

As with most of the methods in this source-code module, a connection to the database is created and opened. A Command object specifying the `sp_QuestionInfoFromText` stored procedure is created. The `sp_QuestionInfoFromText` can be seen below.

```
CREATE PROCEDURE sp_QuestionInfoFromText
    @Text varchar(254),
    @ID int output,
    @CategoryID int output,
    @Enabled int output
AS
    SELECT @ID=ID,@CategoryID=CategoryID,@Enabled=Enabled FROM
        Questions WHERE Text=@Text

    if( @ID IS NULL )
        SELECT @ID = -1
GO
```

Four parameters must be created and set up for the sp_Question-InfoFromText stored procedure. These parameters are `@Text` (for the question text), `@ID` (for the unique question ID), `@CategoryID` (for the category ID that has been assigned to the question), and `@Enabled` (which indicates whether a question is enabled). After the parameters are set up, the `ExecuteNonQuery()` method is called.

Three of the four parameters are marked for output and will contain important information. The question ID, category ID, and enabled flag are all available after the `QuestionInfoFromText` stored procedure has been executed.

The answers must all be obtained from the database. This is done with the `sp_AnswerInfo` stored procedure shown below.

```
CREATE PROCEDURE sp_AnswerInfo
    @ID int
AS
    SELECT Text FROM Answers WHERE QuestionID=@ID
GO
```

Each answer that is retrieved is appended to the Answers TextField object. And all variables, such as `Session("CurrentQuestionID")`, are set so that proper application behavior will result.

Listing 3.10 The `QuestionList_SelectedIndexChanged()` Method

```
Private Sub QuestionList_SelectedIndexChanged(ByVal sender As _
  System.Object, ByVal e As System.EventArgs) Handles _
  QuestionList.SelectedIndexChanged
    Dim lb As ListBox lb = sender

    Dim myConnection As New _
      SqlConnection(Application("DBConnectionString").ToString())

    Try
        myConnection.Open()
      Dim myCommand As New SqlCommand("sp_QuestionInfoFromText", _
          myConnection)
      myCommand.CommandType = CommandType.StoredProcedure

      myCommand.Parameters.Add(New SqlParameter("@Text", _
        SqlDbType.VarChar, 254))
      myCommand.Parameters("@Text").Direction = _
        ParameterDirection.Input
      myCommand.Parameters("@Text").Value = _
        lb.SelectedItem.Value

      myCommand.Parameters.Add(New SqlParameter("@ID", _
        SqlDbType.Int))
      myCommand.Parameters("@ID").Direction = _
        ParameterDirection.Output

      myCommand.Parameters.Add(New SqlParameter("@CategoryID", _
        SqlDbType.Int))
      myCommand.Parameters("@CategoryID").Direction = _
        ParameterDirection.Output

      myCommand.Parameters.Add(New SqlParameter("@Enabled", _
        SqlDbType.Int))
      myCommand.Parameters("@Enabled").Direction = _
        ParameterDirection.Output

      myCommand.ExecuteNonQuery()

      Dim nCatID As Integer = _
        Convert.ToInt32(myCommand.Parameters("@CategoryID").Value)
      Dim nID As Integer = _
```

```
        Convert.ToInt32(myCommand.Parameters("@ID").Value)
    If nID <> -1 Then
        Session("CurrentQuestionID") = nID
        QuestionID.Text = Convert.ToString(nID)
        Question.Text = lb.SelectedItem.Value
        Enabled.Checked = True
    If _
  Convert.ToInt32(myCommand.Parameters("@Enabled").Value)= 0 _
        Then
            Enabled.Checked = False
        End If
        Answers.Text = ""

        myCommand = New SqlCommand("sp_AnswerInfo", _
            myConnection)
        myCommand.CommandType = CommandType.StoredProcedure

        myCommand.Parameters.Add(New SqlParameter("@ID", _
            SqlDbType.Int))
        myCommand.Parameters("@ID").Direction = _
            ParameterDirection.Input
        myCommand.Parameters("@ID").Value = nID

        Dim reader As SqlDataReader = _
            myCommand.ExecuteReader()

        While reader.Read()
            Answers.Text += (reader.GetString(0) + vbCrLf)
        End While

        reader.Close()

        If nCatID < 0 Then
            nCatID = 0
        End If

        CategoryList.SelectedIndex = nCatID
    End If

    myConnection.Close()
Catch ex As Exception
    If myConnection.State = ConnectionState.Open Then
        myConnection.Close()
```

```
         End If
         Message.Text = ex.Message.ToString()
     End Try
End Sub
```

As you can see, the code in the Administer source code is straightforward. It follows a fairly predictable pattern and uses stored procedures for optimal performance.

The Main Survey Application Code

In the project code, you'll find all of the main screen functionality in default.aspx.cs or default.aspx.vb (depending on whether you are using the C# or VB version). This source code module contains all of the methods that perform the administrative functions for the application. Table 3.4 shows what the methods are and describes their purpose.

The `Page_Load()` Method

The `Page_Load()` method performs a fairly powerful procedure. It obtains the data for a question (both the question and all choices) and populates the user interface objects (SurveyQuestion and AnswerList). Although this procedure is powerful, it appears simple because a Web Service is invoked that returns the information.

The code in Listing 3.11 instantiates a `Web Service` class (named `com.aspnet_solutions.www.SurveyItem`), invokes its `GetSurveyData()` method, and receives a populated SurveyData structure that contains all the necessary survey question information.

You might notice that the `GetSurveyData()` method takes two arguments, both of which are −1 here. The first argument lets the caller specify a category ID. That way, a specific category can be selected from. If the value is −1, then the survey question is selected from all categories.

The second argument allows a specific question ID to be asked for. This way, if you want to make sure a certain question is asked, you can pass the question's ID number as the second argument. If this value is −1, it is ignored.

It's important to take a look at the data structures that are used in the application. They can be seen in Listing 3.11.

Table 3.4 The Survey Application Main Page Methods Found in default.aspx.cs and default.aspx.vb

Method	Listing	Description
Page_Load()	3.11	This method executes when the default.aspx page is requested. If the request is not a post back, a survey question is retrieved from the TheSurvey Web Service.
LoginButton_Click	3.12	This is the event handler that is fired when the Login button is clicked. This method takes the user name and password, checks them for a match in the database, and then goes to the Administer.aspx page if a match has been found.
VoteButton_Click	3.13	This is the event handler that is fired when the Vote button is clicked. The Web Service is called upon to register the vote.
ResultsButton_Click	3.14	This is the event handler that is fired when the Results button is clicked. The Web Service is called upon to retrieve the results.

Listing 3.11 The Page_Load() Method

```
If Not IsPostBack Then
    Dim srv As New com.aspnet_solutions.www.SurveyItem()
    Dim data As com.aspnet_solutions.www.SurveyData = _
      srv.GetSurveyData(-1, -1)
    SurveyQuestion.Text = data.strQuestion
    If SurveyQuestion.Text.Length = 0 Then
        SurveyQuestion.Text = data.strError
    End If
    Dim i As Integer
    For i = 0 To data.Answers.Length - 1
        Dim item As New ListItem(data.Answers(i))
        AnswerList.Items.Add(item)
    Next
    QuestionID.Text = Convert.ToString(data.nQuestionID)
End If
```

The *LoginButton_Click()* Method

The LoginButton_Click() method shown in Listing 3.12 checks the database for a match with the user's name and password. It uses a stored procedure named sp_Login that's shown below.

```
CREATE PROCEDURE sp_Login
    @Name varchar(254),
    @Password varchar(254),
    @ID int output
AS
    SELECT @ID=ID FROM Administrators WHERE Name=@Name
        AND Password=@Password

    if( @ID IS NULL )
        SELECT @ID = -1
GO
```

The sp_Login stored procedure takes three parameters: @Name, @Password, and @ID. The @ID parameter will contain the ID of the user if a match was found. If not match was found, the ID will be −1.

If the login was successful, the user is redirected to Administer.aspx. If not, a message stating that the login failed is placed into the Message Label object.

Listing 3.12 The LoginButton_Click() Method

```
Private Sub LoginButton_Click(ByVal sender As System.Object, ByVal e _
  As System.EventArgs) Handles Button1.Click
    Dim myConnection As New _
SqlConnection(Convert.ToString(Application("DBConnectionString")))

    Try
        myConnection.Open()
        Dim myCommand As New SqlCommand("sp_Login", myConnection)
        myCommand.CommandType = CommandType.StoredProcedure

        myCommand.Parameters.Add(New SqlParameter("@Name", _
          SqlDbType.VarChar, 254))
        myCommand.Parameters("@Name").Direction = _
          ParameterDirection.Input
        myCommand.Parameters("@Name").Value = Name.Text
```

```
myCommand.Parameters.Add(New SqlParameter("@Password", _
    SqlDbType.VarChar, 254))
myCommand.Parameters("@Password").Direction = _
    ParameterDirection.Input
myCommand.Parameters("@Password").Value = Password.Text

myCommand.Parameters.Add(New SqlParameter("@ID", _
    SqlDbType.Int))
myCommand.Parameters("@ID").Direction = _
    ParameterDirection.Output

myCommand.ExecuteNonQuery()
myConnection.Close()

Dim nID As Integer = _
    Convert.ToInt32(myCommand.Parameters("@ID").Value)
If nID = -1 Then
    Message.Text = "Login failure"
Else
    Session("AdminID") = nID
    Response.Redirect("Administer.aspx")
End If
Catch ex As Exception
If myConnection.State = ConnectionState.Open Then
    myConnection.Close()
End If
Message.Text = ex.Message.ToString()
End Try
End Sub
```

The *VoteButton_Click()* Method

You would think that the VoteButton_Click() method as shown in Listing 3.13 would be complicated. It's not; it's simple. That's because it calls the Web Service's Vote() method, which takes care of the dirty work of registering the vote in the database.

That's the beauty of using Web Services; your application focus on program logic and not on procedural things that can easily be encapsulated in Web Services. Other situations in which to use a Web Service might include when you want to allow voting from other client applications and when you want to keep vote functionality close to the database server but deploy the larger application across a Web farm.

The code in the `VoteButton_Click()` method starts by setting Button2's `Visible` property to `False`. This helps prevent users from voting more than once (although they could simply reload the page and vote again).

The SurveyMessage Label object is set with a message thanking the user for voting.

The Web Service is instantiated, and the `Vote()` method is called. The `Vote()` method needs two parameters, the answer number (0, 1, 2, and so on) and the question ID number. If you want to skip ahead, the code for the `Vote()` method can be seen in Listing 3.18.

Listing 3.13 The `VoteButton_Click()` Method

```
Private Sub Vote_Click(ByVal sender As System.Object, ByVal e As_
   System.EventArgs) Handles Button2.Click
    Vote.Visible = False
    SurveyMessage.Text = "Thanks for voting!"
    Try
      Dim srv As New com.aspnet_solutions.www.SurveyItem()
      Dim nAnswerNumber As Integer = AnswerList.SelectedIndex
      srv.Vote(Convert.ToInt32(QuestionID.Text), nAnswerNumber)
    Catch ex As Exception
      SurveyMessage.Text = ex.Message.ToString()
    End Try
End Sub
```

The `ResultsButton_Click()` Method

When users click on the Results button, the `ResultsButton_Click()` method is invoked, as shown in Listing 3.14. This method goes to the Web Service for the results that pertain to the currently displayed survey question.

The first thing the method does is instantiate a `Web Service` class. A call to the `GetResults()` method is then made. The only parameter this method requires is the question ID, and this is supplied by converting a hidden field named QuestionID to an integer.

A data structure containing the relevant information is returned from the `GetResults()` method. For details, see Listing 3.15.

Once the survey results have been retrieved, the SurveyMessage Label object is populated with the survey result data.

Listing 3.14 The `Results_Click()` Method

```
Private Sub ResultsButton_Click(ByVal sender As System.Object, ByVal e_
  As System.EventArgs) _
       Handles Button3.Click
    Dim srv As New com.aspnet_solutions.www.SurveyItem()
    Dim res As com.aspnet_solutions.www.SurveyResults = _
       srv.GetResults(Convert.ToInt32(QuestionID.Text))
    If res.strError.Length > 0 Then
       SurveyMessage.Text = res.strError
       Return
    End If
    SurveyMessage.Text = "The results are:<br>" + vbCrLf
    Dim i As Integer
    For i = 0 To res.nCount.Length - 1
       SurveyMessage.Text += (AnswerList.Items(i).Value + ": ")
       Dim strPercent As String = res.dPercent(i).ToString(".00")
       If res.dPercent(i) = 0 Then
           strPercent = "0"
       End If
       SurveyMessage.Text += (strPercent + "%<br>" + vbCrLf)
    Next
End Sub
```

As you can see, the code in the Survey application's main page is simple. This simplicity is a direct result of using a Web Service to encapsulate the survey functionality.

TheSurvey Web Service

In the TheSurvey Web Service project, you'll find all of the Web Service functionality in surveyItem.asmx.cs or surveyItem.asmx.vb (depending on whether you are using the C# or VB version). This source code module contains all the methods that perform the administrative functions for the application. Table 3.5 shows what the methods are and describes their purpose.

The Data Structures

To return all the information necessary to display a survey question on the client machine, the application needs a data structure. A Web Service can return only one thing (via a return statement), and it can't have reference

Table 3.5 The Survey Web Service Methods Found in surveyItem.asmx.cs and surveyItem.aspx.vb

Method	Listing	Description
_GetSurveyData()	3.16	This method creates the survey data. It takes two integer arguments—nCategoryID and nQuestionID—and retrieves the appropriate question and answer data.
GetSurveyData()	3.17	This method simply returns the values that are obtained by calling the _GetSurveyData() method.
Vote()	3.18	This method takes the vote data and records it in the database.
GetResults()	3.19	This method gets the results for the survey question number that's passed in.

(noted by the ref keyword) variables that are passed in (which expect to be populated before a method returns). To solve the problem in which we need to pass back the question, an error (if it occurs), the list of answers, the question ID, and the category ID, we'll collect all of the information into a data structure.

The Web Service also needs to return information pertaining to survey results. For this, another data structure collects the information so that it can be returned as a single data type. The data structure that contains the survey question data is called SurveyData, and it can be seen in Listing 3.15. Also shown in Listing 3.15 is the SurveyResults data structure.

Listing 3.15 The Data Structures Used to Return Information

```
C#
public struct SurveyData
{
    public string strQuestion;
    public string strError;
    public StringCollection Answers;
    public int nQuestionID;
    public int nCategoryID;
}

public struct SurveyResults
{
```

```
    public string strError;
    public int[] nCount;
    public double[] dPercent;
}
```

VB
```
Public Structure SurveyData
    Public strQuestion As String
    Public strError As String
    Public Answers As StringCollection
    Public nQuestionID As Integer
    Public nCategoryID As Integer
End Structure

Public Structure SurveyResults
    Public strError As String
    Public nCount As Integer()
    Public dPercent As Double()
End Structure
```

The _GetSurveyData() Method

The _GetSurveyData() method is marked as private. The publicly callable method is called GetSurveyData(). The real work is done in _GetSurveyData(), and GetSurveyData() simply calls _GetSurveyData() (as shown in Listing 3.16) to return its results.

This was done so that the Web Service can be easily extended at a later time. When I developed the Web Service, I considered returning two versions of the data: one with the question and a list of answers (as is returned now in the GetSurveyData() method), and one that includes user-interface HTML codes so that the client application doesn't have to construct the presentation's objects but can just use what is retrieved from the Web Service.

If you ever extend the Web Service so that you have a method called GetSurveyInHTML() that returns the survey with the appropriate HTML, you can still call the _GetSurveyData() method to get the actual survey data. You can then construct the HTML data in your GetSurveyInHTML() method before returning the HTML data to the client application.

The _GetSurveyData() method has two paths: one when a specific question ID has been given, and the other when the question ID value has been given as −1, which indicates the pool of all questions can be drawn upon. If the first path is taken, the routine calls the sp_QuestionFrom-

ID stored procedure to retrieve the information corresponding to the question ID.

The second path of the _GetSurveyData() method follows this sequence: Find the number of survey questions in the database that match the criteria (either a given category ID or all questions), generate a random number that's in the correct range, and then retrieve the row that matches the random number. To accomplish the first task, a stored procedure named sp_QuestionCount (which is shown below) is called. This procedure requires a single input parameter that indicates the requested category ID. If this parameter value is less than 0, then all categories are selected.

```
CREATE PROCEDURE sp_QuestionCount
    @CategoryID int,
    @Count as int output
AS
    if( @CategoryID < 0 )
        SELECT @Count=Count(*) FROM Questions WHERE Enabled=1
    else
        SELECT @Count=Count(*) FROM Questions WHERE Enabled=1
            AND CategoryID=@CategoryID
GO
```

An instance of the Random class is created to provide random number functionality. A call is made to its Next() method, with a parameter indicating the largest number desired, thus generating the random number. Remember that this number is zero based—it ranges from zero to the record count minus one. The following code shows how the random number is generated:

```
Dim rnd As New Random()
Dim nRandomNumber As Integer = rnd.Next(nCount - 1)
```

With the random number generated, a call to the sp_GetSingle-Question stored procedure can be made (shown below). This stored procedure takes two parameters—the random number and the category ID. Here again, the category ID can be −1, which indicates that all categories can be drawn upon. The random number can't be zero based because the SQL FETCH Absolute command considers the first row to be numbered as 1. For this reason, we add one to the random number when we assign the @RecordNum parameter's value.

```
CREATE PROCEDURE sp_GetSingleQuestion
    @RecordNum int,
    @CategoryID int
AS
    if( @CategoryID >= 0 )
    begin
        DECLARE MyCursor SCROLL CURSOR
            For SELECT Text,ID,CategoryID FROM Questions WHERE
                Enabled=1
                AND CategoryID=@CategoryID
        OPEN MyCursor
        FETCH Absolute  @RecordNum from MyCursor
        CLOSE MyCursor
        DEALLOCATE MyCursor
    end
    else
    begin
        DECLARE MyCursor SCROLL CURSOR
            For SELECT Text,ID,CategoryID FROM Questions WHERE
                Enabled=1
        OPEN MyCursor
        FETCH Absolute  @RecordNum from MyCursor
        CLOSE MyCursor
        DEALLOCATE MyCursor
    end
GO
```

Once we have the question information (which includes the question ID), whether the code took the first or second paths, we can get the answers for this question. The code calls the `sp_AnswerInfo` stored procedure to retrieve all the answers for this survey question. The answers will be in a Sql-DataReader object, and the code just loops through and gets each record.

Listing 3.16 The `_GetSurveyData()` Method

```
Private Function _GetSurveyData(ByVal nCategoryID As Integer, _
  ByVal nQuestionID As Integer) As SurveyData

    ' Create a SurveyData object and set its
    '    properties so the it will contain a
    '    StringCollection object, the question id
    '    and the category id.
```

```vb
Dim sd As SurveyData
sd.strQuestion = ""
sd.strError = ""
sd.Answers = New StringCollection()
sd.nQuestionID = nQuestionID
sd.nCategoryID = nCategoryID

' Create the connection object.
Dim myConnection As New _
  SqlConnection(Application("DBConnectionString").ToString())

Try
    ' Open the connection
    myConnection.Open()

    Dim myCommand As SqlCommand
    Dim reader As SqlDataReader = nothing

    ' If we have a valid question id, perform this code.
    If nQuestionID >= 0 Then
        ' Create a command the will use the sp_QuestionFromID
        '   stored procedure.
        myCommand = New SqlCommand("sp_QuestionFromID", _
          myConnection)
        myCommand.CommandType = CommandType.StoredProcedure

        ' Add a parameter for the question id named @ID
        '   and set the direction and value.
        myCommand.Parameters.Add(New SqlParameter("@ID", _
          SqlDbType.Int))
        myCommand.Parameters("@ID").Direction = _
          ParameterDirection.Input
        myCommand.Parameters("@ID").Value = nQuestionID

        ' Retrieve a recordset by calling the ExecuteReader()
        '   method.
        reader = myCommand.ExecuteReader()

        ' If we got a record, set the question text and
        '   the category id from it.
        If reader.Read() Then
            sd.strQuestion = reader.GetString(0)
            sd.nCategoryID = reader.GetInt32(1)
        End If
```

```
        ' Set the question id and close the reader.
        sd.nQuestionID = nQuestionID
        reader.Close()
Else
        ' This is a new question, so we'll need the count from
        '    the category.
        myCommand = New SqlCommand("sp_QuestionCount", _
            myConnection)
        myCommand.CommandType = CommandType.StoredProcedure

        ' The parameter is CategoryID since we need to specify
        '    the category id.
        myCommand.Parameters.Add(_
            New SqlParameter("@CategoryID", _
            SqlDbType.Int))
        myCommand.Parameters("@CategoryID").Direction = _
            ParameterDirection.Input
        myCommand.Parameters("@CategoryID").Value = -
            nCategoryID

        ' The count will be retrieved, and is therefore set
        '    for output direction.
        myCommand.Parameters.Add(New SqlParameter("@Count", _
            SqlDbType.Int))
        myCommand.Parameters("@Count").Direction = _
            ParameterDirection.Output

        ' Execute the stored procedure by calling the
        '     ExecuteNonQuery() method.
        myCommand.ExecuteNonQuery()

        ' Get the count as in Int32.
        Dim nCount As Integer = _
            Convert.ToInt32(myCommand.Parameters("@Count").Value)

        ' If the count is zero, we have a problem and will
        '    alert the user to the error and return.
        If nCount = 0 Then
            sd.strError = _
                "The sp_QuestionCount procedure returned zero."
            myConnection.Close()
            Return
        End If
```

```vb
' We need a random number from 0 to nCount - 1.
Dim rnd As New Random()
Dim nRandomNumber As Integer = rnd.Next(nCount - 1)


' We're going to call the sp_GetSingleQuestion
'    stored procedure.
myCommand = _
  New SqlCommand("sp_GetSingleQuestion", myConnection)
myCommand.CommandType = CommandType.StoredProcedure


' We need to specify the category id.
myCommand.Parameters.Add(_
  New SqlParameter("@CategoryID", _
  SqlDbType.Int))
myCommand.Parameters("@CategoryID").Direction = _
  ParameterDirection.Input
myCommand.Parameters("@CategoryID").Value = _
  nCategoryID


' We need to specify the record number that we're
'    after.
myCommand.Parameters.Add(_
  New SqlParameter("@RecordNum", _
  SqlDbType.Int))
myCommand.Parameters("@RecordNum").Direction = _
  ParameterDirection.Input
myCommand.Parameters("@RecordNum").Value = _
  nRandomNumber + 1


' Execute the stored procedure by calling the
'    ExecuteReader() method. This returns a recordset.
reader = myCommand.ExecuteReader()


' If we got a record, perform this code.
If reader.Read() Then
    ' Store the question text.
    sd.strQuestion = reader.GetString(0)
    ' Store the question id.
    sd.nQuestionID = reader.GetInt32(1)
    sd.nCategoryID = reader.GetInt32(2)
    ' Store the category id.
```

```
        MyReader.Close()
    End If

    ' We're going to call the sp_AnswerInfo stored procedure.
    myCommand = New SqlCommand("sp_AnswerInfo", myConnection)
    myCommand.CommandType = CommandType.StoredProcedure

    ' Create an id parameter and set its value.
    myCommand.Parameters.Add(New SqlParameter("@ID", _
      SqlDbType.Int))
    myCommand.Parameters("@ID").Direction = _
      ParameterDirection.Input
    myCommand.Parameters("@ID").Value = sd.nQuestionID

    ' Execute the stored procedure by calling the
    '   ExecuteReader() method. This returns a recordset.
    reader = myCommand.ExecuteReader()

    ' For each record, add the string to the StringCollection
    '   object.
    While reader.Read()
        sd.Answers.Add(reader.GetString(0))
    End While
    reader.Close()
Catch ex As Exception
    sd.strError = ex.Message.ToString()
Finally
    If myConnection.State = ConnectionState.Open Then
        myConnection.Close()
    End If
End Try

Return (sd)

End Function
```

The *GetSurveyData()* Method

There isn't much to the GetSurveyData() method. It simply calls the _GetSurveyData() method and returns the results. As discussed earlier in the text, this was done so that the survey generation code could be a private method that other methods (added at a later date) could call upon to retrieve survey data.

Listing 3.17 The `GetSurveyData()` Method

```
<WebMethod()> Public Function GetSurveyData(ByVal nCategory As Integer,_
    ByVal nQuestionID As Integer) As SurveyData
      Return (_GetSurveyData(nCategory, nQuestionID))
End Function
```

The `Vote()` Method

The `Vote()` method is straightforward. It takes the question number and the answer key (which is actually the order of the answer, with a value such as 0, 1, 2, and so on) and calls the `sp_Vote` stored procedure. This stored procedure simply increments that value in the database of the appropriate question, as shown below:

```
CREATE PROCEDURE sp_Vote
      @ID int,
      @Answer int
AS
      UPDATE Answers SET Cnt=Cnt+1 WHERE Ord=@Answer AND
      QuestionID=@ID
GO
```

The actual `Vote()` method creates and opens a database connection (SqlConnection), creates a Command object (SqlCommand), sets up the `@ID` and `@Answer` parameters, and executes the stored procedure (with the `ExecuteNonQuery()` method). The code can be seen in Listing 3.18.

Listing 3.18 The `Vote()` Method

```
<WebMethod()> Public Function Vote(ByVal nQuestionID As Integer,_
    ByVal nAnswerNumber As Integer)
      Dim myConnection As New _
        SqlConnection(Convert.ToString(Application("DBConnectionString")))

      Try
          myConnection.Open()
```

```
      Dim myCommand As New SqlCommand("sp_Vote", myConnection)
      myCommand.CommandType = CommandType.StoredProcedure

      myCommand.Parameters.Add(New SqlParameter("@ID", _
        SqlDbType.Int))
      myCommand.Parameters("@ID").Direction = _
        ParameterDirection.Input
      myCommand.Parameters("@ID").Value = nQuestionID

      myCommand.Parameters.Add(New SqlParameter("@Answer", _
        SqlDbType.Int))
      myCommand.Parameters("@Answer").Direction = _
        ParameterDirection.Input
      myCommand.Parameters("@Answer").Value = nAnswerNumber

      myCommand.ExecuteNonQuery()
      myConnection.Close()
  Catch ex As Exception
      If myConnection.State = ConnectionState.Open Then
          myConnection.Close()
      End If
  End Try
End Function
```

The *GetResults()* Method

The GetResults() method performs three main tasks: It gets a record set with the number of votes for the answers, it creates a list of the raw answer counts in the data structure, and it creates a list of the percentages for each answer in the data structure.

The sp_Results stored procedure is called upon to retrieve the answers, and this stored procedure can be seen below.

```
CREATE PROCEDURE sp_Results
    @ID int
AS
    SELECT Cnt FROM Answers WHERE QuestionID=@ID ORDER BY Ord
GO
```

The next chunk of code that's in the GetResults() method takes care of creating the list of answer counts. These values are the counts for each answer, and they indicate how many times the answers have been voted for.

The last part of the method takes the counts for each answer and calculates the total number of votes for the question. It then goes through and calculates the percentage of votes that each answer has received. The entire GetResults() method can be seen in Listing 3.19.

Listing 3.19 The GetResults() Method

```
<WebMethod()> Public Function GetResults(ByVal nQuestionID As_
   Integer) As SurveyResults
     ' Create a SurveyResults object and initialize some members.
     Dim sr As SurveyResults
     sr.strError = ""
     sr.nCount = Nothing
     sr.dPercent = Nothing

     ' Create the connection object.
     Dim myConnection As New _
       SqlConnection(Convert.ToString(Application("DBConnectionString")))

     Try
         ' Open the connection.
         myConnection.Open()

         ' We're going to call the sp_Results stored procedure.
         Dim myCommand As New SqlCommand("sp_Results", _
           myConnection)
         myCommand.CommandType = CommandType.StoredProcedure

         ' We'll have to specify the ID as a parameter and set its
         '     value.
         myCommand.Parameters.Add(New SqlParameter("@ID", _
           SqlDbType.Int))
         myCommand.Parameters("@ID").Direction = _
           ParameterDirection.Input
         myCommand.Parameters("@ID").Value = nQuestionID

         ' Call the ExecuteReader() method, which returns a
         '     recordset that's contained in a SqlDataReader object.
         Dim reader As SqlDataReader = myCommand.ExecuteReader()

         ' Go through the records and store the new result.
         Dim i As Integer
```

```
Dim nCount As Integer = 0
While reader.Read()
    ' Increment the counter          nCount = nCount + 1

    ' Create a temporary Integer array and copy
    '    the values from the nCount array into it.

    Dim nTempCounts(nCount) As Integer
    For i = 0 To nCount - 2
        nTempCounts(i) = sr.nCount(i)
    Next

    ' Now reinitialize the nCount Integer array to contain
    '    one more than it contains now. Copy the old
    '    values into it.
    sr.nCount(nCount) = New Integer()
    For i = 0 To nCount - 2
        sr.nCount(i) = nTempCounts(i)
    Next
    ' Copy the new value into the newly-created array.
    sr.nCount(nCount - 1) = reader.GetInt32(0)
End While

' We're now going to total up all of the counts.
Dim dTotal As Double = 0
For i = 0 To nCount = 1
    dTotal = dTotal + sr.nCount(i)
Next

' Create a double array for the percents.
sr.dPercent(nCount) = New Double()
' Loop through the list.
For i = 0 To nCount - 1
    ' Either set the percent to zero, or calculate it.
    If dTotal = 0 Then
        sr.dPercent(i) = 0
    Else
        sr.dPercent(i) = (sr.nCount(i) * 100.0) / dTotal
    End If

Next
Catch ex As Exception
    sr.strError = ex.Message.ToString()
```

```
Finally
    If myConnection.State = ConnectionState.Open Then
        myConnection.Close()
    End If
End Try


Return (sr)
End Function
```

Extending and Modifying the Survey Application

I will do some things in the future to make the Survey application even more useful and flexible. I plan to do a couple of things to streamline the source code, too. I'm going to talk about my ideas here, and I might post them on the Web site in the future.

Streamlining the Code

I wrote this chapter so that it was easy to understand. Sometimes, I optimize code and sacrifice code readability as a result. I didn't want that to happen in the chapter examples, so as a result, some code could have been streamlined. The most obvious example in which I could have streamlined code is that for adding parameters to SqlCommand objects. Three lines of code are required to add a parameter along with its value, as shown here:

```
myCommand.Parameters.Add(New SqlParameter("@ID", SqlDbType.Int))
myCommand.Parameters("@ID").Direction = ParameterDirection.Input
myCommand.Parameters("@ID").Value = nQuestionID
```

It would be good to create a helper method named AddParameter() that offers a single line of code to do what is done here in three lines of code. By **helper method,** I'm referring to a method that performs a small amount of functionality, not a full-blown sequence of functionality. We actually need two versions of the AddParameter() method for the Survey application, one for integers and one for strings. The two methods are shown below.

C#
```
void AddParameter( SqlCommand myCommand, string strParamName,
    int nValue )
{
    myCommand.Parameters.Add( new SqlParameter( strParamName,
```

```
        SqlDbType.Int ) );
    myCommand.Parameters[strParamName].Direction =
        ParameterDirection.Input;
    myCommand.Parameters[strParamName].Value = nValue;
}

void AddParameter( SqlCommand myCommand, string strParamName,
    string strValue, int nSize )
{
    myCommand.Parameters.Add( new SqlParameter( strParamName,
        SqlDbType.VarChar, nSize ) );
    myCommand.Parameters[strParamName].Direction =
        ParameterDirection.Input;
    myCommand.Parameters[strParamName].Value = strValue;
}
```

VB

```
Sub AddParameter(ByVal myCommand As SqlCommand,_
    ByVal strParamName As string, ByVal nValue As Integer)
        myCommand.Parameters.Add(New SqlParameter(strParamName, _
            SqlDbType.Int))
        myCommand.Parameters(strParamName).Direction = _
            ParameterDirection.Input
        myCommand.Parameters(strParamName).Value = nValue
End Sub

Sub AddParameter(ByVal myCommand As SqlCommand, _
    ByVal strParamName As string, ByVal strValue as string, _
    ByVal nSize As Integer )
        myCommand.Parameters.Add(New SqlParameter(strParamName,_
            SqlDbType.VarChar, nSize))
        myCommand.Parameters(strParamName).Direction = _
            ParameterDirection.Input
        myCommand.Parameters(strParamName).Value = strValue
End Sub
```

Each of the above methods can be called from Survey application code, thus replacing three lines of code with one. Note one thing, though: These methods add only parameters that have an Input direction.

The following code,

```
myCommand.Parameters.Add(New SqlParameter("@Text", _
    SqlDbType.VarChar, 254))
```

```
myCommand.Parameters("@Text").Direction = ParameterDirection.Input
myCommand.Parameters("@Text").Value = Question.Text

myCommand.Parameters.Add(New SqlParameter("@CategoryID", _
  SqlDbType.Int))
myCommand.Parameters("@CategoryID").Direction = -
  ParameterDirection.Input
myCommand.Parameters("@CategoryID").Value = _
  CategoryList.SelectedIndex

myCommand.Parameters.Add(New SqlParameter("@Enabled", -
  SqlDbType.Int))
myCommand.Parameters("@Enabled").Direction = _
  ParameterDirection.Input
myCommand.Parameters("@Enabled").Value = 0
```

can be replaced with these three lines:

```
AddParameter( myCommand, "@Text", Question.Text, 254 )
AddParameter( myCommand, _
    "@CategoryID", CategoryList.SelectedIndex)
AddParameter( myCommand, "@Enabled", 0 )
```

Using helper methods can reduce the amount of code in your applications. The `AddParameter()` method is a good example of how you can streamline your code with helper methods.

Here are the tradeoffs to consider when you are creating and using helper functions:

- Does the helper method really simplify things? It can actually complicate matters if a lot of parameters must be passed.
- Does the helper method make the code hard to read and thus hard to maintain? If the answer is Yes, then consider avoiding the use of helper functions that make code hard to read, especially if another developer will be maintaining the code.
- Does the helper function reduce the overall amount of code without obfuscating the code's intent? If so, then the use of helper methods is desirable.
- Does the helper function offer reusability so that the functionality can be maintained and bugs can be fixed in a single location? If so, then the user of helper methods is desirable.

Creating a `GetSurveyInHTML()` Method

You might want to create a method in the Web Service that takes a survey question and wraps it in HTML presentation code, by adding the appropriate HTML tags. If doing this would be helpful, then this section will get you started (although you most certainly will change the specifics of the presentation).

The method will start by calling the `_GetSurveyData()` method to retrieve the survey question and answer data. A single string will be returned to the client application that contains all of the HTML data.

The following method shown in Listing 3.20 creates HTML data that renders a survey question:

Listing 3.20 The `GetSurveyInHTML()` Method

C#

```
[WebMethod]
public string GetSurveyInHTML( int nCategoryID, int nQuestionID, string
strVoteURL )
{

    // Create the objects we'll need.
    SurveyData sd = _GetSurveyData( nCategoryID, nQuestionID );
    SurveyResults sr = GetResults( sd.nQuestionID );

    // Create the start of the Html data string.
    string strHTMLData =
      "<form name=\"Survey\" method=\"post\" action=\"" +
      strVoteURL +
      "?ID=4\">\r\n";
    strHTMLData += "<script language=\"javascript\">\r\n";
    strHTMLData += "\tfunction ShowResults()\r\n";
    strHTMLData += "\t{\r\n";
    strHTMLData += "\t\tSurveyResults.innerHTML = ";

    // Loop through each answer.
    for( int i=0; i<sd.Answers.Count; i++ )
    {

// Add the answer, the supporting Html, and the formatted number.
    strHTMLData +=
      ( sd.Answers[i] + ": " + sr.dPercent[i].ToString( ".00" ) +
        "%");
```

```
        if( i < sd.Answers.Count - 1 )
        {
            strHTMLData += "<br>";
        }
        else
        {
            strHTMLData += "\r\n";
        }
    }

    // End this part of the Html.
    strHTMLData += "\t{\r\n";
    strHTMLData += "</script>\r\n";
    strHTMLData += ( "<P>" + sd.strQuestion + "<BR>\r\n" );

    // Loop through each answer again.
    for( int i=0; i<sd.Answers.Count; i++ )
    {
        // Create radio button Html code.
    strHTMLData += ( "<INPUT type=\"radio\" name=\"sr\" value=\"" +
            Convert.ToString( i ) + "\"> " +
            sd.Answers[i] + "<BR>\r\n" );
    }

    // Add the Vote button.
    strHTMLData +=
        "<INPUT type=\"submit\" value=\"Vote\">  " +
        "<INPUT type=\"button\" +
        " onclick=\"ShowResults()\" value=\"Results\"></P>\r\n";
    strHTMLData += "<div id=\"SurveyResults\"></div>\r\n";
    strHTMLData += "</form>\r\n";

    return( strHTMLData );
}
```

VB

```
<WebMethod()> Public Function GetSurveyInHTML(ByVal nCategoryID _
 As _
  Integer, ByVal nQuestionID As Integer, _
  ByVal strVoteURL As String) As String

 ' Create the objects we'll need.
 Dim sd As SurveyData = _GetSurveyData(nCategoryID, nQuestionID)
    Dim sr As SurveyResults = GetResults(sd.nQuestionID)
```

```
' Create the start of the Html data string.
Dim strHTMLData As String = _
   "<form name=Survey method=post action=" + strVoteURL + _
      "?ID=4>" + vbCrLf
strHTMLData += ("<script language=javascript>" + vbCrLf)
strHTMLData += ("function ShowResults()" + vbCrLf)
strHTMLData += ("    {" + vbCrLf)
strHTMLData += "         SurveyResults.innerHTML = "

' Loop through each answer.
Dim i As Integer
For i = 0 To sd.Answers.Count - 1
' Add the answer, the supporting Html, and the formatted number.
      strHTMLData += (sd.Answers(i) + ": " + _
        sr.dPercent(i).ToString(".00") + "%")
      If i < sd.Answers.Count - 1 Then
          strHTMLData += "<br>"
      Else
          strHTMLData += vbCrLf
      End If
Next

' End this part of the Html.
strHTMLData += ("    {" + vbCrLf)
strHTMLData += ("</script>" + vbCrLf)
strHTMLData += ("<P>" + sd.strQuestion + "<BR>" + vbCrLf)

' Loop through each answer again.
For i = 0 To sd.Answers.Count - 1

    ' Create radio button Html code.
    strHTMLData += ("<INPUT type=radio name=sr value=" + _
      Convert.ToString(i) + "> " + _
        sd.Answers(i) + "<BR>" + vbCrLf)
Next

' Add the Vote button.
strHTMLData += _
("<INPUT type=submit value=Vote>  <INPUT type=button" + _
    " onclick=ShowResults() value=Results></P>" + vbCrLf)
strHTMLData += ("<div id=SurveyResults></div>" + vbCrLf)
strHTMLData += ("</form>" + vbCrLf)
```

```
        Return (strHTMLData)
End Function
```

Adding a `ResetResults()` Method

At times, the results for a question need to be reset to zero. This reset might happen on a schedule, or as part of the administrative portion of the application. This section presents a method that can be added to the Web Service to do this, and it can be seen in Listing 3.21.

Listing 3.21 The `ResetResults()` Method

C#
```csharp
[WebMethod]
public string ResetResults( int nQuestionID )
{
SqlConnection myConnection =
 new SqlConnection(
   Convert.ToString(Application["DBConnectionString"]));

    try
    {
        myConnection.Open();
        string strSql =
          "update Answers set Cnt=0 where QuestionID=" +
          Convert.ToString( nQuestionID );
        SqlCommand myCommand =
          new SqlCommand( strSql, myConnection );
        myCommand.ExecuteNonQuery();
        myConnection.Close();
    }
    catch( Exception ex )
    {
        if( myConnection.State == ConnectionState.Open )
        {
            myConnection.Close();
        }
    }
}
```

VB
```vb
<WebMethod()> Public Function ResetResults(ByVal nQuestionID As _
  Integer)
```

```
Dim myConnection As New _
    SqlConnection(Convert.ToString(Application("DBConnectionString")))

Try
    myConnection.Open()
    Dim strSql as string = _
        "update Answers set Cnt=0 where QuestionID=" + _
        Convert.ToString(nQuestionID)
    Dim myCommand As New SqlCommand(strSql, myConnection)
    myCommand.ExecuteNonQuery()
    myConnection.Close()
Catch ex As Exception
    If myConnection.State = ConnectionState.Open Then
        myConnection.Close()
    End If
End Try
End Function
```

Deploying the Survey Application

You must follow a few steps to deploy the Survey application on your server:

1. Start by creating a database named Survey.
2. Then, restore the database that can be obtained from the Web site. (The page that has a link to this download is www.ASPNET-Solutions. com/Chapter_3.htm.) A SQL Script also is available in the same place—you can use it in SQL Query Analyzer to create the database.
3. Next, run Visual Studio .NET. Create a project on the server named Survey for a C# project, or SurveyVB for a VB project. You'll have to make sure you select the appropriate (C# or VB) type of ASP.NET project.
4. Compile the application once it is created.
5. Now, create a project on the server named TheSurvey for a C# project, or TheSurveyVB for a VB project. Here again, you'll have to make sure you select the appropriate (C# or VB) type of ASP.NET Web Service project.
6. Compile the Web Service once it is created.
7. Close the projects in Visual Studio .NET. Not doing so will create a sharing violation for the next steps.

8. Make sure you have downloaded the zipped projects from the Web site. Unzip them (the Survey/SurveyVB application and the The-Survey/TheSurveyVB Web Service) into the default Web site directory (usually c:\inetpub\wwwroot). You will be asked if you want to overwrite existing directories—answer Yes.

9. Open the application project. Check the Global.asax file to make sure that the database connection string matches the connection string for your situation. Compile it. Do the same with the Web Service.

All of this is easy so far, but here's the more difficult part. The application is using a Web Reference to the Web Service on the www.ASPNET-Solutions.com server. That's OK (except that you're using my bandwidth!), but any changes you make to the Web Service will have no effect when your application runs. To fix this, do the following:

10. Delete the Web Reference in your Survey application.

11. Add a Web Reference to your Web Service.

12. Change the references in the code from the class to my Web Service to the class name that wraps your Web Service.

Your Survey application should now be ready to use and ready to modify as you see fit.

Summary

This chapter gives you a starting point for the effective use of ADO.NET. You've learned how to use the SqlConnection, SqlCommand, and SqlDataReader objects. You've also learned how to add parameters to a command and how to call a stored procedure.

A complete and reusable application was introduced to illustrate the ADO.NET topics that were presented. Along the way, best practices and design patterns were presented that will assist you in developing robust applications.

Although this chapter provides 90 percent of what you need for database access, Chapter 4 covers more advanced ADO.NET topics.

Using ADO.NET: Creating a Technical Support Application

In This Chapter:

- Ad Hoc Queries
- The DataAdapter and DataSet Objects
- The Cache API
- The HelpDesk Application
- Extending and Modifying the HelpDesk Application
- Deploying the HelpDesk Application

This chapter teaches additional ADO.NET techniques that you'll commonly use in application development. Whereas the Survey application in Chapter 3 used stored procedures throughout, this chapter and its featured application uses ad hoc queries. The DataAdapter and DataSet objects are discussed because these are extremely useful and flexible data-access objects. The .NET Cache API can cache data obtained from a database, and this in turn speeds up your application performance.

A ready-to-use HelpDesk application illustrates the topics presented in the chapter. The application uses ad hoc queries instead of stored procedures, and it creates the queries with parametric and string concatenating techniques. The HelpDesk application offers users the capability to post problems they're experiencing for the purpose of seeking a resolution. Because a Web-based technical support solution is less expensive than a phone-based solution, this capability might save your company a lot of money. Users can also search on previously entered problems to find resolutions that have already been posted.

Finally, hints on extending and modifying the HelpDesk application follow. These hints give you ways to adapt an already-useful application to your specific needs. A section covers deployment of the HelpDesk application so that you can easily use it in your Web application.

Ad Hoc Queries

An ad hoc query is created dynamically to retrieve information that's required, such as a list of contact addresses; such a query might contain qualifying information that's known, such as a user id. For instance, if your application needed to perform a query to find all orders (in a table named Orders) for a customer with the customer ID of 567, you might use the following SQL query:

```
SELECT * FROM Orders WHERE CustumerID=567
```

Taking that query from SQL to programming code, you might have the following code shown in Listing 4.1:

Listing 4.1 This Code Performs a Query for the Customer ID of 567.

C#
```
SqlConnection objConnection =
new SqlConnection("server=localhost;uid=sa;pwd=;database=SomeDatabase");
try
{
    objConnection.Open();
    SqlCommand objCommand =
      new SqlCommand("SELECT * FROM Orders WHERE CustomerID=567",
      objConnection );
    SqlDataReader reader = objCommand.ExecuteReader();

    // Do something with the data...

    reader.Close();
    objConnection.Close();
}
catch
{
}
finally
{
    if( objConnection.State == ConnectionState.Open )
    {
        objConnection.Close();
    }
}
```

VB

```
Dim objConnection as new _
SqlConnection("server=localhost;uid=sa;pwd=;database=SomeDatabase" )
Try
    objConnection.Open()
    Dim objCommand as new _
      SqlCommand("SELECT * FROM Orders WHERE CustomerID=567", _
      objConnection )
    Dim reader as SqlDataReader = objCommand.ExecuteReader()

    ' Do something with the data...

    reader.Close()
    objConnection.Close()
Catch
Finally
    If objConnection.State = ConnectionState.Open Then
        objConnection.Close()
    End If
End Try
```

Dynamically Created Queries

The preceding code works great if the customer ID is always 567, but that won't usually be the case. Instead, you'll either have to use a bound parameter or dynamically create a string that contains the appropriate SQL for the query.

Let's assume, for the sake of the examples in this section, that the customer ID is contained in a session variable named CID. The session ID may have been assigned at customer login, but in any case, the session variable contains the unique identifier for the customer who's logged on.

Using Parameter Binding

Parameter binding with SQL commands was covered in Chapter 3 in the section entitled "Parameter Binding with SQL Commands." I'd like to show a quick example here, in case you haven't read Chapter 3. The following code shown in Listing 4.2 uses a SqlCommand parameter with which the customer ID value is bound. This arrangement makes creating queries based on dynamic information fairly easy.

Listing 4.2 This Code Performs a Query Based on a Bound Parameter.

C#

```csharp
SqlConnection objConnection =
new SqlConnection("server=localhost;uid=sa;pwd=;database=SomeDatabase");
try
{
    objConnection.Open();
    SqlCommand objCommand =
      new SqlCommand("SELECT * FROM Orders WHERE CustomerID=@CustID",
      objConnection );
    objCommand.Parameters.Add("@CustID", SqlDbType.Int );
    objCommand.Parameters["@CustID"].Direction =
      ParameterDirection.Input;
    objCommand.Parameters["@CustID"].Value =
      Convert.ToInt32( Session["CID"] );
    SqlDataReader reader = objCommand.ExecuteReader();

    // Do something with the data...

    reader.Close();
}
catch
{
}
finally
{
    if( objConnection.State == ConnectionState.Open )
    {
        objConnection.Close();
    }
}
```

VB

```vb
Dim objConnection as new _
SqlConnection("server=localhost;uid=sa;pwd=;database=SomeDatabase" )
Try
    objConnection.Open()
    Dim objCommand as new _
      SqlCommand("SELECT * FROM Orders WHERE CustomerID=@CustID ", _
      objConnection )
    objCommand.Parameters.Add("@CustID", SqlDbType.Int )
    objCommand.Parameters("@CustID").Direction = _
      ParameterDirection.Input
```

```
objCommand.Parameters("@CustID").Value = _
    Convert.ToInt32( Session("CID") )
Dim reader as SqlDataReader = objCommand.ExecuteReader()

' Do something with the data...

    reader.Close()
Catch
Finally
    If objConnection.State = ConnectionState.Open Then
        objConnection.Close()
    End If
End Try
```

Two Clarifications

I've been reading technical books for 25 years, and I have been teaching and speaking for 5 years. Over the years, when I've read technical books, I always seemed to miss something—either it wasn't clear or I just plain missed it. And I see my students go through the same thing. For that reason, I try to anticipate these spots and clarify them. Forgive me if you don't need these two clarifications, but I am guessing that half of you do.

Clarification One is this: The names used for the session variable, the database field, and the parameter do not have to be the same thing. In the above example, the session variable is named `"CID"`, the parameter `"@CustID"`, and the database field `"CustomerID"`. I purposely chose different identifications for each of these objects to emphasize the point that they are different objects and therefore can be named differently. I can't tell you how many students I've had over the years who interchanged session variables with parameters because they had the same name.

Clarification Two is this: C# cannot convert a session variable to an integer because a session variable is an object, and C# won't perform an implicit conversion, but VB will. The C# compiler sees a session variable as a generic object, not knowing what the variable contains (in this case, an integer). VB, however, finds out what's in the session variable and performs the implicit conversion automatically. For instance, the following will cause a compile error in C#:

```
Session["Test"] = 14;
// The following line attempts to implicitly convert an object
//   to an integer. The compiler will not allow this  without a
```

```
//   type cast.
int nTest = Session["Test"];
```

while the following will compile with no difficulty in VB:

```
Session("Test") = 14
Dim nTest as Integer = Session("Test")
```

Why would C# introduce a complexity that VB does not have? The answer has to do with the difference in the languages. VB has always performed implicit conversions, going back to the fact that all variables in VB5 and VB6 were variants (and going back even further, most of the earliest versions of BASIC had a dynamic type system). C# was designed with tighter type safety, and thus requires more explicit coding.

In some ways this dynamic nature makes VB easier and more convenient to use. But this freedom can backfire because the compiler may not catch errant code. Suppose, for example, that your code expects an integer, but the object from which you're getting an integer value contains a string. The compiler won't catch this error, but at runtime an error will be generated. Hopefully, the error will be caught when the software is tested, but C# catches the type conversion error at compile time.

So how do we coerce C# to get an integer value out of a session variable? There are two recommended ways. I normally use the `Convert.ToInt32()` method, which takes an object and converts its contents to an integer. This method is somewhat cumbersome to type, but it's hard to miss what's going on when you read your code. You can alternately use a **type cast** to let the C# compiler know that you intend to convert the contents of the object into an integer. To perform a type cast, place the data type you expect to get in front of the object from which the data will come. The type must be in parentheses, as the following C# examples show:

```
nMyInteger = (int) objSomeObject;
strMyString = (string) objOtherObject;
objThisObject = (ThisObjectType) = objThatObject;
```

The following two C# code snippets give the same final results. One uses `Convert.ToInt32()`, and the other uses a type cast:

```
Example 1
Session["Test"] = 14;
int nTest = Convert.ToInt( Session["Test"] );
```

```
Example 2
Session["Test"] = 14;
int nTest = (int) Session["Test"];

Example 3
int nTest = Session["Test"] as int;

Example 4
int nTest = int.Parse( Session["Test"].ToString() );
```

The last question in all of this is "Why, when VB performs explicit type conversions, did the VB example code in Listing 4.2 use `Convert.ToInt32()`?" Good question. The answer is that I like to be consistent across all languages. I write as much code in VB as in C#. For that reason, the more unified my code can be, the easier it is for me to go back and forth. So you'll see `Convert.ToInt32()` (and other similar conversion methods) throughout the code in this book.

Dynamic SQL in a String

The alternative to parameter binding is to create a string that contains a SQL query. Let's consider, for instance, the query used in Listing 4.1, as shown here:

```
SELECT * FROM Orders WHERE CustomerID=567
```

The customer ID can be any value, depending on who is logged on. We can create a string to reflect this variability. Suppose that the customer ID is contained in a session variable named `CID`. The following code shows how to create a string for the query:

C#
```
string strSql =
  string.Format( "SELECT * FROM Orders WHERE CustomerID={0}",
Session["CID"] );
```

VB
```
Dim strSql As string = string.Format( "SELECT * FROM Orders
WHERE CustomerID={0}",  Session("CID") )
```

The `string.Format()` method uses a string as its first argument, and then a variable number of arguments. The first argument that's a string can contain references to the remaining arguments. For instance, {0} refers to the second argument (that comes after the first string argument). The {0} in the string is replaced by the contents of the second argument. And if a second replacement is to made in the string, it'll be indicated with {1}.

The situation gets a little more difficult when a query string has text data because this must be enclosed between two ' ' characters, as in the following SQL:

```
SELECT * FROM SomeTable WHERE Name='Rick'
```

For SQL that contains text data between single quotes, you must be careful how you structure your SQL string. Suppose that the name we want to use in the query is in a string variable named strName. We can concatenate this variable with other string data to form the SQL string, but we must make sure that the final string encloses the contents of the strName variable with single quotes. The following example shows how to form a query using the contents of a string variable:

C#
```
strName = "George Washington";
// Other code might be here...
string strSql =
  string.Format( "SELECT * FROM Orders WHERE Name='{0}'", strName );
```

VB
```
strName = "George Washington"
' Other code might be here...
Dim strSql As string = _
  String.Format( "SELECT * FROM Orders WHERE Name='{0}'", strName )
```

Parameter Binding vs. Strings

After being presented with two methods of creating ad hoc queries, you're probably wondering which method you should use. It depends. Here are some things to keep in mind to help you decide:

- Parameters require at least two lines of code, and usually three. This requirement might make code sections long if there are a lot of parameters.
- Parameters can make code more readable.

- If there's only one record, parameters can eliminate the need for a data reader. (See Chapter 3 for more details.)
- Queries in strings usually contain less code than the code required for parameter binding.
- Queries in strings can be difficult to read and debug.
- Parameters eliminate a security issue when users type in a name such as `' go Drop Table UserInfo`.

I almost always prefer a SqlDataReader for queries because I find it easier to create and use than using parameters. My students, on the other hand, are usually better off with parameters because they sometimes get confused with single quotes and commas. If you're very comfortable with SQL, you might favor string queries.

If I want to perform a query that retrieves one record with one or two fields, I use parameters. The code's cleaner, and the application doesn't suffer the overhead of a data reader (which makes the program slower).

One last note about parameters vs. strings: If you really want to get performance gains and eliminate the security issues, stored procedures are the way to go. They give you the benefit of having the execution plan pre-built.

The DataAdapter and DataSet Objects

The DataAdapter and DataSet objects offer a great deal of flexibility. They not only let you retrieve data in a flexible manner, but they also give you the opportunity to change data and update the database. This section talks about these two important objects.

The DataSet Object

The DataSet object is the core component of ADO.NET. The DataSet object is best described as a collection of disconnected recordsets that contain a hierarchy of table, row, and column data. A major difference between DataSet objects and a group of disconnected recordsets is that the DataSet internally keeps track of the relationships between tables. With a DataSet, the information requested is cached on the client and disconnected from the server. As a result, the DataSet has no knowledge of its data sources, so separate objects have to pass information between the DataSet and the data source.

Using the disconnected model minimizes resources for open connections and server load. A typical use of a DataSet would include the following steps:

1. Populate a DataSet from a database.
2. Modify the data in the DataSet.
3. Create a new DataSet object that contains only the modified information from the first DataSet.
4. Check for errors in the second DataSet.
5. Fix any errors.
6. Update the DataSet back to the database.
7. Accept or reject the modifications made to the DataSet.

Another important distinction of the DataSet from its ADO Recordset predecessor is the DataSet's capability to track changes as they are made to its internal data and provide error handling on a row-by-row basis. In the previous ADO Recordset model, changes were made and passed back to the server. The recordset would either succeed or fail. Now, with the DataSet model, row errors can be trapped before the data is passed back to the database.

NOTE: One of the most challenging feats for a developer working with ADO.NET will be using the disconnected DataSet model. ADO.NET uses this model for two main reasons: First, scalability reduces the demands placed on database servers, and second, it has XML support. Using XML enables DataSet objects to be independent of databases or a query language, leaving the data bound to a user-defined interface.

DataAdapter

The DataAdapter object is much like the Command object, but it is used specifically to access and manipulate information in a DataSet. The Command object has only one `CommandText` property, whereas the DataAdapter contains four properties: `SelectCommand`, `InsertCommand`, `DeleteCommand` and `UpdateCommand`. The DataAdapter also contains two methods for receiving and sending data to a database. The `Fill()` method populates a DataSet, whereas the `Update()` method sends data from the DataSet back to the data source.

The `Fill()` Method

The `Fill()` method uses two parameters to populate a DataSet: the DataSet object and the name of the table to associate with the data begin loaded. Listings 4.3 through 4.6 are examples of using a DataAdapter object and filling a DataSet with the `Fill()` method.

Listing 4.3 SQL Implementation—Visual Basic Example

```
Dim objConnection as new _
  SqlConnection("server=localhost;uid=sa;pwd=;database=pubs")
Dim objDataAdapter as new _
  SqlDataAdapter("SELECT * FROM Authors",objConnection)
Dim objDataSet as new DataSet
objDataAdapter.Fill(objDataSet,"Authors")
```

Listing 4.4 SQL Implementation—C# Example

```
SqlConnection objConnection = new
  SqlConnection("server=localhost;uid=sa;pwd=;database=pubs");
SqlDataAdapter objDataAdapter =
  new SqlDataAdapter("SELECT * FROM Authors",objConnection);
DataSet objDataSet = new DataSet();
objDataAdapter.Fill(objDataSet,"Authors");
```

Listing 4.5 OLE DB Implementation—Visual Basic Example

```
Dim objConnection as new _
  OleDbConnection("Provider=SQLOLEDB;Data Source=localhost;
uid=sa;pwd=;Initial Catalog=pubs")
Dim objDataAdapter as new _
  OleDbDataAdapter("SELECT * FROM Authors",objConnection)
Dim objDataSet as new DataSet
objDataAdapter.Fill(objDataSet,"Authors")
```

Listing 4.6 OLE DB Implementation—C# Example

```
OleDbConnection objConnection = new
  OleDbConnection("Provider=SQLOLEDB;Data " +
    Source=localhost;uid=sa;pwd=;Initial Catalog=pubs");
OleDbDataAdapter objDataAdapter =
```

```
new OleDbDataAdapter("SELECT * FROM Authors",objConnection);
DataSet objDataSet = new DataSet();
objDataAdapter.Fill(objDataSet,"Authors");
```

Right away you will notice several differences between the `Fill()` method and a managed provider implementation of returning data. First, the connection to the database is not specifically opened or closed. The `Fill()` method encapsulates these calls, so the connection is automatically handled. After the data is returned, the data is cached in the DataSet and the connection terminated, thus the disconnected DataSet model.

Second, the `Fill()` method populates a table named `Authors` in the DataSet. Because the table was not predefined in the DataSet before the `Fill()` method was called, the SqlClient and OleDb DataAdapter objects automatically create the table schema if one is not predefined. If a table schema is created before the table is loaded in the DataSet, the DataSet uses the defined one. Therefore, if an Authors table schema exists before the `Fill()` method is executed, the DataAdapter simply fills the existing defined schema. If you use the `FillSchema()` method, the DataSet's schema is forced to match the schema of the database.

Because no physical relationships exist between the DataSet and the DataAdapter, the DataAdapter can be used to fill any number of DataSet instances. For example, I could add another table to the examples in Listings 4.3 through 4.6 by using the following code:

```
Dim objConnection as new
  SqlConnection("server=localhost;uid=sa;pwd=;database=pubs")
Dim objDataAdapter as new SqlDataAdaoter("SELECT * FROM Authors",
  objConnection)
Dim objDataSet as new DataSet
objDataAdapter.Fill(objDataSet,"Authors")
objDataAdapter.CommandText = "SELECT * FROM Publishers"
objDataAdapter.Fill(objDataSet,"Publishers")
```

The DataSet now contains two different tables—one Authors table and one Publishers table—with completely different structures and data.

The `Update()` Method

The `Update()` method is used to send data from the DataSet back to the data source. Just like the `Fill()` method, the `Update()` method also requires two parameters: the DataSet object and the table name reference.

The connection handling is done automatically. Listing 4.7 uses the `Fill()` method example, modifies some of the rows, and passes the results back to the database.

Listing 4.7 Modifying Data with the `Fill()` Method—Visual Basic Example

```
<%@ Import Namespace="System.Data" %>
<%@ Import Namespace="System.Data.SqlClient" %>
<html>
<head>
<script language="VB" runat="server" ID=Script1>

Sub Page_Load(Sender as Object, E as EventArgs)
  Dim objConnection as _
    new SqlConnection("server=localhost;uid=sa;pwd=;database=pubs")
  Dim objDataAdapter as _
    new SqlDataAdapter("SELECT * FROM Authors", objConnection)

  Dim objDataSet as DataSet

  objDataAdapter.Fill(objDataSet,"Authors")

  Dim objDataView as DataView
  objDataView = new DataView(objDataSet.Tables("Authors"))
  ShowData(objDataView)

  objDataSet.Tables("Authors").Rows(0)("au_fname") = "John"
  objDataSet.Tables("Authors").Rows(0)("au_lname") = "Doe"
  objDataSet.Tables("Authors").Rows(1)("au_fname") = "Jane"
  objDataSet.Tables("Authors").Rows(1)("au_lname") = "Doe"
  objDataAdapter.Update(objDataSet,"Authors")

End Sub

Sub ShowData (objDataView as DataView)

  Dim I as integer
  Response.Write("<table border=1>")
  Response.Write("<th>au_id</th><th>au_fname</th>" + _
    "<th>au_lname</th><th>address</th><th>city</th><th>state</th>" + _
    "<th>zip</th><th>phone</th><th>contract</th>")
```

```
for I = 0 to objDataView.Count - 1
  Response.Write("<tr><td>")
  Response.Write(objDataView(I)("au_id").ToString)
  Response.Write("</td><td>")
  Response.Write(objDataView(I)("au_fname").ToString)
  Response.Write("</td><td>")
  Response.Write(objDataView(I)("au_lname").ToString)
  Response.Write("</td><td>")
  Response.Write(objDataView(I)("address").ToString)
  Response.Write("</td><td>")
  Response.Write(objDataView(I)("city").ToString)
  Response.Write("</td><td>")
  Response.Write(objDataView(I)("state").ToString)
  Response.Write("</td><td>")
  Response.Write(objDataView(I)("zip").ToString)
  Response.Write("</td><td>")
  Response.Write(objDataView(I)("phone").ToString)
  Response.Write("</td><td>")
  Response.Write(objDataView(I)("contract").ToString)
  Response.Write("</td></tr>")
  Next
  Response.Write("</table><br>")
End Sub
</script>
</head>
</html>
```

Listing 4.8 Using the `ShowData()` Method—C# Example

```
void page_load(Object Sender, EventArgs e)
  SqlConnection objConnection =
    new SqlConnection( "server=localhost;uid=sa;pwd=;database=pubs" );
  SqlDataAdapter objDataAdapter =
    new SqlDataAdapter( "SELECT * FROM Authors", objConnection );

  DataSet objDataSet = new DataSet();

  objDataAdapter.Fill( objDataSet,"Authors" );

  int nIndex = objDataSet.Tables.IndexOf( "Authors" );

  // The following assume that two rows of data exist.
  objDataSet.Tables[nIndex].Rows[0]["au_fname"] = "John";
```

```
objDataSet.Tables[nIndex].Rows[0]["au_lname"] = "Doe";
objDataSet.Tables[nIndex].Rows[1]["au_fname"] = "Jane";
objDataSet.Tables[nIndex].Rows[1]["au_lname"] = "Doe";\
objDataAdapter.Update(objDataSet,"Authors");

Dim objDataView as DataView;
objDataView = new DataView(objDataSet.Tables("Authors"));
ShowData(objDataView);
End Sub
```

If I change the first and last names of the first two rows of data and then call the `Update()` method, the data is changed in the database table. To show the modified data, I create a DataView object, and the `ShowData()` method writes the data to the browser.

Another feature of the `Update()` method is its capability to automatically generate commands to complete the `Update` call if the `Insert`, `Update`, or `Delete` commands are not defined. A SQL `Update` statement is generated based on the rows modified. A DiffGram is an XML format used to identify current and original versions of data elements. The DataSet uses the DiffGram format to load and persist its contents, and to serialize its contents for transport across a network connection. When a DataSet is written as a DiffGram, it populates the DiffGram with all the necessary information to accurately recreate the contents, though not the schema, of the DataSet, including column values from both the `Original` and `Current` row versions, row error information, and row order.

Table Mappings

The DataAdapter contains a table-mapping method that enables the data-source table names to be mapped to table names used by the DataSet. Likewise, the returned DataTableMappingCollection object contains a `ColumnMappings` property that enables column names to be mapped as well. The `TableMappings()` method becomes very useful if you have a SQL command or stored procedure that returns multiple `SELECT` statements. The following example performs two `select` statements in a single SQL command:

```
Dim objConnection as new _
   SqlConnection("server=localhost;uid=sa;pwd=;database=pubs")
Dim objDataAdapter as new _
```

```
SqlDataAdapter("SELECT * FROM Authors;SELECT * FROM Publishers", _
   objConnection)
```

```
objDataSetCOmmand.TableMappings.Add("Table","Authors")
objDataSetCOmmand.TableMappings.Add("Table_1","Publishers")
Dim objDataSet as DataSet _
  objDataSetCommand.FillDataSet(objDataSet)
```

Using the `TableMappings` property of the `DataAdapter` object, you can assign specific table names to each `SELECT` statement. Each `SELECT` statement is assigned a default name for the result, starting with `Table`. After the first `SELECT`, each additional mapping requires a sequence number as the source table name.

DataSet Parameter Binding

The use of parameter binding with a DataAdapter is very similar to the managed provider's Command object implementation. The only additional item of consideration with parameter binding is the DataRowVersion used to bind each parameter. Each parameter needs five pieces of information to be bound correctly. These components are parameter name, data type, direction, SourceData, and SourceVersion. The first three elements work exactly like the managed provider's Command object. Now I'll explain the other two.

The `SourceData` parameter tells the DataAdapter which column is to be used when passing data to the data source.

The SourceVersion specifies which version of row information in the DataSet should be used for binding. A DataTable can keep track of changes as data changes are made to its internal rows. Data can be in one of four different states at any given time. Table 4.1 describes these states (which are source version values).

Table 4.1 The Four States Possible for Data

State	Description
Original	Is the version of a row as it was first added to the table.
Default	Is the default version of a row.
Current	Contains any changes that have been made to the row.
Proposed	Represents the state moving from original data to current data. A row moves into this state when the row's `BeginEdit()` method is called.

The next example demonstrates how to bind parameters to a DataAdapter. In this example, shown in Listings 4.9 and 4.10, I need to create two SQL statements: one for the initial DataSet load and another to update the DateSet using the `UpdateCommand` property when the `Update()` method is called.

Notice in the example that I have created my own `update` command to update changes to the Authors table. I have created two SQL statements for the DataAdapter object: one for the initial DataSet load and another to update the DateSet when the `Update()` method is called. Because I defined an explicit `UpdateCommand`, the `Update()` method uses this explicit command instead of dynamically creating one.

Next, I create the parameter bindings to the names in the update statement. The first and last names are bound using the `DataRowVersion.Current` property of the table to capture the modified values. I set the `ID` parameter to use the `DataRowVersion.Original` property. Because this value was not altered, the `Current` version would have worked just as well. However, if I had changed its value and it was the table's Primary Key, I would need to use the `Original` row version to find a match.

Last, I modify the first two rows of data and call the `Update()` method.

Listing 4.9 Two SQL Statements Get the Job Done in This VB Example.

```
Sub Page_Load()

    Dim objConnection as new _
       SqlConnection("server=localhost;uid=sa;pwd=;database=pubs")
    Dim objDataAdapter as new _
       SqlDataAdapter("SELECT * FROM Authors",objConnection)
    objDataAdapter.UpdateCommand = _
       New SqlCommand("Update Authors set au_fname=@Fname," + _
          "au_lname=@Lname WHERE au_id=@ID",objConnection)

    Dim objDataSet as DataSet
    objDataSet = new DataSet()

    objDataAdapter.Fill(objDataSet,"Authors")

    Dim objDataView as DataView
    objDataView = new DataView(objDataSet.Tables("Authors"))
    ShowData(objDataView)
```

```
objDataSet.Tables("Authors").Rows(0)("au_fname") = "yyyy"
objDataSet.Tables("Authors").Rows(0)("au_lname") = "Smith"
objDataSet.Tables("Authors").Rows(1)("au_fname") = "Jane"
objDataSet.Tables("Authors").Rows(1)("au_lname") = "Smith"

objDataAdapter.UpdateCommand.Parameters.Add(_
   new SqlParameter("@Fname",SqlDBType.Varchar,20))
objDataAdapter.UpdateCommand.Parameters("@Fname").Direction = _
   ParameterDirection.Input
objDataAdapter.UpdateCommand.Parameters("@Fname").SourceColumn = _
   "au_fname"
objDataAdapter.UpdateCommand.Parameters("@Fname").SourceVersion = _
   DataRowVersion.Current

objDataAdapter.UpdateCommand.Parameters.Add(_
   new SQLParameter("@Lname",SqlDBType.Varchar,40))
objDataAdapter.UpdateCommand.Parameters("@Lname").Direction = _
   ParameterDirection.Input
objDataAdapter.UpdateCommand.Parameters("@Lname").SourceColumn = _
   "au_lname"
objDataAdapter.UpdateCommand.Parameters("@Lname").SourceVersion = _
   DataRowVersion.Current

objDataAdapter.UpdateCommand.Parameters.Add(_
   new SQLParameter("@ID",SqlDBType.Varchar,11))
objDataAdapter.UpdateCommand.Parameters("@ID").Direction = _
   ParameterDirection.Input
objDataAdapter.UpdateCommand.Parameters("@ID").SourceColumn = _
   "au_id"
objDataAdapter.UpdateCommand.Parameters("@ID").SourceVersion = _
   DataRowVersion.Original

objDataAdapter.Update(objDataSet,"Authors")

End Sub


Sub ShowData (objDataView as DataView)

   Dim I as integer
   Response.Write("<table border=1>")
   Response.Write("<th>au_id</th><th>au_fname</th>" + _
     "<th>au_lname</th><th>address</th><th>city</th><th>state</th>" + _
       "<th>zip</th><th>phone</th><th>contract</th>")
```

```
for I = 0 to objDataView.Count - 1
    Response.Write("<tr><td>")
    Response.Write(objDataView(I)("au_id").ToString)
    Response.Write("</td><td>")
    Response.Write(objDataView(I)("au_fname").ToString)
    Response.Write("</td><td>")
    Response.Write(objDataView(I)("au_lname").ToString)
    Response.Write("</td><td>")
    Response.Write(objDataView(I)("address").ToString)
    Response.Write("</td><td>")
    Response.Write(objDataView(I)("city").ToString)
    Response.Write("</td><td>")
    Response.Write(objDataView(I)("state").ToString)
    Response.Write("</td><td>")
    Response.Write(objDataView(I)("zip").ToString)
    Response.Write("</td><td>")
    Response.Write(objDataView(I)("phone").ToString)
    Response.Write("</td><td>")
    Response.Write(objDataView(I)("contract").ToString)
    Response.Write("</td></tr>")
Next
Response.Write("</table><br>")
End Sub
```

Listing 4.10 Two SQL Statements Get the Job Done in This C# Example.

```
void Page_Load()
{
    SqlConnection objConnection =
      new SqlConnection( "server=localhost;uid=sa;pwd=;database=pubs");
    SqlDataAdapter objDataAdapter = new SqlDataAdapter();
    objDataAdapter.SelectCommand =
      new SqlCommand("SELECT * FROM Authors",objConnection);
    objDataAdapter.UpdateCommand = new SqlCommand(
      "Update Authors set au_fname=@Fname," +
      "au_lname=@Lname WHERE au_id=@ID",objConnection);

    DataSet objDataSet = new DataSet();
    objDataAdapter.Fill(objDataSet,"Authors");

    DataView objDataView;
    objDataView = new DataView(objDataSet.Tables["Authors"]);
```

```
    ShowData(objDataView);

    objDataSet.Tables["Authors"].Rows[0]["au_fname"] = "John";
    objDataSet.Tables["Authors"].Rows[0]["au_lname"] = "Smith";
    objDataSet.Tables["Authors"].Rows[1]["au_fname"] = "Jane";
    objDataSet.Tables["Authors"].Rows[1]["au_lname"] = "Smith";

    objDataAdapter.UpdateCommand.Parameters.Add(
        new SqlParameter("@Fname",SqlDbType.VarChar,20));
    objDataAdapter.UpdateCommand.Parameters["@Fname"].Direction =
        ParameterDirection.Input;
    objDataAdapter.UpdateCommand.Parameters["@Fname"].SourceColumn =
        "au_fname";
    objDataAdapter.UpdateCommand.Parameters["@Fname"].SourceVersion =
        DataRowVersion.Current;

    objDataAdapter.UpdateCommand.Parameters.Add(
        new SqlParameter("@Lname",SqlDbType.VarChar,40));
    objDataAdapter.UpdateCommand.Parameters["@Lname"].Direction =
        ParameterDirection.Input;
    objDataAdapter.UpdateCommand.Parameters["@Lname"].SourceColumn =
        "au_lname";
    objDataAdapter.UpdateCommand.Parameters["@Lname"].SourceVersion =
        DataRowVersion.Current;

    objDataAdapter.UpdateCommand.Parameters.Add(
        new SqlParameter("@ID",SqlDbType.VarChar,11));
    objDataAdapter.UpdateCommand.Parameters["@ID"].Direction =
        ParameterDirection.Input;
    objDataAdapter.UpdateCommand.Parameters["@ID"].SourceColumn =
        "au_id";
    objDataAdapter.UpdateCommand.Parameters["@ID"].SourceVersion =
        DataRowVersion.Original;

    objDataAdapter.Update(objDataSet,"Authors");
}

void ShowData (DataView objDataView)
{
    Response.Write("<table border=1>");
    Response.Write("<th>au_id</th><th>au_fname</th>" +
        "<th>au_lname</th><th>address</th><th>city</th><th>state</th>" +
        "<th>zip</th><th>phone</th><th>contract</th>");
```

```
for(int i=0;i<objDataView.Count - 1;i++)
{
    Response.Write("<tr><td>");
    Response.Write(objDataView[i]["au_id"].ToString());
    Response.Write("</td><td>");
    Response.Write(objDataView[i]["au_fname"].ToString());
    Response.Write("</td><td>");
    Response.Write(objDataView[i]["au_lname"].ToString());
    Response.Write("</td><td>");
    Response.Write(objDataView[i]["address"].ToString());
    Response.Write("</td><td>");
    Response.Write(objDataView[i]["city"].ToString());
    Response.Write("</td><td>");
    Response.Write(objDataView[i]["state"].ToString());
    Response.Write("</td><td>");
    Response.Write(objDataView[i]["zip"].ToString());
    Response.Write("</td><td>");
    Response.Write(objDataView[i]["phone"].ToString());
    Response.Write("</td><td>");
    Response.Write(objDataView[i]["contract"].ToString());
    Response.Write("</td></tr>");
}
Response.Write("</table><br>");
}
```

The Cache API

Many of my classic ASP applications use session and application variables to store data that's used often. This approach can dramatically improve an application's performance because database queries (and other methods of data retrieval) can be done at session or application start, and not every time the application needs the data. Of course, you have to make sure you're loading data that's actually used enough to warrant the pre-loading.

This method only works with data that's constant. If you cache data that changes often, it will not be current and thus not valid when your application uses it. With clever classic ASP programming, however, an application can watch for changes in data that change infrequently without incurring too much overhead.

Of course, there's a price for caching data—that price is called memory. For every piece of cached data, a chunk of memory is committed for as long as the data is cached. You probably wouldn't cache your entire product catalog, but you would very likely cache something small, such as a list of states with which a selection list is populated.

The ASP.NET Cache object offers much more than the session and application variable caching that was so popular in classic ASP programming. Cached objects can expire in several ways, giving you great flexibility. Three methods, `Add()`, `Insert()`, and `Remove()`, offer an easier way to manipulate items. And you can even find out what type of object is cached with the `GetType()` method.

This section will show you how to use the Cache object, and this in turn will offer you a great way to improve your application's performance.

Cache objects maintain state on a per-domain basis. That means each domain can share cached data between various applications that reside inside of the domain, and between all the users in the domain.

Enumerating Cache Items

We'll first take a look at enumerating the cached objects that a server is maintaining for the domain. Each page has a `Cache` property. As the application walks through the list of Cache items, DictionaryEntry objects are returned for each cached object found. The DictionaryEntry object has a `Key` property, which can be used to obtain the object contents from the Cache object. Listing 4.11 shows code that enumerates the items that are currently cached in the domain.

Listing 4.11 This Code Shows All Objects That Are Cached in the Current Domain.

C#

```
string strCacheContents;
string strName;

strCacheContents = "<b>The ASP.NET application cache
contains:</b><br/>";
foreach( DictionaryEntry objItem in Cache )
{
    strName = objItem.Key.ToString();
    // Skip System-created cache objects and look for ones
    //   that were created by applications.
    if( strName.Substring( 0, 7 ) != "System.")
    {
        strCacheContents = strName + " + " + Cache[strName].ToString() +
```

```
        "<br/>";
        Response.Write( strCacheContents );
    }
}
```

VB

```
Dim strCacheContents As String
Dim objItem As DictionaryEntry
Dim strName as String

strCacheContents = "<b>The ASP.NET application cache contains:</b><br/>"
For Each objItem In Cache
    strName = objItem.Key
    If Left(strName, 7) <> "System." Then
        strCacheContents = "key=" & strName & "<br />"
        Response.Write(strCacheContents)
        strCacheContents = "value=" & Convert.ToString(objItem.Value) & _
            "<br/>"
        Response.Write(strCacheContents)
    End If
Next
```

Expiration Types

There are two types of Cache expiration: absolute and sliding. **Absolute expiration** causes a Cache object to expire after a specific time has elapsed, such as five minutes. If you want some data to expire once a day to reflect changes that may have to go into effect, you can set the expiration time for 24 hours.

Sliding expiration causes a Cache object to expire after the object hasn't been accessed for a certain time period. If a Cache object has a sliding expiration of 15 minutes, it won't expire until it hasn't been accessed for 15 minutes. For an example, see the code snippet labeled "Cache Example 1."

Adding, Inserting, and Removing Cache Items

The Cache object provides three methods that make manipulating objects easy: these are the Add(), Insert(), and Remove() methods. This section talks about these three methods.

The `Add()` Method

The `Add()` method adds the specified item to the Cache object with dependencies and expiration and priority policies. The method uses seven arguments: key, value, dependencies, absolute expiration, sliding expiration, priority, and a removal callback. The key is a string that identifies the object that you're placing into the cache, such as `"ListOfStates"`. If a key with this name already exists in the cache, the `Add()` method will fail.

The `value` parameter can be any object that you want to place in the cache. The `dependency` parameter contains either a file or a key dependency. If, for instance, you have a key dependency of `"ListOfCounties"` and the Cache object with the key `"ListOfCounties"` expires, any key that you add with this as a dependency will expire also.

The `priority` parameter determines the urgency with which cached items are evicted from the list. The higher the priority, the closer to the exact expiration time that an object is likely to be removed from the cache. Table 4.2 shows the priorities that can be used.

Table 4.2 Priorities for Cache Objects

Priority	Description
AboveNormal	Cache items with this priority level are less likely to be deleted as the server frees system memory than those assigned a `Normal` priority.
BelowNormal	Cache items with this priority level are more likely to be deleted from the cache as the server frees system memory than items assigned a `Normal` priority.
Default	The default value for a cached item's priority is `Normal`.
High	Cache items with this priority level are the least likely to be deleted from the cache as the server frees system memory.
Low	Cache items with this priority level are the most likely to be deleted from the cache as the server frees system memory.
Normal	Cache items with this priority level are likely to be deleted from the cache as the server frees system memory only after those items with `Low` or `BelowNormal` priority. This is the default.
NotRemovable	The cache items with this priority level will not be deleted from the cache as the server frees system memory.

The last parameter for the Add() method allows you to specify a delete to handle an object's expiration. This doesn't apply to ASP.NET applications because they do not contain code that can be called as a delegate between page requests.

The following example demonstrates how to add an item to the cache with an absolute expiration five minutes from the current time, no sliding expiration, a priority of high, and no notification delegate.

Cache Example 1

C#

```
Cache.Add( "MyName", objSomeObject, null, DateTime.Now.AddMinutes( 15 ),
  null, CacheItemPriority.High, null );
```

VB

```
Cache.Add("MyName", objSomeObject, Nothing, _
  DateTime.Now.AddMinutes( 15 ), Nothing, _
  CacheItemPriority.High, Nothing)
```

The Insert() Method

The Insert() method puts an object into the cache but overwrites any objects currently in the cache with the same key. You would use the Insert() method if you wanted to update an object in the cache.

The following example shows how to use one of the overloaded versions of Insert(). It caches a DSN connection string for two minutes from the current time, using sliding expiration. This particular example provides a callback method that is fired when the Cache object expires.

C#

```
Cache.Insert( "DSN", connectionString, null, DateTime.Now.AddMinutes(2),
  TimeSpan.Zero, CacheItemPriority.High, onRemove );
```

VB

```
Cache.Insert("DSN", connectionString, Nothing, _
  DateTime.Now.AddMinutes(2), TimeSpan.Zero,_
  CacheItemPriority.High, onRemove )
```

The Remove() Method

The Remove() method requires a single parameter, the key. This method removes the object from the cache that matches the key.

The following example demonstrates how you can remove an item from your application's Cache object:

C#
```
Cache.Remove( "timestamp" );
```

VB
```
Cache.Remove( "timestamp" )
```

RECOMMENDED PRACTICE: The above code, though, suggests a problem that could arise when you're using named Cache objects. You could inadvertently mistype in one place in your code, and then things won't work. The following could prevent typos in your code:

C#
```
public const String CacheObjectName = "timestamp";
Cache.Remove( CacheObjectName );
```

VB
```
public const CacheObjectName As String = "timestamp"
Cache.Remove( CacheObjectName )
```

Using Cache Items

The `Get()` method retrieves an object given a key. If the object isn't found in the cache, a `null` is returned (or `Nothing` in VB). The `GetType()` method returns the runtime type of the object.

The HelpDesk Application

The HelpDesk application can be used to support your products online. This application lets users search through problems that have been posted and read the resolutions to the problems. Users also can post new problems, for which you can find and post resolutions. This application can save your company a tremendous amount of money because if your support staff is competent and conscientious, the online Help Desk will reduce your phone support costs immensely.

The HelpDesk application can be separated into two distinct sections. The first section is what all users see, including the screens with which they can search for problems and their resolutions. The second distinct part of

Table 4.3 The HelpDesk Methods Found in Listings 4.12 through 4.21

Method	Listing	Source Code File	Description
`Page_Load()`	4.12	Default.aspx.cs	This method is fired when the default.aspx file is loaded. It simply takes the user name and the time that user was last on, which are contained in session variables, and displays this information on the screen.
`Logout_Click()`	4.12	Default.aspx.cs	This method logs the user out from the HelpDesk application.
`SearchID_Click()`	4.12	Default.aspx.cs	This method takes a problem ID, which the user has specified, and searches for it.
`ViewID_Click()`	4.13	Default.aspx.cs	This method takes an ID the user has specified and searches for the related property. Only users who have submitted the searchable ID can use this method.
`Search_Click()`	4.13	Default.aspx.cs	This method simply redirects to the ViewProblem list page, with a parameter specifying the search criteria.
`AddParameter()` (1)	4.14	Login.aspx.cs	This method simply adds a parameter to a SqlCommand object. With this method, the amount of code used later in the application will be reduced.
`AddParameter()` (2)	4.14	Login.aspx.cs	This method adds a parameter to a SqlCommand object. As with the first `AddParameter()` method, it reduces the amount of code in the application. Unlike the previous `AddParameter()` method, this method assumes that no size is specified for the parameter.

(continued)

Table 4.3 The HelpDesk Methods Found in Listings 4.12 through 4.21 (*cont.*)

Method	Listing	Source Code File	Description
Login_Click()	4.14	Login.aspx.cs	This method let users log in and sets the various session variables that will be used later in the application.
Page_Load()	4.15	ShowIncident. aspx.cs	This method requires a parameter that indicates the incident ID, searches for this ID in the database, and puts the information into the user interface objects so that the user can interact with the information.
Page_Load()	4.16	SubmitProblem. aspx.cs	This method is called when the SubmitProblem page is loaded. It may or may not have an incident ID supplied to it in the form of a query string parameter. If it does, this information is placed into the user interface objects. If it doesn't, the user interface objects are blank, and the user can type in the specifics for a new problem.
MainMenu_Click()	4.17	SubmitProblem .aspx.cs	This method simply redirects to the main page.
UpdateEmail()	4.17	SubmitProblem. aspx.cs	This method updates a user's e-mail address in the database if it is necessary.
Save_Click()	4.17	SubmitProblem. aspx.cs	This method saves the problem information to the database. It may update an existing record, or it may create a new record.
DisplayList()	4.18	ViewProblem-List.aspx.cs	This method queries the database for incidents and displays a list of them from which the user can select.

Table 4.3 The HelpDesk Methods Found in Listings 4.12 through 4.21 (*cont.*)

Method	Listing	Source Code File	Description
`Page_Load()`	4.19	Admin-Administrators.aspx.cs	This method calls the `PopulateAdministratorList()` method. It also checks to make sure that the person logged on has administrative rights.
`Populate-AdministratorList()`	4.19	Admin-Administrators.aspx.cs	This method queries the database and binds the data with a data list so that the user can see and interact with the results.
`MainMenu_Click()`	4.19	Admin-Administrators.aspx.cs	This method simply redirects to the main page.
`AdminMenu_Click()`	4.19	Admin-Administrators.aspx.cs	This method simply redirects to the Admin menu main page.
`Update_Click()`	4.20	Admin-Administrators.aspx.cs	This method updates information for an administrator.
`Delete_Click()`	4.20	Admin-Administrators.aspx.cs	This method deletes an administrator from the database.
`New_Click()`	4.20	Admin-Administrators.aspx.cs	This method creates a new administrator record.
`Administrators_SelectedIndex-Changed()`	4.21	Admin-Administrators.aspx.cs	This method is fired when the user selects an administrator in the data list. The method populates all of the other related fields.

this program is the administrative section, where a person with administrative rights can come to administer various activities related to the program, such as adding administrative accounts and entering the resolution for problems.

A number of source code modules make up the HelpDesk application. Table 4.3 shows the important methods comprising the application, the listing the methods are in, the source code modules in which they can be found, and a description. Not every source code module is shown in this chapter because many of them are similar and need not be explained separately. All the pages that are similar fall into the administrative section of the application. I have shown, in Listings 4.19, 4.20, and 4.21, the Admin-Administrators source code module, which is almost identical to the other administrative modules.

Listing 4.12 contains three of the methods from Default.aspx.cs that are important. The `Page_Load()` method simply takes information from two session variables, `UserName` and `LastOn`, and displays them on the screen so it is easy to see who has logged on and what the last date/time of logon is. The `LogIn_Click()` method uses the `FormsAuthentication` class to log the user in. This application uses `FormAuthentication`, and the `SignOut()` method is used to actually log a user out. Once the user has been signed out, he is redirected to the login page.

The `SearchID_Click()` method is fired when a user clicks on a search ID button. The first thing this method does is take a look at the editable text field with the identifier of `LookupID`. If no data is in this field, then no search can be carried out. When that is the case, an error message is displayed in the page, and the return is performed. Later in this method, the data that is found in the `LookUpID` field is converted into an integer. If the data in the text field isn't numeric (for instance, if the user typed in her name or something else like that) then an exception will be thrown, caught, and no action will be taken. However, if the `LookUpID` field is successfully converted to an integer value, the user will be redirected to the ShowIncident page, and the converted IncidentID will be carried as a parameter, which will be retrieved with the `QueryString()` method.

RECOMMENDED PRACTICE: You might normally expect a user to enter a numeric value when that is called for in the user interface, but to take it as a given that he will is not a good idea. If the user types in something that is not numeric, and you try to evaluate the data with one of the `Convert` methods, doing so could very well and probably will throw an exception.

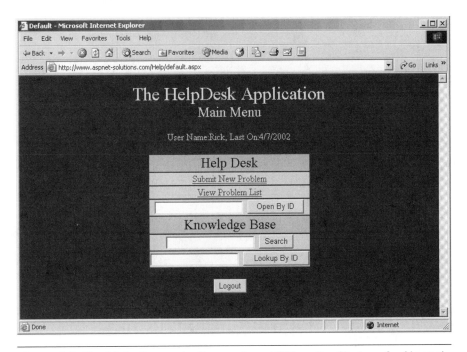

Figure 4.1 The Main Screen Is Compact and Offers the Choices for Normal Users.

You can protect yourself from this in two ways. The first is to use a validator that contains a regular expression that matches only numerics. This validator will not let users proceed with non-numerics in the field.

Additionally, you should catch any exceptions that might be thrown when they're being converted from a text field to numeric data.

You can see the HelpDesk application's main screen in Figure 4.1. It is clear and easy to understand.

Listing 4.12 Methods in Default.aspx.cs

```
private void Page_Load(object sender, System.EventArgs e)
{
    UserInfo.Text =
      "User Name:" + Convert.ToString( Session["UserName"] ) +
      ",   Last On:" +
      Convert.ToDateTime( Session["LastOn"] ).ToString();
}
```

```
private void Logout_Click(object sender, System.EventArgs e)
{
    FormsAuthentication.SignOut();
    Response.Redirect( "Login.aspx" );
}


private void SearchID_Click(object sender, System.EventArgs e)
{
    if( LookupID.Text.Trim().Length == 0 )
    {
        ErrorMessage.Text = "There is nothing in the ID field.<br>";
        return;
    }

    try
    {
        int nIncidentID = Convert.ToInt32( LookupID.Text.Trim() );
        Response.Redirect( "ShowIncident.aspx?IncidentID=" +
            Convert.ToString( nIncidentID ) );
    }
    catch( Exception ex )
    {
        ErrorMessage.Text = ex.Message.ToString() + "<br>";
    }
}
```

The code in Listing 4.13 contains the rest of the methods from Default.aspx.cs. The ViewID_Click() method first makes sure that the ID field contains data. If it does not, then the program displays an error message and simply returns.

A SqlConnection object is created, and the connection string is obtained from the Application("DBConnectString") object. The try/catch block is set up so that exceptions resulting from numeric parse errors and database errors will be caught and errors displayed. The first thing inside the try block is a conversion from the OpenID field into an integer, which represents the ID of the incident that is to be viewed.

This code includes a chunk of database-related code. The SqlConnection object is opened, a command is created (which is a select for the incident table), and a SqlDataReader is obtained from the SqlCommand object's ExecuteReader() method. Then the SqlDataReader is used to see whether any matching records exist, and if so, the user ID is obtained from the SqlDataReader object. This piece is important because the user who is logged on must match the user ID which matches the incident object. This requirement is so that users who do not create this particular incident cannot edit it. Once the query has been performed, the Sql-DataReader and the SqlConnection objects are closed. If no record was found, an error message is displayed for the page and a return is performed.

The session ID that contains the user type is then evaluated using `Convert.ToInt32()` method. If the user type is 1, the user that is logged on has administrative rights. If the user type is 0, this user has no administrative rights, and the incident creator ID must match the logged user's ID.

If the person logged on does not have administrative rights, and the incident ID does not match the user ID, then an error message is displayed to the user, and a return is performed. If everything matches up, though, the user is redirected to the submit problem page, or the incident will be displayed and offer the user the capability to edit.

The `Search_Click()` method simply redirects the user to the ViewProblemList page. If the search criteria is carried to the ViewProblemList page as a parameter, and then it is used in the query.

Listing 4.13 Methods in Default.aspx.cs

```
private void ViewID_Click(object sender, System.EventArgs e)
{
    if( OpenID.Text.Trim().Length == 0 )
    {
        ErrorMessage.Text = "There is nothing in the ID field.<br>";
        return;
    }

  SqlConnection objConnection = new
    SqlConnection( Convert.ToString( Application["DBConnectString"] ) );

    try
    {
        int nIncidentID = Convert.ToInt32( OpenID.Text.Trim() );

        objConnection.Open();
        SqlCommand objCommand =
          new SqlCommand( "SELECT UserID FROM Incident WHERE ID=" +
            Convert.ToString( nIncidentID ), objConnection );
        SqlDataReader reader = objCommand.ExecuteReader();
```

```
            bool bFound = reader.Read();
            int nUserID = Convert.ToInt32( reader["UserID"] );
            reader.Close();
            objConnection.Close();

            if( !bFound )
            {
                ErrorMessage.Text =
                  "No match was found for the entered ID.<br>";
                return;
            }

            if( Convert.ToInt32( Session["UserType"] ) == 1 )
            {
                Response.Redirect( "SubmitProblem.aspx?IncidentID=" +
                  Convert.ToString( nIncidentID ) );
            }

            if(Convert.ToInt32( Session["UserID"] ) != nUserID )
            {
                ErrorMessage.Text =
                  "The current user cannot edit that problem.<br>";
                return;
            }

            Response.Redirect( "SubmitProblem.aspx?IncidentID=" +
              Convert.ToString( nIncidentID ) );
        }
    catch( Exception ex )
    {
        if( objConnection.State == ConnectionState.Open )
        {
            objConnection.Close();
        }
        ErrorMessage.Text = ex.Message.ToString() + "<br>";
    }
}

private void Search_Click(object sender, System.EventArgs e)
{
    Response.Redirect( "ViewProblemList.aspx?SearchCriteria=" +
      SearchSpec.Text );
}
```

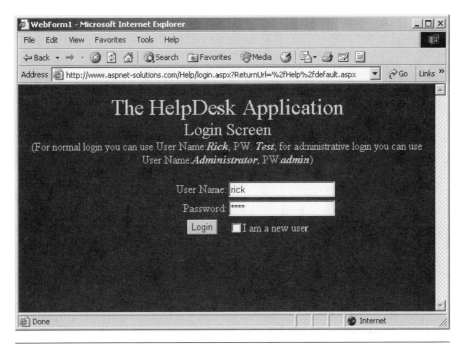

Figure 4.2 Before Using the HelpDesk Application, You Must Log In.

Listing 4.14 has code that can be found in a Login.aspx.cs file. It is important to know that this program uses forms authentication, and that the user must log in, as shown in Figure 4.2.

There are two `AddParameter()` methods. These methods make it easy to add parameters to SqlCommand objects. Using these two methods reduces the amount of code in this source module. Less code makes not only for a more efficient assembly because smaller chunks of code execute faster but also makes understanding and maintaining the code easier. The first `AddParameter()` method lets you specify the size of the parameter type. Doing this is important for types that have variable lengths, such as `varchar` and `nvarchar` (as opposed to integers, which are 4 bytes). The second `AddParameter()` method does not let you specify the size, and it works great when you are using integers and things that always have a constant size. Both of these methods set the parameter direction for output. This setting is perfectly fine for the code found in the `Login_Click()` method because it doesn't need to add parameters for any other direction except output.

Next, we will take a look at the `Login_Click()` method. This method creates a SqlConnection object and gets the connect string from the application variable that we have already created in this application. A `try/catch` block makes sure that any exceptions that are thrown are caught, and that means the error messages are displayed to users. First, the connection is opened. Next, a SQL string is created based on the user name found in the `UserName` editable text field. The SqlCommand object is created, and then six parameters are added. These parameters are `@Password`, `@ID`, `@UserType`, `@LastOn`, `@Name`, and `@Email`. After adding these parameters, the SqlCommand object `ExecuteNonQuery()` method is called.

Some local variables I declared are used in this method. They will contain the user ID, the user type, the date that the user was last on, the user name, and the user e-mail address. If the user has checked the new user checkbox in the user interface, then we execute code that creates a new record. This is the first code that is seen after the local variables are declared. The first thing that is done is to check the ID field that was returned from the query. If the ID is found, then this indicates the user name already exists in the database. If that is the case, the connection is closed, and we bail out of the method with a return. If, however, the user name is not found in the database, a new record is created using a SQL `Insert` command. The ID that was retrieved is then stored in the local ID variable for use later in the code, and the user name is stored in the `Session["UserName""]` variable.

If the user is trying to log on and has not checked the new user box, a chunk of code is executed that checks the user's credentials against the database information. If the ID field is `null`, then a matching record was not found. When this is the case, an error message is shown to the user and a return is performed.

The password is retrieved from the query that was performed earlier in this method, and if the password does not match the password the user typed in, the user is alerted to the mismatch, the connection object is closed, and we bail out of the method with a return. If the user name has been found and the password matches, then all the information needed is retrieved from the parameters of the Command object. The last piece of database code that is performed is to update the date when the user has been logged on. This update is done so that we always know the last time of day that the user was logged on.

The last piece of code performed in this method is to set session variables so that they contain the relevant information. This information includes the user ID, the user type, the date the user was last on, the user name, and the user e-mail address. Finally, the user is redirected to the Default.aspx page. Because this application uses forms authentication, this redirect is done using the forms authentication class.

Listing 4.14 Methods in Login.aspx.cs

```
private void AddParameter( ref SqlCommand objCommand, string strName,
SqlDbType Type, int nSize )
{
    objCommand.Parameters.Add( strName, Type, nSize );
    objCommand.Parameters[strName].Direction =
      ParameterDirection.Output;
}

private void AddParameter( ref SqlCommand objCommand, string strName,
SqlDbType Type )
{
    objCommand.Parameters.Add( strName, Type );
    objCommand.Parameters[strName].Direction =
      ParameterDirection.Output;
}

private void Login_Click(object sender, System.EventArgs e)
{
  SqlConnection objConnection = new
    SqlConnection( Convert.ToString( Application["DBConnectString"] ) );

    try
    {
        objConnection.Open();

        string strSql =
            "SELECT @ID=ID,@UserType=UserType,@Password=Password, " +
            "@LastOn=DateLastOn,@Name=Name,@Email=Email " +
            "FROM UserInfo WHERE Name='" + UserName.Text.Trim() + "'";
        SqlCommand objCommand = new SqlCommand( strSql, objConnection );
        AddParameter( ref objCommand, "@Password", SqlDbType.VarChar,
          254 );
        AddParameter( ref objCommand, "@ID", SqlDbType.Int );
        AddParameter( ref objCommand, "@UserType", SqlDbType.Int );
        AddParameter( ref objCommand, "@LastOn", SqlDbType.DateTime );
        AddParameter( ref objCommand, "@Name", SqlDbType.VarChar, 254 );
        AddParameter( ref objCommand, "@Email", SqlDbType.VarChar,
          254 );
        objCommand.ExecuteNonQuery();

        int nID, nUserType = 0;
        DateTime objLastOn = DateTime.Now;
```

```
string strUserName = "";
string strEmail = "";

if( NewUser.Checked )
{
    if( !Convert.IsDBNull( objCommand.Parameters["@ID"].Value ))
    {
        ErrorMessage.Text =
          "The user name you entered already exists.";
        objConnection.Close();
        return;
    }

    strSql = "INSERT INTO UserInfo (Name,Password) VALUES('" +
        UserName.Text.Trim() + "','" + Password.Text.Trim() +
        "') SELECT @ID=@@IDENTITY";
    objCommand = new SqlCommand( strSql, objConnection );
    AddParameter( ref objCommand, "@ID", SqlDbType.Int );
    objCommand.ExecuteNonQuery();

    nID = Convert.ToInt32( objCommand.Parameters["@ID"].Value );
    strUserName = UserName.Text;
}
else
{
    if( Convert.IsDBNull( objCommand.Parameters["@ID"].Value ) )
    {
        ErrorMessage.Text =
          "The user name you entered does not exist.";
        objConnection.Close();
        return;
    }

  string strPassword =
    Convert.ToString( objCommand.Parameters["@Password"].Value);
    if( strPassword.ToUpper() != Password.Text.Trim().ToUpper())
    {
        ErrorMessage.Text =
          "The password you entered is incorrect.";
        objConnection.Close();
        return;
    }
```

```
        nID = Convert.ToInt32( objCommand.Parameters["@ID"].Value );
        nUserType =
         Convert.ToInt32( objCommand.Parameters["@UserType"].Value);
        objLastOn =
         Convert.ToDateTime( objCommand.Parameters["@LastOn"].Value);
        strUserName =
         Convert.ToString( objCommand.Parameters["@Name"].Value );
        strEmail =
         Convert.ToString( objCommand.Parameters["@Email"].Value );

        objCommand =
          new SqlCommand( "update UserInfo set DateLastOn='" +
          DateTime.Now.ToShortDateString() + "'", objConnection );
        objCommand.ExecuteNonQuery();
      }

    objConnection.Close();
    Session["UserID"] = nID;
    Session["UserType"] = nUserType;
    Session["LastOn"] = objLastOn;
    Session["UserName"] = strUserName;
    Session["Email"] = strEmail;
    FormsAuthentication.RedirectFromLoginPage( UserName.Text,false);
  }
  catch( Exception ex )
  {
    ErrorMessage.Text = ex.Message.ToString();
  }
  finally
  {
    if( objConnection.State == ConnectionState.Open )
    {
        objConnection.Close();
    }
  }
}
```

The code show in Listing 4.15 is from the ShowIncident.aspx.cs file. In the `Page_Load()` method, the first thing that happens is that the value contained in the query string `IncidentID` is converted to an integer. This integer will represent the database ID that will uniquely identify this par-

Table 4.4 Methods for the Application

Method	Listing	Source Code File	Description
Page_Load()	4.12	Default.aspx.cs	This method is fired when the default.aspx file is loaded. It simply takes the user name and the time that user was last logged in, which are contained in session variables, and displays this information on the screen.
Logout_Click()	4.12	Default.aspx.cs	This method logs the user out from the HelpDesk application.
SearchID_Click()	4.12	Default.aspx.cs	This method takes a problem ID, which the user has specified, and searches for it.
ViewID_Click()	4.13	Default.aspx.cs	This method takes an ID the user has specified and searches for the related property. Only users who have submitted the searchable ID can use this method.
Search_Click()	4.13	Default.aspx.cs	This method simply redirects to the ViewProblem list page, with a parameter specifying the search criteria.
AddParameter() (1)	4.14	Login.aspx.cs	This method simply adds a parameter to a SqlCommand object. By using this method the amount of code used later in the application will be reduced.
AddParameter() (2)	4.14	Login.aspx.cs	This method adds a parameter to a SqlCommand object. As with the first AddParameter() method, it reduces the amount of code in the application. This method, unlike the previous AddParameter() method, assumes that no size is specified for the parameter.

(continued)

Table 4.4 Methods for the Application (*cont.*)

Method	Listing	Source Code File	Description
Login_Click()	4.14	Login.aspx.cs	This method lets users log in and sets the various session variables that will be used later in the application.
Page_Load()	4.15	ShowIncident.aspx.cs	This method takes a parameter that indicates the incident ID, searches for that ID in the database, and puts the information into the user interface objects so that the user can interact with the information.
Page_Load()	4.16	SubmitProblem.aspx.cs	This method is called when the SubmitProblem page is loaded. The page may or may not have an incident ID, which is supplied to it in the form of a query string parameter. If it does, this information is placed into the user interface objects. If it doesn't, the user interface objects are blank, and the user can type in the specifics for a new problem.
MainMenu_Click()	4.17	SubmitProblem.aspx.cs	This method simply redirects to the main page.
UpdateEmail()	4.17	SubmitProblem.aspx.cs	This method updates a user's e-mail address in the database if it is necessary.
Save_Click()	4.17	SubmitProblem.aspx.cs	This method saves the problem information to the database. It may update a current record ,or it may create a new record.
DisplayList()	4.18	ViewProblem-List.aspx.cs	This method queries the database for incidents and displays a list of them from which the user can select.

(continued)

Table 4.4 Methods for the Application (*cont.*)

Method	Listing	Source Code File	Description
Page_Load()	4.19	Admin-Administrators.aspx.cs	This method calls the PopulateAdministrator-List() method. It also checks to make sure that the person logged on has administrative rights.
Populate-Administrator-List()	4.19	Admin-Administrators.aspx.cs	This method queries the database and binds the data with a data list so that the user can see and interact with the results.
MainMenu_Click()	4.19	Admin-Administrators.aspx.cs	This method simply redirects to the main page.
AdminMenu_Click()	4.19	Admin-Administrators.aspx.cs	This method simply redirects to the Admin menu main page.
Update_Click()	4.20	Admin-Administrators.aspx.cs	This method updates information for an administrator.
Delete_Click()	4.20	Admin-Administrators.aspx.cs	This method deletes an administrator from the database.
New_Click()	4.20	Admin-Administrators.aspx.cs	This method creates a new administrator record.
Administrators_SelectedIndex-Changed	4.21	Admin-Administrators.aspx.cs	This method is fired when the user selects an administrator in the data list. The method populates all the other related fields.

ticular incident. A hidden text field named `problem ID` will maintain this value for later use. You can see this text field being assigned the value that the incident ID contains. A SqlConnection is created and a `try/catch` block follows. The SqlConnection is opened with the `Open()` method, and a string that contains the query is informed. Essentially, the query will select user ID location, phone, title, description, and resolution from the database incident corresponding to this ID. A SqlCommand object is created with the query string. And, finally, a SqlDataReader is obtained by executing the SqlCommand object's `ExecuteReader()` method.

If a record has been found, then the `SqlDataReader.read()` method will return `True` and code will execute that populates the user interface object with the information found in the database. For instance, the problem title, the description, and the resolution are retrieved from the database and placed in user-interface elements. The location and phone information are also retrieved and placed into a string variable that will be used shortly. A new query is made to retrieve information about the particular user who submitted this problem. The user information is queried from the UserInfo table, and if a match is found, this information, along with the location and phone information, forms the information in the form that will identify the submitter and all pertinent information. The `catch` block closes the SqlConnection object and shows the user the error message.

Listing 4.15 Methods in ShowIncident.aspx.cs

```
private void Page_Load(object sender, System.EventArgs e)
{
    int nIncidentID =
      Convert.ToInt32( Request.QueryString["IncidentID"] );
    ProblemID.Text = Convert.ToString( nIncidentID );
    SqlConnection objConnection = new
      SqlConnection( Convert.ToString( Application["DBConnectString"]));

    try
    {
        objConnection.Open();

        string strSql =
           "SELECT UserID,Location,Phone,Title,Description,Resolution" +
           "FROM Incident WHERE ID=" +
           Convert.ToString( nIncidentID );
        SqlCommand objCommand = new SqlCommand( strSql, objConnection );
        SqlDataReader reader = objCommand.ExecuteReader();
        if( reader.Read() )
        {
            ProblemTitle.Text = Convert.ToString( reader["Title"] );
            Description.Text =
              Convert.ToString( reader["Description"] );
```

```
        string strResolution = Convert.ToString( reader["Title"] );
        if( strResolution.Length == 0 )
        {
            strResolution = "None yet...";
        }
        Resolution.Text = strResolution;
        string strLocation = Convert.ToString( reader["Location"] );
        string strPhone = Convert.ToString( reader["Phone"] );

        int nUserID = Convert.ToInt32( reader["UserID"] );
        reader.Close();
        string strUserName = "";
        string strEmail = "";

        strSql = "SELECT Name,Email FROM UserInfo WHERE ID=" +
          Convert.ToString( nUserID );
        objCommand = new SqlCommand( strSql, objConnection );
        reader = objCommand.ExecuteReader();
        if( reader.Read() )
        {
            strUserName = Convert.ToString( reader["Name"] );
            strEmail = Convert.ToString( reader["Email"] );
        }
        reader.Close();

        Submitter.Text = strUserName + ", Email:" + strEmail +
          ", Location:" + strLocation +
          ", Phone:" + strPhone;

    }
    else
    {
        reader.Close();
        ProblemTitle.ForeColor = Color.Red;
        ProblemTitle.Text = "No records found!";
    }
    objConnection.Close();
}
catch( Exception ex )
{
    if( objConnection.State == ConnectionState.Open )
    {
        objConnection.Close();
```

```
        }
        ProblemTitle.ForeColor = Color.Red;
        ProblemTitle.Text = ex.Message.ToString();
    }
}
```

Listing 4.16 shows the code that is called when the SubmitProblem page is loaded. The code is actually performed only the first time through and not for any subsequent post backs. The first thing the code does is retrieve an ID from the query string that was passed into the page. Then it retrieves the user name and e-mail addresses from two session variables that were previously set.

The database code is fairly simple. A SqlConnection object is created and then opened. A SqlCommand object is created with a simple query that retrieves the ID and name columns from the Category table. The record set that is returned will be contained in a SqlDataReader object, and this DataReader object will then be bound to the category list box that is part of the user interface. Another SqlCommand object is created that retrieves all the departments from the database. The record set contained in the departments is then bound to the department list box that is also part of the user interface.

If the variable `IncidentId` is greater than 0, this means that there was an IncidentId passed in the query string. An entire block of code is performed if that is the case. This block of code retrieves the information related to this incident from the database and then populates the user interface objects with the information.

A SqlCommand object is created in which the query that retrieves the correct indicant from the database is created. The reader's `Execute-Reader()` method is called, and a SqlDataReader object is returned. If the data reader's `Read()` method returns `True`, this means a record was returned and is part of a record set. If that is the case, then the fields from the record set will be used to populate the user interface object for the page.

Two small details must be attended to for the user interface to correctly reflect the retrieved information. The Category drop-down list must be set to the correct category in which this incident belongs, and the Department drop-down list must be set to correctly reflect the department to which this incident belongs. You can see two for loops, each of which sets the correct item in a category list and a department list, respectively.

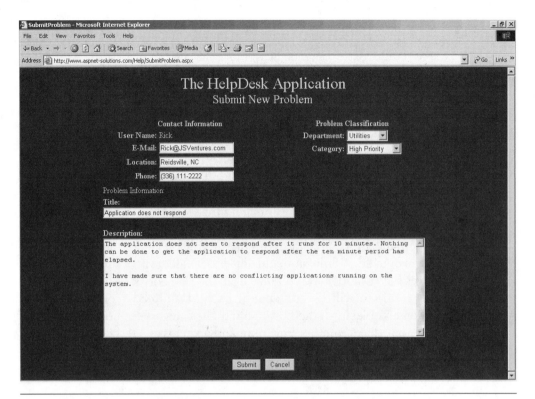

Figure 4.3 Users Can Submit Problems for Resolution.

You can see in Figure 4.3 the submission screen with which users can submit or edit problems.

Listing 4.16 Methods in SubmitProblem.aspx.cs

```
private void Page_Load(object sender, System.EventArgs e)
{
    if( !IsPostBack )
    {

        int nIncidentID =
          Convert.ToInt32( Request.QueryString["IncidentID"] );

        UserName.Text = Convert.ToString( Session["UserName"] );
        Email.Text = Convert.ToString( Session["Email"] );
```

```
SqlConnection objConnection = new
 SqlConnection(Convert.ToString(Application["DBConnectString"]));
  try
  {
      objConnection.Open();

      SqlCommand objCommand = new
        SqlCommand( "SELECT ID,Name FROM Category",objConnection);
      SqlDataReader reader = objCommand.ExecuteReader();
      Category.DataTextField = "Name";
      Category.DataValueField = "ID";
      Category.DataSource = reader;
      Category.DataBind();
      reader.Close();

      objCommand = new
        SqlCommand("SELECT ID,Name FROM Department",objConnection);
      reader = objCommand.ExecuteReader();
      Department.DataTextField = "Name";
      Department.DataValueField = "ID";
      Department.DataSource = reader;
      Department.DataBind();
      reader.Close();

      if( nIncidentID > 0 )
      {
          ScreenTitle.Text = "Edit Problem";
          Button1.Text = "Update";
          ForUpdate.Text = "1";
          IncidentID.Text = Convert.ToString( nIncidentID );

          objCommand = new SqlCommand(
            "SELECT Title,Location,Resolution,Phone, " +
            "CatID,DeptID,Description FROM Incident WHERE ID=" +
             Convert.ToString( nIncidentID ), objConnection );
          reader = objCommand.ExecuteReader();

          if( reader.Read() )
          {
              Title.Text = Convert.ToString( reader["Title"] );
              Location.Text =
                Convert.ToString( reader["Location"] );
```

```
        Phone.Text = Convert.ToString( reader["Phone"] );
        Description.Text =
          Convert.ToString( reader["Description"] );
        Resolution.Text =
          Convert.ToString( reader["Resolution"] );

        int nCatID = Convert.ToInt32( reader["CatID"] );
        int DeptID = Convert.ToInt32( reader["DeptID"] );

       for( int i=0; i<Category.Items.Count; i++ )
       {
        if(Convert.ToInt32(Category.Items[i].Value)==nCatID)
           {
              Category.SelectedIndex = i;
              break;
           }
       }

      for( int i=0; i<Department.Items.Count; i++ )
      {
       if(Convert.ToInt32(Department.Items[i].Value)==nCatID)
          {
             Department.SelectedIndex = i;
             break;
          }
      }

     }
     reader.Close();
    }

    objConnection.Close();
   }
   catch
   {
       if( objConnection.State == ConnectionState.Open )
       {
          objConnection.Close();
       }
   }
  }
 }
}
```

The code in Listing 4.17 is used to respond to user events from the SubmitProblem page. The first message you see is from the `MainMenu_Click()` method. This message simply redirects to the main menu page.

The `UpdateEmail()` method takes a look at the e-mail address that the user has entered. It saves this e-mail address to the database for this particular user. It is important to note, though, that the `UpdateEmail()` method is not called unless the e-mail address is blank or the user has made a change in his e-mail address.

The `Save_Click()` method is the one in which a great deal of the work is done. First, it takes a look at the query string named NE. This query string will indicate whether or not the page is read-only. Actually, "NE" stands for "no edit." If this particular page has been called and is set for no edit, at this point the user is redirected to the main page.

A SqlConnection object is created and then opened. Right below where you see the SqlConnection object being opened, you will see that the e-mail address is examined to see whether it is either blank or has changed. If it has changed, then the `UpdateEmail()` method is called.

A hidden text field named `ForUpdate` indicates whether or not this particular incident record can be updated. If it can't be updated, then a new record must be created. You can see in the code when a new record is created because the SQL statement uses the insert command.

After the query string has been created, a SqlCommand object is created, and an `ID` parameter is added so that the newly created identity field, which represents the ID value, can be returned after the SQL command has been executed. Moving down a few lines, you can see where an update statement has been created. This code updates an incident record rather than creating a new incident record. You can see that the SQL string is created, a SqlCommand object is created, and the Command object's `ExecuteNonQuery()` method is called. The user is then redirected to a page ThanksForNew. This page acknowledges the user's interaction and thanks him.

Listing 4.17 Methods in SubmitProblem.aspx.cs

```
private void MainMenu_Click(object sender, System.EventArgs e)
{
    Response.Redirect( "Default.aspx" );
}
```

```
private void UpdateEmail( SqlConnection objConnection, string strEmail )
{
    Session["Email"] = strEmail;
    string strSql = "Update UserInfo set Email='" +
        strEmail + "' WHERE ID=" +
        Convert.ToString( Session["UserID"] );
    SqlCommand objCommand = new SqlCommand( strSql, objConnection );
    objCommand.ExecuteNonQuery();
}

private void Save_Click(object sender, System.EventArgs e)
{

    if( Convert.ToInt32( Request.QueryString["NE"] ) == 1 )
    {
        Response.Redirect( "default.aspx" );
    }

    ErrorMessage.Text = "";

    SqlConnection objConnection =
      new SqlConnection(
        Convert.ToString( Application["DBConnectString"] ) );

    try
    {
        objConnection.Open();

        if( Convert.ToString( Session["Email"] ).Length == 0 &&
            Email.Text.Trim().Length > 0 )
        {
            UpdateEmail( objConnection, Email.Text.Trim() );
        }

        int nIncidentID;

        if( ForUpdate.Text == "0" )
        {
            string strSql =
                "INSERT INTO Incident (UserID,CatID,DeptID, " +
                "Location,Phone,Title,Description) VALUES (" +
                Convert.ToString( Session["UserID"] ) + "," +
                Category.SelectedItem.Value + "," +
```

```
                    Department.SelectedItem.Value + ",'" +
                    Location.Text.Replace( "'", "`" ) + "','" +
                    Phone.Text + "','" +
                    Title.Text.Replace( "'", "`" ) + "','" +
                    Description.Text.Replace( "'", "`" ) +
                    "') SELECT @ID=@@IDENTITY";

                SqlCommand objCommand =
                    new SqlCommand( strSql, objConnection );
                objCommand.Parameters.Add( "@ID", SqlDbType.Int );
                objCommand.Parameters["@ID"].Direction =
                    ParameterDirection.Output;
                objCommand.ExecuteNonQuery();

                nIncidentID =
                    Convert.ToInt32( objCommand.Parameters["@ID"].Value );
            }
            else
            {
                string strSql = "Update Incident Set CatID=" +
                    Category.SelectedItem.Value + ",DeptID=" +
                    Department.SelectedItem.Value + ",Location='" +
                    Location.Text.Replace( "'", "`" ) + "',Phone='" +
                    Phone.Text + "',Title='" +
                    Title.Text.Replace( "'", "`" ) + "',Description='" +
                    Description.Text.Replace( "'", "`" ) + "',Resolution='"+
                    Resolution.Text.Replace( "'", "`" ) + "')";

                SqlCommand objCommand =
                    new SqlCommand( strSql, objConnection );
                objCommand.ExecuteNonQuery();

                nIncidentID = Convert.ToInt32( IncidentID.Text );
            }

        objConnection.Close();
        Response.Redirect( "ThanksForNew.aspx?IncidentID=" +
            Convert.ToString( nIncidentID ) );
    }
    catch( Exception ex )
    {
        if( objConnection.State == ConnectionState.Open )
        {
```

```
        objConnection.Close();
    }
    ErrorMessage.Text = ex.Message.ToString() + "<br>";
  }
}
```

Listing 4.18 contains the `DisplayList()` method. This method is used in the ViewProblemList page to display a list of all problems that are currently in the database. A SqlConnection object is created and then opened. A query string is placed into a variable named `strSql`. If a search string was passed in (and this is from a query string named `SearchCriteria`), then this will become part of the SQL string with which the query will be made. This allows the same code to be used with or without a given search string.

The SqlCommand object is created, and then its `ExecuteReader()` method is called. A SqlDataReader contains the data set that was returned, and this is used to iteratively create the list from which the user can make a selection.

Listing 4.18 Methods in ViewProblemList.aspx.cs

```
public void DisplayList()
{
  SqlConnection objConnection =
    new SqlConnection(Convert.ToString(Application["DBConnectString"]));

    try
    {
        objConnection.Open();

        string strSql = "SELECT Title,ID FROM Incident ORDER BY Title";
        string strSearch =
          Request.QueryString["SearchCriteria"].Trim().Replace("'","`");
        if( strSearch.Length > 0 )
        {
            strSql =
              "SELECT Title,ID FROM Incident where(Description like '%"+
              strSearch +
              "%' or Resolution like '%" + strSearch +
              "%' or Title like '%" + strSearch +
              "%') ORDER BY Title";
        }
```

```
SqlCommand objCommand = new SqlCommand( strSql, objConnection );
SqlDataReader reader = objCommand.ExecuteReader();

bool bResultsFound = false;
while( reader.Read() )
{
    bResultsFound = true;
    Response.Write( "<tr><td>" + reader["Title"].ToString() +
        "</td><td><a href=\"ShowIncident.aspx?IncidentID=" +
        reader["ID"].ToString() +
        "\">View</a></td></td>\r\n" );
}

if( !bResultsFound )
{
    Response.Write( "<tr><td>There were no " +
        "results found</td><td> </td></td>\r\n" );
}

objConnection.Close();
}
catch( Exception ex )
{
    if( objConnection.State == ConnectionState.Open )
    {
        objConnection.Close();
    }
    Response.Write( "<tr><td>" + ex.Message.ToString() +
        "</td></tr>" );
}
}
```

Users who are logged on with administrative rights are brought to a different screen by default once they log on. As you can see in Figure 4.4, this menu offers four buttons plus the opportunity to go back to the main page. This screen offers users four choices for administering the HelpDesk application. They can add, edit, and delete administrators; add categories; add departments; and edit incidences.

The four pages with which administrators can administer the application are similar, if not practically identical, to each other. For this reason, I am showing you only the code in the AdminAdministrators page.

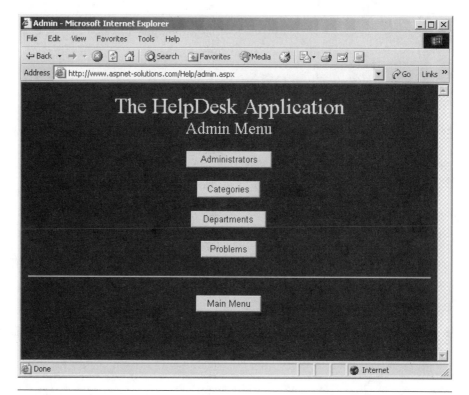

Figure 4.4 If You Log In As an Administrator, You Are Brought to a Different Screen than Normal Users.

The first thing that happens when the AdminAdministrators page is loaded is that a session variable that contains the user type is checked to make sure that the user has administrative rights. If she doesn't, then she is redirected to a page called Unauthorized.aspx. If she does have the right, and this is not a post back, then the `PopulateAdministratorList()` method is called. This method populates a DataList that contains all current administrators for the application.

The `PopulateAdministratorList()` method is fairly simple. This method creates and opens a SqlConnection object. It creates a Sql-Command object to retrieve all the information about users who have administrative rights. The returned SqlDataReader object is then bound to the data list named AdministratorList. You can see the AdminAdministrator screen in Figure 4.5.

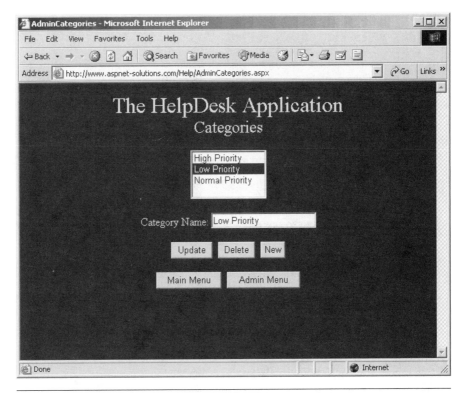

Figure 4.5 The Administrative Screens Are All Similar, and Each Offers Maintenance for Different Application Sets of Information.

Listing 4.19 Methods in AdminAdministrators.aspx.cs

```
private void Page_Load(object sender, System.EventArgs e)
{
    if( Convert.ToInt32( Session["UserType"] ) != 1 )
    {
        Response.Redirect( "Unauthorized.aspx" );
    }

    if( !IsPostBack )
    {
        PopulateAdministratorList();
    }
}
```

```csharp
private void PopulateAdministratorList()
{
  SqlConnection objConnection =
    new SqlConnection(Convert.ToString(Application["DBConnectString"]));
    try
    {
        objConnection.Open();

        SqlCommand objCommand =
          new SqlCommand( "SELECT Name,ID FROM UserInfo WHERE " +
          "UserType=1 ORDER BY Name",
          objConnection );
        SqlDataReader reader = objCommand.ExecuteReader();
        AdministratorList.DataTextField = "Name";
        AdministratorList.DataValueField = "ID";
        AdministratorList.DataSource = reader;
        AdministratorList.DataBind();
        reader.Close();
        objConnection.Close();
    }
    catch( Exception ex )
    {
        if( objConnection.State == ConnectionState.Open )
        {
            objConnection.Close();
        }
        ErrorMessage.Text = ex.Message.ToString();
    }
}

private void MainMenu_Click(object sender, System.EventArgs e)
{
    Response.Redirect( "Default.aspx" );
}

private void AdminMenu_Click(object sender, System.EventArgs e)
{
    Response.Redirect( "Admin.aspx" );
}
```

Listing 4.20 contains the methods that fire when the user clicks any of the Update, the Delete, or the New buttons. The Update_Click()

method updates a record in the database. It retrieves the information from the user interface (and this includes the administrator name and password) and then simply updates the database with the newly edited information.

The `Delete_Click()` method deletes the currently selected administrator from the database. It does this by creating a SqlConnection object and opening it. It then creates a SqlCommand object and forms a query based on the current ID. After the method performs the SQL command, the user interface objects are cleared out to indicate that the user is no longer there. The `New_Click()` method simply sets all the user interface objects so that they are empty and can receive the information for a new administrator. The method also sets the AdministratorListSelectedIndex to −1 so that when the page is displayed none of the items in the administrator list will be selected.

Listing 4.20 Methods in AdminAdministrators.aspx.cs

```
private void Update_Click(object sender, System.EventArgs e)
{
    ErrorMessage.Text = "";

    int nID = Convert.ToInt32( AdministratorList.SelectedItem.Value );
    string strSql;
    if( nID <= 0 )
    {
        strSql =
            "INSERT INTO UserInfo (Name,Password,UserType) VALUES ('" +
            UserName.Text + "','" +
            Password.Text + "',1)";
    }
    else
    {
        strSql = "Update UserInfo set Name='" + UserName.Text +
            "',Password='" + Password.Text +
            "' WHERE ID=" + Convert.ToString( nID );
    }

    SqlConnection objConnection =
        new SqlConnection(Convert.ToString(Application["DBConnectString"]));

    try
    {
        objConnection.Open();
```

```
        SqlCommand objCommand = new SqlCommand( strSql, objConnection );
        objCommand.ExecuteNonQuery();
        objConnection.Close();

        if( nID <= 0 )
        {
            PopulateAdministratorList();
            UserName.Text = "";
            Password.Text = "";
            AdminID.Text = "0";
        }

        ErrorMessage.Text =
          "Administrative user has been updated/added";
    }
    catch( Exception ex )
    {
        if( objConnection.State == ConnectionState.Open )
        {
            objConnection.Close();
        }
        ErrorMessage.Text = ex.Message.ToString();
    }
}

private void Delete_Click(object sender, System.EventArgs e)
{
    ErrorMessage.Text = "";

    int nID = Convert.ToInt32( AdministratorList.SelectedItem.Value );
    if( nID <= 0 )
    {
        ErrorMessage.Text = "There is no currently selected user";
        return;
    }

  SqlConnection objConnection =
    new SqlConnection(Convert.ToString(Application["DBConnectString"]));

    try
    {
        objConnection.Open();
```

```
        SqlCommand objCommand =
          new SqlCommand( "DELETE FROM UserInfo WHERE ID=" +
            Convert.ToString( nID ),
            objConnection );
        objCommand.ExecuteNonQuery();
        objConnection.Close();

        PopulateAdministratorList();
        UserName.Text = "";
        Password.Text = "";
        AdminID.Text = "0";

        ErrorMessage.Text = "Administrative user has been deleted";
    }
    catch( Exception ex )
    {
        if( objConnection.State == ConnectionState.Open )
        {
            objConnection.Close();
        }
        ErrorMessage.Text = ex.Message.ToString();
    }
}


private void New_Click(object sender, System.EventArgs e)
{
    AdministratorList.SelectedIndex = -1;
    UserName.Text = "";
    Password.Text = "";
    AdminID.Text = "0";
    ErrorMessage.Text =
      "Enter information for new administrative user and click Update";
}
```

Listing 4.21 contains a single method named Administrator_
SelectedIndexChanged(). This method gets the ID and user name
from the currently selected item in the administrator list object. Using this
information, it retrieves the password from the database that corresponds to
this particular user. It then populates all the user interface objects with the
information for the selected administrator, which then gives the user the
opportunity to edit all this information.

Listing 4.21 Methods in AdminAdministrators.aspx.cs

```
private void Administrators_SelectedIndexChanged(object sender,
  System.EventArgs e)
{
    ErrorMessage.Text = "";

    AdminID.Text =
      Convert.ToString( AdministratorList.SelectedItem.Value );
    UserName.Text =
      Convert.ToString( AdministratorList.SelectedItem.Text );

  SqlConnection objConnection =
    new SqlConnection(Convert.ToString(Application["DBConnectString"]));

    try
    {
        objConnection.Open();

        SqlCommand objCommand =
          new SqlCommand( "SELECT Password FROM UserInfo WHERE ID=" +
            AdminID.Text,
            objConnection );
        SqlDataReader reader = objCommand.ExecuteReader();
        if( reader.Read() )
        {
            Password.Text = Convert.ToString( reader["Password"] );
        }
        else
        {
            Password.Text = "";
        }
        reader.Close();
        objConnection.Close();

    }
    catch( Exception ex )
    {
        if( objConnection.State == ConnectionState.Open )
        {
            objConnection.Close();
        }
```

```
      ErrorMessage.Text = ex.Message.ToString();
   }
}
```

Extending and Modifying the HelpDesk Application

Right now, the HelpDesk application doesn't use the department as part of the search criteria. Including the department as part of the search criteria is the first enhancement I'd suggest.

Deploying the HelpDesk Application

You must follow a few steps to deploy the Survey application on your server:

1. Start by creating a database named HelpDesk.
2. Then, restore the database, which can be obtained from the www.ASPNET-Solutions.com Web site. (The page with a link to this download is www.ASPNET-Solutions.com/Chapter_4.htm.)
3. Next, run Visual Studio .NET.
4. Create a project on the server named Help for a C# project, or HelpVB for a VB project. You'll have to make sure you select the appropriate (C# or VB) type of ASP.NET project.
5. Compile the application once it is created.
6. Open the application project. Check the Global.asax file to make sure that the database connection string matches the connection string for your situation. Compile the application.

Your HelpDesk application should now be ready to use and ready to modify as you see fit.

Summary

As we saw in Chapter 3, ADO.NET makes interacting with a database easy. And in this chapter, we've seen how flexible ADO.NET can be when you're using ad hoc queries. This chapter presented ADO.NET topics such as the

DataSet object that weren't covered in Chapter 3, and then went on to create a HelpDesk application.

The HelpDesk application can be used as-is in your Web site, or it can be modified to better suit your needs. The application is straightforward and lends itself well to modifications. Please visit the www.ASPNET-Solutions.com forums and participate in the discussions so that all readers will know what you've done with your version.

CHAPTER 5

Databound Controls: Building a Scheduling Application

In This Chapter:

- Databound Controls
- Schedule Application
- Deployment and Customization

This chapter will teach you how to use databound controls and how to add dynamic data to a non-databound control, the calendar control. It's easy to bind data to controls such as DataLists and Repeaters, but binding data to controls that don't natively support databinding is a different matter. The use of these controls and binding data to them will then be demonstrated in a scheduling application. The scheduling application also demonstrates a simple data-access layer where the actual accessing of the database is done through calls to a class that controls access to the database.

The scheduling application is a simple calendar application with a contact list that can easily be extended for your own needs.

Databound Controls

The .NET Framework includes a number of databound controls. These controls allow you to use data from a data source to easily populate the control. The data source can be any of a number of different types of objects, depending upon the control. Here is a list of the controls that are considered databound controls.

- ListBox
- DropDownList

- RadioButtonList
- CheckBoxList
- Repeater
- DataList
- DataGrid

These controls are considered databound because a DataSet, a Data-Reader, or an Array can be assigned to a control and then bound. Normally this is done by setting the `DataSource` property to the collection of data that you want to bind to, and then calling the `DataBind()` method.

ListBox, DropDownList, RadioButtonList, and CheckBoxList

The simplest of the databound controls are the list controls. These controls are all identical in terms of how they are used because the data binding is implemented in a common base class called `ListControl`. Using these controls is quite simple; just do the following:

1. If you are using Visual Studio .NET, you can drag a ListControl from the Toolbox; otherwise, you will need to add the control to your .aspx page.

2. In the code behind, assign the data source to the `DataSource` property of the control. Normally this data source is a DataSet, DataTable, or a DataReader, but it can be an array or even a custom collection.

3. Set the `DataTextField` and `DataValueField` properties to the name of the column in the DataTable that contains the data to be used as the display text and value of the list control entries.

4. Call the `DataBind()` method of the list control.

Here is an example of how to do this. Our data will be a list of country names and country codes. For the example I'm assuming that we have a DataReader already set up. It will have two columns, Country and Country-Code. This data will be loaded into a DropDownList.

The .aspx code looks like this:

```
<asp:DropDownList
  id="CountryList"
```

```
  style="Z-INDEX: 101; LEFT: 88px;
    POSITION: absolute; TOP: 152px"
  runat="server"
  DataTextField="Country"
  DataValueField="CountryCode">
</asp:DropDownList>
```

The code to initialize the data in the `Page_Load` event handler looks like this:

```
Dim objConnection As New SqlConnection
'Setup and Open Connection Here

Dim objCommand As New SqlCommand
Dim objReader As SqlDataReader

objCommand.CommandText = _
"SELECT Country,CountryCode FROM tblCountryList"
objCommand.Connection = objConnection
objCommand.ExecuteReader(CommandBehavior.CloseConnection)
Me.CountryList.DataSource = objReader
Me.DataBind()
```

It is important to note that the reader will be closed by the `Data-Bind()` method. You can't perform additional queries on a connection with an opened reader. If you call the ExecuteReader with the `Command-Behavior.CloseConnection` parameter, the connection will be automatically closed when the reader is closed. If you do not call ExecuteReader with this parameter, you will need to be sure and close the connection manually.

The Repeater Control

The Repeater control is the most basic of the iterative databound controls. This has its advantages and disadvantages. The advantage is that the Repeater control does not have an inherent look. There is no default layout or display methodology. This makes is possible for you to do whatever you want with it. The disadvantage is that it takes more work to do something simple.

Templates

The Repeater control uses templates to define how things are displayed. Each template is used to define different portions of the Repeater control's data. Here is a list of the templates used by the repeater controls and what the template is used for:

- **ItemTemplate**—This template is used to define the content and layout for each item in the data assigned to the DataSource property. This item can be a row in a DataTable, or an element of an array. This is the only required template.
- **AlternatingItemTemplate**—This template is like the ItemTemplate, but, if it is specified, it is used to render every other element. This allows you to easily give a different appearance to alternating rows. If it is not defined, the ItemTemplate is used.
- **HeaderTemplate**—This template is for elements that are rendered before any of the databound rows are rendered. If it is not defined, a header is not rendered.
- **FooterTemplate**—This template is for elements that are rendered after any databound rows are rendered. If it is not defined, a footer is not rendered.
- **SeparatorTemplate**—This template is for elements that render between each row. If it is not defined, a separator is not rendered.

When the Repeater control renders itself, it starts by rendering the HeaderTemplate, followed by an ItemTemplate alternating with the AlternatingItemTemplate if it is defined for each data row to be rendered. The Repeater control renders a SeparatorTemplate between each of the ItemTemplate or AlternatingItemTemplate data. Finally, the FooterTemplate is rendered.

Data Binding

The Repeater must be bound to a data source prior to using it. If it is not bound to a data source, nothing will be rendered. Data is bound to the Repeater control by assigning a data source to the `DataSource` property and then calling the `DataBind()` method. Any class that implements the ICollection or the IEnumerable interfaces can be used as a data source. Common data sources include the `DataTable` class and the `SqlDataReader` class. Other classes such as the `Array` class or the `ArrayList` class can also be used as a data source.

Events

The Repeater control supports three Repeater-specific events: the `Item-Created` event, the `ItemDataBound` event, and the `ItemCommand` event. The `ItemCreated` event is fired after the contents of the ItemTemplate are created, but before they are databound. This event should be handled if you want to make changes to the controls inside the ItemTemplate that don't rely on the data in the template.

The `ItemDataBound` is fired after the data binding is done but before the item is rendered on the page. This event should be handled if you need to make changes based on the data being bound. This would include things such as changing the style of the displayed text based upon what text is being displayed, or changing a label control to a link control if the text being bound to it is a URL.

The `ItemCommand` event is fired if any of the contained controls fire a `Command` event. This allows you to handle events from things such as buttons without specifically attaching an event handler to every item that is rendered.

Example

Let's look at an example. The example will be taken from the contact portion of the scheduling application where an alphabet list is provided to filter the contacts alphabetically.

Here is the .aspx code to define the repeater:

```
<asp:Repeater id="ctlAlphaList" runat="server"
  EnableViewState="False">
  <ItemTemplate>
    <td>
    <asp:LinkButton Runat="server" ID="Alpha"
      CommandName="CHANGE"
      CommandArgument='
      <%# DataBinder.Eval(Container.DataItem, "Name")
      %>'>
      <%# DataBinder.Eval(Container.DataItem, "Name") %>
      </asp:LinkButton></td>
  </ItemTemplate>
</asp:Repeater>
```

The following code behind code is called to load the data in to the Reader.

Listing 5.1 The `CountItem` Class

```
' This class counts the items in a control.
Private Class CountItem
    Public Sub New(ByVal strName As String, ByVal nValue As Integer)
        m_Name = strName
        m_Value = nValue
    End Sub

    ' Private variables
    Private m_Name As String
    Private _Value As Integer

    Public ReadOnly Property Name()
        Get
            Return m_Name
        End Get
    End Property

    Public ReadOnly Property Value()
        Get
            Return m_Value
        End Get
    End Property

Private Sub LoadAlphaList()
    Dim objCounts() As CountItem
    Dim I As Integer
    Dim isValidReader As Boolean
    Dim objReader As IDataReader
    Dim strName As String

    objCounts = Array.CreateInstance(GetType(CountItem), 27)
    objCounts(0) = New CountItem("All - ", _
        Page.AuthUser.ContactCount)

    objReader = Page.AuthUser.ContactAlphaCountsReader
    isValidReader = objReader.Read()

    For I = 1 To 26
        strName = Chr(Asc("A") + I - 1)
        If isValidReader Then
            ' AlphaInx is the column with the X increment.
```

```
            If objReader.Item("AlphaInx") = I Then
                ' ContactCount is the column that counts the contacts.
                objCounts(I) = New CountItem(strName, _
                    objReader.Item("ContactCount"))
                isValidReader = objReader.Read()
            Else
                objCounts(I) = New CountItem(strName, 0)
            End If
        Else
            objCounts(I) = New CountItem(strName, 0)
        End If
    Next
    objReader.Close()

    Me.ctlAlphaList.DataSource = objCounts
    Me.ctlAlphaList.DataBind()
End Sub
End Class
```

In this case, the data is first loaded into an array of custom objects. The array is the set to be the Repeater's data source.

DataList

The DataList control is a flexible control for displaying information from a DataSource. Like the Repeater control, it does not force you to use a given structure for displaying your data, but it allows more flexibility because you can specify different templates for selected items and for items that are being edited. With the DataList control, you can also specify styles to be applied to any of the templates.

If you don't wish to specify your own structure, you can set the RepeatLayout property to RepeatLayout.Table to display the data in a table. If you choose to use the table layout provided by the DataList control, it is assumed that each item is to be rendered in a single cell of the table, which means your table will have only a single column or row, depending upon the setting of the RepeatDirection property. If your data item is actually a row from a data source with multiple data fields, you will need to specify your own layout rather then using the built-in table layout if you wish each field in the row to be displayed in its own cell.

Templates

The DataList control uses templates to define how it is displayed. Each template is used to define different portions of the DataList control's data. Here is a list of the templates used by the repeater controls and what each template is used for:

- **ItemTemplate**—This template is used to define the content and layout for each item in the data assigned to the `DataSource` property. This item can be a row in a DataTable, or an element of an array. This is the only required template.
- **AlternatingItemTemplate**—This template is like the ItemTemplate, but, if it is specified, it is used to render every other element. This allows you to easily give a different appearance to alternating rows. If it is not defined, the ItemTemplate is used.
- **EditItemTemplate**—If this template is defined, it provides the content and layout for the item currently being edited. If it is not defined, the ItemTemplate is used.
- **SelectedItemTemplate**—If this template is defined, it provides the content and layout for the item currently selected. If it is not defined, the ItemTemplate is used.
- **HeaderTemplate**—This template is for elements that are rendered before any of the databound rows are rendered. If it is not defined, a header is not rendered.
- **FooterTemplate**—This template is for elements that are rendered after any databound rows are rendered. If it is not defined, a footer is not rendered.
- **SeparatorTemplate**—This template is for elements that render between each row. If it is not defined, a separator is not rendered.

When the DataList control renders itself, it starts by rendering the HeaderTemplate, followed by an ItemTemplate alternating with the AlternatingItemTemplate if it is defined for each data row to be rendered. The Repeater control renders a SeparatorTemplate between each of the ItemTemplate or AlternatingItemTemplate data. Finally the FooterTemplate is rendered. If an item is being edited, then the EditItemTemplate will be rendered instead of the ItemTemplate. If an item is selected, then the SelectedItemTemplate will be rendered instead of the ItemTemplate.

Style Properties

One of the big advantages of the DataList control over the Repeater control is the capability to set styles that match each of the templates. These styles are not rendered specifically on the matching template but are rendered where the template would be used if it existed. This allows you to do things such as specify alternating background colors without specifying an Alternating-ItemTemplate. Here is a list of the style properties that can be defined:

- **AlternatingItemStyle**—Specifies the style for alternating items. This style is alternated even if an AlternatingItemTemplate is not specified.
- **EditItemStyle**—Specifies the style for the item being edited.
- **FooterStyle**—Specifies the style for the footer.
- **HeaderStyle**—Specifies the style for the header.
- **ItemStyle**—Specifies the style for normal items.
- **SelectedItemStyle**—Specifies the style for the selected item.
- **SeparatorStyle**—Specifies the style for the separator.

Data Binding

Like the Repeater control, the DataList control must be bound to a data source prior to using it. If it is not bound to a data source, nothing will be rendered. Data is bound to the DataList control by assigning a data source to the `DataSource` property and then calling the `DataBind()` method. Any class that implements the `IEnumerable` interface can be used as a data source. This means that common data sources such as the `DataTable` class and the `SqlDataReader` class, as well as other classes such as the `Array` class or the `ArrayList` class, can be used as data sources.

Events

The DataList control has a number of events that can be handled. These events allow you to customize the DataList control in a variety of situations.

- **CancelCommand**—This event occurs when a button with its `CommandID` property set to `Cancel` is pressed.
- **DeleteCommand**—This event occurs when a button with its `CommandID` property set to `Delete` is pressed.

- **EditCommand**—This event occurs when a button with its `CommandID` property set to `Edit` is pressed.
- **ItemCommand**—This event occurs when any button is clicked for an item.
- **ItemCreated**—This event occurs after an item is created but prior to it being databound.
- **ItemDataBound**—This event occurs after an item is databound.
- **SelectedIndexChanged**—This event occurs when the selected index is changed.
- **UpdateCommand**—This event occurs when a button with its `CommandID` property set to `Update` is pressed.

Schedule Application

Now that the basics of databound controls have been covered, it is time to apply this by building a schedule/contact application. Most simple applications can be thought of as a two-layer problem. There is the user interface, which is what you want the user to see, and the data access, which is how data is stored. Most of the programming work is in hooking up the visual layer to the underlying data layer. More complex applications will also have the so-called business logic layer. Our scheduling application is a fairly straightforward presentation of data, so it can be built easily without a business logic layer. I will, however, spend a little time discussing what kind of additions to this application would be most easily accomplished by adding a business logic layer.

Application Overview

Before getting into the design details for each layer, let's define the application to be developed. Our application is to be a basic scheduling application with a contact manager. Each user will have her own schedule and contacts. Because this application is intended to be available for trial on the book's Web site, users will need to be able to register themselves. The data for this application will be stored in a SQL Server database, and to demonstrate a best practice way of accessing the data, all data access will be done through stored procedures. Style sheets are used as much as possible for setting the style elements to maintain consistency across the application.

User Interface Design

When designing an application, I often start with the user interface design and then determine what kinds of data I need from what I want displayed. This is not always the best design method for all applications; for some applications, the data requirements are well known, and it is easier to do the database design first and then figure out a way to display the data in a manner that is clear to the end user. In this application, though, let's start with the user interface.

When I was designing this application, two areas were clearly necessary. There needed to be a section with the schedule and a section for the contacts. What wasn't so clear was what to do with the login and registration. In the end, I decided to break the application into the following three pages:

- **Home Page**—This is where the login and registration occur, and, in the case of this application, it also contains an explanation of the application.
- **Schedule Page**—This page is where the schedule is displayed.
- **Contact Page**—This page is where the contacts are displayed.

The three pages are connected with a simple menu bar. Each page is just that: a single .aspx page. Changes of what is displayed on each of the pages are done by implementing portions of each page as a user control and changing its visibility depending upon whether or not it needs to be displayed.

Designing with User Controls

User controls are a quick way of encapsulating user interface portions of your program in a way that is reusable. There are a couple of big disadvantages to user controls that limit their overall usefulness. These are the necessity to have an .ascx file and the corresponding inability to compile a user control to only a .dll file, and the inability to share a user control across Web applications. The second disadvantage is, in my experience, the biggest one.

Alternatively, user controls are easy to create because they are basically encapsulated .aspx pages. They are most useful for componentizing portions of an application when they will be used only in that application. If a control was to be used across a number of applications, it might be better to spend the extra time and create a custom control. Custom controls are covered in more detail in Chapter 15, "Server Controls and HttpModules."

The biggest thing about user controls is not how to use them, but when to use them. Currently, Visual Studio .NET does not provide as much support for user controls as I would really like. Specifically, when a user control is placed on another control, Visual Studio .NET does not render it visually so that you can see how it looks. Visual Studio .NET also does not automatically add an access variable in the code-behind file, and, at least when developing in C#, you must do all event hook-ups by hand. Although future versions of Visual Studio .NET may address some of these issues, currently it is quite tedious to nest user controls to any great extent if there are any data dependencies, because you must either handle events, pass data into the nested user controls in the `Page_Load()` method, or place the necessary data items in the .aspx page. The last method is the easiest, but it creates a dependency on the underlying page, which reduces the reusability of the code.

So when do you use them? Normally, you use a user control when your content logically fits together and you are likely to reuse that content in multiple places throughout an application but not across applications. It is also easier to implement portions of a page as a user control when the control is visible only part of the time because it is logically cleaner and easier to deal with than trying to place it all on the .aspx page. Generally, I try to avoid nesting user controls as much as possible, but I do use them to a great extent.

In this scheduling application, I use a number of user controls, and their usage pretty much follows my usage guidelines listed above. The menu is encapsulated into a user control because it is needed on all three pages. Other items that are logically grouped together for display purposes and functionality are also encapsulated into user controls. If I have some HTML that is conditionally displayed with no code-behind element, and it is not used on multiple pages, I normally place it in a Panel server control rather then in its own user control.

Home Page

This is the starting page for the application. It is where the user logs in or registers. It uses the following user controls:

- MenuModule
- LoginModule
- RegisterModule

The LoginModule user control is displayed when the user is not logged in, and the RegisterModule user control is displayed if the user presses the Register button on the LoginModule user control.

If the user is logged in, then only the MenuModule user control is displayed, in addition to the HTML that is part of the home.aspx page.

Schedule Page

This page displays all the scheduling information. The user can select between a monthly view and a daily view. A set of three small calendars are used to select dates more quickly. This page uses the following user controls:

- MenuModule
- DayModule
- MonthModule
- ScheduleEditModule
- SmallMonth

Of these user controls, the SmallMonth user control is the only one that doesn't really follow my rules for when to use user controls. The three small month calendars were encapsulated in a user control for logic reasons rather then visual reasons. The DayModule user control illustrates the use of a DataList server control, and the MonthModule user control shows how to bind data to a Calendar server control.

Contact Page

This page displays all the contact information. The user can see the contacts filtered by the first letter of the last name, or all at once. Contacts can be added, edited, and deleted. This page uses the following user controls:

- MenuModule
- ContactEdit
- ContactView

This page is the one on which it could have been easy to overuse user controls. I was going to place the contact list on its own user control, but I decided that no real advantage would have been gained. The contact list is a DataGrid server control, and the alphabetical selection is done using a Repeater server control.

Designing a Data Access Layer

Now that you have an overview of the user-interface aspects of the scheduling application, let's take a closer look at the data access layer.

The data structure in the application is fairly simple. There are three tables, defined as follows:

- tblUser—This table contains the information about the user, including the username and password used to log in to the application.
- tblContact—This table contains information needed for each contact. It is linked with a foreign key relationship to tblUser.
- tblAppointment—This table contains information needed for each appointment. It too is linked with a foreign key relationship to tblUser.

Before going any further, I want to say that I hate repetitious programming. It really annoys me to spend hours typing almost the exact same code over and over. Nowhere is that more true than when writing a data-access layer. Many data-access layers that I have seen repeat much of the same code over and over when they're writing classes that contain and load the data for a specific type of data. My solution to this problem has usually been to write a base class that handles all of the actual data access. This class is used as the base class for all of the data objects that I then use.

When designing a base class for this purpose, I try very hard to keep all the code that actually accesses the database in this class. This way, when I use my data object, I don't have to think about things such as opening connections, loading data, and so on. This is all done automatically by the base class. Let's look at a sample data-access class to show what I mean. Here is a code snippet that shows the usage of the appointment data item. It loads the appointment data item with its data from the AppointmentID that is used as the primary key for tblAppointment.

```
Dim objAppointment As New AppointmentItem

objAppointment.ID=2
'objAppointment is now loaded with the data for the row in
'tblAppointment with AppointmentID equal to 2.
```

Wow! That was easy. With two lines of code, I could get the data for my data object. Now consider this: The data was loaded with a parameterized call to a stored procedure. To do this without a data-access layer would involve 20 lines to 30 lines of code. Now many data-access layers provide similar ease of retrieving data. Normally, though, they shift the code to the data-access item's class, in this case, the `AppointmentItem` class. As more data-access classes are created in larger projects, this is still quite a bit of work. Let's look at the implementation of the `AppointmentItem` class. Listing 5.2 shows the `AppointmentItem` data-access class. The class has an attribute named `ItemDef` that keeps appointment IDs.

Listing 5.2 `AppointmentItem` Data-Access Class—AppointmentItem.vb

```
Imports System.Data
<ItemDef ("Appointment", "AppointmentID")> _
Public Class AppointmentItem
    ' Inherits the base class for data.
    Inherits DataBase

    'Public Property Accessors
    Public ReadOnly Property AppointmentID() As Integer
        Get
            Return GetFieldData("AppointmentID")
        End Get
    End Property

    Public Property UserID() As Integer
        Get
            Return GetFieldData("UserID")
        End Get
        Set(ByVal Value As Integer)
            SetFieldData("UserID",Value)
        End Set
    End Property

    Public Property TimeStart() As DateTime
        Get
            Return GetFieldData("TimeStart")
        End Get
        Set(ByVal Value As DateTime)
            SetFieldData("TimeStart",Value)
        End Set
    End Property
```

```
Public Property TimeEnd() As DateTime
    Get
        Return GetFieldData("TimeEnd")
    End Get
    Set(ByVal Value As DateTime)
        SetFieldData("TimeEnd",Value)
    End Set
End Property

Public Property Title() As String
    Get
        Return GetFieldData("Title")
    End Get
    Set(ByVal Value As String)
        SetFieldData("Title",Value)
    End Set
End Property

Public Property Note() As String
    Get
        Return GetFieldData("Note")
    End Get
    Set(ByVal Value As String)
        SetFieldData("Note",Value)
    End Set
End Property

Public ReadOnly Property User() As UserItem
    Get
        Dim objReader As IDataReader

        objReader = ExecDataReader("sp_User_GetByID")
        If objReader.Read() Then
            LoadDataRecord(objReader)
        Else
            Throw New Exception("Invalid UserID")
        End If
        objReader.Close()
    End Get
End Property
End Class
```

As you can see, in this case, the `AppointmentItem` class is not very complex, and it barely has enough code to retrieve and store data. The class that does all the actual work in my data access layer is the `DataBase` class, which is the base class of the `AppointmentItem` class.

The DataBase Class

The `DataBase` class as it has been implemented provides a number of helper functions that reduce the amount of coding necessary to access the database. One of these functions can be seen in the preceding `AppointmentItem` class in the implementation of the `User` property. Look at the call to ExecDataReader.

```
objReader = ExecDataReader("sp_User_GetByID")
```

Nowhere do you see any data being passed to the `Exec-DataReader()` method. This is because the `ExecDataReader()` method does a number of things. First, it uses the static `DeriveParameters()` method from the SqlCommandBuilder to determine what parameters are necessary for the stored procedure call. Then, if there are no other parameters passed to the `ExecDataReader()` method, it uses the names of the parameters to try to match the parameters with the property data of the data object. So because my stored procedure looks like this:

```
ALTER PROCEDURE dbo.sp_User_GetByID
  (
    @UserID int
  )
AS
  Select * FROM [tblUser] WHERE [UserID]=@UserID
  RETURN
```

and the `AppointmentItem` class has a data property named `UserID`, the data from the property will be placed in the parameter for the stored procedure call. If you need to pass data that is not a property in the data-item class, you can pass the extra data directly in the method call. So the following statement is equivalent to the previous call to ExecDataReader:

```
objReader = ExecDataReader("sp_User_GetByID",UserID)
```

When passing the data directly to the `ExecDataReader()` method, you need to be aware of a couple of things. The parameters are matched in order according to how they are defined in the stored procedure, and the number of parameters must match the number of parameters in the stored procedure. There are equivalent `ExecNonQuery()` and `ExecScalar()` methods to match the `Execute()` methods of an `SqlCommand` class.

Table 5.1 Public Interface

Name	Type	Description
ConnectionString	Property	This property is a string that contains the connection string to the data source to be used. This connection string is retrieved from the ConnectionString entry in the appSettings section in the web.config file.
dbConnection	Property	This property returns an SqlConnection object that is initialized with the ConnectionString.
ExecDataReader	Method	This method calls a stored procedure and returns the results in a SqlDataReader. The parameters for the stored procedure can either be passed as parameters to this method, or else be matched by name to the data stored in the derived data class.
ExecNonQuery	Method	This method calls a stored procedure and does not return any results. The parameters for the stored procedure can either be passed as parameters to this method, or else be matched by name to the data stored in the derived data class.
ExecScalar	Method	This method calls a stored procedure and returns the results as a scalar value in an object. The parameters for the stored procedure can either be passed as parameters to this method, or else be matched by name to the data stored in the derived data class.
GetFieldData	Method	Returns the data for a specified field.
SetFieldData	Method	Sets the data for a specified field.
ID	Property	Returns the value of the Primary key data field.
Update	Method	Updates the database with the data in the current data object. If the ID is 0, then a new record is inserted.
Delete	Method	Deletes the current record from the database.

Before looking at the actual code of the DataBase class, let's look at the properties and methods that are provided. Table 5.1 details the public methods and properties of this class.

Listing 5.3 shows the complete code listing for the DataBase class.

Listing 5.3 DataBase Class Listing—DataBase.vb

```
Imports System.Data
Imports System.Data.SqlClient
Imports System.Diagnostics
Imports System.Reflection

Public Class DataBase
    Private m_FieldData As New NameObjectCollection
    Private _m_ConnectionString As String
    Private m_dbConnection As SqlConnection

    Public Sub New()
        ResetData()
    End Sub

    Private Sub ResetData()
        _FieldData.Clear()
    End Sub

    ' This property contains the connection string.
    Public ReadOnly Property ConnectionString() As String
        Get
            Dim configurationAppSettings As _
                System.Configuration.AppSettingsReader = _
                New System.Configuration.AppSettingsReader
                m_ConnectionString = _
                CType(configurationAppSettings. _
                GetValue("ConnectionString", _
                GetType(System.String)), String)
            Return _ConnectionString
        End Get
    End Property

    Public ReadOnly Property dbConnection() As SqlConnection
        Get
            If (IsNothing(m_dbConnection)) Then
```

```vb
            m_dbConnection = _
                New SqlConnection(m_ConnectionString)
        End If

        Return m_dbConnection
    End Get
End Property


Private Sub AddParameters( _
    ByVal objCommand As SqlCommand, _
    ByVal objValues() As Object)

    Dim objValue As Object
    Dim I As Integer
    Dim objParameter As SqlParameter

    objCommand.Parameters.Clear()
    SqlCommandBuilder.DeriveParameters(objCommand)

    I = 0
    For Each objParameter In objCommand.Parameters
        If objParameter.Direction = ParameterDirection.Input _
            Or objParameter.Direction = _
            ParameterDirection.InputOutput Then

            objValue = objValues(I)
            objParameter.Value = objValue
            I = I + 1
        End If
    Next
End Sub


Private Sub AddFieldParameters _
    (ByVal objCommand As SqlCommand)

    Dim objParameter As SqlParameter

    objCommand.Parameters.Clear()
    SqlCommandBuilder.DeriveParameters(objCommand)

    For Each objParameter In objCommand.Parameters
        objParameter.Value = _
            _FieldData.Item(objParameter.ParameterName. _
```

```vb
            Substring(1))
        Next
    End Sub

    Public Function ExecDataReader _
        (ByVal strStoredProc As String, _
        ByVal ParamArray objValues() As Object) _
        As SqlDataReader

        Dim objCommand As SqlCommand
        Dim objReader As SqlDataReader

        objCommand = New SqlCommand

        objCommand.CommandText = strStoredProc
        objCommand.CommandType = CommandType.StoredProcedure
        objCommand.Connection = dbConnection

        Try
            objCommand.Connection.Open()
            If (objValues.Length = 0) Then
                AddFieldParameters(objCommand)
            Else
                AddParameters(objCommand, objValues)
            End If
            objReader = objCommand. _
                ExecuteReader(CommandBehavior.CloseConnection)
        Catch ex As Exception
            If objCommand.Connection.State.Open Then
                objCommand.Connection.Close()
            End If
        End Try

        Return objReader
    End Function

    Public Sub ExecNonQuery _
        (ByVal strStoredProc As String, _
        ByVal ParamArray objValues() As Object)

        Dim objCommand As SqlCommand

        objCommand = New SqlCommand
```

```
    objCommand.CommandText = strStoredProc
    objCommand.CommandType = CommandType.StoredProcedure
    objCommand.Connection = dbConnection

    Try
        objCommand.Connection.Open()
        If (objValues.Length = 0) Then
            AddFieldParameters(objCommand)
        Else
            AddParameters(objCommand, objValues)
        End If
        objCommand.ExecuteNonQuery()
    Catch ex As Exception
        Throw ex
    Finally
        If objCommand.Connection.State.Open Then
            objCommand.Connection.Close()
        End If
    End Try
End Sub

Public Function ExecScalar _
    (ByVal strStoredProc As String, _
    ByVal ParamArray objValues() As Object)

    Dim objCommand As SqlCommand
    Dim objReturn As Object

    objCommand = New SqlCommand
    objCommand.CommandText = strStoredProc
    objCommand.CommandType = CommandType.StoredProcedure
    objCommand.Connection = dbConnection

    Try
        objCommand.Connection.Open()
        If (objValues.Length = 0) Then
            AddFieldParameters(objCommand)
        Else
            AddParameters(objCommand, objValues)
        End If
        objReturn = objCommand.ExecuteScalar()
    Catch ex As Exception
        Throw ex
```

```
    Finally
        If objCommand.Connection.State.Open Then
            objCommand.Connection.Close()
        End If
    End Try


    Return objReturn
End Function


Private m_ItemDefData As ItemDefAttribute
Public Function GetItemDefData() As ItemDefAttribute
    If IsNothing(m_ItemDefData) Then
        m_ItemDefData = CType(Attribute.GetCustomAttribute( _
            Me.GetType(), GetType(ItemDefAttribute)), _
            ItemDefAttribute)
    End If


    Return m_ItemDefData
End Function


Public Function GetFieldData _
    (ByVal strProperty As String) As Object
    Return _FieldData.Item(strProperty)
End Function


Public Sub SetFieldData _
    (ByVal strProperty As String, ByVal Value As Object)
    _FieldData.Item(strProperty) = Value
End Sub


Public Sub LoadDataRecord(ByVal objRecord As IDataReader)
    Dim objItem As Object
    Dim strKey As String
    Dim I As Integer


    Dim objRowDef As DataTable
    objRowDef = objRecord.GetSchemaTable()


    For I = 0 To objRowDef.Rows.Count - 1
        strKey = objRowDef.Rows.Item(I).Item(0)


        Try
            objItem = objRecord.Item(strKey)
```

```vb
              If Not objItem.GetType.IsInstanceOfType( _
                  GetType(System.DBNull)) Then
                  _FieldData.Item(strKey) = objItem
              End If
          Catch ex As Exception
          End Try
      Next
End Sub

Public Property ID() As Integer
    Get
        Return _FieldData.Item(GetItemDefData().PrimaryKey)
    End Get
    Set(ByVal Value As Integer)
        Dim objReader As SqlDataReader
        Dim strItem = GetItemDefData.Name

        If Value > 0 Then
            ' Note that the stored procedure name follows
            '   a pattern for its naming.
            objReader = ExecDataReader _
                ("sp_" & strItem & "_GetByID", Value)
            If objReader.Read() Then
                LoadDataRecord(objReader)
            Else
                Throw New Exception("Invalid ID")
            End If
        Else
            ResetData()
        End If

        objReader.Close()
    End Set
End Property

Public Sub Update()
    Dim strItem As String
    Dim strProc As String

    strItem = GetItemDefData.Name

    If ID = 0 Then
        strProc = "sp_" & strItem & "_Insert"
```

```
            _FieldData.Item(GetItemDefData().PrimaryKey) = _
                ExecScalar(strProc)
        Else
            strProc = "sp_" & strItem & "_Update"
            ExecNonQuery(strProc)
        End If
    End Sub

    Public Sub Delete()
        Dim strItem = GetItemDefData.Name
        ExecNonQuery("sp_" & strItem & "_Delete")
    End Sub
End Class

<AttributeUsage(AttributeTargets.Class, _
    Inherited:=True, AllowMultiple:=False)> _
Public Class ItemDefAttribute
    Inherits System.Attribute

    'Private fields
    Private m_Name As String
    Private m_PrimaryKey As String

    Public Sub New _
        (ByVal Name As String, ByVal PrimaryKey As String)
        M_Name = Name
        m_PrimaryKey = PrimaryKey
    End Sub

    Public ReadOnly Property Name() As String
        Get
            Return m_Name
        End Get
    End Property

    Public ReadOnly Property PrimaryKey() As String
        Get
            Return m_PrimaryKey
        End Get
    End Property
End Class
```

There are a number of assumptions that need to be kept in mind if you use this as the base class for your data access classes. They are as follows:

- The `ItemDefAttribute` must be applied to any dependant data-access classes. Its two parameters are the name of data access item in the way you want to use it in stored procedures and the primary key field name for this table.
- Create the four mandatory stored procedures for each data table.
- Each of the data properties in the data-access class must be named identically to the field names in your data table.

There is a mandatory stored procedure for each of the following actions: Deleting, Inserting, Updating and Retrieving a record by its primary key ID value. Following is an SQL listing of all four stored procedures for the `AppointmentItem` class: The stored procedures are named `sp_Name_Action`, where `Name` is the name of the data-access class as defined in the ItemDefAttribute that was applied to the class, and `Action` is one of `Update`, `Insert`, `Delete`, or `GetByID`.

```
CREATE PROCEDURE dbo.sp_Appointment_Insert
(
  @UserID int,
  @TimeStart datetime,
  @TimeEnd datetime,
  @Title varchar(500),
  @Note varchar(2000)
)
AS
  INSERT INTO [tblAppointment]
    VALUES(@UserID,@TimeStart,@TimeEnd,@Title,@Note)
  SELECT Convert(int,@@IDENTITY) AS [AppointmentID]
  RETURN

CREATE PROCEDURE dbo.sp_Appointment_Update
(
  @AppointmentID int,
  @UserID int,
  @TimeStart datetime,
  @TimeEnd datetime,
  @Title varchar(500),
  @Note varchar(2000)
```

```
)
AS
   Update [tblAppointment]
   Set [UserID]=@UserID,[TimeStart]=@TimeStart,
      [TimeEnd]=@TimeEnd,[Title]=@Title,[Note]=@Note
   WHERE [AppointmentID]=@AppointmentID
   RETURN

CREATE PROCEDURE dbo.sp_Appointment_Delete
(
   @AppointmentID int
)
AS
   DELETE FROM [tblAppointment] WHERE [AppointmentID]=@AppointmentID
   RETURN

ALTER PROCEDURE dbo.sp_Appointment_GetByID
   (
      @AppointmentID int
   )
AS
   Select * FROM [tblAppointment] WHERE [AppointmentID]=@AppointmentID
   RETURN
```

Developing a data-access layer in this way requires more work when developing the initial base class, but the subsequent reuse of that class and the reduced effort in developing the rest of the data access layer make it well worthwhile.

The Business Logic Layer

The first thing many of you may wonder is why I didn't develop a business logic layer for this application. The answer is simple: I don't do any business logic-type things to my data. In this application, the data is selected and then displayed. There is nothing being processed with the data. So where might you use a business logic layer? If you were to extend the application to allow meetings, with multiple people receiving notifications, and having best time scheduling within a range of dates and times, then you would want to implement this logic in a business logic layer. At this point, you are starting to do much more then just retrieve and store data. I feel that business logic layers should not be developed just to have them, but they should be developed where there is a need for them.

Implementation Details

Rather then trying to place all the code for this application here, I will discuss in detail only the code that is related to the main topic of this chapter; namely, databound server controls. With this in mind, we will look first at the Contact.aspx page.

In the Contact.aspx page, the server controls in question are located on the page and not on a user control. The user controls on this page are only for entering and editing contact data.

Listing 5.4 Contact.aspx.vb—Contact Page Code-Behind File

```
Public Class Contact
    Inherits System.Web.UI.Page

    Public WithEvents ctlContactEdit As ContactEdit
    Public WithEvents ctlContactView As ContactView

#Region " Web Form Designer Generated Code "

    'This call is required by the Web Form Designer.
    <System.Diagnostics.DebuggerStepThrough()> Private Sub _
      InitializeComponent()

    End Sub
    Protected WithEvents pnlMain As System.Web.UI.WebControls.Panel
    Protected WithEvents Panel1 As System.Web.UI.WebControls.Panel
    Protected WithEvents ctlAlphaList As _
      System.Web.UI.WebControls.Repeater
    Protected WithEvents ctlContactGrid As _
      System.Web.UI.WebControls.DataGrid
    Protected WithEvents btnAddContact As _
        System.Web.UI.WebControls.LinkButton
    Protected WithEvents Panel2 As System.Web.UI.WebControls.Panel

    'NOTE: The following placeholder declaration is required by the Web
    '  Form Designer.
    'Do not delete or move it.
    Private designerPlaceholderDeclaration As System.Object
```

```
    Private Sub Page_Init(ByVal sender As System.Object, ByVal e As _
        System.EventArgs) Handles MyBase.Init
            'CODEGEN: This method call is required by the Web Form Designer
            'Do not modify it using the code editor.
            InitializeComponent()
    End Sub

#End Region

    Public ctlMenuModule As MenuModule
    Private m_AuthUser As UserItem

    Private Sub Page_Load(ByVal sender As System.Object, _
        ByVal e As System.EventArgs) Handles MyBase.Load
        ctlMenuModule.CurrentMenu = "Contact"
        If Not IsPostBack Then
            State = ContactState.Normal
        End If


        Me.LoadAlphaList()
        Me.LoadContactGrid()
    End Sub

    Public ReadOnly Property AuthUser() As UserItem
        Get
            If IsNothing(m_AuthUser) Then
                m_AuthUser = New UserItem
                m_AuthUser.LoadByUsername(Me.User.Identity.Name)
            End If


            Return m_AuthUser
        End Get
    End Property

    Public Enum ContactState
        Normal = 0
        Edit = 1
        View = 2
    End Enum

    Public Property State() As ContactState
        Get
```

```vb
        If IsNothing(ViewState("ContactState")) Then
            ViewState("ContactState") = ContactState.Normal
        End If
        Return CType(ViewState("ContactState"), ContactState)
    End Get
    Set(ByVal Value As ContactState)
        ViewState("ContactState") = Value

        If Value = ContactState.Normal Then
            ctlContactEdit.Visible = False
            ctlContactView.Visible = False

        ElseIf Value = ContactState.Edit Then
            ctlContactEdit.Visible = True
            ctlContactView.Visible = False

        ElseIf Value = ContactState.View Then
            ctlContactEdit.Visible = False
            ctlContactView.Visible = True

        End If
    End Set
End Property


Private Class CountItem

    Private m_Name As String
    Private m_Value As Integer

    Public Sub New(ByVal strName As String, _
        ByVal nValue As Integer)
        m_Name = strName
        m_Value = nValue
    End Sub

    Public ReadOnly Property Name()
        Get
            Return m_Name
        End Get
    End Property

    Public ReadOnly Property Value()
        Get
            Return m_Value
```

```vbnet
        End Get
    End Property
End Class

Private Sub LoadAlphaList()
    Dim objCounts() As CountItem
    Dim I As Integer
    Dim isValidReader As Boolean
    Dim objReader As IDataReader
    Dim strName As String

    objCounts = Array.CreateInstance(GetType(CountItem), 27)
    objCounts(0) = _
        New CountItem("All - ", Page.AuthUser.ContactCount)

    objReader = Page.AuthUser.ContactAlphaCountsReader
    isValidReader = objReader.Read()

    For I = 1 To 26
        strName = Chr(Asc("A") + I - 1)
        If isValidReader Then
            If objReader.Item("AlphaInx") = I Then
                objCounts(I) = New CountItem(strName, _
                    objReader.Item("ContactCount"))
                isValidReader = objReader.Read()
            Else
                objCounts(I) = New CountItem(strName, 0)
            End If
        Else
            objCounts(I) = New CountItem(strName, 0)
        End If
    Next
    objReader.Close()

    Me.ctlAlphaList.DataSource = objCounts
    Me.ctlAlphaList.DataBind()
End Sub

Private Sub LoadContactGrid()
    Dim objReader As IDataReader

    If AlphaSelect = "ALL" Then
        objReader = Page.AuthUser.ContactsReader
    Else
```

```
        objReader = Page.AuthUser.GetContactsByFirstLetter _
            (AlphaSelect)
    End If

    Me.ctlContactGrid.DataSource = objReader
    Me.ctlContactGrid.DataBind()
End Sub

Private Property AlphaSelect() As String
    Get
        If IsNothing(ViewState.Item("AlphaSelect")) Then
            ViewState.Item("AlphaSelect") = "ALL"
        End If

        Return ViewState.Item("AlphaSelect")
    End Get
    Set(ByVal Value As String)
        If Value.Length > 3 Then
            ViewState.Item("AlphaSelect") = _
                Value.Substring(0, 3).ToUpper()
        Else
            ViewState.Item("AlphaSelect") = Value
        End If

        LoadAlphaList()
        LoadContactGrid()
    End Set
End Property

Public Shadows Property Page() As Contact
    Get
        Return CType(MyBase.Page, Contact)
    End Get
    Set(ByVal Value As Contact)
        MyBase.Page = Value
    End Set
End Property

Private Sub ctlAddContact_Click(ByVal sender As Object, _
    ByVal e As System.EventArgs) Handles btnAddContact.Click

    State = ContactState.Edit
    ctlContactEdit.ContactID = 0
End Sub
```

```
Private Sub ctlContactGrid_ItemCommand( _
    ByVal source As Object, _
    ByVal e As DataGridCommandEventArgs) _
    Handles ctlContactGrid.ItemCommand

    If e.CommandName = "EditItem" Then
        Me.State = ContactState.View
        Me.ctlContactView.ContactID = _
            Convert.ToInt32(e.CommandArgument)
        Me.ctlContactView.DataBind()
    End If
End Sub

Private Sub ctlAlphaList_ItemCommand( _
    ByVal source As Object, _
    ByVal e As RepeaterCommandEventArgs) _
    Handles ctlAlphaList.ItemCommand

    If e.CommandName = "CHANGE" Then
        Me.AlphaSelect = e.CommandArgument
    End If
End Sub
End Class
```

On the Contact page, user controls are used to collect and display the detailed data about the contact. There are two user controls, ContactEdit and ContactView. ContactEdit is also used for new contacts. The visibility of these controls is set depending upon whether or not it should be displayed.

The ContactEdit user control is a good example of a self-contained editing control. Listing 5.5 details this control. The code of other similar controls will not be shown here.

Listing 5.5 ContactEdit.ascx.vb—Code-Behind File for User Control to Edit Contact Data

```
Public Class ContactEdit
    Inherits System.Web.UI.UserControl

#Region " Web Form Designer Generated Code "

    'This call is required by the Web Form Designer.
    <System.Diagnostics.DebuggerStepThrough()> Private Sub _
      InitializeComponent()
```

```
    Dim configurationAppSettings As _
      System.Configuration.AppSettingsReader = _
        New System.Configuration.AppSettingsReader
    Me._Contact = New ScheduleVB.ContactItem
End Sub


Protected WithEvents Panel1 As System.Web.UI.WebControls.Panel
Protected WithEvents lblEdit As System.Web.UI.WebControls.Label
Protected WithEvents Label1 As System.Web.UI.WebControls.Label
Protected WithEvents Label2 As System.Web.UI.WebControls.Label
Protected WithEvents Label3 As System.Web.UI.WebControls.Label
Protected WithEvents Label4 As System.Web.UI.WebControls.Label
Protected WithEvents Label5 As System.Web.UI.WebControls.Label
Protected WithEvents Label6 As System.Web.UI.WebControls.Label
Protected WithEvents Label7 As System.Web.UI.WebControls.Label
Protected WithEvents Label8 As System.Web.UI.WebControls.Label
Protected WithEvents Panel2 As System.Web.UI.WebControls.Panel
Protected WithEvents btnUpdate As System.Web.UI.WebControls.Button
Protected WithEvents btnCancel As System.Web.UI.WebControls.Button
Protected WithEvents RequiredFieldValidator1 As _
    System.Web.UI.WebControls.RequiredFieldValidator
Protected WithEvents editLastName As _
    System.Web.UI.WebControls.TextBox
Protected WithEvents editFirstName As _
    System.Web.UI.WebControls.TextBox
Protected WithEvents editMiddleName As _
    System.Web.UI.WebControls.TextBox
Protected WithEvents editEmail As System.Web.UI.WebControls.TextBox
Protected WithEvents editWorkPhone As _
    System.Web.UI.WebControls.TextBox
Protected WithEvents editHomePhone As _
    System.Web.UI.WebControls.TextBox
Protected WithEvents editCellPhone As _
    System.Web.UI.WebControls.TextBox
Protected WithEvents editFax As _
    System.Web.UI.WebControls.TextBox
Protected WithEvents RegularExpressionValidator1 As _
      System.Web.UI.WebControls.RegularExpressionValidator
Protected WithEvents RegularExpressionValidator2 As _
    System.Web.UI.WebControls.RegularExpressionValidator
Protected WithEvents RegularExpressionValidator3 As _
    System.Web.UI.WebControls.RegularExpressionValidator
Protected WithEvents RegularExpressionValidator4 As _
```

```
        System.Web.UI.WebControls.RegularExpressionValidator
    Protected WithEvents RegularExpressionValidator5 As _
        System.Web.UI.WebControls.RegularExpressionValidator

    'NOTE: The following placeholder declaration is required by the Web
    '    Form Designer.
    'Do not delete or move it.
    Private designerPlaceholderDeclaration As System.Object

    Private Sub Page_Init(ByVal sender As System.Object, ByVal e As _
        System.EventArgs) Handles MyBase.Init
        'CODEGEN: This method call is required by the Web Form Designer
        'Do not modify it using the code editor.
        InitializeComponent()
    End Sub

#End Region

    Private m_ContactID As Integer
    Protected m_Contact As ScheduleVB.ContactItem

    Private Sub Page_Load(ByVal sender As System.Object, _
        ByVal e As System.EventArgs) Handles MyBase.Load
        'Put user code to initialize the page here
    End Sub

    Public Overloads Sub DataBind()
        Me.editLastName.Text = ContactObj.LastName
        Me.editMiddleName.Text = ContactObj.MiddleName
        Me.editFirstName.Text = ContactObj.FirstName
        Me.editEmail.Text = ContactObj.Email
        Me.editWorkPhone.Text = ContactObj.WorkPhone
        Me.editHomePhone.Text = ContactObj.HomePhone
        Me.editCellPhone.Text = ContactObj.CellPhone
        Me.editFax.Text = ContactObj.Fax
    End Sub

    Private Sub btnUpdate_Click(ByVal sender As System.Object, _
        ByVal e As System.EventArgs) Handles btnUpdate.Click
        ContactObj.LastName = Me.editLastName.Text
        ContactObj.MiddleName = Me.editMiddleName.Text
        ContactObj.FirstName = Me.editFirstName.Text
        ContactObj.Email = Me.editEmail.Text
```

```
            ContactObj.WorkPhone = Me.editWorkPhone.Text
            ContactObj.HomePhone = Me.editHomePhone.Text
            ContactObj.CellPhone = Me.editCellPhone.Text
            ContactObj.Fax = Me.editFax.Text
            ContactObj.UserID = Page.AuthUser.ID

            ContactObj.Update()
            Response.Redirect("Contact.aspx")
        End Sub


        Private Sub btnCancel_Click(ByVal sender As System.Object, _
            ByVal e As System.EventArgs) Handles btnCancel.Click
            Page.State = Contact.ContactState.Normal
        End Sub


        Public Shadows Property Page() As Contact
            Get
                Return CType(MyBase.Page, Contact)
            End Get
            Set(ByVal Value As Contact)
                MyBase.Page = Value
            End Set
        End Property


        Public Property ContactID() As Integer
            Get
                If IsNothing(ViewState.Item("ContactID")) Then
                    ViewState.Item("ContactID") = 0
                End If

                Return ViewState.Item("ContactID")
            End Get
            Set(ByVal Value As Integer)
                ViewState.Item("ContactID") = Value
                If Value = 0 Then
                    lblEdit.Text = "Add Contact"
                Else
                    lblEdit.Text = "Edit Contact"
                End If
            End Set
        End Property


        Public ReadOnly Property ContactObj() As ContactItem
            Get
```

```
        If IsNothing(m_Contact) Then
            m_Contact = New ContactItem
        End If
        If ContactID > 0 And _Contact.ID <> ContactID Then
            m_Contact.ID = ContactID
        End If

        m_Contact.UserID = Page.AuthUser.ID
        Return m_Contact
    End Get
  End Property
End Class
```

The MonthModule user control shows how to display custom data in a calendar control. To get the calendar to look the way I wanted it to, I had to insert a `div` tag around the date, and then use a style sheet to position it properly. Shortened appointment titles are then displayed below the date. Listing 5.6 show the details of this user control.

Listing 5.6 MonthModule.ascx.vb—Code-Behind File for User Control to Display Month View

```
Public Class MonthModule
    Inherits System.Web.UI.UserControl

#Region " Web Form Designer Generated Code "

    'This call is required by the Web Form Designer.
    <System.Diagnostics.DebuggerStepThrough()> Private Sub _
      InitializeComponent()

    End Sub
    Protected WithEvents ctlBigCalendar As _
        System.Web.UI.WebControls.Calendar
    Protected WithEvents Panel1 As System.Web.UI.WebControls.Panel

    'NOTE: The following placeholder declaration is required by the Web
    '    Form Designer.
    'Do not delete or move it.
    Private designerPlaceholderDeclaration As System.Object

    Private Sub Page_Init(ByVal sender As System.Object, ByVal e As _
        System.EventArgs) Handles MyBase.Init
```

```
            'CODEGEN: This method call is required by the Web Form Designer
            'Do not modify it using the code editor.
            InitializeComponent()
        End Sub

#End Region

    Private Sub Page_Load(ByVal sender As System.Object, _
        ByVal e As System.EventArgs) Handles MyBase.Load
        _Page = Page

        Me.ctlBigCalendar.SelectedDate = Page.SelectedDate
        Me.ctlBigCalendar.VisibleDate = Page.SelectedDate
    End Sub

    Private Sub ctlBigCalendar_DayRender(ByVal sender As Object, _
        ByVal e As System.Web.UI.WebControls.DayRenderEventArgs) _
        Handles ctlBigCalendar.DayRender

        Dim objReader As IDataReader
        Dim objAppointment As New AppointmentItem
        Dim I As Integer

        e.Cell.Controls.AddAt(0, _
            New LiteralControl("<div class='CalendarDate'>"))
        e.Cell.Controls.Add(New LiteralControl("</div>"))
        I = 0

        objReader = Me.Page.AuthUser.GetAppointmentsByDate(e.Day.Date)
        While (objReader.Read())
            Dim objLabel As New LinkButton
            Dim strTitle As String

            If I > 0 Then
                e.Cell.Controls.Add(New LiteralControl("<br>"))
            End If

            objAppointment.LoadDataRecord(objReader)
            strTitle = objAppointment.Title
            If strTitle.Length > 13 Then
                strTitle = strTitle.Substring(0, 10) & "..."
            End If
            objLabel.Text = strTitle
```

```
            objLabel.ToolTip = _
                objAppointment.TimeStart.ToShortTimeString() & _
                "~" & _
                objAppointment.TimeEnd.ToShortTimeString() & _
                ": " & _
                objAppointment.Title
            e.Cell.Controls.Add(objLabel)

            I = I + 1
        End While
        objReader.Close()

    End Sub

    Private WithEvents _Page As New Schedule
    Public Shadows Property Page() As Schedule
        Get
            Return CType(MyBase.Page, Schedule)
        End Get
        Set(ByVal Value As Schedule)
            MyBase.Page = Value
        End Set
    End Property

    Private Sub _Page_SelectedDateChanged(ByVal sender As Object, _
        ByVal e As System.EventArgs) _
        Handles _Page.SelectedDateChanged

        Me.ctlBigCalendar.SelectedDate = Page.SelectedDate
        Me.ctlBigCalendar.VisibleDate = Page.SelectedDate
    End Sub

    Private Sub ctlBigCalendar_SelectionChanged(ByVal sender As Object, _
        ByVal e As System.EventArgs) _
        Handles ctlBigCalendar.SelectionChanged

        Page.SelectedDate = ctlBigCalendar.SelectedDate
    End Sub
End Class
```

The DayModule user control gives another example of how a Repeater server control can be used. Listing 5.7 shows the details of this module.

Listing 5.7 DayModule.ascx.vb—Code-Behind File for User Control to Display Day View

```
Imports System.Collections.Specialized

Public Class DayModule
    Inherits System.Web.UI.UserControl

#Region " Web Form Designer Generated Code "

    'This call is required by the Web Form Designer.
    <System.Diagnostics.DebuggerStepThrough()> Private Sub _
        InitializeComponent()

    End Sub
    Protected WithEvents Panel1 As System.Web.UI.WebControls.Panel
    Protected WithEvents ctlDay As System.Web.UI.WebControls.Repeater
    Protected WithEvents Time As System.Web.UI.WebControls.Label

    'NOTE: The following placeholder declaration is required by the Web
    '   Form Designer.
    'Do not delete or move it.
    Private designerPlaceholderDeclaration As System.Object

    Private Sub Page_Init(ByVal sender As System.Object, ByVal e As _
        System.EventArgs) Handles MyBase.Init
        'CODEGEN: This method call is required by the Web Form Designer
        'Do not modify it using the code editor.
        InitializeComponent()
    End Sub

#End Region

    Private m_StartTime As DateTime
    Private m_EndTime As DateTime
    Private m_Increment As TimeSpan
    Private m_ItemCount As Integer
    Private m_Appointments As IDataReader
```

```
Private m_HasAppointment As Boolean
Private m_NextAppointment As AppointmentItem
Protected WithEvents m_Page As Schedule


Private Sub Page_Load(ByVal sender As System.Object, _
    ByVal e As System.EventArgs) Handles MyBase.Load
    m_StartTime = New DateTime(1, 1, 1, 8, 0, 0)
    m_EndTime = New DateTime(1, 1, 1, 18, 0, 0)
    m_Increment = New TimeSpan(0, 30, 0)
    m_ItemCount = 20
    m_Page = Page

    LoadData()
End Sub

Public Shadows Property Page() As Schedule
    Get
        Return CType(MyBase.Page, Schedule)
    End Get
    Set(ByVal Value As Schedule)
        MyBase.Page = Value
    End Set
End Property

Public Sub LoadNextAppointment()
    If IsNothing(m_Appointments) Then
        m_Appointments = m_Page.AuthUser. _
            GetAppointmentsByDate(m_Page.SelectedDate)
    End If
    If Not m_Appointments.IsClosed Then
        m_HasAppointment = m_Appointments.Read()
        If m_HasAppointment Then
            m_NextAppointment = New AppointmentItem
            m_NextAppointment.LoadDataRecord(m_Appointments)
        Else
            m_Appointments.Close()
        End If
    End If
End Sub

Public Sub LoadData()
```

```
    Dim dtCurTime As System.DateTime
    Dim strTimeList As New StringCollection
    Dim I As Integer

    m_Appointments = Nothing
    LoadNextAppointment()

    dtCurTime = m_StartTime
    I = 0

    While (dtCurTime < m_EndTime)
        strTimeList.Add(dtCurTime.ToShortTimeString())
        dtCurTime = dtCurTime.Add(m_Increment)
        I = I + 1
    End While

    Me.ctlDay.DataSource = strTimeList
    Me.ctlDay.DataBind()

    If Not m_Appointments.IsClosed Then
        m_Appointments.Close()
    End If
End Sub

Private Sub ctlDay_ItemDataBound(ByVal sender As Object, _
    ByVal e As RepeaterItemEventArgs) _
    Handles ctlDay.ItemDataBound

    Dim objAppointments As Panel
    Dim objItem As RepeaterItem
    Dim dtCurrent As New DateTime
    Dim nAptCount As Integer
    objItem = e.Item

    If (objItem.ItemType = ListItemType.Item) Or _
        (objItem.ItemType = ListItemType.AlternatingItem) _
        Then

        dtCurrent = _DateTime.Parse(_Page.SelectedDate. _
            ToShortDateString() & " " & objItem.DataItem)
        objAppointments = _
            CType(objItem.FindControl("pnlAppointments"), _
            Panel)
```

```
        If _HasAppointment Then
            nAptCount = 0
            While (_NextAppointment.TimeStart < _
                dtCurrent.Add(Me._Increment) And _
                m_HasAppointment)

                Dim objLink As New LinkButton
                objLink.Text = m_NextAppointment.TimeStart. _
                    ToShortTimeString() & " - " & _
                    m_NextAppointment.TimeEnd. _
                    ToShortTimeString() & ": " & _
                    m_NextAppointment.Title

                objLink.ToolTip = m_NextAppointment.Note
                objLink.CommandName = "EditAppointment"
                objLink.CommandArgument = _
                    m_NextAppointment.ID.ToString()
                AddHandler objLink.Command, _
                    AddressOf ctlDay_ItemCommand

                If nAptCount > 0 Then
                    objAppointments.Controls.Add( _
                        New LiteralControl("<br>"))
                End If
                objAppointments.Controls.Add(objLink)

                LoadNextAppointment()
                nAptCount = nAptCount + 1
            End While
        End If

        If nAptCount = 0 Then
            objAppointments.Controls.Add( _
                New LiteralControl(" "))
        End If
    End If
End Sub

Private Sub ctlDay_ItemCommand(ByVal source As Object, _
    ByVal e As System.Web.UI.WebControls.CommandEventArgs)

    If e.CommandName = "EditAppointment" Then
        Page.ctlEditModule.AppointmentID = _
```

```
            Convert.ToInt32(e.CommandArgument)
        End If
    End Sub

    Private Sub _Page_SelectedDateChanged(ByVal sender As Object, _
        ByVal e As System.EventArgs) _
        Handles _Page.SelectedDateChanged

        LoadData()
    End Sub
End Class
```

Deployment and Customization

The deployment of this application is straightforward. First, copy all the Web files into a folder in the Web root directory. Next, attach a copy of the SQL database to the database server you wish to access. Finally, change the ConnectionString in the appSettings section of the web.config file to one that will allow access to the database.

This application has a lot of potential for further customizations. Adding a multiuser scheduling feature that would allow a best time/date to be automatically chosen would be my favorite, but there are many other possible features that can be added.

Summary

In this chapter, you've learned how to build an entire scheduling application. One of the main things we touched on was databinding to a control with custom databinding. This application also uses SQL Server effectively by accessing stored procedures.

After reading this chapter, you should be able to write custom controls that are derived from the standard ASP.NET server controls. This will give you flexibility as you design and write your own controls based on the standard controls.

CHAPTER 6

The Microsoft Forum Application

In This Chapter:

- Using Embedded Server Controls in Iterative Databound Controls
- The Database
- The Repeater Demo
- The DataList Demo
- The DataGrid Demo

Microsoft went the extra mile to provide some great applications that are examples of how to get the most out of the .NET Framework, and especially ASP.NET. This chapter shows the Microsoft Forum application, and then talks about one specific technique that's used—how to use embedded server controls in iterative databound controls.

The Microsoft Forum application is freely available from www.ASP.net, where you can follow the links to Source Projects, and then to ASP.NET Forums. I have the application installed on www.ASPNET-Solutions.com, as you can see in Figure 6.1.

Using Embedded Server Controls in Iterative Databound Controls

In this section, I'll show you how to get more functionality from iterative databound controls such as Repeaters, DataLists, and DataGrids. With the extra functionality comes a richer user interface, which will ultimately yield a better application. Applications that have smooth user interfaces almost always work better because users more easily grasp their functionality.

To pull this enhancement off, server controls such as Labels, CheckBoxes, and DropDownLists can be embedded into iterative databound

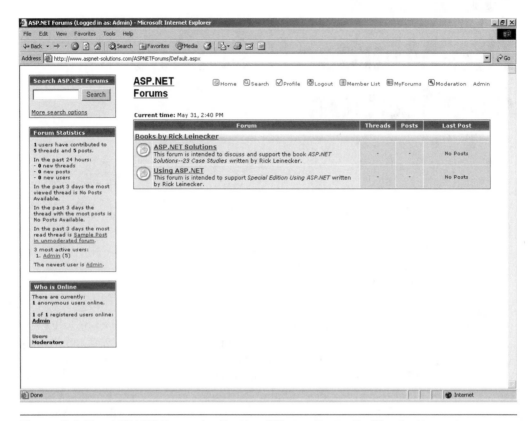

Figure 6.1 The ASP.NET Forum Application Offers a Fantastic Way for Users to Communicate.

controls. Getting access to the embedded controls is easy, thus making the iterative databound controls very flexible.

The scenario is this: You've convinced your boss to let you develop the next Web application with ASP.NET. He's reluctant, but one of the selling points is the iterative databound controls, including Repeaters, DataLists, and DataGrids. These three databound controls differ from other databound controls such as the DropDownList or ListBox because they're iterative. Iterative controls loop through a data source to which they're bound and apply HTML templates to each row of data.

OK; so three weeks have passed, and your boss comes by to see the work in progress. One of the pages has a Repeater object that's been bound to a recordset that was retrieved from the database. The application looks great, and he's really impressed with the small amount of code it took to get the result. He asks for a change, though. You need to be able to select each row with a checkbox so that users can select any number of items for processing.

You get busy and scour the Repeater documentation. There must be something about checkboxes. But hours of research are fruitless, and you throw up your hands in despair. Maybe a Repeater wasn't the object type you should have used. You take a look at the DataList and DataGrid objects, hoping to find the solution, but no such luck. No checkboxes are built into the iterative databound controls.

Hold on, though; there is hope. Server controls such as CheckBoxes, Labels, and TextBoxes can all be embedded within ASP.NET iterative databound controls. With the right approach, the Repeater in the already-developed ASP.NET application can be easily changed to give users the capability to select the items in the list. This section talks about embedding server controls in iterative databound controls, and shows some example programs that'll help you understand.

ASP.NET iterative databound controls give you an easy way to display lists of data from a data source. They also offer flexibility because you can add server controls such as Labels and CheckBoxes to the declarative constructs, such as ItemTemplates, that go in the .aspx file. The section is broken into three parts: a Repeater demo, a DataList demo, and a DataGrid demo.

For each demo, I'll talk about the declaration of the objects that reside in the .aspx file. This declaration includes things such as ItemTemplates and Columns.

For each demo, I'll also go through the code that's behind it. We'll rely heavily on the `FindControl()` method. This method obtains object references to the server controls that we want to access.

All code snippets are presented in C# and VB. The complete demo project can be downloaded as either a C# or a VB project.

The Database

If you have SQL Server 2000 installed, chances are you have the database that's used for the demos in this section. It's the pubs database that's used. (The pubs database is installed as a sample database by default with a SQL Server 2000 installation.) Because this database is so common, I haven't included any mechanisms to recreate it. The three tables that are used are the authors, publishers, and employees tables.

The Repeater Demo

This demo binds the authors table to a Repeater, allows users to select items with checkboxes, and then creates a list of selected names when the OK button is clicked. You can see the demo as it first appears in Figure 6.2.

The User Interface

There is some incidental text, but to build the meat of the user interface, I first placed a Repeater onto the screen and named it Authors. Below the Repeater, I put a Label that doubles as an error-report mechanism and the destination for the list of selected authors—this object is named ErrorMessage. Below the Label is a button that fires an event handler.

The Repeater has three columns when it renders: one for the author's name, one for the author's phone, and one for the author's contact. Three

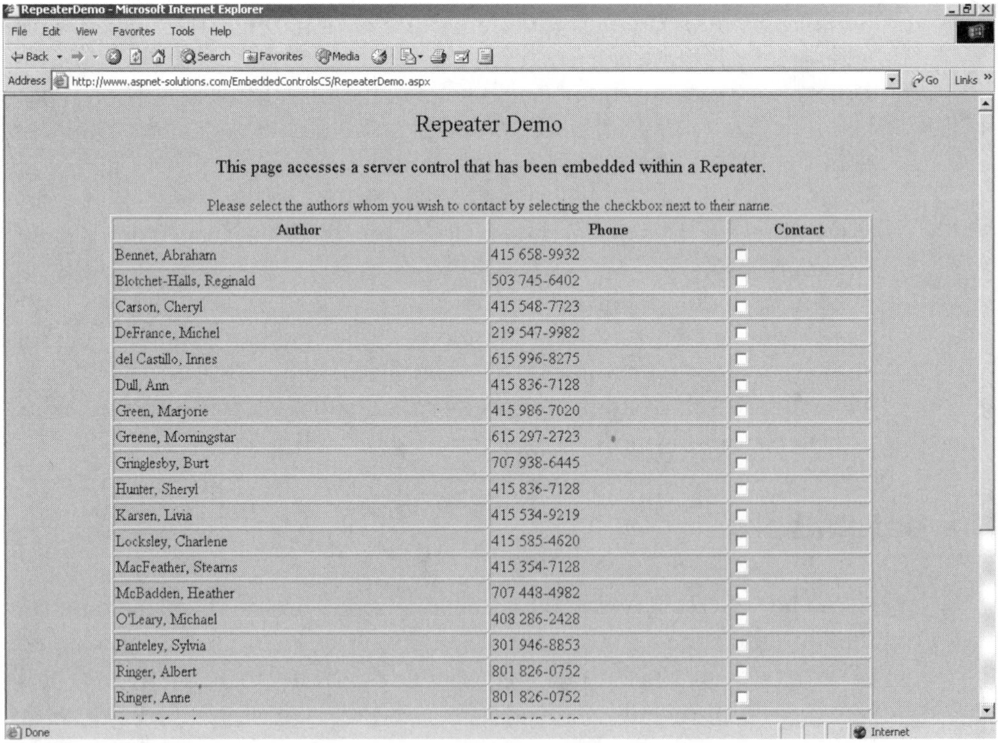

Figure 6.2 The Repeater Demo Shows a Checkbox for Each Row.

templates are used in the Repeater: a HeaderTemplate, an ItemTemplate, and a FooterTemplate. The following code shows a simplified version of the Repeater. We'll get to the details shortly.

```
<asp:repeater id="Authors" runat="server">
  <HeaderTemplate>
    <table border="1" width="80%">
      <tr>
        <th>
          Author
        </th>
        <th>
          Phone
        </th>
        <th>
          Contact
        </th>
      </tr>
  </HeaderTemplate>
  <ItemTemplate>
    <tr>
    <td>
     <asp:Label id="Name" runat="server"
       text='Populate name data here' />
    </td>
    <td>
     <asp:Label id="Phone" runat="server"
       text='Populate phone data here' />
    </td>
    <td>
     <asp:CheckBox runat="server" id="Schedule" />
     </td>
    </tr>
  </ItemTemplate>
  <FooterTemplate>
    </table>
  </FooterTemplate>
</asp:repeater>
```

If you look at the HeaderTemplate in the code above, you'll see the start of a table and three table headings. Repeaters do not generate the table start tag, so you must put it either in the HeaderTemplate or before the Repeater starts.

Take a look at the FooterTemplate next. It contains just the table end tag.

The ItemTemplate has three columns (within `<td></td>` tags). The first column contains the author name, and the name data will be in a Label object named Name. The second column contains the author phone, and the phone data will be in a Label object named Phone. The third column contains a CheckBox object that users can select.

That's the nickel tour of the Repeater's templates. The next thing you need to know is how to populate the Labels with the name and phone data. There are several ways to do it, but the way I find easiest and most maintainable is with the following syntax:

```
DataBinder.Eval(Container.DataItem, "fieldname")
```

The code above, though, must be within the `<%#` and `%>` symbols to indicate that it's code, as follows:

```
<%# DataBinder.Eval(Container.DataItem, "fieldname") %>
```

This syntax inserts the contents of the named field into the Repeater template. The following is the complete .aspx code for the Repeater:

```
<asp:repeater id="Authors" runat="server">
  <HeaderTemplate>
    <table border="1" width="80%">
      <tr>
        <th>
          Author
        </th>
        <th>
          Phone
        </th>
        <th>
          Contact
        </th>
      </tr>
  </HeaderTemplate>
  <ItemTemplate>
    <tr>
    <td>
     <asp:Label id="Name" runat="server"
      text='<%# DataBinder.Eval(Container.DataItem, "au_lname") +
        ", " + DataBinder.Eval(Container.DataItem, "au_fname")' />
```

```
      </td>
      <td>
       <asp:Label id="Phone" runat="server"
         text='<%# DataBinder.Eval(Container.DataItem, "Phone") %>' />
      </td>
      <td>
       <asp:CheckBox runat="server" id="Schedule" />
      </td>
     </tr>
   </ItemTemplate>
   <FooterTemplate>
     </table>
   </FooterTemplate>
</asp:repeater>
```

NOTE: When you place Label objects onto an ASP.NET form and set the text in the Property window, the text content that you specified will appear between the `<asp:Label>` and `</asp:Label>` tags. Let's say, for example, that you have a Label object named Address. You put the text **1234 Main Street** into the text field of the property window. If you go the HTML view and look at the code, you'll see something like the following:

```
<asp:Label id="Address" runat="server">1234 Main Street</asp:Label>
```

Then, to access the text contents in code, you simply use the `Label.Text` property. I ran into a small dilemma that I couldn't solve when I added the code as follows to populate the Label objects (as you would expect to do):

```
<asp:Label id="Phone" runat="server">
   <%# DataBinder.Eval(Container.DataItem, "Phone") %>
</asp:Label>
```

When I tried to retrieve the contents by accessing the `Label.Text` property, they were invariably empty. But when I set the Label's **Text** attribute as follows, it worked perfectly:

```
<asp:Label id="Phone" runat="server"
   Text='<%# DataBinder.Eval(Container.DataItem, "Phone") %>'>
</asp:Label>
```

To make matters even stranger, the **Text** attribute of a Label object doesn't come up with `autocomplete`, as do all other available attributes.

NOTE: The Code behind the Repeater Demo
There are two methods in the code that we'll talk about. The first is the Page_Load() method, in which the Repeater is bound to a recordset. The second method is the button handler event that's fired when the user clicks the button labeled OK.

All of the demos require the System.Data.SqlClient namespace because all the samples use SQL Server. Toward the top of each source code module, you'll see the following:

C#
```
using System.Data.SqlClient;
```

VB
```
Imports System.Data.SqlClient
```

The Page_Load() Method of the Repeater Demo

The code for the Page_Load() method follows. A discussion of the code is immediately below it.

C#
```
private void Page_Load(object sender, System.EventArgs e)
{

  // Only populate the Repeater if this is not a post back.
  if( !IsPostBack )
  {

    // Create a connection object.
    SqlConnection objConnection =
     new SqlConnection("server=localhost;database=pubs;uid=sa;pwd=");

    // Use a try/catch/finally construct to
    //   gracefully handle errors.
    try
    {
      // Open the connection.
      objConnection.Open();

      // Create the command object. We'll select all
      //   author first and last name along with phone.
```

```
    SqlCommand objCommand =
      new SqlCommand( "SELECT au_lname,au_fname,phone FROM authors " +
      "ORDER BY au_lname,au_fname",
      objConnection );

    // Populate a reader.
    SqlDataReader objReader = objCommand.ExecuteReader();

    // Set the Repeater's data source and then
    //   call the DataBind() method.
    Authors.DataSource = objReader;
    Authors.DataBind();

    // Close the reader.
    objReader.Close();

  }
  catch( Exception ex )
  {
    // Display the error message to the reader.
    ErrorMessage.Text = ex.Message.ToString();
  }
  finally
  {
    // See if the connection is open.
    if( objConnection.State == ConnectionState.Open )
    {
      // Close it if it is open.
      objConnection.Close();
    }
  }
  }
}
```

VB
```
Private Sub Page_Load(ByVal sender As System.Object, _
  ByVal e As System.EventArgs) Handles MyBase.Load
    ' Only populate the Repeater if this is not a post back.
    If Not IsPostBack Then
    ' Create a connection object.
     Dim objConnection As _
      New SqlConnection("server=localhost;database=pubs;uid=sa;pwd=")

       ' Use a try/catch/finally construct to
       '   gracefully handle errors.
```

```
Try
    ' Open the connection.
    objConnection.Open()

 ' Create the command object. We'll select all
 '    author first and last name along with phone.
 Dim objCommand As _
  New SqlCommand( _
     "SELECT au_lname,au_fname,phone FROM authors " + _
     "ORDER BY au_lname,au_fname", _
     objConnection)

    ' Populate a reader.
    Dim objReader As SqlDataReader = objCommand.ExecuteReader()

    ' Set the Repeater's data source and then
    '    call the DataBind() method.
    Authors.DataSource = objReader
    Authors.DataBind()

    ' Close the reader.
    objReader.Close()

Catch ex As Exception
    ' Display the error message to the reader.
    ErrorMessage.Text = ex.Message.ToString()
Finally
    ' See if the connection is open.
    If objConnection.State = ConnectionState.Open Then
        ' Close it if it is open.
        objConnection.Close()
    End If
End Try
    End If
End Sub
```

This code performs a pretty straightforward retrieval of data with which the Repeater is bound. First, a connection to the database is created by creating a SqlConnection object and then calling its `Open()` method. Any code that can throw an exception is within a `try` block. The `try`/`catch`/

finally construct allows the code to be robust and handle any errors that might arise. If everything goes well, all of the code in the try block is executed, followed by the code in the finally block. If an exception is thrown at any point in the try block, execution proceeds to the catch block, after which the finally block will be executed.

All of the connection strings in this section have a blank password for the sa SQL Server account. I've removed these so that the password is blank so that my server remains secure. It is a bad idea, however, to have a blank password for the sa account. For one thing, this leaves a security hole open. For another thing, there is a worm (named DispId) that could strike your server.

Once the connection has been established to the database, a Sql-Command object must be created. This object gives us the capability to execute a query on the database and get a recordset back. The recordset will be contained in a SqlDataReader object. The following SQL will be executed:

```
SELECT au_lname,au_fname,phone FROM authors ORDER BY au_lname,au_fname
```

A call to the SqlCommand.ExecuteReader() method returns a populated SqlDataReader object. The Repeater is now bound to the data by setting the Repeater.DataSource property to the SqlDataReader, and then calling the Repeater.DataBind() method.

The ExamineRepeater_Click() Method of the Repeater Demo

The code for the ExamineRepeater_Click() method follows. It is fired when users click the OK button. A discussion of the code is immediately below it.

C#
```
private void ExamineRepeater_Click(object sender, System.EventArgs e)
{

  // Clear the Label so that we start with an empty string.
  //   (The label that's used to show database exception
  //   messages is also used to display the results.)
  ErrorMessage.Text = "";
```

```
// Loop through the items in the Authors object (which is
//   a Repeater).
foreach( Control control in Authors.Controls )
{
  // Make sure we have a line that's not a header or footer.
  if( ((RepeaterItem)control).ItemType == ListItemType.Item ||
    ((RepeaterItem)control).ItemType == ListItemType.AlternatingItem )
  {
    // Find the CheckBox object so that we know if this item
    //   was selected.
    CheckBox cb = (CheckBox)control.FindControl( "Schedule" );
    if( cb.Checked )
    {
      // Find the Label objects from which we'll get the
      //   text.
      Label Name = (Label)control.FindControl( "Name" );
      Label Phone = (Label)control.FindControl( "Phone" );

      // Concatenate the text from the Name and Phone
      //   Labels onto the Label that will hold the results.
      ErrorMessage.Text +=
        ( Name.Text + " -- " + Phone.Text + "<br>\r\n" );
    }
  }
}
```

VB

```
Private Sub ExamineRepeater_Click(ByVal sender As System.Object, _
  ByVal e As System.EventArgs) Handles ExamineRepeater.Click

    ' Clear the Label so that we start with an empty string.
    '   (The label that's used to show database exception
    '   messages is also used to display the results.)
    ErrorMessage.Text = ""

    ' Loop through the items in the Authors object (which is
    '   a Repeater).
    Dim i As Integer
    For i = 0 To Authors.Controls.Count - 1
        Dim item As RepeaterItem = Authors.Controls(i)
```

```
      ' Make sure we have a line that's not a header or footer.
   If item.ItemType = ListItemType.Item Or _
         item.ItemType = ListItemType.AlternatingItem Then

            ' Find the CheckBox object so that we know if this item
            '    was selected.
            Dim cb As CheckBox = item.FindControl("Schedule")
            If cb.Checked Then
               ' Find the Label objects from which we'll get the
               '    text.
               Dim Name As Label = item.FindControl("Name")
               Dim Phone As Label = item.FindControl("Phone")

               ' Concatenate the text from the Name and Phone
               '    Labels onto the Label that will hold the results.
               ErrorMessage.Text += _
                  (Name.Text + " -- " + Phone.Text + "<br>" + vbCrLf)
            End If
         End If
      Next
End Sub
```

Let's start with one thing: you can't directly access the server controls. For instance, the following code will not compile:

C#
```
string strText = ServerLabelControl.Text;
```

VB
```
Dim strText as String = ServerLabelControl.Text
```

These controls are not accessible at the page level because of the implementation of ASP.NET templates. Each template runs in a separate naming container that makes it impossible for the common language runtime processing the ASP.NET page to retrieve the controls that are in the templates. This setup is so that we can duplicate named controls on the same page working in their respective naming containers.

The code in the `ExamineRepeater_Click()` method starts off by emptying the ErrorMessage Label object so that it can be used to hold a cumulative listing of the selected names. The code then iterates through the Controls collection in the Authors Repeater object. Note that in C# a foreach loop is used, while in VB a For/Next loop is used. That's because VB does not have a foreach loop.

We make sure that each control in the collection is either an ItemTemplate or an AlternatingItemTemplate. If we don't perform this check, we might be inadvertently looking at the HeaderTemplate and FooterTemplate, in which case the FindControl() method will return a null (or Nothing in VB) because the control won't be found.

Next, we get an object reference to the CheckBox that's in the current row. This is done with the FindControl() method. I've extracted the lines (for C# and VB) that find the CheckBox objects, and they are here:

C#
```
CheckBox cb = (CheckBox)control.FindControl( "Schedule" );
```

VB
```
Dim cb As CheckBox = item.FindControl("Schedule")
```

A simple check to the CheckBox.Checked property lets us know whether it is checked. If it's not, we won't do anything else during this iteration of the loop. If it is checked, though, we'll go on to get object references to the Labels that are in the Repeater, as follows:

C#
```
Label Name = (Label)control.FindControl( "Name" );
Label Phone = (Label)control.FindControl( "Phone" );
```

VB
```
Dim Name As Label = item.FindControl("Name")
Dim Phone As Label = item.FindControl("Phone")
```

Once object references to the Labels have been retrieved, it's a simple matter to concatenate their Text properties to the ErrorMessage.Text property. You can see the application below in Figure 6.3, after several rows have been selected and the OK button has been pressed:

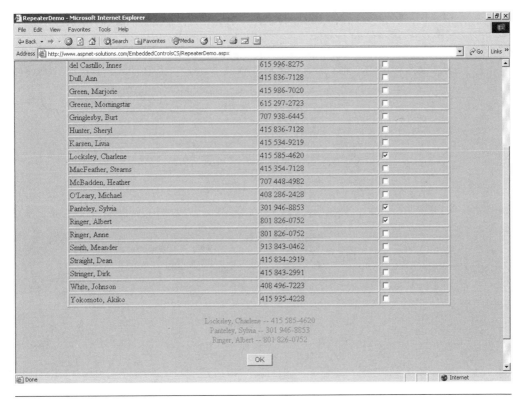

Figure 6.3 You Can See the Rows That Were Selected.

The DataList Demo

This demo binds the publishers table to a DataList, allows users to select a color with which the publisher name will be rendered, and then redraws the list with the newly selected colors. You can see the demo below, in Figure 6.4, as it first appears .

The User Interface

At the heart of the user interface is a DataList object named Publishers. Below the DataList is a Label named ErrorMessage that's used to alert users to any exception messages that have been caught. And below that is a Button that fires an event handler.

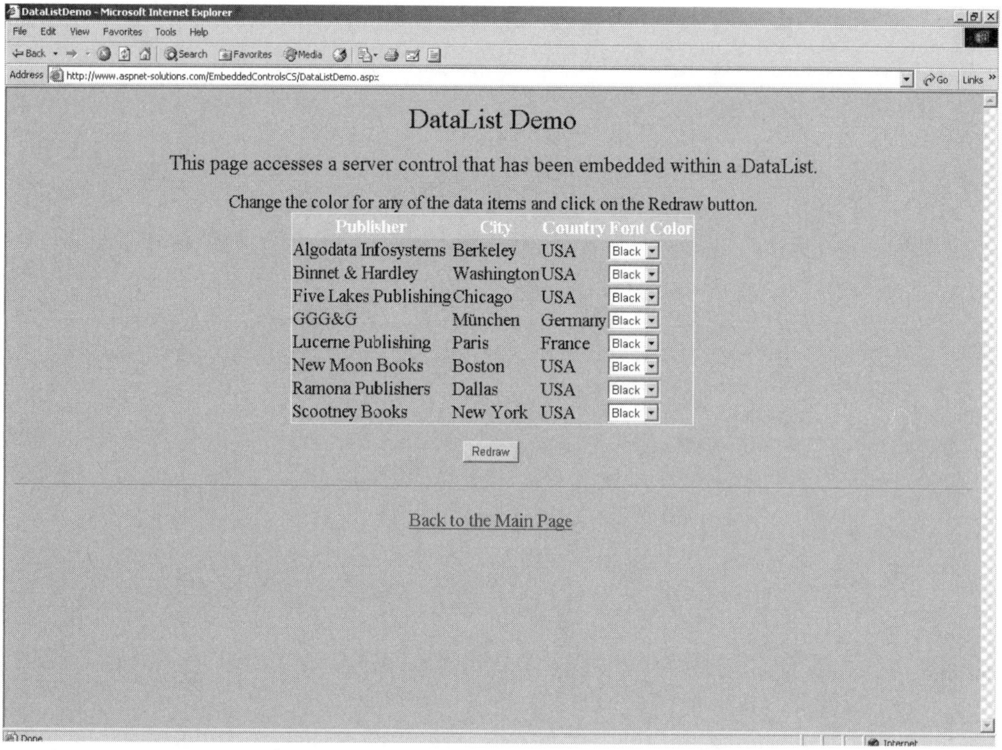

Figure 6.4 The DataList Demo Shows How to Use Embedded Server Controls in a DataList.

The DataList has four columns when it renders: one for the publisher's name, one for the publisher's city, one for the publisher's country, and one for the list of colors. Within the DataList are two server controls: a Label named pub that contains the list of publishers, and a DropDownList named StyleSelector that contains a list of colors. The DataList code from the .aspx file is below. A discussion of the code follows the code listing.

```
<asp:datalist id="Publishers" runat="server" BorderWidth="1">
  <HeaderTemplate>
    <tr>
      <th bgcolor="Thistle">
        <font color="white">Publisher</font>
      </th>
      <th bgcolor="Thistle">
```

```
      <font color="white">City</font>
    </th>
    <th bgcolor="Thistle">
      <font color="white">Country</font>
    </th>
    <th bgcolor="Thistle">
      <font color="white">Font Color</font>
    </th>
  </tr>
</HeaderTemplate>
<ItemTemplate>
  <tr>
    <td>
      <asp:Label id="pub" Runat="server"
      Text='<%# DataBinder.Eval(Container.DataItem, "pub_name") %>' />
    </td>
    <td>
      <%# DataBinder.Eval(Container.DataItem, "city") %>
    </td>
    <td>
      <%# DataBinder.Eval(Container.DataItem, "country") %>
    </td>
    <td>
      <asp:DropDownList ID="StyleSelector" Runat="server">
        <asp:ListItem>Black</asp:ListItem>
        <asp:ListItem>Red</asp:ListItem>
        <asp:ListItem>Green</asp:ListItem>
        <asp:ListItem>Blue</asp:ListItem>
      </asp:DropDownList>
    </td>
  </tr>
</ItemTemplate>
</asp:datalist>
```

First, notice that there are no `<table>` or `</table>` tags. That's because DataLists automatically render these. In the code above, the HeaderTemplate contains the table row for the table's heading. It renders as follows in Figure 6.5:

The code that produced the table heading is as follows:

```
<tr>
  <th bgcolor="Thistle">
```

Publisher	City	Country Font Color

Figure 6.5 The Table Has a Heading.

```
    <font color="white">Publisher</font>
  </th>
  <th bgcolor="Thistle">
    <font color="white">City</font>
  </th>
  <th bgcolor="Thistle">
    <font color="white">Country</font>
  </th>
  <th bgcolor="Thistle">
    <font color="white">Font Color</font>
  </th>
</tr>
```

The ItemTemplate has four columns. The first column contains the publisher name in a Label named pub. It's populated with the `Data-Binder.Eval(Container.DataItem, "pub_Name")` expression. The entire Label code is as follows:

```
<asp:Label id="pub" Runat="server"
  Text='<%# DataBinder.Eval(Container.DataItem, "pub_name") %>' />
```

The second and third column simply use the `DataBinder.Eval()` method to populate the columns with data. The data is not included in a server control, and the second and third columns contain no server controls.

The fourth column contains a DropDownList with four colors. The color selection determines the color with which the publisher name (in the first column) is rendered. The DropDownList code is as follows:

```
<asp:DropDownList ID="StyleSelector" Runat="server">
  <asp:ListItem>Black</asp:ListItem>
  <asp:ListItem>Red</asp:ListItem>
  <asp:ListItem>Green</asp:ListItem>
  <asp:ListItem>Blue</asp:ListItem>
</asp:DropDownList>
```

The Code behind the DataList Demo

There are two methods behind the DataList demo that we'll take a look at. The first is the `Page_Load()` method, and the second is the `RedrawData-List_Click()` method. Both methods are described in the next two sections.

The `Page_Load()` Method Of The DataList Demo

The code for the `Page_Load()` method follows. A discussion of the code is immediately below it.

C#
```
private void Page_Load(object sender, System.EventArgs e)
{

  // Only populate the Repeater if this is not a post back.
  if( !IsPostBack )
  {

  // Create a connection object.
  SqlConnection objConnection =
    new SqlConnection("server=localhost;database=pubs;uid=sa;pwd=");

    // Use a try/catch/finally construct to
    //   gracefully handle errors.
    try
    {
      // Open the connection.
      objConnection.Open();

      // Create the command object. We'll select all
      //   publisher name, city, and country.
      SqlCommand objCommand =
       new SqlCommand( "SELECT pub_name,city,country FROM publishers " +
         "ORDER BY pub_name",
         objConnection );

      // Populate a reader.
      SqlDataReader objReader = objCommand.ExecuteReader();

      // Set the DataLists's data source and then
      //   call the DataBind() method.
      Publishers.DataSource = objReader;
      Publishers.DataBind();
```

```
      // Close the reader.
      objReader.Close();


    }
    catch( Exception ex )
    {
      // Display the error message to the reader.
      ErrorMessage.Text = ex.Message.ToString();
    }
    finally
    {
      // See if the connection is open.
      if( objConnection.State == ConnectionState.Open )
      {
        // Close it if it is open.
        objConnection.Close();
      }
    }
  }
}
```

VB

```
Private Sub Page_Load(ByVal sender As System.Object, _
  ByVal e As System.EventArgs) Handles MyBase.Load

    ' Only populate the DataList if this is not a post back.
    If Not IsPostBack Then
    ' Create a connection object.
     Dim objConnection As _
      New SqlConnection("server=localhost;database=pubs;uid=sa;pwd=s")

        ' Use a try/catch/finally construct to
        '   gracefully handle errors.
        Try
            ' Open the connection.
            objConnection.Open()

            ' Create the command object. We'll select all
            '   publisher name, city, and country.
           Dim objCommand  as _
            new SqlCommand( _
              "SELECT pub_name,city,country FROM publishers "+_
               "ORDER BY pub_name", _
               objConnection )
```

```
    ' Populate a reader.
    Dim objReader As SqlDataReader = objCommand.ExecuteReader()

    ' Set the DataList's data source and then
    '    call the DataBind() method.
    Publishers.DataSource = objReader
    Publishers.DataBind()

    ' Close the reader.
    objReader.Close()

Catch ex As Exception
    ' Display the error message to the reader.
    ErrorMessage.Text = ex.Message.ToString()
Finally
    ' See if the connection is open.
    If objConnection.State = ConnectionState.Open Then
        ' Close it if it is open.
        objConnection.Close()
    End If
End Try
    End If
End Sub
```

As with the `Page_Load()` method for the Repeater demo, this code performs a pretty straightforward retrieval of data with which the Repeater is bound. Again, a connection to the database is created by creating a Sql-Connection object and then calling its `Open()` method. And as per the recommended practice, the main code is within a `try` block. The `try/catch/finally` construct allows the code to be robust and handle any errors that might arise. If everything goes well, all of the code in the `try` block is executed, followed by the code in the `finally` block. If an exception is thrown at any point in the `try` block, execution proceeds to the `catch` block, after which the `finally` block will be executed.

Once the connection has been established to the database, a SqlCommand object must be created. This gives us the capability to execute a query on the database and get a recordset back. The recordset will be contained in a SqlDataReader object. The following SQL will be executed:

```
Select pub_name,city,country from publishers order by pub_name
```

A call to the `SqlCommand.ExecuteReader()` method returns a populated SqlDataReader object. The Repeater is now bound to the data by setting the `DataList.DataSource` property to the SqlDataReader, and then calling the `DataList.DataBind()` method.

The *RedrawDataList_Click()* Method Of the DataList Demo

The code for the `RedrawDataList_Click()` method follows. It is fired when users click the Redraw button. A discussion of the code is immediately below it.

C#
```csharp
static Color[] color =
{
  Color.Black, Color.Red,
  Color.Green, Color.Blue
};


private void RedrawDataList_Click(object sender, System.EventArgs e)
{

  // Loop through the items in the Publishers object (which is
  //    a DataList).
  foreach( Control control in Publishers.Controls )
  {
    // Make sure we have a line that's not a header or footer.
    if( ((DataListItem)control).ItemType == ListItemType.Item ||
      ((DataListItem)control).ItemType == ListItemType.AlternatingItem )
    {
      // Find the DropDownList object so that we know what
      //    was selected.
      DropDownList dl =
        (DropDownList)control.FindControl( "StyleSelector");

      Label Pub = (Label)control.FindControl( "pub" );
      Pub.ForeColor = color[dl.SelectedIndex];

    }
  }
}
```

VB
```vb
Dim colr() As Color = {Color.Black, Color.Red, _
    Color.Green, Color.Blue}
```

```
Private Sub RedrawDataList_Click(ByVal sender As System.Object, _
  ByVal e As System.EventArgs) Handles RedrawDataList.Click

    ' Loop through the items in the Publishers object (which is
    '   a DataList).
    Dim i As Integer
    For i = 0 To Publishers.Controls.Count - 1
        Dim item As DataListItem = Publishers.Controls(i)
        ' Make sure we have a line that's not a header or footer.
        If item.ItemType = ListItemType.Item Or _
          item.ItemType = ListItemType.AlternatingItem Then
            ' Find the DropDownList object so that we know what
            '   was selected.
            Dim dl As DropDownList = item.FindControl("StyleSelector")

            Dim Pub As Label = item.FindControl("pub")
            Pub.ForeColor = colr(dl.SelectedIndex)
        End If
    Next
End Sub
```

The code in the listings above is similar to the code in the Repeater demo that was fired in response to clicking the OK button. The first thing that you'll see in the listing, though, is an array of Color objects. These four objects are used to set the Label's color based on the DropDownList's index (more on this shortly).

Next, you'll see the loops. In C#, a `foreach` loop is used; in VB, a `For/Next` loop is used. These loops go through each of the Control objects that are in the Publishers.Controls collection. A check is made to be sure that we're looking at either an ItemTemplate or an Alternating-ItemTemplate. We don't want to inadvertently examine the HeaderTemplate. Once we're sure that we're looking at either an ItemTemplate or an AlternatingItemTemplate, we retrieve an object reference to the Drop-DownList object with the `FindControl()` method, as follows:

C#
```
DropDownList dl = (DropDownList)control.FindControl( "StyleSelector");
```

VB
```
Dim dl As DropDownList = item.FindControl("StyleSelector")
```

NOTE: Using the `FindControl()` method in C# and VB is different. For starters, the `FindControl()` method returns a generic Control object—which could be one of many types of controls, such as Labels, DropDownLists, and TextBoxes. In VB, objects that are returned from the `FindControl()` method can easily be assigned to objects such as DropDownLists or Labels. VB does not check at compile time to see whether the object types match; it just assumes that you know what you're doing, and that the object types will match at runtime. But at runtime, if they differ, an exception will be thrown, and you'll have to deal with it at that time.

In C#, however, the compiler checks to make sure the object types match. The following code will not compile:

```
DropDownList dl = control.FindControl( "StyleSelector");
```

In this case, we have to coerce the compiler to continue and convince it we are sure that the object types will match. We use a typecast to let the compiler know that we are sure the object types will match. If, however, at runtime they don't match, an exception will be thrown, and you'll have to deal with it. The following code typecasts the previous C# example so that it compiles:

```
DropDownList dl = (DropDownList)control.FindControl( "Style-
Selector");
```

The next thing to do is retrieve an object reference to the Label. The following code shows how this is done:

C#
```
Label Pub = (Label)control.FindControl( "pub" );
```

VB
```
Dim Pub As Label = item.FindControl("pub")
```

Last, the color of the Label is set to reflect the current selection. This is done by using the DropDownList.SelectedIndex as an index into the `color` (for C#) or `colr` (for VB) arrays (the reason for the name change is that VB is case insensitive and `color` will match the `Color` enumeration in VB). For instance, if Red is selected, then the `DropDownList.SelectedIndex` property will contain the value of 1. This will act as an index for the array containing the Color objects. The following breaks the code down:

C#
```
// Red is selected. This is the second choice, or an index value 1.
// dl.SelectedIndex contains the value of 1.
// color[1] contains the value Color.Red.
// color[dl.SelectedIndex] also contains the value Color.Red
// Pub.ForeColor = Color.Red is the result.
Pub.ForeColor = color[dl.SelectedIndex];
```

VB
```
' Red is selected. This is the second choice, or an index value 1.
' dl.SelectedIndex contains the value of 1.
' colr(1) contains the value Color.Red.
' colr(dl.SelectedIndex) also contains the value Color.Red
' Pub.ForeColor = Color.Red is the result.
Pub.ForeColor = colr(dl.SelectedIndex)
```

Figure 6.6 shows the DataList with different colors that have been selected.

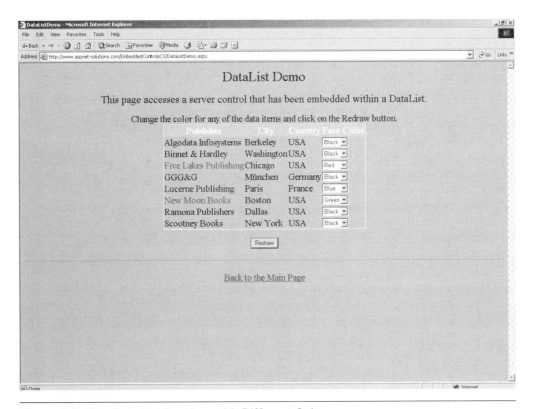

Figure 6.6 This DataList Renders with Different Colors.

The DataGrid Demo

This demo binds the employees table to a DataGrid, allows users to click a Send button, and then e-mails a notification about the employee to the e-mail address in a TextBox. You can see the demo below as it first appears.

The User Interface

At the heart of the user interface is a DataGrid named Employees. Below the DataGrid is a Label named ErrorMessage that's used to alert users to any exception messages that have been caught. And below that is a TextBox named Email into which users type an email address.

The DataGrid has three columns when it renders: one for the employee's name, one for the employee's hire date, and one for a Send button. Within the DataGrid is a server control: a Label named Name that contains the employees's name. The DataGrid code from the .aspx file is below. A discussion of the code follows the code.

```
<asp:datagrid id="Employees" runat="server" AutoGenerateColumns="False">
  <Columns>
    <asp:TemplateColumn runat="server" HeaderText="Name">
      <ItemTemplate>
        <asp:Label ID="Name" Runat="server"
          Text='<%# DataBinder.Eval(Container.DataItem, "lname") +
          ", " + DataBinder.Eval(Container.DataItem, "fname") %>' />
      </ItemTemplate>
    </asp:TemplateColumn>
    <asp:BoundColumn DataField="hire_date"
      DataFormatString="{0:MM/dd/yyyy}" HeaderText="Hire Date" />
    <asp:ButtonColumn CommandName="select" HeaderText="Send Email"
      DataTextField="lname" DataTextFormatString="Send" />
  </Columns>
</asp:datagrid>
```

Unlike Repeaters and DataLists, Column tags are used instead of ItemTemplate and AlternatingItemTemplate tags. Within the Column tag are three other tags: an asp:TemplateColumn, an asp:BoundColumn, and an asp:ButtonColumn tag. These three tags function in different ways, as you'll see.

The asp:TemplateColumn tag lets you use an ItemTemplate tag, as with Repeaters and DataLists. The ItemTemplate tag has a Label object inside of it, just as the Repeater and DataList demos did. The Label is named Name, and it is populated with the last and first name of the employee.

The asp:BoundColumn provides an easy way to describe a column that'll appear in the DataGrid. Its attributes let you set the data field, the header text, and how to format the data. Being able to format the data using the string formatting options is a big help when you need to carefully manage the formatting.

The asp:ButtonColumn lets you add a button that users can use to make a selection that can fire an event. This particular button fires the `Employees_SelectedIndexChanged()` method (seen later).

The Code behind the DataGrid Demo

There are two methods behind the DataGrid demo that we'll take a look at. The first is the `Page_Load()` Method, and the second is the `Employees_SelectedIndexChanged()` method. Both methods are described in the next two sections.

NOTE: In addition to the System.Data.SqlClient namespace, this demo also requires the System.Web.Mail namespace because of the use of the mail objects. Toward the top of each source code module, you'll see the following:

C#
```
using System.Web.Mail;
```

VB
```
Imports System.Web.Mail
```

The Page_Load() Method of the DataGrid Demo

The code for the `Page_Load()` method follows. A discussion of the code is immediately below it.

C#
```
private void Page_Load(object sender, System.EventArgs e)
{

    // Only populate the DataGrid if this is not a post back.
    if( !IsPostBack )
    {
```

```
// Create a connection object.
SqlConnection objConnection =
 new SqlConnection("server=localhost;database=pubs;uid=sa;pwd=");

// Use a try/catch/finally construct to
//   gracefully handle errors.
try
{
  // Open the connection.
  objConnection.Open();

  // Create the command object. We'll select all
  //   author first and last name along with phone.
  SqlCommand objCommand =
    new SqlCommand( "SELECT lname,fname,hire_date FROM employee " +
    "ORDER BY lname,fname",
    objConnection );

  // Populate a reader.
  SqlDataReader objReader = objCommand.ExecuteReader();

  // Set the DataGrid's data source and then
  //   call the DataBind() method.
  Employees.DataSource = objReader;
  Employees.DataBind();

  // Close the reader.
  objReader.Close();

}
catch( Exception ex )
{
  // Display the error message to the reader.
  ErrorMessage.Text = ex.Message.ToString();
}
finally
{
  // See if the connection is open.
  if( objConnection.State == ConnectionState.Open )
  {
    // Close it if it is open.
    objConnection.Close();
  }
```

```
   }
  }
}
```

VB
```vb
Private Sub Page_Load(ByVal sender As System.Object, _
  ByVal e As System.EventArgs) Handles MyBase.Load

    ' Only populate the DataGrid if this is not a post back.
    If Not IsPostBack Then
     ' Create a connection object.
     Dim objConnection As _
      New SqlConnection("server=localhost;database=pubs;uid=sa;pwd=")

        ' Use a try/catch/finally construct to
        '   gracefully handle errors.
        Try
            ' Open the connection.
            objConnection.Open()

            ' Create the command object. We'll select all
            '    author first and last name along with phone.
            Dim objCommand As _
             New SqlCommand( _
               "SELECT lname,fname,hire_date FROM employee " + _
               "ORDER BY lname,fname", _
              objConnection)

            ' Populate a reader.
            Dim objReader As SqlDataReader = objCommand.ExecuteReader()

            ' Set the DataGrid's data source and then
            '    call the DataBind() method.
            Employees.DataSource = objReader
            Employees.DataBind()

            ' Close the reader.
            objReader.Close()

        Catch ex As Exception
            ' Display the error message to the reader.
            ErrorMessage.Text = ex.Message.ToString()
        Finally
```

```
        ' See if the connection is open.
        If objConnection.State = ConnectionState.Open Then
            ' Close it if it is open.
            objConnection.Close()
        End If
    End Try
  End If
End Sub
```

As with the `Page_Load()` method for the Repeater demo, this code performs a pretty straightforward retrieval of data with which the Repeater is bound. First, a connection to the database is created by creating a Sql-Connection object and then calling its `Open()` method. Any code that can throw an exception is within a `try` block. The `try/catch/finally` construct allows the code to be robust and handle any errors that might arise. If everything goes well, all of the code in the `try` block is executed, followed by the code in the `finally` block. If an exception is thrown at any point in the `try` block, execution proceeds to the `catch` block, after which the `finally` block will be executed.

Once the connection has been established to the database, a SqlCommand object must be created. This gives us the capability to execute a query on the database and get a recordset back. The recordset will be contained in a SqlDataReader object. The following SQL will be executed:

```
SELECT lname,fname,hire_date FROM employee ORDER BY lname,fname
```

A call to the `SqlCommand.ExecuteReader()` method returns a populated SqlDataReader object. The Repeater is now bound to the data by setting the `DataGrid.DataSource` property to the SqlDataReader, and then calling the `DataGrid.DataBind()` method.

The `Employees_SelectedIndexChanged()` Method of the DataGrid Demo
The code for the `Employees_SelectedIndexChanged()` method follows. It is fired when users click on the Send button. A discussion of the code is immediately below it.

C#

```
private void Employees_SelectedIndexChanged(object sender,
System.EventArgs e)
{
    // Get the employee name.
```

```csharp
string strName =
  ((Label)Employees.Items[Employees.SelectedIndex].FindControl(
  "Name")).Text;

// Create the message body.
string strMessage = "This is a message that was sent by " +
  "the DataGrid demo program. The employee that is being " +
  "referred to is " + strName;

try
{
  // Send the email.
  SmtpMail.SmtpServer = "mail.server.com";
  SmtpMail.Send( "DataGrid Demo <Joe@server.com>",
    Email.Text, "Notification about employee", strMessage );

  // Alert the user to the success.
  ErrorMessage.Text = "Your message was sent at " +
    Convert.ToString( DateTime.Now );
}
catch( Exception ex )
{
  ErrorMessage.Text = ex.Message.ToString();
}
}
```

VB
```vb
Private Sub Employees_SelectedIndexChanged(ByVal sender As
System.Object, _
  ByVal e As System.EventArgs) Handles Employees.SelectedIndexChanged
    ' Get the employee name.
    Dim Name As Label = _
      Employees.Items(Employees.SelectedIndex).FindControl("Name")
    Dim strName As String = Name.Text

    ' Create the message body.
    Dim strMessage as String = "This is a message that was sent by " + _
      "the DataGrid demo program. The employee that is being " + _
      "referred to is " + strName

    Try
        ' Send the email.
        SmtpMail.SmtpServer = "mail.server.com"
```

```
        SmtpMail.Send("DataGrid Demo <Joe@server.com>", _
        Email.Text, "Notification about employee", strMessage)

        ' Alert the user to the success.
        ErrorMessage.Text = "Your message was sent at " + _
          Convert.ToString( DateTime.Now )
    Catch ex As Exception
        ErrorMessage.Text = ex.Message.ToString()
    End Try
End Sub
```

The `Employees_SelectedIndexChanged()` method starts off by retrieving the e-mail address that the user (hopefully) typed in the e-mail TextBox. The next thing it does is to create the message text for the e-mail. The employee name is used in the creation of the message body.

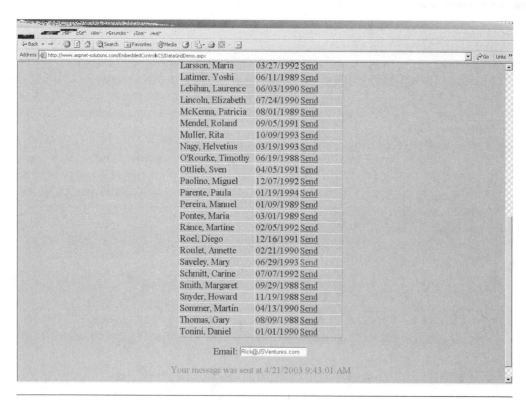

Figure 6.7 This Part of the Application Sends E-mails.

Next, the `SmtpMail` class is used to send an e-mail message. I should point out that, technically, setting the `SmtpServer` property isn't necessary. Where this is important, though, is in the security restrictions of most mail servers. On my network, without setting this to our mail server, the e-mails could not be delivered.

Finally, if everything goes well, the user is alerted to the successful sending of the e-mail message. Notice, though, that the `SmtpMail` code is within a `Try/Catch` construct. That's because `SmtpMail` code can throw an exception. You can see the demo after an e-mail has been sent in Figure 6.7.

Summary

Using server controls within iterative databound controls offers more flexibility and power than simple static HTML controls. This chapter has shown you how to use such controls in your own programs. Now you can increase the power of your user interfaces tremendously.

In this chapter, you've learned about using and populating iterative databound controls. We've spent a good deal of time learning about the `FindControl()` method and how it can be used to retrieve data from the control rows. Your applications will be far more powerful when you harness the power of server controls within the iterative databound controls.

CHAPTER 7

Using Session State: Building a Classifieds Application

In This Chapter:

- Using Application and Session Variables
- Synchronization
- Using the Cache Object
- The Classifieds Application

This chapter talks about several topics. Among them are session state, application state, caching, and using cookies. With all these topics, the intention is to preserve some information about the application and a particular session. **Session state** can include things such as user's selected colors, user information, or user selections (such as ordering information). **Application state**, or information, might include things such as a counter of how many visitors the site has had today, or maybe even something as simple as the date and time. **Cached** objects can be pretty much anything, but they are used to improve the performance of a Web application by keeping commonly used data in memory. To discuss using cookies requires a brief introduction to the concept of **state**.

HTTP is a stateless protocol. Let's look at what this means. A client makes a request by providing the HTTP server with some data such as IP address, browser type, and operating system. The server grinds on that data and creates some output. At that point, the client and server disconnect from each other. Any new client requests require that the client provide more information for the server to act. This is why we say that HTTP is stateless.

Using cookies is one way to maintain some state. But clients can prevent cookies from being saved by altering the browser settings—and when this happens, using cookies to maintain state is impossible. ASP.NET pro-

269

vides an even better mechanism for maintaining a certain amount of state between a client and a server, and this mechanism has two distinct categories. In the first category, state can be maintained as application variables. Application state affects all users; session state affects individual users. ASP.NET lets you remember things based on individuals or based on everything. **Application variables** hold data from the time the application starts until the application ends. That is not to say that data doesn't change; it is to say that data is maintained in whatever state it happens to be for the life of the application. Another category of variables that can maintain state are called **session variables**. These variables contain information about the current session. For example, if a user prefers that all of his backgrounds be blue, a session variable can indicate this. And if a user is identified with some sort of ID, this information also can be kept in a session variable.

In this chapter, you are going to learn about several topics related to maintaining state. Of course, application and session variables will be important topics. We will have to talk about synchronizing access to these variables because there will be times when only one client session can access or change the value of a state variable at any given time.

Using Application and Session Variables

Application and session variables work similarly, with each having a dictionary of objects. Keys (which must be strings) identify each object in the dictionary. The keys are normal text strings that give a name to each object in the dictionary. For example, I might have a user ID object and I name it UserID. The following simple example shows how an integer value of 12 can be stored in a session variable named UserID:

C#
```
Session["UserId"] = 12;
```

VB
```
Session("UserId") = 12
```

It is just as easy to set a session variable to contain a string. The following examples show how to set session variables in C# and VB to a string containing the name John Doe:

C#
```
Session["UserName"] = "John Doe";
```

VB
```
Session("UserName") = "John Doe"
```

Session variables can also contain any sort of object that you want to store. To store an object in a session variable, you simply figure out what key name you want to give a session variable, and then assign that name to the object. The following examples show how to assign an object into a session variable in C# and in VB:

C#
```
Session["SomeGreatObject"] = MyObject;
```

VB
```
Session("SomeGreatObject") = MyObject
```

To create and assign values to an application variable, you do exactly the same thing. Application variables, though, usually apply to the entire application and are thus more global in nature. One of the more common application variables people use is for traffic counters. The following examples show how to increment a counter in C# and in VB. Note that the customary unary increment operator is not available in C# as you might expect it to be on application and session variables. That is because in C# language, the application variable is seen as an object rather than a value type. The example includes two notes you should pay heed to.

C#
```
Application["Counter"] = (int)Application["Counter"] + 1;
```

Note that the following code will generate the error: *No such operator '++' defined for type 'object'*

```
Application["Counter"]++;
```

Note also that the following code will generate the error: *Operator '+' cannot be applied to operands of type 'object' and 'int'*

```
Application["Counter"] = Application["Counter"] + 1;
```

VB
```
Application("Counter") = Application("Counter") + 1
```

It is sometimes important to check the variable to see whether it exists. Many times, the application or the session hasn't created a variable yet, and you can't access a variable until it has been created. Until a variable has been created, it doesn't exist and the program throws an exception when you try to access such a variable. In C#, you check to see whether a variable is equal to `null`, and in VB you check to see whether it is equal to `Nothing` (with a statement such as my `OBJ==null` or `OBJ=Nothing`). The following code shows how to check session and application variables in both C# and VB to see whether they exist or have not yet been created:

C#
```
// Check an application variable for null
if( Application["SomeKey"] == null )
{
    // Do something here to initialize the variable
}

// Check a session variable for null
if( Session["SomeKey"] == null )
{
    // Do something here to initialize the variable
}
```

VB
```
' Check an application variable for null
If Application("SomeKey") = Nothing Then
    ' Do something here to initialize the variable
End If

' Check a session variable for null
If Session("SomeKey") = Nothing Then
    ' Do something here to initialize the variable
End If
```

Application variables are really global variables for an entire ASP.NET application. These variables are available for every user who is currently accessing the application except those who are accessing the application across a Web farm. You should always carefully consider the impact of storing anything as a global variable. Keep the following in mind:

- Resources that application variables consume
- Concurrency and synchronization
- Scalability implications of using application variables
- Life cycle implications of using application variables

You also want to keep session data to a minimum, if possible—especially when a site is a high-traffic site. Session variables as implemented by default take up system memory resources for as long as a session is active. If your site gets hit from 10,000 unique users in a minute, for example, and your session lasts for 20 minutes, you could be storing session data for 200,000 users. If the data stored were 100 bytes, your session would use 20MB of your system memory. If the data stored were 1000 bytes, the session data would be 200MB. As you can see, this use of system resources can easily get out of hand.

Resources That Application Variables Consume

The memory occupied by a variable stored within application variables isn't released until the value is either removed or replaced. Keeping items in application variables that are not used very often is not a good idea. For example, if you store a recordset that is 10MB or so, and you don't use it very often, this storage is an expensive use of these resources.

Concurrency and Synchronization

Multiple running threads within an application cannot simultaneously access values stored within application variables. This means that you must be careful about accessing these variables. You must ensure that an object stored in an application object is free threaded (able to be accessed from multiple threads) and contains built-in synchronization support. If you don't do that, and an object in an application is not free threaded, you must provide your own synchronization. To do this, use the `Lock()` and `Unlock()` methods.

Scalability Implications of Using Application Variables

You might be forced at times to use locks that protect global resources. Code that runs on multiple threads and accesses these global resources will ultimately end up contending for the resources. This situation causes the operation system to block some threads while others access the resource. A server bearing a heavy load can cause severe thread thrashing (wherein different threads spend inordinate amounts of time waiting for their chance to perform operations) on the system, which can significantly affect the performance of your Web application.

Life Cycle Implications of Using Application Variables

Developers should be aware that .NET applications can be torn down and destroyed at any moment during application execution. This destruction could be the result of crashes, code updates, scheduled process restarts, and other things. Global data stored in application state is not durable; it is lost when the host containing it is destroyed. Developers who want to store a state that survives these types of failures should store either in a database or some sort of other durable storage. (We'll discuss using the Cache API in the section that comes later entitled "Using the Cache Object.")

Synchronization

In many cases, it is important to synchronize access to application variables. Especially with things such as counters, you want only one thread to access an application variable and alter its contents at any given time. Suppose you have an application counter, and its accuracy is important. Now suppose that two different clients increment the variable at exactly the same time. Will the counter be two more than the original, or just one? No way exists to guarantee the behavior once simultaneous access happens.

Session variables do not succumb to the same problem because there is only one client access at a time to any session variable. The following code shows how to ensure that only a single thread can modify the contents of an application variable. The code calls the `Lock()` method, alters the variable, and then calls the `Unlock()` method.

C#
```
Application.Lock();
Application["SomeKey"] = (int)Application["SomeKey"] + 1;
Application.Unlock();
```

VB
```
Application.Lock()
Application("SomeKey") = Application("SomeKey") + 1
Application.Unlock()
```

Using the Cache Object

When Microsoft designed ASP.NET, one of its main goals was to give ASP.NET great performance. One way Microsoft offers ASP.NET developers the capability to increase performance is by offering a Cache API. A Cache object can store any type of information or data so that it can be used at any time within an ASP.NET application. This means that for data such as recordsets, the database does not have to be queried to use the data; the data can simply be retrieved from the Cache object.

The Cache object is simple to use. If you want to use this basic functionality, then the syntax is identical to using the application and session variables, as show below:

C#
```
Cache["SomeData"] = "This or that";
```

VB
```
Cache("SomeData") = "This or that";
```

But using the simple Cache object syntax doesn't give you the kind of flexibility that the Cache object is intended to provide. As a matter of fact, the simplified use of the Cache object is no more beneficial than using an application or session variable. A Cache object, though, will be global to your entire application, which means that the simplified cache syntax will give you the same results as using an application variable.

To really use the Cache object's extended features, you should add data with the `Add()` method. The `Add()` method requires seven parameters. The first parameter is the key, which is how you name the data that you are saving. The second parameter is the item that is to be added to the cache. The third parameter gives you the capability to add dependencies to the Cache object. A dependency can be either a file or another cache key. When either the file changes or the cache that is referenced by the key changes, the added Cache object becomes invalid and is removed from the cache. If you don't want to pin any dependencies on the cache data you are adding, you simply make the third parameter `null` in C# or `Nothing` in VB. The fourth parameter specifies an automatic expiration time, at which point the object expires and is removed from the cache. If you don't want an automatic expiration (for instance, if you want a sliding expiration), then you should make this parameter `null` for C# or `Nothing` for VB. The fifth parameter gives you the opportunity to provide a sliding expiration, which indicates how long after the last access to this Cache object a time-out will occur. The difference between an absolute and sliding expiration is this: An absolute expiration will occur regardless of any access that is made to cache data, while a sliding expiration begins its countdown after each access to a cached piece of data. Table 7.1 shows the CachePriority enumeration. These values are what you use to set the priority of a cache item. The seventh and last parameter gives you the opportunity to provide a call-back function so that your code can be notified when and if an object is removed from the cache. You will make this last parameter `null` in ASP.NET applications.

I'd like to give you a few examples now of using a `Cache.Add()` method. The following code adds a data reader (named OBJReader) to the cache. The key with which it will identify this data is named `Categories`. For this example, this is a SqlDataReader that contains a list of categories from a SQL database. No dependencies are specified as the third argument, and it is `null` or `Nothing`. An absolute expiration of 20 seconds is specified by passing as the fourth argument a date object with 20 seconds added to it. No sliding expiration is specified, the cache item priority is high, and there is no call back.

Table 7.1 The CacheItemPriority Enumeration

Member Name	Description
AboveNormal	Cache items with this priority level are less likely to be deleted as the server frees system memory than those assigned a `Normal` priority.
BelowNormal	Cache items with this priority level are more likely to be deleted from the cache as the server frees system memory than items assigned a `Normal` priority.
Default	The default value for a cached item's priority is `Normal`.
High	Cache items with this priority level are the least likely to be deleted from the cache as the server frees system memory.
Low	Cache items with this priority level are the most likely to be deleted from the cache as the server frees system memory.
Normal	Cache items with this priority level are likely to be deleted from the cache as the server frees system memory only after those items with `Low` or `BelowNormal` priority. This is the default.
NotRemovable	The cache items with this priority level will not be deleted from the cache as the server frees system memory.

C#
```
Cache.Add("Categories", objReader, null, Date.Now.AddSeconds(20),
  null, CacheItemPriority.High, null);
```

VB
```
Cache.Add("Categories", objReader, Nothing, Date.Now.AddSeconds(20), _
  Nothing, CacheItemPriority.High, Nothing)
```

The next code example adds the same SqlDataReader to the cache and identifies it by the key named categories. It does not specify any dependencies or an absolute expiration. It does, however, specify a sliding expiration with a TimeSpan object that is passed in to the fifth argument. In this case, the TimeSpan is specified to 20 minutes, which will cause the data to time out in 20 minutes. The cache item priority is set to high, and, again, no call back is specified.

C#
```
Cache.Add("Categories", objReader, null, null,
  new TimeSpan(0, 0, 20, 0, 0), CacheItemPriority.High, null);
```

VB
```
Cache.Add("Categories", objReader, Nothing, Nothing, _
  new TimeSpan(0, 0, 20, 0, 0), CacheItemPriority.High, Nothing)
```

The Classifieds Application

This section shows and explains the code used in the classified application. Table 7.2 is a convenient reference so you can easily find any method that is part of the application, the source code module in which the method resides, the listing number, and a short description of the method. This information will help you as you study the program.

NOTE: There is a link to the Classifieds application from the www.ASPNET-Solutions.com Web site. Follow the links to Chapter Examples, and then choose Chapter 7. Or go directly to http://www.aspnet-solutions.com/chapter_7.htm. You also can download the complete project for both the C# and VB languages from this page.

Table 7.2 The Classifieds Application Methods

Method Name	Code Module	Listing Number	Description
OutputColor()	All code modules	7.1	This method outputs the background color into the HTML stream.
GetColor()	All code modules	7.1	This method retrieves or creates a cookie that contains the background color.
Page_Load()	Default.aspx.cs	7.2	This method initializes the user interface for the application's main page. Specifically, it sets the color selector object (PageColor) to indicate the currently set color, and it populates the category list (CategoryList).
EditItem_Click()	Default.aspx.cs	7.3	This method redirects to the EditItem page.
AddItem_Click()	Default.aspx.cs	7.3	This method redirects to the AddItem page.
SearchItem_Click()	Default.aspx.cs	7.3	This method redirects to the SearchItem page.
PageColor_Selected-IndexChanged	Default.aspx.cs	7.4	This method responds to a change in the selected color. It stores the choice into the persistent cookie.
Page_Load()	AddItem.aspx.cs	7.7	This method initializes the user interface for the AddItem screen.
AddIt_Click()	AddItem.aspx.cs	7.7	This method fires when the user clicks the Add It button. This method creates a new record with the user information in the database.

Table 7.2 The Classifieds Application Methods (*cont.*)

Method Name	Code Module	Listing Number	Description
Cancel_Click()	AddItem.aspx.cs	7.7	This method cancels the item-adding process and redirects to the main application page (Default .aspx).
PopulateCategory-List()	EditItem.aspx.cs	7.8	This method populates the items in the category selector object (CategoryList).
RetrieveItem_Click()	EditItem.aspx.cs	7.8	This method retrieves data for an item and populates the user interface with the data.
Delete_Click()	EditItem.aspx.cs	7.8	This method deletes an item from the database.
Page_Load()	SearchItem.aspx.cs	7.9	This method performs a SQL query and outputs the results to the user interface.
MainPage_Click()	SearchItem.aspx.cs	7.9	This method redirects to the application's main page.
Page_Load()	ViewItem.aspx.cs	7.10	This method performs a SQL query, retrieves the data, and populates the user interface so that users can see a particular classified item.
Page_Load()	Thanks.aspx.cs	7.11	This method thanks the user for adding an item, and shows the item ID for future reference.
MainPage_Click()	Thanks.aspx.cs	7.11	This method redirects the user to the main application page.
Session_Start()	Global.asax	7.12	This method maintains the counter and day variables.

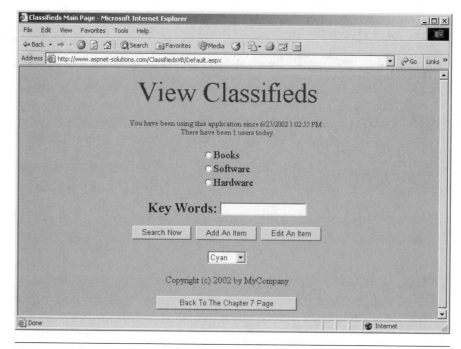

Figure 7.1 The Main Classifieds Application Screen Allows Users to Search For, Add, or Edit Items.

When the Classifieds application first runs, users get the choice to search for, add, or edit items, as shown in Figure 7.1.

The first thing I need to point out are the `Imports` statements (or `using` statements for C#) that must be in the source code. These statements are shown below, and they include the namespaces for SQL database access, code for retrieving configuration from the Web.Config file, and code that uses the Cache API.

C#

```
using System.Data.SqlClient;
using System.Configuration;
using System.Web.Caching;
```

VB

```
Imports System.Data.SqlClient
Imports System.Configuration
Imports System.Web.Caching
```

Retrieving the Background Color

We're going to start off in this application by taking a look at some code that is common to all source code modules in the application. This code enables the application, in a cookie, to keep track of the user's selected background color. Actually, two cookies maintain the background color; one cookie is the actual color name, and the other cookie is the index of the selected color within the drop-down list that can be seen in the user interface in the main page.

The code for doing the cookie information retrieval can be seen in Listing 7.1. The code includes two methods: the OutputColor() method and the GetColor method. The OutputColor() method retrieves the cookie that is identified by the key named ClassifiedsColor. The value that the code gets comes directly from the GetColor() method. This method returns a string that contains the named color. The named color is output into the HTML stream with the Response.Write() method. Once output into the HTML stream, this value becomes part of the bgcolor attribute found in the body tag.

The GetColor() method first attempts to retrieve the cookie that is identified by the key named ClassifiedsColor. If this key cannot be found, then a cookie with the key ClassifiedsColor is created, and the default values of Cyan and 0 are added. Cyan is the named color, and 0 is the index of the drop down list. The AppendCookie() method is then called with the newly created cookie, and it will then persist. If the cookie was found, then the value is retrieved out of the cookie and returned as a string to the caller.

Listing 7.1 Code Common to All Modules That Retrieve and Output the HTML Background Color

```
Public Sub OutputColor()
    Response.Write(GetColor())
End Sub

Private Function GetColor() As String
    If Request.Cookies("ClassifiedsColor") Is Nothing Then
        Dim Cookie As HttpCookie = _
            New HttpCookie("ClassifiedsColor")
        Cookie.Values.Add("Color", "Cyan")
        Cookie.Values.Add("Index", "0")
        Response.AppendCookie(Cookie)
        Return "Cyan"
    Else
```

```
        Dim Cookie As HttpCookie = _
            Request.Cookies("ClassifiedsColor")
        Return Convert.ToString(Cookie.Values.Get("Color"))
    End If
End Function
```

Initializing the User Interface

The main page is named Default.aspx. A number of items must be initialized in this page's `Page_Load()` method. It is important to note that no user-interface initialization is required if this method is being called in response to a post back. So before any user interface initialization is done in this method, the `IsPostBack` property is checked so that the initialization won't be done again unnecessarily.

The first thing that happens is that the code checks for the existence of the `ClassifiedsColor` cookie. If this cookie exists, then the index value is retrieved so that the drop-down list box can be set to the correct color. That is, the drop-down list will correctly reflect whatever color the background is currently set to. The next thing that is done is to get the list of categories. This is done in one of two ways, either retrieving the list from the cache, or querying the database for the list. You will notice that the code acts as if the cached list exists. It assigns the category `List.DataSource` property from the `Cache.Get()` method. It then calls the `DataBind()` method and returns. If, however, the cache data does not exist, an exception will be thrown and the SQL code which is directly below will be executed.

The SQL code is fairly straightforward. A new Connection object is created to the database. The Connection object is opened, a new command is created with the simple SQL `select` that will retrieve all the categories, and then a SQLDataReader object is retrieved by calling the command's `ExecuteReader()` method.

The SqlDataReader object is added to the cache and identified with the key named `Categories`. A 20-second absolute expiration is specified, so this DataList will expire in 20 seconds. Once the SqlDataReader is retrieved, the CategoryList object (which is part of the user interface) is bound to the data.

Listing 7.2 The `Page_Load()` Method in Default.aspx.cs, in Which the User Interface Is Initialized.

```
Private Sub Page_Load(ByVal sender As System.Object, _
  ByVal e As System.EventArgs) Handles MyBase.Load
```

```
If Not IsPostBack And _
  (Not Request.Cookies("ClassifiedsColor") Is Nothing) Then
    Dim Cookie As HttpCookie = _
        Request.Cookies("ClassifiedsColor")
    PageColor.SelectedIndex = _
        Convert.ToInt32(Cookie.Values.Get("Index"))
End If


If Not IsPostBack Then

    ' Programming for success, guarding against failure.
    Try
        CategoryList.DataTextField = "Name"
        CategoryList.DataValueField = "ID"
        CategoryList.DataSource = Cache.Get("Categories")
        CategoryList.DataBind()
        Return
    Catch
    End Try

  Dim objConnection As New _
   SqlConnection(ConfigurationSettings.AppSettings("ConnectString"))
  Try
        objConnection.Open()
        Dim objCommand As New _
            SqlCommand("Select * from Categories", objConnection)
        Dim objReader As SqlDataReader = objCommand.ExecuteReader()

        Cache.Add("Categories", objReader, Nothing, _
            Date.Now.AddSeconds(20), Nothing, _
            CacheItemPriority.High, Nothing)

        CategoryList.DataTextField = "Name"
        CategoryList.DataValueField = "ID"
        CategoryList.DataSource = objReader
        CategoryList.DataBind()
        ObjReader.Close()
    Catch ex As Exception
        ErrorMessage.Text = ex.Message.ToString()
    Finally
        If objConnection.State = ConnectionState.Open Then
            objConnection.Close()
        End If
```

```
        End Try
    End If
End Sub
```

Responding to Users in the Main Page

Three buttons for the main page take the user to different pages. The first page is in response to the Edit Item button, the second page in response to the Search Item button, and the third page in response to the Add Item button.

The `EditItem_Click()` method does two things. First, it sets a session variable name with the key of `EditItem` to `Nothing` (or `null` in C#).

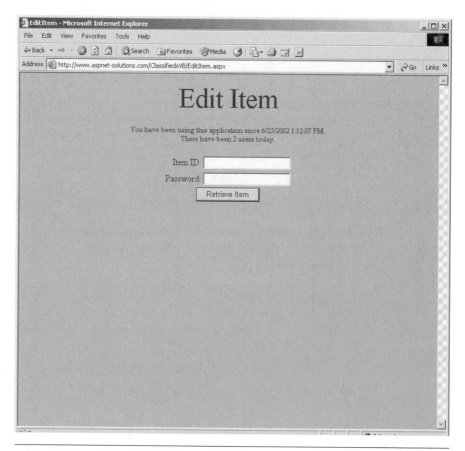

Figure 7.2 You Must Enter ID and Password Before You Can Edit an Item.

This session variable is used to remember which item the user is currently editing. How this session variable is used will become clear in later code, found in listing 7.8. But for now, it will suffice to say that we want to make sure that we start off fresh with nothing in this variable. The `Response.Redirect()` method is then called, going to the EditItem.aspx page. Before an item can be edited, though, an ID and password must be entered, as shown in Figure 7.2.

The `SearchItem_Click()` method starts off by creating a session variable and assigning it the value from the selected item in the category list. This value, from the database, will be the actual category ID that corresponds to the selected category name. If no value has been selected, an exception will be thrown; and when the exception is caught, this session variable will be

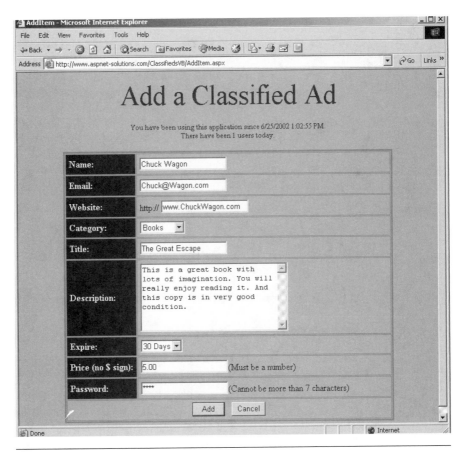

Figure 7.3 Adding an Item Is Easy with the Simple User Interface.

set to −1 so that code later on in the program will know that a category was not selected. Another session variable named `SearchCriteria` is created and contains any key words that the user typed in. The `Response.Redirect()` method is called, taking the user to the SearchItem.aspx page.

The `AddItem_Click()` method simply redirects the user to the AddItem.aspx page, as shown in Figure 7.3.

Listing 7.3 Button Handlers for the Application's Main Page

```
Private Sub EditItem_Click(ByVal sender As System.Object, _
  ByVal e As System.EventArgs) Handles EditItem.Click
    Session("EditItem") = Nothing
    Response.Redirect("EditItem.aspx")
End Sub

Private Sub SearchItem_Click(ByVal sender As System.Object, _
  ByVal e As System.EventArgs) Handles SearchItem.Click
    Try
        Session("CategoryID") = _
            Convert.ToInt32(CategoryList.SelectedItem.Value)
    Catch
        Session("CategoryID") = -1
    End Try
    Session("SearchCriteria") = KeyWords.Text
    Response.Redirect("SearchItem.aspx")
End Sub

Private Sub AddItem_Click(ByVal sender As System.Object, _
  ByVal e As System.EventArgs) Handles AddItem.Click
    Response.Redirect("AddItem.aspx")
End Sub
```

User Color Selection

The method that responds to the user's color selection from the main page is `PageColor_SelectedIndexChanged()`. This method can be seen in Listing 7.4. If the method can already find a cookie named `ClassifiedsColor`, it retrieves this cookie, asks the color, and then asks the index of the selected item in the drop-down list. The `Response.AppendCookie()` method is then called to add this cookie to the current page. If the cookie does not exist, then a new cookie is created. The color and index values are added, and the expiration of this cookie is set to `DateTime.MaxValue`. Setting the expiration to this value in essence means that the cookie will never expire. This means that any time the user comes back to this application, the cookie will persist and be loaded again. The last thing that happens is a call to the `Response.AppendCookie()` method.

Listing 7.4 Code That Responds to User Color Selection

```
Private Sub PageColor_SelectedIndexChanged( _
  ByVal sender As System.Object, _
  ByVal e As System.EventArgs) Handles PageColor.SelectedIndexChanged
    If Request.Cookies("ClassifiedsColor") Is Nothing Then
        Dim Cookie As HttpCookie = New HttpCookie("ClassifiedsColor")
        Cookie.Values.Add("Color", PageColor.SelectedItem.Value)
        Cookie.Values.Add("Index", _
          Convert.ToString(PageColor.SelectedIndex))
        Response.AppendCookie(Cookie)
    Else
        Dim Cookie As HttpCookie = Request.Cookies("ClassifiedsColor")
        Cookie.Values.Set("Color", PageColor.SelectedItem.Value)
        Cookie.Values.Set("Index", _
          Convert.ToString(PageColor.SelectedIndex))
        Cookie.Expires = DateTime.MaxValue
        Response.AppendCookie(Cookie)
    End If
End Sub
```

Displaying the Session Start Time and the Application Counter

The code that displays the start time of the user session and the value found in the application-counter variable can be seen in Listing 7.5. Unlike most of the other code in the listings within this chapter, this code is from the .aspx file. It was relatively easy to put this code inline, so that is what was done. Doing this makes the program a little simpler than having the code behind methods.

You can see that the `Response.Write()` method is called to output the start time and the counter directly into the HTML stream.

Listing 7.5 Common User Interface Code That Displays the Session Start Time and the Application Counter

```
<p align="center"><FONT color="blue" size="2">You have been using
  this application since
  <%Response.Write(Session("StartTime").ToString())%>.<br>
  There have been
  <%Response.Write(Application("Counter"))%>
  users today. </FONT>
</p>
```

Retrieving the `Database Connection` String from Web.Config

Many of the applications that I create keep the database connection string in the Global.asax file. I had a system with such an application that I delivered to a client in the Atlanta area. When I got to the client's location, I found that the computer had a naming conflict with another computer on his network. I then changed the name of the computer and hooked it up.

Unfortunately, the name change in the computer caused the database connection string to stop working. Without a copy of Visual Studio to recompile, I could have been in a big mess because changing the Global.asax.cs file with a text editor did not result in the application picking up the new `connect` string. Although I would have assumed the application would pick up the string, it didn't, and the application did not work.

I was, however, able to recover. I had brought my development box with me, and I simply recompiled the application on the development box and copied it over.

This example points out one weakness of keeping information such as database connection strings in the Global.asax file. The strings cannot easily be edited with a text editor so that the application will pick up the changes. For this reason, there are many cases in which similar information should be kept in the Web.Config file, from which the application can retrieve it.

The Classifieds application keeps its database connection string in the Web.Config file. The pertinent part of the Web.Config file can be seen in Listing 7.6. The following code shows how to retrieve the string that will contain the configuration data named `ConnectString` from the Web.Config file.

```
ConfigurationSettings.AppSettings("ConnectString")
```

Listing 7.6 The Web.Config Section That Contains the Connection String

```xml
<?xml version="1.0" encoding="utf-8" ?>
<configuration>
  <appSettings>
    <add key="ConnectString"
      value="data source=localhost;initial catalog=Classifieds;persist
security info=False;user id=sa;pwd=;packet size=4096" />
  </appSettings>

...

</configuration>
```

Adding an Item to the Classifieds Database

Listing 7.7 shows the code that is used that can be found in the AddItem.aspx.cs file. This code is all related to adding items into the Classifieds database.

The `Page_Load()` method simply populates the CategoryList DropDrownList object. If the recordset that contains the list of categories can be found in a cache, then the CategoryList object is populated from this. Otherwise, the code drops down, queries the database, and from the retrieved recordset, populates the CategoryList DropDownList object.

The user fills out a large number of user-interface items before submitting the new classified ad. The `AddIt_Click()` method can be seen just below the `Page_Load()` method in Listing 7.7. The method starts off by creating a new database connection object. It then creates an ExpirationDate object, which is contained in a DateTime object. It does this by obtaining the current date and time and using the `AddDays()` method to add however many days have been selected for this classifieds item to expire.

The database connection is opened, and a SQL string is created based on all the information that the user has entered in the form's editable fields. At the end of the SQL string, you should notice that a special syntax retrieves the identity value once the record has been created. The ID (which is the identity value) is used below, and this retrieves the value into the stored procedure parameter named `@ID`. Once the query has been created, a SqlCommandObject is instantiated, the `@ID` parameter is added, its direction set, and the `ExecuteNonQuery()` method is called. The ID parameter then is retrieved into an integer, thus remembering the `item's` ID that was created as an identify field (this happens when a row is inserted into the database).

The clean-up work in this method is to simply close the connection and redirect to the Thanks.aspx page. While the method is redirecting to this Thanks.aspx page, for convenience, the item's title, expiration, and ID are sent as command-line parameters. If for some reason the database code throws an exception, then the exception message will be displayed in the ErrorMessageLabel object.

The last method in this listing is the `Cancel_Click()` method. This method simply redirects to the main page and does not save any information.

Listing 7.7 The Code Found in AddItem.aspx.cs. This Code Initializes the User Interface, Saves the New Data, and Redirects to the Main Page.

```
Private Sub Page_Load(ByVal sender As System.Object, _
  ByVal e As System.EventArgs) Handles MyBase.Load
    If Not IsPostBack Then
        Try
            CategoryList.DataTextField = "Name"
            CategoryList.DataValueField = "ID"
            CategoryList.DataSource = Cache.Get("Categories")
            CategoryList.DataBind()
            Return
        Catch
        End Try


        Dim objConnection As New _
            SqlConnection(ConfigurationSettings.AppSettings(_
              "ConnectString"))
        Try
            objConnection.Open()
            Dim objCommand As New _
                SqlCommand("Select * from Categories", objConnection)
            Dim objReader As SqlDataReader = objCommand.ExecuteReader()
            CategoryList.DataTextField = "Name"
            CategoryList.DataValueField = "ID"
            CategoryList.DataSource = objReader
            CategoryList.DataBind()
        Catch ex As Exception
```

```vb
                ErrorMessage.Text = ex.Message.ToString()
            Finally
                If objConnection.State = ConnectionState.Open Then
                    objConnection.Close()
                End If
            End Try
        End If
End Sub

Private Sub AddIt_Click(ByVal sender As System.Object, _
    ByVal e As System.EventArgs) Handles AddIt.Click
    Dim objConnection As New _
        SqlConnection( _
          ConfigurationSettings.AppSettings("ConnectString"))
    Try
        Dim objDateExpires As DateTime = _
            DateTime.Now.AddDays( _
              Convert.ToInt32(Expire.SelectedItem.Value))

        objConnection.Open()

        Dim strSql As String = _
            "Insert into Item (Name,Category,Email,URL,Title," + _
            "Description,DateExpires,Price,Password) VALUES (" + _
            "'" + Name.Text.Replace("'","") + "'," + _
            "'" + CategoryList.SelectedItem.Text + "'," + _
            "'" + Email.Text.Replace("'","") + "'," + _
            "'" + URL.Text.Replace("'","") + "'," + _
            "'" + Title.Text.Replace("'","") + "'," + _
            "'" + Description.Text.Replace("'","") + "'," + _
            "'" + objDateExpires.ToShortDateString() + "'," + _
            "'" + Price.Text.Replace("'","") + "'," + _
            "'" + Password.Text.Replace("'","") + "'" + _
            ") select @ID=@@IDENTITY"

        Dim objCommand As New SqlCommand(strSql, objConnection)
        objCommand.Parameters.Add("@ID", SqlDbType.Int)
        objCommand.Parameters("@ID").Direction = _
          ParameterDirection.Output
        objCommand.ExecuteNonQuery()
        Dim nItemID As Integer = _
            Convert.ToInt32(objCommand.Parameters("@ID").Value)
```

292 Chapter 7 Using Session State: Building a Classifieds Application

```
            Response.Redirect("Thanks.aspx?Title=" + Chr(34) + _
                Title.Text + Chr(34) + "&Expiration=" + _
                objDateExpires.ToShortDateString() + "&ItemID=" + _
                Convert.ToString(nItemID))

        Catch ex As Exception
            ErrorMessage.Text = ex.Message.ToString()
        Finally
            If objConnection.State = ConnectionState.Open Then
                objConnection.Close()
            End If
        End Try
    End Sub


    Private Sub Cancel_Click(ByVal sender As System.Object, ByVal e As
    System.EventArgs) Handles Cancel.Click
        Response.Redirect("Default.aspx")
    End Sub
```

Editing an Item in the Classifieds Database

The code for editing an item has a lot of similarity to the code for adding an item. That's because the user interface is almost identical for both processes, and the information contained in the user interface objects must be written to the database.

Retrieving the Item to Be Edited

First, the `PopulateCategoryList()` method takes what's in the cache and populates the CategoryList DropDownList object. If the cache doesn't have anything in it, a new query is made, from which the CategoryList object is populated.

A method named `RetrieveItem_Click()` fires in response to the Retrieve Item button. In general, this method retrieves data from the database and populates the user interface objects. The item that is retrieved is based on the Item ID `TextBox` field into which users enter an item ID. The `RetrieveItem_Click()` method creates a database connection and opens it. It then creates a SQL string that selects an item's data based on the item ID that was entered. If the item exists in the database (and this will be `true` when the SqlDataReader's `Read()` method is `True`), the information will be taken from the recordset and placed into the user interface objects.

You might notice that a session variable named EditItem is set to a value of 1. This setting is so that the application will know later on whether an item is being edited or added. This value of 1 indicates that an item is being edited.

Once the data has been stored in the user interface objects, typical clean-up code follows. The SqlDataReader object is closed, and then the SqlConnection object is closed.

Deleting an Item

Also seen in Listing 7.8 is the Delete_Click() method. In general, this method deletes an item from the database.

The Delete_Click() method first creates and opens a database connection. Then, a SQL string is created that will delete the correct item. A SqlCommand object is created and its ExecuteNonQuery() method called, followed by some clean-up code. The clean-up code consists of setting the EditItem session variable to Nothing (or null in C#), clearing the ItemID and Password fields, and closing the database connection.

Listing 7.8 This Is the Code That Supports Item Editing Functionality. It Consists of Initializing the User Interface, Retrieving an Item's Data, Saving Updates to an Item, and Deleting an Item.

```
Private Sub PopulateCategoryList()
    Try
        CategoryList.DataTextField = "Name"
        CategoryList.DataValueField = "ID"
        CategoryList.DataSource = Cache.Get("Categories")
        CategoryList.DataBind()
        Return
    Catch
    End Try

    Dim objConnection As New _
      SqlConnection(ConfigurationSettings.AppSettings("ConnectString"))
    Try
        objConnection.Open()
        Dim objCommand As New _
          SqlCommand("Select * from Categories", objConnection)
        Dim objReader As SqlDataReader = objCommand.ExecuteReader()
        CategoryList.DataTextField = "Name"
        CategoryList.DataValueField = "ID"
```

```vb
        CategoryList.DataSource = objReader
        CategoryList.DataBind()
    Catch ex As Exception
        ErrorMessage.Text = ex.Message.ToString()
    Finally
        If objConnection.State = ConnectionState.Open Then
            objConnection.Close()
        End If
    End Try
End Sub

Private Sub RetrieveItem_Click(ByVal sender As System.Object, _
  ByVal e As System.EventArgs) Handles RetrieveItem.Click
    Dim objConnection As New _
      SqlConnection(ConfigurationSettings.AppSettings("ConnectString"))
    Try
        objConnection.Open()
        Dim strSql As String = "select * from Item where ID=" + _
            ItemID.Text.Replace("'","") + _
            " and Password='" + Password.Text.Replace("'","") + "'"
        Dim objCommand As New SqlCommand(strSql, objConnection)
        Dim objReader As SqlDataReader = objCommand.ExecuteReader()

        If objReader.Read() Then
            Session("EditItem") = 1
            PopulateCategoryList()
            Name.Text = Convert.ToString(objReader("Name"))
            Dim i As Integer
            For i = 0 To CategoryList.Items.Count - 1
                If CategoryList.Items(i).Text = _
                    Convert.ToString(objReader("Category")) Then
                    CategoryList.SelectedIndex = i
                End If
            Next
            Email.Text = Convert.ToString(objReader("Email"))
            URL.Text = Convert.ToString(objReader("URL"))
            Title.Text = Convert.ToString(objReader("Title"))
            Description.Text = _
              Convert.ToString(objReader("Description"))
            Expires.Text = Convert.ToString(objReader("DateExpires"))
            Price.Text = Convert.ToString(objReader("Price"))
            PW.Text = Convert.ToString(objReader("Price"))
        End If
```

```
        objReader.Close()
    Catch ex As Exception
        ErrorMessage.Text = ex.Message.ToString()
    Finally
        If objConnection.State = ConnectionState.Open Then
            objConnection.Close()
        End If
    End Try
End Sub

Private Sub Delete_Click(ByVal sender As System.Object, _
   ByVal e As System.EventArgs) Handles Delete.Click
    Dim objConnection As New _
      SqlConnection(ConfigurationSettings.AppSettings("ConnectString"))
    Try
        objConnection.Open()
        Dim strSql As String = "Delete Item where ID=" + _
            ItemID.Text
        Dim objCommand As New SqlCommand(strSql, objConnection)
        objCommand.ExecuteNonQuery()

        Session("EditItem") = Nothing
        ItemID.Text = ""
        Password.Text = ""

    Catch ex As Exception
        ErrorMessage.Text = ex.Message.ToString()
    Finally
        If objConnection.State = ConnectionState.Open Then
            objConnection.Close()
        End If
    End Try
End Sub
```

Searching for an Item

When users search for an item, the application must do a search of the database, and then, if the item is found, display the matches. Listing 7.9 shows the code that does this search. The code performs a query and then binds the data to a DataList object so that the user can easily make a selection, as shown in Figure 7.4.

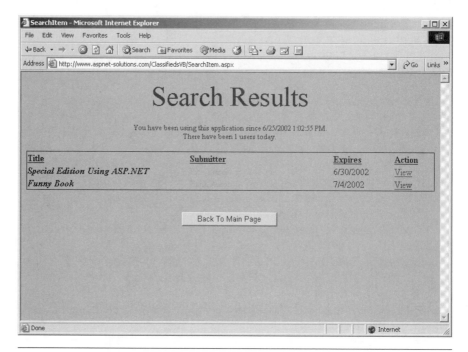

Figure 7.4 When a User Searches for Items, They Are Displayed in the Search Results Screen.

The first thing the `Page_Load()` method in Listing 7.9 does is to instantiate and open a database connection. A SQL string is then created, based on the `SearchCriteria` session variable. This session variable is used to form a query that looks at the Description field and the Title field. If the search criteria matches any text found in either field, the item will be placed into the result set.

Users may also have selected a category from the user interface on the main page. If they did, the value will be contained in a session variable named `CategoryID`. If this value is positive (`>=0`), then the SQL query will be adjusted so that the category ID will be a part of the query.

The last thing the query must do is take the item expiration date into account. It does this by appending a clause to the SQL query string that makes sure that the expiration date has not occurred.

A SqlDataReader object is returned from a `SqlCommand Execute-Reader()` method. The recordset is then databound to the DataList named ResultList.

Listing 7.9 This Code Supports the Item Search Functionality. In It Are Methods to Initialize the User Interface (Which Involves a SQL Query), and a Button Handler to Redirect to the Application Main Page.

```
Private Sub Page_Load(ByVal sender As System.Object, _
  ByVal e As System.EventArgs) Handles MyBase.Load
    If Not IsPostBack Then
        Dim objConnection As New _
            SqlConnection(_
              ConfigurationSettings.AppSettings("ConnectString"))
        Dim strSql As String = _
            "select Title,Name,DateExpires,ID from Item where (" + _
            "Description like '%" + _
            Convert.ToString(Session("SearchCriteria")) + "%' " + _
            "OR Title like '%" + _
            Convert.ToString(Session("SearchCriteria")) + "%')"

        Dim nCategoryID As Integer = _
            Convert.ToInt32(Session("CategoryID"))
        If nCategoryID >= 0 Then
            strSql += (" and Category in (select Name from " + _
            Categories "where ID=" + Convert.ToString(nCategoryID) + ")")
        End If

        strSql += (" and DateExpires >= '" + _
          DateTime.Now.ToShortDateString() + "'")

        Try
            objConnection.Open()

            Dim objCommand As New SqlCommand(strSql, objConnection)
            Dim objReader As SqlDataReader = objCommand.ExecuteReader()

            ResultList.DataSource = objReader
            ResultList.DataBind()

        Catch
        Finally
            If objConnection.State = ConnectionState.Open Then
                objConnection.Close()
            End If
        End Try
```

```
      End If
End Sub

Private Sub MainPage_Click(ByVal sender As System.Object, _
   ByVal e As System.EventArgs) Handles MainPage.Click
      Response.Redirect("Default.aspx")
End Sub
```

Viewing a Classified Ad

Users view a classified item within the ViewItem.aspx page. This page displays the item from the `Page_Load()` method. This method expects an item ID to be contained in a session variable named ItemID. After it queries the database for the item, the database information is placed into the user interface.

The `Page_Load()` method first creates and opens a database connection. A SQL query string is then formed with which a SqlCommand object is created. The `ExecuteReader()` method returns a SqlDataReader object, which contains all of the necessary item information. Finally, the user-interface

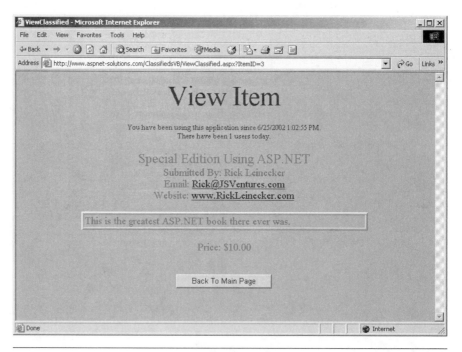

Figure 7.5 Links Are Offered So That Users Can E-mail a Seller or Go to a URL.

objects are populated from the returned DataSet. Links to item URLs and e-mails make it easy for viewers to get more information, as shown in Figure 7.5.

Listing 7.10 This Code Allows Users to View a Classified Item. It Consists of a SQL Query to Retrieve the Data, Populate the User Interface, and Respond to a Button That Redirects to the Main Application Page.

```
Private Sub Page_Load(ByVal sender As System.Object, _
  ByVal e As System.EventArgs) Handles MyBase.Load
    If Not IsPostBack Then
        Dim objConnection As New _
          SqlConnection(_
            ConfigurationSettings.AppSettings("ConnectString"))
        Try
            objConnection.Open()
            Dim objCommand As New SqlCommand("Select * from Item " + _
                "where ID=" + _
                Request.QueryString("ItemID"), objConnection)
            Dim objReader As SqlDataReader = objCommand.ExecuteReader()
            If objReader.Read() Then
                Title.Text = Convert.ToString(objReader("Title"))
                Name.Text += Convert.ToString(objReader("Name"))
                Dim strEmail As String = _
                  Convert.ToString(objReader("Email"))
                If strEmail.Length > 0 Then
                    Name.Text += ("<br>Email: <a href=mailto:" + _
                    strEmail + _
                    ">" + strEmail + "</a>")
                End If
                Dim strURL As String = _
                  Convert.ToString(objReader("URL"))
                If strURL.Length > 0 Then
                    Name.Text += ("<br>Website: <a href=" + Chr(34) + _
                        strURL + Chr(34) + ">" + strURL + "</a>")
                End If
                Price.Text += Convert.ToString(objReader("Price"))
                Description.Text = _
                    Server.HtmlEncode(_
                        Convert.ToString(objReader("Description")))
            End If
            objReader.Close()
        Catch ex As Exception
```

```
                ErrorMessage.Text = ex.Message.ToString()
        Finally
            If objConnection.State = ConnectionState.Open Then
                objConnection.Close()
            End If
        End Try
    End If
End Sub

Private Sub MainPage_Click(ByVal sender As System.Object, _
  ByVal e As System.EventArgs) Handles MainPage.Click
    Response.Redirect("Default.aspx")
End Sub
```

Giving Feedback After an Item Has Been Added

The code in Listing 7.11 displays information to the user about the classified add item that she has just added. The code that populates the Label objects that display the information can be found in the `Page_Load()` method.

The `MainPage_Click()` method simply redirects the user to the Default.aspx page. The `AnotherAd_Click()` method redirects the user to the AddItem.aspx page. You can see this part of the application in Figure 7.6, in which the user is given information about the item that she just added.

Listing 7.11 This Code Thanks the User for Adding an Item.

```
Private Sub Page_Load(ByVal sender As System.Object, _
  ByVal e As System.EventArgs) Handles MyBase.Load
    Title.Text = Request.QueryString("Title")
    Expiration.Text = Request.QueryString("Expiration")
    ItemID.Text = Request.QueryString("ItemID")
End Sub

Private Sub MainPage_Click(ByVal sender As System.Object, _
  ByVal e As System.EventArgs) Handles MainPage.Click
    Response.Redirect("Default.aspx")
End Sub

Private Sub AnotherAd_Click(ByVal sender As System.Object, ByVal e As
System.EventArgs) Handles AnotherAd.Click
    Response.Redirect("AddItem.aspx")
End Sub
```

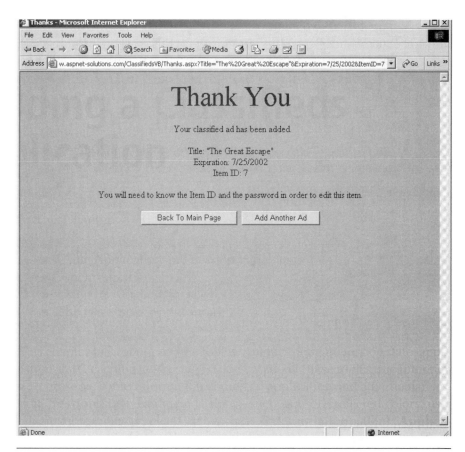

Figure 7.6 Users Will Need to Remember the Item IDs and Their Passwords if They Want to Edit an Item at a Later Time.

Maintaining the Counter and Day Variables

The code that maintains the session start time and the application counter variables can be seen in Listing 7.12. Setting the session `StartTime` variable is easy. All that must be done is to set the variable equal to `Date-Time.Now`. The application `Counter` variable, however, is slightly more complicated. The first thing that must be done is to check for its existence. If it doesn't exist, then a value of 0 is assigned to it. And one very important detail, even before this is done, is to use the `Application.Lock()` method. The `Application.Lock()` method must be called before any access is made to this application variable. Once you are sure that the application variable exists, then you will able to increment the variable in code that follows. But before you do this, you will also make sure that the application day variable exists. If it doesn't, you simply create it by assigning a `DateTime.Now.Day()` method to it. The last thing you do in this method is to call the `Application.Unlock()` method so that other threads will have access to this code.

Listing 7.12 This Code, Which Can Be Found in the Global.asax file, Maintains the Counter and Day Variables.

```
Sub Session_Start(ByVal sender As Object, ByVal e As EventArgs)
    Session("StartTime") = DateTime.Now
    Application.Lock()
    If Application("Counter") Is Nothing Then
        Application("Counter") = 0
    End If
    If Application("Day") Is Nothing Then
        Application("Day") = DateTime.Now.Day()
    End If
    Application("Counter") = Application("Counter") + 1
    If DateTime.Now.Day() <> Application("Day") Then
        Application("Day") = DateTime.Now.Day()
        Application("Counter") = 1
    End If
    Application.UnLock()
End Sub
```

Summary

This chapter has shown you how to use application and session variables, along with other useful features such as Cache objects and cookies. These features will allow your applications to maintain a certain amount of state, both for the user and session, in the application itself.

This chapter has also given you a useful application that you can use in many of your Web sites. Many times, users enjoy posting items they want to sell, or looking through items they might want to buy. I would like to see what you can do with this application, so if you use it and modify it, please send me an e-mail so that I can see what you have done.

CHAPTER 8

Creating Custom Server Controls: Building an Online Store

In This Chapter:

- Home Page
- The Store Database
- Server Controls
- Product List Page
- Product Detail Page
- Review and Add Page
- Search Results Page
- Shopping Cart Page

This chapter features an application that was written by the developers at Microsoft. It's called The IBuySpy Store. This application is different from the IBuySpy application in Chapter 18 because that is a portal, not a store. An online store's primary purpose is to display and sell products, while a portal's main purpose is to organize and present information. This application, though, is chocked full of recommended practices that the Microsoft developers feel strongly about.

The IBuySpy Store was probably created when the Microsoft developers had been imbibing in too much Jolt cola. You can buy anything from a fake moustache translator to a pocket protector rocket pack. Its purpose, though, is to simulate a Web-based catalog sales application. The items are categorized, and users can browse through the items in each category. If they find something they like, they can add it to their shopping cart. When they've found everything they need to become the spy of their dreams, they can check out and pay for their items. Of course, the sales are not real, and no credit card transactions really occur.

If users don't want to browse through the items, they can search for something by typing in a keyword. They can even review the items, similar to writing those book reviews on Amazon. Just to show the proper techniques, the final order information is checked for an account number, an e-mail address, and a password.

For authenticated users, there's an "instant order" feature whereby orders can be placed and tracked. This mechanism is built into a Web Service that can be used from another application. This means that you could easily extend the ordering and tracking functionality to a third-party application. For more information about creating and using Web services, see Chapter 14.

The IBuySpy Store application is written in ASP.NET. It does, however, use several server controls, or components, such as the one that encapsulates the menus. The controls provide a way to easily reuse functionality from one page to another. A complete description of these server controls can be found in the section entitled "Server Controls."

The database engine used is SQL Server. All of the product information and transaction information is stored in the database. Most of the access is done through stored procedures, which are encapsulated in the reusable components that we've talked about. A complete discussion of the database can be found in the section entitled "The Store Database."

Home Page

The application's home page is contained in the Default.aspx file. Most of the page consists of static HTML. There are, however, three components that are referenced by this page that encapsulate the real work. These components are for the header, menu, and popular items.

A single server component Label object named WelcomeMsg is on the home page. This object contains the user's full name if he has at one time logged in at this machine. When a user logs in, a cookie persists his full name on the client machine. The following code shows how the WelcomeMsg object is created from the cookie. It checks for the existence of a cookie named IBuySpy_FullName, and if it is found, the value in it is placed into the `WelcomeMsg.Text` property.

```
void Page_Load(Object sender, EventArgs e) {

  // Customize welcome message if personalization cookie is present
  if (Request.Cookies["IBuySpy_FullName"] != null) {
    WelcomeMsg.Text =
       "Welcome " + Request.Cookies["IBuySpy_FullName"].Value;
  }
}
```

The Classifieds application in Chapter 7 uses cookies more extensively. If you haven't read Chapter 7 and want more information about cookies, read through that chapter.

TIP: It's sometimes easier to use session variables than cookies. Session variables can require a bit less code, and they usually seem easier to use. But the choice of whether to use cookies or session variables isn't a simple one.

Session variables expire after a set period of time (20 minutes by default). This may be the desired behavior if you don't want users to keep your Web application open indefinitely. Cookies can time out, but they don't have to (you can set their `Expires` property to `DateTime.MaxValue`). This is the first part of the decision: value persistence.

Another consideration is that session variables require server resources such as memory and CPU cycles. Cookies require client memory and CPU cycles. If you are concerned with your server's resources, you might want to consider cookies instead of session variables.

Scalability is enhanced with cookies (over session variables) because more users don't require more server resources—the work is on the client machine. One issue of which you need to be aware is the reluctance of some users to allow cookies on their machines. You'll have to 1) insist that users allow cookies, 2) use another mechanism such as session variables, or 3) dynamically choose the mechanism at runtime according to whether a user's browser allows cookies.

The application's home page looks like a typical e-commerce site. It lists product categories, a featured product, and a list of popular products. You can see the home page in Figure 8.1

Just to make sure you can see where the three components are located on the screen, Figure 8.2 shows their locations.

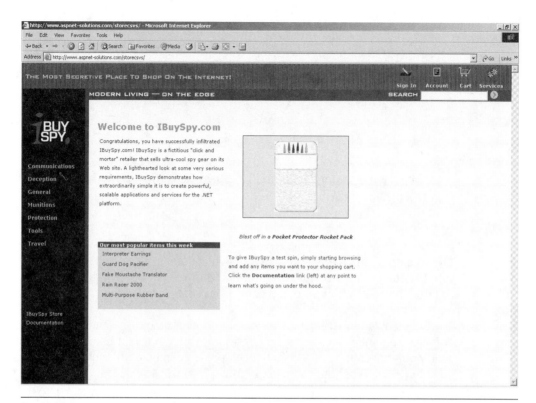

Figure 8.1 The Main Page Shows Product Categories, a Featured Product, and a Popular Items List.

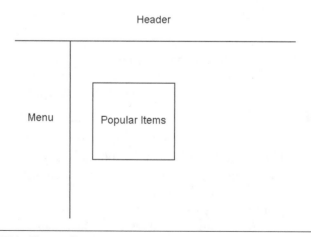

Figure 8.2 This Figure Shows the Location of the Three Components.

Because this is the page that's seen most frequently in the IBuySpy Store application, performance is important. For this reason, two of the components, the Menu and the PopularItems components, are cached. They query the database once every hour for the content that they display. Chapter 4 talks at length about the Cache API. Refer to this chapter for a complete explanation. Caching saves tremendously on the CPU time that would have been spent querying the database without it.

Another big performance gain (that we've already talked about some) is the fact that the personalization is done with a client-side cookie. This way, the user's name will appear on the page with very little server-side processing.

The Store Database

The IBuySpy Store application uses SQL Server as the database for its records. In total, there are seven tables that contain the store's information. Following is a description of each table.

Categories—This table contains the names of each category. It has only two fields: `CategoryID` and `CategoryName`. `CategoryID` is a primary key (and also an identity column), and `CategoryName` contains the name of the category, such as Communications and Deception.

Customers—This table contains information about customers. It has four fields: `CustomerID`, `FullName`, `EmailAddress`, and `Password`. `CustomerID` is a primary key (and also an identity column); and `FullName`, `EmailAddress`, and `Password` contain the user's information.

OrderDetails—This table contains information about order items for orders that have been placed. It has four fields: `OrderID`, `ProductID`, `Quantity`, and `UnitCost`. `OrderID` is an integer key that uniquely identifies the order number; `ProductID` is an integer key that uniquely identifies the product number; `Quantity` is an integer that contains the number of this particular product that was ordered; and `UnitCost` is a money field that contains the price of the item at the time that the order was placed.

Orders—This table contains information about a specific order. It has four fields: `OrderID`, `CustomerID`, `OrderDate`, and `ShipDate`. `OrderID` is an integer key (and also an identity column) that uniquely identifies the order number; the `CustomerID` contains the ID of the customer who placed the order; the `OrderData` field contains the date that the order was place (and is automatically assigned when a row is created by using `getdate()` for the default value); and the `ShipDate` field contains the date that the order was shipped (and is automatically assigned when a row is created by using `getdate()` for the default value).

Products—This table contains information about a specific product. It has seven fields: `ProductID`, `CategoryID`, `ModelNumber`, `ModelName`, `ProductImage`, `UnitCost`, and `Description`. `ProductID` is an integer key that uniquely identifies the product (and is an identity key); `CategoryID` is an integer field that identifies the category; `ModelNumber` is a text string that contains the product model number; `ModelName` is a text string that contains the product name; `ProductImage` contains the image file name that is displayed; `UnitCost` contains the cost for a single product; and `Description` is a text description of the product.

Reviews—This table contains user/customer reviews for each product. It has six fields: `ReviewID`, `ProductID`, `CustomerName`, `CustomerEmail`, `Rating`, and `Comments`. `ReviewID` is an integer key that uniquely identifies the review (and also an identity column); `ProductID` is an integer that associates the review with a product; `CustomerName` contains the name of the customer; `CustomerEmail` contains the email of the customer; `Rating` is an integer that contains the rating value that the customer assigned the product; and `Comments` contains the text that the customer entered when reviewing the product.

ShoppingCart—This table contains the shopping cart contents for customers. It has five fields: `RecordID`, `CartID`, `Quantity`, `ProductID`, and `DateCreated`. `RecordID` is an integer key that uniquely identifies the shopping cart record (and is an identity column); `CartID` contains the name of the cart; `Quantity` contains the number of a particular product that's in the shopping cart; `ProductID` identifies the product that's in the cart for this record; and `DateCreated` contains the date that this shopping cart record was created (and is automatically assigned when a row is created by using `getdate()` for the default value).

The relationships between the tables can be seen on Figure 8.3.

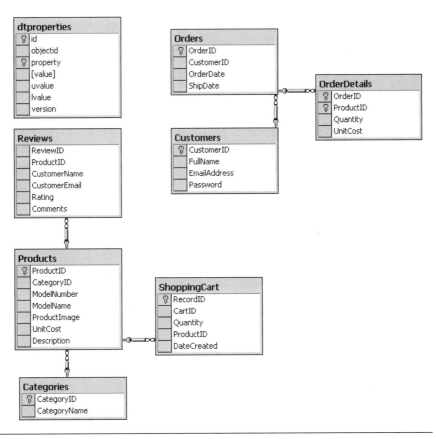

Figure 8.3 This Is a Diagram of the Database Schema.

Server Controls

Custom server controls, sometimes known as *user controls,* encapsulate user-interface functionality. They are implemented just like regular .aspx pages, except that they usually don't have some of the wrapping HTML tags, such as `<html>` and `<body>`. That's because they're almost always used from within another .aspx page that already has these wrapping HTML tags. As with regular .aspx pages, there is still a `Load` and `Unload` event that can be used to maintain data.

Most user controls are contained in .ascx files as this is the file extension for them. This differentiates them from regular .aspx files.

Custom controls can be used from a page by registering them with a unique prefix and name, and specifying the source file. A register tag is placed at the top of the .aspx file to register custom controls, as follows:

```
<%@ Register TagPrefix="IBuySpy" TagName="Menu" Src="_Menu.ascx" %>
```

This control can be declared and used within the .aspx page as follows:

```
<IBuySpy:Menu id="MyMenu" runat="server" />
```

The public properties can all be set from within the .aspx page, as you can see above where the `id` property is set to contain the value of `"MyMenu"`.

Also Bought

This user control displays products that others who bought a particular item have bought. It's a good way to offer additional products that customers might buy. For instance, if they buy the moustache translator, there's a good chance that they'll buy the interpreter earrings. The control can be found in the _AlsoBought.ascx and _AlsoBought.ascx.cs files (_AlsoBought.ascx and _AlsoBought.ascx.vb for the VB version).

This control relies on a component named ProductsDB, and this component is located in the Components directory in a file named ProductsDB.cs (or ProductsDB.vb for the VB version). The ProductsDB component performs queries that are related to the products. Table 8.1 shows the methods and their descriptions.

The .ascx page of the AlsoBought user control contains a Repeater with an ID named alsoBoughtList. This Repeater is decorated so that it looks attractive, and it has header and footer templates (HeaderTemplate and FooterTemplate). The ItemTemplate contains a HyperLink that will be bound to the data. This will create hyperlinks that go to the ProductDetails.aspx page.

The .ascx.cs (or .ascx.vb for the VB version) file contains the code that uses the ProductsDB component. In the `Page_Load()` method, a ProductsDB object named productCatalogue is instantiated. A call to the `ProductsDB.GetProductsAlsoPurchased()` method returns the lists of products that were also purchased by people who purchased this particular item. (The `ProductID` is passed as a parameter to the `GetProductsAlsoPurchased()` method.) The Repeater object's `DataSource` property is set to the SqlDataReader object that is returned.

Table 8.1 The Methods for the ProductsDB Component

Method	Return Type	Description
`GetProduct Categories()`	`SqlDataReader`	The `GetProductCategories()` method returns a DataReader that exposes all product categories (and their CategoryIDs) within the IBuySpy Products database. The `SqlDataReader-Result` structure also returns the SQL connection, which must be explicitly closed after the data from the DataReader is bound into the controls.
`GetProducts()`	`SqlDataReader`	The `GetProducts()` method returns a structure containing a forward-only, read-only DataReader. This displays all products within a specified product category. The `SqlDataReaderResult` structure also returns the SQL connection, which must be explicitly closed after the data from the DataReader is bound into the controls.
`GetProductDetails()`	`ProductDetails`	The `GetProductDetails()` method returns a `ProductDetails` structure containing specific details about a specified product within the IBuySpy Products Database.
`GetProductsAlso Purchased()`	`SqlDataReader`	The `GetPGetProductsAlso-Purchasedroducts()` method returns a structure containing a forward-only, read-only DataReader. This displays a list of other products also purchased with a specified product. The `SqlDataReaderResult` structure also returns the SQL connection, which must be explicitly closed after the data from the DataReader is bound into the controls.

(continued)

Table 8.1 The Methods for the ProductsDB Component (*cont.*)

Method	Return Type	Description
GetMostPopular ProductsOfWeek()	SqlDataReader	The GetMostPopularProductsOf-Week() method returns a structure containing a forward-only, read-only DataReader containing the most popular products of the week within the IBuy-Spy Products database. The SqlData-ReaderResult structure also returns the SQL connection, which must be explicitly closed after the data from the DataReader is bound into the controls.
SearchProduct Description()	SqlDataReader	The SearchProductDescriptions() method returns a structure containing a forward-only, read-only DataReader. This displays a list of all products whose name and/or description contains the specified search string. The SqlData-ReaderResult structure also returns the SQL connection, which must be explicitly closed after the data from the DataReader is bound into the controls.

Then, the Repeater's `DataBind()` method is called. Finally, if there are no items in the recordset, the Repeater is hidden by setting the Repeater's `Visible` property to `false`. Listing 8.1 shows the AlsoBought user control's `Page_Load()` method in C# and VB.

Listing 8.1 The `Page_Load()` method for the AlsoBought User Control

C#

```
private void Page_Load(object sender, System.EventArgs e)
{

  // Obtain list of products that people who "also bought" an item have
  // purchased.  Databind to list control
  IBuySpy.ProductsDB productCatalogue = new IBuySpy.ProductsDB();

  alsoBoughtList.DataSource =
    productCatalogue.GetProductsAlsoPurchased(ProductID);
```

```
alsoBoughtList.DataBind();

// Hide the list if no items are in it
if (alsoBoughtList.Items.Count == 0)
{
    alsoBoughtList.Visible = false;
}
}
```

VB
```
Sub Page_Load(ByVal sender As Object, ByVal e As EventArgs)

    ' Obtain list of products that people who "also bought" an item have
    ' purchased.  Databind to list control
    Dim productCatalogue As IBuySpy.ProductsDB = New IBuySpy.ProductsDB()

    alsoBoughtList.DataSource = _
        productCatalogue.GetProductsAlsoPurchased(ProductID)
    alsoBoughtList.DataBind()

    ' Hide the list if no items are in it
    If alsoBoughtList.Items.Count = 0 Then
        alsoBoughtList.Visible = False
    End If
End Sub
```

Header

The Header user control is used at the top of each page in the IBuySpy Store application. This control is very simple because all it contains is static HTML. None of the data-access components are used, and no other user controls are used. The control can be found in the _Header.ascx and _Header.ascx.cs files (_Header.ascx and _Header.ascx.vb for the VB version).

Menu

This user control creates a menu of all product categories in the database. This forms the left-hand navigation of the product catalog pages. The control can be found in the _Menu.ascx and _Menu.ascx.cs files (_Menu.ascx and _Menu.ascx.vb for the VB version).

The .ascx page contains a DataList named MyList. This object will contain the product categories as hyperlinks.

The .ascx.cs file (or the .ascx.vb file for the VB version) contains the code that gets the data, and it databinds to the MyList object. It's in the Page_Load() method. As with the AlsoBought user control, the Menu control relies on the ProductDB component. (See Table 8.1 for details about this class's methods.)

The Page_Load() method is simple. It first attempts to retrieve an HTML parameter named Selection. If this parameter is found, the DataList object's SelectedIndex property is set to this value. The next thing that is done is to instantiate a ProductsDB component. The ProductsDB.GetProductCategories() method is used to retrieve a SqlDataReader object, which is then used to set the DataList's DataSource property. Finally, a call to the DataList's DataBind() method completes the process. Listing 8.2 shows the C# and VB source code for the Menu user control's Page_Load() method.

Listing 8.2 This Page_Load() Method Populates the DataList with the Product Categories.

C#

```csharp
private void Page_Load(object sender, System.EventArgs e) {

  // Set the curent selection of list
  String selectionId = Request.Params["selection"];

  if (selectionId != null) {
    MyList.SelectedIndex = Int32.Parse(selectionId);
  }

  // Obtain list of menu categories and databind to list control
  IBuySpy.ProductsDB products = new IBuySpy.ProductsDB();

  MyList.DataSource = products.GetProductCategories();
  MyList.DataBind();
}
```

VB

```vb
Sub Page_Load(ByVal sender As Object, ByVal e As EventArgs)

  ' Set the curent selection of list
  Dim selectionId As String = Request.Params("selection")
```

```
If Not selectionId Is Nothing Then
  MyList.SelectedIndex = CInt(selectionId)
End If

' Obtain list of menu categories and databind to list control
Dim products As IBuySpy.ProductsDB = New IBuySpy.ProductsDB()

MyList.DataSource = products.GetProductCategories()
MyList.DataBind()

End Sub
```

There's one important note regarding the Menu control. It is cached and refreshes only every hour (or 3,600 seconds). This is a significant performance win because the database access can really add up if the application is heavily trafficked. The following directive is placed at the top of the _Menu.ascx page (but below the Control directive). The **VaryByParam** attribute allows you to vary the cached output, depending on the GET query string or form POST parameters.

```
<%@ OutputCache Duration="3600" VaryByParam="selection" %>
```

Popular Items

This user control displays the five most popular items, and it is a way to *suggest sell*—a technique popular in today's retail environment. It's kind of like when you walk into McDonalds and don't order French fries; many times, the person taking your order will ask if you want French fries. This is known as *suggest selling* because it suggests a purchase that the buyer hasn't made. Many times the items that are suggested are ones that are common, or ones that are on special. The control can be found in the _PopularItems.ascx and _PopularItems.ascx.cs files (_PopularItems.ascx and _PopularItems.ascx.vb for the VB version).

The user-interface part of this control features a Repeater. This Repeater is populated in the control's Page_Load() method. The data will become part of a HyperLink that's in the DataList that has as its destination the ProductDetails.aspx page. This gives users a way to see the details about these popular items.

The Page_Load() method uses the ProductsDB component to retrieve the list of popular items from the database. After instantiating a ProductsDB component, the ProductsDB.GetMostpopularProd-

uctsOfWeek() method, which returns a SqlDataReader object, is called.
The SqlDataReader is assigned to the DataList's DataSource property. A
call to the DataList.DataBind() method finishes things up. There is
one final detail, though. If the recordset is empty, the DataList is hidden by
setting its Visible property to false. The Page_Load() method can
be seen in Listing 8.3.

Listing 8.3 The Page_Load() Method That Populates the DataList Object for the
PopularItems User Control

C#
```
private void Page_Load(object sender, System.EventArgs e) {

  // Obtain list of favorite items
  IBuySpy.ProductsDB products = new IBuySpy.ProductsDB();

  // Databind and display the list of favorite product items
  productList.DataSource = products.GetMostPopularProductsOfWeek();
  productList.DataBind();

  // Hide the list if no items are in it
  if (productList.Items.Count == 0) {
    productList.Visible = false;
  }
}
```

VB
```
Sub Page_Load(ByVal sender As Object, ByVal e As EventArgs)

  ' Obtain list of favorite items
  Dim products As ProductsDB = New ProductsDB()

  ' Databind and display the list of favorite product items
  productList.DataSource = products.GetMostPopularProductsOfWeek()
  productList.DataBind()

  ' Hide the list if no items are in it
  If productList.Items.Count = 0 Then
    productList.Visible = False
  End If

End Sub
```

The PopularItems user control does partial-page output caching at one-hour intervals. This enables the application to avoid having to read the database on each request to a page containing this user control, thus dramatically improving performance. The following directive can be seen at the top of the PopularItems.ascx page (although you must include the **VaryByParam** attribute in any @ OutputCache directive, you can set its value to None if you do not want to use the functionality it provides):

```
<%@ OutputCache Duration="3600" VaryByParam="None" %>
```

Review List

This user control displays a list of customer reviews. The control can be found in the _ReviewList.ascx and _ ReviewList.ascx.cs files (_ReviewList. ascx and _ReviewList.ascx.vb for the VB version).

The user interface object that's used to display the list is a DataList. It is declared in the .ascx file and populated in the .ascx.cs (or .ascx.vb file for the VB version).

Product List Page

The Product List page is contained in the ProductList.aspx file. The user is brought to this page in response to a selection from the Menu user control in the Home page (Default.aspx). When you first install the application, the categories available are Communications, Deception, General, Munitions, Protection, Tools, and Travel. The Product List page displays all products in a selected category.

For performance, this page is cached and refreshes every 100 minutes (6,000 seconds).

When users go from the Home page to the Product List page, there are two HTML parameters that carry important values. The first is named CategoryID and contains the category ID with which the database can be queried for the products in the selected category. The second is named Selection, and this simply remembers the selection number in the Menu user control. The following URL shows a category ID of 14 and a selection of 0:

```
ProductsList.aspx?CategoryID=14&selection=0
```

The user interface object that's used to display the products is a Data-List. The ProductsList.aspx file has an ItemTemplate that declaratively describes the data values that will be bound to the DataList object, as shown here:

```
<ItemTemplate>
  <table border="0" width="300">
    <tr>
      <td width="25">
      </td>
      <td width="100" valign="middle" align="right">
        <a href='ProductDetails.aspx?productID=<%#
DataBinder.Eval(Container.DataItem, "ProductID") %>'>
          <img src='ProductImages/thumbs/<%#
DataBinder.Eval(Container.DataItem, "ProductImage") %>'
            width="100" height="75" border="0">
        </a>
      </td>
      <td width="200" valign="middle">
        <a href='ProductDetails.aspx?productID=<%#
DataBinder.Eval(Container.DataItem, "ProductID") %>'>
          <span class="ProductListHead">
            <%# DataBinder.Eval(Container.DataItem, "ModelName") %>
          </span>
          <br>
        </a>
        <span class="ProductListItem"><b>Special Price: </b>
          <%# DataBinder.Eval(Container.DataItem, "UnitCost", "{0:c}") %>
        </span>
        <br>
        <a href='AddToCart.aspx?productID=<%# DataBinder.Eval(Container.
DataItem, "ProductID") %>'>
          <span class="ProductListItem"><font color="#9D0000">
            <b>Add To Cart<b></font></span>
        </a>
      </td>
    </tr>
  </table>
</ItemTemplate>
```

You should notice that within the DataList's ItemTemplate, an Add To Cart link has been implemented. When this is clicked, the product item is added to the user's shopping cart. The product ID is passed to the AddTo-Cart.aspx page as an HTML parameter named ProductID.

RECOMMENDED PRACTICE: A similar functionality could have been added by using an ImageButton that posts back to the ProductsList.aspx page, but there are reasons for implementing it the way it's currently being done.

The AddToCart.aspx page can be used from two different places, thus giving better reuse of the code. The AddToCart.aspx page is called from the ProductsList.aspx, ProductDetails.aspx, and ProductSearch.aspx pages.

Posting back to the ProductsList.aspx page with different parameter values would defeat the page caching that's been implemented because there would need to be a cache entry with a unique parameter string for each page. So instead of posting back with different parameters, the post backs are made with the data not being contained in parameters.

The DataList object is bound to data in the Page_Load() method. The code is simple. It starts by parsing the CategoryID parameter into an integer. It then instantiates a ProductsDB object. The recordset is assigned to the DataList's DataSource property with a call to the ProductsDB. GetProducts() method (which takes an integer argument specifying the category ID). And last, a call to the DataList's DataBind() method finishes it up. The C# and VB source code can be seen in Listing 8.4.

Listing 8.4 The Page_Load() Method That Binds All Products in a Category to a DataList

C#
```
void Page_Load(Object sender, EventArgs e) {

  // Obtain categoryId from QueryString
  int categoryId = Int32.Parse(Request.Params["CategoryID"]);

  // Obtain products and databind to an asp:datalist control
  IBuySpy.ProductsDB productCatalogue = new IBuySpy.ProductsDB();

  MyList.DataSource = productCatalogue.GetProducts(categoryId);
  MyList.DataBind();
}
```

VB
```
Sub Page_Load(ByVal sender As Object, ByVal e As EventArgs)
```

```
' Obtain categoryId from QueryString
Dim categoryId As Integer = CInt(Request.Params("CategoryID"))

' Obtain products and databind to an asp:datalist control
Dim productCatalogue As IBuySpy.ProductsDB = New IBuySpy.ProductsDB()

MyList.DataSource = productCatalogue.GetProducts(categoryId)
MyList.DataBind()

End Sub
```

Product Detail Page

The Product Detail page displays the details about a specific product. The product displayed is the one corresponding to the `ProductID` parameter that was carried from the ProductsList.aspx page. All of the code is contained in the `Page_Load()` method.

The `Page_Load()` method starts by converting the `ProductID` parameter into an integer. It then instantiates a ProductsDB object. A ProductDetails structure is obtained by calling the `ProductsDB.GetProductDetails()` method with the product ID as an argument to the method. The user interface objects are then populated. Table 8.2 shows the user interface objects that are populated.

Table 8.2 The User Interface Objects That Display the Product Details

Identifier	Type	Description
Desc	Label	This holds the product description text.
UnitCost	Label	This holds the single unit cost for the product.
ModelName	Label	This holds the name of the product.
ModelNumber	Label	This holds the catalog number of the product.
ProductImage	Image	This contains the product image that will be displayed.
addToCart	HyperLink	This links the product to the AddToCart.aspx page.
ReviewList	User Control	This is a user control that contains the list of reviews.
AlsoBoughtList	User Control	This is a user control that contains the list of items that user who bought this product also bought.

Once the product data is fetched from the database, it is pushed into a number of server controls on the page. Most of these server controls are standard ASP.NET ones (Labels, Images, Hyperlinks, and so on). Two of the server controls, however, are custom IBuySpy user controls that we have written to encapsulate the Review List of a product, as well as a list of products that people who bought the current product Also Bought. Note that these user controls can be programmatically manipulated (property sets/gets, methods called, events sunk and raised) just like any other standard server control. They provide a very nice way to encapsulate and reuse functionality, as well as to cleanly partition work among multiple developers.

Listing 8.5 shows the `Page_Load()` method in C# and VB.

Listing 8.5 The `Page_Load()` Method That Populates the User Interface Objects for the Product Detail Page

C#
```csharp
void Page_Load(Object sender, EventArgs e) {

    // Obtain ProductID from QueryString
    int ProductID = Int32.Parse(Request.Params["ProductID"]);

    // Obtain Product Details
    IBuySpy.ProductsDB products = new IBuySpy.ProductsDB();
    IBuySpy.ProductDetails myProductDetails =
      products.GetProductDetails(ProductID);

    // Update Controls with Product Details
    desc.Text = myProductDetails.Description;
    UnitCost.Text = String.Format("{0:c}", myProductDetails.UnitCost);
    ModelName.Text = myProductDetails.ModelName;
    ModelNumber.Text = myProductDetails.ModelNumber.ToString();
    ProductImage.ImageUrl = "ProductImages/" +
      myProductDetails.ProductImage;
    addToCart.NavigateUrl = "AddToCart.aspx?ProductID=" + ProductID;
    ReviewList.ProductID = ProductID;
    AlsoBoughtList.ProductID = ProductID;
}
```

VB
```vb
Sub Page_Load(ByVal sender As Object, ByVal e As EventArgs)
```

```
' Obtain ProductID from QueryString
Dim ProductID As Integer = CInt(Request.Params("ProductID"))

' Obtain Product Details
Dim products As IBuySpy.ProductsDB = New IBuySpy.ProductsDB()
Dim myProductDetails As IBuySpy.ProductDetails = _
  products.GetProductDetails(ProductID)

' Update Controls with Product Details
desc.Text = myProductDetails.Description
UnitCost.Text = String.Format("{0:c}", myProductDetails.UnitCost)
ModelName.Text = myProductDetails.ModelName
ModelNumber.Text = myProductDetails.ModelNumber.ToString()
ProductImage.ImageUrl = "ProductImages/" & _
  myProductDetails.ProductImage
addToCart.NavigateUrl = "AddToCart.aspx?ProductID=" & ProductID
ReviewList.ProductID = ProductID
AlsoBoughtList.ProductID = ProductID

End Sub
```

Review and Add Page

The Review and Add page (ReviewAdd.aspx) enables customers to enter their own reviews of a product. This page appears when a user clicks the Review this Product image link on a product detail page (ProductsDetails.aspx). The link is not actually part of the product detail page. Instead, it is part of the ReviewList user control (_ReviewList.ascx) that is incorporated into the page.

The ReviewAdd.aspx page is brought up in response to users clicking the Review this Product link. The ID of the product to review is passed to this page in the query string. For example, if the user wants to add a review of the Mighty, Mighty Pen, the URL to display this page would be the following:

```
ReviewAdd.aspx?productID= 371.
```

The page logic is encapsulated in two event handlers, the Page_Load() method and an event handler for the Click event of an Image-

Button control. The `Page_Load()` method obtains the specified `Pro-ductID` parameter using the Params collection of the page's Request object. The Params collection contains all query-string, form-field, cookie, and server variables sent from a client during an HTTP request. This is the typical API through which page developers access arguments when they're doing page-to-page navigation transfers.

After converting the `ProductID` into an `Integer`, the `Page_Load()` method creates an instance of the `ProductDB` class and calls its `GetProductDetails()` method, passing it the product ID. This method internally uses the `ProductDetail` stored procedure to fetch the `ModelName` field of the product.

The code in the `Page_Load()` method is wrapped in a conditional code block that executes only if `Page.IsPostBack` is `false`. This check determines whether the page is being accessed for the first time or whether it is being displayed because the user clicked the Submit button (which causes the page to post back to the server). The `Page.IsPostBack` property provides us with an easy way to ensure the page fetches only product information the first time the page is being displayed.

The `ReviewAddBtn_Click()` method is fired when a user clicks the Submit Image button on the page. This handler illustrates an important feature of ASP.NET pages and server controls: Although the click actually occurs in the browser, the method runs on the server, after the page has been posted back.

All the logic required to fire the Click method on the server, and there to find and execute the correct method, is built into the page and control framework. No client-side script, ActiveX controls, Java applets, or any other special processing is required to make this happen. It works with all browsers, including Internet Explorer, Netscape, and Opera.

The `ReviewAddBtn_Click()` method calls the `AddReview()` method of the `ReviewsDB` class, which in turn calls the `ReviewsAdd` stored procedure to save the user's review in the IBuySpy database. All values are HTML encoded before the method is called. This provides protection against a common hacker technique, which is to embed image and anchor links within posted text values that, when later rendered on a page, end up displaying remote images (with pass-through links) on the page.

The page requires that users enter a name and e-mail address. If you look at the source for the ReviewAdd.aspx page, you'll see that there is no input validation code. Instead, we use the built-in ASP.NET validation controls, which enable you to declaratively specify validation constraints on any input control.

ASP.NET comes with built-in validation controls to handle almost any validation requirement: the RequiredField, CompareValidator, Regular-ExpressionValidator, RangeValidator, and CustomValidator controls. (Chapter 2 discusses data validation in much more detail.) You can put a validation control anywhere on a page and declaratively link it to a target input control using the validator's `ControlToValidate` property. You can optionally specify a `Text` property that displays in place of the validation control if the input data fails the validation test. If necessary, you can use multiple validators to "chain" validation logic for a single control (for example, a field is required and must meet a specified pattern).

The validation controls can perform client-side validation, which provides immediate feedback to the user. The validators also perform their check in server code, so if the browser does not support DHMTL, or if client-side scripting is disabled, the validation check is still performed. No code changes are required to enable either scenario—all logic required to handle the checks on both basic and DHTML-compatible browsers is built into the controls themselves.

If you are using validation controls, your server code can determine whether the user's input passed the check by testing the `IsValid` property of the validation control. Additionally, you can check the page's `IsValid` property; this property is an aggregate of the `IsValid` properties of all the validators on the page. If any one validation has detected a failure, the page's `IsValid` property is set to `false`.

Only if all controls on the page are valid will we go ahead and add the product review. If one of the input fields is invalid, then the page will simply be redisplayed again, with the validation controls automatically taking care of displaying the appropriate error message to the user.

Search Results Page

The SearchResults.aspx page displays a list of all products whose names or descriptions match specified search criteria. This page appears when a user clicks the Search button that appears at the top of most pages in IBuySpy. The search form itself is not actually part of the page; instead, it is part of the Header user control (_Header.ascx) that is incorporated into the page.

The ProductsList page logic is encapsulated entirely within its `Page_ Load()` method. This event handler is called when the page is accessed by a browser client. The `Page_Load()` method obtains the text clause to search the product database using the Params collection of the page's Request object.

After parsing the `CategoryID` parameter into an integer value, the `Page_Load()` method instantiates a `ProductDB` class and calls the `GetProducts()` method. It gives the `GetProducts()` method an integer argument representing the category ID.

The product collection is displayed using a DataList server control. The DataList server control contains a user-defined ItemTemplate that describes what each item in the list should look like. The data values returned from the `ProductsDB.GetProducts()` method are populated into the DataList by setting its `Datasource` property, and then calling its `DataBind()` method. When `DataBind()` is called, the DataList will iterate over the DataSource and render a copy of the ItemTemplate for each row, populating data from the row.

Shopping Cart Page

The ShoppingCart.aspx page enables customers to view the current state of their shopping carts. They can also change quantities and remove items. To change quantities, users change the value in a text box, and then click the Update Your Shopping Cart button. If they are finished shopping, they can click the Final Check Out button.

The stored procedure that retrieves the information is named `ShoppingCartList` and can be seen below:

```
CREATE Procedure ShoppingCartList
(
    @CartID nvarchar(50)
)
AS

SELECT
    Products.ProductID,
    Products.ModelName,
    Products.ModelNumber,
    ShoppingCart.Quantity,
    Products.UnitCost,
    Cast((Products.UnitCost * ShoppingCart.Quantity) as money)
      as ExtendedAmount
```

```
FROM
    Products,
    ShoppingCart

WHERE
    Products.ProductID = ShoppingCart.ProductID
AND
    ShoppingCart.CartID = @CartID

ORDER BY
    Products.ModelName,
    Products.ModelNumber
```

The logic for this page is encapsulated in three event handlers: the `Page_Load()` method, the `UpdateBtn_Click()` method for the Update button, and the `CheckoutBtn_Click()` method for the Check Out button. The page includes some internal methods used to maintain the shopping cart information.

Shopping cart information is maintained in the IBuySpy database. When users add items to their cart, the application is actually writing records to the database. To keep track of which items belong to which cart, the application tags each record with a cart ID, which is created in the `ShoppingCartDB` class, either from the user's login name, or, if the user has not yet logged in, from a dynamically generated GUID.

When the ShoppingCart.aspx page is first displayed, the `Page_Load()` method calls the internal `PopulateShoppingCartList()` method to populate the shopping cart. That method first checks that there are items in the cart. If not, an error is displayed by setting the text of a Label control.

The shopping cart items are displayed in a DataGrid control, which includes built-in support for headers and footers, embedded controls in a column, alternating item display (the gray bar), and databinding.

The `PopulateShoppingCartList()` method obtains a collection of all items in the user's shopping cart by calling the `GetItems()` method of the `ShoppingCartDB` class. The `GetItems()` method in turn uses the `ShoppingCartList` stored procedure to retrieve the items from the database.

Once the collection of items is retrieved, it is bound to the DataGrid control by setting the control's `DataSource` property. Data is copied from the collection to the grid by calling the grid's `DataBind()` method, which causes a grid to loop through the data source to generate a row for each item. The layout of each item is determined by a set of individual column definitions in the DataGrid control.

When users click the Update Your Shopping Cart button, it invokes the `UpdateBtn_Click()` method, which in turn calls the `UpdateShoppingCartDatabase()` method to write the shopping cart items back into the database. After the update, the `UpdateBtn_Click()` method calls the same `PopulateShoppingCartList()` method used when the page is first displayed, to refresh the shopping cart grid on the page. The update is performed by looping through the Items collection of the DataGrid control. Each item corresponds logically to a row in the grid. To get the value of an individual control in an item, the process calls the Items collection's `FindControl()` method, which is a shorthand way to locate a control that might be in any column. For each item, the update process determines whether to remove or update that item in the shopping cart.

If the user clicks the Final Check Out button, it invokes the `CheckoutBtn_Click()` method. This method performs an update of the cart to make sure the database is current, and then redirects the client to the Checkout.aspx page.

A possible optimization would be to store the original (pre-update) quantity value of each row in a hidden field of the grid. Doing so would enable us to determine whether the Quantity text box value had changed and would allow us to call the `UpdateItem()` method of the `ShoppingCartDB` class only if the quantity value of that specific row had actually changed. As currently implemented, the page updates every item and refreshes the grid each time the user clicks the Update Your Shopping Cart button, even if there is no change.

Summary

The IBuySpy Store application is a great example of how to create an online store using ASP.NET. It's a simple application, yet it does a lot.

The output caching is a great example of squeezing extra performance out of ASP.NET applications. And the use of user controls illustrates how to effectively create reusable components for applications.

You might be interested in locating a white paper that has additional information, at http://www.asp.net/ibuyspy/IBuySpy%20Store%20Whitepaper.doc. A forum on www.asp.net also supports a discussion about the store.

CHAPTER 9

Using XML: Creating a Guest Book Application

In This Chapter:

- .NET XML Architecture
- XmlTextReader
- XmlTextWriter
- XslTransform
- Writing a Guest Book Application

This chapter covers XML and how to effectively use XML in .NET applications. The first thing you need to know is why you should use XML. After all, Web applications have been written now for years, and no one has had to worry about XML. One of the main reasons you need to consider using XML is that Web applications have now gotten much more complicated, and XML represents data in a new way. Because XML is so good at representing data, writing large enterprise Web applications is a lot easier.

XML adds type and structure to information with the Extensible Schema Definition (XSD) mechanism. This information in the past may have been some sort of HTML data, or some sort of query result from a database. The point is, though, that information can be stored anywhere on the Internet, and XML plus a data description in XSD adds structure to this information. XML also enables data from multiple sources to be aggregated into a single unit of information. This aggregated information will contain XML-specific structure information. For instance, a C++ data structure can be represented as the following XML snippet:

C++ Data
```
struct POINT
{
    int x;
    int y;
} spot = { 20, 40 };
```

XML Data

```
<spot type='POINT'>
    <x>20</x>
    <y>40</y>
</spot>
```

XML is a set of specifications from the World Wide Web Consortium (W3C); XPath, XSL, XSD, and XML are the family of specifications that are of most interest. These specifications are publicly available at www.w3.org/tr. Anyone can contribute and comment and implement these standards. Microsoft followed these standards as it developed the .NET XML classes.

.NET XML Architecture

.NET contains an entire XML Framework. This Framework comprises a number of classes that make it easy for you to implement and work with XML in your applications. Because .NET is so reliant on XML, Microsoft spent a great deal of time making these classes robust, easy to use, and very performant (i.e., it performs well in terms of CPU and execution time). As I have said before, these classes all follow the W3C specification for XML, and they are an evolution to MSXML, which you may have already used.

Much of .NET actually uses XML for its native data representation. Examples of this can be seen in ASP.NET and Web Services (which rely on SOAP), and you can even see XML in the automatic source-code comments that are added when you create classes with Visual Studio .NET. XML is also an integral part of ADO.NET and SQL Server 2000.

The .NET XML classes enable you to easily work with relational data and hierarchical data. The classes provide a unified programming model.

NOTE: The .NET XML Framework can be found in several namespaces. The core types are contained in System.Xml. The XPath and Xslt types can be found in System.Xml.XPath and System.Xml.Xsl. Another important namespace is System.Xml.Serialization. To use these classes, you must import the correct namespaces through the `using` directive, as follows:

```
using System.Xml;
using System.Xml.Xpath;
using System.Xml.Xsl;
using System.Xml.Serialization;
```

At the core of the .NET Framework XML classes are two abstract classes: `XmlReader` and `XmlWriter`. `XmlReader` provides a fast, forward-only, read-only cursor for processing an XML document stream. `XmlWriter` provides an interface for producing XML document streams that conform to the W3C's XML recommendations. Applications that need to process XML documents use `XmlReader`, whereas applications that want to create XML documents use `XmlWriter`. Both classes imply a streaming model that doesn't require an expensive in-memory cache. This makes them both attractive alternatives to the classic DOM approach.

The `XmlReader` and `XmlWriter` classes are abstract base classes. They define functionality that all derived classes must support. At present, three implementations of `XmlReader` are included in the .NET Framework: `XmlTextReader`, `XmlNodeReader`, and `XslReader`. The implementation of `XmlWriter` is in the .NET Framework. It is `XmlTextWriter`. The `XmlTextReader` and `XmlTextWriter` classes support reading from and writing to text-based streams. `XmlNodeReader` is used for in-memory DOM trees. One of the biggest advantages of this design is that custom readers and writers can be developed to extend the built-in functionality. I expect to see many of these extended classes appear on the Internet and in newsgroups as developers extend the classes to meet their needs and share the classes with others.

XmlTextReader

The `XmlTextReader` class is derived from the `XmlReader` class. `XmlReader` provides a fast-forward-only cursor for reading XML documents. It simplifies XML by providing some well-defined methods. `XmlReader` also implements a pull model that has several advantages over the more common push model. First and foremost, the pull model is easier to use. It is just easier for developers to think about `while` loops than complicated state machines. The `XmlReader` demo program compares using the pull model to using the push model. Although contextual state management is still a challenge with the pull model, it is easier to deal with through procedural techniques that are more natural for most developers.

The pull model can also offer improved performance through a variety of techniques. The `XmlReader` class makes efficient use of character buffers. In the end, the pull model offers a more familiar programming model, along with performance benefits.

This section talks about the `XmlTextReader` class and shows some examples of using it. Take a look at the simple XML file in Listing 9.1, which includes three book authors and book titles. We're going to use this file to demonstrate `XmlReader`.

Listing 9.1 An XML File Representing Authors and Books

```
<?xml version="1.0" encoding="utf-8" ?>
<library>
 <book>
  <author>Ernest Hemingway</author>
  <title>For Whom the Bell Tolls</title>
 </book>
 <book>
  <author>Dean Coontz</author>
  <title>Watchers</title>
 </book>
 <book>
  <author>Tom Clancy</author>
  <title>The Cardinal Of The Kremlin</title>
 </book>
</library>
```

I have created an example, which you can see at www.ASPNET-Solutions.com. After you get to the Web site, go to the chapter examples, and then select Chapter 9. One of the first examples is entitled XmlReader. Click the XmlReader link to see the example that I have prepared to demonstrate as simple use of `XmlReader`.

The first thing you should do is click the Read and Render Xml File button. When you click the button, an `XmlReader` goes out and reads the Simple.xml file that you saw in Listing 9.1 and renders it on the screen.

The source code for this example is shown in Listing 9.2. The code is very simple. First, `XmlTextReader` is instantiated using the constructor, which takes a single argument. This argument is a string, which indicates the XML file that will be opened and read. Notice that I am using the `Request.MapPath()` method, so that what gets past to the `XmlTextReader` constructor will be a fully qualified path.

My .aspx file has a text label that I am going to use for display purposes. I will read in the XML, and, if the note type is `text`, I will put the value into the label with a `<br>` at the end of it. The `<br>` ensures that each XML item that is read in is on a single line. You can see this part of the application in Figure 9.1.

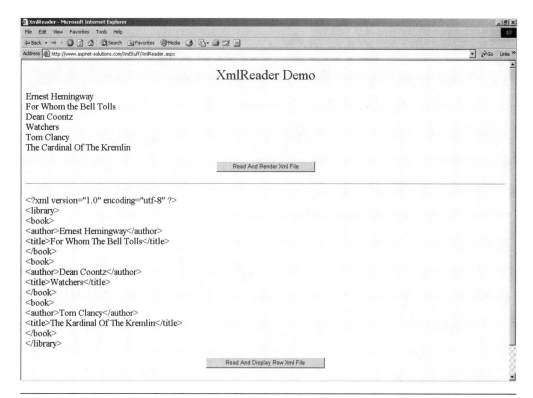

Figure 9.1 This Page Reads and Renders an XML Ril, and Also Shows the Raw XML.

One of the most important things you need to note is the `while`. You will see `while reader.read` do something. The `Reader.Read()` method reads through the XML data until there is no more data left. This provides an extremely easy, straightforward, and understandable way to process and read XML files.

Listing 9.2 The C# Source Code That Demonstrates a Simple Example Using XML Text Reader

C#

```csharp
public void ShowXmlRead_Click(System.Object sender, System.EventArgs e)
{
    XmlTextReader Reader =
      new XmlTextReader( Request.MapPath( "Simple.xml" ) );

    Label1.Text = "";
```

```
    while( Reader.Read() )
    {
        if( Reader.NodeType == XmlNodeType.Text )
        {
            Label1.Text += ( Reader.Value + "<br>\r\n" );
        }
    }
}
```

VB
```
Private Sub ShowXmlRead_Click(ByVal sender As System.Object, _
  ByVal e As System.EventArgs) Handles Button1.Click
    Dim Reader As New XmlTextReader(Request.MapPath("Simple.xml"))

    Label1.Text = ""

    While Reader.Read()
        If Reader.NodeType = XmlNodeType.Text Then
            Label1.Text += ( Reader.Value + "<br>\r\n" )
        End If
    While End
End Sub
```

I have also created, on the same Web page, a simple program that reads to the XML data file, as is, and displays it on the screen. This way, users can see what the actual XML looks like that was used to create the rendering with XmlTextEditor. You can see this code in Listing 9.3.

If you look at the code, you will notice I don't use any XML classes. I actually used the .NET StreamReader and file classes to read in the wrong XML from the disk file. I did this so that there would be no processing of XML and users could see the raw XML data.

Listing 9.3 Here Is the C# Code That Is Used to Display Raw XML Text.

C#
```
public void DisplayRaw_Click(System.Object sender, System.EventArgs e)
{
    Label2.Text = "";

    try
    {
        StreamReader reader =
```

```
        File.OpenText(Request.MapPath("SimpleXml.txt"));
        // Label2 eventually renders as a <span> in the HTML.
        Label2.Text += "<pre>";
        while( reader.Peek() != -1 )
        {
            Label2.Text += ( Server.HtmlEncode( reader.ReadLine() ) +
                "<br>\r\n" );
        }
        Label2.Text += "</pre>";
        reader.Close();
    }
    catch( Exception ex )
    {
        Label2.Text = ex.Message.ToString();
    }

}
```

VB
```
Private Sub DisplayRaw_Click(ByVal sender As System.Object, _
  ByVal e As System.EventArgs) Handles Button1.Click
    Label2.Text = ""

    Try
        StreamReader reader = _
          File.OpenText(Request.MapPath("SimpleXml.txt"))
        ' Label2 eventually renders as a <span> in the HTML.
        While reader.Peek() != -1
            Label2.Text += "<pre>"
            Label2.Text += ( Server.HtmlEncode( reader.ReadLine() ) + _
                "<br>\r\n" );
            Label2.Text += "</pre>"
        End While
        reader.Close()
    Catch ex As Exception
        Label2.Text = ex.Message.ToString()
    End Try

End Sub
```

The XmlTextReader, which is derived from XmlReader, provides you with an easy, clean way to parse data from XML files. It supports other types of input streams, though, such as those from a database. It also provides data valuation and resolution of external entities. `XmlTextReader` is easy to use. You should probably take a few moments to create a simple program of your own to familiarize yourself with using the class.

XmlTextWriter

`XmlTextWriter` is derived from the `XmlWriter` class. `XmlWriter` is the abstract class that defines the basic functionality required to produce document streams conforming to the W3C's XML recommendations. `XmlWriter` completely shields applications from the complexities of producing XML document streams by enabling them to work with a well-organized API. Producing a document with `XmlWriter` is very similar to producing documents via SAX. Currently there is one implementation of `XmlWriter`: `XmlTextWriter`. These implementations are just like reader versions, only they work in the opposite directions.

`XmlWriter` makes it possible to write out all standard constructs such as elements, attributes, and processing instructions. It does this using the corresponding methods. Some of these methods include `WriteStart-Document()`, `WriteStartElement()`, and `WriteProcessingInstruction()`. `XmlWriter` also provides methods for writing out typed elements and attributes through the `WriteElement()` and `WriteAttribute()` methods.

The source code for this entire part of the application can be seen in Listing 9.4. This part of the application can be seen running in Figure 9.2. You need to notice that the first thing I do is create an XmlTextWriter object. I pass the file name as an argument to the constructor. This actually creates the XML file before any data is written. I also set the formatting to be indented. If I don't do this, the entire XML file will be one long line with no carriage returns; it then becomes hard to read in any kind of text editor. If your file needs to be opened up or edited with anything besides `XmlTextReader`, you need to be sure you set the Formatting property to `Formatting.Indented`.

The first thing you need to do to create an XML file is to call the `WriteStart()` document method. This prepares the `XmlTextWriter` for creating a new document. I then call the `WriteComment()` method, but this is optional, and you may not need to do this in your particular application. Another optional method I call is the `WriteProcessing()` instruction. To create the elements and write the data into these elements, I use a combination of the `WriteStartElement()` method, the `WriteString()` method, and the `WriteEndElement()` method. These

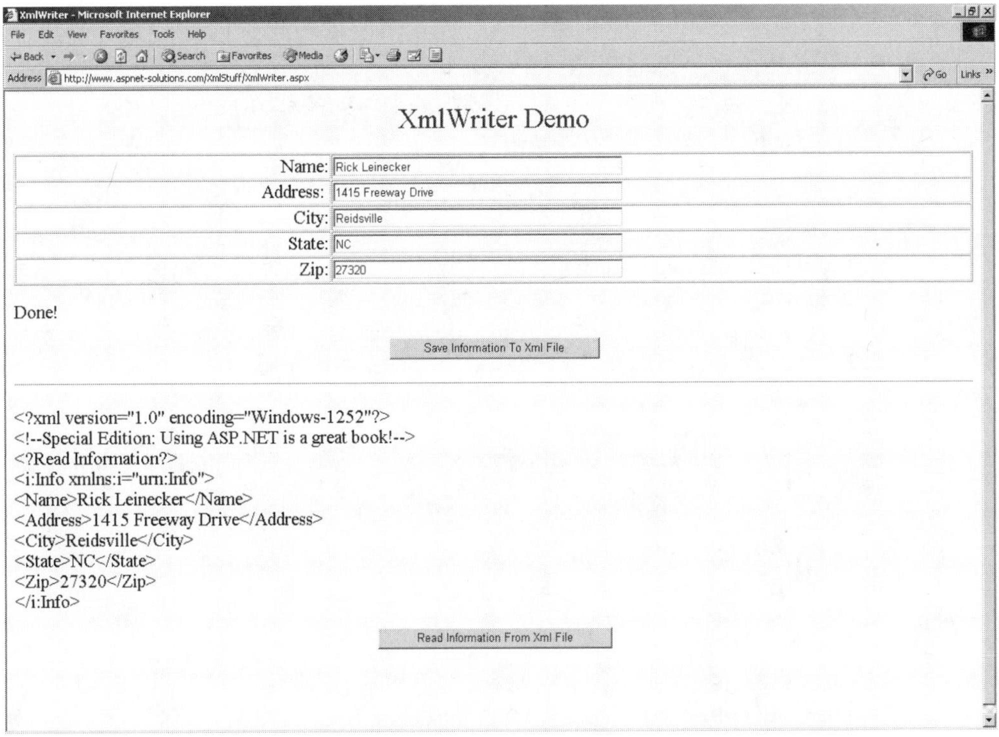

Figure 9.2 This Page Shows How to Use `XmlWriter` to Create and Write to an XML File.

methods create the elements, write the data to them, and then close them up. Because I have five elements, I made this set of calls five times: once for the name, once for the address, once for the city, once for the state, and once for the Zip code. The last thing I had to do was call the `WriteEndDocument()` method. This closed off the document internally and prepared it for writing to disk. When I finally called the `Close()` method, all the XML data that was contained in the `XmlTextWriter` class was saved out to disk.

Listing 9.4 The C# Source Code That Demonstrates a Simple Example Using XML Text Reader

C#
```
public void UseTextReader_Click(System.Object sender,
  System.EventArgs e)
{
```

```
try
{
    XmlTextWriter Writer =
        new XmlTextWriter( Request.MapPath( "SimpleInfo.xml" ),
        System.Text.Encoding.Default );

    Writer.Formatting = Formatting.Indented;

    Writer.WriteStartDocument();
    Writer.WriteComment( "Addison-Wesley is a great publisher!" );
    Writer.WriteProcessingInstruction( "Read", "Information" );
    Writer.WriteStartElement( "i", "Info", "urn:Info" );

    Writer.WriteStartElement( "Name", "" );
    Writer.WriteString( TextBox1.Text );
    Writer.WriteEndElement();

    Writer.WriteStartElement( "Address", "" );
    Writer.WriteString( TextBox2.Text );
    Writer.WriteEndElement();

    Writer.WriteStartElement( "City", "" );
    Writer.WriteString( TextBox3.Text );
    Writer.WriteEndElement();

    Writer.WriteStartElement( "State", "" );
    Writer.WriteString( TextBox4.Text );
    Writer.WriteEndElement();

    Writer.WriteStartElement( "Zip", "" );
    Writer.WriteString( TextBox5.Text );
    Writer.WriteEndElement();

    Writer.WriteEndDocument();

    Writer.Close();

    Label1.Text = "Done!";
}
catch( Exception ex )
{
    Label1.Text = ex.Message.ToString();
```

```
      }
}
```

VB
```
Private Sub UseTextReader_Click(ByVal sender As System.Object, _
  ByVal e As System.EventArgs) Handles Button1.Click

    Try
        Dim Writer As New _
          XmlTextWriter(Request.MapPath("SimpleInfo.xml"), _
         System.Text.Encoding.Default)

        Writer.Formatting = Formatting.Indented

        Writer.WriteStartDocument()
        Writer.WriteComment("Addison-Wesley is a great publisher ")
        Writer.WriteProcessingInstruction("Read", "Information")
        Writer.WriteStartElement("i", "Info", "urn:Info")

        Writer.WriteStartElement("Name", "")
        Writer.WriteString(TextBox1.Text)
        Writer.WriteEndElement()

        Writer.WriteStartElement("Address", "")
        Writer.WriteString(TextBox2.Text)
        Writer.WriteEndElement()

        Writer.WriteStartElement("City", "")
        Writer.WriteString(TextBox3.Text)
        Writer.WriteEndElement();

        Writer.WriteStartElement("State", "")
        Writer.WriteString(TextBox4.Text)
        Writer.WriteEndElement()

        Writer.WriteStartElement("Zip", "")
        Writer.WriteString(TextBox5.Text)
        Writer.WriteEndElement()

        Writer.WriteEndDocument()

        Writer.Close()
```

```
        Label1.Text = "Done!"
    Catch ex As Exception
        Label1.Text = ex.MessageToString()
    End Try
End Sub
```

This example also includes a button that enables you to view the raw XML text file. The method I created that does this doesn't use any of the XML classes. It simply opens the file, reads in the lines, and displays them in a label. You can see this code in Listing 9.5. In this code, I created a stream reader by calling the file `OpenText()` method, reading through the file one line at a time, and then closing it.

Listing 9.5 This Code Reads In the XML File and Displays It in Raw Format.

C#

```
public void Display_Click(System.Object sender, System.EventArgs e)
{
    Label2.Text = "<pre>";

    try
    {
        StreamReader reader =
          File.OpenText(Request.MapPath("SimpleInfo.xml"));
        while( reader.Peek() != -1 )
        {
            Label2.Text += ( Server.HtmlEncode( reader.ReadLine() ) +
              "<br>\r\n" );
        }
        reader.Close();
        Label2.Text += "</pre>";
    }
    catch( Exception ex )
    {
        Label2.Text = ex.Message.ToString();
    }

}
```

VB

```
Private Sub Display_Click(ByVal sender As System.Object, _
  ByVal e As System.EventArgs) Handles Button1.Click
```

```
Label2.Text = ""

Try
    StreamReader reader = _
      File.OpenText(Request.MapPath("SimpleInfo.xml"))
    While reader.Peek() <> -1
        Label2.Text += ( Server.HtmlEncode( reader.ReadLine() ) + _
          "<br>\r\n" );
    End While
    reader.Close()

Catch ex As Exception
    Label2.Text = ex.Message.ToString()
End Try

End Sub
```

The XML data that is written to disk is a very simple file. This file can be seen in Listing 9.6.

Listing 9.6 This Is the Simple XML File That Was Saved Out from the Code in Listing 9.5.

```xml
<?xml version="1.0" encoding="Windows-1252"?>
<!--Special Edition: Using ASP.NET is a great book!-->
<?Read Information?>
<i:Info xmlns:i="urn:Info">
   <Name>Rick</Name>
   <Address>123</Address>
   <City>5t</City>
   <State>ef</State>
   <Zip>asdf</Zip>
</i:Info>
```

I have created an example on www.ASPNET-Solutions.com. The example allows a user to type in a query. It then searches through XML files to try to find a match or matches for the user's query. You can see this example running in Figure 9.3.

The source code for this example can be seen in Listing 9.7. To accomplish the query, I first created an XmlDocument object. I then loaded the document using the Load() method. And as you can see by the source

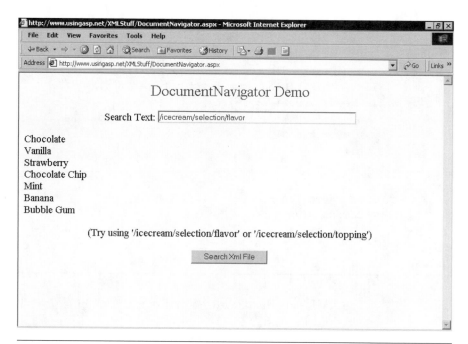

Figure 9.3 You Can Perform Queries in an XML File with the `DocumentNavigator` Class.

code listing, the `Load()` method takes a single argument, which is a string containing the file name. You may want to notice that once again I used the `Request.MapPath()` method to provide a fully qualified file name to the method.

After loading the XML file, I created a DocumentNavigator object. Then I used the `Select()` method to do the query. The `Select()` method takes a single argument, which is the string containing the query that must be used. I then looped through by using the `MoveToNextSelected()` method and displayed each match for the query found. Bear in mind that the XML document contains ice cream, so to have a successful query, the user needs to enter something such as chocolate or vanilla.

Listing 9.7 This C# Code Performs a Query on the XML Data.

C#
```
public void Match_Click(System.Object sender, System.EventArgs e)
{
```

```
    try
    {
        XmlDocument doc = new XmlDocument();
        doc.Load(Request.MapPath("IceCream.xml"));
        DocumentNavigator nav = new DocumentNavigator(doc);
        nav.Select(TextBox1.Text);

        bool bFound = false;
        Label1.Text = "";

        while( nav.MoveToNextSelected())
        {
            Label1.Text += ( nav.InnerText + "<br>\n\r" );
            bFound = true;
        }

        if( !bFound )
        {
            Label1.Text = "No matches found!";
        }
    }
    catch( Exception ex )
    {
        Label1.Text = ex.Message.ToString();
    }

}
```

VB

```
Public Sub Match_Click(ByVal sender As System.Object, _
  ByVal e As System.EventArgs)

    Try
        XmlDocument doc = new XmlDocument()
        doc.Load(Request.MapPath("IceCream.xml"))
        Dim nav As New DocumentNavigator(doc)
        nav.Select(TextBox1.Text)

        Dim bFound as bool = False
        Label1.Text = ""

        While nav.MoveToNextSelected()
            Label1.Text += ( nav.InnerText + "<br>\n\r" )
```

```
        bFound = True
    End While

    If not bFound Then
        Label1.Text = "No matches found!"
    End If

Catch ex As Exception
    Label1.Text = ex.Message.ToString()
End Try

End Sub
```

The `XmlDocument` and `XmlNavigator` classes provide you with a rich and powerful capability to perform queries on XML documents. They are easy to use and you will quickly be using them to add powerful functionality to your applications.

XslTransform

XSL, or XSLT, as it will be referred to in this section, stands for extensible style sheet language transformation. XSLT is a formatting language. It is based on template rules, which specify how XML documents should be processed. Although conventional programming languages are often sequential, template rules can be based in any order because XSLT is a declarative language. The style sheet declares what output should be produced when a pattern in the XML document is matched.

For example, a style sheet could declare that when the XSL transformation engine finds a `NAME` element, it should add markup by calling the name template. You can see a simple example of what this name template might look like in the following code:

```
<xsl:template match="NAME">
    ...
</xsl:template>
```

I have created an example that can be found on www.UsingASP.NET. It takes a simple XML file and renders it using an `XslTransform`. You can see the final rendered output in Figure 9.4.

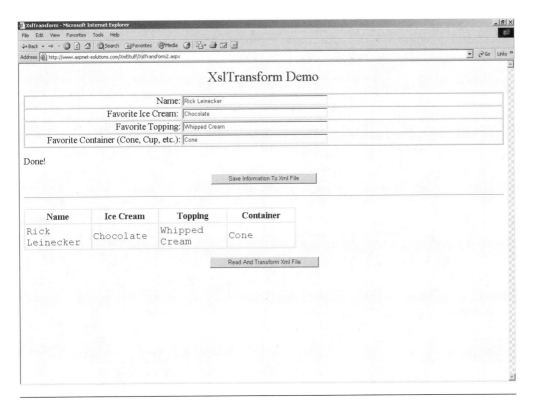

Figure 9.4 A Simple XML File Is Saved and Then Rendered with an XSLTransform.

The XSLT file for this example is not very complicated. It can be seen in Listing 9.8. You can see in the example that the XML will be rendered in a table. Note the XSLT construct with the for-each syntax. This will cause each set of matching patterns in the XML file to be rendered as a row in the table.

Listing 9.8 This Simple XSL Transform File Is What Determines How the XML Data Will Be Rendered.

```
<xsl:stylesheet version='1.0'
xmlns:xsl='http://www.w3.org/1999/XSL/Transform'>
    <xsl:template match="/">
    <style>
        .value { width:"25%";font-family:courier new; font-size:.8em;
white-space=pre;}
```

```
  </style>
  <table border="1" cellspacing="0" cellpadding="3"
    bordercolor="gainsboro" width="100%">
      <tr>
          <th>Name</th>
          <th>IceCream</th>
          <th>Topping</th>
          <th>Container</th>
      </tr>
      <xsl:for-each select='info/entry'>
          <tr>
              <td class="value"><xsl:value-of select='name'/></td>
              <td class="value"><xsl:value-of select='icecream'/></td>
              <td class="value"><xsl:value-of select='topping'/></td>
              <td class="value">
                  <xsl:value-of select='container'/></td>
          </tr>
      </xsl:for-each>
  </table>
  </xsl:template>

</xsl:stylesheet>
```

The XML file that is used to create the display on the screen is extremely simple. It has four data elements: name, ice cream, topping, and container. You could increase the number of entries by doing a copy and paste on the entry tag and editing them to create additional names, ice creams, toppings, and containers. This simple XML file can be seen in Listing 9.9.

Listing 9.9 This Is the Simple XML File, Which Will Be Rendered on the Screen.

```
<?xml version="1.0" encoding="Windows-1252"?>
<info>
  <entry>
    <name>Rick Leinecker</name>
    <icecream>Chocolate</icecream>
    <topping>Whipped Cream</topping>
    <container>Waffle Cone</container>
  </entry>
</info>
```

In this example, I also gave users the capability to change or edit the simple XML file. The source code can be seen in Listing 9.10. You can see this code in Listing 9.7. In this code I create an `XmlTextWriter`, as I did before in the section explaining `XmlTextWriter`. I then took the data that the users typed in in the HTML form and saved it out to an XML file. In this way, when users click the button to see the XML file, they can actually see information that they themselves have typed in.

Listing 9.10 This C# Code Saves the User Input to the XML File.

C#
```csharp
public void Transform_Click(System.Object sender, System.EventArgs e)
{

    try
    {
        XmlTextWriter Writer =
            new XmlTextWriter( Request.MapPath( "IceCreamInfo.xml" ),
            System.Text.Encoding.Default );

        Writer.Formatting = Formatting.Indented;

        Writer.WriteStartDocument();

        Writer.WriteStartElement( "info" );
        Writer.WriteStartElement( "entry" );

        Writer.WriteStartElement( "name", "" );
        Writer.WriteString( TextBox1.Text );
        Writer.WriteEndElement();

        Writer.WriteStartElement( "icecream", "" );
        Writer.WriteString( TextBox2.Text );
        Writer.WriteEndElement();

        Writer.WriteStartElement( "topping", "" );
        Writer.WriteString( TextBox3.Text );
        Writer.WriteEndElement();

        Writer.WriteStartElement( "container", "" );
        Writer.WriteString( TextBox4.Text );
        Writer.WriteEndElement();
```

```
        Writer.WriteEndDocument();

        Writer.Close();

        Label1.Text = "Done!";
    }
    catch( Exception ex )
    {
        Label1.Text = ex.Message.ToString();
    }

}
```

VB

```
Public Sub Transform_Click(ByVal sender As System.Object,
  ByVal e As System.EventArgs)

    Try

        Dim Writer As New _
            XmlTextWriter(Request.MapPath("IceCreamInfo.xml"), _
            System.Text.Encoding.Default );

        Writer.Formatting = Formatting.Indented

        Writer.WriteStartDocument()

        Writer.WriteStartElement("info")
        Writer.WriteStartElement("entry")

        Writer.WriteStartElement("name", "")
        Writer.WriteString(TextBox1.Text)
        Writer.WriteEndElement()

        Writer.WriteStartElement("icecream", "")
        Writer.WriteString(TextBox2.Text)
        Writer.WriteEndElement()

        Writer.WriteStartElement("topping", "")
        Writer.WriteString(TextBox3.Text)
        Writer.WriteEndElement()
```

```
Writer.WriteStartElement("container", "")
Writer.WriteString(TextBox4.Text)
Writer.WriteEndElement()

Writer.WriteEndDocument()

Writer.Close()

Label1.Text = "Done!"

Catch ex As Exception ex
    Label1.Text = ex.Message.ToString()
End Try

End Sub
```

The code that renders the XML can be seen in Listing 9.11. An XmlDocument object is created. Then the XmlDocument's `Load()` method is used to load the IcecreamInfo.Xml file. Next, an XslTransform object is created and its `Load()` method is called to load the XSL file. A `DocumentNavigator` class is created, which is used for the transform. Finally, the XslTransform object's `Transform()` method is called to carry out the transform.

Listing 9.11 The Following C# Code Loads the XML File and Does the XSLT Transform.

C#
```
public void Button2_Click(System.Object sender, System.EventArgs e)
{
    Label2.Text = "";

    try
    {
        StringBuilder builder = new StringBuilder("");
        StringWriter writer = new StringWriter(builder);

        XmlDocument doc = new XmlDocument();
        doc.Load( Request.MapPath( "IceCreamInfo.xml" ) );

        XslTransform tr = new XslTransform();
        tr.Load( Request.MapPath( "SimpleTransform.xsl" ) );
```

```csharp
            DocumentNavigator nav = new DocumentNavigator( doc );
            tr.Transform( nav, null, writer );

            for( int i=0; i<builder.Length; i++)
            {
                Label2.Text += builder[i];
            }

        }
    catch( Exception ex )
    {
        Label2.Text = ex.Message.ToString();
    }

}
```

VB

```vb
Public Sub Button2_Click(ByVal sender As System.Object, _
  ByVal e As System.EventArgs)

    Label2.Text = ""

    Try
        Dim builder As New StringBuilder("")
        Dim writer As New StringWriter(builder)

        Dim doc As New XmlDocument()
        doc.Load(Request.MapPath("IceCreamInfo.xml"))

        Dim rs As New XslTransform()
        tr.Load(Request.MapPath("SimpleTransform.xsl"))
        Dim nav As New DocumentNavigator(doc)
        tr.Transform(nav, null, writer)

        Dim i As Integer
        For i = 0 To builder.Length - 1
            Label2.Text += builder(i);
        Next

    Catch ex As Exception
        Label2.Text = ex.Message.ToString()
    End Try

End Sub
```

The combination of XML and XSLT provide you with a very powerful way to render XML data to the output. And beyond that, when you use XSLT, changing the XSLT data and modifying the rendering is extremely simple. Although it might take you some time to get up to speed using XSLT, it will be well worth the effort. For more information on XSLT transforms I suggest you visit www.WebMoney.com.

Writing a Guest Book Application

XML can be used as something more than a means of describing and packaging data. By walking through a fully functional Guest Book application I explain how to combine XML with XSL and ASP.NET to write Web-based applications.

The first impression most developers get after reading about XML is that it sounds great, but that they don't know exactly how it is useful. In this section, I show you how a little XML knowledge combined with ASP.NET and XSL can be used to create a Guest Book application for your Web site.

Guest books are a simple function of most Web sites. Easily broken down into an XML structure by analyzing the type of information you want to record from visitors, XML is very handy when handling information such as the following in a Web site:

- Visitor's name
- Visitor's e-mail address
- Visitor's home page
- Visitor's country
- Message

It's also important to record the time and date that the message was left in the guest book. You can take advantage of ASP.NET to get the "real" server time and record this information.

A regular XML document to record time and date could be this:

```
<guestbook>
  <entry date="03/11/00 00:03:53">
    <name>Rick Leinecker</name>
    <email>rick@there.now</email>
    <homepage>http://www.infinitevision.NET</homepage>
```

```
    <country>US</country>
    <comment>This is the only comment in the Guest Book</comment>
  </entry>
</guestbook>
```

From the example, you can see that I can record all the information under each Entry node in the XML document. This is a simple XML document, and it doesn't really need a document type definition (DTD) to show its structure (or for processing purposes). Guestbook (the document node) can hold many entry nodes, which will eventually make up the entire guest book.

Recording It All

Now that you've seen how I'm going to record the guest book entries in an XML file, it's time to investigate the mechanism that will enable this data to

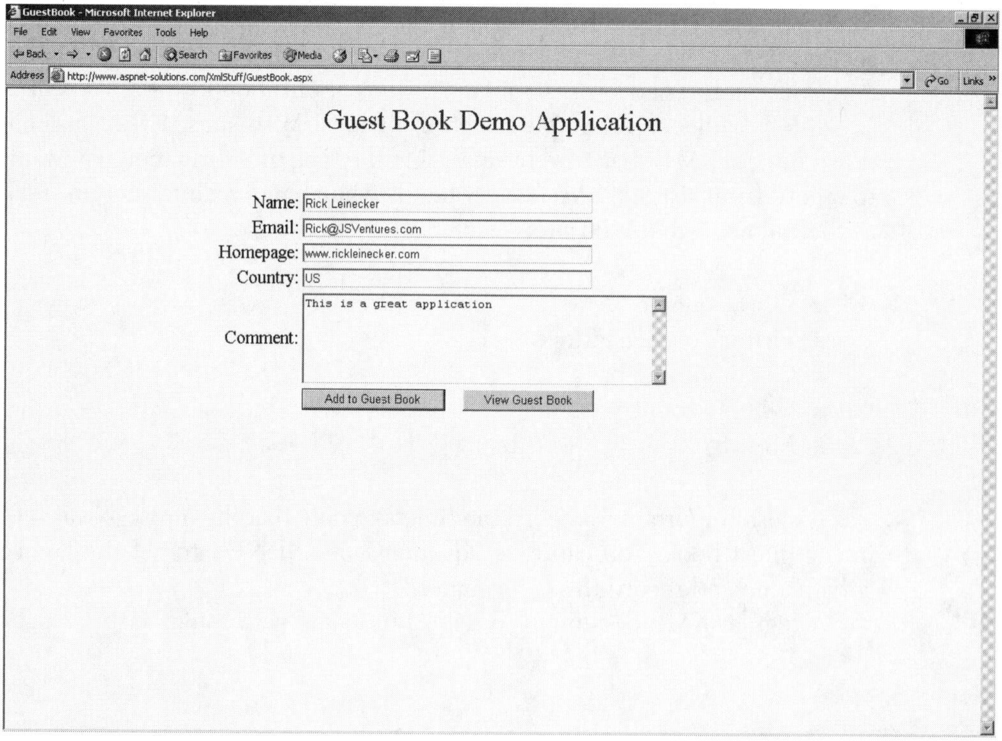

Figure 9.5 This Page Enables the User to Add Entry Information to the Guest Book.

be recorded. Figure 9.5 is a good example of a guest book form where the user inputs information.

The majority of guest books are made of a standard HTML form that posts a CGI script (or in some cases, an ASP.NET page). The example ASP.NET application takes the input from a ASP.NET text box and the controls, and then creates the XML objects on the server.

Follow these steps when you use ASP.NET code to record and store the data by retrieving the information from the user-interface controls:

1. Create an XmlDocument object.
2. Load the current XML document (with the existing entries) into the XmlDocument object.
3. Create an XmlDocumentFragment object.
4. Populate the XmlDocumentFragment object with the text box data that the user entered.
5. Append the XmlDocumentFragment to the document.
6. Save the document.

To retrieve the values from the text box controls, I used the following:

- `Name.Text`
- `Email.Text`
- `Homepage.Text`
- `Country.Text`
- `Comments.Text`

Listing 9.12 shows the ASP.NET code to save the user data. In using this code on your Web site, you should place checks to change any of the recorded data (filter out profanities, hide or "munge" visitor e-mail addresses, and so on).

Listing 9.12 The C# Code That Saves the User Information to the XML File.

C#
```
public void Button1_Click(Object Source, EventArgs e)
{

    try
    {
```

```csharp
XmlDocument doc = new XmlDocument();
doc.Load( Request.MapPath( "gbook.xml" ) );

XmlDocumentFragment newVisitor = doc.CreateDocumentFragment();

newVisitor.InnerXml = "<entry date=\"" +
    DateTime.Now.Format("mm/dd/yyyy hh:mm tt",
      DateTimeFormatInfo.InvariantInfo) + "\">\r\n" +
    "\t<name>" + Name.Text + "</name>\r\n" +
    "\t<email>" + Email.Text + "</email>\r\n" +
    "\t<homepage>" + Homepage.Text + "</homepage>\r\n" +
    "\t<country>" + Country.Text + "</country>\r\n" +
    "\t<comment>" + "<![CDATA[" + Comments.Text +
    "]]></comment>\r\n" +
    "</entry>\r\n";

XmlElement root = doc.DocumentElement;
root.AppendChild( newVisitor );
doc.Save( Request.MapPath( "gbook.xml" ) );

Message.Text = "Done!";

Name.Text = "";
Email.Text = "";
Homepage.Text = "";
Country.Text = "";
Comments.Text = "";
}
catch( Exception ex )
{
    Message.Text = ex.Message.ToString();
}

}
```

VB

```vb
Public Sub Button1_Click(ByVal Source As Object, ByVal e As EventArgs)

    Try

        Dim doc As New XmlDocument()
        doc.Load(Request.MapPath("gbook.xml"))
```

```
    Dim newVisitor As XmlDocumentFragment  = _
      doc.CreateDocumentFragment()

    newVisitor.InnerXml = "<entry date=\"" + _
        DateTime.Now.Format("mm/dd/yyyy hh:mm tt", _
          DateTimeFormatInfo.InvariantInfo) + "\">\r\n" + _
        "\t<name>" + Name.Text + "</name>\r\n" + _
        "\t<email>" + Email.Text + "</email>\r\n" + _
        "\t<homepage>" + Homepage.Text + "</homepage>\r\n" + _
        "\t<country>" + Country.Text + "</country>\r\n" + _
        "\t<comment>" + "<![CDATA[" + Comments.Text + _
        "]]></comment>\r\n" + _
        "</entry>\r\n"

    Dim root As XmlElement = doc.DocumentElement
    root.AppendChild(newVisitor)
    doc.Save(Request.MapPath("gbook.xml"))

    Message.Text = "Done!"

    Name.Text = ""
    Email.Text = ""
    Homepage.Text = ""
    Country.Text = ""
    Comments.Text = ""

  Catch ex As Exception
    Message.Text = ex.Message.ToString()
  End Sub

End Try
```

I have now recorded the visitor information and message inside an XML document stored on the Web server.

Displaying the Guest Book Entries

In the future, all Internet browsers will let us view XML and process it using XSL on the client browser. Right now, though, Internet Explorer 5.0 and above are the only browsers that will do this. You have to process the

XML on the server and convert its contents to HTML so that visitors can view the guest book.

Using the `XslTransform` class, I need to transform the `XmlDocument` class to process the XML file.

When users visit this example application, they first see one main page. For convenience, I have added a button that enables them to go to the page where the guest book can be viewed. I actually could have placed all the `view` code in this page, but then I would have had that code in two different pages. So, instead, I redirect users who click this button to the view page, as shown in the following code:

C#
```
public void Button2_Click(Object Source, EventArgs e)
{

    Response.Redirect( "WebForm6.aspx" );

}
```

VB
```
Public Sub Button2_Click(ByVal source As Object, _
  ByVal e As EventArgs)

    Response.Redirect("WebForm6.aspx")

End Sub
```

The .aspx code that can be found in the page where users go to view the text book is very simple. It is some simple HTML with one additional line. That additional line makes a call to the `LoadAndRender()` method, and the `load` and `render` do everything necessary to render the guest book to the display. Now this is a perfect example in which code is separated from the actual HTML. This is one of the strong points that ASP.NET brings to the table. The capability to separate code from HTML is something that is long overdue and will be an asset for developers.

```
<%@ Page language="c#" Codebehind="WebForm6.cs" AutoEventWireup="false"
  Inherits="XmlExamples.WebForm6" %>

<html>
  <head>
```

```
    <meta name="GENERATOR" Content="Microsoft Visual Studio 7.0">
    <meta name="CODE_LANGUAGE" Content="C#">
  </head>
  <body>

<% LoadAndRender(); %>

  </body>
</html>
```

You can see the application displayed in the guest book in Figure 9.6. It loads in the XML document and does an XSLT transform.

The rendering is done in the `LoadAndRender()` method. This method creates an XmlDocument object, loads the XML data into the XmlDocument object, creates an XslTransform object, loads the XSL file, and

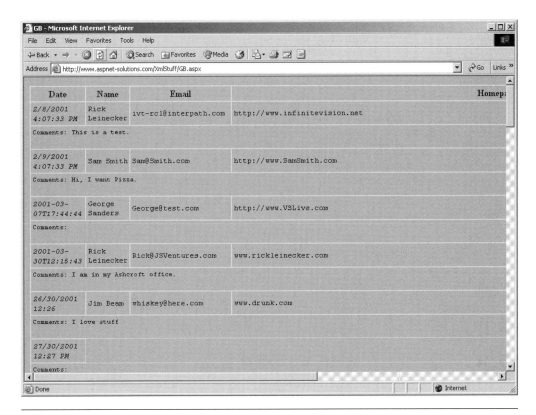

Figure 9.6 An XSL Transform Is Used to Display the Guest Book.

then does the transform. One thing you should look at is the XslTransform object's `Transform()` method. The third argument passed to this method is `Response.Output`. This causes the transform output to go directly to the HTTP stream if you specify `Response.Output` as the destination.

C#
```csharp
public void LoadAndRender()
{
    try
    {
        m_strText = "";

        XmlDocument doc = new XmlDocument();
        doc.Load( Request.MapPath( "gbook.xml" ) );

        XslTransform tr = new XslTransform();
        tr.Load( Request.MapPath( "gbook.xsl" ) );
        DocumentNavigator nav = new DocumentNavigator( doc );
        tr.Transform( nav, null, Response.Output );

    }
    catch( Exception ex )
    {
        Response.Write( ex.Message.ToString() );
    }

}
```

VB
```vb
Public Sub LoadAndRender()

    Try

        m_strText = ""

        Dim doc As New XmlDocument()
        doc.Load(Request.MapPath("gbook.xml"))

        Dim tr As New XslTransform()
        tr.Load(Request.MapPath("gbook.xsl"))
        Dim nav As New DocumentNavigator(doc)
        tr.Transform(nav, null, Response.Output)
```

```
Catch ex As Exception
    Response.Write( ex.Message.ToString() )
End Try

End Sub
```

Summary

I hope that you can take this Guest Book application and use it on your Web site. It works fairly well and can easily be modified to suit your needs. Working through this process will teach you a great deal about using XML and XSLT transforms in your applications. When you do use this, whether or not you modify it, It would be great to see what you have done. Please e-mail me at Rick@jsventures.com and let me know that you have used it so that I can take a look at what you've done.

In this chapter, you've learned how to use the `XmlReader`- and `Xml-Writer`-derived classes. We've created two applications that use them, and we show how to best put them into use. These two applications can easily be used on your own Web site.

CHAPTER 10

Dynamic Charts and Graphs

In This Chapter:

- Dynamic Images
- Getting Started with Dynamic Images in ASP.NET
- The `Graph2D` Class
- Using the `Graph2D` Class
- Enhancing the `Graph2D` Class

Over the years, I've written a lot of software that saves statistical information to a database. Right now I'm maintaining some Internet filtering software, and the recorded statistics are an essential part of the application. There's one catch, though. Staff from the human resource department are the ones who need to see the statistics. There is a wide chasm between what technical types, such as network administrators, and the human resources staff can tolerate in terms of document formats. Text-based reports, lists of URLs, and data without explicit relationships just don't cut it outside the realm of IT professionals.

For this reason, I created a graphical reporting class with which I can easily display two-dimensional data. I hear some of you right now: "Why not use Crystal Reports since it's already a part of Visual Studio .NET, and you don't have to create your own class?" Good question. In fact, using Crystal Reports is how I started out.

The version of Crystal Reports I used had a lot of bugs. By the time you read this they should be fixed (I hope). In addition, I didn't have as much control as I wanted. I was constantly asking, "How can I make this look and act exactly as I want it to?" My challenge was kind of like using the data-bound controls—they are easy to use and flexible, but it seems like you have to work really hard to do something that's outside the box.

Another thing about Crystal Reports is that you must pay a licensing fee to distribute it. Depending on your situation, the licensing fee might price you out of the market.

With my graphing class, I was able to provide exactly what the human resource types wanted—understandable graphs that clearly depict the relevant information. The graphical reporting class relies on GDI+ (the latest rendition of Microsoft's Graphics Device Interface) to render the data into an image. Using GDI+ to create dynamic images is presented in the next section.

Dynamic Images

This section will teach you how to create dynamic images that you can use in your ASP.NET applications. Graphics and imaging are an area that I have found most developers to be somewhat lacking in. I am not really sure why this is; probably because most developers end up creating database applications, or applications with complicated user interfaces. When I started programming in the early '80s, the user-interface elements that are so common today did not exist. So that meant that you had to draw your own objects.

With that said, though, you still need to ask yourself why you would want to create dynamic images for your ASP.NET applications. After all, we have the modern user-interface objects. And there is DHTML, which offers many of the graphical techniques that you might desire. But DHTML is not the panacea it is claimed to be. Different browsers respond in different ways, and even different browser versions respond in different ways. In fact, a good piece of DHTML code will not work at all on some browsers. I was sitting next to a friend of mine at the Authors' Summit that Microsoft invited us to in the summer of 2000. When speakers started talking about the GDI+ technology and what you could do with it in an ASP.NET, my friend turned to me and said, "Why would I need that? DHTML does everything they are talking about." Well, the fact is, DHTML doesn't do everything that GDI+ does, and GDI+ doesn't rely on a browser version to work correctly.

So what types of things could you do with dynamic images? Well, there are some marvelous answers to that question. You can create charts and graphs to display data that users might want to see, as I've done for this chapter's application. For instance, if you are tracking a certain stock, you can easily represent its movement with a graphical chart that is generated on demand. And this generated chart will reflect the current information about that particular stock, such as its current price, its PE (performance evaluation), and its high and low. This graphic representation gives users a much more pleasant experience than just seeing a bunch of numbers in some sort of table. People would almost always rather see something represented graphically than in a text-based table.

Besides applications that depict charts and graphs, you can envision a raft of scientific applications. These applications might show astronomical data in the form of charts, they might show star charts for the evening, they might show weather maps, or they might show some sort of engineering model. There is almost no end to what kinds of scientific and engineering applications you could create if you could dynamically generate images from a Web-based application.

Some of you at this moment are saying, "Well, I have been doing this for years. I have an ASP-based application that dynamically generates images." And I could say the same thing, because I have an application on www.ekid-place.com that allows users to create certificates online. The certificates are generated using some COM objects on the server end that takes the user's input and creates the resulting certificate image. I also have an interesting interactive application on the same Web site that lets users create graffiti-like images. These images are then dynamically rendered on the server side, saved to disk, and indexed in a database. The entire application is fairly complicated, but it illustrates that even without ASP.NET and GDI+, you can dynamically create images in a server-side ASP application. But to do both of those applications I just described took a lot of work. I had to do all the imaging myself, I had to write, test, and debug the COM objects, and then I had to work out a lot of details along the way. ASP.NET with its GDI+ components makes the entire process much easier. And that is what this chapter will talk about—how to use these ASP.NET features to quickly and effectively create applications with dynamic images.

Getting Started with Dynamic Images in ASP.NET

Before you can create any images or use any graphics commands, you need to decide what you will be drawing to. In a stand-alone application, you will draw to the one of the application's windows. Those of you who have been doing Windows programming for a while now, either in VB or C++, will be familiar with the notion of a device context. A **device context** is a Windows object that describes a device to which you will draw. The device might be a window, a printer, a disk file, or any other item that is suitable for drawing.

Because your ASP.NET application will not have a window in the classic sense to which it can draw, you will have to create some other object to which you will draw. In this chapter, we will be using bitmaps, and these bitmaps are encapsulated in a `Bitmap` class. So all of the code samples in this chapter will begin by creating an object to which we will draw that will be a Bitmap object. Actually it would be more correct to refer to this as a **surface**. This is a similar concept to the DirectX notion, in which all operations in DirectX are done to a surface. So for the rest of this chapter, I won't refer to a device context, but rather I will refer to either a Bitmap or a surface as the destination for all of our drawing operations.

A number of Bitmap object constructors are available to you. But in this chapter I will use the constructor that accepts a width and a height, each as integers, and pixel format argument; and a constructor that accepts a file name and loads an image from a disk file. A **pixel format argument** is an enumeration that can be seen in Table 10.1.

The follow code fragment creates a Bitmap object that is 300 pixels wide and 200 pixels high. It specifies a format of 24 bits per pixel (BPP) in an RGB color space. I tend to use 24-bit images because most JPEG images are 24 BPP. When I generate dynamic images using 24 BPP, I usually get a more accurate rendering when I compare the created Bitmap object to saved JPEG images.

Table 10.1 The PixelFormat Enumeration

Name	Description
Alpha	The pixel data contains alpha values that are not premultiplied.
DontCare	No pixel format is specified.
Format16bppArgb1555	The pixel format is 16 bits per pixel. The color information specifies 32,768 shades of color, of which 5 bits are red, 5 bits are green, 5 bits are blue, and 1 bit is alpha.
Format16bppGrayScale	The pixel format is 16 bits per pixel. The color information specifies 65,536 shades of gray.
Format16bppRgb555	The pixel format is 16 bits per pixel. The color information specifies 32,768 shades of color, of which 5 bits are red, 5 bits are green, and 5 bits are blue.
Format16bppRgb565	The pixel format is 16 bits per pixel. The color information specifies 32,768 shades of color, of which 5 bits are red, 6 bits are green, and 5 bits are blue.

Table 10.1 The PixelFormat Enumeration (*cont.*)

Name	Description
Format24bppRgb	The pixel format is 24 bits per pixel. The color information specifies 16,777,216 shades of color, of which 8 bits are red, 8 bits are green, and 8 bits are blue.
Format32bppArgb	The pixel format is 32 bits per pixel. The color information specifies 16,777,216 shades of color, of which 8 bits are red, 8 bits are green, and 8 bits are blue. The 8 additional bits are alpha bits.
Format32bppPArgb	The pixel format is 32 bits per pixel. The color information specifies 16,777,216 shades of color, of which 8 bits are red, 8 bits are green, and 8 bits are blue. The 8 additional bits are premultiplied alpha bits.
Format32bppRgb	The pixel format is 32 bits per pixel. The color information specifies 16,777,216 shades of color, of which 8 bits are red, 8 bits are green, and 8 bits are blue. The remaining 8 bits are not used.
Format48bppRgb	The pixel format is 48 bits per pixel. The color information specifies 16,777,216 shades of color, of which 8 bits are red, 8 bits are green, and 8 bits are blue. The 8 additional bits are alpha bits. The remaining 8 bits are not used.
Format64bppArgb	The pixel format is 64 bits per pixel. The color information specifies 281,474,976,710,656 shades of color, of which 16 bits are red, 16 bits are green, and 16 bits are blue. The 16 additional bits are alpha bits.
Format64bppPArgb	The pixel format is 64 bits per pixel. The color information specifies 281,474,976,710,656 shades of color, of which 16 bits are red, 16 bits are green, and 16 bits are blue. The 16 additional bits are premultiplied alpha bits.
GDI	The pixel data contains GDI colors.
Indexed	The pixel data contains color-indexed values, which means the values are an index to colors in the system color table, as opposed to individual color values.
Max	The maximum value for this enumeration.
PAlpha	The pixel format contains premultiplied alpha values.
Undefined	The pixel format is undefined.

C#

```
Bitmap newBitmap = new Bitmap( 300, 200, PixelFormat.Format24bppRgb );
```

VB

```
Dim newBitmap As New Bitmap(300, 200, PixelFormat.Format32bppRgb)
```

Once you have created a Bitmap object you then need to obtain a Graphics object that references that Bitmap object. This is similar to getting a device context in Visual Basic or Visual C++ programming. And it is almost identical to what you do in Java. In Java, you have an object named exactly the same thing, Graphics. In Java, you make a method call to get-Graphics(), and then you use the Graphics object for all draw operations. In ASP.NET, for a Bitmap object as we have created, you use the static FromImage() method. The FromImage() method takes as an argument that is our Bitmap object to which we want to draw, and returns a Graphics object, which references the Bitmap object. We use this Graphics object then for all our subsequent drawing operations. You can see in the next line how we have obtained a Graphics object from our newly created Bitmap object.

C#

```
Graphics g = Graphics.FromImage( newBitmap );
```

VB

```
Dim g As Graphics = Graphics.FromImage(newBitmap)
```

It is time now to create an example application. This example is written in VB, creates a Bitmap object that is 300 pixels wide and 200 pixels high, and draws four rectangles to the Bitmap object. This Bitmap object is then displayed in a browser window.

I need to spend a short time now talking about pens and brushes. You cannot simply select a color, make some sort of call to the graphics API, and have your draw operation be performed in that color. To draw a line or a line-related object in a certain color, you must create a Pen object. Pen objects are created with attributes such as a specified color, a width, and a style (such as dotted, dashed, or other). Then, when you draw a line, you use a Pen object that you have created to let GDI+ know how to draw the line. For instance, if you want to draw a solid red line, you would first create a pen and specify that it would be red and the style would be solid. You would then call the Graphics object's DrawLine() method and specify your newly created line. The following code shows how to create a red pen and then draw a line using this newly created red pen:

C#
```
Pen pen = new Pen( Color.Red );
// Draw a line from the x,y point 10,14 to the point 100,225
g.DrawLine( pen, 10, 14, 100, 225 );
// Or the following if you prefer...
g.DrawLine( pen, new Point( 10, 14 ), new Point( 100, 225 ) );
```

VB
```
Dim pen as new Pen( Color.Red )
' Draw a line from the x,y point 10,14 to the point 100,225
g.DrawLine( pen, 10, 14, 100, 225 )
' Or the following if you prefer...
g.DrawLine( pen, New Point( 10, 14 ), New Point( 100, 225 ) )
```

The same idea holds true if you want to draw shapes that are solid in nature, such as a filled rectangle or a filled ellipse. Instead of a Pen, though, you must create a SolidBrush, and the SolidBrush will indicate the color with which you want to draw. The following example shows how to create a SolidBrush and draw a rectangle with it:

C#
```
SolidBrush blueBrush = new SolidBrush( Color.Blue );
// Draw a filled rectangle that starts at the x,y coordinate 0,0
//   that is 150 pixels wide and 100 pixels high.
g.FillRectangle( blueBrush, 0, 0, 150, 100 );
```

VB
```
Dim blueBrush as new SolidBrush( Color.Blue )
' Draw a filled rectangle that starts at the x,y coordinate 0,0
'   that is 150 pixels wide and 100 pixels high.
g.FillRectangle( blueBrush, 0, 0, 150, 100 )
```

And now, let's complete our discussion of creating simple Bitmap objects, obtaining a Graphics object, and then drawing to the Graphics object. Take a look at the application in Figure 10.1. This application draws four rectangles to a created Bitmap object, and then sends the Bitmap object out to the browser or display. The source code for the creation of the Bitmap object can be seen in Listing 10.1.

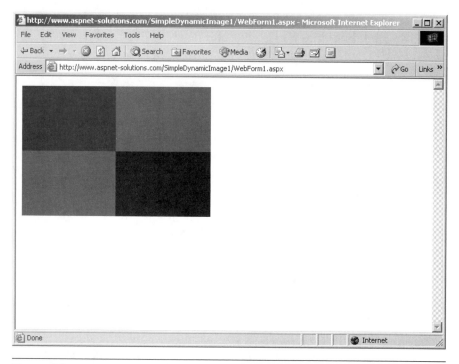

Figure 10.1 This Simple Application Creates a Bitmap, and Then Draws Four Rectangles.

Listing 10.1 Simple Code That Creates and Draws to a Bitmap Object.

```
Dim newBitmap As New Bitmap(300, 200, PixelFormat.Format24bppRgb)
Dim g As Graphics = Graphics.FromImage(newBitmap)

Dim blueBrush As New SolidBrush(Color.Blue)
Dim redBrush As New SolidBrush(Color.Red)
Dim greenBrush As New SolidBrush(Color.Green)
Dim blackBrush As New SolidBrush(Color.Black)

g.FillRectangle(blueBrush, 0, 0, 150, 100)
g.FillRectangle(redBrush, 150, 0, 150, 100)
g.FillRectangle(greenBrush, 0, 100, 150, 100)
g.FillRectangle(blackBrush, 150, 100, 150, 100)

newBitmap.Save(Response.OutputStream, ImageFormat.Jpeg)
```

I need to make several comments about the preceding code, and, more specifically, about the call to the `Save()` method in the last line in Listing 10.1. The first thing you need to notice is that I sent the image to the Response object. The result of this will be to simply send the image bits directly to the browser, without saving or loading them to and from disk. The only thing that the browser will get will be the image bits; it will get no HTML. It will be just as if you loaded an image in your browser outside the context of HTML. I also point out that I used this code inside of the `Web-form` class's `Page_Load()` method. If I had created a method such as a `DrawBitmap()` method, and then called it somewhere within the HTML creation process, it would have output what looked like garbage into the HTML stream, as shown in Figure 10.2.

The code in Listing 10.1 could be simplified somewhat. The following two lines create a blue brush and draw a rectangle:

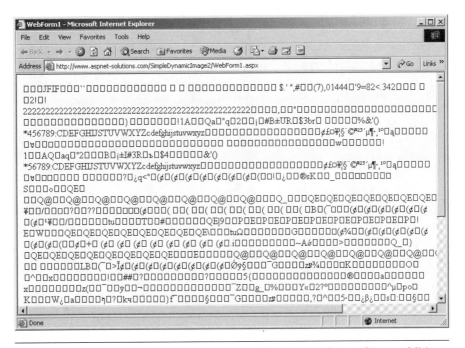

Figure 10.2 Here the Image Was Output to Response.OutputStream Midway into the HTML Rendering Process.

C#
```
SolidBrush blueBrush = new SolidBrush( Color.Blue );
g.FillRectangle( blueBrush, 0, 0, 150, 100 );
```

VB
```
Dim blueBrush As New SolidBrush(Color.Blue)
g.FillRectangle(blueBrush, 0, 0, 150, 100)
```

A shorter (and possibly more understandable) way to write equivalent code is this:

C#
```
g.FillRectangle( new SolidBrush( Color.Blue ), 0, 0, 150, 100 );
```

VB
```
g.FillRectangle(New SolidBrush(Color.Blue), 0, 0, 150, 100)
```

This abbreviation works well if you're only going to use the blue brush once. If, however, you're going to use it more than once, there's no reason to continually create blue brushes with the new operator because doing so will put more pressure on the server's CPU and memory resources.

RECOMMENDED PRACTICE: If you intend to use a GDI+ object more than once, the following code is not efficient because a new brush is created for each FillRectangle() method:

C#
```
g.FillRectangle( new SolidBrush( Color.Blue ), 0, 0, 150, 100 );
g.FillRectangle( new SolidBrush( Color.Blue ), 101, 0, 150, 100 );
g.FillRectangle( new SolidBrush( Color.Blue ), 201, 0, 150, 100 );
g.FillRectangle( new SolidBrush( Color.Blue ), 301, 0, 150, 100 );
```

VB
```
g.FillRectangle(New SolidBrush(Color.Blue), 0, 0, 150, 100)
g.FillRectangle(New SolidBrush(Color.Blue), 101, 0, 150, 200)
g.FillRectangle(New SolidBrush(Color.Blue), 201, 0, 150, 300)
g.FillRectangle(New SolidBrush(Color.Blue), 301, 0, 150, 400)
```

Consider changing the code so that a blue brush is created only once, as follows:

C#
```
SolidBrush blueBrush = new SolidBrush( Color.Blue );
g.FillRectangle( blueBrush, 0, 0, 150, 100 );
```

```
g.FillRectangle( blueBrush, 101, 0, 150, 100 );
g.FillRectangle( blueBrush , 201, 0, 150, 100 );
g.FillRectangle( blueBrush, 301, 0, 150, 100 );
```

VB
```
Dim blueBrush As New SolidBrush(Color.Blue)
g.FillRectangle(blueBrush, 0, 0, 150, 100)
g.FillRectangle(blueBrush, 101, 0, 150, 200)
g.FillRectangle(blueBrush, 201, 0, 150, 300)
g.FillRectangle(blueBrush, 301, 0, 150, 400)
```

On a 700MHz machine, the first code was executed 10,000 times in 4.3696 seconds, while the second code was executed 10,000 times in 3.785 seconds.

Another thing I want to point out is the image-format enumerator that was used in the `Save()` method. The image-format enumerator gives you the capability to save your image in a variety of formats, including BMP, GIF, JPEG, PNG, and TIFF, among others. Table 10.2 lists the formats that are available to you in the image format enumerator.

RECOMMENDED PRACTICE: You must be careful when you choose an image format for your save operations. Different formats will give you different results. For instance, JPEG files are great for photographic images, but they are not very good when your images are sharp and crisp. If your images

Table 10.2 The ImageFormat Enumerations.

Identifier	Description
Bmp	Specifies the bitmap image format (BMP).
Emf	Specifies the enhanced Windows metafile image format (EMF).
Exif	Specifies the Exchangeable Image Format (EXIF).
Gif	Specifies the Graphics Interchange Format (GIF) image format.
Icon	Specifies the Windows icon image format.
Jpeg	Specifies the Joint Photographic Experts Group (JPEG) image format.
MemoryBmp	Specifies a memory bitmap image format.
Png	Specifies the W3C Portable Network Graphics (PNG) image format.
Tiff	Specifies the Tag Image File Format (TIFF) image format.
Wmf	Specifies the Windows metafile (WMF) image format.

are sharp and crisp and you save in the JPEG format, you will notice unexplainable artifacts that make the image look less than perfect. GIF images are very good when the desired rendering must be sharp and crisp. But GIF is limited to colors with an 8-bit pixel depth, which limits you to a total of 256 colors in a given image. What that means is that if you have drawn to a Bitmap object in a color that is not available in a saved GIF image, those colors will be mapped in a way that may be somewhat undesirable. For instance, if you draw a color in a shade of green that cannot be found in the standard GIF file-format palette, then your green color will be dithered in a way that most closely approximates the color with which you drew. But it won't look like what you had originally drawn or had expected it to look.

So if your image is counting on some specific colors that are not a part of the standard GIF palette, then you need to consider using JPEG. Alternatively, if your image needs to be crisp and sharp, then you must select GIF. The decision is not always an easy one because you might want some of the benefits that each format has to offer.

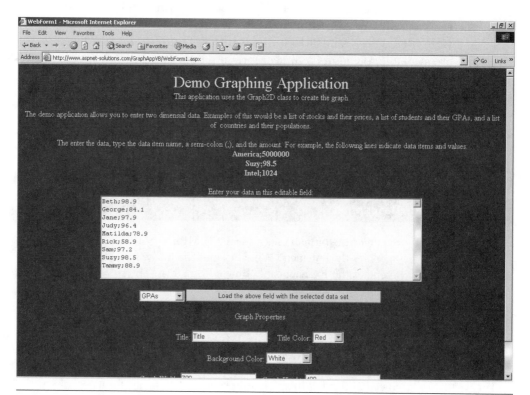

Figure 10.3 The Application Allows You to Enter Data That Will Then Be Rendered Graphically.

As you can see from reading this section, creating and saving images dynamically is an easy process with the .NET framework. ASP.NET applications can easily use the base classes to create images that will enhance the user's experience.

The `Graph2D` Class

The class that I created to encapsulate the graphing methodology is called `Graph2D`. Three steps are required to use the `Graph2D` class: instantiate the class, add data, and render the graph. The following code snippet shows the bare necessities for creating a graph image that saves to disk. More detail for these methods will be given shortly.

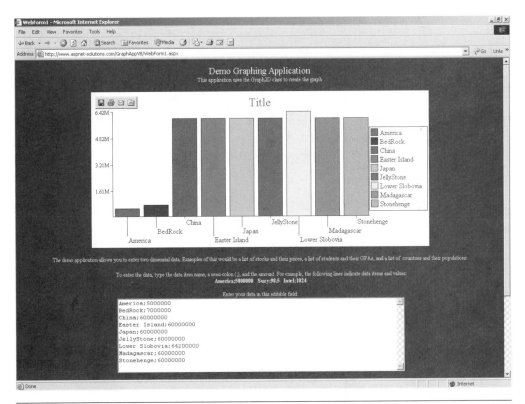

Figure 10.4 The Graph Presents an Easy-to-Understand Depiction of the Data.

C#
```
Graph2D graph = new Graph2D();
String strFilename;
graph.AddPair( "Rick", 50 );
graph.AddPair( "Sam", 60 );
strFilename = graph.Render( Request.MapPath( "" ) );
```

VB
```
Dim graph as new Graph2D()
Dim strFilename as String
graph.AddPair("Rick", 50)
graph.AddPair("Sam", 60)
strFilename = graph.Render(Request.MapPath(""))
```

The presentation code must use the file name that's returned from the Render() method. The file name can either be assigned to an ASP.NET server object, such as the Image or ImageButton objects, or output to the HTML stream with a call to the Response.Write() method.

I've written an application that uses the Graph2D class. The application lets users type in data pairs (column name and value), and then render and display the graph. You can see the text box into which users enter data in Figure 10.3.

Once the user clicks the Render the Graph button, the graph is rendered, saved to disk, and displayed at the top of the page. You can see the rendered graph in Figure 10.4.

Two namespaces must be imported with the Imports (or using for C#) directive. These are the System.Collections.Specialized namespace (for the StringCollection class) and the System.Drawing.Imaging namespace (for the PixelFormat enumerator). The following shows the code that must be added to applications:

C#
```
using System.Collections.Specialized;
using System.Drawing.Imaging;
```

VB
```
Imports System.Collections.Specialized
Imports System.Drawing.Imaging
```

All the methods for the GraphAppVB application and the Graph2D class can be found in Table 10.3. This table lists the method names, the

Table 10.3 The Graph2D Methods

Method Name	Code Module	Listing Number	Description
`AddPair()`	Graph2D.vb	10.3	This method adds data to the lists.
`Render()`	Graph2D.vb	10.4	This method creates a Bitmap object and calls the helper methods, which all together render the graph.
`DrawTitle()`	Graph2D.vb	10.5	This method draws the graph title.
`DrawLegend()`	Graph2D.vb	10.6	This method draws the graph legend.
`DrawBounds()`	Graph2D.vb	10.7	This method draws the bound lines of the graph.
`DrawData()`	Graph2D.vb	10.8	This method draws the data and represents the values as graph bars.
`DrawScale()`	Graph2D.vb	10.9	This method draws the graph scale at the left side of the graph.
`Width()`, `Height()`, `BackgroundColor()`, `TitleColor()`, `TitleSize()`, `Title()`	Graph2D.vb	10.10	These are the property methods for the `Graph2D` class.
`InsertGraphLink()`	WebForm1.aspx.cs	10.11	This method outputs the link for the rendered graph image.
`LoadData_Click()`	WebForm1.aspx.cs	10.12	This method responds to a button click and populates the text box with data.
`RenderGraph()`	WebForm1.aspx.cs	10.13	This method instantiates a `Graph2D` class, sets its properties, and calls its Render() method.

code module in which the methods are contained, the listing number in this chapter, and a short description. This information will help you as you read through the code, and especially when you reference the methods.

Member Variables and Default Values

A number of `Graph2D` member variables all maintain the state of the instantiated object. These variables—such as `m_strTitle` (for the graph title), `m_BackgroundColor` (for the graph background color), and `m_nCategoryCount` (for the count of categories). include information about how the graph will be drawn.

Two very important member variables contain the data: the column name and value. These member variables are `m_DataNames` and `m_dDataValues`. Table 10.4 is a handy reference to the member variables. The table lists the variable type, name, description, and default value. Many of the member variables can be set using the `Graph2D` properties.

Listing 10.2 contains all the code that declares and initializes the `Graph2D` member variables.

Listing 10.2 The `Graph2D` Member Variables and Their Initialization

```
' Global colors with which we'll draw the graph bars.
Dim m_Colors() As Color = { _
    Color.Red, Color.Blue, Color.Green, Color.Magenta, _
    Color.Cyan, Color.Brown, Color.Yellow, Color.OliveDrab, _
    Color.Salmon, Color.Orange, Color.Gray, Color.Indigo, _
    Color.Lime, Color.PaleGoldenrod, Color.SteelBlue, _
    Color.YellowGreen}

' The next two members will contain the data element names and
' values.
Dim m_DataNames As New StringCollection()
Dim m_dDataValues() As Double

' Information with which we'll draw the title.
Dim m_strTitle As String = "Title"
Dim m_TitleColor As Color = Color.Red
Dim m_nTitleSize As Integer = 20
Dim m_strTitleFontFamily As String = "Times New Roman"

' Overall image width and height.
Dim m_nWidth As Integer = 780
Dim m_nHeight As Integer = 400
```

Table 10.4 The `Graph2D` Member Variables

Type	Name	Description	Default
`Color()`	`m_Colors`	This array determines the colors with which the rectangles will be drawn. There are 16 colors in the array, so the code must ensure that only values from 0 to 15 are used.	As show in Listing 10.3
`String-Collection`	`m_DataNames`	This collection contains the name for each data element.	No default data
`Double()`	`m_dDataValues`	This array contains the actual data values for each element.	No default data
`String`	`m_strTitle`	This is the string that will be used to draw the graph title.	`"Title"`
`Color`	`m_TitleColor`	This is the color with which the title will be drawn.	`Color.Red`
`Integer`	`m_nTitleSize`	This contains the size with which the title font will be created.	20
`String`	`m_strTitle-FontFamily`	This string contains the name of the font family with which the title font will be created.	`"Times New Roman"`
`Integer`	`m_nWidth`	The width of the chart in pixels.	780
`Integer`	`m_nHeight`	The height of the chart in pixels.	400
`Integer`	`m_nLegendX`	The x-position (within the chart) of the left side of the legend.	0
`Integer`	`m_nLegendBox-Width`	The width in pixels of the legend box.	0
`Font`	`m_objLegend-Font`	The Font object that is used to draw legend text.	No default creation
`Pen`	`m_objBlackPen`	A black pen that is used to draw lines in the graph.	`New Pen (Color.Black)`
`SolidBrush`	`m_objBlack-Brush`	A black brush that is used to draw rectangles in the graph.	`New Solid-Brush(Color.Black)`
`Color`	`m_Background-Color`	The background color for the graph.	`Color.White`
`Integer`	`m_nCategory-Count`	The number of categories (or bars) in the chart.	0
`Double`	`m_dMaxValue`	The greatest (maximum) value of all elements in the m_Data-Values array.	0

```
' Information about the legend position and size.
Dim m_nLegendX As Integer = 0
Dim m_nLegendBoxWidth As Integer = 0
Dim m_objLegendFont As Font
Dim m_nLegendTextHeight As Integer = 0

' Black pen and brush for use throughtout.
Dim m_objBlackPen As New Pen(Color.Black)
Dim m_objBlackBrush As New SolidBrush(Color.Black)

' The default background color.
Dim m_BackgroundColor As Color = Color.White

' Number of categories and maximum data value;
Dim m_nCategoryCount As Integer = 0
Dim m_dMaxValue As Double = 0
```

Adding Data

No graph in the world is any good without data. While designing the class, I went through several ideas, most of which provided a `DataSource` property and a `DataBind()` method, as do many of the databound controls. This combination was convenient in many cases, but it didn't offer the flexibility I wanted. For that reason, I elected to simply provide a method with which calling code can add data pairs one at a time.

The `AddPair()` method shown in Listing 10.3 takes two arguments: the element name as a string and the element value as a double. The element name is placed into the m_DataNames StringCollection object, while the element value is placed into the m_dDataValues double array.

It's easy to add a string to the StringCollection object with an `Add()` method that adds a string to the collection. The array of doubles, however, is another matter. In the `AddPair()` method, a new array of the correct size is created, its members are initialized to the values currently in the m_dDataValues array, the new value is set in the last array element, and the m_dDataValues variable is set to the newly created array.

Listing 10.3 The `AddPair()` Method Adds Data to the Lists.

```
' Add a pair: element name and value.
Public Function AddPair(ByVal strDataName As String, _
  ByVal dDataValue As Double)
```

```
    m_DataNames.Add(strDataName)
    m_nCategoryCount = m_nCategoryCount + 1
    Dim dDataValues(m_DataNames.Count) As Double
    m_DataNames.CopyTo(dDataValues, 0)
    dDataValues(m_DataNames.Count - 1) = dDataValue
    m_dDataValues = dDataValues
End Function
```

Rendering

The Render() method creates a Bitmap object, and then calls the Draw-Title(), DrawLegend(), DrawBounds(), DrawData(), and DrawScale() helper functions. The last thing this method does is to save the image to disk. This section breaks the Render() method down and describes it in detail.

Creating the Bitmap

The Render() method shown in Listing 10.4 is called once the data has been added to the Graph2D class and any properties have been set. The method expects a single string argument that contains the path into which the image will be saved. For the image to be saved, the directory must have the appropriate permissions.

The first thing that happens in the Render() method is that a file name is created based on the current clock ticks. This is an easy way to create a unique file name. However, for high-volume use, you should use an Application variable to absolutely guarantee a unique number. I show the change that you'd have to make using the Application variable in the section entitled "Enhancing the Graph2D Class."

CAUTION: The directory into which the rendered graph is to be saved must have the necessary permissions so that the image can be written to disk. Consult with your network administrator, but, if possible, you should give full control for the IUSR_SERVER and IWAM_SERVER accounts. You must at a minimum have read and write permissions.

A Bitmap object is created with the width and height that are contained in the m_nWidth and m_nHeight variables. A Graphics object is obtained from the Bitmap object using the Graphics.FromImage()

method. The Bitmap object is set to the background color (found in m_BackgroundColor) by drawing a rectangle.

Last, the five helper methods are called, the image is saved to disk, and the file name is returned to the calling code.

Listing 10.4 The Render() Method Creates a Bitmap and Then Calls the Helper Methods, Which All Together Render the Graph.

```
' This method renders the graph to a disk file. It requires the path
'   to the directory into which the file will be saved such as
'   c:\inetpub\project\images It is also required that the directory
'   grants write rights to the asp.net process.
Public Function Render(ByVal strSavePath As String)
      ' The image name is based on the system ticks. For high volume
      '   use, ensure this is unique with an Application variable.
      Dim strName As String = Convert.ToString(DateTime.Now.Ticks)

      ' Create the canvas bitmap, get a Graphics object, and
      '   initialize to the default background color.
      Dim objBitmap As New Bitmap(m_nWidth, m_nHeight, _
        PixelFormat.Format24bppRgb)
      Dim g As Graphics = Graphics.FromImage(objBitmap)
      g.FillRectangle(New SolidBrush(m_BackgroundColor), 0, 0, _
        m_nWidth, m_nHeight)

      ' Call helper methods to draw the title, legend, bounding lines,
      '   data, and scale.
      DrawTitle(g)
      DrawLegend(g)
      DrawBounds(g)
      DrawData(g)
      DrawScale(g)

      ' Save the image to disk.
      objBitmap.Save(strSavePath + "\\GraphImages\\Graph" + _
        strName + ".gif", ImageFormat.Gif)

      ' Return the image name.
      Return (strName)
End Function
```

Drawing the Title

Drawing the title on the graph could be as easy as making a call to the DrawString() method at the upper-left corner of the bitmap. The result wouldn't look very nice, though; what we really need to do is center the title at the top of the graph.

Conceptually, the process is simple, but I have never taught a class in which a significant percentage of the students didn't have trouble understanding. Here's my best description of the conceptual processes.

Find the midpoint of the graph along the x-axis. This can be found in the Graph2D class with the expression m_nWidth / 2. Now you must find out how many pixels wide the title text is. A method named MeasureString() returns a SizeF object, in which the width and height of a text string is contained. Once you have the width of the string, you need to calculate half of that width, because that's the x-coordinate at which you'll draw the string. You calculate half of the string width in the DrawTitle() method with the expression sz.Width / 2. Figure 10.5 shows the calculations graphically.

Listing 10.5 The DrawTitle() Method Draws the Graph Title.

```
' Draw the graph title.
Private Sub DrawTitle(ByVal g As Graphics)
    Dim objTitleFont As New Font(m_strTitleFontFamily, m_nTitleSize)
    Dim sz As SizeF = g.MeasureString(m_strTitle, objTitleFont)

    Dim x As Integer = (m_nWidth / 2) - (sz.Width / 2)
    Dim y As Integer = 10
```

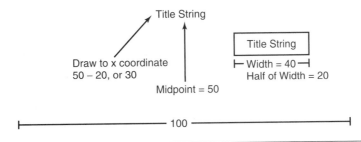

Figure 10.5 This Figure Shows How the Calculations Allow a String to Be Centered.

```
    g.DrawString(m_strTitle, objTitleFont, _
        New SolidBrush(m_TitleColor), x, y)
End Sub
```

Drawing the Legend

The graph legend is drawn at the right side of the graph. For each data column, a color box indicates the color with which that column was drawn. This detail helps users identify the data and what it represents. The method that draws the legend is named `DrawLegend()` and can be found in Listing 10.6.

The first thing that happens in this method is that a Font object is created with which the legend text will be drawn. The size will be 12 points unless there are 20 data items or more, in which case the size will be 9 points. This option lets the legend adjust for a lot of entries by making the font size smaller.

It's important to find out how long the longest string is (that is, how many pixels wide). We can't really draw the box around the legend area until we know how big the box must be. And we don't know how big the box must be until we know how wide the widest string is. Similarly to what we did in the `DrawTitle()` method (Listing 10.5), we use the `MeasureString()` method to get the pixel width of each string. The widest string is recorded in the `nLegendTextWidth` variable, and the string height is recorded in the `m_nLegendTextHeight` variable.

With the widest string width, we calculate the legend box width by adding 16 pixels and 8 pixels: 16 pixels for the colored rectangles and 8 pixels for some padding space. We also check to make sure there's a minimum size.

With the legend box width and height, we next calculate the x- and y-coordinates to which the legend box rectangle will be drawn. The legend box values are recorded in some member variables because the size and position of the legend box will affect how other things on the graph are drawn.

A simple loop goes through each category. A filled rectangle is drawn and then outlined in black, and the text string with the column name is drawn to the left of the rectangles.

Listing 10.6 The `DrawLegend()` Method Draws the Graph Legend and Stores Its Position so That the Rest of the Graph Can Be Correctly Drawn.

```
' Draw the graph legend.
Private Sub DrawLegend(ByVal g As Graphics)
    ' Create the legend font. If there are more than 20 categories,
```

```
' we'll need to make the font smaller.
' "Times New Roman" is contained in m_strFontName by default.
If m_nCategoryCount < 20 Then
        m_objLegendFont = New Font(m_strFontName, 12)
Else
    m_objLegendFont = New Font(m_strFontName, 9)
End If

' Find the max width and for the strings
Dim nLegendTextWidth As Integer = 0
Dim i As Integer
For i = 0 To m_nCategoryCount - 1
    Dim s As SizeF = _
      g.MeasureString(m_DataNames(i), m_objLegendFont)
    If s.Width > nLegendTextWidth Then
        nLegendTextWidth = s.Width
    End If
    If s.Height > m_nLegendTextHeight Then
        m_nLegendTextHeight = s.Height
    End If
Next

' Calculate the width of the legend box. (We add 8 and 16
'    for the margin within the legend (8) and the margin between
'    the legend and the edge of the bitmap (16).)
Dim nLegendBoxWidth As Integer = nLegendTextWidth + 8 + 16

' Make sure the legend text height is at least 16.
If m_nLegendTextHeight < 16 Then
    m_nLegendTextHeight = 16
End If

' Calculate the height of the legend box.
Dim nLegendBoxHeight As Integer = m_nLegendTextHeight
nLegendBoxHeight *= m_nCategoryCount
nLegendBoxHeight += 8

' Calculate the upper left corner of the legend box.
Dim nLegendX As Integer = m_nWidth - nLegendBoxWidth - 4
Dim nLegendY As Integer = (m_nHeight - nLegendBoxHeight) / 2

' Record into a class member the left size of the legend box.
m_nLegendX = nLegendX
m_nLegendBoxWidth = nLegendBoxWidth
```

```
' Draw the legend box.
g.DrawRectangle(New Pen(Color.Black), _
    nLegendX, nLegendY, _
  nLegendBoxWidth, nLegendBoxHeight)

' Draw the category item boxes.
For i = 0 To m_nCategoryCount - 1
    ' Calculate x and y.
    Dim x As Integer = nLegendX + 4
    Dim y As Integer = nLegendY + 4 + i * m_nLegendTextHeight

    ' Draw the colored rectangle.
    g.FillRectangle(New SolidBrush(m_Colors(i And 15)), _
     x, y, _
     16, 16)
    ' Draw a black border.
    g.DrawRectangle(m_objBlackPen, x, y, 16, 16)

    ' Draw the text.
    g.DrawString(m_DataNames(i), _
      m_objLegendFont, m_objBlackBrush, (x + 18), y)

Next

If m_nCategoryCount >= 20 Then
    m_nLegendX -= 20
End If

End Sub
```

Drawing the Bounds

The graph has two lines. One goes along the left side of the data, and the other runs below the data. These two lines help frame the data and make it easier to view. The code in Listing 10.7 shows the DrawBounds() method that draws these two lines.

Listing 10.7 Drawing the Bounding Lines Is Simple, and the Code in the DrawBounds() Method is Short.

```
' Draw the bounding lines (left and bottom).
Private Sub DrawBounds(ByVal g As Graphics)
    Dim nChartBottom As Integer = m_nHeight - 70
```

```
' Draw the left and bottom lines
g.DrawLine(m_objBlackPen, 50, 45, 50, m_nHeight - 70)
g.DrawLine(m_objBlackPen, 50, nChartBottom, _
    m_nLegendX, m_nHeight - 70)
End Sub
```

Drawing the Data

Drawing the data is the main course of the `Graph2D` class. It's the featured element and as such is the most prominent item, appearing in the central portion of the graph. The method that does the work is named `Draw-Data()` and can be seen in Listing 10.8.

The first thing that must be done to draw the data is to find the maximum of all data values. Finding this value is essential because the largest value should occupy the entire vertical distance available. In other words, we'll use the maximum value, and the bar that's drawn for that value will go from the bottom of the graph to the top of the graph. All other data values will then be scaled in the proper proportion.

We then need to know how wide each column should be. To find this information, we simply take the graph width (minus the legend and some other space) and divide by the number of columns.

With the bar width and maximum data values calculated, the code loops through and draws each column. First, the height of the column bar is calculated. Then the x- and y-coordinates where the rectangle will be drawn are calculated.

There might be times when the height of a rectangle is zero. That value would result when a data value is zero, or is very small in comparison with the other data values. No rectangle is drawn when that is the case, and the calculated height of the rectangle is zero. But when the rectangle has a positive height, the rectangle is drawn in the appropriate color and then outlined in black.

The text string that names the column is drawn next. The text is drawn underneath the rectangles, and a line is then drawn connecting the text to the rectangle.

A variable named `nLabelY` is used to draw the text strings at different y values. Doing this prevents the strings from overwriting each other, thus making the graph impossible to read. The `nLabelY` variable is incremented and can have a value ranging from 0 through 2.

Listing 10.8 The `DrawData()` Method Does the Real Work by Calculating and Drawing the Bars That Represent the Data Values.

```
' Draw the data bars.
Private Sub DrawData(ByVal g As Graphics)
    Dim nChartBottom As Integer = m_nHeight - 70

    ' Figure out the max value.
    m_dMaxValue = 0
    Dim nMaxIndex As Integer = 0

    Dim i As Integer
    For i = 0 To m_nCategoryCount - 1
        If m_dMaxValue < m_dDataValues(i) Then
            m_dMaxValue = m_dDataValues(i)
            nMaxIndex = i
        End If
    Next

    ' The legend is always 48, so we pad with 2 pixels
    '    and subtract 50.
    Dim nBarWidth As Integer = _
      ((m_nLegendX - 50) / m_nCategoryCount)
    Dim nLabelY As Integer = 2

    Dim dHeight As Double = m_nHeight
    ' The area above the graph where the title resides plus
    '    the area below the graph where the labels reside is
    '    a total of 115 pixels.
    Dim dHeightForBars As Double = m_nHeight - 115

    For i = 0 To m_nCategoryCount - 1
        Dim nBarHeight As Integer = _
          ((m_dDataValues(i) * _
          ((dHeightForBars / dHeight) * m_nHeight)) / _
          m_dMaxValue)
        ' 55 pixels gives enough room for a space to the left of the
        '    graph plus the graph line.
        Dim x As Integer = 55 + i * nBarWidth
        Dim y As Integer = nChartBottom - nBarHeight

        If nBarHeight > 0 Then
            ' 10 pixels is a pleasing space to have between the bars.
```

```
        g.FillRectangle(New SolidBrush(m_Colors(i And 15)), _
            x, y, nBarWidth - 10, nBarHeight)
        g.DrawRectangle(m_objBlackPen, _
            x, y, nBarWidth - 10, nBarHeight)
    End If


    ' 66 pixels allows the height to be drawn below the graph's
    '    title at the top.
    g.DrawString(m_DataNames(i), _
        m_objLegendFont, m_objBlackBrush, _
        x + (nBarWidth - 10) / 2, _
        m_nHeight - 66 + nLabelY * m_nLegendTextHeight)

    Dim xx As Integer = x + (nBarWidth - 10) / 2


    ' The numbers 66 and 70 were found to give the best
    '    appearance through testing.
    g.DrawLine(m_objBlackPen, _
     xx, m_nHeight - 66 + nLabelY * m_nLegendTextHeight, _
     xx, m_nHeight - 70)

    nLabelY = nLabelY - 1

    If nLabelY < 0 Then
        nLabelY = 2
    End If
    Next
End Sub
```

Drawing the Scale and Saving

To the left side of the graph is the scale. This scale indicates the relative values for the data columns so that users can quickly estimate their values. The code that draws the scale is contained in a method named `DrawScale()` and can be seen in Listing 10.9.

If the data value is from 0 through 999, the value will be displayed as it is. If the value is from 1,000 through 999,999, the value will be displayed in thousands (the original value divided by 1,000) and a `K` symbol will appear to the right of the numeric value. If the value is from 1,000,000 through 999,999,999, then the value will be displayed in millions (the original value divided by 1,000,000) and an `M` symbol will appear to the right of the numeric value. The same principle applies to values in the billions.

An integer variable named nStep contains the calculated height for the three scale marks that will be drawn. The value of this variable is essentially the height of the data divided by four.

A loop counts from 0 to 3 and draws the scale marks and values.

Listing 10.9 The DrawScale() Method Makes It Easy for the User to Understand the Relative Values.

```
' Draw the scale to the left.
Private Sub DrawScale(ByVal g As Graphics)
    Dim dDivisor As Double = 1
    Dim strModifier As String = ""
    Const dBillions As double = 1000000000
    Const dMillions As double = 1000000
    Const dThousands As double = 1000

    ' Billions...
    If m_dMaxValue >= dBillions Then
        strModifier = "B"
        If m_dMaxValue >= dBillions Then
            dDivisor = dBillions
        ElseIf m_dMaxValue >= dBillions Then
            dDivisor = dBillions
        Else
            dDivisor = dBillions
        End If
        ' Millions...
    ElseIf m_dMaxValue >= dMillions Then
        strModifier = "M"
        If m_dMaxValue >= dMillions Then
            dDivisor = dMillions
        ElseIf m_dMaxValue >= dMillions Then
            dDivisor = dMillions
        Else
            dDivisor = dMillions
        End If
        ' Thousands...
    ElseIf m_dMaxValue >= dThousands Then
        strModifier = "K"
        If m_dMaxValue >= dThousands Then
            dDivisor = dThousands
```

```
        ElseIf m_dMaxValue >= dThousands Then
            dDivisor = dThousands
        Else
            dDivisor = dThousands
        End If
    End If

    ' The values in the following calculation give the best
    '    appearance to the graph.
    Dim nStep As Integer = (((m_nHeight - 70) - 45) / 4)
    Dim objScaleFont As New Font("Times New Roman", 9)

    Dim i As Integer
    For i = 0 To 3
        ' Since the graph's left margin line is at pixel 50,
        '    we'll draw from that point to the left 5 pixels (45-50).
        '    We'll start drawing at the top at pixel 46.
        g.DrawLine(m_objBlackPen, 45, 46 + nStep * i, 50, _
            46 + nStep * i)
        Dim dThisNumber As Double = _
            ((m_dMaxValue / dDivisor) / 4) * (4 - i)
        Dim strNumber As String = _
            dThisNumber.ToString("0.00") + strModifier
        Dim sz As SizeF = g.MeasureString(strNumber, objScaleFont)
        g.DrawString(strNumber, objScaleFont, m_objBlackBrush, _
            45 - sz.Width, 46 + nStep * i - (sz.Height / 2))
    Next
End Sub
```

Graph2D Properties

A number of Graph2D properties can be used to alter the appearance of the graph. These properties can be seen in Listing 10.10, and they include Width, Height, BackgroundColor, TitleColor, TitleSize, and Title. For a more detailed description of the member variables that correspond to these properties, refer to Table 10.4.

Listing 10.10 This Listing Shows the Property Methods for the Graph2D Class.

```
Property Width() As Integer
    Get
        Width = m_nWidth
```

```
        End Get
    Set(ByVal Value As Integer)
        m_nWidth = Value
    End Set
End Property


Property Height() As Integer
    Get
        Height = m_nHeight
    End Get
    Set(ByVal Value As Integer)
        m_nHeight = Value
    End Set
End Property


Property BackgroundColor() As Color
    Get
        BackgroundColor = m_BackgroundColor
    End Get
    Set(ByVal Value As Color)
        m_BackgroundColor = Value
    End Set
End Property


Property TitleColor() As Color
    Get
        TitleColor = m_TitleColor
    End Get
    Set(ByVal Value As Color)
        m_TitleColor = Value
    End Set
End Property


Property TitleSize() As Integer
    Get
        TitleSize = m_nTitleSize
    End Get
    Set(ByVal Value As Integer)
        m_nTitleSize = Value
    End Set
End Property


Property Title() As String
    Get
```

```
        Title = m_strTitle
    End Get
    Set(ByVal Value As String)
        m_strTitle = Value
    End Set
End Property
```

Using the Graph2D Class

The Graph2D class is easy to use. Simply instantiate it, add the data, set any properties that need to be set, and call its Render() method. This section shows how an application named GraphAppVB uses the Graph2D class.

Displaying the Rendered Image

The graph image has to be displayed in the HTML page in one way or another. I chose to output an <IMG> tag with the Response.Write() method. The application keeps the file name for the current image in a session variable named Graph. If the session variable is not nothing (null in C#), then the file name is output so that the HTML rendering engine will display it. This code can be seen in Listing 10.11 in a method named InsertGraphLink().

Listing 10.11 The InsertGraphLink() Method Outputs a Link for the Rendered Image.

```
Public Sub InsertGraphLink()
    If Session("Graph") <> Nothing Then
        Response.Write("<IMG SRC=GraphImages/Graph" + _
        Convert.ToString(Session("Graph")) + ".gif>")
    End If
End Sub
```

Inserting Data into the TextBox

Because this demo application isn't meant to tax its users, it has some pre-loaded data. I didn't want users to have to type in lots of data just to see the graph appear. Of course, users can type in their own data, but doing so is not necessary.

The `LoadData_Click()` method fires when the user clicks the Load Data button, and it can be seen in Listing 10.12. This method simply sets the GraphData TextBox object to contain some data.

Listing 10.12 When the User Clicks the Load Data Button, This Method Is Fired, and the Selected Set of Default Data Is Loaded into the Text Box.

```
Private Sub LoadData_Click(ByVal sender As System.Object, _
  ByVal e As System.EventArgs) Handles LoadData.Click
    Select Case DataSelection.SelectedIndex
        Case 0
            GraphData.Text = _
                "Beth;98.9" + vbCrLf + _
                "George;84.1" + vbCrLf + _
                "Jane;97.9" + vbCrLf + _
                "Judy;96.4" + vbCrLf + _
                "Matilda;78.9" + vbCrLf + _
                "Rick;58.9" + vbCrLf + _
                "Sam;97.2" + vbCrLf + _
                "Suzy;98.5" + vbCrLf + _
                "Tammy;88.9"
        Case 1
            GraphData.Text = _
                "America;5000000" + vbCrLf + _
                "BedRock;7000000" + vbCrLf + _
                "China;60000000" + vbCrLf + _
                "Easter Island;60000000" + vbCrLf + _
                "Japan;60000000" + vbCrLf + _
                "JellyStone;60000000" + vbCrLf + _
                "Lower Slobovia;64200000" + vbCrLf + _
                "Madagascar;60000000" + vbCrLf + _
                "Stonehenge;60000000"
        Case 2
            GraphData.Text = _
                "Acme;47" + vbCrLf + _
                "ExpenseCo;63" + vbCrLf + _
                "Generic;15" + vbCrLf + _
                "IBM;25" + vbCrLf + _
                "Intel;24" + vbCrLf + _
                "JSVentures;12" + vbCrLf + _
                "Microsoft;30" + vbCrLf + _
                "PBS;43" + vbCrLf + _
```

```
                        "ProxyShield;4" + vbCrLf + _
                        "SmithCo;53"
        End Select
    End Sub
```

Rendering the Graph

The GraphAppVB application calls on a method named `RenderGraph()` that can be seen in Listing 10.13. This method could be simple if no Graph2D properties were set. But it starts (after instantiating a Graph2D object) by taking information from the user interface objects and setting the Graph2D properties.

The data is parsed from the GraphData TextBox. Each data pair is separated by a carriage return/line-feed pair, and the data name and value are separated by a semi-colon (`;`). Each data name and value are added to the Graph2D object.

Finally, the `Render()` method is called, which draws the graph and saves it to disk.

Listing 10.13 The `RenderGraph()` Method Takes the Properties That Have Been Set in the User Interface, Puts Them into an Instantiated Graph2D Object, and Calls the Graph2D's `Render()` Method.

```
Private Sub RenderGraph_Click(ByVal sender As System.Object, _
  ByVal e As System.EventArgs) Handles RenderGraph.Click
    Dim graph As New Graph2D()

    ' Set graph properties...
    graph.Title = GraphTitle.Text
    Dim TitleColor As Color() = {Color.Red, Color.Green, _
      Color.Blue, Color.Green}
    graph.TitleColor = TitleColor(TitleColors.SelectedIndex)
    Dim BackgroundColor As Color() = {Color.White, Color.Yellow, _
      Color.Cyan, Color.LightGray, Color.LightGreen}
    graph.BackgroundColor = _
      BackgroundColor(BackgroundColors.SelectedIndex)
    graph.Width = Convert.ToInt32(GraphWidth.Text)
    graph.Height = Convert.ToInt32(GraphHeight.Text)

    Dim separator As Char() = {ChrW(126)}
    Dim strData As String() = _
      GraphData.Text.Replace(vbCrLf, "~").Split(separator, 200)
```

```
    Dim i As Integer
    For i = 0 To strData.Length - 1
        Dim SemiColonSeparator As Char() = {ChrW(59)}
        Dim strPair As String() = strData(i).Split(SemiColonSeparator,
2)
        If strPair(0) <> Nothing And _
            strPair(0).Length > 0 And _
            strPair(1) <> Nothing And _
            strPair(1).Length > 0 Then
            graph.AddPair(strPair(0), Convert.ToDouble(strPair(1)))
        End If
    Next
    Session("Graph") = graph.Render(Request.MapPath("."))
End Sub
```

Enhancing the `Graph2D` Class

I'd like to present two enhancements that you might consider for your version of the `Graph2D` class. The first enhancement is the ability to guarantee unique file names, even in high-traffic situations. The next is the ability to change the type of graph that's rendered.

To ensure a unique graph number, even for high-volume use, replace the following:

```
Dim strName As String = Convert.ToString(DateTime.Now.Ticks)
```

with

```
Lock()
If Application("GraphNumber") = nothing Then
  Application("GraphNumber") = 0
End If
Dim strName As String =
Convert.ToString(Application("GraphNumber"))
Application("GraphNumber") = _
  Convert.ToInt32(Application("GraphNumber")) + 1
  ' Wrap if we get the 1000000.
  If Application("GraphNumber") > 1000000 Then
    Application("GraphNumber") = 0
  End If
Unlock()
```

I mentioned earlier in this chapter that I use the `Graph2D` class in an application that I currently support. One of the ways I added some dazzle for the human resources people who use it was to allow them to see a vertical bar graph, a horizontal bar graph, a line graph, and a pie graph. I'm including the horizontal rendering here in Listing 10.14 so that you can see what you need to do to add additional renderings. I would have included all the renderings from my application in this class, but my class requires some specific implementation dependencies.

You can see the horizontal bar graph in Figure 10.6.

Listing 10.14 These Methods Make It Possible to Render the Graph with Horizontal Bars Rather Than Vertical Bars.

```
' Draw the bounding lines (left and bottom).
Private Sub DrawBounds2(ByVal g As Graphics)
    Dim nChartBottom As Integer = m_nHeight - 70
```

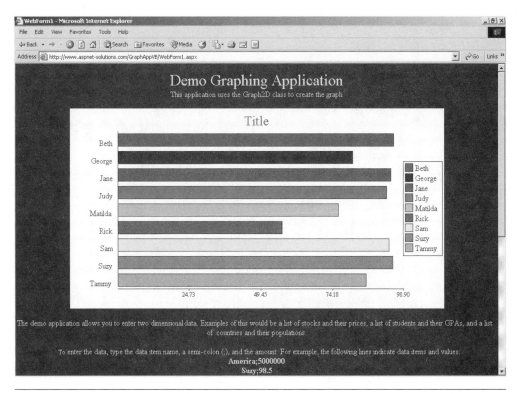

Figure 10.6 The Bars Can Go Horizontally with Some Modification to the Code.

```
    ' Draw the left and bottom lines
    g.DrawLine(m_objBlackPen, 100, 45, 100, m_nHeight - 70)
    g.DrawLine(m_objBlackPen, 100, m_nHeight - 40, _
       m_nLegendX, m_nHeight - 40)
End Sub

' Draw the data bars.
Private Sub DrawData2(ByVal g As Graphics)
    Dim nChartBottom As Integer = m_nHeight - 70

    ' Figure out the max value.
    m_dMaxValue = 0
    Dim nMaxIndex As Integer = 0

    Dim i As Integer
    For i = 0 To m_nCategoryCount - 1
        If m_dMaxValue < m_dDataValues(i) Then
            m_dMaxValue = m_dDataValues(i)
            nMaxIndex = i
        End If
    Next

    Dim nBarHeight As Integer = ((m_nHeight - 85) / m_nCategoryCount)
    For i = 0 To m_nCategoryCount - 1
        Dim nBarWidth As Integer = _
           (m_dDataValues(i) * (m_nLegendX - 100 - 20)) / m_dMaxValue
        Dim x As Integer = 100
        Dim y As Integer = 50 + i * nBarHeight
        If nBarWidth > 0 Then
            g.FillRectangle(New SolidBrush(m_Colors(i And 15)), _
                x, y, nBarWidth, nBarHeight - 10)
            g.DrawRectangle(m_objBlackPen, _
                x, y, nBarWidth, nBarHeight - 10)
        End If
        Dim s2 As SizeF = _
            g.MeasureString(m_DataNames(i), m_objLegendFont)
        g.DrawString(m_DataNames(i), m_objLegendFont, m_objBlackBrush, _
            x - s2.Width - 5, y + (s2.Height / 2))
    Next
End Sub

' Draw the scale to the left.
Private Sub DrawScale2(ByVal g As Graphics)
```

```
Dim dDivisor As Double = 1
Dim strModifier As String = ""

' Billions...
If m_dMaxValue >= 1000000000 Then
    strModifier = "B"
    If m_dMaxValue >= 100000000000 Then
        dDivisor = 100000000000
    ElseIf m_dMaxValue >= 10000000000 Then
        dDivisor = 10000000000
    Else
        dDivisor = 1000000000
    End If
    ' Millions...
ElseIf m_dMaxValue >= 1000000 Then
    strModifier = "M"
    If m_dMaxValue >= 100000000 Then
        dDivisor = 100000000
    ElseIf m_dMaxValue >= 10000000 Then
        dDivisor = 10000000
    Else
        dDivisor = 1000000
    End If
    ' Thousands...
ElseIf m_dMaxValue >= 1000 Then
    strModifier = "K"
    If m_dMaxValue >= 100000 Then
        dDivisor = 100000
    ElseIf m_dMaxValue >= 10000 Then
        dDivisor = 10000
    Else
        dDivisor = 1000
    End If
End If

Dim nStep As Integer = ((m_nLegendX - 100) / 4)
Dim objScaleFont As New Font("Times New Roman", 9)

Dim i As Integer
For i = 0 To 3
    g.DrawLine(m_objBlackPen, 100 + (4 - i) * nStep, _
      m_nHeight - 40, 100 + (4 - i) * nStep, m_nHeight - 43)
    Dim dThisNumber As Double = _
```

```
      ((m_dMaxValue / dDivisor) / 4) * (4 - i)
    Dim strNumber As String = _
      dThisNumber.ToString("0.00") + strModifier
    Dim sz As SizeF = g.MeasureString(strNumber, objScaleFont)
    g.DrawString(strNumber, objScaleFont, m_objBlackBrush, _
      100 + (4 - i) * nStep - sz.Width / 2, m_nHeight - 46)
  Next
End Sub
```

Summary

The capability to dynamically create images is truly a monumental addition to ASP.NET. And the creation of the Graph2D class in this chapter illustrates just how easy it is to create a useful class.

You can easily enhance the Graph2D class, or create your own. Please let us know at www.ASPNET-Solutions.com if you create your own class, and we'll post it for others if you want.

CHAPTER 11

Animated Banners

In This Chapter:

- Anatomy of a GIF Image
- The `AnimatedGif` Class
- Using the `AnimagedGif` Class

It seems as if every Web page has at least one banner that promotes a product or a service. Banners are kind of like the billboards we drive by—they've become part of the landscape. And in spite of any annoyance we might feel, they're an effective way to reach consumers. Without any effectiveness, advertisers wouldn't pay to sponsor banners. (Of course, we could talk about that period from 1998 through 2001, during which advertisers paid far more than they should have in the now-famous irrational exuberance about the Internet's potential.)

Almost all the banners that dot the Web page landscape are GIF images, many of them animated. The .NET Framework provides a fantastic array of image creation, manipulation, and saving methodology. I first learned about all this at a summit on the Microsoft campus. The possibility of creating animated GIF banners programmatically really excited me. I asked several of the speakers how to create and save animated GIFs. Their responses were all similar: You can do it, but they didn't know exactly how. Finally, Rob Howard agreed to find the answer and let me know via e-mail. Two weeks, and lots of e-mails from various engineers at Microsoft later, I had an answer. Creating and saving animated GIFs is not possible with the current GIF codec. Bummer!

So I've kept my desire alive ever since. I did some research into the format of animated GIF files and realized there is a way to do it with the .NET classes as a starting point. I wrote a class named `AnimagedGif` that can be used to save a series of GIF images as a single animation. This chapter talks about this class and how you can easily use it in your applications.

Anatomy of a GIF Image

A single-frame GIF file breaks down into two major parts: the header and the image data. A multiframe GIF file is similar, except that it can include any number of sets of image data after the header. Of course, I've left out some important details in the name of overview, but we'll get to them shortly.

Indexed Image Data

GIF images have, at most, an 8-bit color resolution. With 8 bits, there can be, at most, 256 colors.

GIF image data does not itself represent RGB values. This would be impossible because each of the three components of an RGB triple requires 8 bits, and thus a total of 24 bits for the entire value. Instead, the GIF image data is an index into a palette that defines up to 256 RGB values, as Figure 11.1 shows.

You need to know about the GIF indexed image data for several reasons. One reason is the general understanding of the format. Another is that, knowing this, you can easily see why the format is limited to 256 colors. I need to point out here that all GIF images don't have the same palettes—each and every one can have a different palette. The last of my three reasons for knowing how GIF data is laid out is that if you want to set a transparent color, you do it with an indexed value and not an RGB value. We'll talk more about this later.

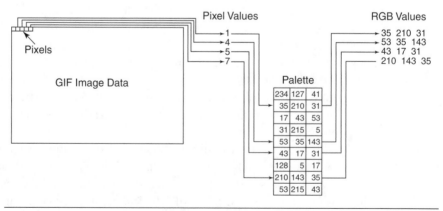

Figure 11.1 Each Pixel in a GIF Image's Data Is Actually an Index into a Palette That Can Contain Up to 256 colors.

GIF Data Compression

OK, let's say you open a GIF file with a disk editor and want to look at the data. You want to get a look at some of the data indices. Although this is a nice thought, it won't work because GIF image data is compressed by a technique know as LZW (which stands for Lempel, Ziv, and Welch—the original creators). So the image data will look completely unintelligible.

There have been times when I wanted to see the data indices for a GIF image. I resorted to running the debugger and examining the memory contents of an image object, or to saving the image to disk as a BMP file. In the .NET Framework, it's a lot easier to save a GIF image as a BMP and then look at it with a disk editor.

The GIF Header

The GIF header provides a descriptor of the image. The header contains the width and height of the screen (which 99.9 percent of the time is the same as the width and height of the image); some flags indicating palette information, such as whether there is a global palette and, if so, how large it is; a background color; and an aspect ratio value. Table 11.1 shows the layout of the GIF header.

Table 11.1 The GIF Header

Section	Bytes	Description
Signature	3 + 3	"GIF" + "87a" or "GIF" + "89a".
Logical Screen Descriptor	7 + Palette Entries × 3	This section globally describes the image.
	2	Width of logical screen.
	2	Height of logical screen.
	1	Screen and color information: Bits 0–2: size of global palette Bit 3: 1 if palette is sorted Bits 4–6: color resolution Bit 7: 1 if global palette exists
	1	Background color.
	1	Aspect ratio.
	Number of palette entries × 3	Global palette.

The Local Image Descriptor

Because GIF files can have more than one image, it's important that each image can be described independently. For this reason, the GIF format provides the Local Image Descriptor section for each image in the file. This section describes the image that follows. It includes x and y positions, width and height, and palette information. You can see a description of the Local Image Descriptor in Table 11.2.

The Graphics Control Extension

The earlier GIF format is identified by the signature "GIF87a", while the later version that we use today is identified by the signature "GIF89a". The newer version allows additional information that adds flexibility to the for-

Table 11.2 The Local Image Descriptor

Section	Bytes	Description
Image Description		This section describes how an image is stored in a file.
	1	Block type (will be 0x2c).
	2	X position of image on screen.
	2	Y position of image on screen.
	2	Width of image.
	2	Height of image.
Local Color Palette (optional)		This is a color palette for this local image. In this way, a different palette can be supplied for each image in an animation. This palette, though, is optional.
	1	Screen and color information: Bit 0: 1 if there is a local palette Bit 1: 1 if image is interlaced Bit 2: 1 if palette is sorted Bit 3: reserved, always 0 Bits 4–7: size of local palette
	Number of local palette entries × 3	Local palette data.
Image data	Unknown	Compressed image data (indexes into the palette).

Table 11.3 The Graphics Control Extension Block

Bytes	Description
1	Hex 21 indicates the start of an extension block.
1	Hex F9 indicates the extension block is a Graphics Control Extension.
1	Size of the information.
1	Information about what the decoder should do after the image is displayed.
	Bit 0: 1 if there is a transparent color.
	Bit 1: 1 if the decoder should wait for user input.
	Bit 2: 1 to leave graphics on screen alone.
	Bit 3: 1 to erase graphic to background color.
	Bit 4: 1 to restore previous image.
	Bits 5–7: reserved, always 0.
2	Delay in 100ths of a second.
1	Treat this palette color as transparent.

mat, including the capabilities to make an image transparent and to animate a set of images.

The Graphics Control Extension is used in the `AnimatedGif` class to provide transparency and animation delay information. Extension blocks can have a variable size, but the Graphics Control Extension variety has four bytes of data. Table 11.3 shows the Graphics Control Extension Block.

The `AnimatedGif` Class

The `AnimatedGif` class has two methods that are called and several properties that can be set. This section explains how the code works. In essence, though, the calling code simply adds Bitmap objects to an instantiated class using the `AddFrame()` method, and then creates the animated GIF file by calling the `CreateAnimation()` method.

The `AnimatedGif` class is used in a demo program named Dynamic-BannerCS (and a VB version named DynamicBannerVB). This code can be seen in the section titled "Using the `AnimatedGif` Class."

Structures

To simplify the gathering and grouping of information, several structures are used. One structure contains the GIF header information, one the local

Table 10.4 The `AnimatedGif` Structures

Struct Name	Description
`GifHeader`	Contains the information from the file's GIF header; some calculated values, such as the variable `nColorTableEntries`; some Boolean values; and the global color table (if it exists).
`GraphicsControlExtension`	Contains information that will be written to the destination file, such as the delay value and transparency index.
`LocalImageDescriptor`	Contains information from the file's Local Image Descriptor section for each image.

image description, and one a graphics-control extension block. These structures are described in Table 10.4

Listing 11.1 contains the struct definitions that are used in the `AnimagedGif` class.

Listing 11.1 The `AnimatedGif` Structures

```
struct GifHeader
{
    private byte[] _Signature;
    public byte[] Signature
    {
      get
      {
        return( _Signature );
      }
      set
      {
        if( value.Length == 3 )
        {
          _Signature = value;
        }
      }
    }
    private byte[] _Version;
    public byte[] Version
    {
```

```
      get
      {
        return( _Version );
      }
      set
      {
        if( value.Length == 3 )
        {
          _Version = value;
        }
      }
    }
    public short nScreenWidth, nScreenHeight;
    public byte Packed;
    public byte BackgroundColor;
    public byte AspectRatio;
    public int nSizeOfGCT;
    public int nColorTableEntries;
    public bool bColorTableSortFlag;
    public int nColorResolution;
    public bool bGlobalColorTableFlag;
    public byte[] GCT;
};

struct GraphicsControlExtension
{
    public byte Introducer;
    public byte Label;
    public byte BlockSize;
    public byte Packed;
    public short nDelayTime;
    public byte ColorIndex;
    public byte Terminator;
};

struct LocalImageDescriptor
{
    public byte Separator;
    public short nLeft, nTop, nWidth, nHeight;
    public byte Packed;
    public bool bLocalColorTableFlag;
    public bool bInterlaceFlag;
    public bool bSortFlag;
```

```
        public int nSizeLCT;
        public int nColorTableEntries;
        public byte[] LCT;
};
```

Member Variables

The `AnimatedGif` class doesn't have that many member variables. This limited number works because two of the member variables are structs that themselves contain a number of variables describing the image. These member variables can be seen along with their descriptions in Table 10.5.

Table 10.5 The `AnimatedGif` Member Variables

Variable Name	Type	Default Value	Description
strFilename-Fragment	string	None	This string variable contains the file name fragment for the destination file.
m_nFrameCount	Int	0	This integer variable contains the frame count for the class.
m_nTransparent-ColorIndex	Int	−1	This integer variable contains a value for the transparent index. If it is −1, then no transparent index will be saved to the destination file.
m_gh	GifHeader	new GifHeader()	This struct contains information from the file's GIF header, including some calculated values. It also contains the global color table if it exists.
m_ld	LocalImage-Descriptor	new LocalImage-Descriptor()	This struct contains information for an individual image.
m_nDelayValue	Int	50	This integer variable contains the delay value for each frame.

The member variable declarations as found in the `AnimatedGif` class can be seen in Listing 11.2.

Listing 11.2 The Member Variables

```
string m_strFilenameFragment;
int m_nFrameCount = 0;
int m_nTransparentColorIndex = -1;
GifHeader m_gh = new GifHeader();
LocalImageDescriptor m_ld =
    new LocalImageDescriptor();
int m_nDelayValue = 50;
```

An Overview of the Methods

Table 10.6 contains a handy reference to the methods found both in the `AnimatedGif` class and the demo program that uses the class.

Table 10.6 The `AnimatedGif` Methods

Method Name	Access	Code Module	Listing Number	Description
ReadHeader()	Private	AnimatedGif.cs	11.3	Reads the GIF header from a file, calculates values such as the number of color entries, and loads the color palette if it exists.
WriteHeader()	Private	AnimagedGif.cs	11.3	Writes the GIF header to the destination file, including the global color table if it exists.
ReadLocalImage-Descriptor()	Private	AnmatedGif.cs	11.4	Reads the Local Image Descriptor for an image from a file.
				(continued)

Table 10.6 The AnimatedGif Methods (*cont.*)

Method Name	Access	Code Module	Listing Number	Description
WriteLocalImage-Descriptor()	Private	AnmatedGif.cs	11.4	Writes the Local Image Descriptor for an image to the destination file.
WriteGraphics-ControlExtension()	Private	AnmatedGif.cs	11.5	Writes the Graphics Control Extension to the destination file.
WriteLoopControl()	Private	AnmatedGif.cs	11.6	Writes the loop control data to the destination file.
AnimatedGif()	Public	AnimatedGif.cs	11.7	The Animated-Gif constructor. This simply forms the file name fragment.
AddFrame()	public	AnimatedGif.cs	11.7	Accepts a Bitmap object and adds it to the animation queue.
CreateAnimation()	Public	AnimatedGif.cs	11.8	Creates an animated GIF file from the list of images that was added with the Add-Frame() method.
TransparentColor-Index()	Public property	AnimatedGif.cs	11.9	Property that sets the transparent color index.
TransparentColor()	Public property	AnimatedGif.cs	11.9	Property that takes a Color class and matches its RGB values to a value in the palette.

Table 10.6 The AnimatedGif Methods (*cont.*)

Method Name	Access	Code Module	Listing Number	Description
`DelayValue()`	Public property	AnimatedGif.cs	11.9	The delay value with which each animation frame will wait until the next frame is displayed.
`OutputBanner-Image()`	Public	WebForm1.aspx	11.10	Outputs the `<IMG>` tag into the HTML stream.
`RenderBanner_Click()`	Public	WebForm1.aspx	11.11	Fired when the user clicks the Render Banner button.

Reading and Writing the GIF Header

Reading the GIF header data is simple. Using the `ReadBytes()` method of the BinaryReader, the signature, version, width, height, flag byte (named `Packed`), background color, and aspect ratio are all read in. Once these values are read in, the code goes on to break the `Packed` variable apart. The lower 3 bits contain the size of the global color table, which can later be used to calculate the exact number of bytes in the global color table with this formula:

```
gh.nColorTableEntries = ( 1 << ( gh.nSizeOfGCT + 1 ) );
```

If a global color table exists, it is read in the `ReadHeader()` method.

The `WriteHeader()` method is simpler than the `ReadHeader()` method because it doesn't have to perform any calculations; it simply writes out the data using the `Write()` method. The `ReadHeader()` and `WriteHeader()` methods can be seen in Listing 11.3.

Listing 11.3 Reading and Writing the GIF Header

```
private void ReadHeader( BinaryReader reader,
    ref GifHeader gh, ref int nFileBytes )
{
```

```
        gh.Signature = reader.ReadBytes( 3 );
        gh.Version = reader.ReadBytes( 3 );
        gh.nScreenWidth = reader.ReadInt16();
        gh.nScreenHeight = reader.ReadInt16();
        gh.Packed = reader.ReadByte();
        gh.BackgroundColor = reader.ReadByte();
        gh.AspectRatio = reader.ReadByte();
        nFileBytes -= 13;
        gh.nSizeOfGCT = (int) ( gh.Packed & 0x07 );
        gh.nColorTableEntries = 0;
        gh.bColorTableSortFlag =
            (bool) ( ( gh.Packed & 0x8 ) != 0 );
        gh.nColorResolution =
            (int) ( ( gh.Packed & 0x70 ) >> 4 );
        gh.bGlobalColorTableFlag =
            (bool) ( ( gh.Packed & 0x80 ) != 0 );
        if( gh.bGlobalColorTableFlag )
        {
            gh.nColorTableEntries =
                ( 1 << ( gh.nSizeOfGCT + 1 ) );
            gh.GCT =
                reader.ReadBytes( gh.nColorTableEntries * 3 );
            nFileBytes -=
                ( gh.nColorTableEntries * 3 );
        }
    }


    private void WriteHeader( BinaryWriter writer, GifHeader gh )
    {
        writer.Write( gh.Signature );
        writer.Write( gh.Version );
        writer.Write( gh.nScreenWidth );
        writer.Write( gh.nScreenHeight);
        writer.Write( gh.Packed );
        writer.Write( gh.BackgroundColor );
        writer.Write( gh.AspectRatio );

        if( gh.bGlobalColorTableFlag )
        {
            writer.Write( gh.GCT );
        }
    }
```

Reading and Writing the Local Image Descriptor

Reading a Local Image Descriptor is easy, but just as with the GIF header, the ReadLocalImageDescriptor() method performs some calculations. Besides assigning values to some Boolean values, it calculates the size of the color table toward the end of the ReadLocalImageDescriptor() method. The local palette is also read in if it exits.

Because it makes no calculations but simply writes data to disk, the WriteLocalImageDescriptor() method is simpler than the ReadImageDescriptor() Method. Both of these methods can be seen in Listing 11.4.

Listing 11.4 Reading and Writing the Local Image Descriptor

```
private void ReadLocalImageDescriptor( BinaryReader reader,
    ref LocalImageDescriptor ld, ref int nFileBytes )
{
    ld.Separator = reader.ReadByte();
    ld.nLeft = reader.ReadInt16();
    ld.nTop = reader.ReadInt16();
    ld.nWidth = reader.ReadInt16();
    ld.nHeight = reader.ReadInt16();
    ld.Packed = reader.ReadByte();
    nFileBytes -= 10;
    ld.bLocalColorTableFlag =
        (bool) ( ( ld.Packed & 0x01 ) != 0 );
    ld.bInterlaceFlag =
        (bool) ( ( ld.Packed & 0x02 ) != 0 );
    ld.bSortFlag =
        (bool) ( ( ld.Packed & 0x04 ) != 0 );
    ld.nSizeLCT = (int) ( ( ld.Packed & 0xe ) >> 5 );
    ld.nColorTableEntries = 0;
    if( ld.bLocalColorTableFlag )
    {
        ld.nColorTableEntries =
            1 << ( ld.nSizeLCT + 1 );
        ld.LCT =
            reader.ReadBytes( ld.nColorTableEntries * 3 );
        nFileBytes -= ( ld.nColorTableEntries * 3 );
    }
}
```

```
private void WriteLocalImageDescriptor( BinaryWriter writer,
    LocalImageDescriptor ld )
{
    writer.Write( ld.Separator );
    writer.Write( ld.nLeft );
    writer.Write( ld.nTop );
    writer.Write( ld.nWidth );
    writer.Write( ld.nHeight );
    writer.Write( ld.Packed );

    if( ld.bLocalColorTableFlag )
    {
        writer.Write( ld.LCT );
    }
}
```

Writing the Graphics Control Extension and the Loop Control

For the `AnimatedGif` class, the Graphics Control Extension indicates a delay value for the animation and a transparent color if the calling code set one. You can see the `WriteGraphicsControlExtension()` method in Listing 11.5. It simply writes the values for the GraphicsControlExtension structure to disk.

Listing 11.5 Writing the Graphics Control Extension

```
private void WriteGraphicsControlExtension( BinaryWriter writer,
    GraphicsControlExtension gce )
{
    writer.Write( gce.Introducer );
    writer.Write( gce.Label );
    writer.Write( gce.BlockSize );
    writer.Write( gce.Packed );
    writer.Write( gce.nDelayTime );
    writer.Write( gce.ColorIndex );
    writer.Write( gce.Terminator );
}
```

By default, GIF animations stop animating once they reach the last frame. A special control block must be written to the file for the animations to continuously restart at the beginning. Listing 11.6 shows the looping control block being written to disk. I got this information from www. Netscape.com because it was nowhere to be found on the Microsoft Web site.

Listing 11.6 Writing the Loop Control

```
private void WriteLoopControl( BinaryWriter writer )
{
    byte[] bc = new byte[] { 0x21, 0xff, 0x0b, (byte)'N',
        (byte)'E', (byte)'T', (byte)'S', (byte)'C',
        (byte)'A', (byte)'P', (byte)'E', (byte)'2',
        (byte)'.', (byte)'0', 3, 1, 0, 0, 0 };
    writer.Write( bc );
}
```

Adding Frames

Once an `AnimatedGif` class has been instantiated, any number of frames can be added. The frames are added by passing a Bitmap object to the `AddFrame()` method.

The Bitmap is then saved as a GIF image that will eventually be combined with all the others into the single animated image. It's important to note that a directory must exist with the necessary permissions into which these images can be saved. For this reason, a path is passed into the `AddFrame()` method so that it will save to the correct directory.

The complete file name, including the path, is formed as the first order of business in the `AddFrame()` method. The file name is composed of the save path, the file name fragment that was formed in the `AnimatedGif` constructor (which is actually based on the current clock ticks), the frame number, and the .gif extension.

Next, the image is saved by calling the Bitmap's `Save()` method. The frame count contained in the `m_nFrameCount` variable is incremented so that the class knows how many frames it has, and so that it knows how to form the next file name.

Later on, we'll talk about the properties that deal with the transparent color (or index) of the animation. But I need to point out that the `Set-TransparentColor()` method requires that we have a color palette with which the specified color can be matched. For this reason, before we leave the `AddFrame()` method, we need to load the palette. This is done by calling the `ReadHeader()` and `ReadLocalImageDescriptor()`

methods. Why call both methods? Because neither is guaranteed: you can have a global or a local palette.

The code in Listing 11.7 starts off with the `AnimatedGif()` constructor. In this code you can see the file name fragment being formed based on the system clock ticks. The `AddFrame()` method can also be seen in this listing.

Listing 11.7 The `AnimatedGif()` Constructor and the `AddFrame()` Method

```
public AnimatedGif()
{
    m_strFilenameFragment = "AnimationFrames" +
        Convert.ToString( DateTime.Now.Ticks );
}

public void AddFrame( Bitmap img, string strSavePath )
{
    string strFilename = strSavePath + "\\" +
        m_strFilenameFragment +
        Convert.ToString( m_nFrameCount ) +
        ".gif";

    img.Save( strFilename, ImageFormat.Gif );
    m_nFrameCount++;

    if( m_nFrameCount == 1 )
    {
        FileStream fs =
            new FileStream( strFilename, FileMode.Open );
        int nFileBytes = (int) fs.Length;
        BinaryReader reader = new BinaryReader( fs );

        ReadHeader( reader, ref m_gh, ref nFileBytes );

        byte[] bt = reader.ReadBytes( 8 );
        nFileBytes -= 8;

        ReadLocalImageDescriptor( reader, ref m_ld,
            ref nFileBytes );

        fs.Close();
    }
}
```

Creating the Animation

The animated GIF file is created by loading each GIF file that was saved in the `AddFrame()` method and saving it all to one big animated GIF file, as shown in Listing 11.8. I'll talk about a few other details in this section.

First, the file name for the animated GIF file is formed. The name starts with the file name fragment and then concatenates the string `"_Complete.gif"`.

FileStream and BinaryWriter objects are instantiated so that the output file can be written. A flag indicating when the first frame has been written is set to `False` so that the code knows when the first frame is about to be written. This step is important because a Graphics Control Extension and a Loop Control must be written before any images are written.

A `for` loop counts through each frame that was saved. A file name for the frame image is formed, and FileStream and BinaryReader objects are created with which the file data can be read.

First, the GIF header is read. Of course, this was already done when the first frame was saved, but the data must be read anyway. Another 8 bytes are read because the Microsoft GIF images always contain a single Graphics Control Extension that the code simply discards.

The LocalImageDescriptor is read from the source file, and then the image data is read. You might note that when the image data is read, a determination is made of whether or not the image currently being read is the last. If it is not, the code reads one less byte than is available because the last byte is a terminator character and indicates the end of image data. If we have this data in the buffer and write it out into the complete GIF animation file, the decoder will stop when it sees the terminator. For this reason, the code reads in (and subsequently writes out) only the terminator byte for the last image.

Once the code is done with the file, the FileStream object is closed, and the file is deleted. You could actually change the code so that the files aren't deleted. This change would let you call the `CreateAnimation()` method more than once because the individual frame images would still exist. You'd want to delete these frames somehow, though, possibly in some sort of `Finalize()` method.

If the image that was just read in is the first image, the GIF header must be written out to the destination file. The Loop Control is also written out because this is the proper place.

A Graphics Control Extension is created for each image that's to be written. The Graphics Control Extension is written to the destination file by calling the `WriteGraphicsControlExtension()` method.

The last two things that are done for each image are to write the Local-ImageDescriptor and the image data. Finally, the FileStream object for the output file is closed. The string that contains the file name for the newly created animation image is returned so that the calling code knows where the file is. Note that the file returned does not contain the full path, but simply the file name itself.

Listing 11.8 Creating the Animation

```
public string CreateAnimation( string strSavePath )
{

    // Create the destination file string.
    string strFilename = m_strFilenameFragment +
        "_Complete.gif";

    // Create the file and get a writer from it.
    FileStream fs = new FileStream( strSavePath + "\\" +
        strFilename, FileMode.CreateNew );
    BinaryWriter writer = new BinaryWriter( fs );
    bool bWriteFirst = false;

    // Loop through each frame.
    for( int i=0; i<m_nFrameCount; i++ )
    {
        // Create the string that contains the file for this
        //    frame.
        string strSaveFile = strSavePath + "\\" +
            m_strFilenameFragment + Convert.ToString( i ) +
            ".gif";
        // Open the file for reading and get a BinaryReader object.
        FileStream fs2 = new FileStream( strSaveFile, FileMode.Open );
        int nFileBytes = (int) fs2.Length;
        BinaryReader reader = new BinaryReader( fs2 );

        // Call the method that reads the GIF header.
        ReadHeader( reader, ref m_gh, ref nFileBytes );

        // Read the Graphics Control Block, but we don't use it.
        byte[] bt = reader.ReadBytes( 8 );
        nFileBytes -= 8;
```

```csharp
// Call the method that reads the Local Image Descriptor.
ReadLocalImageDescriptor( reader, ref m_ld,
    ref nFileBytes );

// Unless this is the last frame, we'll omit the
//    separator byte.
if( i < m_nFrameCount - 1 )
{
    nFileBytes--;
}
// Read the image data.
byte[] ImageData = reader.ReadBytes( nFileBytes );

// Close this file and delete it.
fs2.Close();
File.Delete( strSaveFile );

// We have to write the header for the first frame.
if( !bWriteFirst )
{
    bWriteFirst = true;
    WriteHeader( writer, m_gh );
    WriteLoopControl( writer );
}

// Here we create the Graphics Control Extension
//    indicating the delay value for this frame.
GraphicsControlExtension gce =
    new GraphicsControlExtension();
gce.Introducer = 0x21;
gce.Label = 0xf9;
gce.BlockSize = 4;
gce.Packed = 8;
gce.nDelayTime = (byte) m_nDelayValue;
gce.ColorIndex = 0;
gce.Terminator = 0;
if( m_nTransparentColorIndex >= 0 )
{
    gce.ColorIndex =
        (byte) m_nTransparentColorIndex;
    gce.Packed = 9;
}
```

```
        // Write the Graphics Control Extension and the
        //   Local Image Descriptor.
        WriteGraphicsControlExtension( writer, gce );
        WriteLocalImageDescriptor( writer, m_ld );
        // Write the image data.
        writer.Write( ImageData );
    }

    // Close the output file.
    fs.Close();

    // Return the file name.
    return( strFilename );
}
```

The Properties

Two properties (`TransparentColorIndex` and `DelayValue`) can be set, and also one helper method that makes it easy to set the transparent color index by passing a Color value. One thing to note, though, is that the `SetTransparentColor()` method finds the first RGB match for the specified color. If more than one palette entry contains the same RGB values, there is no guarantee that the transparent index will be correct.

Listing 11.9 The `AnimatedGif` Properties

```
public int TransparentColorIndex
{
    get
    {
        return( m_nTransparentColorIndex );
    }
    set
    {
        m_nTransparentColorIndex = TransparentColorIndex;
    }
}

public void SetTransparentColor(Color col)
{
    for( int i=0; i<m_gh.nColorTableEntries; i++ )
```

```
    {
        if( col.R == m_gh.GCT[i*3] &&
            col.G == m_gh.GCT[i*3+1] &&
            col.B == m_gh.GCT[i*3+2] )
        {

            m_nTransparentColorIndex = i;
            break;
        }
    }
}


public int DelayValue
{
    get
    {
        return( m_nDelayValue );
    }
    set
    {
        m_nDelayValue = DelayValue;
    }
}
```

Using the AnimatedGif Class

The AnimatedGif class is easy to use. All you need to do is instantiate the class, add frames, create the animation, and then use the file name in whatever way is appropriate. I've created a simple demo program that illustrates this class's use. Users simply type in a text string, and a series of frames are created with the text string at various positions in the GIF image. In Figure 11.2, you can see the demo program as it appears when it first starts.

Once the user clicks on the Render Banner button, the animation is created, and the animated image appears on the screen, as shown in Figure 11.3.

Listing 11.10 shows the <IMG> tag being output to the HTML stream. The file name is held in a session variable that won't exist until the animation has been created.

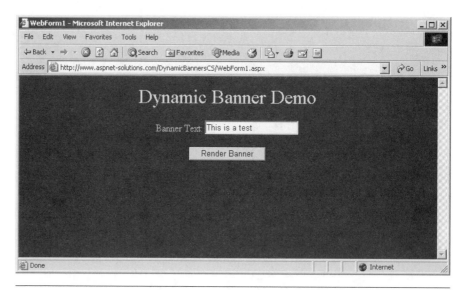

Figure 11.2 The Demo Program Has a Simple User Interface.

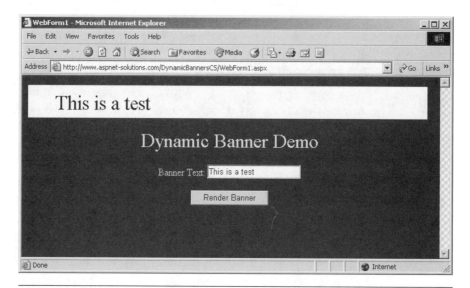

Figure 11.3 The Animated Banner Is Simple, but This Demo Program Gives You the Idea of How to Use the AnimatedGif Class.

Listing 11.10 Outputing the Banner Image Tag into the HTML Stream

```
public void OutputBannerImage()
{
    if( Session["Banner"] != null )
    {
        Response.Write( "<IMG SRC=\"BannerImages/" +
            Convert.ToString( Session["Banner"] ) + "\">" );
    }
}
```

Listing 11.11 shows the process for creating the animation. First, an AnimatedGif object is created. Next, a series of images is created and added to the `AnimatedGif` class. Last, the animation is created with the `CreateAnimation()` method.

Listing 11.11 Rendering the Banner

```
private void RenderBanner_Click(object sender, System.EventArgs e)
{
    AnimatedGif anim = new AnimatedGif();

    for( int i=0; i<10; i++ )
    {
        Bitmap objBitmap = new Bitmap( 668, 53,
            PixelFormat.Format24bppRgb );
        Graphics g = Graphics.FromImage( objBitmap );
        g.FillRectangle( new SolidBrush( Color.Red ), 0, 0, 668, 53 );
            g.DrawString( BannerText.Text, new Font( "Times New Roman",
                15 ),
            new SolidBrush( Color.White ), i * 10, 10 );

        anim.AddFrame( objBitmap, Request.MapPath( "BannerImages" ) );
    }

    Session["Banner"] =
        anim.CreateAnimation( Request.MapPath( "BannerImages" ) );
}
```

Summary

The `AnimatedGif` class might be extremely useful to you, especially if you want to create customized banners in real time that catch the user's attention.

This class would be difficult to create without the great GDI+ methodology that the .NET Framework provides. Using the `Bitmap.Save()` method saves a lot of development time and code.

Microsoft has obtained a license from Unisys to use the GIF file format and other LZW technologies that are covered by the Unisys-owned U.S. and foreign patents in a number of Microsoft products. However, this license does not extend to third-party developers who use Microsoft development products or toolkits to develop applications. As a third-party developer, you need to determine whether you need to obtain a license from Unisys to use the GIF format or the LZW technologies.

A little knowledge of the GIF file format will provide all the code needed to put the individual images together into one big animated GIF file—that, plus some knowledge of the .NET IO namespace!

CHAPTER 12

Using NT Services: An Ad Banner Management Application

In This Chapter:

- The BannerBuddy Application
- Writing and Deploying Windows Services in .NET

I can't tell you how many times I've told a project manager that it would be better to build an in-house solution, only to have a piece of technology dumped in my lap that I was forced to use. Let me describe a situation that all developers have found themselves in. Your team is just now starting on a big project. You're in a meeting, and the project manager tells you that your company has licensed some technology that will save development time. All you have to do is download the files (along with the documentation files) and get started. Oh, and by the way, here's a name and phone number of a contact for someone in the licensor's organization. You say, "Great! I'm saved from developing a piece of technology that would have been very difficult to create."

You eagerly open the zip file file and take a look. The documentation is two pages of unintelligible ramblings. The example programs not only attempt to show you how to use the API, but they have thrown in every programming trick known to man. And they're interwoven with each other like spaghetti. This makes it almost impossible to figure anything out.

You finally manage to get something working, but it doesn't really work right. You cry "Uncle" and reach for the phone number. After three days of phone tag, the guy you talk to says "Oh, yeah; that's a problem we've been meaning to fix. Here's a workaround." The rest of the project is a series of workarounds.

Where is this discussion headed? Well, there are ad banner management systems out there. Some of them work pretty well. But some don't. I licensed one for $1,000 (per domain), and it was not too hot. When I contacted tech support to alert them to a problem, they swore that it wasn't a problem for the first three rounds, and then they finally recreated it on their end. I couldn't get it to do what I wanted and threw up my hands. That's when I decided to create BannerBuddy, an ad banner management system that can easily be modified.

In this chapter, you'll learn about maintaining hit counter and click counter statistics. You'll also learn about creating an NT Service to send out statistical information to advertisers.

There's another advantage to BannerBuddy: It's free. Almost all of the systems out there are licensed on a per-domain basis. This gets expensive if you have a number of domains.

The BannerBuddy Application

The BannerBuddy application has several distinct parts: a SQL Server 2000 database that maintains all information, a Web Service that creates the HTML for the ad banner, an administrative application, and an NT Service that e-mails statistics to advertisers. This section describes the entire application except for the NT Service. The section entitled "Writing and Deploying NET Services in .NET" describes how to create and use NT Services. The section following entitled "The BannerBuddy Service" then discusses the NT Service that e-mails statistics to advertisers.

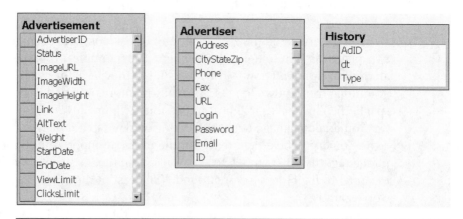

Figure 12.1 The BannerBuddy Database Schema

The Database

The database used is SQL Server 2000. You can download a script from http://www.ASPNET-Solutions.com/Chapter_12.htm that will create the database, or you can download the backed-up database. The database contains three tables: Advertiser, Advertisement, and History. The Advertiser table keeps all of the information related to an advertiser, including contact information. The Advertisement table keeps all information about an advertisement, including the banner image URL and statistics. The History table keeps a record of the ad impressions and clicks. Figure 12.1 shows the BannerBuddy database schema.

Displaying a Banner

The advertisements all have a weight value. The greater the weight, the more likely it is that an advertisement will be shown. The weight of each individual advertisement is relative to the total of all other advertisement weights. Although there are no hard, fast ranges, I suggest values from 1 to 100. The higher the value, the more often an ad appears. In this way, you can cause more important ad banners to appear more often. You can also charge more for customers with greater weights.

Figuring out how to use the weight values to select which ad banner appears next took some thought. The `Views` field keeps track of how many views an advertisement has had. The `ViewLimit` field keeps track of how many views an advertisement will have when it expires. These two fields can be used to gauge the previous display preponderance of each advertisement.

The stored procedure that calculates and returns the next ad can be seen in Listing 12.1. It starts by getting a total of the `ViewLimit` field for all active (or unexpired) advertisements. The following line from the stored procedure shows this:

```
select @all=sum(ViewLimit) from Advertisement where Status=0
```

A calculated field named `Parts` is then created by taking the difference between the `Weight` field of the ads divided by the total of the `ViewLimit` fields, and the `Views` field of the ads divided by the total of the `ViewLimits` field. The following shows the creation of this value:

```
Parts=((Weight/@all)-(Views/@all))
```

Listing 12.1 The Stored Procedure Selects the Next Advertisement Based on the Weight of All Advertisements and Their History.

```
CREATE PROCEDURE sp_GetNextAd
AS
  declare @all float
  select @all=sum(ViewLimit) from Advertisement where Status=0
  select ID,ImageURL,ImageWidth,ImageHeight,
    Link,AltText,Parts=((Weight/@all)-(Views/@all))
    from Advertisement where Status=0 order by Parts desc
GO
```

Another important part of the advertisement logic is expiring the advertisements when they've exceeded values in the ViewLimit, ClicksLimit, or EndDate fields. A trigger performs this housekeeping chore, and it can be seen in Listing 12.2. The trigger sets the Status field to 1 if the Views field catches up with the ViewLimit field, the Clicks field catches up with the ClicksLimit field, or the current date has exceeded the EndDate field. There are five fields that determine when an advertisement expires: EndDate, Clicks, ClicksLimit, Views, and ViewLimit. Advertisements need a way to expire based on the arrangements that have been made with advertisers. For instance, if the advertisement should expire at a certain date, then the EndDate field must be checked to ensure that the advertisement expires when appropriate. And the combinations of the Views/ViewLimit and Clicks/ClicksLimit fields give the software the opportunity to place a cap on the number of views and the number of clicks.

RECOMMENDED PRACTICE: The status field contains an integer value rather than a string containing values such as done and open. Queries on integer values are faster than queries on strings, so the performance of the queries is increased.

Listing 12.2 The Trigger That Expires Advertisements and Resets the Weight Accumulation

```
CREATE TRIGGER tr_ExpireAd ON Advertisement
  AFTER UPDATE
AS
  If Update(Views) or Update(Clicks)
  Begin
    Update Advertisement set Status=1
```

```
    where Views>=ViewLimit or Clicks>=ClicksLimit or EndDate<getdate()
  declare @ID int
  select @ID = -1
  select @ID=ID from Advertisement
    where WeightAccumulation<Weight and Status=0
  if @ID=-1
    Update Advertisement set WeightAccumulation=0 and Status=0
End
```

The code that creates the HTML for the ad banner can be found in a Web Service named TheAdBannerCS (or TheAdBannerVB for the VB version). The code makes a single method named NextAd() available for consumption. The NextAd() method, shown in Listing 12.3, calls the sp_Get-NextAd stored procedure, and then creates the HTML for the ad banner.

The NextAd() method starts off by creating a connection to the database, and the connection is then opened. A SqlCommand object is created and set so that the sp_GetNextAd stored procedure will be called. A Sql-DataReader object is returned from the SqlCommand.Execute-Reader() method. Some default values are stored in local string variables for items such as the image URL, image width, and image height.

If a record is returned from the stored procedure, then the default values are replaced with the values from the first record returned, as follows:

```
// Get the information from the recordset that we'll need.
nAdID = Convert.ToInt32( objReader["ID"] );
strImageURL = Convert.ToString( objReader["ImageURL"] );
strImageWidth = Convert.ToString( objReader["ImageWidth"] );
strImageHeight = Convert.ToString( objReader["ImageHeight"] );
strLink = Convert.ToString( objReader["Link"] );
strAltText = Convert.ToString( objReader["AltText"] );
```

Another stored procedure is called to update the Views field in the database. To do this, another SqlCommand object is created, and its Exe-cuteNonQuery() method is called. The AdID is required for the stored procedure to know which advertisement to update, so the stored procedure takes a single integer parameter with this value.

The HTML is created by concatenating the values into a single string, as follows:

```
strImageInfo = "<a href='" +
  ConfigurationSettings.AppSettings["ClickAccepter"] +
```

```
"?AdID=" + Convert.ToString( nAdID ) +
"&Link=" + strLink +
"'><IMG SRC='" + strImageURL +
"' AltText='" + strAltText +
"' Width='" + strImageWidth +
"' Height='" + strImageHeight +
"'></a>";
```

Finally, cleanup is performed. The data reader is closed, and the connection is closed.

Listing 12.3 The Web Service That Creates the Ad Banner HTML Code

```
[WebMethod]
public string NextAd()
{
  string strImageInfo = "";

  // Create the database connection object.
  SqlConnection objConnection =
    new SqlConnection(
      ConfigurationSettings.AppSettings["ConnectString"] );

  try
  {
    // Open the database connection.
    objConnection.Open();

    // Create the command object. Set it for the
    //   sp_GetNextAd stored procedure.
    SqlCommand objCommand = new SqlCommand( "sp_GetNextAd",
      objConnection );
    objCommand.CommandType = CommandType.StoredProcedure;

    // Execute the reader and get the recordset.
    SqlDataReader objReader = objCommand.ExecuteReader();

    // Set some default values in case we don't get a recordset.
    int nAdID = 0;
    string strImageURL = "http://www.nowhere.com/image.jpg";
    string strImageWidth = "600";
    string strImageHeight = "60";
```

```
string strLink = "http://www.ASPNET-Solutions.com";
string strAltText = "No banner record was found";

// Read a record.
if( objReader.Read() )
{
  // Get the information from the recordset that we'll need.
  nAdID = Convert.ToInt32( objReader["ID"] );
  strImageURL = Convert.ToString( objReader["ImageURL"] );
  strImageWidth = Convert.ToString( objReader["ImageWidth"] );
  strImageHeight = Convert.ToString( objReader["ImageHeight"] );
  strLink = Convert.ToString( objReader["Link"] );
  strAltText = Convert.ToString( objReader["AltText"] );

  // Close the reader.
  objReader.Close();

  // Create the command object. Set it for the
  //   sp_UpdateAdViews stored procedure.
  objCommand = new SqlCommand( "sp_UpdateAdViews",
    objConnection );
  objCommand.CommandType = CommandType.StoredProcedure;

  // We need to give it a parameter of the Ad ID. This
  //   way it can retrieve the correct ad information.
  objCommand.Parameters.Add( "@ID", SqlDbType.Int );
  objCommand.Parameters["@ID"].Direction = ParameterDirection.Input;
  objCommand.Parameters["@ID"].Value = nAdID;

  // Execute the SP.
  objCommand.ExecuteNonQuery();
}
else
{
  // Close the reader.
  objReader.Close();
}

strImageInfo = "<a href='" +
  ConfigurationSettings.AppSettings["ClickAccepter"] +
  "?AdID=" + Convert.ToString( nAdID ) +
  "&Link=" + strLink +
  "'><IMG SRC='" + strImageURL +
```

```
      "' AltText='" + strAltText +
      "' Width='" + strImageWidth +
      "' Height='" + strImageHeight +
      "'></a>";
  }
  catch( Exception ex )
  {
    strImageInfo = ex.Message.ToString();
  }
  finally
  {
    // If the database connection is open,
    //    close it.
    if( objConnection.State == ConnectionState.Open )
    {
      objConnection.Close();
    }
  }
  return( strImageInfo );
}
```

The code that must be inserted into applications to display an ad banner is simple. It just instantiates an instance of the Web Service, calls the NextAd() method, and sends the data out with the Response.Write() method. This method is as follows:

```
public void InsertAdBanner()
{
  // Instantiate the Web service wrapper class.
  com.aspnet_solutions.www.TheAdBanner1 sv =
    new com.aspnet_solutions.www.TheAdBanner1();
  // Output the new ad to the HTML stream.
  Response.Write( sv.NextAd() );
}
```

Responding to Banner Clicks

If a user clicks a banner, then the click needs to be recorded. A stored procedure handles the logic for doing this, and it is named sp_UpdateAd-Clicks, shown in Listing 12.4. This stored procedure also inserts a record into the History table.

Listing 12.4 The Stored Procedure That Updates Advertisement View and Click Counts

```
CREATE PROCEDURE sp_UpdateAdClicks
   @ID int
AS
   update Advertisement set Clicks=Clicks+1 where ID=@ID
   insert into History (AdID,Type) VALUES (@ID,1)
GO
```

There's a page named AcceptClick.aspx that is the destination of all banner clicks. This page records the click, and then redirects to the true destination page. The code behind this page can be seen in Listing 12.5.

The `Page_Load()` method in Listing 12.5 creates and opens a database connection. It then creates a SqlCommand object with which it will access the `sp_UpdateAdClicks` stored procedure. The stored procedure takes a single parameter of the advertisement ID. This ID arrives at the page as a query parameter and is converted to an integer with the following code:

```
Convert.ToInt32( Request.QueryString["AdID"] )
```

Once the stored procedure is executed, the database connection is closed. Finally, the user is redirected to the true destination URL with the `Response.Redirect()` method.

Listing 12.5 The AcceptClick.aspx.cs Source Code. This Code Is Called in Response to a User's Banner Click.

```
private void Page_Load(object sender, System.EventArgs e)
{

  // Create the database connection object.
  SqlConnection objConnection =
    new SqlConnection(
      ConfigurationSettings.AppSettings["ConnectString"] );

  try
  {
    // Open the database connection.
    objConnection.Open();
```

```
// Create the command object. Set it for the
//   sp_GetNextAd stored procedure.
SqlCommand objCommand = new SqlCommand( "sp_UpdateAdClicks",
  objConnection );
objCommand.CommandType = CommandType.StoredProcedure;

// We need to give it a parameter of the Ad ID. This
//   way it can retrieve the correct ad information.
objCommand.Parameters.Add( "@ID", SqlDbType.Int );
objCommand.Parameters["@ID"].Direction = ParameterDirection.Input;
objCommand.Parameters["@ID"].Value =
  Convert.ToInt32( Request.QueryString["AdID"] );

// Execute the SP.
objCommand.ExecuteNonQuery();
}
catch
{
}
finally
{
  // If the database connection is open,
  //   close it.
  if( objConnection.State == ConnectionState.Open )
  {
    objConnection.Close();
  }
}

// Redirect to the destination URL.
Response.Redirect( Request.QueryString["Link"] );
}
```

Administering Banners

There has to be a way to add and edit information. And the information you need to add and edit includes advertisement records and advertiser records. The first page I'll talk about adds and edits advertisement information. This page can be seen in Figure 12.2, and the code for it can be seen in Listing 12.6.

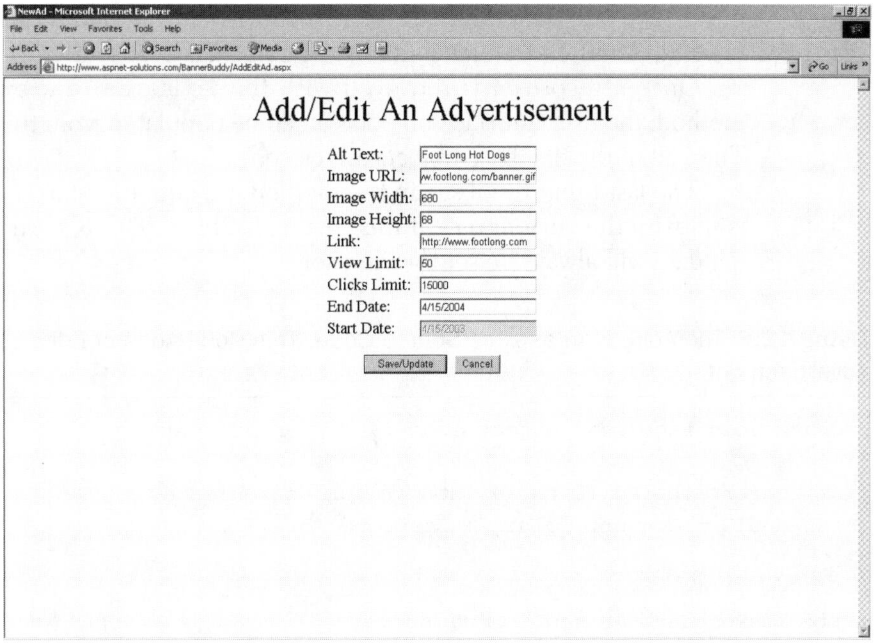

Figure 12.2 This Is the Page for Adding and Editing Advertisements.

In Listing 12.6, the `Page_Load()` method of the AddEditAd.aspx.cs source code module can be seen. The first thing in this method is the conversion of the `AdID` session variable into an integer variable. This makes it easier to use the `AdID` value.

If we're not in a post back, meaning this is the first time the page is being rendered, we'll need to populate the user interface objects. We'll also do this only if the page is being used for editing an advertisement and not for adding a new one. The `AdID` variable will be `-1` if it's a new add, so this value is checked before performing the code that populates the user interface. I selected the value of `-1` because the `ID` field in the table starts at `1`. If you modify the software and/or table in any way, make sure that an ID of `-1` will always be an invalid ID.

To populate the user interface objects, a database connection is created and then opened. Next, a SqlCommand object is created for accessing the `sp_GetAdInfo` stored procedure. This stored procedure can be seen in Listing 12.7 (along with the `sp_GetAdvertiserInfo` stored proce-

dure). The `SqlCommand.ExecuteReader()` method is called, returning a SqlDataReader that contains the correct advertisement's data.

Once a recordset is retrieved with the `SqlDataReader.Read()`
method, the user interface objects can all be populated from the recordset.
Then all of the database objects are closed.

The last thing you'll see in the method is where the StartDate TextBox
is set with the current date if this isn't a post back. This is so that the starting date will always be set for the user.

Listng 12.6 The AddEditAd.aspx.cs Source Code. This Code Adds or Edits an
Advertisement.

```
private void Page_Load(object sender, System.EventArgs e)
{
  // Convert the Ad ID to an integer for convenience.
  int nAdID = Convert.ToInt32( Session["AdID"] );

  // See if we need to populate the user interface.
  if( !IsPostBack && nAdID >= 0 )
  {
    // Create the database connection object.
    SqlConnection objConnection =
      new SqlConnection(
        ConfigurationSettings.AppSettings["ConnectString"] );

    try
    {
      // Open the database connection.
      objConnection.Open();

      // Create the command object. Set it for the
      //   sp_GetAdInfo stored procedure.
      SqlCommand objCommand = new SqlCommand( "sp_GetAdInfo",
        objConnection );
      objCommand.CommandType = CommandType.StoredProcedure;

      // We need to give it a parameter of the Ad ID. This
      //   way it can retrieve the correct ad information.
      objCommand.Parameters.Add( "@ID", SqlDbType.Int );
      objCommand.Parameters["@ID"].Direction =
          ParameterDirection.Input;
      objCommand.Parameters["@ID"].Value = nAdID;
```

```csharp
      // Execute the reader and get the recordset.
      SqlDataReader objReader = objCommand.ExecuteReader();

      // Read a record.
      if( objReader.Read() )
      {
        // Set all the user interface objects from the
        //   recordset.
        AltText.Text = Convert.ToString( objReader["AltText"] );
        ImageURL.Text = Convert.ToString( objReader["ImageURL"] );
        ImageWidth.Text =
            Convert.ToString( objReader["ImageWidth"] );
        ImageHeight.Text =
            Convert.ToString( objReader["ImageHeight"] );
        Link.Text = Convert.ToString( objReader["Link"] );
        ViewLimit.Text = Convert.ToString( objReader["ViewLimit"] );
        ClicksLimit.Text =
            Convert.ToString( objReader["ClicksLimit"] );
        // We'll make sure to convert the DateTime objects
        //   into short date strings.
        EndDate.Text =
          Convert.ToDateTime(
              objReader["EndDate"] ).ToShortDateString();
        StartDate.Text =
          Convert.ToDateTime(
              objReader["StartDate"] ).ToShortDateString();
      }
    }
    catch( Exception ex )
    {
      // Alert the user to the error.
      ErrorMessage.Text = ex.Message.ToString();
    }
    finally
    {
      // If the database connection is open,
      //   close it.
      if( objConnection.State == ConnectionState.Open )
      {
        objConnection.Close();
      }
    }
  }
}
```

```
// We come here when this is a new record.
else if( !IsPostBack )
{
  // Populate the start date field with today's date.
  StartDate.Text = DateTime.Now.ToShortDateString();
}
}
```

Listing 12.7 The Stored Procedures That Get Advertisement, Advertisers' Information, Advertisement History, and a List of Advertisements.

```
CREATE PROCEDURE sp_GetAdInfo
  @ID int
AS
  select * from Advertisement where ID=@ID
GO


CREATE PROCEDURE sp_GetAdvertiserInfo
  @ID int
AS
  select * from Advertiser where ID=@ID
GO


CREATE PROCEDURE sp_GetHistory
  @Start DateTime,
  @End DateTime
AS
  select dt,Hour=DATEPART(hh,dt) from history
    where dt>=@Start and dt<=@End order by dt desc
GO


CREATE PROCEDURE sp_GetListOfAds
AS
  select AltText,ID from Advertisement order by AltText
GO
```

The code in Listing 12.8 shows the code behind the Default.aspx page. The Page_Load() method populates the AdList user interface object from the database. It gives users an easy way to select an advertisement that they might want to edit. The Page_Load() method populates the AdList object only when the method is not called in response to a post back. At that time, a database connection is created and opened. A SqlCommand object is created for accessing the `sp_GetListOfAds` stored procedure. The `SqlCommand.ExecuteReader()` method is called, returning a recordset of all the ads. The recordset is then bound to the AdList ListBox object. If there are no records found, the AdList object is hidden.

The `NewAd_Click()` method is fired when the user clicks the New Ad button. This method simply redirects to the AddEditAd.aspx page after setting the `AdID` session variable to −1. When the `AdID` session variable is −1, it indicates to the AddEditAd.aspx page that it's a new add and not an edited ad.

The `EditInfo_Click()` method just redirects to the EditAdvertiser.aspx page.

The `AdList_SelectedIndexChanged()` method fires when the user clicks an ad in the list. The first thing this method does is to set the `AdID` session variable so that the AddEditAd.aspx page will know what advertisement should be edited. Control is then redirected to the AddEditAd.aspx page.

The `Logout_Click()` method signs out using the `FormsAuthentication.SignOut()` method, and then redirects to the Login.aspx page.

The `InsertAdBanner()` method was discussed earlier. It invokes the Web Service that creates the HTML for the ad banner. This data is then inserted into the HTML stream with the `Response.Write()` method.

The `Reports_Click()` method redirects to the reports page.

Listing 12.8 The Default.aspx.cs Source Code. This Is the Controlling Module for the Application.

```
private void Page_Load(object sender, System.EventArgs e)
{
  if( !IsPostBack )
  {
    // Create the database connection.
    SqlConnection objConnection =
      new SqlConnection(
          ConfigurationSettings.AppSettings["ConnectString"] );

    // Create a reader and set it to null.
    SqlDataReader objReader = null;

    try
    {
```

```
// Open the database connection.
objConnection.Open();

// Create the command object and set it
//   for the sp_GetListOfAds SP.
SqlCommand objCommand =
  new SqlCommand( "sp_GetListOfAds", objConnection );
objCommand.CommandType = CommandType.StoredProcedure;

// Execute the reader and get the recordset.
objReader = objCommand.ExecuteReader();

// Set the DataList properties: the DataSource,
//   the DataTextField, the and DataValueField.
AdList.DataSource = objReader;
AdList.DataTextField = "AltText";
AdList.DataValueField = "ID";
// Bind the data.
AdList.DataBind();

// If there are no records, hide the
//   DataList object.
if( AdList.Items.Count == 0 )
{
  AdList.Visible = false;
  EditAnAd.Visible = false;
}
}
catch( Exception ex )
{
  // Alert the user to the error.
  ErrorMessage.Text = ex.Message.ToString();
}
finally
{
  // If the reader is non-null we'll
  //   need to close it.
  if( objReader != null )
  {
    objReader.Close();
  }
  // If the database connection is open,
  //   close it.
```

```
        if( objConnection.State == ConnectionState.Open )
        {
          objConnection.Close();
        }
      }
    }
}


private void NewAd_Click(object sender, System.EventArgs e)
{
  // Set the session variable to -1 to indicate
  //   a new ad.
  Session["AdID"] = -1;
  Response.Redirect( "AddEditAd.aspx" );
}


private void EditInfo_Click(object sender, System.EventArgs e)
{
  Response.Redirect( "EditAdvertiser.aspx" );
}


private void AdList_SelectedIndexChanged(object sender, System.EventArgs e)
{
  // Set the session variable to the Ad ID for the
  //   selected ad.
  try
  {
    Session["AdID"] = Convert.ToInt32( AdList.SelectedItem.Value );
  }
  catch
  {
    ErrorMessage.Text = "You did not make a selection.";
  }
  Response.Redirect( "AddEditAd.aspx" );
}


private void Logout_Click(object sender, System.EventArgs e)
{
  // Log out.
  FormsAuthentication.SignOut();
  Response.Redirect( "Login.aspx?Force=1" );
}
```

```
public void InsertAdBanner()
{
  // Instantiate the Web service wrapper class.
  com.aspnet_solutions.www.TheAdBanner1 sv =
    new com.aspnet_solutions.www.TheAdBanner1();
  // Output the new ad to the HTML stream.
  Response.Write( sv.NextAd() );
}


private void Reports_Click(object sender, System.EventArgs e)
{
  Response.Redirect( "Reports.aspx" );
}
```

The code in Listing 12.9 shows the code for the EditAdvertiser.aspx.cs source code module. The `Page_Load()` method populates the information from the database. It calls the `sp_GetAdvertiserInfo` stored prodedure shown in Listing 12.7. It starts off by creating a database connection and then opening it. A SqlCommand object is then created for accessing the `sp_GetAdvertiserInfo` stored procedure. The `AdvertiserID` is used as a parameter for the `sp_GetAdvertiserInfo` stored procedure (the parameter name is `@ID`).

When the `SqlCommand.ExecuteReader()` method is called, it returns a recordset with the advertiser's information. This is used to populate the user interface objects.

The `AddParameter()` method is used to simplify adding parameters to a SqlCommand object. This method is called from the `SaveUpdate_Click()` method. It just uses the `SqlCommand.Parameters.Add()` method to add the parameter, it sets the parameter direction, and then it sets the parameter value.

The `SaveUpdate_Click()` method fires when the user clicks the Save/Update button. It starts by creating and opening a database connection. It creates a SqlCommand object with which the `sp_UpdateAdvertiser` stored procedure will be accessed. The `@ID` parameter is added and its value set. Then, eight parameters are added by using the `AddParameter()` helper method. The parameters (which are all strings) that are added are `@Name`, `@Password`, `@Address`, `@CityStateZip`, `@Phone`, `@Fax`, `@Email`, and `@URL`. Finally, the `SqlCommand.ExecuteNonQuery()` method is called to execute the stored procedure. You can see the EditAdvertiser.aspx page in Figure 12.3.

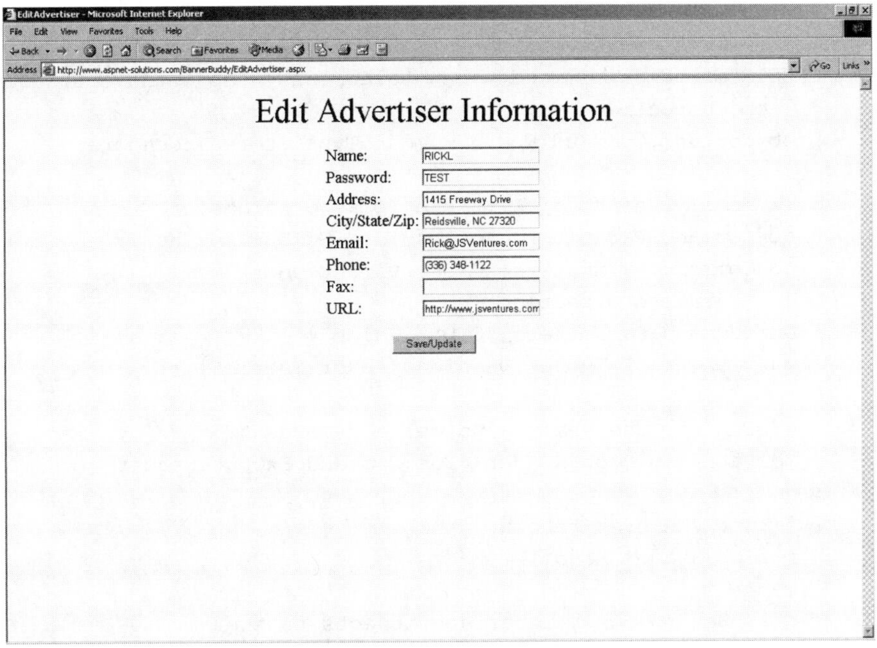

Figure 12.3 You Can Edit the Advertiser Information with This Screen.

The `sp_GetAdvertiserInfo` stored procedure can be seen in Listing 12.9.

Listing 12.9 The EditAdvertiser.aspx.cs source code. This code allows an advertiser's information to be edited.

```
private void Page_Load(object sender, System.EventArgs e)
{
  if( !IsPostBack )
  {
    // Create the database connection object.
    SqlConnection objConnection =
      new SqlConnection(
        ConfigurationSettings.AppSettings["ConnectString"] );

    try
    {
      // Open the database connection.
      objConnection.Open();
```

```
// Create the command object and set for
//  the sp_GetAdvertiserInfo SP.
SqlCommand objCommand = new SqlCommand( "sp_GetAdvertiserInfo",
  objConnection );
objCommand.CommandType = CommandType.StoredProcedure;

// We'll need to give it the ID as a parameter.
objCommand.Parameters.Add( "@ID", SqlDbType.Int );
objCommand.Parameters["@ID"].Direction =
    ParameterDirection.Input;
objCommand.Parameters["@ID"].Value =
    Convert.ToInt32( Session["AdvertiserID"] );

// Execute the reader and get a recordset.
SqlDataReader objReader = objCommand.ExecuteReader();

// Get the first record.
if( objReader.Read() )
{
  // Set the user interface objects to the
  //   appropriate data.
  Name.Text = Convert.ToString( objReader["Login"] );
  Password.Text = Convert.ToString( objReader["Password"] );
  Email.Text = Convert.ToString( objReader["Email"] );
  Phone.Text = Convert.ToString( objReader["Phone"] );
  Fax.Text = Convert.ToString( objReader["Fax"] );
  URL.Text = Convert.ToString( objReader["URL"] );
  Address.Text = Convert.ToString( objReader["Address"] );
  CityStateZip.Text =
      Convert.ToString( objReader["CityStateZip"] );
  }
}
catch( Exception ex )
{
  // Alert the user to the error.
  ErrorMessage.Text = ex.Message.ToString();
}
finally
{
  // If the database connection is opened,
  //   close it.
  if( objConnection.State == ConnectionState.Open )
  {
```

```
      objConnection.Close();
    }
  }
  }
}


// Helper method that adds a string parameter to a command object.
private void AddParameter( ref SqlCommand objCommand, string strValue,
string strParamName, int nSize )
{
  // Add the parameter.
  objCommand.Parameters.Add( strParamName, SqlDbType.NVarChar, nSize );
  // Set the direction.
  objCommand.Parameters[strParamName].Direction =
    ParameterDirection.Input;
  // Store the value.
  objCommand.Parameters[strParamName].Value = strValue;
}

private void SaveUpdate_Click(object sender, System.EventArgs e)
{
  // Create the database connection object.
  SqlConnection objConnection =
    new SqlConnection(
      ConfigurationSettings.AppSettings["ConnectString"] );

  // Assume pessimism for success.
  bool bSuccess = false;

  try
  {
    // Open the database connection.
    objConnection.Open();

    // Convert the Advertiser ID into an integer for convenience.
    int nAdvertiserID = Convert.ToInt32( Session["AdvertiserID"] );

    // Create the command object and set for the
    //    sp_UpdateAdvertiser SP.
    SqlCommand objCommand = new SqlCommand( "sp_UpdateAdvertiser",
      objConnection );
    objCommand.CommandType = CommandType.StoredProcedure;
```

```
    // We'll need to give it the ID as a parameter.
    objCommand.Parameters.Add( "@ID", SqlDbType.Int );
    objCommand.Parameters["@ID"].Direction = ParameterDirection.Input;
    objCommand.Parameters["@ID"].Value = nAdvertiserID;

    // Call the AddParameter() helper method to add the
    //   parameters and set the data.
    AddParameter( ref objCommand, Name.Text, "@Name", 150 );
    AddParameter( ref objCommand, Password.Text, "@Password", 150 );
    AddParameter( ref objCommand, Address.Text, "@Address", 150 );
    AddParameter( ref objCommand, CityStateZip.Text, "@CityStateZip",
      150 );
    AddParameter( ref objCommand, Phone.Text, "@Phone", 150 );
    AddParameter( ref objCommand, Fax.Text, "@Fax", 150 );
    AddParameter( ref objCommand, Email.Text, "@Email", 150 );
    AddParameter( ref objCommand, URL.Text, "@URL", 150 );

    // Execute the query.
    objCommand.ExecuteNonQuery();

    // Indicate success.
    bSuccess = true;
  }
  catch( Exception ex )
  {
    // Alert the user to the error.
    ErrorMessage.Text = ex.Message.ToString();
  }
  finally
  {
    // Close the database connection if it's
    //   open.
    if( objConnection.State == ConnectionState.Open )
    {
      objConnection.Close();
    }
  }
  // If successful, go back to the main page.
  if( bSuccess )
  {
    Response.Redirect( "Default.aspx" );
  }
}
```

Listing 12.10 The Stored Procedures That Update Advertisements and Advertisers.

```
CREATE PROCEDURE sp_UpdateAdvertiser
  @Name nvarchar(150),
  @Password nvarchar(150),
  @Address nvarchar(150),
  @CityStateZip nvarchar(150),
  @Phone nvarchar(25),
  @Fax nvarchar(25),
  @URL nvarchar(300),
  @Email nvarchar(250),
  @ID int
AS
  update Advertiser set Login=@Name,Password=@Password,Address=@Address,
CityStateZip=@CityStateZip,Phone=@Phone,Fax=@Fax,URL=@URL,Email=@Email
where ID=@ID
GO

CREATE PROCEDURE sp_UpdateAd
  @AltText nvarchar(300),
  @ImageURL nvarchar(300),
  @ImageWidth int,
  @ImageHeight int,
  @Link nvarchar(300),
  @ViewLimit int,
  @ClicksLimit int,
  @EndDate DateTime,
  @ID int out
AS
  Update Advertisement set AltText=@AltText,ImageURL=@ImageURL,
ImageWidth=@ImageWidth,ImageHeight=@ImageHeight,Link=@Link,ViewLimit
=@ViewLimit,ClicksLimit=@ClicksLimit,EndDate=@EndDate where ID=@ID
GO
```

Writing and Deploying Windows Services in .NET

Windows Services (formerly called NT Services) are applications that perform a set of tasks behind the scenes. They allow optimal performance and convenience. If a service fails, Windows can automatically restart it, leaving your application available 24/7.

Windows Services are also independent of the logged-on user, and they run under an identity that the machine administrator can select. Your service can be run in the background, regardless of whether a user is logged into Windows. This can be a mission-critical capability.

In times past, writing Windows Services required advanced knowledge of C and the Windows APIs. To use Visual Basic, a C++ "wrapper" had to be constructed. With Visual Studio .NET, you can write powerful Windows Services, in the language of your choice, with no more effort than writing other applications.

Writing a Windows Service in Visual Studio .NET

To demonstrate the ease of writing a service in Visual Studio .NET, let's create a sample service. Our new service will delete the contents of the C:\TEMP folder on a timed basis. It will also notate this event in the EventLog (accessible in the Event Viewer).

To begin, we'll select File, then New, and then Project from the Visual Studio .NET IDE menu. The project type we'll be selecting is Windows Service, and I named the project Service1, as shown in Figure 12.4.

A Windows Service cannot be run without being installed on the test machine. Fortunately, Microsoft has automated this process. You must add an installer. To do this, follow these steps:

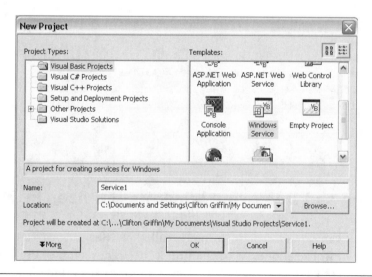

Figure 12.4 Select "Windows Service" in the Project Selector.

1. In the design view of Service1.vb, select Add Installer.
2. Open the properties for ServiceProcessInstaller1.
3. Set the account setting to Local System to ensure that you run the service with the proper credentials. This actually allows the application to run under the "Run as part of the operating system" privilege. Be careful because a poorly written NT Service running under this account can do some real damage.
4. Open the properties for ServiceInstaller1 as well.
5. Change the ServiceName and DisplayName to SampleServiceVB.

NOTE: You can also set the `StartType` property. This dictates whether the service is disabled by default, requires manual starting, or starts automatically with Windows. You'll want to select this based on your project's demands.

The next thing we'll do is add a timer. Go back to the Design view of Service1.vb, and add a Timer from the tool box. Open the properties for the new timer, and set the interval to `1000`, which will be 10 seconds.

In Service1.vb design mode, right click and select View Code. You will see there are two preset methods here: `OnStart()` and `OnStop()`. The `OnStart()` method fires when the service runs. The `OnStop()` method fires when necessary to cleanly stop the service when a stop request is received.

The work of this service will be performed in two methods: `Delete-Files()` and `WriteLog()`. We'll create those methods now by adding empty methods to the code module, as follows:

C#
```csharp
public void DeleteFiles()
{
}
public void WriteLog(string LogEntry)
{
}
```

VB
```vb
Public Sub DeleteFiles()

End Sub
```

```
Public Sub WriteLog(ByVal LogEntry As String)
End Sub
```

The first method, `DeleteFiles()`, will perform the temp file deletion. The second method will receive the text of a log entry passed in and
write the entry out.

Add the following code to the `DeleteFiles()` method:

C#

```
try
{
    // Delete temporary files
    foreach( string strFile in Directory.GetFiles( "C:\\temp" ) )
    {
        File.Delete( strFile );
    }
    // Send log entry info to WriteLog function
    WriteLog( "Files deleted on: " + DateTime.Now.TimeOfDay.ToString() );
}
catch( Exception ex )
{
        WriteLog( "Error:" + ex.ToString() );
}
```

VB

```
Try
    ' Delete temporary files
    Dim strFile As String
    For Each strFile In Directory.GetFiles("C:\temp")
        File.Delete(strFile)
    Next
    ' Send log entry info to WriteLog function
    WriteLog("Files deleted on: " & CStr(TimeOfDay))
Catch ex As Exception
    WriteLog("Error:" & e.ToString())
End Try
```

To protect against unforeseen errors, I inserted the code in a `try/`
`catch` block. The code declares a string and uses `For Each` to gather the
list of files for deletion. It then uses this array to delete the files, one by one.
Consider this a hard-wired `while` statement.

NOTE: Subdirectories and their contents will not be deleted with this code. Because this is for demonstration purposes, the simplest method was chosen.

C#

```
WriteLog( "Files deleted on: " +
DateTime.Now.TimeOfDay.ToString() );
```

VB

```
WriteLog("Files deleted on: " &
DateTime.Now.TimeOfDay.ToString())
```

The above code provides the necessary information as a string to the `WriteLog()` method. In the code that follows, a custom log is being created named ServiceCS. This log can be read, just like the Application, System, and Security logs, by selecting ServiceCS in the tree control of Event Viewer. Here is the code that should be added to the `WriteLog()` method:

C#

```
// Check for existence of current log
if( !EventLog.SourceExists( "ServiceCS" ) )
{
  EventLog.CreateEventSource( "ServiceCS","ServiceCS Log" );
}
EventLog.Source = "SampleServiceCS";
// Write entry
EventLog.WriteEntry( "ServiceCS Log", LogEntry,
 EventLogEntryType.Information );
```

VB

```
' Create event log
Dim Log As New EventLog()
' Check for existents of current log
If Not Log.SourceExists("SampleServiceVB") Then
    Log.CreateEventSource("SampleServiceVB", "SampleServiceVB Log")
End If
Log.Source = "SampleServiceVB"
'Write entry
Log.WriteEntry("SampleServiceVB Log", LogEntry,
  EventLogEntryType.Information)
```

This gathers the string passed into LogEntry and writes out an appropriate log entry with the data.

C#

```
if( !EventLog.SourceExists( "ServiceCS" ) )
{
  EventLog.CreateEventSource("ServiceCS","ServiceCS Log");
}
```

VB

```
Dim Log As New EventLog()
' Creates new EventLog object.
If Not Log.SourceExists("SampleServiceVB") Then
   Log.CreateEventSource("SampleServiceVB", "SampleServiceVB Log")
End If
```

The following code checks for an existing log. If there isn't any, we create one.

C#

```
EventLog.Source = "SampleServiceVB";
// Write entry
EventLog.WriteEntry( "ServiceCS Log", LogEntry, EventLogEntryType.
Information );
```

VB

```
Log.Source = "SampleServiceVB"
' Write entry
Log.WriteEntry("SampleServiceVB Log", LogEntry, EventLogEntryType.
Information)
```

And last, we set the `Source` property of our Log object to our created Log entitled SampleServiceVB. We then write out the appropriate Log Entry.

This takes care of deleting the files and writing to the log file; but until we add a timer action, none of this will happen.

Back in Design view of Service1.VB, double-click Timer1. Add `DeleteFiles()` to this new function. It should look like this:

C#

```
private void timer1_Elapsed(object sender,
  System.Timers.ElapsedEventArgs e)
```

```
{
  DeleteFiles();
}
```

VB
```
Private Sub Timer1_Elapsed(ByVal sender As System.Object, _
  ByVal e As System.Timers.ElapsedEventArgs) Handles Timer1.Elapsed
    DeleteFiles()
End Sub
```

Deployment

Because a service is a special application, it cannot be run by simply double-clicking it from File Explorer. This is where our ServiceInstaller comes into play.

From the Build menu, select Build Solution. Ensure that it finishes without errors. To install the service, open up the command prompt by clicking Start >Run. Type **cmd** in the box, and press OK.

Switch directories to C:\WINDOWS\Microsoft.NET\Framework\ v1.0.3705. The exact directory will be different, depending upon the installed version of the .NET Framework and your version of Windows.

RUNNING THE `InstallUtil` PROGRAM: InstallUtil is contained in the CLR Framework directory. It opens up the assembly, looks for

Figure 12.5 Command Prompt

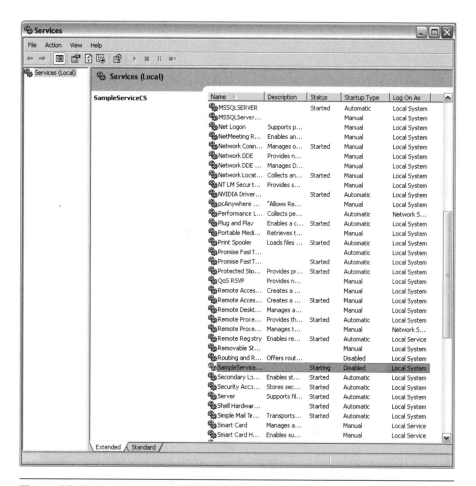

Figure 12.6 Services Control Panel

Installer derived classes, and runs the entry points in some order to install the item without requiring the user to build an MSI (see Figure 12.5).

Once you're in the proper directory, type **InstallUtil "c:\My Documents\Visual Studio Projects\Service1\bin\service1.exe"**. The actual path to your executable will vary on your setup. Pressing enter will register the service with Windows.

To start the service, open up the Services control panel from Administrative Tools in the Control Panel as shown in Figure 12.6. Click your new service and press the Play button above. WARNING: This will—as specified in the program—delete the contents of the C:\Temp folder. Be sure your directory is free of important files OR select a different directory in the application and redeploy.

To stop the service, press the Stop button.

To view the created log, open up the Event Viewer under Administrative Tools in the Control Panel.

The BannerBuddy Service

I created an NT Service that sends out e-mails once a day to advertisers to let them know their statistics. The code is simple and can be seen in Listing 12.11. It simply formats the numerical data for each day and time so that it can easily be read.

Listing 12.11 The NT Service Code for Sending Out E-mails to Advertisers

```
public void SendReports()
{
 // Create the database connection.
 SqlConnection objConnection =
  new SqlConnection( "data source=localhost;initial
catalog=Bannerbuddy;" +
      "persist security info=False;user id=sa;pwd=" );

 // Create a reader and set it to null.
 SqlDataReader objReader = null;

 try
 {
  // Open the database connection.
  objConnection.Open();

  // Create the command object.
  SqlCommand objCommand =
   new SqlCommand( "select ID from Advertiser", objConnection );

  // Execute the reader and get the recordset.
  objReader = objCommand.ExecuteReader();

  while( objReader.Read() )
  {
   string strEmail;
```

```
    string strEmailContent =
      FormatReportInfo( Convert.ToInt32( objReader["ID"] ),
      ref strEmail );

  MailMessage message = new MailMessage();
  message.Body = strEmailContent;
  message.BodyFormat = MailFormat.Html;
  message.From = "BannerBuddy<Reports@ASPNET-Solutions.com>";
  message.Subject = "BannerBuddy Report";
  SmtpMail.SmtpServer = "mail.aspnet-solutions.com";
  message.To = strEmail;
  SmtpMail.Send ( message );
  }


 objReader.Close();
}
catch( Exception ex )
{
 // Alert the user to the error.

 // Check for existents of current log
 if( !EventLog.SourceExists( "BannerBuddy" ) )
 {
  EventLog.CreateEventSource( "ServBannerBuddyiceCS","BannerBuddy Log" );
 }
 EventLog.Source = "BannerBuddyServiceCS";
 // Write entry
 EventLog.WriteEntry( "BannerBuddy Log", ex.Message.ToString(),
  EventLogEntryType.Information );

}
finally
{
 // If the reader is non-null we'll
 //   need to close it.
 if( objReader != null )
 {
  objReader.Close();
 }
 // If the database connection is open,
 //   close it.
 if( objConnection.State == ConnectionState.Open )
```

```
    {
      objConnection.Close();
    }
  }
}
```

Summary

There you have it: a complete advertising banner system with source code. If it isn't exactly what you want, get in there and make the changes you need. And it might even be just what you need without modifications.

In this chapter, you've learned several important things. One is how to maintain statistics in a database. The important statistics are the `Clicks/ClicksLimit` and `Views/VewLimit` fields.

Another very important thing you saw was how to perform some fairly complex calculations in a stored procedure. This was done in the `sp_GetNextAd` stored procedure because the weights of all advertisements are considered for selecting the next advertisement.

The last important thing talked about was creating an NT Service. The NT Service that was created for this application sends out e-mails with statistics for the advertisements.

CHAPTER 13

Effective Use of the .NET Networking Classes

In This Chapter:

- Using the `Dns` Class
- Using the `WebClient` Class
- Using the `WebRequest` and `WebResponse` Classes
- Using the `WebProxy` Class
- NTLM Authentication
- SSL Communication
- Posting Data
- System.Net Errors

At times, you will need to request data from other Web servers within your ASP.NET application. At first, this idea might seem strange. After all, we have been talking about using Web services to get data from other servers. Although Web services are extremely useful and represent the current recommended way for obtaining data from other servers, not all servers will offer Web services to your application.

For instance, a page on another server might present data or information of some sort, and you would like to retrieve this information for use in your application. If this is an older server that does not support Web services, you might need to employ some more pedestrian data-retrieval methods. Essentially, you would request the Web page in which the data resides, then you would process the Web page and extract the data. This technique is commonly known as **data scraping**, in which you retrieve a Web page and extract data that you would like to use in your application. One important note, though, is that you must have permission before you can legally scrape data from another Web site. Make sure, before you use data from someone else's Web site, that you have the necessary permissions.

The System.Net namespace provides a simple programming interface to many of the protocols found in today's networks. This namespace includes `WebRequest`, `WebResponse`, `Dns`, `WebProxy`, and many

Table 13.1 The Commonly Used .NET Networking Classes

Class	Description
WebRequest	This class makes a request to a Uniform Resource Identifier.
WebResponse	This class provides a response from a Uniform Resource Identifier.
Dns	This class provides simple domain name resolution functionality.
WebProxy	This class contains HTTP proxy settings for the WebRequest class.

other types of classes with which you can easily write networking applications. This namespace enables you to develop applications that use Internet resources, and the classes encapsulate them in such a way that you don't have to worry about the specific details of doing the networking. Table 13.1 gives a brief description of these classes.

Using the Dns Class

The Internet Domain Name System (DNS) is the general system with which networking applications can retrieve information about specific hosts on a network, usually on the Internet. This information includes host names, domain names, and IP addresses. The Dns class that comes with the .NET Framework is a static class. You can't instantiate the class before using it because all of its members are static.

When the Dns methods return information, it is always in the form of an IPHostEntry object. For instance, the following line retrieves host information based on a domain name.

```
IPHostEntry HostInfo = Dns.GetHostByName( "www.somedomain.com" );
```

The IPHostEntry object contains all the information that DNS can obtain about a given host. This object includes a list of addresses (because any given host can have more than one address), aliases, and the host name. After you get the IPHostEntry object, you should use the first IP address in the list. It is rare to have more than one IP address for a domain, but it is possible—that's why under most circumstances you'll just use the first address in the list. This is the most common thing you will do with an IPHostEntry object. The most useful way to get an IP address is in the form of an unsigned integer (32 bits). The following code shows how to retrieve the first IP address from an IPHostEntry object that has an unsigned 32-bit integer:

```
uint nIPAddress = Convert.ToUInt32( HostInfo.AddressList[0].Address;
```

To represent an IP address in a string, you must convert each of the bytes in the 32-bit integer to a value that will be placed in a string variable. The following code shows how to set a string to reflect an IP address that is contained in an unsigned integer:

```
string strSomeString = Convert.ToString( nIPAddress & 0x000000ff ) +
  "." + Convert.ToString( ( nIPAddress & 0x0000ff00 ) >> 8 ) + "." +
  Convert.ToString( ( nIPAddress & 0x00ff0000 ) >> 16 ) + "." +
  Convert.ToString( ( nIPAddress & 0xff000000 ) >> 24 );
```

You can also use the `IPAddress` class to directly output an IP address as a string with the `ToString()` method, as follows:

```
string strSomeString = myIPAddress.ToString();
```

You have already seen how to get an IP address from a domain name. You can do the reverse as well. You can get a host name from an IP address, because DNS does a reverse lookup on an IP address and resolves the address to a domain name. The following code shows how to retrieve a domain name from an IP address. Note that the first thing that happens is that an IPHostEntry object is created. This object will contain the host name that the method returns.

```
IPHostEntry HostInfo = Dns.GetHostByAddress( "208.242.41.232" );
string strSomeString = HostInfo.HostName;
```

I have created an application to demonstrate the topics in this chapter. The name of the application is NetworkingDemoApplication. I have created individual pages to demonstrate the individual topics. And to show you the Dns class in action, I have created a page named DnsDemos. When the page first executes, it retrieves the host name and IP address of the current machine. It also gives users the opportunity to type in a domain name and do a resolution. And in another text box, users can type in an IP address and get a reverse resolution. This application can be seen in Figure 13.1.

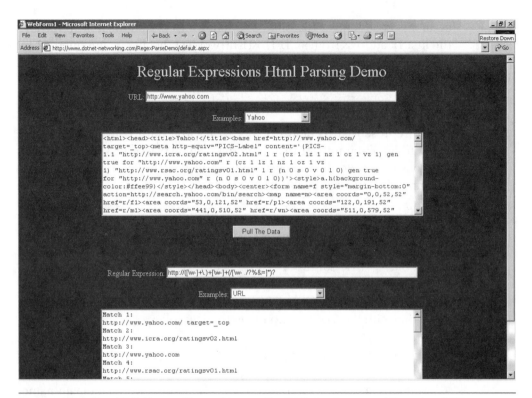

Figure 13.1 The DNS Demo Shows How to Do DNS Lookups and Reverse DNS Lookups.

The source code for the DNSDemos page can be seen in listing 13.1. Actually, this is not the .aspx source code, but the C# code that is behind the DnsDemo.aspx file.

Listing 13.1 The Source Code for the DNS Demo Portion of the Networking Demo Application

```
private void Page_Load(object sender, System.EventArgs e)
{
  try
  {
    HostName.Text = Dns.GetHostName();
    IPHostEntry Host = Dns.GetHostByName( HostName.Text );

    IPAddress.Text=Host.AddressList[0].ToString();
  }
```

```
    catch
    {
    }
}


private void Button1_Click(object sender, System.EventArgs e)
{
    try
    {
        IPHostEntry Host = Dns.GetHostByName( DomainNameIn.Text );

        IPFromDomain.Text=Host.AddressList[0].ToString();
    }
    catch( Exception ex )
    {
        IPFromDomain.Text = ex.Message.ToString();
    }
}


private void Button2_Click(object sender, System.EventArgs e)
{
    try
    {
        IPHostEntry Host = Dns.GetHostByAddress( IPAddressIn.Text );
        DomainFromIP.Text = Host.HostName;
    }
    catch( Exception ex )
    {
        DomainFromIP.Text = ex.Message.ToString();
    }
}


private void Button3_Click(object sender, System.EventArgs e)
{
    Response.Redirect( "MainMenu.aspx" );
}
```

When you look at the source code, notice the Page_Load() method. In the Page_Load() method, the first thing that happens is that the Dns.GetHostName() method is called. This method returns the host name of the server on which the application is running. The next line of code uses this name, the host name, to retrieve an IPHostEntry object in which the IP address is contained.

The second line of code in the `Page_Load()` method calls the `Dns.GetHostByName()` method, whereas the third line in the `Page_Load()` method retrieves the first IP address from the IPHostEntry object as an unsigned integer. The last thing that happens in the `Page_Load()` method is that the 32-bit integer is converted into a string, and the string represents the IP address of the server. This string will be stored into a label named `IPAddress` in the .aspx file. The user can then view the IP address.

The `Button_Click()` method is fired when the user wants to perform a lookup on a domain name. In other words, the user types a domain name, and this code looks up that domain name's IP address. The code first calls the `Dns.GetHostByName()` method, which returns an IPHostEntry object. The next thing it does is to retrieve the unsigned 32-bit integer of the first IP address. Finally, it converts the 32-bit IP address into a string value, which is then easily read by the user. You might notice, too, that any exceptions that are thrown are caught in the error message displayed on the screen.

The last method in the code in Listing 13.1 is the `Button2_Click()` method. This method fires when the user wants to do a reverse lookup on an IP address. In other words, if in the second editable text field the user types something such as **208.242.41.135**, this program goes out and finds the domain name of that IP address. It does so by calling the `Dns.GetHostByAddress()` method, which returns an IPHostEntry object. The IPHostEntry object has a property named `HostName` that contains the host name that resulted from the reverse lookup.

The `Dns` class has several other useful methods; most notably, the ones that enable you to do asynchronous lookups. Because this book does not cover the C# and VB languages in great detail, we have not covered issues of threading and thread synchronization. For that reason, it is impractical to cover these additional methods at this time. The `Dns` class supports synchronous and asynchronous methods of retrieving data. The synchronous methods are as easy to use as the `Dns` class methods that we have already discussed, and the asynchronous methods are easy as long as you understand .NET threading and synchronization.

Using the `WebClient` Class

The `WebClient` class provides common methods for sending data to and receiving data from a resource identified by a URL. Underneath the covers, the `WebClient` class uses the `WebRequest` class (which is covered in more detail later in this chapter) to provide access to Internet resources. For this reason, the WebClient class is easier to use than the WebRequest class because it encapsulates the WebRequest class at a higher level and abstracts much of the detail out.

The WebClient class has four methods for performing data transfer. They are the OpenWrite() method, which sends a stream to the resource; the UploadData() method, which sends a byte array to the resource and returns the byte array with any response; the Upload-File() method, which sends a local file to the resource and returns a byte array with any response; and the UploadValues() method, which sends a name value collection to the resource.

Three other methods are even easier to use than the four just mentioned. These are the DownloadData() method, which downloads data from a resource and returns a byte array; the DownloadFile() method, which downloads data from a resource to a local file; and the OpenRead() method, which returns the data from the resource as a stream.

I have created a page in the NetworkingDemoApplication named Web-ClientDemo. This page enables users to retrieve a Web page with either the OpenRead() method or the DownloadFile() method. You can see the application in Figure 13.2.

The code shown ahead in Listing 13.2 is what is behind the .aspx file that you can see in Figure 13.2. There are two buttons that users can click. The first button takes the resource identifier (and this is some kind of URL) that the user specifies and retrieves the data. The data is placed into a text box.

In Listing 13.2 you should first see the ReadData_Click() method. The method starts off by setting a Label1.Text so that it is empty. The next line instantiates a WebClient object. This object is used to read the data from the remote server. You can then see where the OpenRead() method is called. The single argument to the OpenRead() method is the URL that the user has given. The OpenRead() method returns a Stream object.

Listing 13.2 The Source Code for the WebClient Demo

```
private void ReadData_Click(object sender, System.EventArgs e)
{
    try
    {
        Label1.Text = "";
        WebClient client = new WebClient();
```

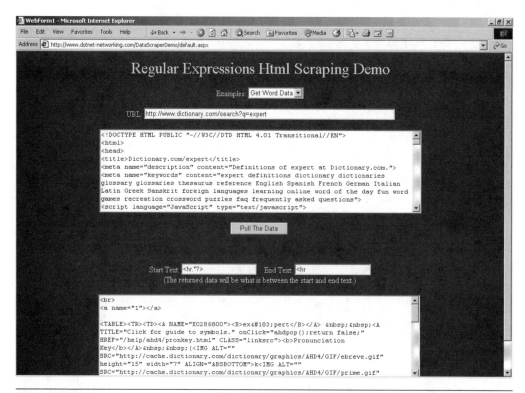

Figure 13.2 The `WebClient` Class Lets You Easily Download Data from the Web.

```
        Stream response = client.OpenRead( URL1.Text );
        Content1.Text = "";
        Content1.Visible = true;
        int nByteData;
        do
        {
            nByteData = response.ReadByte();
            if( nByteData > 0 )
            {
                Content1.Text += Convert.ToChar( nByteData );
            }
        } while( nByteData > 0 );
        response.Close();
    }
    catch( Exception ex )
    {
        Content1.Visible = false;
```

```
            Label1.Text = ex.Message.ToString();
        }
    }
}

private void Button2_Click(object sender, System.EventArgs e)
{
    try
    {
        Label2.Text = "";
        WebClient client = new WebClient();
        string strDest =
            Request.MapPath( @"TempFiles\Temp" +
            Convert.ToString( DateTime.Now.Millisecond +
                DateTime.Now.Second * 1000 )
            + ".tmp" );
        client.DownloadFile( URLSource.Text, strDest );
        FileDest.Text = strDest;
        Label2.Text = "Done!";
    }
    catch( Exception ex )
    {
        Label2.Text = ex.Message.ToString();
    }
}
```

The text box that is used to display data that has been retrieved is named `Content1`. Its `Text` property is cleared and set to be empty before the retrieval process starts. The text box should be empty in case there is some sort of retrieval error and an exception is thrown. The text box's `Visible` property is set to `true`. Initially, the `Visible` property is set to `false`, and the text box cannot be seen until a file is successfully retrieved.

A simple do/while construct retrieves the data one byte at a time and then appends that byte of data to the text box's `Text` property. This way, all the retrieved data will be placed into the text box so the user can view it. After all the data is read, the Stream object is closed. Note that if an exception is thrown, the text box's `Visible` property is set to `false` and the exception error message is output to the message label so that the user can see the error that was generated.

You can then see the `Button2_Click()` method. This method starts off in much the same way as the `Button1_Click()` method did. The label's `Text` properties are emptied and a `WebClient` class is created. The next thing that happens, though, is that a string is created that contains a destination path for the file. This is necessary because the `DownloadFile()` method requires a destination file name on the local hard drive. The application contains a directory named TempFiles, which has the necessary permissions so that these temporary files can be written. The `WebClient` class's `DownloadFile()` method is then called, which downloads the file to the server and not the client. This method requires two arguments: the source URL and the destination file name. These are both passed as string arguments. As a convenience to users, the temporary file name is displayed in a read-only text box on the Web Form. Then, the status label (named `Label2`) indicates that the transfer is done. If for some reason an error occurs and an exception is thrown, the status label reflects the error message.

Using the `WebRequest` and `WebResponse` Classes

A combination of `WebRequest` and `WebResponse` classes can be used to request data from Internet resources, and then to read the response. To do these actions, the first thing you must do is create a WebRequest object, as the following code shows you:

```
WebRequest wReq = WebRequest.Create( "http://www.SomeDomain.com/" );
```

The .NET Framework provides protocol-specific WebRequest and WebResponse objects for resources that begin with HTTP, HTTPS, and FILE. To access other protocols, you must implement protocol-specific descendants of WebRequest and WebResponse. This chapter deals only with HTTP and HTTPS data.

The next thing you should do is to set any properties required to perform the data retrieval request that you want. For instance, you may need to set the credentials so that your request authenticates to the server, or you may need to set the proxy server so that your request goes through the correct proxy server. Both these items are covered later on in this chapter.

In most cases, the WebRequest instance itself is sufficient to send and receive data. The following code shows how to use a WebRequest object to get a WebResponse object:

```
WebResponse wResp = wReq.GetResponse();
```

You can also find out when the resource was last updated. This information might be important if you want to retrieve data so that the time-sensitive data can be accurately evaluated. The following code shows you how to check the date of a resource:

```
if( wResp is HttpWebResponse )
{
    DateTime Updated = (HttpWebResponse)wResp)).LastModified;
}
```

You can also get access to the HTTP headers that are contained within the WebResponse object. These headers might include the server, the content type, the content length, and so forth. The following example shows you how to retrieve the server header from the headers collection:

```
string server = wResp.Headers["Server"];
```

In Listing 13.3, code that uses a WebRequest and a WebResponse object shows you how to retrieve data over the Internet. The WebRequest object is created based on a URL (and the URL specification is in a string named strURL). A WebResponse object is obtained by calling the Web-Request GetResponse() method. A Stream object is created, the encoding is specified, and a StreamReader object is also created. Then some fairly simple code lets you retrieve the entire contents of the resource. In the case of this example, nothing is done with the data; it is simply assigned to a string. But in most cases, you would be storing the data to a disk file or some sort of a user interface object.

Listing 13.3 Using WebRequest and WebResponse Objects to Retrieve Data

```
try
{
    WebRequest req = WebRequest.Create( strURL );
    WebResponse result = req.GetResponse();
    Stream ReceiveStream = result.GetResponseStream();
    Encoding encode = System.Text.Encoding.GetEncoding( "utf-8" );
    StreamReader sr = new StreamReader( ReceiveStream, encode );

    Char[] ReadBuffer = new Char[256];
    int nCount = sr.Read( ReadBuffer, 0, 256 );
```

Table 13.2 The TransportType Enumeration

Member name	Description
All	All transport types.
Connectionless	The transport type is connectionless, such as UDP.
ConnectionOriented	The transport is connection-oriented, such as TCP.
Tcp	TCP transport.
Udp	UDP transport.

```
    while( nCount > 0 )
    {
        String str = new String( ReadBuffer, 0, nCount );
        nCount = sr.Read( ReadBuffer, 0, 256 );
    }
}
catch( Exception )
{
    // Handle the exception here
}
```

I have created a page in MyNetworkingDemo application named WebRequestDemo.

You have a number of choices with regard to the transport type when you retrieve information. The default is `All`, which allows retrieval using all transport types. But you can be specific in the types you allow with the enumeration seen in Table 13.2.

Using the `WebProxy` Class

There may be times when your application needs to communicate through a proxy server. When this is true, it would be advisable to use the `WebProxy` class so you can have control over the communication. You can specify the name of the proxy server, the port through which you will be communicating, and whether to bypass the proxy server for local communications. The following code snippet shows how you can use the `WebProxy` class to make a Web request:

```
WebProxy proxyObject = new WebProxy( "http://MyProxyServer:80/", true );
WebRequest req = WebRequest.Create( "http://www.SomeDomain.com" );
req.Proxy = proxyObject;
```

When the Proxy object is created, the name of the proxy server (in this case, MyProxyServer), the port number (80), and whether to bypass the proxy for local servers (`true` in this case) are specified. The second line of this example creates a WebRequest object. The third line sets the Web-Request object's proxy field to the newly created Proxy object. This setting causes the WebRequest to go through the proxy server that was specified in the creation of the WebProxy object.

A more complete example can be seen in Listing 13.4. This example creates a WebProxy object and pulls data from a remote URL. A couple of string variables used in this example need some explanation. The first is `strProxyName`. This is a string that should contain the name of a proxy server. The other string variable that I am using in this example is `strURL`. This string contains the URL identifier for the data that you want to retrieve.

Listing 13.4 Using a WebProxy Object to Exercise Control over the Data Retrieval Operation

```
try
{
    WebProxy ProxyObj = new WebProxy( strProxyName, 80 );

    // Disable Proxy use when the host is local i.e. without periods.
    ProxyObj.BypassProxyOnLocal = true;

    // Now actually take over the global with new settings,
    // all new requests
    // use this proxy info
    GlobalProxySelection.Select = ProxyObj;

    WebRequest req = WebRequest.Create( strURL );
    WebResponse result = req.GetResponse();
    Stream ReceiveStream = result.GetResponseStream();
    Encoding encode = System.Text.Encoding.GetEncoding( "utf-8" );
    StreamReader sr = new StreamReader( ReceiveStream, encode );

    Char[] ReadBuffer = new Char[256];
    int nCount = sr.Read( ReadBuffer, 0, 256 );
```

```
    while( nCount > 0 )
    {
        String str = new String( ReadBuffer, 0, nCount );
        nCount = sr.Read( ReadBuffer, 0, 256 );
    }

}
catch( Exception )
{
    // Handle the exception here
}
```

If you look at the code in Listing 13.4, you will see that the first thing that happens is that the WebProxy object is created. The next thing that is done is to specify that the proxy server is bypassed access the local host. Then the global proxy settings for this machine are set to be the same as the WebProxy object that was just created. A WebRequest object is then created based on the URL in the strURL string. A WebResponse object is created that will be used to obtain any data that is sent back. A Stream object is then created, which provides flexibility because Stream objects offer a lot of choices when deciding how to process data. In Listing 13.4, you will see a simple do/while loop that reads in data and assigns the character data to a string. In this case, the code is not doing anything with the data except simply reading it in, although most applications do some useful work with the information.

NTLM Authentication

Many Web resources are protected by some sort of authentication scheme. This section examines retrieving data from Web resources that require NTLM authentication. Essentially, a NetworkCredential class needs to be created. The NetworkCredential class constructor requires a username and password in the domain. The NetworkCredential class can then be assigned to the WebRequest object that is used to perform any kind of Web request. This combination then satisfies the authentication requirements of the remote server. The code in Listing 13.5 shows how to use authentication when requesting data from a remote server.

Listing 13.5 Authenticating a User Before the Data Is Retrieved

```
try
{
    WebRequest req = WebRequest.Create( strURL );
    NetworkCredential sc =
     new NetworkCredential( strUsername, strPassword, strDomain );
    req.Credentials = sc;
    WebResponse result = req.GetResponse();
    Stream ReceiveStream = result.GetResponseStream();
    Encoding encode = System.Text.Encoding.GetEncoding( "utf-8" );
    StreamReader sr = new StreamReader( ReceiveStream, encode );

    Char[] ReadBuffer = new Char[256];
    int nCount = sr.Read( ReadBuffer, 0, 256 );

    while( nCount > 0 )
    {
        String str = new String( ReadBuffer, 0, nCount );
        nCount = sr.Read( ReadBuffer, 0, 256 );
    }

}
catch( Exception )
{
    // Handle the exception here
}
```

SSL Communication

You may need to communicate over a secure connection. If you do, chances are that you will be using the Secure Sockets Layer (SSL). The example in Listing 13.6 shows you how to make requests using SSL because the user is simply using HTTPS.

Listing 13.6 Requesting Data via SSL

```
try
{
    WebRequest req = WebRequest.Create( "https://www.SecureServer.com" );
```

```
    WebResponse result = req.GetResponse();
    Stream ReceiveStream = result.GetResponseStream();
    Encoding encode = System.Text.Encoding.GetEncoding( "utf-8" );
    StreamReader sr = new StreamReader( ReceiveStream, encode );

    Char[] ReadBuffer = new Char[256];
    int nCount = sr.Read( ReadBuffer, 0, 256 );

    while( nCount > 0 )
    {
        String str = new String( ReadBuffer, 0, nCount );
        nCount = sr.Read( ReadBuffer, 0, 256 );
    }
}
catch( Exception )
{
    // Handle the exception here
}
```

Posting Data

Many times, you might want to include data in your Web request that must be posted to a remote server. This data is likely to include form data that you want to post to a server, and this form data must be processed before any data can be returned. The code in Listing 13.7 shows you how to add POST data to your WebRequest.

Listing 13.7 This Code Shows How to Post Data in a Request.

```
try
{
    WebRequest req = WebRequest.Create( strURL );
    req.Method = "POST";
    req.ContentType = "application/x-www-form-urlencoded";

    byte[] SomeBytes = null;
    SomeBytes = Encoding.UTF8.GetBytes( strPostData );
    req.ContentLength = SomeBytes.Length;
    Stream newStream = req.GetRequestStream();
    newStream.Write( SomeBytes, 0, SomeBytes.Length );
    newStream.Close();
```

```
    WebResponse result = req.GetResponse();
    Stream ReceiveStream = result.GetResponseStream();
    Encoding encode = System.Text.Encoding.GetEncoding("utf-8");
    StreamReader sr = new StreamReader( ReceiveStream, encode );

    Char[] ReadBuffer = new Char[256];
    int nCount = sr.Read( ReadBuffer, 0, 256 );

    while( nCount > 0 )
    {
        String str = new String( ReadBuffer, 0, nCount );
        nCount = sr.Read( ReadBuffer, 0, 256 );
    }
}
catch( Exception ex )
{
    // Handle the exception here
}
```

System.Net Errors

It is important that you be able to correctly identify anything that goes wrong with your networked applications. For that reason, this entire section is dedicated to presenting a comprehensive guide to System.Net errors. Table 13.3 contains all the HttpStatusCode enumeration values. These values don't necessarily represent errors, but in many cases they do. This table presents the status codes that can be returned from networking method calls.

Table 13.4 contains the WebExceptionStatus enumeration. All exceptions that the System.Net methods throw can be found in this table. These are the values that you must check when your System.Net throws an exception.

Table 13.3 The HttpStatusCode Enumeration

Member Name	Description
Accepted	Equivalent to HTTP status 202. Accepted indicates that the request has been accepted for further processing. *(continued)*

Table 13.3 The HttpStatusCode Enumeration (*cont.*)

Member Name	Description
Ambiguous	Equivalent to HTTP status 300. Ambiguous indicates that the requested information has multiple representations. The default action is to treat this status as a redirect and follow the contents of the Location header associated with this response. If the Http-WebRequest.AllowAutoRedirect property is false, Ambiguous causes an exception to be thrown. Ambiguous is a synonym for MultipleChoices.
BadGateway	Equivalent to HTTP status 502. BadGateway indicates that an intermediate proxy server received a bad response from another proxy or the originating server.
BadRequest	Equivalent to HTTP status 400. BadRequest indicates that the server could not understand the request. BadRequest is sent when no other error is applicable, or if the exact error is unknown or does not have its own error code.
Conflict	Equivalent to HTTP status 409. Conflict indicates that the request could not be carried out because of a conflict on the server.
Continue	Equivalent to HTTP status 100. Continue indicates that the client may continue with its request.
Created	Equivalent to HTTP status 201. Created indicates that the request resulted in a new resource that was created before the response was sent.
ExpectationFailed	Equivalent to HTTP status 417. Expectation-Failed indicates that an expectation given in an Expect header could not be met by the server.
Forbidden	Equivalent to HTTP status 403. Forbidden indicates that the server refuses to fulfill the request.
Found	Equivalent to HTTP status 302. Found indicates that the requested information is located at the URI specified in the Location header. The default action when this status is received is to follow the Location header associated with the response. When the original request method is POST, the redirected request uses the GET method. If the HttpWebRequest.AllowAutoRedirect property is false, Found causes an exception to be thrown. Found is a synonym for Redirect.

Table 13.3 The HttpStatusCode Enumeration (*cont.*)

Member Name	Description
GatewayTimeout	Equivalent to HTTP status 504. GatewayTimeout indicates that an intermediate proxy server timed out while waiting for a response from another proxy or the originating server.
Gone	Equivalent to HTTP status 410. Gone indicates that the requested resource is no longer available.
HttpVersionNotSupported	Equivalent to HTTP status 505. HttpVersion-NotSupported indicates that the server does not support the requested HTTP version.
InternalServerError	Equivalent to HTTP status 500. InternalServer-Error indicates that a generic error has occurred on the server.
LengthRequired	Equivalent to HTTP status 411. LengthRequired indicates that the required Content-length header is missing.
MethodNotAllowed	Equivalent to HTTP status 405. MethodNot-Allowed indicates that the request method (POST or GET) is not allowed on the requested resource.
Moved	Equivalent to HTTP status 302. Moved indicates that the requested information has been moved to the URI specified in the Location header. The default action when this status is received is to follow the Location header (the location that it specifies) associated with the response. When the original request method was POST, the redirected request uses the GET method. If the HttpWebRequest.AllowAutoRedirect property is false, Moved causes an exception to be thrown. Moved is a synonym for MovedPermanently.
MovedPermanently	Equivalent to HTTP status 301. MovedPermanently indicates that the requested information has been moved to the URI specified in the Location header. The default action when this status is received is to follow the Location header associated with the response. If the HttpWebRequest. AllowAutoRedirect property is false, Moved-Permanently causes an exception to be thrown. MovedPermanently is a synonym for Moved.

(continued)

Table 13.3 The HttpStatusCode Enumeration (*cont.*)

Member Name	Description
MultipleChoices	Equivalent to HTTP status 300. MultipleChoices indicates that the requested information has multiple representations. The default action is to treat this status as a redirect and follow the contents of the Location header (the location that is specified) associated with this response. If the HttpWebRequest.AllowAutoRedirect property is false, MultipleChoices causes an exception to be thrown. MultipleChoices is a synonym for Ambiguous.
NoContent	Equivalent to HTTP status 204. NoContent indicates that the request has been successfully processed and that the response is intentionally blank.
NonAuthoritative-Information	Equivalent to HTTP status 203. Non-AuthoritativeInformation indicates that the returned meta information is from a cached copy instead of the originating server and therefore may be incorrect.
NotAcceptable	Equivalent to HTTP status 406. NotAcceptable indicates that the client has indicated with Accept headers that it will not accept any of the available representations of the resource.
NotFound	Equivalent to HTTP status 404. NotFound indicates that the requested resource does not exist on the server.
NotImplemented	Equivalent to HTTP status 501. NotImplemented indicates the server does not support the requested function.
NotModified	Equivalent to HTTP status 304. NotModified indicates that the client's cached copy is up-to-date. The contents of the resource are not transferred.
OK	Equivalent to HTTP status 200. OK indicates that the request succeeded and the requested information is in the response. This is the most common status code to receive.
PartialContent	Equivalent to HTTP status 206. PartialContent indicates that the response is a partial response, as requested by a GET request that includes a byte range.

Table 13.3 The HttpStatusCode Enumeration (*cont.*)

Member Name	Description
PaymentRequired	Equivalent to HTTP status 402. PaymentRequired is reserved for future use.
PreconditionFailed	Equivalent to HTTP status 412. Precondition-Failed indicates that a condition set for this request failed, and the request cannot be carried out. Conditions are set with conditional request headers such as If-Match, If-None-Match, or If-Unmodified-Since.
ProxyAuthentication-Required	Equivalent to HTTP status 407. Proxy-AuthenticationRequired indicates that the requested proxy requires authentication. The Proxy-authenticate header contains the details of how to perform the authentication.
Redirect	Equivalent to HTTP status 302. Redirect indicates that the requested information is located at the URI specified in the Location header. The default action when this status is received is to follow the Location header associated with the response. When the original request method was POST, the redirected request uses the GET method. If the HttpWebRequest.AllowAutoRedirect property is false, Redirect causes an exception to be thrown. Redirect is a synonym for Found.
RedirectKeepVerb	Equivalent to HTTP status 307. RedirectKeepVerb indicates that the request information is located at the URI specified in the Location header. The default action when this status is received is to follow the Location header (redirect to the location it specifies) associated with the response. When the original request method is POST, the redirected request also uses the POST method. If the HttpWebRequest.AllowAutoRedirect property is false, RedirectKeepVerb causes an exception to be thrown. RedirectKeepVerb is a synonym for TemporaryRedirect.

(continued)

Table 13.3 The HttpStatusCode Enumeration (*cont.*)

Member Name	Description
RedirectMethod	Equivalent to HTTP status 303. `RedirectMethod` automatically redirects the client to the URI specified in the `Location` header as the result of a `POST`. The request to the resource that the `Location` header specifies is made with a `GET`. If the `HttpWebRequest.AllowAutoRedirect` property is `false`, `RedirectMethod` causes an exception to be thrown. `RedirectMethod` is a synonym for `SeeOther`.
RequestedRangeNot-Satisfiable	Equivalent to HTTP status 416. `Requested-RangeNotSatisfiable` indicates that the range of data requested from the resource cannot be returned, either because the beginning of the range is before the beginning of the resource, or the end of the range is after the end of the resource.
RequestEntityTooLarge	Equivalent to HTTP status 413. `RequestEntityTooLarge` indicates that the request is too large for the server to process.
RequestTimeout	Equivalent to HTTP status 408. `RequestTimeout` indicates that the client did not send a request within the time the server was expecting the request.
RequestUriTooLong	Equivalent to HTTP status 414. `RequestUriTooLong` indicates that the URI is too long.
ResetContent	Equivalent to HTTP status 205. `ResetContent` indicates that the client should reset (not reload) the current resource.
SeeOther	Equivalent to HTTP status 303. `SeeOther` automatically redirects the client to the URI specified in the `Location` header as the result of a `POST`. The request to the resource that the `Location` header specifies is made with a `GET`. If the `HttpWebRequest.AllowAutoRedirect` property is `false`, `SeeOther` causes an exception to be thrown. `SeeOther` is a synonym for `RedirectMethod`.
ServiceUnavailable	Equivalent to HTTP status 503. `ServiceUnavailable` indicates that the server is temporarily unavailable, usually due to high load or maintenance.

Table 13.3 The HttpStatusCode Enumeration (*cont.*)

Member Name	Description
SwitchingProtocols	Equivalent to HTTP status 101. Switching-Protocols indicates that the protocol version or protocol is being changed.
TemporaryRedirect	Equivalent to HTTP status 307. Temporary-Redirect indicates that the requested information is located at the URI specified in the Location header. The default action when this status is received is to follow the Location header (or redirect to what is specified) associated with the response. When the original request method is POST, the redirected request also uses the POST method. If the HttpWebRequest.AllowAuto-Redirect property is false, TemporaryRedirect causes an exception to be thrown. Temporary-Redirect is a synonym for RedirectKeepVerb.
Unauthorized	Equivalent to HTTP status 401. Unauthorized indicates that the requested resource requires authentication. The WWW-Authenticate header contains the details of how to perform the authentication.
UnsupportedMediaType	Equivalent to HTTP status 415. Unsupported-MediaType indicates that the request is an unsupported type.
Unused	Equivalent to HTTP status 306. Unused is a proposed extension to the HTTP/1.1 specification that is not fully specified.
UseProxy	Equivalent to HTTP status 305. UseProxy indicates that the request should use the proxy server at the URI specified in the Location header.

Table is excerpted from MSDN and is copyrighted by Microsoft.

Table 13.4 The WebExceptionStatus Enumeration

Member Name	Description
ConnectFailure	The remote service point could not be contacted at the transport level.
ConnectionClosed	The connection was prematurely closed.
KeepAliveFailure	The connection for a request that specifies the Keep-alive header was closed unexpectedly.
NameResolutionFailure	The name-resolver service could not resolve the host name.
Pending	An internal asynchronous request is pending.
PipelineFailure	This member supports the .NET Framework infrastructure and is not intended to be used directly from your code.
ProtocolError	The response received from the server was complete but indicated a protocol-level error. For example, an HTTP protocol error such as 401 Access Denied would use this status.
ProxyNameResolutionFailure	The name-resolver service could not resolve the proxy host name.
ReceiveFailure	A complete response was not received from the remote server.
RequestCanceled	The request was canceled, the `WebRequest.Abort` method was called, or an unclassifiable error occurred. This is the default value for `Status`.
SecureChannelFailure	An error occurred in a secure channel link.
SendFailure	A complete request could not be sent to the remote server.
ServerProtocolViolation	The server response was not a valid HTTP response.
Success	No error was encountered.
Timeout	No response was received during the time-out period for a request.
TrustFailure	A server certificate could not be validated.

Table is excerpted from MSDN and is copyrighted by Microsoft.

Summary

In this chapter, you have learned about the System.Net namespace. You have looked at using the Dns class, classes that send and receive data, and classes that configure how data retrieval will be carried out. These classes all encapsulate networking functionality and make networking easy to do. All the implementation details of difficult networking operations are taken care of for you.

The basics have all been presented in this chapter. But as you use these options in your applications, you will find more and more richness in the System.Net namespace, richness that has not been covered in this chapter. As your networking applications become more complex, your demand for more complex operations will increase. But this chapter is a great place to start with the System.Net namespace.

CHAPTER 14

Effective Use of Networking and Regular Expressions: Mining Data

In This Chapter:

- Regular Expressions
- Example Programs That Use Regular Expressions
- Web Services Overview
- SOAP
- Discovery
- Creating Web Services
- Consuming Web Services
- Web Service Security
- Web Service Transactions
- Data Scraping Web Services

Web Services are one of the most exciting things to be introduced to .NET. Web Services have the potential for changing everything that you do in your Web development. They can simplify your development tasks and they can also provide you with opportunities that previously would have been very difficult to carry out.

This chapter talks about Web Services, showing you what they are, what you would use them for, and walking you through their creation and use.

Regular Expressions

The Perl programming language has long been revered by many CGI programmers for its ability to quickly and effortlessly extract or replace substrings within a body of text. Not too long ago, you could probably ask any

Perl guru to name the top three advantages of his language, and you would unwillingly receive a detailed lecture on the power of regular expressions. Well, those days are surely over, and there wouldn't be any mention of regular expressions in this chapter if they were still considered a Perl advantage. You can now think of your Perl friends as excellent resources when you need to perform a string parsing operation with .NET technology—that is, if they will even talk to you about .NET.

For the newcomer, the term **regular expressions** refers to an extremely rich set of informally standardized pattern-matching tools that removes every last bit of drudgery from the text-parsing process. Do you need to extract phone numbers that may be written with or without parentheses or hyphens from a 359K document? These days, you can grab them all at a cost of about five lines of code. Let's face it—nobody has time to iterate through characters and track positions in a string just to find a lousy Zip code that might be written any of several different ways. Learn to use regular expressions, and you will not only save yourself countless hours and headaches when you are retrieving and parsing data while networking, but you will forever change your approach to the parsing of text.

This section covers some of the tools included in the System.Text.RegularExpressions namespace and how those tools can be used to greatly simplify your networking applications. We'll start with a simple example using the Regex and Match objects, followed by a crash course on regular expressions tools and syntax. Then, we'll use the very same tools to perform search-and-replace operations. Finally, you'll practice writing regular expressions with a Web application that allows you to extract information from the source code of any Web page you have a URL for.

Using Regular Expressions to Match Sub-Strings

Suppose you're a programmer for a Bob's Used Cars, a large used-car dealership. An agreement has recently been set up in which Bob's Used Cars has agreed to purchase at a discount all vehicles accepted for trade-in by Tom's Auto Mall, a new-car dealership. At the end of each month, Bob's Used Cars will be sent a URL pointing to a report of all trade-ins received under the agreement, with the report formatted like the sample shown below.

```
Used Cars Received
Week of 3/8/2002
Lot ID:   1742-208
Make:     Saturn
Model:    SL1
```

```
Year:      1999
Price:     $10,294

Lot ID:    2283-517
Make:      Honda
Model:     Accord
Year:      1993
Price:     $3,309

Lot ID:    2413-502
Make:      Nissan
Model:     Maxima
Year:      1990
Price:     $4700
```

Your job is to develop an application that will retrieve the data from the Tom's Auto Mall Web server, convert it to HTML, and present the HTML on the Bob's Used Cars Web site. To keep all focus on the functionality provided by the RegularExpressions namespace, let's assume that you have already made your application retrieve the report and are ready to pass it as string parameter to the HTML conversion function we'll create.

To get the ball rolling, we'll create a Regex object that can be used to extract the value of one field. We'll get this working properly, and then we'll modify the regular expression to extract and format the remaining fields as well. (If this is confusing, skip down to read the section entitled "A Taste of Regular Expressions.")

C#
```csharp
private string ConvertToHtml( string strData )
{
    String strExpr = "Lot ID:\\s+(?<lot_id>.*)";

    Regex regEx = new Regex( strExpr );
}
```

VB
```vb
Private Function ConvertToHtml( ByVal strData as string ) as string
    Dim strExpr as string = "Lot ID:\\s+(?<lot_id>.*)"
    Dim regEx as new Regex( strExpr )
End Sub
```

Now you have a Regex object that can eventually be used to extract the Lot ID from one or more records, but for now, it doesn't do anything you can actually benefit from. So to make your effort worthwhile, you must tell the Regex object to process a string using your regular expression. This can be done simply by passing the string you want processed to the `Match()` method of the Regex object, as follows:

C#
```
Match regExMatch = regEx.Match( strData );
```

VB
```
Dim regExMatch as Match = regEx.Match( strData )
```

That's all there is to it, really. You probably never thought parsing a string could be so simple! Now, all you have to do is check the Match object to see whether a match was found by evaluating the Boolean `Success` property. If a match was found, you will extract the value of group `"lot_id"` and append that value to `strHtml`. Then, just tell the Match object to look for another match by calling its `NextMatch()` method.

C#
```
while( myMatch.Success )
{
    strHtml += myMatch.Groups["lot_id"].Value + "<BR>\r\n";
    myMatch = myMatch.NextMatch();
}
```

VB
```
While myMatch.Success
    strHtml += myMatch.Groups["lot_id"].Value + "<BR>\r\n"
    myMatch = myMatch.NextMatch()
End While
```

The `NextMatch()` method of the Match object is a particularly helpful method because it allows you to iterate through every occurrence of a match in a string without having to keep track of your position within the string. If you ran the program in the example, you would get the following output:

```
1742-408
2283-517
2413-502
```

Here's the entire method:

C#

```csharp
private string ConvertToHtml( string strData )
{
    string strHtml = ""; // value to be returned

    // store the regular expression
    string strExpr = "Lot ID:\\s*(?<lot_id>.*)";

    // create and initialize a Regex object
    Regex regEx = new Regex( strExpr );

    // perform the initial match
    Match myMatch = regEx.Match( strData );

    while( myMatch.Success ) // while match found
    {
        // add match group "lot_id" to return value
        strHtml += myMatch.Groups["lot_id"].Value + "<BR>\r\n;

        // attempt to match again
        myMatch = myMatch.NextMatch();
    }

    return strHtml;
}
```

VB

```vb
Private Function ConvertToHtml(ByVal strData As String) As String
    Dim strHtml As String = "" ' value to be returned

    ' store the regular expression
    Dim strExpr As String = "Lot ID:\\s*(?<lot_id>.*)"

    ' create and initialize a Regex object
    Dim regEx As New Regex(strExpr)

    ' perform the initial match
    Dim myMatch As Match = regEx.Match(strData)

    While myMatch.Success
        ' add match group "lot_id" to return value
        strHtml += myMatch.Groups("lot_id").Value + "<BR>\r\n"
```

```
        ' attempt to match again
        myMatch = myMatch.NextMatch()

    End While

    Return strHtml
End Function
```

If you have never used regular expressions before, you may be wondering exactly what just happened, so let's look at the regular expression itself in just a little more detail. To be completely honest, you will probably have a much clearer understanding of this material on your second time through, and especially after you have had some time to play around with some different regular expressions formulas. But just to get you started thinking about regular expressions, Table 14.1 shows a breakdown of the formula we just used.

To avoid some frustration, keep in mind that any escape sequences that are not known to the C# compiler and that you include in your regular expression will cause problems. Remember to escape the preceding back-

Table 14.1 The Regular Expressions Used in the Example

Component	Explanation
Full Expression:	`Lot ID:\s*(?<lot_id>.*)`
Lot ID:	Simply tells the parser to match `"Lot ID:"`.
\s*	Tells the parser to match zero or more whitespace characters
.*	Tells the parser to match zero or more characters. In this case, the dot (`.`) will match anything but a carriage return or line feed, so `.*` effectively gives you the rest of the line after `"Lot ID:"` and zero or more spaces. There are options you can pass to the Regex constructor that control the behavior of the dot in a regular expression that we'll discuss later.
(?<lot_id>.*)	Tells the parser to match `.*` and store the result of `.*` so that it may be referenced by the name `"lot_id."` A match group is always enclosed in parentheses. Notice that `?<lot_id>` names the group, while any results of the match criteria that follow are placed in the group. If it were possible to write this as a C# expression, it might be written as `lot_id = .*;`

slash for metacharacters, such as the \s, and use \\s in your regular expression string.

We'll add some additional ammo to our regular expressions arsenal a little later, but for now, let's modify the above example to extract all fields from the automobile report and return an HTML table. Here's an expression we could pass to the Regex object's constructor:

C#
```
string strExpr =
    "Lot ID:\\s*(?<lot_id>.*)\r\n" +
    "Make:\\s*(?<make>.*)\r\n" +
    "Model:\\s*(?<model>.*)\r\n" +
    "Year:\\s*(?<year>.*)\r\n" +
    "Price:\\s*(?<price>.*)";
```

VB
```
Dim strError as string = _
    "Lot ID:\\s*(?<lot_id>.*)\r\n" + _
    "Make:\\s*(?<make>.*)\r\n" +  _
    "Model:\\s*(?<model>.*)\r\n" +  _
    "Year:\\s*(?<year>.*)\r\n" + _
    "Price:\\s*(?<price>.*)"
```

As you can see, the regular expression ends up masking a record contained in the actual data. This particular example requires a mask that is fairly readable, but with more general regular expressions, you may have to do some intense studying to figure out exactly what the expression is attempting to match. For example, a regular expression to match an e-mail address would look like this:

```
\w+([-+.]\w+)*@\w+([-.]\w+)*\.\w+([-.]\w+)*
```

Unless you're at least mildly experienced with regular expressions, the above line probably looks like something a comic book character might say in a fit of rage. If this is the case, don't worry; it will all make sense once you have had a little more exposure.

Here is the finished method you could use to present the data from the Tom's Auto Mall report in an HTML table:

C#
```
private string ConvertToHtml( string strData )
```

```
{
    string strHtml;
    // The string for the expression.
    string strExpr =
        "Lot ID:\\s*(?<lot_id>.*)\r\n" +
        "Make:\\s*(?<make>.*)\r\n" +
        "Model:\\s*(?<model>.*)\r\n" +
        "Year:\\s*(?<year>.*)\r\n" +
        "Price:\\s*(?<price>.*)";

    // Create the Regex object and do the match.
    Regex regEx = new Regex( strExpr );
    Match myMatch = regEx.Match( strData );

    // Start the HTML string.
    strHtml = "<table border=\"1\">\r\n";

    while( myMatch.Success )
    {
        // Add another row of data.
        strHtml +=
            "\t<tr>\r\n" +
            "\t\t<td>" + myMatch.Groups["lot_id"].Value + "</td>\r\n" +
            "\t\t<td>" + myMatch.Groups["make"].Value + "</td>\r\n" +
            "\t\t<td>" + myMatch.Groups["model"].Value + "</td>\r\n" +
            "\t\t<td>" + myMatch.Groups["year"].Value + "</td>\r\n" +
            "\t\t<td>" + myMatch.Groups["price"].Value + "</td>\r\n" +
            "\t</tr>\r\n";

        // Find the next match.
        myMatch = myMatch.NextMatch();
    }

    // End the HTML table.
    strHtml += "</table>\r\n";

    return strHtml;
}

VB
Private Function ConvertToHtml(ByVal strData As String) As String
    Dim strHtml As String = ""
```

```
Dim strExpr As String = _
    "Lot ID:\\s*(?<lot_id>.*)\r\n" + _
    "Make:\\s*(?<make>.*)\r\n" + _
    "Model:\\s*(?<model>.*)\r\n" + _
    "Year:\\s*(?<year>.*)\r\n" + _
    "Price:\\s*(?<price>.*)"

Dim regEx As New Regex(strExpr)
Dim myMatch As Match = regEx.Match(strData)

strHtml = "<table border=1>\r\n"

While myMatch.Success
    strHtml += _
        "\t<tr>\r\n" + _
        "\t\t<td>" + myMatch.Groups("lot_id").Value + "</td>\r\n" + _
        "\t\t<td>" + myMatch.Groups("make").Value + "</td>\r\n" + _
        "\t\t<td>" + myMatch.Groups("model").Value + "</td>\r\n" + _
        "\t\t<td>" + myMatch.Groups("year").Value + "</td>\r\n" + _
        "\t\t<td>" + myMatch.Groups("price").Value + "</td>\r\n" + _
        "\t</tr>\r\n"
    myMatch = myMatch.NextMatch()
End While

strHtml += "</table>\r\n"

Return strHtml

End Function
```

That's it. The result of this function is now a string containing an HTML table that neatly displays all the cars that have been purchased from the new-car dealership in the past month. What a large benefit for such a minute amount of code.

A Taste of Regular Expressions

Now that you've learned to process regular expressions in C#, it will help to have some basic knowledge of regular expressions themselves. Table 14.2 is a limited dictionary containing some of the more common regular expressions metacharacters and their meanings. Table 14.3 offers a few examples of regular expressions syntax.

Table 14.2 Common Regular Expressions

Metacharacters	Meanings
\w	Matches an alphanumeric character, including the underscore.
\W	Matches a non-alphanumeric character.
\d	Matches a digit character.
\D	Matches a non-digit character.
\s	Matches a whitespace character.
\S	Matches a non-whitespace character.
.	Using default options, matches any single character except a carriage return or line-feed.
*	Modifies preceding character or grouping of characters to match zero or more times. For example, \w* would match zero or more alphanumeric characters. (Possible Matches: "", "A", "Apple")
+	Modifies preceding character or grouping of characters to match one or more times. For example, \d+ would match one or more digits. (Possible Matches: "0", "093", "0479")
[ ]	Brackets specify a collection of characters to be matched. For example, the regular expression [aeiou] would match any vowel.
Min-Max	Specifies a range of characters to be matched. Ranges are specified with a hyphen between the minimum and maximum values ("A-Z", "a-z", "0-9") and must be contained in a bracketed grouping. A range is also treated as a single character and can be used with single characters in bracketed groups. For example, [0-9A-Fa-f] or [0-9A-Fabcdef] would match any single hexadecimal digit.
^	Represents the beginning of the string.
$	Represents the end of a string.
?	Matches preceding character zero or more times. When used after a + or *, this character causes the match to be less "greedy." For example, .* would match an entire line, but .*?</font> would match only text preceding the literal "</font>". The ? character is also used to define a group name in C#. For example, (?<my_group>\w+) would match a sequence of one or more alphanumeric characters and store the match in a group called "my_group."
{n}	Matches preceding character or grouping exactly *n* times.
{n1, n2}	Matches preceding character or grouping a minimum of *n1* times and a maximum of *n2* times.
{n, }	Matches preceding character or grouping a minimum of *n* times.
\metacharacter	Escapes a metacharacter. Because characters such as the plus sign, dollar sign, and period have special meaning to the Regex parser, use \+, \$, \. when you want to match those characters in a string.

Table 14.3 Regular Expressions that are Built into Visual Studio .NET

Regular Expression	Syntax
US Zip+4	`(?<zip_five>\d{5})\D+(?<zip_four>\d{4})`
US Phone No.	`(?<area_code>\d{3})\D+(?<prefix>\d{3})\` `D+(?<suffix>\d{4})`
Currency	`\$(?<dollars>\d*)\.(?<cents>\d{2})`

As mentioned earlier in the chapter, Perl's unrivaled support of regular expression pattern-matching has long been one of the major reasons for its popularity as a language. Fortunately, most regular expressions parsers, such as the one provided by the System.Text.RegularExpressions namespace, behave very similarly to Perl's, so you can easily dig up a wealth of regular expressions dictionaries and examples on the Internet, such as at www.regxlib.com. Just be sure to test your formulas in C# and not assume that they will all translate perfectly.

The Search-And-Replace Operation

Now that you've seen how regular expressions easily extract information from a string, you'll be delighted to find out that replacing substrings is even simpler.

In this cheesy, but appropriate example, you'll see how regular expressions can literally be used to take the work out of networking. This example is so simple that we won't even create a new method.

Create a new ASP/C# Web application and place a label named lblReplace and a button named btnReplace on a WebForm. For the btnReplace control's event handler, place the following code:

C#
```
private void btnReplace_Click(object sender, System.EventArgs)
{
    // create new regex object to match 'work'
    Regex regEx = new Regex("work");
    // replace any matches of 'work' with ''
    lblReplace.Text = regEx.Replace("Networking", "");
}
```

VB
```
Private Function btmReplace_Click( ByVal sender as object, ByVal e as
System.EventArgs )
```

```
    ' create new regex object to match 'work'
    Dim regEx as new Regex( "work" )
    ' replace any matches of 'work' with ''
    lblReplace.Text = regEx.Replace("Networking", "")
End Function
```

Run the application. When you press the button, the label should display "Neting" to show that you've literally taken the work out of networking.

You'd probably rarely want to take a word out of another word as shown in the example, but suppose your company is a member of a business legal association that requires each member company to dedicate a portion of its Web site to providing uniform and specific information. The association distributes an HTML template that must be used if the member companies are to remain in compliance. You are frustrated because the association keeps changing its layout and has been e-mailing you nearly every other day to notify you that an updated template is available.

Fortunately for you, the association posts the template on its Web site and maintains the same information, but it just can't decide on the look and feel of the documents. Rather than manually downloading the page, opening it in Notepad, and inserting the same information you've been inserting for the past two weeks, you decide to dole the task out to your new friend, the Regex object.

Let's assume the HTML page looks like the sample below, and that you have already downloaded it and stored the data in a string called str-LegalData. Again, we'll keep it simple so we can focus on the important points. Notice that the creators of the template have conveniently placed any text to be replaced inside brackets.

```
<HTML>
<HEAD><TITLE>[Company Name] - Legal Web Watchers Association</TITLE>
<BODY>
   <H1>[Company Name] - Company Profile</H1>
   <P>Number of Employees: [Employee Count]</P>
   <P>Rate of Turnover in 2001: [Turnover Rate]</P>
</BODY>
</HTML>
```

All you have to do is create a method to accept a field name, a value to replace the field with, and the target string containing the template data.

C#
```
private void ReplaceLegalField( string strFieldName,
   string strFieldValue, ref string strData )
```

```
{
    Regex strExpr = new Regex("\\[" + strFieldName + "\\]");
    strData = strExpr.Replace( strData, strFieldValue );
}
```

VB
```
Private Function ReplaceLegalField(ByVal strFieldName as string, _
 ByVal strFieldValue as string,
    ByRef strDate as String)
    Dim strExpr as new Regex("\\[" + strFieldName + "\\]" )
    StrData = strExpr.Replace( strData, strFieldValue )
End Function
```

Now, simply call the method once for each field. Remember that str-LegalData holds the template you downloaded from the association's Web site.

C#
```
ReplaceLegalField("Company Name", "Parsing, Inc.", strLegalData);
ReplaceLegalField("Employee Count", "64", strLegalData );
ReplaceLegalField("Turnover Rate", "14.2%", strLegalData );
```

VB
```
ReplaceLegalField("Company Name", "Parsing, Inc.", strLegalData)
ReplaceLegalField("Employee Count", "64", strLegalData )
ReplaceLegalField("Turnover Rate", "14.2%", strLegalData )
```

That's it! Now, the value of strLegalData is as follows:

```
<HTML>
<HEAD><TITLE>Parsing, Inc. - Legal Web Watchers Association</TITLE>
<BODY>
  <H1>Parsing, Inc. – Company Profile</H1>
  <P>Number of Employees: 64</P>
  <P>Rate of Turnover in 2001: 14.2%</P>
</BODY>
</HTML>
```

Keep in mind that you are downloading and processing this document in realtime, so you won't have to bother with it ever again, unless the association adds, deletes, or renames a field. Of course, you'd probably want to grab the data you're plugging into the fields from a location outside the program.

The addition of regular expressions capabilities to the world of object-oriented programming is sure to be a big relief for those who have long been frustrated when useful scripting languages such as Perl have been so annoyingly convenient for one or two applications.

Example Programs That Use Regular Expressions

We've created two Web-based example programs that show how to use the Regex classes on retrieved HTML data. The two programs are shown and explained in the next two sections.

Regular Expressions Html Parsing Demo

This program allows users to enter a URL and a regular expression. The data from the URL is retrieved when the Pull The Data button is clicked. The pulled data will show up in the TextField object.

Once the HTML data has been retrieved from the URL, regular expression parsing can be performed on the data. Users can enter any regular expression, click the Parse button, and see all matches that were found in the TextField below the regular expression field.

You can see this application running in Figure 14.1.

Several predefined URLs and regular expressions can be selected. For instance, you can see www.Yahoo.com and parse all e-mail addresses by making these selections in the DropDownList objects. This makes it easier to get an idea of how the program works without having to think too much.

Pulling HTML Data

HTML data is retrieved in response to clicking the Pull The Data button. When users click this button, an event is fired that calls the `Button1_Click()` method, as shown in Listing 14.1.

NOTE: The complete code for this application can be found via links from www.ASPNET-Solutions.com/chapter_14.htm. There are two versions, one for C# and one for VB. You can also view the code for both via links at the bottom of each page of the application.

This program can be run from a link on the same page.

Pulling the HTML data is very simple and relies on the `WebClient` class. For a detailed understanding of this class, refer to Chapter 13 and the section entitled "Using the `WebClient` Class."

After a WebClient object is instantiated, the URL is obtained from the URLText TextField object. The user may or may not have preceded the URL with the "`http://`" protocol (or scheme) specifier. We check for it because the DownloadData() method requires it. If we don't find it, we'll add it.

Once we're sure we have a URL preceded with "`http://`", the `DownloadData()` method is called. This method returns an array of bytes, which are then used to populate the HtmlData TextField object. This is the user interface object that resides on the ASP.NET page with which the user interacts.

If an exception is thrown, the HtmlData object will contain the exception message.

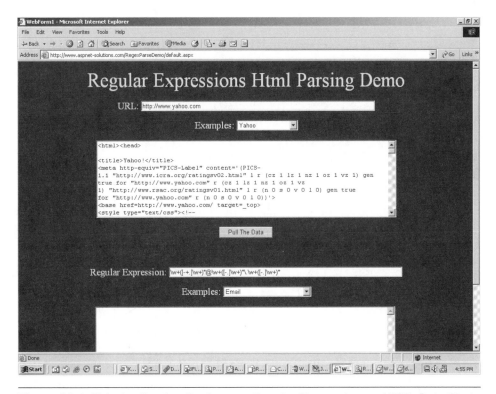

Figure 14.1 This Application Performs a Regular Expression on HTML Data That Has Been Retrieved.

Listing 14.1 This Code Retrieves Data from a URL.

```
private void Button1_Click(object sender, System.EventArgs
{
    try
    {
        WebClient wc = new WebClient();
        byte[] data;
        string strURL;
        if( URLText.Text.ToUpper ().Substring( 0, 7 ) != "HTTP://" )
        {
            strURL = "http://" + URLText.Text;
        }
        else
        {
            strURL = URLText.Text;
        }
        data = wc.DownloadData( strURL );
        HtmlData.Text = Encoding.ASCII.GetString( data );
    }
    catch( Exception ex )
    {
        HtmlData.Text = ex.Message.ToString();
    }
}
```

Parsing HTML Data

Listing 14.2 shows how the application parses the data using the regular expression that the user entered. The first part of the code considers the options that the user has selected by testing the state of the four CheckBox objects that are on the page. For each one that's selected, the enumeration value is ORed to form the combined value for all selected options. The object named options contains this value.

A Regex object is created using the user-supplied regular expression and the RegexOptions object that resulted from the user option choices.

With the Regex object created, the parsing is done by calling the Matches() method with the HTML data string as the only parameter. This method returns a collection of Match objects, and these are contained in a MatchCollection object.

Once the MatchCollection object has been obtained, it's a simple matter to walk through the collection and emit the results for each match. The ParsedData TextField object is appended for each match with the text for each match. The text is in the `Value` property.

Listing 14.2 This Code Parses the Data with the User-Provided Regular Expression.

```
private void Button2_Click(object sender, System.EventArgs
{
    try
    {
        RegexOptions options = RegexOptions.None;
        if( IgnoreCase.Checked )
        {
            options |= RegexOptions.IgnoreCase;
        }
        if( Singleline.Checked )
        {
            options |= RegexOptions.Singleline;
        }
        if( Multiline.Checked )
        {
            options |= RegexOptions.Multiline;
        }
        if( IgnorePatternWhitespace.Checked )
        {
            options |= RegexOptions.IgnorePatternWhitespace;
        }
        Regex re = new Regex( RegexText.Text, options );
        MatchCollection mc = re.Matches( HtmlData.Text );

        int nCount = 0;
        ParsedData.Text = "";
        foreach( Match m in mc )
        {
            nCount++;
            ParsedData.Text += ( "Match " + nCount + ":\r\n" + m.Value +
                "\r\n" );
        }

    }
    catch( Exception ex )
```

```
    {
        ParsedData.Text = ex.Message.ToString();
    }
}
```

Housekeeping Tasks

I've found that most people want to use a demonstration program without having to think too hard. This is especially true for this demo and people new to regular expressions. For this reason, the demo program has some predefined choices that make it easy to use. The URLs that are predefined are http://www.yahoo.com, http://www.microsoft.com, and http://www.ASPNET-Solutions.com. The regular expressions that are predefined are Email, URL, U.S. Phone Number, U.S. Social Security, and U.S. Zip Code.

The code in Listing 14.3 shows the event handlers that fire when users select something from the DropDownList objects that contain the predefined choices.

Listing 14.3 These Two Methods Allow Users to Take Advantage of Some Predefined Choices.

```
private void ExampleExpressions_SelectedIndexChanged(object sender,
    System.EventArgs
{
    RegexText.Text = ExampleExpressions.SelectedItem.Value;
    if( RegexText.Text == "(Custom)" )
    {
        RegexText.Text = "";
    }
}

private void URLExamples_SelectedIndexChanged(object sender,
    System.EventArgs
{
    URLText.Text = ExampleURLs.SelectedItem.Value;
    if( URLText.Text == "(Custom)" )
    {
        URLText.Text = "";
    }
}
```

Regular Expressions Html Scraping Demo

This program allows users to enter a URL and two text fragments. The text fragments represent the start and end text of the data you want to extract. The data from the URL is retrieved when the Pull The Data button is clicked. The pulled data will show up in the TextField object.

Once the HTML data has been retrieved from the URL, the desired data can be extracted. Users can enter any starting and ending text, click the Scrape button, and see the scraped text in the TextField below the Starting and Ending TextField objects.

Several predefined URLs and Starting and Ending text fragments can be selected. For instance, you can select Get Word, Get Weather, and Get Quote. This makes it easier to get an idea of how the program works without having to think too much.

You can see this application running in Figure 14.2.

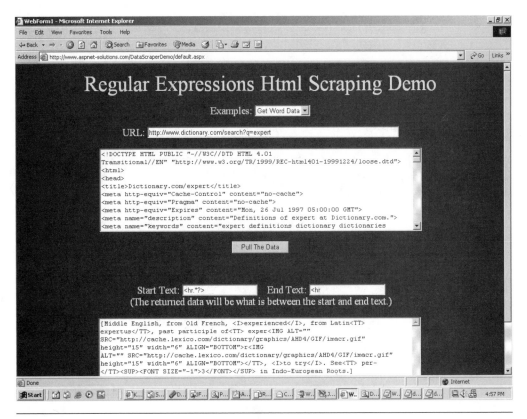

Figure 14.2 This Application Scrapes Data from HTML Data That Has Been Retrieved.

Pulling HTML Data

This code works identically to the code in Listing 14.1. HTML data is retrieved in response to clicking the Pull The Data button. When users click this button, an event is fired that calls the `Button1_Click()` method, as shown in Listing 14.4.

WEB CONTENT: The complete code for this application can be found via links from www.ASPNET-Solutions.com/chapter_14.htm. There are two versions, one for C# and one for VB. You can also view the code for both via links at the bottom of each page of the application.

This program can be run from a link on the same page.

Listing 14.4 This Code Retrieves Data from a URL.

```
private void Button1_Click(object sender, System.EventArgs
{
try
    {
        WebClient wc = new WebClient();
        byte[] data;
        string strURL;
        if( URLText.Text.ToUpper().Substring( 0, 7 ) !=
            "HTTP://" )
        {
                strURL = "http://" + URLText.Text;
        }
        else
        {
                strURL = URLText.Text;
        }
        data = wc.DownloadData( strURL );
        HtmlData.Text = Encoding.ASCII.GetString( data );
    }
    catch( Exception ex )
    {
        HtmlData.Text = ex.Message.ToString();
    }
}
```

Extracting Text From HTML Data

Listing 14.5 shows how the application extracts text based on the Starting and Ending text that the user enters. Unlike the previous example wherein users could provide their own options, this demo is hard-coded to use the `IgnoreCase` and `Singleline` options. These are necessary for the application to work correctly.

A Regex object is created using a regular expression that is created by combining the starting text, some regular expression code, and the ending text.

With the Regex object created, the extraction is done by calling the `Match()` method with the HTML data string as the only parameter. This method returns a single Match object. The extracted text will be contained in the `Groups[].Value` property.

Listing 14.5 This Code Extracts Data Based on Starting and Ending Text Fragments.

```
private void Button2_Click(object sender, System.EventArgs
{
try
        {
                Regex re = new Regex( StartText.Text +
                    "(?<MYDATA>.*?(?=" + EndText.Text + "))",
                    RegexOptions.IgnoreCase | RegexOptions.Singleline );
                Match m = re.Match( HtmlData.Text );

                ScrapedData.Text = m.Groups["MYDATA"].Value;


        }
        catch( Exception ex )
        {
                ScrapedData.Text = ex.Message.ToString();
        }
}
```

More Housekeeping Tasks

The code in Listing 14.6 shows the event handler that fires when users select something from the DropDownList objects that contain the predefined choices.

Listing 14.6 Some Predefined Choices Can Make the Demonstration of the Program Simple.

```
private void DropDownList1_SelectedIndexChanged(object sender,
    System.EventArgs
{
        switch( Convert.ToInt32( Examples.SelectedItem.Value ) )
        {
                case 0:
                        URLText.Text = "";
                        StartText.Text = "";
                        EndText.Text = "";
                        break;
                case 1:
                        URLText.Text =
                          "http://www.dictionary.com/search?q=expert";
                        StartText.Text = "<hr.*?>";
                        EndText.Text = "<hr";
                        break;
                case 2:
                        URLText.Text =
                          "http://www.weather.com/weather/local/27320";
                        StartText.Text = "<B> Reidsville, NC ";
                        EndText.Text = "</table>.*?</table>";
                        break;
                case 3:
                        URLText.Text =
                          "http://www.quotations.com/american.htm";
                        StartText.Text = "<font ";
                        EndText.Text = "<p>";
                        break;
        }
}
```

Web Services Overview

What would you use a Web Service for? Well, that is a fair enough question. Web Services are used to program the Web. Web Services represent a way to abstract a Universal Resource Identifier (URI) and access it across the Web on another server. If this doesn't seem clear, keep reading, and you will understand it as I explain and talk about Web Services.

The Simple Object Application Protocol (SOAP) is what Web Services use to communicate across the Internet. This protocol is described in more detail in the section entitled "SOAP."

Why Are Web Services Useful?

Imagine you have some sort of an e-commerce Web site, and you have a partner that provides you with content. Or you might provide your partner with some sort of content, or you have some other interaction. Web Services give you an easy way to integrate with partners. I will give some examples of this shortly.

Web Services are very easy to program. They are also based on standards. The fundamental protocol on which they are based is HTTP; all the SOAP information uses this protocol as its basis. Then, the data is contained within a SOAP envelope, which is also a standard that has been submitted to the W3C (World Wide Web Consortium). Within the SOAP envelope is XML, and XML is the standard that is becoming very popular and widely adopted for Internet data representation.

Another reason you would want to implement Web Services is they can be easily upgraded on one server without affecting the applications that call them. If server A contains a Web Service, I can easily change it as long as I don't change the calling and return parameters. And I can do this without any knowledge of or effect on server B, which calls methods in my Web Service on server A.

Real-World Scenarios for Using Web Services

I would like to talk for a minute about when you would use a Web Service. Although I can think of many examples, I'll cover just a few here. I'm sure that with a little effort you can come up with your own.

Suppose I have a Web site on which I want to serve up news content to users. The news content comes from a server located somewhere else on the Internet. A Web Service provides the easiest programming model for a Web application to retrieve and consume content from across the Web.

Although I have carried out tasks before that pull in data and content from other Web servers, doing so hasn't always been easy. It has taken me several days to do this, and then several more days to debug the material I received; and making changes was sometimes difficult. In the end, this process might have taken me anywhere from four to five days of programming. With a Web Service, I can consume content from a remote server in about two hours. That's because WSDL describes the data format such that the Web service automates the parsing.

Credit-card authorization of course comes to mind. A Web Service makes the ideal method of doing credit-card authorization. From one server you can easily hit another server and authorize a credit card with just several lines of programming code.

Centralization of user information is another option that Web Services provide. You might have a user who has a set of information that is associated with that user. A Web Service can enable multiple Web Services to retrieve and use information about a given user. Of course this assumes that there is proper security clearance and the proper authorization credentials, which should have been created on the Web server.

Web Services enable you to create a killer ad server (MSDN has an example of this as part of the ColdStorage sample). Imagine being able to provide user information, such as a user's preferences, and an ad server serves up a targeted ad toward that particular user. Say, for instance, that I am on a Web site and somehow I have let it be known that I like golf. As a matter of fact, I may have indicated on the Web site that I am looking for a new set of clubs. Rather than just rotate through a bunch of ads, I can call a Web Service and let the Web Service know that I like or have an interest in golf, and the Web Service serves up a targeted ad with golf clubs or golf accessories.

SOAP

SOAP is a way to send messages across the wire. One computer can use SOAP to send a block of data, say for instance a billing record, to another computer. When using SOAP, both computers understand the protocol and can send and receive the data using it.

The SOAP acronym starts with Simple, and that's one of the key things it delivers. If you've ever worked with DCOM to communicate to remote servers, you know that DCOM is anything but simple—as a matter of fact, it's pretty ugly. I realize that some readers have been using DCOM for years and are very comfortable with it. I had a student who fit this description, and the two of us had a spirited debate about whether Web Services using SOAP offered a better alternative than DCOM. If you're in this camp, I respect your opinion but respectfully disagree.

SOAP is based on XML. The data that is carried in a SOAP package is always represented by XML. If you plan to do much with SOAP, you may want to take a look at the XML specification or do some reading to understand the basics of XML. You might also want to look at the XSD specification, which sometimes causes more confusion than XML.

SOAP works with any operating system because it doesn't rely in any way on operating systems. It's a protocol on its own merit that dictates no hardware, operating system, or language specifications.

SOAP is also built on standards and therefore can easily be implemented by anyone. First, it relies on HTTP to send data across the wire. Second, it relies on XML to represent the data. And third, it relies on the SOAP specification so that every implementer will be in compliance and able to communicate with all other implementers. You can get the SOAP specification at HTTP://msdn.microsoft.com/workshop/XML/general/soap-spec.asp.

SOAP Packages

SOAP data is sent in a well-organized manner as it goes across the Internet. This section shows you the hierarchy of SOAP packages.

Because all SOAP packages are sent within an HTTP message, the first part of a SOAP message is the HTTP header. Information in the section usually contains the domain name, the keyword POST, the Content-Type specification, and other optional information.

After the HTTP header comes the SOAP envelope. This encompasses the entire SOAP message. It's kind of like what's inside the box that arrived at your doorstep. It's all the important stuff you need (the actual data). The address label on the front of the box (the HTTP header) can almost always be discarded.

The SOAP envelope starts off with a SOAP header (which is optional). This is different from the HTTP header. It contains information about the routing of the data (such as the domain name and the size of the content), and it contains information related to the data, such as a transaction ID.

The SOAP body is also in the SOAP envelope after the SOAP header, and it contains the data. Figure 14.3 shows a diagram of SOAP messages.

SOAP Data

In this section, I'm going to show you some captured SOAP packages, to give you an idea of what they look like.

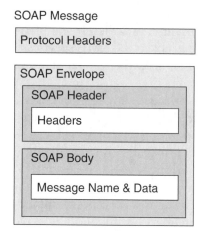

SOAP Message

Protocol Headers

SOAP Envelope

SOAP Header

Headers

SOAP Body

Message Name & Data

Figure 14.3 This Figure Shows the Hierarchy of SOAP Data as It's Sent over the Wire.

A simple SOAP request might look like the following (the HTTP header is in gray):

```
POST /StockQuote HTTP/1.1
Host: www.stockquoteserver.com
Content-Type: text/XML; charset="utf-8"
Content-Length: 323
SOAPAction: Some-Namespace-URI#GetLastTradePrice
<SQ:Envelope
    xmlns:SQ="http://schemas.xmlsoap.org/soap/envelope/"
    SQ:encodingStyle="http://schemas.xmlsoap.org/soap/encoding/">
  <SQ:Body>
    <m:GetLastTradePrice xmlns:m="Some-Namespace-URI">
      <symbol>DIS</symbol>
    </m:GetLastTradePrice>
  </SQ:Body>
</SQ:Envelope>
```

A simple SOAP response might look like the following (the HTTP header is in gray):

```
HTTP/1.1 200 OK
Content-Type: text/XML; charset="utf-8"
Content-Length: nnnn
```

```
<SP:Envelope XMLns:SP="http://schemas.XMLsoap.org/soap/envelope/"
    SP:encodingStyle="http://schemas.XMLsoap.org/soap/encoding/">
  <SP:Body>
    <m:GetLastTradePriceResponse
  XMLns:m="Some-Namespace-URI">
      <Price>34.5</Price>
    </m:GetLastTradePriceResponse>
  </SP:Body>
</SP:Envelope>
```

Discovery

There is a process wherein a discovery process can be performed on Web Services. The process is known as **discovery** (sometimes **XML discovery**), and its target is always a URL. A client process can find what Web Services exist on a server, what its capabilities are, and how to interact with it.

Given the URL to a server with Web Services, or the URL to a Web Service itself, files can be retrieved that are related to the extant Web Services. These files might include service descriptions (which use the Web Service Description Language, or WSDL), XSD schemas, or discovery documents (usually in the form of .disco files). Given the returned information, a proxy stub that is capable of accessing the Web Service can be created.

Let's try it out on one of the Web Services that are on www.ASPNET-Solutions.com. First, though, you need to be able to run disco.exe from a command prompt on your system. The file is usually contained in the c:\Program Files\Microsoft Visual Studio .NET\Bin directory (along with a lot of other useful Framework utilities). You can type in the full path each time you run the program (not a pleasant thought), copy the utilities to a directory that's easier to type (also not an optimal option), or add c:\Program Files\Microsoft Visual Studio .NET\Bin to your system's path. I chose the latter, and I did this by selecting the System icon from Control Panel. From the Advanced tab, I clicked on the Environmental Variables. It was then easy to access the Path variable and add the additional directory. Then, when running the Framework utilities, you won't need to type in the full path. You could also use the Visual Studio .NET command prompt.

When you type in **disco** from the command prompt, you'll see the options that are available. For this example, we'll just enter the URL that we want to perform discovery on, and the files will be saved to the current directory by default.

There's a Web Service (which we'll talk about later in this chapter) that can be found at the URL http://www.ASPNET-Solutions.com/Pharm-FromNDC/Service1.asmx. If we add the parameter WSDL to the URL request, the disco program will generate a WSDL document on the local hard drive, along with a .discomap file.

From a command line, enter the following:

```
disco http://www.ASPNET-Solutions.com/PharmFromNDC/Service1.asmx?WSDL
```

The program will query the Web Service and create two files in the current directory. One will be named results.discomap and the other will be named service1.wsdl. The results.discomap file can be seen in Listing 14.7.

Listing 14.7 The results.discomap File Resulting from Performing Discovery on the PharmFromNDC Web Service

```
<?xml version="1.0" encoding="utf-8"?>
<DiscoveryClientResultsFile xmlns:xsd="http://www.w3.org/2001/XMLSchema"
    xmlns:xsi="http://www.w3.org/2001/XMLSchema-instance">
  <Results>
    <DiscoveryClientResult
      referenceType="System.Web.Services.Discovery.ContractReference"
      url="http://www.ASPNET-Solutions.com/pharmfromndc/service1.
asmx?WSDL"
      filename="service1.wsdl" />
  </Results>
</DiscoveryClientResultsFile>
```

Looking at the .discomap file, you can see that it is XML. The XML version is included, along with the location of this version's specifications, on www.w3.org. Between the <Results> tags are the .NET Framework Namespace that's used for Web Service discovery, the URL from which the discovery was obtained, and the local file name that contains the WSDL contact information.

The .wsdl file is where you can find out information about the Web Service: its methods, properties, and use. Listing 14.8 contains the service1.wsdl file.

Listing 14.8 The service1.wsdl File Resulting from Performing Discovery on the PharmFromNDC Web Service

```xml
<?xml version="1.0" encoding="utf-8"?>
<definitions xmlns:http="http://schemas.xmlsoap.org/wsdl/http/"
xmlns:soap="http://schemas.xmlsoap.org/wsdl/soap/"
xmlns:s="http://www.w3.org/2001/XMLSchema"
xmlns:s0="http://tempuri.org/"
xmlns:soapenc="http://schemas.xmlsoap.org/soap/encoding/"
xmlns:tm="http://microsoft.com/wsdl/mime/textMatching/"
xmlns:mime="http://schemas.xmlsoap.org/wsdl/mime/"
targetNamespace="http://tempuri.org/"
xmlns="http://schemas.xmlsoap.org/wsdl/">
  <types>
    <s:schema elementFormDefault="qualified"
      targetNamespace="http://tempuri.org/">
      <s:element name="GetPharm">
        <s:complexType>
          <s:sequence>
            <s:element minOccurs="0" maxOccurs="1" name="strNDC" type="s:
string" />
          </s:sequence>
        </s:complexType>
      </s:element>
      <s:element name="GetPharmResponse">
        <s:complexType>
          <s:sequence>
            <s:element minOccurs="0" maxOccurs="1" name="GetPharmResult"
type="s:string" />
          </s:sequence>
        </s:complexType>
      </s:element>
      <s:element name="string" nillable="true" type="s:string" />
    </s:schema>
  </types>
  <message name="GetPharmSoapIn">
    <part name="parameters" element="s0:GetPharm" />
  </message>
```

```
<message name="GetPharmSoapOut">
  <part name="parameters" element="s0:GetPharmResponse" />
</message>
<message name="GetPharmHttpGetIn">
  <part name="strNDC" type="s:string" />
</message>
<message name="GetPharmHttpGetOut">
  <part name="Body" element="s0:string" />
</message>
<message name="GetPharmHttpPostIn">
  <part name="strNDC" type="s:string" />
</message>
<message name="GetPharmHttpPostOut">
  <part name="Body" element="s0:string" />
</message>
<portType name="Service1Soap">
  <operation name="GetPharm">
    <input message="s0:GetPharmSoapIn" />
    <output message="s0:GetPharmSoapOut" />
  </operation>
</portType>
<portType name="Service1HttpGet">
  <operation name="GetPharm">
    <input message="s0:GetPharmHttpGetIn" />
    <output message="s0:GetPharmHttpGetOut" />
  </operation>
</portType>
<portType name="Service1HttpPost">
  <operation name="GetPharm">
    <input message="s0:GetPharmHttpPostIn" />
    <output message="s0:GetPharmHttpPostOut" />
  </operation>
</portType>
<binding name="Service1Soap" type="s0:Service1Soap">
  <soap:binding transport="http://schemas.xmlsoap.org/soap/http"
style="document" />
  <operation name="GetPharm">
    <soap:operation soapAction="http://tempuri.org/GetPharm" style=
"document" />
    <input>
      <soap:body use="literal" />
    </input>
    <output>
```

```
        <soap:body use="literal" />
      </output>
    </operation>
  </binding>
  <binding name="Service1HttpGet" type="s0:Service1HttpGet">
    <http:binding verb="GET" />
    <operation name="GetPharm">
      <http:operation location="/GetPharm" />
      <input>
        <http:urlEncoded />
      </input>
      <output>
        <mime:mimeXml part="Body" />
      </output>
    </operation>
  </binding>
  <binding name="Service1HttpPost" type="s0:Service1HttpPost">
    <http:binding verb="POST" />
    <operation name="GetPharm">
      <http:operation location="/GetPharm" />
      <input>
        <mime:content type="application/x-www-form-urlencoded" />
      </input>
      <output>
        <mime:mimeXml part="Body" />
      </output>
    </operation>
  </binding>
  <service name="Service1">
    <port name="Service1Soap" binding="s0:Service1Soap">
      <soap:address location="http://www.ASPNET-Solutions.com/
pharmfromndc/service1.asmx" />
    </port>
    <port name="Service1HttpGet" binding="s0:Service1HttpGet">
      <http:address location="http://www.ASPNET-Solutions.com/
pharmfromndc/service1.asmx" />
    </port>
    <port name="Service1HttpPost" binding="s0:Service1HttpPost">
      <http:address location="http://www.ASPNET-Solutions.com/
pharmfromndc/service1.asmx" />
    </port>
  </service>
</definitions>
```

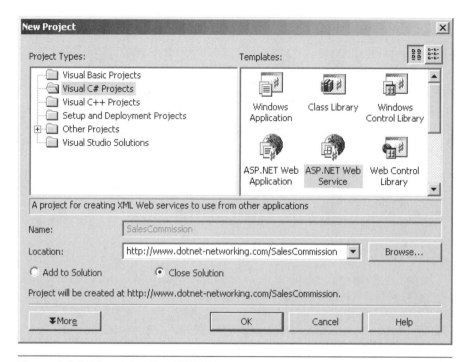

Figure 14.4 Visual Studio .NET Offers a Wizard for Web Service Creation.

Creating Web Services

With Visual Studio .NET, creating Web Services couldn't be easier. A Web Service Wizard is available to make the entire process simple. All you need to do is create a new project (VB, C#, or C++), select Web Service (for VB and C#, this will be labeled ASP.NET Web Service), enter a project name, and create the service with the OK button. Figure 14.4 shows the Wizard dialog box as it appears.

The Wizard creates a simple method for you named `HelloWorld()`. It's commented out, but it can easily be used by removing the `//` characters at the beginning of each line of the `HelloWorld()` method. This gives you a good idea of how to structure Web methods. Below is the code that the Wizard adds to C# projects:

```
// WEB SERVICE EXAMPLE
// The HelloWorld() example service returns the string Hello World
// To build, uncomment the following lines then save and build the
```

```
// project
// To test this web service, press F5

//        [WebMethod]
//        public string HelloWorld()
//        {
//            return "Hello World";
//        }
```

I'll point out several things about the `HelloWorld()` method. First, it is decorated with a `[WebMethod]` attribute. This takes care of the communications details for you. Actually, there is a great deal of code that this injects into your compiled program on your behalf. All of the SOAP conversion code, all of the communication code, and other boiler plate methods are injected by simply adding the `[WebMethod]` attribute. Not all of your methods need this attribute—only the ones that must be discoverable by the discovery process.

You need to notice that the `HelloWorld()` method is marked as `public`. WebMethods that are not marked `public` cannot be discovered via the discovery process, and, more importantly, they can't be called. Make sure that methods that must be discovered and accessed have the `[Web-Method]` attribute and are marked `public`.

This method returns a string object. WebMethods can return just about any kind of object you want. There are a few exceptions, such as SqlReader objects, but the exceptions are few.

The method can also take just about any kind of objects as arguments, too. The `HelloWorld()` method takes no arguments, but Web Services that we'll create later on will take arguments.

As you would imagine, Visual Basic Web Services look slightly different from C# Web Services. The VB version of the sample `HelloWorld()` method can be seen below. Note that VB attributes look a little different from C# attributes. The attribute you can see is in the form `<WebMethod()>`.

```
' WEB SERVICE EXAMPLE
' The HelloWorld() example service returns the string Hello World.
' To build, uncomment the following lines then save and build the
project.
' To test this web service, ensure that the .asmx file is the start page
' and press F5.
'
'<WebMethod()> Public Function HelloWorld() As String
```

```
'  HelloWorld = "Hello World"
' End Function    ' WEB SERVICE EXAMPLE
' The HelloWorld() example service returns the string Hello World.
' To build, uncomment the following lines then save and build the
' project.
' To test this web service, ensure that the .asmx file is the start page
' and press F5.
'
```

Sales Commission Web Service

As an example, I've created a Web Service that calculates sales commissions. Many companies will encapsulate functionality such as sales commissions in Web Services because it offers a single point to which all applications can go to perform the task. If, for any reason, the logic needs to be updated, there is only one place that it must be updated. All applications that use the Web Service won't be affected functionally.

WEB CONTENT: The complete code for this application can be found via links from www.ASPNET-Solutions.com/chapter_14.htm. There are two versions, one for C# and one for VB. You can also access the Web Service from your client application at the URL http://www.ASPNET-Solutions.com/SalesCommission/service1.asmx?WSDL.

There is an application that demonstrates using this Web Service, and it can be run from a link on the same page.

When I think about what Web Services have to offer, it reminds me of what COM offered. You get a way to reuse components, along with a way to maintain contacts with previous applications.

The sales commission Web Service takes the name of a salesperson, and returns her rate of commission. To keep this first example clear, it doesn't do any database access. The values are hard-coded into an array. A production implementation will obviously keep the values in a database.

All of the code (with the exception of one method that we'll talk about later) can be seen in Listing 14.9. An array named dCommissionRates contains the rates for the salespeople. There are only four in the list, thus only four values. The first value (at index 0), actually is −1. This value will be returned in case a salesperson's name can't be found.

The callable WebMethod is named GetCommissionRate(). It takes a single string argument containing the sales person's name. It returns a double representing the rate (in percent) of commission. The GetCommissionRate() method simply calls the GetSalesPerson() method to get an index representing the person's position in a list. If the value returned is −1, the name wasn't found.

The GetSalesPersonIndex() method gets a list of all sales people from the GetSalesForceList() method. The contents of this list are then compared to the name that was passed into the GetCommissionRate() method. When a match is found, the index is returned.

Listing 14.9 This Is the Code for the SalesCommission Web Service.

```
static double[] dCommissionRates =
{
    -1.0, 5.0, 6.2, 4.8, 9.3
};


[WebMethod]
public double GetCommissionRate( string strName )
{
    int nIndexOfName = GetSalesPersonIndex( strName.ToUpper() );

    return( dCommissionRates[nIndexOfName+1] );
}


int GetSalesPersonIndex( string strName )
{

    StringCollection SalesForceList = GetSalesForceList();
    for( int i=0; i<SalesForceList.Count; i++ )
    {
        if( strName == SalesForceList[i].ToUpper() )
        {
            return( i );
        }
    }

    return( -1 );

}


StringCollection GetSalesForceList()
{
```

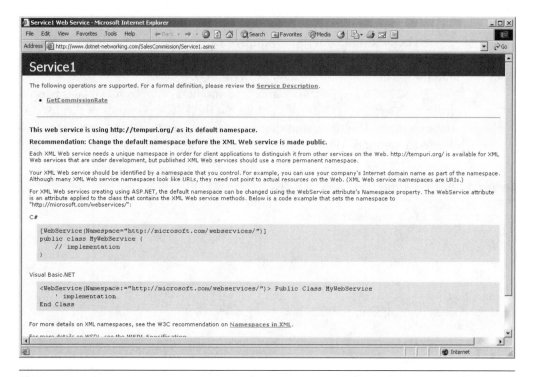

Figure 14.5 Public Methods That Have a [WebMethod] Attribute Show Up for Public Consumption.

```
StringCollection SalesForceList = new StringCollection();
string[] Names = {"John Doe", "Sally Schmoh",
    "Jim Smith", "Suzy Miller"};
SalesForceList.AddRange( Names );

return( SalesForceList );
}
```

Once Web Services are compiled in Visual Studio .NET, they can be executed. This is possible even though Web Services can't execute directly and have no user interface. Visual Studio .NET creates an interface page for you that makes it easy to call the Web Service methods. This page appears when you execute the Web Service, and any public method that has the [WebMethod] attribute will show up in a list of methods that can be called, as you can see in Figure 14.5.

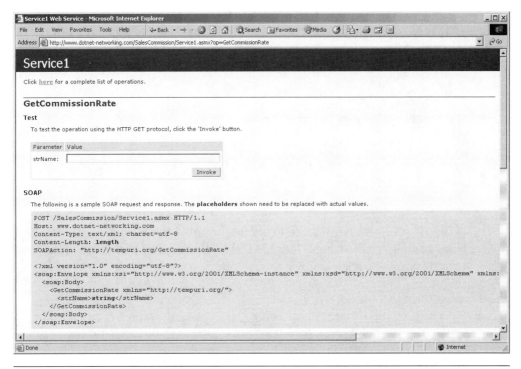

Figure 14.6 When a Method Is Invoked That Requires Parameters, You'll Get a User Interface with Which You Can Supply the Parameters.

When methods are invoked, a page appears into which you can supply parameters. Each parameter that is required will have a text box into which the parameter value can be entered, as shown in Figure 14.6.

Web Services natively exchange data as XML. For this reason, when you click the Invoke button to call into the method, the result is shown as XML data. By typing in **John Doe**, we should get the commission rate of 5 as a return value. The following XML shows the XML that results from this Web Service when the salesperson John Doe has been entered and the commission rate of 5 is returned:

```
<?xml version="1.0" encoding="utf-8" ?>
<double xmlns="http://tempuri.org/">5</double>
```

There's one other thing that would be important for applications that use this Web Service. That is the capability to get a list of salespeople. Client applications could populate selection boxes so that the names wouldn't have to be typed in manually. Returning a StringCollection object does the trick, as you can see for the `GetSalesForce()` method below. This method is public and marked with a `[WebMethod]` attribute, so it is discoverable.

```
[WebMethod]
StringCollection GetSalesForce()
{

    return( GetSalesForceList() );

}
```

The `GetSalesForce()` method returns the StringCollection object as a sequence of strings. The XML that the `GetSalesForce()` method returns can be seen below:

```
<?xml version="1.0" encoding="utf-8"?>
<ArrayOfString xmlns:xsd="http://www.w3.org/2001/XMLSchema" xmlns:xsi=
"http://www.w3.org/2001/XMLSchema-instance" xmlns="http://tempuri.org/">
  <string>John Doe</string>
  <string>Sally Schmoh</string>
  <string>Jim Smith</string>
  <string>Suzy Miller</string>
</ArrayOfString>
```

Pharmacy Web Service

I have a background in pharmaceutical software. One of the most essential pieces information that pharmaceutical applications need is information relating to a given pharmaceutical item. Drugs are uniquely identified by a National Drug Code (NDC) number. Given this number, all information about a drug can be obtained.

WEB CONTENT: The complete code for this application can be found via links from www.ASPNET-Solutions.com/chapter_14.htm. There are two versions, one for C# and one for VB. You can also access the Web Service from your client application at the URL http://www.ASPNET-Solutions.com/ PharmFromNDC/service1.asmx?WSDL.

There is an application that demonstrates using this Web Service, and it can be run from a link on the same page.

Only one method comprises this Web Service. It is named Get-Pharm(), and it can be seen in Listing 14.10. It receives a single string parameter that contains the NDC number of a drug. It then returns a string containing the name, strength, and dosage form for the drug.

The first thing the method does is create a SqlConnection object. This takes care of the database connection functionality. An application variable named Application["DBConnnectString"] is initialized in Global.asax and has the complete connection string.

There's a try/catch block so that exceptions can be handled. Inside the try, the SqlConnection object (which is named myConnection) is opened. A SqlCommand object is created next, and it is created with a SQL string that selects information from the DrugList table. The following is an example of the SQL that might be formed from an NDC number:

```
select * from DrugList where NDC=' 1238000021'
```

The command object is executed so that a recordset will be returned. The method that's called is ExecuteReader(), which returns a Sql-Reader object. The SqlReader object is a read-only, forward-only recordset. And this is perfect for what we need because we're simply going to look for a matching record.

If there is a matching record, the reader.Read() method will return true. Then the column data can be used to create the return value string. Care must be take to check for null columns since the DrugList table allows some fields to be null. The IsDBNull() method is what's used here to check for null values. If the data for any column is null, no action is taken. Otherwise, the information is concatenated onto the return string.

The SqlReader and SqlConnection objects are closed, and the string data is returned. In the case of an exception, the exception message is returned.

Listing 14.10 This Is the Code for the PharmFromNDC Web Service.

```
[WebMethod]
public string GetPharm( string strNDC )
{
  // Create the connection object.
  SqlConnection myConnection =
    new SqlConnection( Convert.ToString( Application["DBConnectString"]
) );
```

```
try
{
  // Open the connection.
  myConnection.Open();

  // Create the command with the SQL.
  SqlCommand myCommand = new SqlCommand(
    "select * from DrugList where NDC='" +
    strNDC + "'", myConnection );

  // Execute and get a recordset.
  SqlDataReader reader = myCommand.ExecuteReader();

  string strReturnData = "Error: No Matching Record";

  // Check the data for name and other information.
  if( reader.Read() )
  {
    strReturnData = reader["Name"].ToString();
    if( !reader.IsDBNull( 4 ) )
    {
      strReturnData += ( " " + reader.GetString( 4 ) );
    }
    if( !reader.IsDBNull( 5 ) )
    {
      strReturnData += ( " " + reader.GetString( 5 ) );
    }
    if( !reader.IsDBNull( 6 ) )
    {
      strReturnData += ( " " + reader.GetString( 6 ) );
    }
  }
  reader.Close();
  return( strReturnData );
}
catch( Exception ex )
{
  return( "Error: " + ex.Message.ToString() );
}
finally
{
  if( myConnection.State == ConnectionState.Open )
  {
    myConnection.Close();
```

```
    }
  }
}
```

This Web Service can be tested from within Visual Studio .NET. When invoked with a valid NDC number, the returned XML will contain information for the pharmaceutical product that matches the NDC number. The NDC 1238000021 returned the following XML:

```
<?xml version="1.0" encoding="utf-8"?>
<string xmlns="http://tempuri.org/">NITROUS OXIDE 99.5 % GAS</string>
```

Consuming Web Services

When you add a Web reference, Visual Studio .Net is actually creating a wrapper class that encapsulates all of the SOAP code. This section talks about doing this. Figure 14.7 shows how to add a Web Reference, Figure

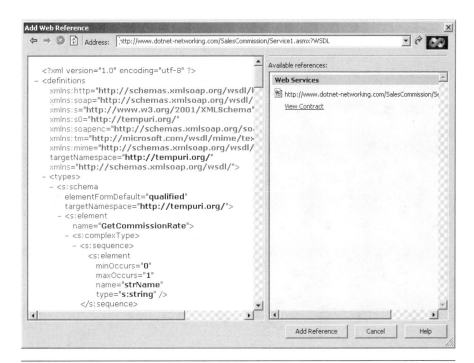

Figure 14.7 When You Add a Web Reference, the Web Service Will Return a WSDL Contract.

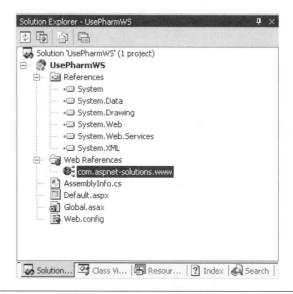

Figure 14.8 The Web Reference Shows Up in the Solution Explorer Window.

Figure 14.9 This Application Shows How Easy It Is to Use a Web Service from an Application.

Figure 14.10 This C# Windows Application Uses a Web Service Easily.

14.8 shows the Web Reference in the Solution Explorer Window, and Figure 14.9 shows using a Web Reference from an ASP.NET application, and Figure 14.10 shows using a Web Reference from a stand-alone application.

```
private void Page_Load(object sender, System.EventArgs
{
  if( !IsPostBack )
  {
    com.dotnet_networking.www.Service1 svc =
      new com.dotnet_networking.www.Service1();

    string[] Names = svc.GetSalesForce();
    NameList.DataSource = Names;
    NameList.DataBind();
  }
}

private void Button1_Click(object sender, System.EventArgs
{
  com.dotnet_networking.www.Service1 svc =
    new com.dotnet_networking.www.Service1();

  double dCommissionRate =
    svc.GetCommissionRate( NameList.SelectedItem.Value );

  CommissionRate.Text = "Commission Rate: " +
```

```
          Convert.ToString( dCommissionRate ) + "%";
}

private void button1_Click(object sender, System.EventArgs
{
  com.dotnet_networking.www.Service1 svc =
    new com.dotnet_networking.www.Service1();

  PharmInfo.Text = svc.GetPharm( NDC.Text );
}
```

Web Service Security

It isn't long into a discussion about Web Services that I'm asked about security. In one class I taught, this question came up within five minutes. (This question, though, usually comes from UNIX developers because they love to taunt Microsoft developers after the many Windows security issues.)

Although it's well and good to make Web Services discoverable and easily used, this may not be the best thing for your enterprise application. Consider, for instance, a credit-card authorization Web Service. If it is openly discoverable and usable from anywhere on the Web, anyone can use it, whether for legitimate or unscrupulous purposes. For this reason, Web Services must be protected in many cases.

There are some security issues for Web Services: authentication, authorization, message integrity, and non-repudiation. **Authentication** is the process of validating identity based on credentials. **Authorization** determines whether an identity has access to a given resource. In this section, we'll deal with authentication, and how to verify a user's credentials.

For secure authentication and data transfer, SSL can be used with a Web Service the same as with Web pages. The two things necessary for this to happen are an SSL certificate that has been properly installed on the server and access to the Web Service with the https:// protocol specifier (instead of http://).

A Web Service must be made to require authentication, or any client request will be granted without the need for credential authentication. This is most easily done from the Internet Service Manager console. To require authentication, right click the Web Service directory and select Properties. Click the Directory Security tab, and click the Edit button in the section entitled "Anonymous access and authentication control." Deselect the "Anonymous access" check box, as shown in Figure 14.11.

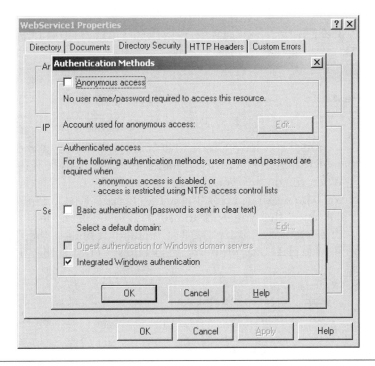

Figure 14.11 You Must Deselect the "Anonymous access" Check Box for Internet Information Server to Require Authentication.

The client code with which you access Web Services that require authentication will need some additions over the simple "instantiate and use" code we've seen to this point in the chapter. First, a CredentialCache object must be created. This object is what ASP.NET uses to transport groups of credentials when authenticating to Web resources. The following code shows the creation of a CredentialCache object:

C#
```
CredentialCache credentialCache = new CredentialCache();
```

VB
```
Dim credentialCache as new CredentialCache()
```

A NetworkCredential object must then be created and must contain the user credentials that will be used to authenticate. The following code creates a NetworkCredential object with credentials:

C#
```
NetworkCredential credentials = new NetworkCredential("Administrator",
"rocknet2","WORKGROUP");
```

VB
```
Dim credentials as new NetworkCredential("Administrator","rocknet2",
"WORKGROUP")
```

Once you have CredentialCache and NetworkCredential objects, you need to add the NetworkCredentials object to the CredentialCache object. When you do this, you'll need to specify the URL for the resource to which you'll be seeking access, the authentication type, and the NetworkCredential object that you want to use. The following code shows how to call the `CredentialCache.Add()` method. It obtains the URL from the Web Service class `Url` property. It specifies NTLM authentication.

C#
```
credentialCache.Add(new Uri(svc.Url), "NTLM", credentials);
```

VB
```
credentialCache.Add(new Uri(svc.Url), "NTLM", credentials)
```

The last thing you must do before making calls to the Web Service's methods is the set the Web Service class's `Credentials` property. Simply assign it the CredentialCache object that you created. The following code shows how to do this, and a complete C# example can be seen in Listing 14.11:

C#
```
svc.Credentials = credentialCache;
```

VB
```
svc.Credentials = credentialCache
```

Listing 14.11 Here You Can See the Complete Process for Instantiating a Web Service, Creating the Credentials Objects, and Calling a Web Service Method.

```
// Create a new instance of the Web Service class.
localhost.Service1 svc = new localhost.Service1();

// Create a new instance of CredentialCache.
CredentialCache credentialCache = new CredentialCache();
```

```
// Create a new instance of a NetworkCredential object.
NetworkCredential credentials = new NetworkCredential("Administrator",
"rocknet2","WORKGROUP");

// Add the NetworkCredential to the CredentialCache.
credentialCache.Add(new Uri(svc.Url), "NTLM", credentials);

// Add the CredentialCache to the Web Service class credentials.
svc.Credentials = credentialCache;

// Call the method on the proxy class.
string strResult = svc.HelloWorld();
```

Web Service Transactions

ADO.NET fully supports transactions, but Web Services offer an easy way
to roll an entire Web Service method into a single transaction. It's as simple
as adding additional information to the **[WebMethod]** attribute. The following code shows how to specify that a Web Service method will be a part
of a single transaction:

C#
```
[ WebMethod(TransactionOption=TransactionOption.RequiresNew)]
```

VB
```
< WebMethod(TransactionOption:=TransactionOption.RequiresNew)>
```

Once you have specified that a Web Service method will participate
as a single transaction, you can expect that any exception that is thrown
will abort the transaction and roll back all operations that preceded the
exception.

I've created an example Web Service that uses the default Hello-
World() method to demonstrate using transactions. It deletes a table that
exists in a database, and then it tries to delete another table that doesn't
exist in the database. Because the second delete fails, the first delete is not
committed, and the table is never deleted. The code for the Hel-
loWorld() method can be seen in Listing 14.12.

Listing 14.12 This Web Service Method Is Contained in a Single Transaction.

```
[ WebMethod(TransactionOption=TransactionOption.RequiresNew)]
public string HelloWorld()
{
    SqlConnection myConnection =
        new SqlConnection( "server=localhost;uid=sa;pwd=;database=pubs" );
    SqlCommand myCommand = new SqlCommand( "delete Table1", myConnection
);
    myConnection.Open();
    myCommand.ExecuteNonQuery();

    myCommand = new SqlCommand( "delete Table55", myConnection );
    myCommand.ExecuteNonQuery();

    return "Hello World";
}
```

Data Scraping Web Services

Data scraping is the technique of extracting useful data from Web resources. It is one of the coolest things that you can do with the System.Net namespace—go out on the Web, get some data, and then use it.

Before we get too far, I need to point out that you need permission to do this. You can't just go to a Web site, get its content (whether or not it explicitly says it has a copyright), and then use it. But there are a great number of legitimate uses for this process.

Imagine that your company has some legacy Web sites where you can't get direct access to the underlying data. But it may be important for you to use the data in your application. You can make requests to the legacy Web application, scrape the data, and use it as needed. In this case, you're leveraging your company's data, and you don't have to worry about or bear the expense of interfacing with the data source.

Another thing you can do is scrape information from .gov Web sites. The data contained on these sites is owned by the government, and therefore it is public domain and can be used in your application.

A typical data-scraping session goes like this: Data is downloaded from a Web resource such as a Web site, it is stored (in memory or on disk) in a convenient form such as in a string object, the desired information is extracted, and the extracted information is used.

You might be asking, "What makes a Web Service a desirable mechanism for scraping data?" Good question, considering your application could easily do the information scraping within its own code. The two main reasons a Web Service is desirable for creating data-scraping processes is that they can be used by multiple applications in disparate locations, and a single Web Service can be updated if the format of the Web resource changes and thus breaks the data-scraping process.

The entire Web Service can be seen in Listing 14.13. I'll describe how it works here.

The externally callable method is called `GetWeather()`. It returns a string collection to the client application that contains three strings. The first string is the temperature; the second, the barometric pressure; and the third, the humidity. It takes no arguments from the client application, although a more complete weather scraper would need information such as a Zip code.

The `GetWeather()` method does three things. It pulls the Web data by calling the `PullHtmlData()` method. It extracts the desired data by calling the `ParseHtmlData()` method. And, finally, it adds the temperature, pressure, and humidity strings in the StringCollection object that will be returned to the client application.

The `PullHtmlData()` method instantiates and uses a WebClient object with which it will download the data. A call to the `WebClient.DownloadData()` method returns an array of bytes, which are then converted to a string object. If an exception is thrown, the `PullHtmlData()` method will return `false`, indicating an error.

The `ParseHtmlData()` method relies heavily on the `Regex` class to scrape the data from the HTML. (For more information about regular expressions and parsing HTML data, see Chapter 10.) This method first creates a Regex object from the downloaded HTML data, and it sets it to ignore case and treat the data as a single line. The regular expression that is used pulls all data between the `<b>` and `</b>` tags. For the page that was downloaded (which is located at www.DotNet-Networking.com/Weather/default.aspx), this works perfectly. For other situations, a different extraction expression is needed. By the way, you have explicit permission to use this Web page to get weather data.

Once the `Regex.Matches()` method is called, it's a simple matter to walk through the list of Match objects and get the data. The first string will be the temperature; the second, the barometric pressure; and the third, the humidity.

Listing 14.13 This Web Service Scrapes Weather Data and Returns It to Be Used by the Client Application.

```
bool PullHtmlData(ref string strHtmlData)
{
    try
    {
        WebClient wc = new WebClient();
        byte[] data;
        data =
            wc.DownloadData( Convert.ToString( Application["WeatherPage"]
) );
        strHtmlData = Encoding.ASCII.GetString( data );
        return( true );
    }
    catch( Exception ex )
    {
        strHtmlData = ex.Message.ToString();
        return( false );
    }
}


bool ParseHtmlData( string strHtmlData, ref string strTemp,
    ref string strPressure, ref string strHumidity )
{
    try
    {
        Regex re = new Regex( strHtmlData,
            RegexOptions.Singleline | RegexOptions.IgnoreCase );
        MatchCollection mc = re.Matches( "<b>(?<MYDATA>.*?(?=</b>))" );

        int nCount = 0;
        foreach( Match m in mc )
        {
            switch( nCount )
            {
                case 0:
                    strTemp = m.Groups["MYDATA"].Value;
                    break;
                case 1:
                    strPressure = m.Groups["MYDATA"].Value;
                    break;
```

```
            case 2:
                strHumidity = m.Groups["MYDATA"].Value;
                break;
        }
        nCount++;
    }

}
catch( Exception ex )
{
    return( false );
}

return( true );
}


[WebMethod]
public StringCollection GetWeather()
{
    string strTemp = "", strPressure = "", strHumidity = "";
    string strHtmlData = "";
    StringCollection WeatherInfo = new StringCollection();

    if( !PullHtmlData( ref strHtmlData ) )
    {
        return( WeatherInfo );
    }

    if( !ParseHtmlData( strHtmlData, ref strTemp,
        ref strPressure, ref strHumidity ) )
    {
        return( WeatherInfo );
    }

    WeatherInfo.Add( strTemp );
    WeatherInfo.Add( strPressure );
    WeatherInfo.Add( strHumidity );

    return( WeatherInfo );
}
```

Summary

Web Services, in conjunction with the System.Net namespace, offer a powerful tool in your development arsenal. They follow standard protocols based on HTTP, SOAP, and XML—and this makes them universal. They are easy to create with Visual Studio .NET and the Wizards that it offers. They are easy to consume because of the discovery process and the support that Visual Studio .NET brings to the table.

Web Services are secure, too. You wouldn't want to open up Web Services to anyone who might discover their location. And the transactional support that can be added to the **[WebMethod]** attribute makes this part of every robust database application an easy matter to implement.

When it comes time to get and use data from Web resources, there's no match for the networking classes combined with the regular expressions classes as part of a Web Service. This technique will take its place as one of the coolest and most useful combinations of the .NET technology.

A good book to read for regular expressions is *Mastering Regular Expressions*, 2nd edition by Friedl (O'Reilly, 2002). This book is a great reference, and it teaches the subject pretty well, too.

CHAPTER 15

Server Controls and HttpModules: Creating a Feedback Tracking Module

In This Chapter:

- Custom Server Controls
- The Comment Tracking Control
- HttpModules
- Add Comment Tracking Automatically
- Deploying the Application

This chapter teaches you how to write custom server controls and how to add content to pages automatically using HttpModules. The sample application that we will build is a server control that tracks feedback about specific ASP.NET pages. Rather then adding this control to each page that we want to track, we will build an HttpModule that automatically places the control on every page within an application. This way, we can add or remove the feedback tracking control from every page by changing only a couple of lines in the web.config file.

HttpModules allow you to handle events generated by the `HttpApplication` class in a global manner. HttpModules are similar to ISAPI filters but are much easier to design and implement. With an HttpModule, you can do processing on a request at various stages of the request. Because an HttpModule is a global object, it is used to do things that affect most if not all of the .aspx files in your application. Here is a partial list of things that can be done with an HttpModule:

- File and user authentication.
- Maintain a collection of objects to be used by a given user (similar to the Session object).
- Add a message to the bottom of every page that returns HTML data.
- Encrypt data for pages of a certain type.
- Centralize error logging for an application.

An HttpModule has two basic purposes. It provides event handlers for events generated by the Application object, and it can generate events that can be handled by your Global.asax file or the code file behind the Global.asax file. Both of these purposes will be discussed in detail.

Custom Server Controls

Custom server controls provide a way of encapsulating server-side code with client-side HTML and scripting into a single logical unit. They allow you to develop a reusable object with a public interface consisting of properties, methods, and events that can be used by dragging and dropping the object when doing design with a visual designer.

Custom Controls and User Controls

.NET provides for two types of developer-created server controls: custom server controls and user controls. This chapter will focus on the custom server controls, but I think it is important to understand the difference between the two types of server controls and when each should be used.

User controls are in many ways much easier to develop than custom controls. User controls can be designed in Visual Studio .NET using the visual designer, while the visual portion of custom controls must be coded entirely by hand. Despite this, custom controls are in many ways superior to user controls and have the following advantages:

- Custom controls compile to their own .dll file and can be used across applications. User controls are limited to a single application.
- Custom controls require no additional files beyond the .dll file and are completely compiled. They render themselves using the developer's language of choice, whereas a user control is rendered using HTML stored in an .ascx file. User controls must be deployed as an

.ascx file, and the source code in the .ascx file will be visible to anyone with rights to view the files on the Web server.

■ Custom controls can display a design-time user interface that mimics what will be displayed at runtime. User controls are always rendered as a generic gray box.

■ Custom controls can be sized visually. User controls can be sized only by setting properties such as height, width, and absolute position.

■ Code to handle events exposed by custom controls can be largely generated automatically by Visual Studio .NET. You will need to add all code by hand to handle an event exposed by a user control.

The only real advantages user controls have over custom controls are that they are easier to implement, and they are potentially easier to make changes to. The following recommendation should be carefully considered.

RECOMMENDED PRACTICE: One should use a user control when reuse is only across a project (it's a time-constraint thing). When the control is used in a second project, take a few hours and turn it into a custom control.

User controls are generally used when you need a control that is specific to a given application and will probably be used only a few times. Custom controls are used when you need a control to be used across many applications. Because for this chapter we are developing an application that is intended to be used across many applications, we will develop it as a custom server control.

Custom Server Control Basics

Even if you've never created a server control, server controls should not be new because you will have used the ones provided as part of the .NET Framework. What may not be clear is that there are two basic types of custom control. There are *render* controls, which produce their output by writing HTML directly to an output stream, and there are *composite* controls, which produce their output by keeping a collection of child controls and calling the `Render()` method of each of its child controls in turn when it needs to render itself.

The basics of creating either a render or a composite control are the same. Creating a custom control requires that you do two things:

1. Derive your control from the `System.Web.UI.WebControls.WebControl` class or a class derived from it.
2. Override either the `CreateChildControls()` method, or the `Render()` method to generate your output.

The method you choose to override depends on what type of server control you are creating. If you are creating a composite control, you would normally override the `CreateChildControls()` method. If you are creating a render control, you would normally override the `Render()` method. It is also possible to create a hybrid control by overriding both the `CreateChildControl()` method and the `Render()` method.

Render Controls

A render control is a control that does not contain any other server controls and outputs only HTML. Implementing a control this way usually results in better performance than a composite control provides, but it is harder to implement extended functionality. This control is defined by overriding the `WebControl` base class's `Render()` method. Listing 15.1 shows a simple render control.

Listing 15.1 Simple Render Control

```
Imports System.ComponentModel
Imports System.Web.UI

Public Class WebCustomControl1
    Inherits System.Web.UI.WebControls.WebControl

    Dim _text As String
    Property [Text]() As String
        Get
            Return _text
        End Get

        Set(ByVal Value As String)
            _text = Value
        End Set
    End Property

    Protected Overrides Sub Render(ByVal output _
    As System.Web.UI.HtmlTextWriter)
```

```
        output.Write([Text])
    End Sub
End Class
```

Most applications will use composite controls rather then render controls because you can use the additional functionality of an existing server control without having to re-implement the details of the control. This is especially true because the .NET platform includes server controls for so many basic controls. For this reason, render controls will not be discussed in detail, and the remainder of the chapter will concentrate on composite controls.

Composite Controls

By far the more common in my experience, composite controls allow you to use the functionality of existing server controls to make up your control. To create a composite control, you need to override the CreateChild-Controls() method of the WebControl class and add all of the contained controls to the Controls collection. Text or HTML can be added by using a LiteralControl. Listing 15.2 shows a simple composite control with a single label as a contained control. The output would be the same as that for the render control example.

Listing 15.2 Simple Composite Control

```
Imports System.ComponentModel
Imports System.Web.UI

Public Class WebCustomControl1
    Inherits System.Web.UI.WebControls.WebControl

    Dim _text As String
    Property [Text]() As String
        Get
            Return _text
        End Get

        Set(ByVal Value As String)
            _text = Value
        End Set
    End Property
```

```
Protected Overrides Sub CreateChildControls()
    Dim label As New Label
    label.Text = Me.Text

    Me.Controls.Add(label)
End Sub
End Class
```

INamingContainer Interface

Many times you need to have several instances of a control you created on the same page. This can be a problem if you are assigning unique IDs to the controls contained in a composite control. To get around this problem, the .NET Framework has defined an interface called INamingContainer. This is a marker interface that has no methods or properties that need to be implemented. Controls that implement this interface will automatically concatenate the ID of the child control with the ID of the parent control to generate unique IDs for all controls on the page. Following is an example of how to implement this interface.

C#
```
public class MyControl : WebControl,INamingContainer
{
    // Class implementation goes here
}
```

VB
```
Public Class WebCustomControl1
    Inherits System.Web.UI.WebControls.WebControl
    Implements INamingContainer
'Class implementation goes here
End Class
```

You will also need to implement this interface if you wish to handle any events of contained server controls.

Handling Events from Contained Controls

Composite controls allow you to easily handle the events of contained controls and generate events for your control. It is important to note here that you must implement the INamingContainer interface as described in the preceding section.

Event handling is a straightforward two-step process. First, define a function to handle the event. Second, add the event handler to the event to be handled. Following is an example of how to handle an event for a contained control.

C#
```
Button objButton=new Button();
objButton.Text="Press Me";
objButton.ID="Button1";
objButton.Click+=new EventHandler(OnButton_Click);
Controls.Add(objButton);
```

VB
```
Dim objButton AS new Button()
objButton.Text="Press Me"
objButton.ID="Button1"
AddHandler objButton.Click,AddressOf OnButton_Click
Controls.Add(objButton)
```

The event-handler function needs to be defined using the .NET standard format for event handlers.

C#
```
private void OnButton_Click(Object sender, EventArgs e)
{
   // Event handling code goes here
}
```

VB
```
Private Sub OnButton_Click(ByVal sender As Object, _
   ByVal e As EventArgs) Handles Button.Click
' Event handling code goes here
End Sub
```

Other than what has been shown, the complexity of the composite control lies mainly in what you are trying to do. Because of this, we are going to show how controls are created by creating the controls necessary for this chapter's example.

The Comment Tracking Control

The comment tracking control is intended to track comments about ASP.NET pages that are under development. Because the comments need to be associated with the different people making them, each user needs to be able to log in. In this control, there is a registration page where anyone can register to make comments on the page. After registering, users will be able to log in at anytime.

Using a module such as this is important in a number of situations. One in particular that I recall is when a client wanted to have staff submit comments for a newly developed Web application. This control provided the perfect mechanism for them to do so.

Because this control is not intended to be used on a production site, the people with knowledge of the URL are likely to be the ones evaluating the site implementation, or the site will be hosted on a development server that is not accessible to the public. In either case, security is not too big of an issue for allowing anyone to register; but if this control were adapted for use on a pubic site, further study of the security issues involved would be necessary. For more discussion of security issues, read the section in Chapter 18 entitled "Security" (page 657).

Control Overview

The comment control handles all facets of commenting. They are the login state, the register state and the comment viewing state. In reality, each state is implemented by a separate server control. Because none of these embedded controls is intended to be used separately, I will just consider them different states of the comment control until I get into the implementation details.

Login State

When a user first accesses a page that has a comment control on it, the comment control is in the login state. Reviewers are required to log in or register prior to seeing other comments. This was intended to get everyone to register and log in. Figure 15.1 shows the comment control when it is first displayed for login.

As you can see, to the left of the control data there is a button, Hide Comments. If this button is pressed, instead of displaying the comment

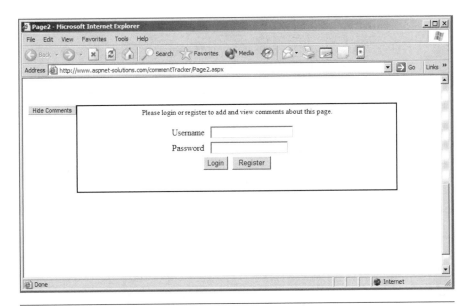

Figure 15.1 Comment Control in Login Mode

control, only a button, Show Comments, is displayed. This allows the person viewing the page to hide the comments if they cover part of the page being evaluated. This feature is available no matter what state the comment control is in, and it will persist across different pages.

The comment control in the login state has two buttons, the Login button, and the Register button. These buttons do pretty much what you would expect them to. The Login button submits the username and password for authentication, and the Register button changes what is displayed in the comment control to a registration page.

Registration State

The first time someone is evaluating a page, he will need to register. Figure 15.2 shows the comment control in its registration state.

Because this control is intended to be used during the development of the site before it is live, security of the comments being made was less of an issue than making it easy for the reviewers to register and log in. Because of this, the `username` is the only required field. If the reviewer wants to display a name other than the `username` with his comments, he should fill in the display name.

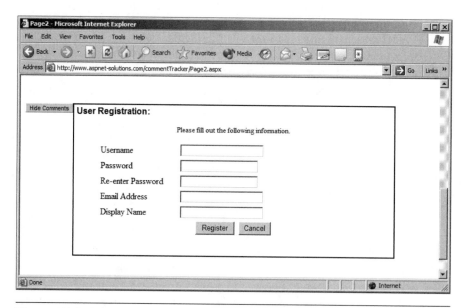

Figure 15.2 Comment Control in Registration Mode

Commenting State

Once a reviewer has logged in, he will see the comment control in its most common state, the commenting state. Figure 15.3 shows the comment control in its commenting state.

Once a reviewer has logged in, the commenting control has three areas. At the top is a page note. If the person logging in has developer rights, she will see a small Edit button here. The developer can add or modify the note by clicking the Edit button. All other users can only read the note.

Following the note is a list of the comments. A user can edit but not delete any of his own comments. At the bottom is an entry field to enter new comments into. The developer has some additional functionality. The developer can reply to any of the comments and have the reply immediately below the comment. All others can only enter new comments. The comments are listed in order of entry. The developer can reply to comments so that if the comment is an action item, such as fixing the color on the page or something, the developer can reply that it has been done, or why it wasn't done, and anyone reading the comments can see whether or not an issue was resolved.

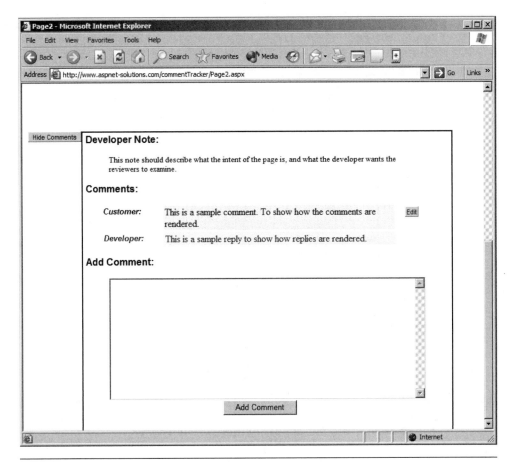

Figure 15.3 Comment Control in Commenting Mode

User Types

The comment control has three different kinds of users: developers, local users, and customers. Developers are the people who are implementing the site. A developer has the ability to edit the page notes and reply to any comment. A local user would be like an in-house site reviewer or tester. Comments entered by this type of user could not be seen by the customer users. This way, in-house testers can add comments/suggestions without the final customer being able to see them. Figure 15.4 shows the comment control as the developer sees it.

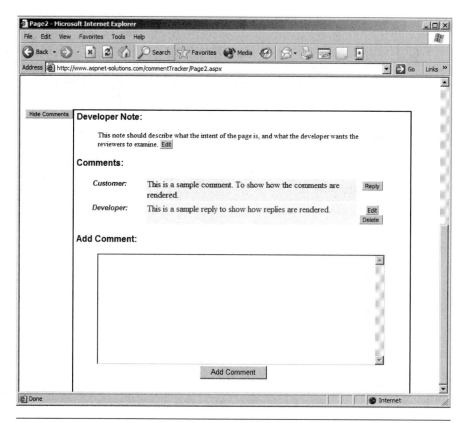

Figure 15.4 Comment Control for the Developer

Implementation

To implement the control, I actually used four different custom controls. There is one control each for each of the states, and a master control that determines which of the other three controls is displayed. Following is a list of the controls that make up the commenting control:

- **CommentCtl**—This is the master control that you use. It displays one of the following controls, depending upon the current state.
- **CommentLoginCtl**—This control displays the initial login.
- **CommentRegisterCtl**—This control displays the registration form.

■ **CommentDisplayCtl**—This control displays the actual comments once the user has logged in.

Now let's look at each of these controls in detail.

CommentCtl

The first thing to look at is the public interface because that is what a user of the control will need to understand. Table 15.1 shows the public interface methods and properties.

Even though CommentCtl is the only one of the controls that has a truly public interface that can be set by the user, the contained controls also have some of the same properties. The contained controls' interface values are set by this control. The way the control is structured, you can't use the contained controls independently from CommentCtrl.

Next, let's look at the methods that are called to create the control. Table 15.2 shows the private and protected methods used to create the control.

Next we will look at the private properties used by the control. Table 15.3 shows the private properties used in this control.

Table 15.1 Public Interface

Name	Type	Description
ConnectionString	Property	This property is a string that contains the OleDb connection string to the data source containing the comment data.
Revision	Property	This property is an integer containing the revision. The comments are displayed by revision, and only the comments for the indicated revision are displayed.
CssFile	Property	This property contains the name of the .css file that contains the css classes necessary to format the control. Using a separate .css file (rather than relying on the styles of the surrounding page) gives you much more control over the appearance.

Table 15.2 Control Creation Methods

Name	Type	Description
CreateChildControls()	Method	This method starts the process of creating the control. All other methods are called from this one.
HandleState()	Method	This method is called to determine which of the other controls will be displayed.
DisplayShowButton()	Method	This method is called when the main portion of the control is hidden and only a button with the label Show Comments is displayed. If this button is pressed, the main portion of the control will be displayed.
DisplayHideButton()	Method	This method is called when the main portion of the control is displayed with the addition of a button labeled Hide Comments. If this button is pressed, the main portion of the control will be hidden so that any portion of the page behind the control can be seen.
DisplayLogin()	Method	This method displays the CommentLoginCtl control.
DisplayRegister()	Method	This method displays the CommentRegisterCtl control.
DisplayStd()	Method	This method displays the CommentDisplayCtl control, which is where the actual comments are displayed.
AddLiteral()	Method	This method adds a LiteralControl to the Controls collection. The text to be added is passed in an argument.

Finally, we will look at the event handlers used in this control. These events are generated by the contained control being displayed. With this control, each of the events fired results in a change of state, which changes the control that is currently being displayed. Table 15.4 shows the event handlers used in this control.

Now let's look at the actual implementation of this control. Listing 15.3 provides a complete source listing of the control.

Table 15.3 Private Properties

Name	Type	Description
State	Property	This property is an enumeration that contains the state of the control.
Compact	Property	This is a Boolean value that indicates whether the control is to be rendered in its compact mode, which displays only a button labeled Show Comments, or whether it is to be rendered normally.
Reload	Property	This is a Boolean value that indicates whether the page needs to be immediately reloaded. The page is normally reloaded every time there is a post back. This property indicates that the page is to be reloaded without resubmitting the previous data.

Table 15.4 Event Handlers

Name	Type	Description
OnShowButton_Click()	Event Handler	This method is used to handle the Click event of the button that shows or hides the main portion of the control.
OnLoggedin()	Event Handler	This method handles the Loggedin event from the CommentLoginCtl control. This event is raised when the user has successfully logged in.
OnRegister	Event Handler	This method handles the Register event from the CommentLoginCtl control. This event is raised when the Register button is pressed when the CommentLoginCtl is displayed.
OnRegistered	Event Handler	This method handles the Registered event from the CommentRegisterCtl control. This event is fired when a new user has successfully registered.
OnCancel	Event Handler	This method handles the Cancel event from the CommentRegisterCtl control. This event is fired when the Cancel button is pressed on the registration form.

Listing 15.3 Comment control—CommentCtl.cs

```
using System;
using System.Web.UI;
using System.Web.UI.WebControls;
using System.ComponentModel;
using System.Configuration;
using System.Collections.Specialized;

namespace Comment
{
    ' State enumerations.
    enum enumState
    {
        stateLogin=1,
        stateRegister=2,
        stateStd=3
    };

    /// <summary>
    /// This is the main comment control, it manages which of
    ///  the other controls are displayed
    /// </summary>
    [DefaultProperty("DataSource"),
        ToolboxData
            ("<{0}:CommentCtl runat=server></{0}:CommentCtl>")]
    public class CommentCtl : WebControl,INamingContainer
    {
        private String m_sUsername;
        private string m_sConnectionString;
        private string m_sCssFile;
        private int m_nRevision;

        // Control Creation Methods
        protected override void CreateChildControls()
        {
            if(Reload)
            {
                Reload=false;
                ' Adding script allows client-side interaction.
                AddLiteral("<script>");
                AddLiteral("window.navigate('"+
                    Page.Request.RawUrl+"')");
```

```
        AddLiteral("</script>");
    }
    else if(Compact)
    {
        DisplayShowButton();
    }
    else
    {
        ' Attempt to retrieve state data.
        if(Page.Request.Cookies["CommentUser"]!=null)
        {
            m_sUsername=
                Page.Request.Cookies["CommentUser"]
                .Value;
            ' There are times when this is not explicitly know.
            State = enumState.stateStd;
        }

        HandleState();
    }
}

private void HandleState()
{
    // Add stylesheet if necessary.
    if(CssFile!="")
    {
        AddLiteral("<link href=\""+CssFile+
            "\" type=\"text/css\" rel=\"stylesheet\">");
    }

    switch (State)
    {
        case enumState.stateLogin :
            DisplayLogin();
            break;

        case enumState.stateRegister :
            DisplayRegister();
            break;

        case enumState.stateStd :
            DisplayStd();
            break;
```

```
            default :
                throw new Exception("Invalid State");
        }
    }


    private void DisplayShowButton()
    {
        // Add stylesheet if necessary.
        if(CssFile!="")
        {
            AddLiteral("<link href=\""+CssFile+
                "\" type=\"text/css\" rel=\"stylesheet\">");
        }

        Button objCompactButton=new Button();
        objCompactButton.Text="Show Comments";
        objCompactButton.CssClass="ShowHideButton";
        objCompactButton.CausesValidation=false;
        objCompactButton.CommandName="Show";
        objCompactButton.ID="Show";
        objCompactButton.Click+=
            new EventHandler(OnShowButton_Click);
        Controls.Add(objCompactButton);
    }


    private void DisplayHideButton()
    {
        // Display Hide Button
        Button objCompactButton=new Button();
        objCompactButton.Text="Hide Comments";
        objCompactButton.CssClass="ShowHideButton";
        objCompactButton.CausesValidation=false;
        objCompactButton.CommandName="Show";
        objCompactButton.ID="Show";
        objCompactButton.Click+=
            new EventHandler(OnShowButton_Click);
        Controls.Add(objCompactButton);
    }


    private void DisplayLogin()
    {
        CommentLoginCtl objCommentLoginCtl=
            new CommentLoginCtl();
```

```
        objCommentLoginCtl.ConnectionString=
            ConnectionString;
        objCommentLoginCtl.Loggedin+=
            new EventHandler(OnLoggedin);
        objCommentLoginCtl.Register+=
            new EventHandler(OnRegister);
        Controls.Add(objCommentLoginCtl);
        DisplayHideButton();
    }

    private void DisplayRegister()
    {
        CommentRegisterCtl objCommentRegisterCtl=
            new CommentRegisterCtl();
        objCommentRegisterCtl.ConnectionString=
            ConnectionString;
        objCommentRegisterCtl.Registered+=
            new EventHandler(OnRegistered);
        objCommentRegisterCtl.Cancel+=
            new EventHandler(OnCancel);
        Controls.Add(objCommentRegisterCtl);
        DisplayHideButton();
    }

    private void DisplayStd()
    {
        CommentDisplayCtl objCommentDisplayCtl=
            new CommentDisplayCtl();
        objCommentDisplayCtl.ConnectionString=
            ConnectionString;
        objCommentDisplayCtl.Revision=Revision;
        objCommentDisplayCtl.Username=m_sUsername;
        Controls.Add(objCommentDisplayCtl);
        DisplayHideButton();
    }

    private void AddLiteral(String sText)
    {
        Controls.Add(new LiteralControl(sText));
    }

    // Private properties start here.
    private enumState State
```

```
    {
        get
        {
            if(Page.Session["State"]==null)
                Page.Session["State"]=enumState.stateLogin;

            return (enumState) Page.Session["State"];
        }
        set
        {
            Page.Session["State"]=value;
        }
    }

    private bool Compact
    {
        get
        {
            if(Page.Session["Compact"]==null)
                Page.Session["Compact"]=false;

            return (bool) Page.Session["Compact"];
        }
        set
        {
            Page.Session["Compact"]=value;
        }
    }

    private bool Reload
    {
        get
        {
            if(Page.Session["Reload"]==null)
                Page.Session["Reload"]=false;

            return (bool) Page.Session["Reload"];
        }
        set
        {
            Page.Session["Reload"]=value;
        }
    }
```

```csharp
// Public properties start here.
public string ConnectionString
{
    get
    {
        return m_sConnectionString;
    }

    set
    {
        m_sConnectionString = value;
    }
}

public int Revision
{
    get
    {
        return m_nRevision;
    }

    set
    {
        m_nRevision = value;
    }
}

public string CssFile
{
    get
    {
        return m_sCssFile;
    }

    set
    {
        m_sCssFile = value;
    }
}

// Event handlers go here
private void OnShowButton_Click
    (Object sender, EventArgs e)
```

```
{
    Compact=!Compact;
    Reload=true;

    Controls.Clear();
    CreateChildControls();
}


private void OnLoggedin(Object sender, EventArgs e)
{
    CommentLoginCtl objLoginCtl=
        (CommentLoginCtl) sender;

    State=enumState.stateStd;
    m_sUsername=objLoginCtl.m_ctlEditUsername.Text;

    // Add the User cookie
    System.Web.HttpCookie objCookie =
        new System.Web.HttpCookie("CommentUser");
    objCookie.Value = m_sUsername;
    Page.Response.Cookies.Add(objCookie);

    Controls.Clear();
    HandleState();
}


private void OnRegister(Object sender, EventArgs e)
{
    State=enumState.stateRegister;

    Controls.Clear();
    HandleState();
}


private void OnRegistered(Object sender, EventArgs e)
{
    CommentRegisterCtl objRegisterCtl=
        (CommentRegisterCtl) sender;

    State=enumState.stateStd;
    m_sUsername=objRegisterCtl.m_ctlEditUsername.Text;
```

```
        // Add the User cookie
        System.Web.HttpCookie objCookie =
            new System.Web.HttpCookie("CommentUser");
        objCookie.Value = m_sUsername;
        Page.Response.Cookies.Add(objCookie);

        Controls.Clear();
        HandleState();
    }

    private void OnCancel(Object sender, EventArgs e)
    {
        State=enumState.stateLogin;

        Controls.Clear();
        HandleState();
    }


  }
}
```

This control is basically a state management engine with two different unrelated sets of states. One set of states manages which of the contained controls is being rendered. The other set of states is whether the controls should be rendered as a button or a complete control.

> **NOTE:** One thing to note here is that the control is positioned absolutely on the page using a style sheet. This means that this control can hide portions of the page. Normally this would be fine becasue we can hide the comment control. The one case in which unexpected results may occur is if the page has a list box, either a drop-down list box or a standard list box. In this case, the list box will render on top of the comment control rather then being hidden by it. This is an inherent problem with Internet Explorer. Before allowing others to review the application, you should go through every page and verify that you have positioned the comment control on the page such that this does not occur.

CommentLoginCtl

The CommentLoginCtl is the control that is displayed by the main CommentCtl control prior to the user logging in. It displays a Username and a Password entry field, and Login and Register buttons. This represents the initial state of our comment control.

Table 15.5 Public Interface

Name	Type	Description
ConnectionString	Property	This property is a string that contains the OleDb connection string to the data source containing the comment data.
m_ctlEditUsername	TextBox	This is a variable that holds a reference to the contained control that contains the username of the user logging in.
M_ctlEditPassword	TextBox	This is a variable that holds a reference to the contained control that contains the password of the user logging in.

Table 15.6 Control Creation Methods

Name	Type	Description
CreateChildControls()	Method	This method starts the process of creating the control. For this control, all this method does is call the CreateLogin() method.
CreateLogin()	Method	This method creates this control.
AddLiteral()	Method	This method adds a LiteralControl to the Controls collection. The text to be added is passed in an argument.

Table 15.7 Event Handlers

Name	Type	Description
OnLoginButton_Click()	Event Handler	This method is used to handle the Click event of the Login button.
OnRegisterButton_Click()	Event Handler	This method is used to handle the Click event of the Register button.

Table 15.8 Events

Name	Type	Description
Loggedin	Event	This event is fired after the Username and Password entered by the user have been confirmed.
Register	Event	This event is fired when the Register button is pressed.

The public interface portion of this control is intended to be used only by the CommentCtl control. Table 15.5 shows the public interface of this control.

Table 15.6 shows the control creation methods.

Table 15.7 shows the event handlers used in this control.

Table 15.8 shows the events generated by this control.

Listing 15.4 contains the source listing for the CommentLoginCtl control.

Listing 15.4 Comment Login Control—CommentLoginCtl.cs

```
using System;
using System.Web.UI;
using System.Web.UI.WebControls;
using System.ComponentModel;
using System.Configuration;
using System.Collections.Specialized;

namespace Comment
{
    public class CommentLoginCtl : WebControl,INamingContainer
    {
        private string m_sConnectionString;
        // Variables that hold references to child controls
        public TextBox m_ctlEditUsername;
        public TextBox m_ctlEditPassword;
        private Label m_ctlLabelLoginError;

        // Public Properties Start Here
        public string ConnectionString
        {
            get
            {
                return m_sConnectionString;
            }

            set
            {
                m_sConnectionString = value;
            }
        }

        // Generated events start here.
        public event EventHandler Loggedin;
        public event EventHandler Register;
```

```
// Control Creation functions start here.
protected override void CreateChildControls()
{
    CreateLogin();
}


private void AddLiteral(String sText)
{
    Controls.Add(new LiteralControl(sText));
}


protected void CreateLogin()
{
    String sTemp;

    // Begin Comment Wrapping Div element
    sTemp="<div align=\"center\"";
    if(CssClass!="")
        sTemp+=" class=\""+CssClass+"\"";
    else
        sTemp+=" class=\"Comment\"";
    if(Width!=Unit.Empty)
        sTemp+=" width=\""+Width.ToString()+"\"";
    if(Height!=Unit.Empty)
        sTemp+=" height=\""+Height.ToString()+"\"";
    sTemp+=">\n";
    AddLiteral(sTemp);

    // Login Message
    AddLiteral("Please login or register to add and "+
        "view comments about    this page.<br><br>");

    // Create Login table
    AddLiteral("<table class=\"LoginTable\" align="+
        "\"center\" border=\"0\" width=\"250\">");

    //Username Field
    AddLiteral("<tr>");
    AddLiteral("<td>Username</td>");
    AddLiteral("<td>");
    m_ctlEditUsername= new TextBox();
    m_ctlEditUsername.ID="Username";
    Controls.Add(m_ctlEditUsername);
```

```
AddLiteral("</td>");
AddLiteral("</tr>");

//Password Field
AddLiteral("<tr>");
AddLiteral("<td>Password</td>");
AddLiteral("<td>");
m_ctlEditPassword= new TextBox();
m_ctlEditPassword.ID="Password";
m_ctlEditPassword.TextMode=TextBoxMode.Password;
Controls.Add(m_ctlEditPassword);
AddLiteral("</td>");
AddLiteral("</tr>");

//Login / Registration Buttons
AddLiteral("<tr>");
AddLiteral("<td colspan=\"2\" align=\"center\">");

// Login Button
Button objLoginButton=new Button();
objLoginButton.Text="Login";
objLoginButton.CssClass="LoginButton";
objLoginButton.CausesValidation=false;
objLoginButton.CommandName="Login";
objLoginButton.ID="Login";
objLoginButton.Click+=
    new EventHandler(OnLoginButton_Click);
Controls.Add(objLoginButton);
AddLiteral("  ");

// Register Button
Button objRegisterButton=new Button();
objRegisterButton.Text="Register";
objRegisterButton.CssClass="RegisterButton";
objRegisterButton.CausesValidation=false;
objRegisterButton.CommandName="Register";
objRegisterButton.ID="Register";
objRegisterButton.Click+=
    new EventHandler(OnRegisterButton_Click);
Controls.Add(objRegisterButton);
AddLiteral("</td>");
AddLiteral("</tr>");
AddLiteral("</table><br><br>");
```

```csharp
        // Add error Message Label
        m_ctlLabelLoginError=new Label();
        m_ctlLabelLoginError.Text=
            "Invalid username or password.";
        m_ctlLabelLoginError.Visible=false;
        m_ctlLabelLoginError.CssClass="ErrorLabel";
        Controls.Add(m_ctlLabelLoginError);

        // End Div element
        AddLiteral("</div>");
    }

    private void OnLoginButton_Click
        (Object sender, EventArgs e)
    {
        //Load Data Objects
        bool bLoggedIn=false;

        CommentDataMgr objCommentDataMgr=
            new CommentDataMgr(ConnectionString);
        bLoggedIn=objCommentDataMgr.Login
            (m_ctlEditUsername.Text,m_ctlEditPassword.Text);
        if(bLoggedIn)
            Loggedin(this,EventArgs.Empty);
        else
            m_ctlLabelLoginError.Visible=true;
    }

    private void OnRegisterButton_Click
        (Object sender, EventArgs e)
    {
        Register(this,EventArgs.Empty);
    }
    }
}
```

CommentRegistrationCtl

The CommentRegistrationCtl is the control that is displayed by the main CommentCtl control if the user pressed the Register button on the CommentLoginCtl control. It displays a registration form.

The public interface portion of this control is intended to be used only by the CommentCtl control. Table 15.9 shows the public interface of this control.

Table 15.9 Public Interface

Name	Type	Description
ConnectionString	Property	This property is a string that contains the OleDb connection string to the data source containing the comment data.
m_ctlEditUsername	TextBox	This is a variable that holds a reference to the contained control that contains the username of the user logging in.
m_ctlEditPassword	TextBox	This is a variable that holds a reference to the contained control that contains the password of the user logging in.

Table 15.10 Control Creation Methods

Name	Type	Description
CreateChildControls()	Method	This method starts the process of creating the control. For this control, all this method does is call the CreateRegistration() method.
CreateRegistration()	Method	This method creates this control.
AddLiteral()	Method	This method adds a LiteralControl to the Controls collection. The text to be added is passed in an argument.

Table 15.11 Event Handlers

Name	Type	Description
OnRegisterButton_Click()	Event Handler	This method is used to handle the Click event of the Register button.
OnCancelButton_Click()	Event Handler	This method is used to handle the Click event of the Cancel button.

Table 15.12 Events

Name	Type	Description
Registered	Event	This event is fired after a valid registration form is submitted.
Cancel	Event	This event is fired when the Cancel button is pressed.

Table 15.10 shows the control creation methods.

Table 15.11 shows the event handlers used in this control.

Table 15.12 shows the events generated by this control.

Listing 15.5 contains the source listing for the CommentRegistrationCtl control.

Listing 15.5 Comment Registration Control—CommentRegistrationCtl.cs

```
using System;
using System.Web.UI;
using System.Web.UI.WebControls;
using System.ComponentModel;
using System.Configuration;
using System.Collections.Specialized;

namespace Comment
{
    public class CommentRegisterCtl :
        WebControl,INamingContainer
    {
        // private variables
        public TextBox m_ctlEditUsername;
        public TextBox m_ctlEditPassword;
        private TextBox m_ctlEditPassword2;
        private TextBox m_ctlEditEmail;
        private TextBox m_ctlEditDisplayName;
        private Label m_ctlLabelUsernameError;
        private Label m_ctlLabelPasswordError;
        private Label m_ctlLabelEmailError;
        private Label m_ctlLabelDisplayNameError;

        private CommentDataMgr m_objCommentDataMgr;
        private string m_sConnectionString;

        protected override void CreateChildControls()
        {
            //Load Data Objects
            m_objCommentDataMgr=
                new CommentDataMgr(ConnectionString);
            CreateRegistration();
        }
```

```csharp
// Public Properties Start Here
public string ConnectionString
{
    get
    {
        return m_sConnectionString;
    }

    set
    {
        m_sConnectionString = value;
    }
}


// Generated events start here.

public event EventHandler Registered;
public event EventHandler Cancel;

private void AddLiteral(String sText)
{
    Controls.Add(new LiteralControl(sText));
}

protected void CreateRegistration()
{
    String sTemp;

    // Begin Comment Wrapping Div element
    sTemp="<div align=\"center\"";
    if(CssClass!="")
        sTemp+=" class=\""+CssClass+"\"";
    else
        sTemp+=" class=\"Comment\"";
    if(Width!=Unit.Empty)
        sTemp+=" width=\""+Width.ToString()+"\"";
    if(Height!=Unit.Empty)
        sTemp+=" height=\""+Height.ToString()+"\"";
    sTemp+=">\n";
    AddLiteral(sTemp);
    AddLiteral("<h1>User Registration:</h1>");
```

```
// Registration Message
AddLiteral("Please fill out the following "+
    "information.<br><br>");

// Create table
AddLiteral("<table class=\"RegistratonTable\" "+
    "align=\"center\" border=\"0\" width=\"500\">");

//Username Field
AddLiteral("<tr>");
AddLiteral("<td width=\"150\">Username</td>");
AddLiteral("<td width=\"150\">");
m_ctlEditUsername= new TextBox();
m_ctlEditUsername.ID="Username";
Controls.Add(m_ctlEditUsername);
AddLiteral("</td>");
AddLiteral("<td  width=\"200\">");

//Username Error Label
m_ctlLabelUsernameError=new Label();
m_ctlLabelUsernameError.Text=
    "Username already exists.";
m_ctlLabelUsernameError.CssClass="ErrorLabel";
m_ctlLabelUsernameError.Visible=false;
Controls.Add(m_ctlLabelUsernameError);
AddLiteral("</td>");
AddLiteral("</tr>");

//Password Field
// Table entries have been added via HTML rather
//   than via objects. This was done in this case
//   because of the table simplicity.
AddLiteral("<tr>");
AddLiteral("<td>Password</td>");
AddLiteral("<td>");
m_ctlEditPassword= new TextBox();
m_ctlEditPassword.ID="Password";
m_ctlEditPassword.TextMode=TextBoxMode.Password;
Controls.Add(m_ctlEditPassword);
AddLiteral("</td>");
AddLiteral("<td>");

//Password Error Label
m_ctlLabelPasswordError=new Label();
```

```
m_ctlLabelPasswordError.Text=
    "Passwords must match.";
m_ctlLabelPasswordError.CssClass="ErrorLabel";
m_ctlLabelPasswordError.Visible=false;
Controls.Add(m_ctlLabelPasswordError);
AddLiteral("</td>");
AddLiteral("</tr>");

//Password2 Field
AddLiteral("<tr>");
AddLiteral("<td>Re-enter Password</td>");
AddLiteral("<td>");
m_ctlEditPassword2= new TextBox();
m_ctlEditPassword2.ID="Password2";
m_ctlEditPassword2.TextMode=TextBoxMode.Password;
Controls.Add(m_ctlEditPassword2);
AddLiteral("</td>");
AddLiteral("<td></td>");
AddLiteral("</tr>");

//Email Field
AddLiteral("<tr>");
AddLiteral("<td>Email Address</td>");
AddLiteral("<td>");
m_ctlEditEmail= new TextBox();
m_ctlEditEmail.ID="Email";
Controls.Add(m_ctlEditEmail);
AddLiteral("</td>");
AddLiteral("<td>");

//Email Error Label
m_ctlLabelEmailError=new Label();
m_ctlLabelEmailError.Text=
    "Email address cannot be blank.";
m_ctlLabelEmailError.CssClass="ErrorLabel";
m_ctlLabelEmailError.Visible=false;
Controls.Add(m_ctlLabelEmailError);
AddLiteral("</td>");
AddLiteral("</tr>");

//DisplayName Field
AddLiteral("<tr>");
AddLiteral("<td>Display Name</td>");
AddLiteral("<td>");
```

```
m_ctlEditDisplayName= new TextBox();
m_ctlEditDisplayName.ID="DisplayName";
Controls.Add(m_ctlEditDisplayName);
AddLiteral("</td>");
AddLiteral("<td>");

//DisplayName Error Label
m_ctlLabelDisplayNameError=new Label();
m_ctlLabelDisplayNameError.Text=
    "Display Name cannot be blank.";
m_ctlLabelDisplayNameError.CssClass="ErrorLabel";
m_ctlLabelDisplayNameError.Visible=false;
Controls.Add(m_ctlLabelDisplayNameError);
AddLiteral("</td>");
AddLiteral("</tr>");

//Register / Cancel Buttons
AddLiteral("<tr>");
AddLiteral("<td colspan=\"3\" align=\"center\">");

// Register Button
Button objRegisterButton=new Button();
objRegisterButton.Text="Register";
objRegisterButton.CssClass="RegisterButton";
objRegisterButton.CausesValidation=false;
objRegisterButton.ID="Register";
objRegisterButton.Click+=
    new EventHandler(OnRegisterButton_Click);
Controls.Add(objRegisterButton);
AddLiteral("  ");

// Cancel Button
Button objCancelButton=new Button();
objCancelButton.Text="Cancel";
objCancelButton.CssClass="CancelButton";
objCancelButton.CausesValidation=false;
objCancelButton.ID="Cancel";
objCancelButton.Click+=
    new EventHandler(OnCancelButton_Click);
Controls.Add(objCancelButton);
AddLiteral("</td>");
AddLiteral("</tr>");
AddLiteral("</table><br><br>");
```

```
    // End Div element
    AddLiteral("</div>");
}


// Event Handlers
private void OnRegisterButton_Click
    (Object sender, EventArgs e)
{
    // Validate Data. This code is used
    //   instead of validation controls because
    //   the complexity of the data validation makes
    //   this a more straightforward approach.
    bool bIsValid=true;

    if(m_ctlEditUsername.Text=="")
    {
        bIsValid=false;
        m_ctlLabelUsernameError.Text=
            "Username cannot be blank.";
        m_ctlLabelUsernameError.Visible=true;
    }

    bool bValid=m_objCommentDataMgr.CheckLogin
        (m_ctlEditUsername.Text);
    if(!bValid)
    {
        m_ctlLabelUsernameError.Text=
            "Username already exists.";
        m_ctlLabelUsernameError.Visible=true;
        bIsValid=false;
    }

    if(m_ctlEditPassword.Text!=m_ctlEditPassword2.Text)
    {
        m_ctlLabelPasswordError.Visible=true;
        bIsValid=false;
    }

    if(m_ctlEditEmail.Text=="")
    {
        m_ctlLabelEmailError.Visible=true;
        bIsValid=false;
    }
```

```
        if(m_ctlEditDisplayName.Text=="")
        {
            m_ctlLabelDisplayNameError.Visible=true;
            bIsValid=false;
        }

        // Done Validating
        if(bIsValid)
        {

            try
            {
                m_objCommentDataMgr.AddUser(
                    m_ctlEditUsername.Text,
                    m_ctlEditPassword.Text,
                    m_ctlEditEmail.Text,
                    m_ctlEditDisplayName.Text,
                    CommentLoginType.Customer);

                //Fire the Registered event
                Registered(this,EventArgs.Empty);
            }
            catch(Exception err)
            {
            }
        }
    }

    private void OnCancelButton_Click
        (Object sender, EventArgs e)
    {
        // Fire the Cancel event.
        Cancel(this,EventArgs.Empty);
    }
    }
}
```

CommentDisplayCtl

The CommentDisplayCtl control is the control that is displayed by the main CommentCtl control after the user has logged in.

The public interface portion of this control is intended to be used only by the CommentCtl control. Table 15.13 shows the public interface of this control.

Table 15.13 Public Interface

Name	Type	Description
ConnectionString	Property	This property is a string that contains the OleDb connection string to the data source containing the comment data.
Username	Property	This property contains the username of the currently logged in user.
Revision	Property	This property contains the revision of the comments being displayed.

Table 15.14 Control Creation Methods

Name	Type	Description
CreateChildControls()	Method	This method starts the process of creating the control.
CreateStdComments()	Method	This method is the main method for generating the comments.
CreateDeveloperNote()	Method	This method displays the developer note. If the user has developer permissions, then the user will be able to edit this note.
CreateCommentSection()	Method	This method displays the comment section of the comment control.
CreateComments()	Method	This method is called to create the comments.
CreateComment()	Method	This method creates each individual comment as well as the Edit, Reply, and Delete buttons for each comment. The Reply and Delete buttons are displayed only for the users with developer permissions.
CreateReplyBox()	Method	This method is called to create an inline edit control to enter the reply.
CreateEditBox()	Method	This method is called to create an inline edit control to edit the comment. Comments can be edited only by the user who initially created it.
CreateCommentButtons()	Method	This method displays the Reply, Delete, and Edit buttons for each comment.
CreateEntryField	Method	This method displays the edit control for new comments.
AddLiteral()	Method	This method adds a LiteralControl to the Controls collection. The text to be added is passed in an argument.

Table 15.15 Event Handlers

Name	Type	Description
SubmitButton_Click()	Event Handler	This method handles the submission of comment text, either an update or a new comment.
EditButton_Click()	Event Handler	This method is called when the Edit button next to a comment is pressed.
EditNote_Click()	Event Handler	This method is called when the Edit button next to the note is pressed. Only a user with developer permissions will have this button.
DeleteButton_Click()	EventHandler	This method is called when the Delete button next to a comment is pressed. Only a user with developer permissions will have this button.
ReplyButton_Click()	EventHandler	This method is called when the Reply button next to a comment is pressed. Only a user with developer permissions will have this button.

Table 15.14 shows the control creation methods.

Table 15.15 shows the event handlers used in this control.

Listing 15.6 contains the source listing for the CommentDisplayCtl control.

Listing 15.6 Comment Display Control—CommentDisplayCtl.cs

```csharp
using System;
using System.Web.UI;
using System.Web.UI.WebControls;
using System.ComponentModel;
using System.Configuration;
using System.Collections.Specialized;
using System.Data;

namespace Comment
{
    public class CommentDisplayCtl : WebControl,INamingContainer
    {
```

```csharp
// Private member data.
private CommentDataMgr m_objCommentDataMgr;
private DataRow m_objLoginRow;
private string m_sUsername;
private string m_sConnectionString;
private int m_nRevision;
private TextBox m_objTextBox;

protected override void CreateChildControls()
{
    //Load Data Objects
    m_objCommentDataMgr=
        new CommentDataMgr(ConnectionString);
    m_objLoginRow=
        m_objCommentDataMgr.LoadLogin(Username);

    // Call the helper method to create the comments.
    CreateStdComments();
}

// Public Properties Start Here
// The Username property.
public string Username
{
    get
    {
        return m_sUsername;
    }

    set
    {
        m_sUsername = value;
    }
}

// This property holds the connection string for the database.
public string ConnectionString
{
    get
    {
        return m_sConnectionString;
    }
```

```csharp
        set
        {
            m_sConnectionString = value;
        }
    }


    // The revision number may be important at a later
    //    date and is supported.
    public int Revision
    {
        get
        {
            return m_nRevision;
        }

        set
        {
            m_nRevision = value;
        }
    }

    // The ID is stored in a session variable in order to
    //    use in other pages.
    private int EditCommentID
    {
        get
        {
            if(Page.Session["EditCommentID"]==null)
                Page.Session["EditCommentID"]=0;

            return (int) Page.Session["EditCommentID"];
        }
        set
        {
            Page.Session["EditCommentID"]=value;
        }
    }

    private int EditNoteID
    {
        get
        {
```

```csharp
            if(Page.Session["EditNoteID"]==null)
                Page.Session["EditNoteID"]=0;

            return (int) Page.Session["EditNoteID"];
        }
        set
        {
            Page.Session["EditNoteID"]=value;
        }
    }
}

private int ReplyCommentID
{
    get
    {
        if(Page.Session["ReplyCommentID"]==null)
            Page.Session["ReplyCommentID"]=0;

        return (int) Page.Session["ReplyCommentID"];
    }
    set
    {
        Page.Session["ReplyCommentID"]=value;
    }
}

// Private helper functions start here.
private void AddLiteral(String sText)
{
    Controls.Add(new LiteralControl(sText));
}

private String FormatForHTML(String sStr)
{
    String sTemp="";

    for(int i=0;i<sStr.Length;++i)
    {
        if(sStr[i]=='\n')
            sTemp+="<br>\n";
        else
            sTemp+=sStr[i];
    }
```

```
        return sTemp;
    }

    private void CreateReload()
    {
        AddLiteral("<script>");
        AddLiteral("window.navigate('"+
            Page.Request.RawUrl+"')");
        AddLiteral("</script>");
    }

    // Functions to create the child controls are here.
    protected void CreateStdComments()
    {
        String sTemp;

        // Begin Comment Wrapping Div element
        sTemp="<div";
        if(CssClass!="")
            sTemp+=" class=\""+CssClass+"\"";
        else
            sTemp+=" class=\"Comment\"";

        if(Width!=Unit.Empty)
            sTemp+=" width=\""+Width.ToString()+"\"";

        if(Height!=Unit.Empty)
            sTemp+=" height=\""+Height.ToString()+"\"";

        sTemp+=">\n";

        AddLiteral(sTemp);
        CreateDeveloperNote();
        CreateCommentSection();
        CreateEntryField();

        // End Div element
        AddLiteral("</div>");
    }

    private void CreateDeveloperNote()
    {
        DataRow objNoteRow=m_objCommentDataMgr.GetNote
            (Page.Request.FilePath,Revision);
```

```
if(EditNoteID==0)
{
    AddLiteral("<div>");
    AddLiteral("<h1>Developer Note:</h1>");
    AddLiteral("<blockquote>");
    AddLiteral(FormatForHTML
        (objNoteRow["NoteText"].ToString()));
    if((int)m_objLoginRow["LoginType"]==
        (int)CommentLoginType.Developer)
    {
        AddLiteral(" ");
        //Edit
        Button objEditButton=new Button();
        objEditButton.Text="Edit";
        objEditButton.CssClass="EditButton";
        objEditButton.CausesValidation=false;
        objEditButton.CommandName="Edit";
        objEditButton.ID="EditNote_"+
            objNoteRow["ID"].ToString();
        objEditButton.CommandArgument=
            objNoteRow["ID"].ToString();
        objEditButton.Command+=
            new CommandEventHandler(EditNote_Click);
        Controls.Add(objEditButton);
    }
    AddLiteral("</blockquote>");
    AddLiteral("</div>");
}
else
{
    AddLiteral("<div>");
    AddLiteral("<h1>Developer Note:</h1>");
    AddLiteral("<blockquote>");

    //Edit Note HTML
    // Text Box
    m_objTextBox= new TextBox();
    m_objTextBox.Height=Unit.Point(100);
    m_objTextBox.Width=Unit.Point(300);
    m_objTextBox.TextMode=TextBoxMode.MultiLine;
    m_objTextBox.ID="EditBox";
    m_objTextBox.Text=
        objNoteRow["NoteText"].ToString();
    Controls.Add(m_objTextBox);
```

```
        AddLiteral("<br>");

        // Submit Button
        Button objSubmitButton=new Button();
        objSubmitButton.Text="Update Note";
        objSubmitButton.CssClass="SubmitButton";
        objSubmitButton.CausesValidation=false;
        objSubmitButton.CommandName="Submit";
        objSubmitButton.ID="Submit";
        objSubmitButton.Click+=
            new EventHandler(SubmitButton_Click);
        Controls.Add(objSubmitButton);

        AddLiteral("</blockquote>");
        AddLiteral("</div>");
    }
}

private void CreateCommentSection()
{
    DataTable objCommentTable;
    objCommentTable=m_objCommentDataMgr.GetComments
        (Page.Request.FilePath,Revision);

    // Write Initial HTML
    AddLiteral("<div>");
    AddLiteral("<h1>Comments:</h1>");

    // Process Individual Comments
    CreateComments(objCommentTable);

    // Write Final HTML
    AddLiteral("</div>");

}

private void CreateComments(DataTable objCommentTable)
{
    int count=objCommentTable.Rows.Count;

    for(int i=0;i<count;++i)
    {
        CreateComment(objCommentTable.Rows[i]);
```

```
        }
    }

    private void CreateComment(DataRow objCommentRow)
    {
        // Write Begin of comment html
        String sTableClass="";
        String sSpacingClass="";
        String sAuthorClass="";
        String sTextClass="";
        String sEditClass="";
        String sButtonClass="";

        if((int)objCommentRow["ReplyToID"]==0)
        {
            sTableClass="CommentTable";
            sSpacingClass="CSpacingCell";
            sAuthorClass="CAuthorCell";
            sTextClass="CTextCell";
            sEditClass="CEditCell";
            sButtonClass="CButtonCell";
        }
        else
        {
            sSpacingClass="CSpacingCell";
            sTableClass="RCommentTable";
            sAuthorClass="RAuthorCell";
            sTextClass="RTextCell";
            sEditClass="CEditCell";
            sButtonClass="CButtonCell";
        }


        AddLiteral("<table border=\"0\" "+
            "class=\""+sTableClass+"\">");
        AddLiteral("<tr>");

        //Spacing cell
        AddLiteral("<td class=\""+sSpacingClass+
            "\" valign=\"top\"></td>\n");

        //Write Author's Name
        AddLiteral("<td class=\""+sAuthorClass+
```

```
            "\" valign=\"top\">\n");
    AddLiteral(objCommentRow["DisplayName"].ToString()+
        ": \n");
    AddLiteral("</td>\n");

    if(EditCommentID!=(int) objCommentRow["ID"])
    {
        AddLiteral("<td class=\""+sTextClass+"\" "+
            "valign=\"top\">\n");

        //Write Comment
        AddLiteral(FormatForHTML
            (objCommentRow["Comment"].ToString()));

        if(ReplyCommentID==(int)objCommentRow["ID"])
            CreateReplyBox(objCommentRow);

        AddLiteral("</td>");
    }
    else // show edit box
    {
        AddLiteral("<td class=\""+sEditClass+
            "\" valign=\"top\">\n");
        CreateEditBox(objCommentRow);
        AddLiteral("</td>");
    }

    //Add Edit/Delete/Reply buttons based on
    //user Level and ID
    AddLiteral("<td class=\""+sButtonClass+
        "\" valign=\"top\">\n");
    if(ReplyCommentID!=(int) objCommentRow["ID"])
        CreateCommentButtons(objCommentRow);
    AddLiteral("</td>");

    // Write Replies
    CreateComments(m_objCommentDataMgr.GetReplies
        ((int) objCommentRow["ID"]));

    //Write End of comment html
    AddLiteral("</tr></table>");
}
```

```
private void CreateReplyBox(DataRow objCommentRow)
{
    // Initial HTML
    AddLiteral("<div>");

    //Edit Comment HTML
    // Text Box
    m_objTextBox= new TextBox();
    m_objTextBox.Height=Unit.Point(100);
    m_objTextBox.Width=Unit.Point(300);
    m_objTextBox.TextMode=TextBoxMode.MultiLine;
    m_objTextBox.ID="EditBox";
    Controls.Add(m_objTextBox);

    AddLiteral("<br>");

    // Submit Button
    Button objSubmitButton=new Button();
    objSubmitButton.Text="Add Reply";
    objSubmitButton.CssClass="SubmitButton";
    objSubmitButton.CausesValidation=false;
    objSubmitButton.CommandName="Submit";
    objSubmitButton.ID="Submit";
    objSubmitButton.Click+=
        new EventHandler(SubmitButton_Click);
    Controls.Add(objSubmitButton);

    // Final HTML
    AddLiteral("</div>");
}

private void CreateEditBox(DataRow objCommentRow)
{
    //Edit Comment HTML
    // Text Box
    m_objTextBox= new TextBox();
    m_objTextBox.Height=Unit.Point(100);
    m_objTextBox.Width=Unit.Point(300);
    m_objTextBox.TextMode=TextBoxMode.MultiLine;
    m_objTextBox.ID="EditBox";
    m_objTextBox.Text=
        objCommentRow["Comment"].ToString();
```

```
    Controls.Add(m_objTextBox);
    AddLiteral("<br>");

    // Submit Button
    Button objSubmitButton=new Button();
    objSubmitButton.Text="Update Comment";
    objSubmitButton.CssClass="SubmitButton";
    objSubmitButton.CausesValidation=false;
    objSubmitButton.CommandName="Submit";
    objSubmitButton.ID="Submit";
    objSubmitButton.Click+=
        new EventHandler(SubmitButton_Click);
    Controls.Add(objSubmitButton);
}

private void CreateCommentButtons(DataRow objCommentRow)
{
    if(EditCommentID==(int)objCommentRow["ID"])
        return;

    AddLiteral(" ");
    if((int)objCommentRow["AuthorID"]==
        (int)m_objLoginRow["ID"])
    {
        // Can edit or delete own message.
        //Edit
        Button objEditButton=new Button();
        objEditButton.Text="Edit";
        objEditButton.CssClass="EditButton";
        objEditButton.CausesValidation=false;
        objEditButton.CommandName="Edit";
        objEditButton.ID="Edit_"+
            objCommentRow["ID"].ToString();
        objEditButton.CommandArgument=
            objCommentRow["ID"].ToString();
        objEditButton.Command+=
            new CommandEventHandler(EditButton_Click);
        Controls.Add(objEditButton);

        //Delete
        if(((CommentLoginType)
            (int)m_objLoginRow["LoginType"])==
            CommentLoginType.Developer)
```

```
        {
            Button objDeleteButton=new Button();
            objDeleteButton.Text="Delete";
            objDeleteButton.CssClass="DeleteButton";
            objDeleteButton.CausesValidation=false;
            objDeleteButton.CommandName="Delete";
            objDeleteButton.ID="Delete_"+
                objCommentRow["ID"].ToString();
            objDeleteButton.CommandArgument=
                objCommentRow["ID"].ToString();
            objDeleteButton.Command+=
                new CommandEventHandler(DeleteButton_Click);
            Controls.Add(objDeleteButton);
        }
    }
    else if(((CommentLoginType)
        (int)m_objLoginRow["LoginType"])==
        CommentLoginType.Developer)
    {
        // Can Reply to a message
        //Reply
        Button objReplyButton=new Button();
        objReplyButton.Text="Reply";
        objReplyButton.CssClass="ReplyButton";
        objReplyButton.CausesValidation=false;
        objReplyButton.CommandName="Reply";
        objReplyButton.ID="Reply_"+
            objCommentRow["ID"].ToString();
        objReplyButton.CommandArgument=
            objCommentRow["ID"].ToString();
        objReplyButton.Command+=
            new CommandEventHandler(ReplyButton_Click);
        Controls.Add(objReplyButton);
    }
}


protected void CreateEntryField()
{
    if(EditCommentID==0 && EditNoteID==0 &&
        ReplyCommentID==0)
    {
        // Initial HTML
```

```
                    AddLiteral("<div align=\"center\">");
                    AddLiteral("<h1>Add Comment:</h1>");
                    AddLiteral("<blockquote>");

                    //New Comment HTML
                    // Text Box
                    m_objTextBox= new TextBox();
                    m_objTextBox.Height=Unit.Point(150);
                    m_objTextBox.Width=Unit.Point(400);
                    m_objTextBox.TextMode=TextBoxMode.MultiLine;
                    m_objTextBox.ID="EditBox";
                    Controls.Add(m_objTextBox);

                    AddLiteral("<br>");

                    // Submit Button
                    Button objSubmitButton=new Button();
                    objSubmitButton.Text="Add Comment";
                    objSubmitButton.CssClass="SubmitButton";
                    objSubmitButton.CausesValidation=false;
                    objSubmitButton.CommandName="Submit";
                    objSubmitButton.ID="Submit";
                    objSubmitButton.Click+=
                        new EventHandler(SubmitButton_Click);
                    Controls.Add(objSubmitButton);

                    // Final HTML
                    AddLiteral("</blockquote>");
                    AddLiteral("</div>");
            }
        }

        // Event handlers
        private void SubmitButton_Click
            (Object sender, EventArgs e)
        {
            // New Comment
            if(EditCommentID==0 && EditNoteID==0)
            {
                if(m_objTextBox.Text!="")
                {
                    m_objCommentDataMgr.AddComment(
                        (int)m_objLoginRow["ID"],
```

```
                    DateTime.Now,
                    ReplyCommentID,
                    Revision,
                    Page.Request.FilePath,
                    m_objTextBox.Text);

                ReplyCommentID=0;
            }
        }
        else if(EditCommentID!=0)
        {
            if(m_objTextBox.Text!="")
            {
                m_objCommentDataMgr.UpdateComment(
                    EditCommentID,
                    m_objTextBox.Text);
            }

            EditCommentID=0;
        }
        else if(EditNoteID!=0)
        {
            m_objCommentDataMgr.UpdateNote
                (EditNoteID,m_objTextBox.Text);

            EditNoteID=0;
        }
        Page.Session["RELOAD"]=true;
        m_objTextBox.Text="";
        Controls.Clear();
        CreateReload();
}

private void EditButton_Click
    (Object sender, CommandEventArgs e)
{
    Button objButton=(Button)sender;
    int nID=Convert.ToInt32
        (objButton.CommandArgument,10);

    EditCommentID=nID;
    EditNoteID=0;
    ReplyCommentID=0;
```

```
        Controls.Clear();
        CreateReload();
}

private void EditNote_Click
    (Object sender, CommandEventArgs e)
{
    Button objButton=(Button)sender;
    int nID=Convert.ToInt32
        (objButton.CommandArgument,10);

    EditCommentID=0;
    EditNoteID=nID;
    ReplyCommentID=0;

    Controls.Clear();
    CreateReload();
}

private void DeleteButton_Click
    (Object sender, CommandEventArgs e)
{
    // Get the comment ID associated with
    // the button that was pushed.
    Button objButton=(Button)sender;
    int nID=Convert.ToInt32
        (objButton.CommandArgument,10);

    // Delete the comment
    m_objCommentDataMgr.DeleteComment(nID);
    Controls.Clear();
    CreateReload();
}

private void ReplyButton_Click
    (Object sender, CommandEventArgs e)
{
    Button objButton=(Button)sender;
    int nID=Convert.ToInt32
        (objButton.CommandArgument,10);

    EditCommentID=0;
    EditNoteID=0;
    ReplyCommentID=nID;
```

```
        Controls.Clear();
        CreateReload();
    }
  }
}
```

HttpModules

At this point, we have a working comment tracking control, but its usefulness is limited in any real-world development. Adding the control to all the ASP.NET pages in a large application can take a lot of time. You would also need to remove the pages before making your application go live, which could potentially add errors to previously tested code. What we need is a way to add the control to every page automatically. This is where HttpModules come in.

An `HttpModule` is a class that, for every page, allows you to handle events that are fired at various stages of the creation of the page. The .NET framework uses HttpModules for authenticating users and managing the session state. The rest of this chapter will show you how to write an HttpModule to manipulate the output of any arbitrary aspx file.

IHttpModule Interface

To write an HttpModule, you need to write a class that implements the IHttpModule interface. The IHttpModule interface is quite simple with only two methods: `Dispose()` and `Init()`. For most modules, only the `Init()` method is of interest, but if you allocate any unmanaged resources that are of module scope, you should free them in the `Dispose()` method.

The `Init()` method is where you normally attach an event handler to any events that you wish to handle.

You should be careful about allocating resources in the `Init()` method because anything allocated and assigned to a class variable will have application scope. This is because HttpModules are created when the application is initialized and destroyed after the application has completed.

Events

There are a number of events that you can handle with an HttpModule. Table 15.16 describes the different events.

Table 15.16 Events Handled by HttpModules

Event	Description
AcquireRequestState	Called before the intrinsic Request object is set up.
AuthenticateRequest	Called to allow authentication of a request.
AuthorizeRequest	Called to allow authorization of a request.
BeginRequest	Called at the beginning of the request before any other processing has been done.
Disposed	Called during the Application object's disposal process, when the application is shutting down.
EndRequest	Called after all processing of the request has been done.
Error	Called if there was an unhandled error during the processing of the request.
PostRequestHandlerExecute	Called after the request handler has finished executing. The request handler is usually a class derived from the System.Web.UI.Page class.
PreRequestHandlerExecute	Called after all pre-request processing (including setting up the intrinsic Request object) has been completed, but before the request handler is called.
PreSendRequestContent	Called before the body of the response is sent.
PreSendRequestHeaders	Called before the response headers are sent.
ReleaseRequestState	Called after the intrinsic Request object's data is released.
ResolveRequestCache	Called after the request cache is resolved.
UpdateRequestCache	Called after the request cache is updated.

If you need to terminate the processing of a page after handling an event, you should call the CompleteRequest() method of the HttpApplication class. If the CompleteRequest() method is not called, then normal processing will continue after your event completes.

Basic HttpModule

Lets now take a look at a simple HttpModule. A complete module will do two things. First, it will implement the IHttpModule interface. Second, it will handle one or more of the events listed in Table 15.16. If it did not handle any of the events, it would never be able to do anything useful. Listing 15.7 shows a basic HttpModule.

Listing 15.7 C# Code for a Minimum Implementation HttpModule

```csharp
public class MyHttpModule : IHttpModule
{
    // Constructor
    public MyHttpModule()
    {
    }

    // Implement IHttpModule Methods
    public void Init(HttpApplication context)
    {
        context.Error += new EventHandler(OnError);
    }
    public void Dispose()
    {
    }

    // Implement the event handler.
    public void OnBeginError(Object sender, EventArgs e)
    {
        HttpApplication app=sender as HttpApplication;
        // Do something here
    }
}
```

Configuration

After an HttpModule has been written, it needs to be registered so that it can be loaded when the Web application starts. To do so, add an entry inside the <HttpModules> section of either the web.config file or the machine.config file. Adding the entry to the web.config file causes the module to load when a specific Web application starts. Adding the entry to the machine.config file causes the module to load when any Web application starts.

The format of entries in the <HttpModules> section is as follows:

```xml
<configuration>
    <system.web>
        <httpModules />
    </system.web>
</configuration>
```

An <add> entry adds a new HttpModule; a <remove> entry will remove an inherited HttpModule (possibly from a higher level web.config or from machine.config); and a <clear> entry will remove all HttpModules. You will need an <add> entry before your module can be used. If you added a module in the machine.config file, you can remove it in the web.config file of a specific Web application using a <remove> entry in the Web application's web.config file. This allows you to load an HttpModule for every Web application except ones that have a <remove> entry in the web.config file.

Adding Comment Tracking Automatically

Now that you've seen the basics of HttpModules, the question arises, How do you change the data in an aspx page? When I first thought about this I looked for an output stream that I could parse and change, but I could not find one anywhere. I approached this problem later, after writing a few custom controls, and it was almost too obvious. You don't have access to an output stream. Instead, you have access to the Controls collection of the page. So to add our comment tracking control to the page, it is enough to search through the Controls collection until you find a good place to add the control.

Listing 15.8 shows the complete HttpModule to automatically add the comment control to the page.

Listing 15.8 Auto-Comment Module—AutoCommentModule.cs

```
using System;
using System.Configuration;
using System.Collections.Specialized;
using System.Web;
using System.Web.UI;

namespace Comment
{
    public class AutoCommentModule : IHttpModule
    {
        public AutoCommentModule()
        {
        }
```

```csharp
// IHttpModule Interface
public void Init(HttpApplication objApplication)
{
    objApplication.PreRequestHandlerExecute+=
        new EventHandler(OnPreRequestHandlerExecute);
}

public void Dispose()
{
}

public void OnPreRequestHandlerExecute(Object objSender,
    EventArgs objArgs)
{
    HttpApplication objApplication=
        (HttpApplication) objSender;
    Page objPage=(Page) objApplication.Context.Handler;

    objPage.Init+=new EventHandler(OnPageInit);
}

public void OnPageInit(Object objSender,EventArgs objArgs)
{
    Page objPage=(Page) objSender;

    // Create our Comment Control
    CommentCtl objCommentCtl=new CommentCtl();
    LoadConfigSettings(objCommentCtl);
    objCommentCtl.ID="AutoComment";

    if(objPage.Session["Reload"]!=null)
    {
        if((bool)objPage.Session["Reload"]==true)
        {
            objPage.Controls.Clear();
            objPage.Controls.Add(objCommentCtl);
            return;
        }
    }

    // Locate the position to add it
    System.Web.UI.ControlCollection objControls=
        objPage.Controls;
```

```
        // Assume that the Form is a top level
        // control in the page.
        for(int i=0;i<objControls.Count;++i)
        {
            if(objControls[i].GetType()==
                typeof(System.Web.UI.HtmlControls.HtmlForm))
            {
                // Add the control
                objControls[i].Controls.
                    AddAt(0,objCommentCtl);
                return;
            }
        }
    }

    private void LoadConfigSettings(CommentCtl objComment)
    {
        NameValueCollection objConfigData =
            ConfigurationSettings.GetConfig("CommentCtl")
            as NameValueCollection;

        for(int i=0;i<objConfigData.Count;++i)
        {
            String sKey=objConfigData.GetKey(i);

            if(sKey == "ConnectionString")
                objComment.ConnectionString=objConfigData[i];
            else if(sKey == "Revision")
                objComment.Revision=
                    Convert.ToInt32(objConfigData[i]);
            else if(sKey == "CssFile")
                objComment.CssFile=objConfigData[i];
        }
    }
  }
}
```

One thing to remember about the comment control is that it does post backs to the server. This is important because it means that the comment control needs to be added inside the Form control that most aspx pages contain.

At first I thought that I wanted it to be added at the end of the last Form control on the page, but after trying that, I found that the page would appear to render, and then after a slight pause the comment control would appear. This was quite annoying, so I moved the comment control to the beginning of the first Form control on the page.

Application Settings

Because this module was intended to be used in a variety of settings, configuration data was placed in a custom section of the web.config file. The following entries need to be made inside the <configuration> section:

```
<configSections>
  <section name="CommentCtl"
    type="System.Configuration.NameValueSectionHandler,
    system, Version=1.0.3300.0, Culture=neutral,
    PublicKeyToken=b77a5c561934e089, Custom=null" />
</configSections>
<CommentCtl>
  <add
    key="ConnectionString"
    value='Provider=Microsoft.Jet.OLEDB.4.0;Password="";
      User ID=Admin;
      Data Source=C:\FullPath\comments.mdb' />
  <add key="Revision" value="1" />
  <add key="CssFile" value="/relativepath/CommentStyle.css" />
</CommentCtl>
```

Additionally, to activate the HttpModule, the following entries need to be made inside the <system.web> section of the web.config file:

```
<httpModules>
  <add name="AutoComment"
  type="Datasphere.Development.WebUI.AutoCommentModule,
    CommentCtl" />
</httpModules>
```

Deploying the Application

This application is fairly easy to deploy. Because all the controls and the HttpModule are in the same library, there is only the one .dll file to deploy. Additionally though, a .css file tcontaining the necessary styles to render the control properly will need to be placed somewhere on the Web server. Here is a complete set of steps to deploy the application:

1. Copy the library's .dll file to the bin folder of the application you wish to add comment tracking.
2. Place the .css file in an accessible location on the web server.
3. Make changes to the web.config file as described in the Application Settings section of this chapter.

The comment control should now appear on every page in your application.

Summary

This chapter has shown you two things. You now know how to write custom controls, and you know how to add content to all .aspx pages in a given application. Additionally, you now have a complete comment tracking application that you can use to solicit feedback while developing custom applications.

We've worked through the concepts of HttpModules, and then we created the application. You should now be able to use this powerful technique in your applications.

CHAPTER 16

Converting Data to Charts: Displaying Data

In This Chapter:

- The DataToGraph Application
- Using the `Graph2D` Class
- The DataToGraph Code
- Deploying the Application
- Extending the Application

Showing data inside a bar graph is a great way to let users easily understand overall trends. Even technical people don't want to look through log files to analyze data. Everyone wants to take one look at a bar chart to get an overall the idea of what a dataset represents.

We spent a good deal of time displaying data in bar charts in Chapter 10. A class named `Graph2D` was used in Chapter 10 to take data and render at as a bar chart. A description of how to use the `Graph2D` class is given in Chapter 10. But this chapter goes a lot further than Chapter 10 and shows how to manipulate data before it is rendered as a bar graph.

You are probably wondering why data needs to be manipulated before it is rendered. There are a number of reasons why this might be so. The data values might have a small variation and their values are far from zero. In this case, you might want to adjust the data by subtracting a value from each of the data values so that the variation in the data is more pronounced and therefore makes trends easier to identify.

You might also want to take advantage of the capability to present data in such a way that it appears to support practically any conclusion. Exaggerating fluctuations, normalizing fluctuations, and performing any number of mathematical operations on the data can be done to alter its appearance. You know the saying: There are lies, damned lives, and statistics.

This chapter uses the `Graph2D` class from Chapter 10, but here we perform mathematical operations on the dataset before they are graphed. This will give you a good idea of what is possible if you plan to use the `Graph2D` class from Chapter 10.

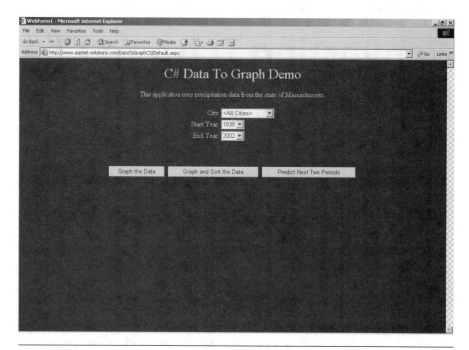

Figure 16.1 You Can Select the City, the Start Year, and the End Year.

Table 16.1 The Methods for the DataToGraphCS Application

Method	Listing	Source Code File	Description
Page_Load()	16.5	Default.aspx.cs	This method initializes the user interface objects, such as the list of cities.
Graph_Click()	16.6	Default.aspx.cs	This method creates a graph based on the unaltered data.
GraphAndClick_Click()	16.7	Default.aspx.cs	This method creates a graph based on the sorted data.
Predict_Click()	16.8	Default.aspx.cs	This method creates a graph that includes two additional predicted values.

The DataToGraph Application

I have created an application that demonstrates using the Graph2D class to represent a rainfall database in various ways. There are three combo boxes in which you can select the query parameters. One drop-down menu contains the cities from which you can select. (The cities are all in the state of Massachusetts.) Another drop-down menu allows you to select the start date of the query. And the third drop-down menu allows you to select the end date of the query. You can see the application in Figure 16.1 as it first appears.

Table 16.1 shows the methods that instantiate and use the Graph2D class. They are all part of the DataToGraph application. This table will provide a handy reference as you use and study the code.

Using the Graph2D Class

The class that I created to encapsulate the graphing class is called Graph2D. There are three required steps to use the class: instantiate the class, add data, and render the graph. The following code snippet shows the bare necessities for creating a graph image that saves to disk. More detail for these methods will be given shortly.

C#
```
Graph2D graph = new Graph2D();
String strFilename;
graph.AddPair( "Rick", 50 );
graph.AddPair( "Sam", 60 );
strFilename = graph.Render( Request.MapPath( "" ) );
```

VB
```
Dim graph as new Graph2D()
Dim strFilename as String
graph.AddPair("Rick", 50)
graph.AddPair("Sam", 60)
strFilename = graph.Render(Request.MapPath(""))
```

The presentation code must use the file name that's returned from the Render() method. The file name can either be assigned to an ASP.NET server object such as Image or ImageButton objects, or output to the HTML stream with a call to the `Response.Write()` method.

Chapter 10 has a complete reference to the `Graph2D` class, including the properties that are available with which you can change its appearance.

The DataToGraph Code

The added code for the DataToGraph application is contained in four methods. They are all shown in Listings 16.1 through 16.4.

The `Page_Load()` Method

The first is the `Page_Load()` method, and this is called each time the page is loaded. Listing 16.1 shows this code. Our code that's contained in the `Page_Load()` method is executed only if the `IsPostBack` property is not `true`. This will be the case the first time the page is requested, but not in response to a post back. This reduces the load on the server because the code needs to be executed only once.

The first thing that happens in the `Page_Load()` method is the creation of a SqlConnection object. The connection string is stored in the Web.config file. This static method can pull configuration information from the Web.Config file, and in this case the connect string is in an element named `ConnectString`.

In Listing 16.1, a SqlReader object is declared and initialized as `null`. This is done so that it will be obvious if an `ExecuteReader()` method has been called. If this method has been called, this object will not be `null`—otherwise it will be `null`.

A `try/catch/finally` construct is used to handle errors. If everything goes well, all of the code inside the `try` block will execute, followed by the execution of everything in the `finally` block. If, for some reason, an exception is thrown by the data access objects, then the `catch` block will be executed. In the `catch` block, the only thing that's done is to display the exception message in a user interface Label object named ErrorMessage.

RECOMMENDED PRACTICE: A `try/catch` construct is understood to be the mechanism to catch and handle exceptions. But I'd like to point out that adding a `finally` clause to the construct is a good idea much of the time. Anytime that some cleanup must occur, whether or not an exception is thrown, a `finally` clause can act as the mechanism to ensure that the cleanup is performed.

Inside of the `try` block, the SqlConnection object's `Open()` method is called. A SqlCommand object is then created with the SQL statement that will retrieve all of the cities in the database. Note that we're qualifying the cities with the `DISTINCT` keyword so that we just get a list of available cities. Each record in the database contains the city name, and if we didn't use the `DISTINCT` keyword, we'd get thousands of cities, most of which would be duplicates.

The name of the user interface object that contains the city names is CityList, and it is a DropDownList object. To populate this list, we call the `ExecuteReader()` method, which returns a SqlDataReader object containing the names of the cities. The SqlDataSet object can be bound to the DropDownList object with the following two lines of code:

C#
```
CityList.DataSource = objReader;
CityList.DataBind();
```

VB
```
CityList.DataSource = objReader
CityList.DataBind()
```

Although this code will bind data from the SqlDataReader to the Drop-DownList object, it won't bind the right data, as shown in Figure 16.2.

You need to specify which field will be bound as the display data, as follows, so that the correct data will appear, as shown in Figure 16.3:

C#
```
CityList.DataValueField = "City";
CityList.DataSource = objReader;
CityList.DataBind();
```

VB
```
CityList.DataValueField = "City"
CityList.DataSource = objReader
CityList.DataBind()
```

We need a way for the user to specify that the query is performed for all cities. To do this, an item is inserted at the top of the list containing the string `"<All Cities>"`. This becomes the default choice because the first item in the list (at the index of zero) is the default choice.

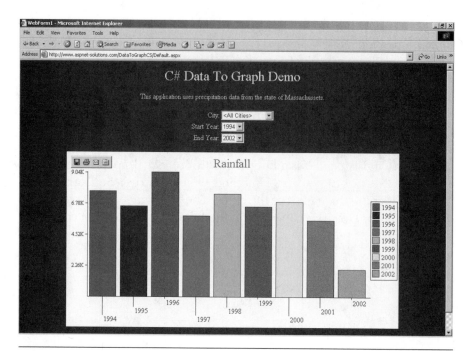

Figure 16.2 Without Binding a Field, the DropDownList Object Will Contain the Record Type.

Before any other SQL commands are executed with this database connection, the SqlDataReader object must be closed. That's because a SqlConnection object can have at most one open data reader. As a matter of fact, with a data reader open, you won't even be able to call an `ExecuteNonQuery()` method without it throwing an exception. If you needed more open data readers, you'd need more open connections.

The next thing that needs to be retrieved from the database is the list of years for which precipitation data exists. A `DISTINCT` keyword is added to the SQL so that the list contains only the unique years that are found. A SqlDataReader object is retrieved using the `ExecuteReader()` method. The StartYearList DropDownList object is set so that the `YR` (year) field populates the list. The `DataSource` property is set, followed by a call to the `DataBind()` method. Now the DropDownList is fully populated.

A SqlDataReader contains a forward-only recordset. Once you have bound it to an object, it will not contain any data and cannot be used again. It would be easy enough to do another database query to get the data for the second DropDownList object, but this would place an unnecessary bur-

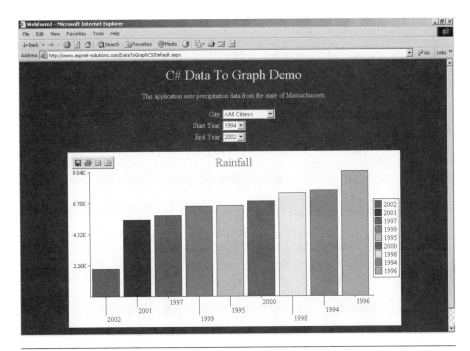

Figure 16.3 The DropDownList Contains the Correct Data.

den on the database. The most efficient way to populate the second Drop-DownList object is to loop through and populate it from the first Drop-DownList, as follows:

```
for( int i=0; i<StartYearList.Items.Count; i++ )
{
  EndYearList.Items.Add( StartYearList.Items[i].Text );
}
```

The finally clause cleans up the database objects. If the SqlDataReader object is not null, then it is closed. If the SqlConnection object is open, then it is closed.

Listing 16.1 The Page_Load() Method

```
private void Page_Load(object sender, System.EventArgs e)
{
  if( !IsPostBack )
```

```
{
SqlConnection objConnection =
new SqlConnection(ConfigurationSettings.AppSettings["ConnectString"]);
  SqlDataReader objReader = null;
  try
  {
   objConnection.Open();
   SqlCommand objCommand =
    new SqlCommand("SELECT DISTINCT City from PrecData order by City",
     objConnection );

    objReader = objCommand.ExecuteReader();
    CityList.DataValueField = "City";
    CityList.DataSource = objReader;
    CityList.DataBind();
    CityList.Items.Insert( 0, new ListItem( "<All Cities>", "" ) );
    objReader.Close();

    objCommand =
      new SqlCommand( "SELECT DISTINCT YR from PrecData order by YR",
       objConnection );
    objReader = objCommand.ExecuteReader();
    StartYearList.DataValueField = "YR";
    StartYearList.DataSource = objReader;
    StartYearList.DataBind();

    for( int i=0; i<StartYearList.Items.Count; i++ )
    {
      EndYearList.Items.Add( StartYearList.Items[i].Text );
    }
    EndYearList.SelectedIndex = EndYearList.Items.Count - 1;
  }
  catch( Exception ex )
  {
    ErrorMessage.Text = ex.Message.ToString();
  }
  finally
  {
    if( objReader != null )
    {
      objReader.Close();
    }
    if( objConnection.State == ConnectionState.Open )
```

```
        {
            objConnection.Close();
        }
    }
  }
}
```

The `Graph_Click()` Method

The `Graph_Click()` method is fired when the user clicks the Graph button. It takes the data from the database, populates an instantiated `Graph2D` class, and then calls the `Graph2D Render()` method. You can see the results in Figure 16.4.

The method starts off by creating a `SqlConnection` string with the connection string retrieved from the Web.Config file. A `try/catch/finally` construct manages exceptions that are thrown by the database objects. If nothing goes wrong, the code in the `try` block is executed. If an

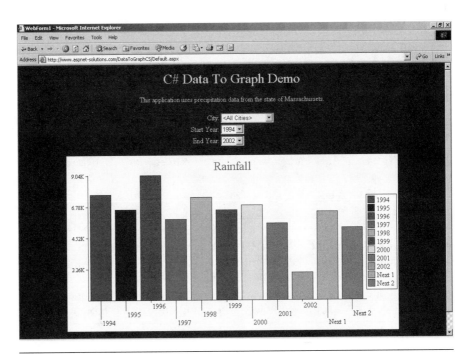

Figure 16.4 The First Button Simply Graphs the Data According to the Selected City and the Data Range.

exception is thrown by one of the database objects, the catch block will simply display the exception message in the user interface Label object named ErrorMessage. Whether or not an exception was thrown, though, the finally block closes the SqlConnection object if it is open.

Inside the try block, the connection is opened. The SQL for this query finds the sum of all of the months for the span of years specified in the Start-YearList and EndYearList objects. The total of all of the sums is in an expression named Value. If a city was selected, then an additional WHERE clause is added so that the city is a constraint for the query. Last, the query specifies that the recordset is grouped by YR (year) and ordered by the YR field.

Because a SqlDataReader is a forward-only dataset, it will not suffice for the calculations that we're going to do. What we need is a DataSet that will contain the entire recordset, with which we can look at any record that we want. In other words, we can look at record 15, record 7, record 31, and then go back to record 15. To do this, we use a SqlDataAdapter object to perform the query and fill a DataSet object. The following code shows how to perform a simple query that fills a DataSet using a SqlDataAdapter object:

C#
```
SqlDataAdapter objDataAdapter =
  new SqlDataAdapter( "SELECT * from MyTable", objConnection );
DataSet objDataSet = new DataSet();
objDataAdapter.Fill( objDataSet, "MyTable" );
objConnection.Close();
```

VB
```
Dim objDataAdapter as _
  new SqlDataAdapter( "SELECT * from MyTable", objConnection )
Dim objDataSet as new DataSet()
objDataAdapter.Fill( objDataSet, "MyTable" )
objConnection.Close()
```

RECOMMEDNED PRACTICE: It's better, whenever possible, to use a disconnected dataset so that the database isn't tied up with too many active connections. This can be done by simply closing the database connection once the dataset is filled. Everything is OK because the data is now in memory, and the code won't be going back to the tables.

Once the DataSet is filled, the number of rows is retrieved and stored in an integer variable named nCount. Immediately after this, a Graph2D class named graph is instantiated.

The one drawback to showing data in a bar graph is that the bars get pretty small if there are more than, say, 20 data values. If there are 20 data values or less, it's a simple matter of storing the data in the Graph2D object. If there are more than 20, though, some manipulation is necessary so that only 20 bars will be shown in the graph. The program deals with that situation this way: When there are more than 20 data values, it averages 2, 3, 4, or more data values into a single value. To find how many values are averaged into a single value, we simply take the number of data values and divide by 20. The following algorithm shows how it's done:

- Calculate the number of years (data values in the recordset) that will be averaged for each bar in the graph by dividing the number of data values by 20 (held in the variable nYearsPerBar).
- Find the number of graph bars by dividing the number of years (data values in the recordset) by the number of years per bar (held in the variable nNumBars).
- If the number of years isn't evenly divisible by the number of years per bar, then we need one more bar for the remainder (we increment nNumBars).

All we have to do now is create a loop that calculates the value for each bar of the graph. Then, we average the next 2, 3, 4, or however many data values. With the averaged value, we now store the data in the Graph2D object.

Once all the data has been added, the Render() method is called. This renders the graph to a disk file. The rendering code is shown here, along with code to set the title to Rainfall:

C#
```
graph.Title = "Rainfall";
GraphImage.Text = "<IMG SRC=\"GraphImages/Graph" +
  graph.Render( Request.MapPath( "." ) ) +
  ".gif\">";
```

VB
```
graph.Title = "Rainfall"
GraphImage.Text = "<IMG SRC=" + Chr( 34 ) + "GraphImages/Graph" +
  graph.Render( Request.MapPath( "." ) ) +
  ".gif" + Chr( 34 ) + ">";
```

Listing 16.2 The `Graph_Click()` Method Performs a Simple Graphing Operation.

```
private void Graph_Click(object sender, System.EventArgs e)
{
 // Create a connection object.
 SqlConnection objConnection =
  new SqlConnection(ConfigurationSettings.AppSettings["ConnectString"]);
  try
  {
    // Open the connection.
    objConnection.Open();

    // Create the SQL string.
    string strSql = "SELECT YR,(SELECT " +
      "Value=(Sum(Jan)+Sum(Feb)+Sum(Mar)+Sum(Apr)+Sum(May)+" +
      "Sum(Jun)+Sum(Jul)+Sum(Aug)+Sum(Sep)+Sum(Oct)+" +
      "Sum(Nov)+Sum(Dece))) from PrecData WHERE YR>=" +
      Convert.ToString( StartYearList.SelectedItem.Text ) +
      " and YR<=" + Convert.ToString( EndYearList.SelectedItem.Text );

    // If the selection is valid, add it to the SQL.
    if( CityList.SelectedIndex > 0 )
    {
      strSql += ( " and City='" + CityList.SelectedItem.Text + "'" );
    }
    // Add the grouping and ordering.
    strSql += " group by YR order by YR";

    // Create the SqlDataAdapter and DataSet, then
    //    populate the dataset with the Fill() method.
    SqlDataAdapter objDataAdapter =
      new SqlDataAdapter( strSql, objConnection );
    DataSet objDataSet = new DataSet();
    objDataAdapter.Fill( objDataSet, "PrecData" );
    objConnection.Close();

    // Find out how many rows are in the dataset.
    int nCount = objDataSet.Tables[0].Rows.Count;
    Graph2D graph = new Graph2D();

    // Here we don't have to adjust for too many entries.
    if( nCount <= 20 )
    {
```

```
  for( int i=0; i<nCount; i++ )
  {
    graph.AddPair(
      Convert.ToString( objDataSet.Tables[0].Rows[i].ItemArray[0] ),
      Convert.ToDouble(objDataSet.Tables[0].Rows[i].ItemArray[1] ));
  }
}
// Here we'll have to do some averaging because there are a lot
//   of entries.
else
{
  // Calculate the years per bar, number of bars,
  //   and the count.
  int nYearsPerBar = nCount / 20;
  int nNumBars = nCount / nYearsPerBar;
  if( nCount % nYearsPerBar != 0 )
  {
    nNumBars++;
  }

  // Loop through for each bar.
  for( int i=0; i<nNumBars; i++ )
  {

    // For this iteration initialize the total, start, and end.
    double dTotal = 0;
    string strStart = "";
    string strEnd = "";

    // Loop through the years in this bar.
    for( int j=0; j<nYearsPerBar; j++ )
    {

      // First year of the bar.
      if( j == 0 )
      {
        strStart =
          Convert.ToString(
          objDataSet.Tables[0].Rows[i*nYearsPerBar+j].ItemArray[0]);
      }

      // Make sure we're in range.
      if( i * nYearsPerBar + j < nCount )
```

```
        {
          // Create the end.
          strEnd =
            Convert.ToString(
              objDataSet.Tables[0].Rows[i*nYearsPerBar+j].ItemArray[0]);
          // Update the total.
          dTotal +=
            Convert.ToDouble(
              objDataSet.Tables[0].Rows[i*nYearsPerBar].ItemArray[1] );
        }
      }
      // Add the data.
      graph.AddPair( strStart + "-" + strEnd, dTotal );
    }
  }

  // Set the graph title and the text for the image link.
  graph.Title = "Rainfall";
  GraphImage.Text = "<IMG SRC=\"GraphImages/Graph" +
    graph.Render( Request.MapPath( "." ) ) +
    ".gif\">";
}
catch( Exception ex )
{
  // Alert the user to the error.
  ErrorMessage.Text = ex.Message.ToString();
}
finally
{
  if( objConnection.State == ConnectionState.Open )
  {
    objConnection.Close();
  }
}
}
```

The `GraphAndSort_Click()` Method

The `GraphAndSort_Click()` method is fired when the user clicks the Graph And Sort button. It retrieves data based on the DropDownList selections, sorts the data, and then adds the data to an instantiated Graph2D object. Figure 16.5 shows a graph with sorted data.

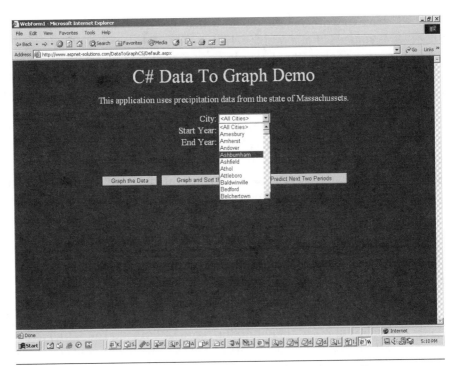

Figure 16.5 You Can Sort the Data with the Graph And Sort Button.

The code in Listing 16.3 that shows the `GraphAndSort_Click()` method starts off similarly to the code in Listing 16.2. The following list outlines the code that is similar to the code in the `Graph_Click()` method in Listing 16.2.

1. A SqlConnection object is created.
2. A string named `strSql` is created with the SQL statement for the database query.
3. A SqlDataAdapter object is created with the string and the SqlConnection, and it is used to populate a DataSet object.
4. The count of rows is retrieved.
5. A Graph2D object is instantiated.

From this point, things change. Instead of populating the Graph2D object, the data is stored in an instantiated ArrayList object. This object has a `Sort()` method, and it will give us a quick and easy way to sort the data.

ArrayList objects are able to sort native data types such a strings, but if we wanted it to support anything special, such as our own structure, we'd have to write a method with which the ArrayList object sorts the data. This is somewhat of a problem because our data consists of a string (the year(s)) and a double (the data value). At first glance, a structure is our best bet to contain the data, but that means we need to write a sorting code.

To avoid having to write our own sorting code, we can convert the data into a string by concatenating the string and the double—but we just have to convert the double to a string. We'll also have to put some sort of separator between the two pieces of data so that we can easily pull them apart later. Because none of the years will use the | character, that'll be the separator character. The formatting for the dValue variable below enables the value to have a consistent formatting regarding the decimal places. Here's how we'll create the single string from both pieces of data:

```
objGraphData.Add( Convert.ToString(
  objDataSet.Tables[0].Rows[i].ItemArray[1] ) + "|" +
  dValue.ToString( "{000000.00000000}" ) );
```

As with the code in Listing 16.2, if there are 20 or fewer data values, we'll simply put them into the ArrayList object. But if there are more than 20 data values, we'll have to average several together to arrive at a bar graph with 20 or fewer bars. The following code calculates the number of years per bar (nYearsPerBar) and the number of bars (nBars) from the count (nCount).

C#
```
int nYearsPerBar = nCount / 20;
int nNumBars = nCount / nYearsPerBar;
if( nCount % nYearsPerBar != 0 )
{
  nNumBars++;
}
```

VB
```
Dim nYearsPerBar as Integer = nCount / 20
Dim nNumBars as Integer = nCount / nYearsPerBar
If nCount MOD nYearsPerBar <> 0 Then
  nNumBars = nNumBars + 1
End If
```

Now, to sort the data, all that we do is call the Sort() method on the ArrayList object (named objGraphData). It's then a simple matter of adding the data to the Graph2D object (named graph), calling the Render() method, and saving the file. Remember, though, that the string has to be split into a string and a double. The following code shows how this is done:

C#
```
for( int i=0; i<objGraphData.Count; i++ )
{
   string[] strData = ((string)objGraphData[i]).Split(
     new char[]{'|'},2);
   graph.AddPair( strData[1], Convert.ToDouble( strData[0] ) );
}
graph.Title = "Rainfall";
GraphImage.Text = "<IMG SRC=\"GraphImages/Graph" +
   graph.Render( Request.MapPath( "." ) ) +
   ".gif\">";
```

VB
```
Dim i as Integer
For i=0 to objGraphData.Count - 1
   String() strData = ((string)objGraphData(i)).Split( _
     New char(){'|'},2)
   graph.AddPair( strData(1), Convert.ToDouble( strData(0) ) );
Next
graph.Title = "Rainfall"
GraphImage.Text = "<IMG SRC=\"GraphImages/Graph" + _
   graph.Render( Request.MapPath( "." ) ) + _
   ".gif\">"
```

Listing 16.3 The `GraphAndSort_Click()` Method Sorts the Data Before Graphing.

```
private void GraphAndSort_Click(object sender, System.EventArgs e)
{
 SqlConnection objConnection =
  new SqlConnection(ConfigurationSettings.AppSettings["ConnectString"]);
  try
  {
    objConnection.Open();
    string strSql = "SELECT YR,(SELECT " +
      "Value=(Sum(JAN)+Sum(Feb)+Sum(Mar)+Sum(Apr)+ " +
      "Sum(May)+Sum(Jun)+Sum(Jul)+Sum(Aug)+Sum(Sep)+" +
      "Sum(Oct)+Sum(Nov)+Sum(Dece))) from PrecData WHERE YR>=" +
```

```
        StartYearList.SelectedItem.Text +
        " and YR<=" + EndYearList.SelectedItem.Text;
    if( CityList.SelectedIndex > 0 )
    {
        strSql += ( " and City='" + CityList.SelectedItem.Text + "'" );
    }
    strSql += " group by YR order by YR";

    SqlDataAdapter objDataAdapter =
        new SqlDataAdapter( strSql, objConnection );
    DataSet objDataSet = new DataSet();
    objDataAdapter.Fill( objDataSet, "PrecData" );

    int nCount = objDataSet.Tables[0].Rows.Count;
    Graph2D graph = new Graph2D();
    ArrayList objGraphData = new ArrayList();

    if( nCount <= 20 )
    {
        for( int i=0; i<nCount; i++ )
        {
            double dValue =
                Convert.ToDouble( objDataSet.Tables[0].Rows[i].ItemArray[0] );
            objGraphData.Add( Convert.ToString(
                objDataSet.Tables[0].Rows[i].ItemArray[1] ) + "|" +
                dValue.ToString( "{000000.00000000}" ) ) );
        }
    }
    else
    {
        int nYearsPerBar = nCount / 20;
        int nNumBars = nCount / nYearsPerBar;
        if( nCount % nYearsPerBar != 0 )
        {
            nNumBars++;
        }
        for( int i=0; i<nNumBars; i++ )
        {
            double dTotal = 0;
            string strStart = "";
            string strEnd = "";
            for( int j=0; j<nYearsPerBar; j++ )
            {
```

```
        if( j == 0 )
        {
          strStart = Convert.ToString(
            objDataSet.Tables[0].Rows[i*nYearsPerBar+j].ItemArray[0]);
        }
        if( i * nYearsPerBar + j < nCount )
        {
          strEnd = Convert.ToString(
            objDataSet.Tables[0].Rows[i*nYearsPerBar+j].ItemArray[0]);
          dTotal += Convert.ToDouble(
            objDataSet.Tables[0].Rows[i*nYearsPerBar].ItemArray[1] );
        }
      }
      objGraphData.Add( dTotal.ToString( "000000.000000"  ) + "|" +
        strStart + "-" + strEnd );
    }
  }

  objGraphData.Sort();
  for( int i=0; i<objGraphData.Count; i++ )
  {
    string[] strData = ((string)objGraphData[i]).Split(
      new char[]{'|'},2);
    graph.AddPair( strData[1], Convert.ToDouble( strData[0] ) );
  }
  graph.Title = "Rainfall";
  GraphImage.Text = "<IMG SRC=\"GraphImages/Graph" +
    graph.Render( Request.MapPath( "." ) ) +
    ".gif\">";
}
catch( Exception ex )
{
  ErrorMessage.Text = ex.Message.ToString();
}
finally
{
  if( objConnection.State == ConnectionState.Open )
  {
    objConnection.Close();
  }
}
}
```

The `Predict_Click()` Method

The `Predict_Click()` method is fired when the user clicks the Predict button. It retrieves data based on the DropDownList selections, sorts the data, and then adds the data to an instantiated Graph2D object. Figure 16.6 shows a graph with predicted data.

The code in Listing 16.4 that shows the `Predict_Click()` method starts off similarly to the code in Listing 16.2. The following list outlines the code that is similar to the code in the `Graph_Click()` method in Listing 16.2:

1. A SqlConnection object is created.
2. A string named `strSql` is created with the SQL statement for the database query.
3. A SqlDataAdapter object is created with the string and the Sql-Connection, and it is used to populate a DataSet object.
4. The count of rows is retrieved.
5. A Graph2D object is instantiated.

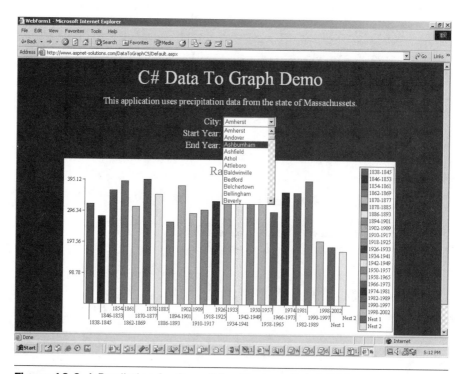

Figure 16.6 A Prediction for Something Such as Rainfall Might Be Important.

Because we're going to add two calculated data values to the graph, we'll check to see whether there are 18 or fewer data values. If so, we'll simply add the 18 data values and then calculate the next 2 values. The next data values are harmonic means of the last data value and the average for all data values. The following code shows how to calculate the first derived data point:

C#

```
double dNext = ( ( dGrandTotal / (double) nCount ) +
  ( dLastTotal / (double) nLastCount ) ) / 2;
graph.AddPair( "Next 1", dNext );
```

VB

```
Dim dNext as Double = ( ( dGrandTotal / (double) nCount ) + _
  ( dLastTotal / nLastCount ) ) / 2
graph.AddPair( "Next 1", dNext )
```

As with the code in Listing 16.2, if there are more than 18 data values, we'll have to average several together to arrive at a bar graph with 18 or fewer bars. The code calculates the number of years per bar (nYearsPer-Bar) and the number of bars (nBars) from the count (nCount).

Once all of the data has been added to the Graph2D object, the Render() method is called, and the bar graph is saved to disk.

Listing 16.4 The `Predict_Click()` Method Predicts the Next Two Data Values.

```
private void Predict_Click(object sender, System.EventArgs e)
{
 SqlConnection objConnection =
  new SqlConnection(ConfigurationSettings.AppSettings["ConnectString"]);
  try
  {
    objConnection.Open();
    string strSql = "SELECT YR,(SELECT " +
      "Value=(Sum(Jan)+Sum(Feb)+Sum(Mar)+Sum(Apr)+Sum(May)+" +
      "Sum(Jun)+Sum(Jul)+Sum(Aug)+Sum(Sep)+Sum(Oct)+" +
      "Sum(Nov)+Sum(Dece))) from PrecData WHERE YR>=" +
      Convert.ToString( StartYearList.SelectedItem.Text ) +
      " and YR<=" + Convert.ToString( EndYearList.SelectedItem.Text );
    if( CityList.SelectedIndex > 0 )
    {
```

```
      strSql += ( " and City='" + CityList.SelectedItem.Text + "'" );
  }
  strSql += " group by YR order by YR";

  SqlDataAdapter objDataAdapter =
    new SqlDataAdapter( strSql, objConnection );
  DataSet objDataSet = new DataSet();
  objDataAdapter.Fill( objDataSet, "PrecData" );

  int nCount = objDataSet.Tables[0].Rows.Count;
  Graph2D graph = new Graph2D();

  if( nCount <= 18 )
  {
    double dGrandTotal = 0;
    double dLastTotal = 0;
    int nLastCount = 0;
    for( int i=0; i<nCount; i++ )
    {
      dGrandTotal +=
        Convert.ToDouble( objDataSet.Tables[0].Rows[i].ItemArray[1] );
      if( i >= nCount - 4 )
      {
       dLastTotal +=
        Convert.ToDouble( objDataSet.Tables[0].Rows[i].ItemArray[1] );
       nLastCount++;
      }
      graph.AddPair( Convert.ToString(
        objDataSet.Tables[0].Rows[i].ItemArray[0] ),
        Convert.ToDouble(objDataSet.Tables[0].Rows[i].ItemArray[1] ));
    }
    double dNext = ( ( dGrandTotal / (double) nCount ) +
      ( dLastTotal / (double) nLastCount ) ) / 2;
    graph.AddPair( "Next 1", dNext );
    dGrandTotal += dNext;
    dLastTotal += dNext;
    dNext = ( ( dGrandTotal / (double) ( nCount + 1 ) ) +
      ( dLastTotal / (double) ( nLastCount + 1 ) ) ) / 2;
    graph.AddPair( "Next 2", dNext );
  }
  else
  {
    double dGrandTotal = 0;
```

```
double dLastTotal = 0;
int nLastCount = 0;
int nYearsPerBar = nCount / 20;
int nNumBars = nCount / nYearsPerBar;
if( nCount % nYearsPerBar != 0 )
{
  nNumBars++;
}
for( int i=0; i<nNumBars; i++ )
{
  double dTotal = 0;
  string strStart = "";
  string strEnd = "";
  for( int j=0; j<nYearsPerBar; j++ )
  {
    if( j == 0 )
    {
      strStart = Convert.ToString(
        objDataSet.Tables[0].Rows[i*nYearsPerBar+j].ItemArray[0] );
    }
    if( i * nYearsPerBar + j < nCount )
    {
      strEnd = Convert.ToString(
        objDataSet.Tables[0].Rows[i*nYearsPerBar+j].ItemArray[0] );
      dTotal += Convert.ToDouble(
        objDataSet.Tables[0].Rows[i*nYearsPerBar].ItemArray[1] );
    }
  }
  dGrandTotal += dTotal;
  if( i >= nNumBars - 4 )
  {
    dLastTotal += dTotal;
    nLastCount++;
  }
  graph.AddPair( strStart + "-" + strEnd, dTotal );
}
double dNext = ( ( dGrandTotal / (double) nCount ) +
  ( dLastTotal / (double) nLastCount ) ) / 2;
graph.AddPair( "Next 1", dNext );
dGrandTotal += dNext;
dLastTotal += dNext;
dNext = ( ( dGrandTotal / (double) ( nCount + 1 ) ) +
  ( dLastTotal / (double) ( nLastCount + 1 ) ) ) / 2;
```

```
      graph.AddPair( "Next 2", dNext );
   }

   graph.Title = "Rainfall";
   GraphImage.Text = "<IMG SRC=\"GraphImages/Graph" +
      graph.Render( Request.MapPath( "." ) ) +
      ".gif\">";
}
catch( Exception ex )
{
   ErrorMessage.Text = ex.Message.ToString();
}
finally
{
   if( objConnection.State == ConnectionState.Open )
   {
      objConnection.Close();
   }
}
}
```

Deploying the Application

There are several ways that you can deploy the application. The first is to download the zip file from the Web site. The links to the C# and VB code can be found at http://www.aspnet-solutions.com/chapter_16.htm. The path to which this archive will be expanded is inetpub\wwwroot\ASPNETSolutionsRoot\DataToGraphCS (or inetpub\wwwroot\ASPNETSolutionsRoot\DataToGraphVB for the VB version).

Once you have the files unzipped, you'll have to go to IIS and create a virtual directory for the project. You can then open the project from Visual Studio .NET as a Web project.

You can also download setup programs that were created with Visual Studio .NET from http://www.aspnet-solutions.com/chapter_16.htm. To use these, simply run them on the Web server.

The database is available as a backed-up database from the same page.

Extending the Application

There are lots of things you can do with this application. The first thing I might suggest is giving users the capability to make the data appear to have fewer and greater fluctuations so that you can show how statistics can be manipulated to make almost any point. I would also suggest using another database for something such as average temperature.

In this chapter, you've learned how to use the Graph2D class for a more advanced application. You've also learned about disconnected datasets and why you'd want to use them. And you've learned how to adjust data for specific needs.

Summary

This chapter has shown you how to use the Graph2D class in a way that goes beyond mere rendering of data. And this is just the beginning. You could do almost anything if you wanted to take the time to figure out how to perform math on the datasets.

Using Dynamic JavaScript: Creating a Personal Idea Organizer

In This Chapter:

- Dynamically Creating JavaScript in ASP.NET
- The BrainStormer Application
- Accepting User Uploads in ASP.NET

I listen to motivational speakers a lot, and my favorite is Tony Robbins. He talks about the importance of organizing your thoughts, and how productive it can make you. Of course, business loves a more productive employee or executive.

I've applied many of Tony's suggestions to my own life. But I always had to carry around the notebook in which I kept my ideas. That's OK if you're organized, but someone like me needs more flexibility. For that reason, I designed and created a Web-based idea-organizer application that I named BrainStormer. This application allows you to access your ideas from anywhere that has an Internet connection, and the ideas get backed up on the server.

One of the innovative and interesting things about the application is its use of dynamic JavaScript. I discovered this by accident as a student when I was experimenting with the Attributes collection of the server controls (which are explained in the section entitled "Server Contols Overview"). You can add JavaScript programmatically with the Attributes collection. And while the examples in this chapter are pretty straightforward, I can imagine some pretty on-the-edge ways to use the idea. For instance, you could add some pop-up help based on the user's current trends or on common things that have happened on the Web server recently.

Dynamically Creating JavaScript in ASP.NET

In this section, I'll show you how to dynamically add JavaScript to server controls. This allows you to easily and powerfully change the behavior of your user interface. Special items can change color when the mouse hovers over them, additional clarification can be provided for specific users, and product information depending on a user's previous buying history can be provided.

The way it's done is with the Attributes collection. All controls derived from WebControl have this collection. It allows you to get and set arbitrary attributes that don't correspond to properties of the control. And in this case, we'll set JavaScript behaviors for events such as onMouseOver and onClick.

It's the Holy Grail: how to make your Web application grab and keep the attention of the user. It used to be easy; just insert an animated GIF image, and you'd easily capture the attention of users. But in this day and age of Flash presentations, an animated GIF image isn't too impressive. The other thing that people quickly learned is that a busy user interface doesn't necessarily make for a good user interface. Color change during a mouse-over is a visual hint that the option can be accessed with a mouse click. When you're performing a lengthy operation, motion on the screen gives the impression that the application is still running.

Another sought-after prize is a rich user interface that provides a lot of information without cluttering up the screen. There are times when you want to add explanatory text for various screen elements, but when you do, applications quickly run out of real estate.

Both of these issues can be effectively addressed with the right JavaScript code. With JavaScript, you can do things such as change text color when the mouse hovers over it, display additional explanatory text when the mouse hovers over special screen elements, and in general, add some eye-catching interactive events.

You may already be asking, "What does this have to do with ASP.NET?" The answer is, "Plenty." For starters, ASP.NET uses JavaScript frequently. For instance, the validation controls that check data users type in work by injecting JavaScript code into the HTML. This injected JavaScript code does the work of validating the user input and notifying users when the data is improper.

In addition, just because you're using ASP.NET server controls doesn't mean you can't use JavaScript. To use JavaScript events such as onMouseOver and onClick with server controls, all you need to do is add the appropriate attributes to the server control. I'll show you more about this in the section entitled "JavaScript Overview."

So far, everything sounds pretty straightforward—you can use JavaScript to enhance your user interface. As my 14-year-old daughter would say, "Duh!" But this article talks about how to dynamically create JavaScript for server controls. This can be very useful if you have special items for which you want to add JavaScript events, but only at certain times. It's also effective to add special explanatory text for some screen items and have the text customized for the current user. For instance, if a user is on a preferred list, and a certain item is on sale on a certain day for preferred users, the item can change in response to this situation.

Server Controls Overview

ASP.NET comes with what are called **server controls**. Server controls aren't ActiveX or COM+ objects, but they are special server objects that can be placed onto an .ASPX page. These controls then render themselves as HTML that's sent to the client machine. Most of the server controls map to an HTML object. For instance, the asp:Button server control renders as an HTML button object.

Most people are already familiar with server controls, so I won't go into detail. I did cover them from a practical aspect in Chapter 2, if you want to refer to that chapter for more information, Server controls are placed into .ASPX code as XML, such as the following:

```
<asp:TextBox id="Test" runat="server"></asp:TextBox>
<asp:Button id="Register" runat="server" Text="Register"></asp:Button>
```

Notice that each server control has attributes that determine the value of the control's properties. When you are programming code behind modules, auto complete shows the properties (and methods) that are available for server controls, as shown in Figure 17.1.

It's also important to note that you can manually add any arbitrary attribute to a server control. Let's say that your application needs a custom attribute named Bozo. You could add this attribute to server controls as follows:

```
<asp:TextBox id="Test" runat="server" Bozo="Me"></asp:TextBox>
<asp:Button id="Register" runat="server" Text="Register"
  Bozo="You"></asp:Button>
```

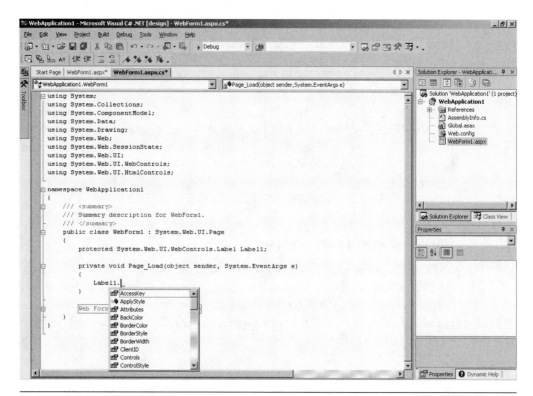

Figure 17.1 Visual Studio .NET Brings Up the List of Methods and Properties for Server Controls.

When the server controls are rendered at the time of the client request, these arbitrary attributes will be part of the rendered HTML object, as follows:

```
<input name="Test" type="text" id="Test" Bozo="Me" />
<input type="submit" name="Register" value="Register" id="Register"
  Bozo="You" />
```

This is an important point because adding the capability to catch JavaScript events for a server control relies on our ability to add arbitrary attributes. We'll talk about this in more detail in the next section.

JavaScript Overview

JavaScript executes on the client computer. It's code that's embedded within the HTML document, and then the client browser executes it. JavaScript has been used extensively for effects that fall under that category known as Dynamic HTML (DHTML). DHTML allows Web developers to provide rich user interfaces that do much more than pedestrian HTML. The HTML tells the browser how to render the user interface, and DHTML/JavaScript allows the user interface to react to user actions.

I'm going to use only three JavaScript events for the demonstration program in this chapter. You could extend the techniques I present, though, to do much more and use the full range of JavaScript events. The three events that we'll see in the demonstration program are onMouseOver, onMouseOut, and onClick.

To enable a JavaScript event for an HTML object, you simply add the event as an attribute to the HTML object, and set it equal to the action that is to be performed when the event is fired. For instance, if you want an alert box to appear when the mouse hovers over an HTML object, you could add the following attribute to the HTML object:

```
onMouseOver="alert('Everyone is happy!');"
```

If the above attribute was added to a button object, it might look like the following:

```
<input type="submit" name="Test" value="Test" id="Test"
   onMouseOver="alert('Everyone is happy!');" />
```

You can add both an onMouseOver and an onMouseOut event. This would allow you to do things such as change the color when the mouse hovers over an HTML object, and have the HTML object restore itself to the original color when the mouse leaves the area. The following code turns the text "Hi There!" to red when the mouse enters the text area and restores the text to black when the mouse leaves the area.

```
<span id="Test1" onmouseover="style.color='red'"
   onmouseout="style.color='black'">Hi there!</span>
```

Adding JavaScript to Server Controls Dynamically

Adding onMouseOver and onMouseOut events to a server control by adding the appropriate attributes to the server control declaration doesn't require any further discussion because it's straightforward, and using these JavaScript events is well documented. My favorite Web site is www.Web-Monkey.com, and my favorite book is Danny Goodman's *Dynamic HTML Reference*, from O'Reilly. It's when we dynamically set the onMouseOver and `onMouseOut` attributes for a server control that some explanation is necessary.

You can get or set any server control attribute with the Attributes collection (which all WebControl-derived controls have). The Attributes collection can't be used for standard server control properties, such as `BorderColor` and `Visible`. The standard server control properties should be accessed in the normal way, such as `TextBox.BorderColor` and `Label.Visible`. But for arbitrary attributes that aren't part of the normal set of properties, you can use the Attributes collection. In other words, the attributes collection is reserved for all attributes that have not been mapped to class properties.

Say, for example, you need to set the `Bozo` attribute to `"Clown"` for a TextField named CircusData. You could use the following code to do this from the code behind:

C#
```csharp
CircusData.Attribute["Bozo"] = "Clown";
```

VB
```vb
CircusData.Attribute("Bozo") = "Clown"
```

When the CircusData object renders, it will appear in the HTML as follows:

```html
<input name="CircusData" type="text
```

This gives you a way to set arbitrary attributes for server controls from your code. With this technique, you can dynamically alter these attributes. It would be rare for you to want to change these attributes programmatically, but there are such cases when you need to alter custom attributes. It gets really interesting when you decide to add JavaScript to the Attributes collection. I'd like to revisit the example that sets some HTML text to red when the mouse enters the text's screen area, which can be found at the end of the "JavaScript Overview" section. Instead of an HTML `<span>` tag, we'll do the same thing with an ASP.NET Label object.

Let's say that the following Label object is in an .aspx file:

```
<asp:Label id="Test1" runat="server">Hi There!</asp:Label>
```

You could make a decision in the code to add JavaScript to turn the code red when the mouse enters the text area, as follows:

```
Test1.Attributes["onMouseOver"] = "style.color='red'";
Test1.Attributes["onMouseOut"] = "style.color='black'";
```

Then, when the Test1 server control was rendered as HTML, you would get the following:

```
<span id="Test1" onMouseOver="style.color='red'"
   onMouseOut="style.color='black'">Hi There!</span>
```

The Dynamic JavaScript Demonstration Application

I've created a demonstration application that shows how to dynamically add JavaScript to server controls. The application offers three pages that each do different things. One page simulates a product catalog in which one

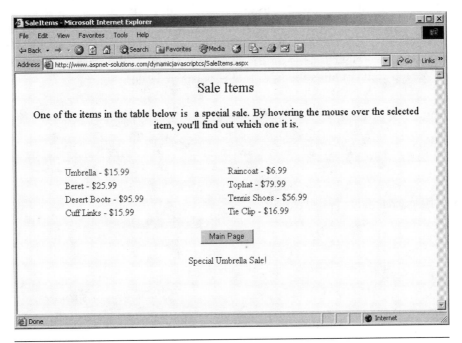

Figure 17.2 When the Mouse Hovers over a Special Item, the Item Changes Colors and Displays Some Text.

The second page of the demonstration application shows how you can give additional information to users about buttons on the screen. Because the extra information is displayed only when users hover over a button, doing this can really give them a lot more information without cluttering up the screen.

of eight items is on special sale. This item will change colors and display extra text when the mouse hovers over it. This technique could be useful if your Web application needed to attract the attention of users in a more subtle way than with a flashing, animated GIF image. This page can be seen in Figure 17.2.

The third page adds JavaScript code to confirm user action, but only if the selected file is a system file. The third page of the demonstration application displays a list box with file names. Some of these are system files, and others are not. The user is provided with the capability to delete any of the files; and before a system file is deleted, a confirmation alert appears. This page can be seen in Figure 17.3.

The SaleItems Code

Behind the SaleItems.aspx page is some fairly simple code, all found in the `Page_Load()` method. It first calls a method named `GetSpecial-SaleIndex()`, which returns an integer value from 0 to 7. Because there are eight Labels on the page, this integer value corresponds to the Label that contains the item that is on special sale.

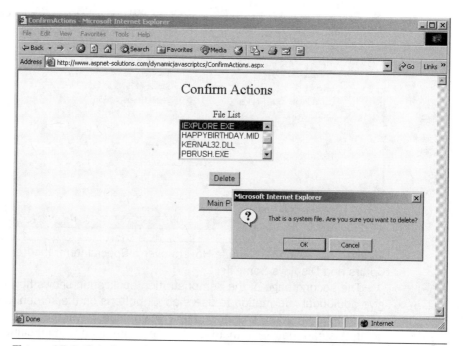

Figure 17.3 This Page Asks for Confirmation before Deleting System Files.

There is a `switch` (for C#) or a `Select` (for VB) in which a small piece of code is executed so that the proper sale item becomes JavaScript-enabled. This is done by adding `onMouseOver` and `onMouseOut` events via the Attributes collection. The `onMouseOver` handler sets the text color for the Label object to `blue`, and then calls a JavaScript method named `SetSpecial()`. The `SetSpecial()` method populates a Label in which the special sale item will appear. The `onMouseOut` handler restores the text color to `black` and calls a JavaScript method named `ClearSpecial()`. The `ClearSpecial()` method simply clears the Label in which the special sale item appeared. The C# version can be seen in Listing 17.1 and is labeled SaleItems.aspx.cs; the VB version can be seen in Listing 17.2 and is labeled SaleItems.aspx.vb.

Listing 17.1 The SaleItems.aspx.cs Source Code

```
int nSpecialSaleIndex = GetSpecialSaleIndex();
switch( nSpecialSaleIndex )
{
  case 0:
    Umbrella.Attributes["onMouseOver"] =
      "style.color='blue'; " +
      "SetSpecial('Umbrella');";
    Umbrella.Attributes["onMouseOut"] =
      "style.color='black'; " +
      "ClearSpecial(); ";
    break;
  case 1:
    Raincoat.Attributes["onMouseOver"] =
      "style.color='blue'; " +
      "SetSpecial('Raincoat');";
    Raincoat.Attributes["onMouseOut"] =
      "style.color='black'; " +
      "ClearSpecial();";
    break;

...

  case 6:
    CuffLinks.Attributes["onMouseOver"] =
      "style.color='blue'; " +
      "SetSpecial('Cuff Links');";
```

```
      CuffLinks.Attributes["onMouseOut"] =
        "style.color='black'; " +
        "ClearSpecial();";
      break;
    case 7:
      TieClip.Attributes["onMouseOver"] =
        "style.color='blue'; " +
        "SetSpecial('Tie Clip');";
      TieClip.Attributes["onMouseOut"] =
        "style.color='black'; " +
        "ClearSpecial();";
      break;
}
```

Listing 17.2 The SaleItems.aspx.vb Source Code

```
Dim nSpecialSaleIndex As Integer = GetSpecialSaleIndex()

Select Case nSpecialSaleIndex
  Case 0
    Umbrella.Attributes("onMouseOver") = _
      "style.color='blue'; " + _
      "SetSpecial('Umbrella');"
    Umbrella.Attributes("onMouseOut") = _
      "style.color='black'; " + _
      "ClearSpecial(); "
  Case 1
    Raincoat.Attributes("onMouseOver") = _
      "style.color='blue'; " + _
      "SetSpecial('Raincoat');"
    Raincoat.Attributes("onMouseOut") = _
      "style.color='black'; " + _
      "ClearSpecial();"

  ...

  Case 6
    CuffLinks.Attributes("onMouseOver") = _
      "style.color='blue'; " + _
      "SetSpecial('Cuff Links');"
    CuffLinks.Attributes("onMouseOut") = _
      "style.color='black'; " + _
```

```
        "ClearSpecial();"
    Case 7
      TieClip.Attributes("onMouseOver") = _
        "style.color='blue'; " + _
        "SetSpecial('Tie Clip');"
      TieClip.Attributes("onMouseOut") = _
        "style.color='black'; " + _
        "ClearSpecial();"
End Select
```

The CustomerService Code

To provide a better simulation, the user needs to type in his name and click the Register button. This way, the program can do a better job simulating feedback to a real, live user. A session variable named Name contains the name the user types in. When the user clicks the Register button, the Register_Click() method is called. This method sets the contents of the session variable, and then calls the SetJavaScriptForName() method (more about this shortly).

The CustomerService page provides three feedback elements for the three main buttons on the screen. When the user hovers over the first button, extra text naming the product that the user last purchased appears to the right of the button.

If you take a look at the Page_Load() method, you'll see that it checks for the existence of a session variable named Name. If this session variable is found, a method named SetJavaScriptForName() is called. This method sets up the dynamic JavaScript in response to the name that has been entered by the user.

The SetJavaScriptForName() method is where most of the work happens for the CustomerService page. At the top is an array of strings from which the extra information for the first button is retrieved. A random number from 0 to 3 determines which of these strings is used in the dynamic JavaScript. For most applications, you'd probably go to a database to get the product that was last purchased.

For the middle button, a text string based on the user's name is created. It might say, for example, "RMA number for Rick." The following code creates the string:

C#
```
string strReturn = "RMA number for " + Session["Name"].ToString();
```

VB
```
Dim strReturn As String = "RMA number for " + Session("Name").ToString()
```

With the `strReturn` string, the RequestReturnAuth Button can then be set so that it contains the JavaScript with which it can display the extra text mentioned above.

The last thing that is done in this method is to create an account number based on the clock ticks. The following line creates the string:

C#
```
string strOrder = "Account number: " +
    Convert.ToString( DateTime.Now.Ticks );
```

VB
```
Dim strOrder As String = "Account number: " + _
    Convert.ToString(DateTime.Now.Ticks)
```

Listing 17.3 shows the C# code for the CustomerService page's code. while Listing 17.4 shows the VB version.

Listing 17.3 CustomerService.aspx.cs

```
private void Page_Load(object sender, System.EventArgs e)
{
  if( Session["Name"] != null )
  {
    SetJavaScriptForName();
  }
}


private void SetJavaScriptForName()
{
  // One of these four strings will be selected
  //    randomly for the first button's extra information.
  string[] ServiceIssues =
  {
    "Regarding your widget",
    "About the credenza you ordered",
    "For your new lawnmower",
    "In reference to your computer"
  };
```

```
// Create a Random object from which we'll get
//    a random number.
Random rnd = new Random();


// Assign a string value to strService from the array
//    of strings based on a random number from 0 to 3.
string strService = ServiceIssues[rnd.Next(0,3)];


// Set the onMouseOver event so that the text for the
//    ServiceIssue Label changes as users hover over the button.
ReportServiceIssue.Attributes["onMouseOver"] =
  "ServiceIssue.innerHTML='" + strService + "'";
// Set the onMouseOut event so that the text for the
//    ServiceIssue Label clears as users leave the button area.
ReportServiceIssue.Attributes["onMouseOut"] =
  "ServiceIssue.innerHTML=''";


// Create the text based on the user's name.
string strReturn = "RMA number for " + Session["Name"].ToString();


// Set the onMouseOver event so that the text for the
//    ReturnAuth Label changes as users hover over the button.
RequestReturnAuth.Attributes["onMouseOver"] =
  "ReturnAuth.innerHTML='" + strReturn + "'";
// Set the onMouseOut event so that the text for the
//    ReturnAuth Label clears as users leave the button area.
RequestReturnAuth.Attributes["onMouseOut"] =
  "ReturnAuth.innerHTML=''";


// Create an account number based on the clock tick.
string strOrder = "Account number: " +
  Convert.ToString( DateTime.Now.Ticks );


// Set the onMouseOver event so that the text for the
//    OrderMore Label changes as users hover over the button.
OrderMoreProduct.Attributes["onMouseOver"] =
  "OrderMore.innerHTML='" + strOrder + "'";
// Set the onMouseOut event so that the text for the
//    OrderMore Label clears as users leave the button area.
OrderMoreProduct.Attributes["onMouseOut"] =
  "OrderMore.innerHTML=''";
}
```

```
private void Register_Click(object sender, System.EventArgs e)
{
  Session["Name"] = Name.Text;
  RegisteredName.Text = "Registered as " + Name.Text;
  Name.Text = "";
  SetJavaScriptForName();
}


private void ReportServiceIssue_Click(object sender, System.EventArgs e)
{
  MessageLabel.Text =
    "Thanks, our efficent staff will attend to the issue.";
}


private void RequestReturnAuth_Click(object sender, System.EventArgs e)
{
  MessageLabel.Text = "The RMA number is 12345ABCDE.";
}


private void OrderMoreProduct_Click(object sender, System.EventArgs e)
{
  MessageLabel.Text = "Your product has been ordered.";
}
```

Listing 17.4 CustomerService.aspx.vb

```
Private Sub Page_Load(ByVal sender As System.Object, _
 ByVal e As System.EventArgs) Handles MyBase.Load
    If Session("Name") <> Nothing Then
        SetJavaScriptForName()
    End If
End Sub


Private Sub SetJavaScriptForName()
    ' One of these four strings will be selected
    '    randomly for the first button's extra information.
    Dim ServiceIssues As String() = _
    { _
     "Regarding your widget", _
     "About the credenza you ordered", _
     "For your new lawnmower", _
     "In reference to your computer" _
    }
```

```vbnet
' Create a Random object from which we'll get
'    a random number.
Dim rnd As New Random()

' Assign a string value to strService from the array
'    of strings based on a random number from 0 to 3.
Dim strService As String = ServiceIssues(rnd.Next(0, 3))

' Set the onMouseOver event so that the text for the
'    ServiceIssue Label changes as users hover over the button.
ReportServiceIssue.Attributes("onMouseOver") = _
    "ServiceIssue.innerHTML='" + strService + "'"
' Set the onMouseOut event so that the text for the
'    ServiceIssue Label clears as users leave the button area.
ReportServiceIssue.Attributes("onMouseOut") = _
    "ServiceIssue.innerHTML=''"

' Create the text based on the user's name.
Dim strReturn As String = "RMA number for " + _
  Session("Name").ToString()

' Set the onMouseOver event so that the text for the
'    ReturnAuth Label changes as users hover over the button.
RequestReturnAuth.Attributes("onMouseOver") = _
  "ReturnAuth.innerHTML='" + strReturn + "'"
' Set the onMouseOut event so that the text for the
'    ReturnAuth Label clears as users leave the button area.
RequestReturnAuth.Attributes("onMouseOut") = _
  "ReturnAuth.innerHTML=''"

' Create an account number based on the clock tick.
Dim strOrder as String = "Account number: " + _
  Convert.ToString( DateTime.Now.Ticks )

' Set the onMouseOver event so that the text for the
'    OrderMore Label changes as users hover over the button.
OrderMoreProduct.Attributes("onMouseOver") = _
    "OrderMore.innerHTML='" + strOrder + "'"
' Set the onMouseOut event so that the text for the
'    OrderMore Label clears as users leave the button area.
OrderMoreProduct.Attributes("onMouseOut") = _
    "OrderMore.innerHTML=''"

End Sub
```

```
Private Sub Register_Click(ByVal sender As System.Object, _
 ByVal e As System.EventArgs) Handles Register.Click
    Session("Name") = Name.Text
    RegisteredName.Text = "Registered as " + Name.Text
    Name.Text = ""
    SetJavaScriptForName()
End Sub

Private Sub ReportServiceIssue_Click(ByVal sender As System.Object, _
 ByVal e As System.EventArgs) Handles ReportServiceIssue.Click
    MessageLabel.Text = _
      "Thanks, our efficent staff will attend to the issue."
End Sub

Private Sub RequestReturnAuth_Click(ByVal sender As System.Object, _
 ByVal e As System.EventArgs) Handles RequestReturnAuth.Click
    MessageLabel.Text = "The RMA number is 12345ABCDE."
End Sub

Private Sub OrderMoreProduct_Click(ByVal sender As System.Object, _
 ByVal e As System.EventArgs) Handles OrderMoreProduct.Click
    MessageLabel.Text = "Your product has been ordered."
End Sub

Private Sub Main_Click(ByVal sender As System.Object, _
 ByVal e As System.EventArgs) Handles Main.Click
    Response.Redirect("Default.aspx")
End Sub
```

The ConfirmActions Code

The ConfirmActions page responds to the Delete button and the FileList
list-box-selection change. When users select a file in the list, JavaScript is
dynamically added to the Delete button if the file that was selected is a system file. This way, when the user clicks the Delete button for a system file,
a confirmation alert will appear with which the user can confirm or reject
the action. Listing 17.5 shows the C# code for the ConfirmActions page,
while Listing 17.6 shows the VB version.

Listing 17.5 The ConfirmActions.aspx.cs Source Code

```
private void Delete_Click(object sender, System.EventArgs e)
{
    MessageLabel.Text = "Done!";
```

```
        try
        {
          FileList.Items.RemoveAt( FileList.SelectedIndex );
        }
        catch
        {
        }
    }

    private void FileList_SelectedIndexChanged(object sender,
     System.EventArgs e)
    {
      MessageLabel.Text = "";
      string strSelected = FileList.SelectedItem.Value;
      // The items that must be confirmed contain
      //   a '*' character.
      if( strSelected.IndexOf( "*" ) >= 0 )
      {
        Delete.Attributes["onClick"] = "return ConfirmDelete();";
      }
      else
      {
        Delete.Attributes["onClick"] = ";";
      }
    }

    private void Main_Click(object sender, System.EventArgs e)
    {
      Response.Redirect( "Default.aspx" );
    }
```

Listing 17.6 The ConfirmActions.aspx.vb Source Code

```
Private Sub FileList_SelectedIndexChanged(ByVal sender As System.Object, _
 ByVal e As System.EventArgs) Handles FileList.SelectedIndexChanged
    MessageLabel.Text = ""
    Dim strSelected As String = FileList.SelectedItem.Value
    If strSelected.IndexOf("*") >= 0 Then
        Delete.Attributes("onClick") = "return ConfirmDelete();"
    Else
        Delete.Attributes("onClick") = ";"
    End If
End Sub
```

```
Private Sub Delete_Click(ByVal sender As System.Object, _
 ByVal e As System.EventArgs) Handles Delete.Click
    MessageLabel.Text = "Done!"
    FileList.Items.RemoveAt(FileList.SelectedIndex)
End Sub

Private Sub Main_Click(ByVal sender As System.Object, _
 ByVal e As System.EventArgs) Handles Main.Click
    Response.Redirect("Default.aspx")
End Sub
```

Dynamically adding JavaScript to server controls is a very useful and powerful technique for enhancing the appearance, usability, and clarity of an ASP.NET Web application. It's easy to do with the Attributes collection that all server controls have.

The BrainStormer Application

I originally wrote the BrainStormer application to help me organize my ideas in a way that I could get to them whenever I have an Internet connection. It has fulfilled my expectations well. Being able to upload an image makes it easy to keep track of visuals that are important. Many people like to create mind maps for their thought processes, and an image can represent a mind map. (For more information on image maps, check out Tony Buzan's book *Mind Mapping* [Thorsons, 2003].) Uploading files is a software developer's addition. I found that the capability to upload code snippets and even complete projects helped me because the files are always available. You must log in to the application, as shown in Figure 17.4.

Once you log in, there is only one screen. The application's main screen allows you to organize your thoughts and ideas, as shown in Figure 17.5.

Categories

Everything is organized into categories. The example in Figure 17.5 has the categories Plan for Vacation, Take Care of Lawn, and Teach My Classes. You can add new categories by entering the category title and then clicking the Add button. You can delete a category by selecting it in the ListBox and then clicking the Delete button.

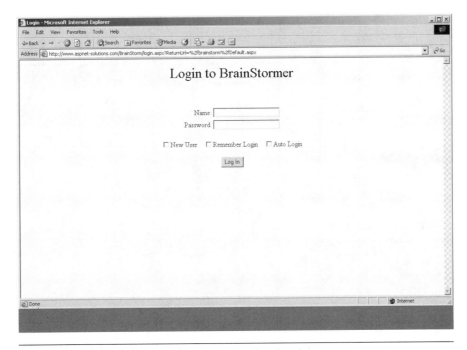

Figure 17.4 You Must First Log In to the Application.

Thoughts

Each category has thoughts. In Figure 17.5, you can see a ListBox in the Thoughts area that contains the thoughts Call Travel Agent and Make Sure the Car Is Serviced. You can add new thoughts by entering the thought and clicking the Add button.

Images

To upload an image, click the Browse button in the Images area, and find the file. Then, for the image, you must enter some descriptive text, which will appear in the ListBox. You can view an image at any time by clicking the image that you want to view, and then clicking the View button.

Files

To upload a file, click the Browse button in the Files area, and find the file. Then, for the file, you must enter some descriptive text, which will appear in the ListBox. You can download a file at any time by clicking the file that you want to download, and then clicking the Download button.

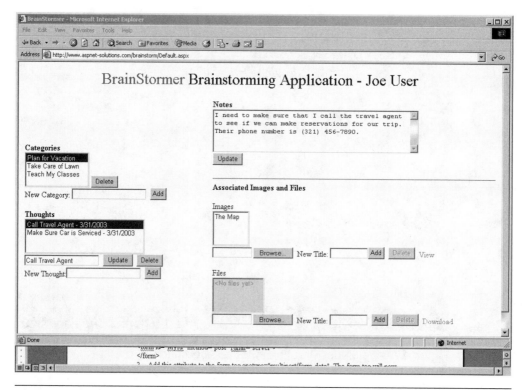

Figure 17.5 In One Screen, You Can Organize All of Your Thoughts and Ideas.

Accepting User Uploads in ASP.NET

Once upon a time, your Web site needed third-party components to allow users to upload files. Now, you can do it all in ASP.NET, without any third-party add-ons. Here's how.

Following are the bare-bones steps to accept user uploads:

1. In an .aspx page, find the form tag. With Visual Studio .NET, this tag is always added automatically. If you're using another tool, make sure that you have the following form tag:

```
<form id="MyId" method="post" runat="server">
</form>
```

2. Add this attribute to the form tag: `enctype="multipart/form-data"`. The form tag will now look like this:

```
<form id="MyId" method="post" runat="server"
enctype="multipart/form-data">
</form>
```

`enctype` determines how the form data is encoded. Whenever data is transmitted from one place to another, there needs to be an agreed-upon means of representing that data.

3. If you're using Visual Studio .NET, open the HTML section of the Toolbox and add a `File` field to the page. If you're not using Visual Studio .NET, manually add the following to the HTML:

```
<INPUT type="file" id="Filename">
```

4. In the `File` field, add a **runat="server"** attribute, as follows:

```
<INPUT type="file" id="Filename" runat="server">
```

In your C# or VB code, you can get the filename from the Filename.PostedFile.FileName property.

5. Save the file to disk (on the server) by using the `Filename.PostedFile.SaveAs()` method.

The destination directory on the server must give the necessary permissions for the save operation. Normally, the ASP.NET account won't have sufficient rights to save a file to disk. The way to fix this is to first create a directory under the application directory, and then give the Everyone group full access.

CAUTION: Make sure that your Web application directory doesn't give full access to the Everyone group. You need to make sure that the hard drive of your server is protected.

This section describes a demo application that accepts user uploads. Figure 17.6 shows the application. You can test the demo application at http://www.aspnet-solutions.com/UploadTest/WebForm1.aspx.

Listings 17.7 and 17.8 show the code that places the file information into the user interface. Listing 17.7 shows the C# code; Listing 17.8 shows the VB code.

Listing 17.7 Placing the File Information into a User Interface Label Object (C#)

```
private void DoIt_Click(object sender, System.EventArgs e)
{
  FileInfo.Text =
```

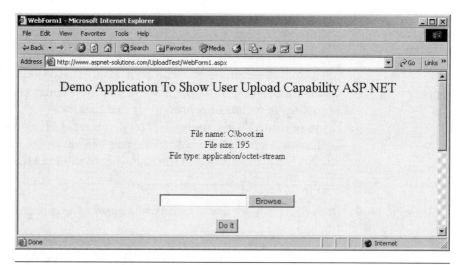

Figure 17.6 This Application Takes a User-Specified File and Shows Information about It.

```
      "File name: " + Filename.PostedFile.FileName + "<br>\r\n" +
      "File size: " + Filename.PostedFile.ContentLength + "<br>\r\n" +
      "File type: " + Filename.PostedFile.ContentType;
}
```

Listing 17.8 Placing the File Information into a User Interface Label Object (VB)

```
Private Sub DoIt_Click(ByVal sender As System.Object, _
  ByVal e As System.EventArgs) Handles DoIt.Click
    FileInfo.Text = _
      "File name: " + Filename.PostedFile.FileName + "<br>" + vbCrLf + _
      "File size: " + Filename.PostedFile.ContentLength + "<br>" + _
      vbCrLf + _
      "File type: " + Filename.PostedFile.ContentType
End Sub
```

As you can see, accepting user uploads from ASP.NET applications is very easy. And you can do it without any third-party add-ons.

Summary

The BrainStormer application could be one of the most valuable things you offer people in your company. It offers the capability to organize ideas, and it will foster creativity because it helps organize ideas.

Uploading files to the server is fairly easy, as we've seen. Uploading files requires a combination of a user interface object and several lines of code to accept the uploaded file. The security issues have been discussed as well.

And adding dynamic JavaScript is a technique that can be useful for many applications. In the BrainStormer application, dynamic JavaScript was used to confirm deletes of items. And in the demo program, dynamic JavaScript was used to confirm important events.

CHAPTER 18

The IBuySpy Portal Application

In This Chapter:

- Application Architecture
- Administering the Portal
- Effective Use of Style Sheets
- Enhancing and Extending the Portal

Imagine creating a portal for your company's Web site that users can clearly understand. Each section, such as insurance benefits or the company calendar, can be accessed with a single click. And the selections are laid out with a Tab metaphor, similar to what is so popular in most Windows software today.

Now imagine that Microsoft created a sample application from which you can simply do some editing, make a few changes, and you're in business with a Web portal. As hard as it is to believe, that's just what Microsoft did. The application is named IBuySpy Portal, and it's ready for you to take and use as you see fit.

The IBuySpy Portal is exemplary in its use of recommended practices. It uses stored procedures, user controls, XML, and many other things that make software development easier, faster, and more robust. Stored procedures execute faster because an execution plan was already created by SQL Server when the stored procedures were created (instead of being created in real-time when executed). Stored procedures can also help reduce the number of attacks that your application is vulnerable to. For a more complete explanation regarding the difference between stored procedures and inline SQL, see Chapter 3.

This chapter explains the workings of the application. We'll talk about the application architecture; its support for multiple browsers, including those on mobile devices; and how to extend the application to add your own functionality. I've created several demonstration programs that isolate some of the things I talk about so that you can more easily understand them.

Application Architecture

The IBuySpy Portal is superbly separated into multiple tiers. This is one of the design goals of distributed applications, and this application accomplishes that design goal admirably. The data tier consists of a SQL Server database and a number of stored procedures. There's an intermediate layer between the application and the stored procedures that provides an abstraction that in turn provides an easy way for the application to access the data tier. This abstraction allows the business logic to be separate from the database-access details. Several of the modules fall into the category of business components because they provide the business logic for the application. Other modules that handle security, configuration, and user interaction comprise the rest of the application. The user interaction is done with Web Forms, and this falls into the category of the presentation layer.

This section talks about the IBuySpy database, the stored procedures that provide data access, the portal settings, the portal tabs, and security. Several demonstration programs have been written to illustrate the discussion topic isolated from the IBuySpy Portal application.

The IBuySpy Database

The database platform used for the IBuySpy application is SQL Server 2000. The database is named Portal. It has 15 tables for the application and 66 stored procedures. All of the application configuration settings are stored in SQL Server. This allows the application to be set up in a server farm because the configuration data can be pulled from a number of servers that are connected to the unique data store. The database schema can be seen in Figure 18.1

TIP: The code for logging users in is in the stored procedure UserLogin. This stored procedure takes the Email and Password as parameters. The problem is that the database is not case sensitive, so it doesn't matter whether the parameters are uppercase or lowercase. Fortunately, you can turn case sensitivity on at the field level. In Enterprise Manager, select the Users table and go into design mode. Select the field you want to set as case sensitive. Select Collation from the Columns tab at the bottom of the design window. On the collation screen, select Windows Collation, Dictionary Sort, and then Case Sensitive. You might want to do this for both the email/password fields and the login/password, which will make them become case sensitive. Normally, though, a recommended practice is to have the login name not case sensitive and the password case sensitive.

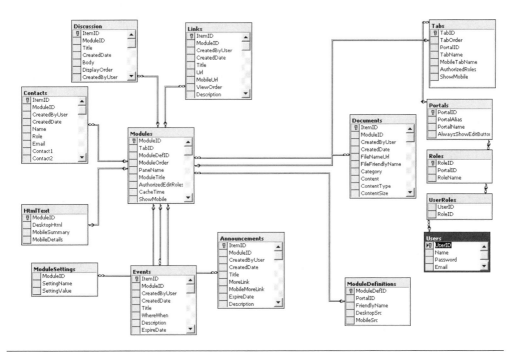

Figure 18.1 A Diagram of the IBuySpy Portal Database Schema

Stored Procedures

Stored procedures are used for all database queries. There are several reasons for this. The first is to separate the data logic from the middle-tier logic. The second is the performance gains that stored procedures provide. The third is the capability to make database changes along with the necessary stored-procedure changes without breaking the application.

Portal Settings

There are a number of settings that determine the behavior and appearance of the portal. They include the portal ID, the portal name, the desktop tabs collection, the mobile tabs collection, and the currently active tab. These settings all reside in a class named `PortalSettings`. This class is placed into the Context object upon each Web request of the portal application.

   The PortalSettings object is placed into the Context upon page request so that the settings are easily accessible from any module that might need the settings. The page request always fires the `Application_BeginRe-`

quest() method found in the Global.asax. That's where the PortalSettings are created and saved. Using this object gives you a great way to access, in the same way, some context that is unique to your application. That's the purpose of the Context.Items collection. It holds your application's request-specific values in a way that is available to every part of your code that participates in the processing of a request.

C#
```
Context.Items.Add( "PortalSettings",
  new PortalSettings( tabIndex, tabId ) );
```

VB
```
Context.Items.Add("PortalSettings", _
  New PortalSettings(tabIndex, tabId))
```

To use the settings that were saved in the Application_BeginRequest() method, we can simply use the HttpContext.Current. Items. HttpContext.Current is a static property that conveniently returns the context for the current request.

C#
```
PortalSettings objSettings =
  HttpContext.Current.Items["PortalSettings"];
```

VB
```
Dim objSettings As PortalSettings = _
  HttpContext.Current.Items("PortalSettings")
```

I created a simple program that shows how to use the Context and HttpContext classes. The program can be accessed from the www.ASP-NET-Solutions.com/Chapter_18.htm page. The C# version is live on the Web site, but both C# and VB versions are available for download.

The application has a simple class named AppSettings with two public string members. They contain the time and date of the request, and the current directory of the application. In the Application_ BeginRequest() method, an AppSettings class is created and added to the Context. In the Page_Load() method of the code behind the Default.aspx page, the AppSettings class is retrieved from the Http-Context.Current.Items collection. A label in the Default.aspx page is then populated with the time and date of the request, and the current directory. You can see the application running in Figure 18.2.

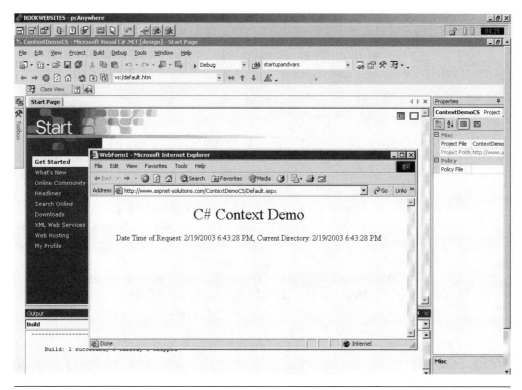

Figure 18.2 The ContextDemoCS Application Running

You're probably wondering why you'd want to use the Context class instead of a Session or Application variable. That's a good question, and its answer involves the persistence of the data. A Context is created for each request and discarded at the end of the request cycle. That means the memory is discarded at the end of the request. OK, so that might not give you a performance boost like a Session or Application variable (the performance boost coming from persistence of data) does, but it gives you the capability to access information throughout in all of the application's modules during the life cycle of the request. If the configuration settings may change often, then it's probably best to discard them after the page request is done anyway.

Portal Tabs

Central to the application's user interface (or presentation layer) is the set of tabs that can be seen in the upper left portion of the screen. When users first open the portal main page, they see five tabs: Home, Employee Info,

Product Info, Discussions, and About the Portal. Clicking these tabs brings a content page into view for the subject that's been selected. The beauty of this system of tabs is that they are very configurable, and different users may see different tabs, depending on what their security role has access to.

A Simple Program with Tabs

To illustrate how the tabs work, I've created a simple application that has a bare-bones set of tabs. This will let you understand how the tabs function outside the user controls. I have another application in the section entitled "A Program with Tabs in a User Control" in which I add the tabs into a user control similar to how it's done in the portal. This will get you closer to a more complete understanding of how the portal is organized. Finally, the Tip on page 678 explains how everything fits together in the IBuySpy Portal application.

The first thing I did was to create a project with a single page named Default.aspx. Because the portal has a table on the main page into which the tabs as well as the content are placed, I pasted the same table into my Default.aspx page.

Into the first table row, I pasted the IBuySpy DataList that contains the tabs. The ItemTemplate tag contains a link back to the Default.aspx page (DesktopDefault.aspx for IBuySpy) with parameters indicating the tab ID and order. The SelectedItemTemplate tag contains the text of the tab (for a more complete explanation see Chapter 5) but does not have a link since that tab is selected. The following code shows the DataList as it appears in my simple program:

```
<asp:datalist id="tabs" cssclass="OtherTabsBg"
     repeatdirection="horizontal" ItemStyle-Height="25"
     SelectedItemStyle-CssClass="TabBg" ItemStyle-BorderWidth="1"
     EnableViewState="false" runat="server">
 <ItemTemplate>
   <a href='<%= Request.ApplicationPath %>
   /Default.aspx?tabindex=<%# Container.ItemIndex %>
   &tabid=<%# ((TabStripDetails) Container.DataItem).TabId %>'
   class="OtherTabs">
   <%# ((TabStripDetails) Container.DataItem).TabName %></a> 
 </ItemTemplate>
 <SelectedItemTemplate>
   <span class="SelectedTab">
  <%# ((TabStripDetails) Container.DataItem).TabName %></span> 
```

```
  </SelectedItemTemplate>
</asp:datalist>
```

I created a class into which the TabStripDetails class was added. The name of the file is Configuration.cs (and Configuration.vb for the VB version). The TabStringDetails class is shown below:

C#
```
public class TabStripDetails
{
   public int        TabId;
   public String     TabName;
   public int        TabOrder;
   public String     AuthorizedRoles;
}
```

VB
```
Public Class TabStripDetails
    Public TabId As Integer
    Public TabName As String
    Public TabOrder As Integer
    Public AuthorizedRoles As String
End Class
```

In the Page_Load() method (which is found in the Default.aspx.cs or Default.aspx.vb files), I added simple code that created four instances of the TabStringDetails class, populated its members, added them to an ArrayList, and then bound the ArrayList to the DataList. In addition, I added some very simple code that displayed in one of the table columns a single sentence of text explaining what content should go in the column. The following code shows how I created the data and bound it to the DataList:

```
// Build list of tabs to be shown to user
ArrayList authorizedTabs = new ArrayList();

// Create a TabStripDetails class
TabStripDetails tab = new TabStripDetails();
// Set the ID to 0 so that the default is the first tab.
tab.TabId = 0;
// Set the text.
tab.TabName = "About Us";
// Set the tab order to 0 so that it starts with the first
```

```
tab.TabOrder = 0;
// Add the object to the ArrayList
authorizedTabs.Add( tab );

// Create a TabStripDetails class
tab = new TabStripDetails();
// Set the ID to 1
tab.TabId = 1;
// Set the text.
tab.TabName = "Catalog";
// Set the tab order.
tab.TabOrder = 1;
// Add the object to the ArrayList
authorizedTabs.Add( tab );

// Create a TabStripDetails class
tab = new TabStripDetails();
// Set the ID to 2
tab.TabId = 2;
// Set the text.
tab.TabName = "Contact Us";
// Set the tab order.
tab.TabOrder = 2;
authorizedTabs.Add( tab );

// Create a TabStripDetails class
tab = new TabStripDetails();
// Set the ID to 3
tab.TabId = 3;
// Set the text.
tab.TabName = "Links";
// Set the tab order.
tab.TabOrder = 3;
// Add the object to the ArrayList
authorizedTabs.Add( tab );

// Get the tabindex - it's a query string but will still evaluate to
zero if this is the first
//   time and there is not query string
int nSelectedIndex = Convert.ToInt32( Request.QueryString["tabindex"] );

// Set the data source to the ArrayList
tabs.DataSource = authorizedTabs;
```

```
// Set the SelectedIndex property to the right value.
tabs.SelectedIndex = nSelectedIndex;
// Bind the data.
tabs.DataBind();

// Add simple text to the content pane.
ContentPane.Visible = true;
switch( nSelectedIndex )
{
  case 0:
    ContentLabel.Text = "This is about us.";
    break;
  case 1:
    ContentLabel.Text = "This is our catalog.";
    break;
  case 2:
    ContentLabel.Text = "This is our contact information.";
    break;
  case 3:
    ContentLabel.Text = "These are recommended links.";
    break;
}
```

The last thing I had to do to get the program working correctly was to create a style sheet in which the IBuySpy Portal styles were re-created. There were several styles that determined the appearances of the tabs, and without the style sheet the tabs didn't have the appearance that they should. I'll talk more about style sheets in the section entitled "Effective Use of Style Sheets."

The simple demo program can be seen at http://www.ASPNET-Solutions.com/TabDemoCS/Default.aspx. This demo allows you to select the tabs, and then it shows some simple text in the table, as shown in Figure 18.3.

A Program with Tabs in a User Control

Now that we've seen a simplified version of the tabs, let's move to something closer to the architecture of the IBuySpy Portal. I created a second demo program in which the tabs are contained in a user control named `TabControl`. This user control is then consumed from the Default.aspx page similar to the IBuySpy Portal.

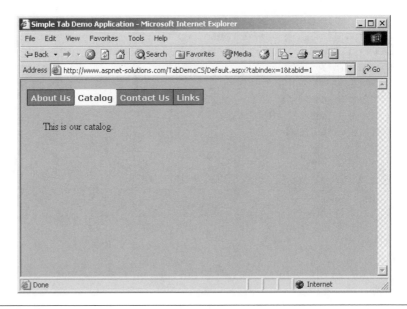

Figure 18.3 This Program Shows How the Tabs Work.

The TabControl.ascx file contains the source code for the user control. The reason for using the ASCX/User Control is that the tab control inherits and extends the TabControl class. At the top of the file are two directives: one to import the TabDemoWithUserControlCS namespace (or TabDemoWithUserControlVB for the VB version), and a Control directive. Below the directives is the DataList, which renders the tabs. The following source code shows the TabControl.ascx file:

```
<%@ Import Namespace="TabDemoWithUserControlCS" %>
<%@ Control Language="c#" AutoEventWireup="false"
    Codebehind="TabControl.ascx.cs"
    Inherits="TabDemoWithUserControlCS.TabControl"
    TargetSchema="http://schemas.microsoft.com/intellisense/ie5"%>

<asp:DataList id="tabs" cssclass="OtherTabsBg"
    repeatdirection="horizontal" ItemStyle-Height="25"
    SelectedItemStyle-CssClass="TabBg" ItemStyle-BorderWidth="1"
    EnableViewState="false" runat="server">
  <ItemTemplate>
       <a href='<%=Request.ApplicationPath%>
      /Default.aspx?tabindex=<%# Container.ItemIndex %>&tabid=
      <%# ((TabStripDetails) Container.DataItem).TabId %>'
```

```
      class="OtherTabs">
      <%# ((TabStripDetails) Container.DataItem).TabName %></a> 
  </ItemTemplate>
  <SelectedItemTemplate>
       <span class="SelectedTab">
      <%# ((TabStripDetails) Container.DataItem).TabName %></span> 
  </SelectedItemTemplate>
</asp:datalist>
```

The `TabControl` user control is then consumed by the Default.aspx page. At the top of the page is a directive registering the user control and specifying the `TagPrefix` and `TagName` attributes, as follows:

```
<%@ Register TagPrefix="demo" TagName="TabControl"
   Src="TabControl.ascx" %>
```

Then, to use the control, it is added declaratively to the .aspx code as any other control, as follows:

```
<demo:TabControl id="Tabs" SelectedTabIndex="0" runat="server" />
```

You can see the TabDemoWithUserControl application in Figure 18.4.

The IBuySpy Tab Architecture

Similarly to the demo application that contains the tabs in a user control, IBuySpy does the same thing. This section talks about the architecture of the presentation layer, especially how the tabs work.

The first thing I need to point out is that there are two default pages: DesktopDefault.aspx for desktop computers that access the portal, and MobileDefault.aspx for mobile devices that access the portal. The file Default.aspx does only one thing: that's redirect to either DesktopDefault.aspx or MobileDefault.aspx, depending on the type of devices that's accessing the portal. This discussion will focus on the desktop files.

The DesktopDefault.aspx page consumes a user control named `Desk-topPortalBanner` (found in the DesktopPortalBanner.ascx file). This user control contains a welcome message, a link to the portal home, a link to the documentation, a site name label, and the tabs. As we've already seen in the two demo programs in this section, the tabs are rendered as part of a `DataList`.

If you take a look at the DesktopPortalBanner.ascx.cs (or Desktop-PortalBanner.ascx.vb for the VB version), you can see how the user inter-

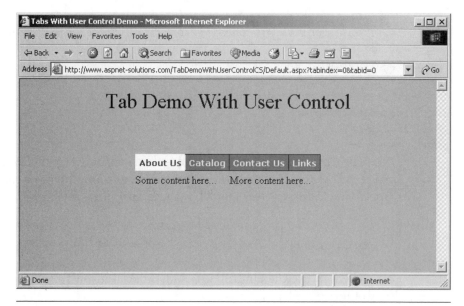

Figure 18.4 This Demo Application Places the Tabs in a User Control.

face objects are populated. The PortalSettings object is first retrieved from the HttpContext, as we've already discussed. From this, the site name (siteName label) is populated. The welcome message (WelcomeMessage label) is populated with the user's identity, which is retrieved from the Context.User.Identity.Name property. The tabs are contained in a collection of TabStripDetail objects, which are all added to an ArrayList object. The ArrayList object is bound to the DataList, and the tabs are then rendered. One thing to note, though, with regard to adding the Tabs to the ArrayList. Before a Tab is added, a check is made to the PortalSecurity.IsInRoles() method to ensure that the user has the right to see the tab.

The Portal Modules

Although the tabs control what content is to be displayed in the main portion of the screen, a set of user controls determines what content appears. The content is rendered by user controls that inherit from the PortalModuleControl base class. This base class gives the necessary communication between the modules and the underlying portal framework. There are 11 built-in portal modules, as shown in Table 18.1.

Table 18.1 The Built-In Content Modules

Control Filename	Description
Announcements.ascx	Contains general announcements for the users.
Contacts.ascx	Gives contact information for the portal company.
Discussion.ascx	Provides a discussion mechanism for users.
Document.ascx	Provides the capability to view documents.
Events.ascx	Displays upcoming events.
HtmlModule.ascx	Empty user control.
ImageModule.ascx	Displays images.
Links.ascx	Shows links.
QuickLinks.ascx	Shows short links.
Signin.ascx	Allows users to log in.
XmlModule.ascx	Displays XML files using an XSLT transform.

We'll talk about creating custom modules and adding them to your portal in the section entitled "Enhancing and Extending the Portal."

Security

The IBuySpy Portal application can be configured for either Forms-based or Windows-based authentication. This is configurable in the Web.config file, as shown below:

Forms-based

```
<authentication mode="Forms">
  <forms name=".ASPXAUTH" protection="All" timeout="60" />
</authentication>
```

Windows-based

```
<authentication mode="Windows" />
<authorization>
    <deny users="?" />
</authorization>
```

For Forms-based authentication, the user names and passwords are validated against the User table in the database. The User table contains `UserID`, `Name`, `Password`, and `Email` fields. The `UserLogin` stored procedure provides the data-access layer with which logins can be attempted. Once a user has been logged in, the `User.Identity.Name` property will contain the user name.

The application also must keep track of which users are in which roles. This allows the application to adjust the presentation layer according to the role that the user is in. For instance, unless a user is in the `Admins` role, the administrative pages won't be displayed. The roles for a user are retrieved from the UserRoles table with the `GetRolesByUser` stored procedure. The calling of the `GetRolesByUser` stored procedure is encapsulated in the `UsersDB` class (found in the Security.cs or Security.vb files).

Immediately after a user has been authenticated, the `Application_ AuthenticateRequest()` method (which is found in the Global.asax file) is called. This method does a number of things that allow the application to easily maintain security. The following is a summary of what happens:

First time

1. Create an instance of the `UsersDB` class.
2. Call the `UsersDB.GetRoles()` method to get an array of strings listing the valid roles for the user.

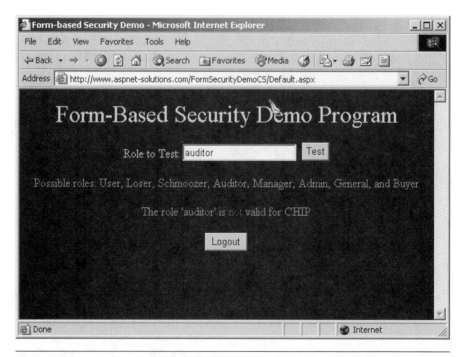

Figure 18.5 This Page Checks the Role That Users Belong To.

3. Create a semicolon-delimited string composed of all roles (such as `'User;Buyer;Seller;'`).
4. Create a cookie authentication ticket.
5. Encrypt the cookie.
6. Send the cookie to the client.

Subsequent times (when a cookie can be loaded)

1. Retrieve the authentication ticket cookie.
2. Decrypt the cookie.
3. Split the `roles` string into an `ArrayList`.

Finally, for both situations, a GenericPrincipal object is instantiated and saved into the `Context`. This can then be accessed from the entire application.

I've created a demonstration application that performs Forms-based authentication, and which also stores roles for the users. It's named FormSecurityDemoCS (or FormSecurityDemoVB for the VB version), and it is shown in Figure 18.5.

The first thing I had to do, so that the application would enforce Forms-based authentication, was to edit the Web.config file, as follows:

```
<authorization>
  <deny users="?" />
</authorization>
<authentication mode="Forms">
  <forms name=".SECURITYDEMO" loginUrl="login.aspx" protection="All"
    timeout="30" path="/">
  </forms>
</authentication>
```

I then created a page named Login.aspx in which users enter their names and passwords to become authenticated. Behind the Login button is a simple method that looks for one of three user name and password pairs. If they are found, the user is authenticated with the `FormsAuthentication.RedirectFromLoginPage()` method. The following in Listing 18.1 shows the `LogUserIn_Click()` method:

Listing 18.1 The Code That Authenticates the User

C#

```csharp
private void LogUserIn_Click(object sender, System.EventArgs e)
{
  // Process the user name and password so
  //    that they're easier to work with.
  string strName = Name.Text.Trim().ToUpper();
  // Security is lowered somewhat since password checking is case
  //    insensitive.
  string strPassword = Password.Text.Trim().ToUpper();

  // Check for our three hard-coded pairs.
  if( ( strName == "JOE" && strPassword == "SMITH" ) ||
    ( strName == "CHIP" && strPassword == "MUNK" ) ||
    ( strName == "CHUCK" && strPassword == "WAGON" ) )
  {
    // Perform the authentication.
    FormsAuthentication.RedirectFromLoginPage( strName, false );
  }
  else
  {
    // Alert user to error.
    ErrorMessage.Text = "Name/Password combination is invalid.";
  }
}
```

VB

```vb
Private Sub LogUserIn_Click(ByVal sender As System.Object, _
  ByVal e As System.EventArgs) Handles LogUserIn.Click
    ' Process the user name and password so
    '    that they're easier to work with.
    Dim strName As String = Name.Text.Trim().ToUpper()
    Dim strPassword As String = Password.Text.Trim().ToUpper()

    ' Check for our three hard-coded pairs.
    If (strName = "JOE" And strPassword = "SMITH") Or _
      (strName = "CHIP" And strPassword = "MUNK") Or _
      (strName = "CHUCK" And strPassword = "WAGON") Then
        ' Perform the authentication.
        FormsAuthentication.RedirectFromLoginPage(strName, False)
    Else
        ' Alert user to error.
        ErrorMessage.Text = "Name/Password combination is invalid."
    End If
End Sub
```

In the Global.asax is a method named `Application_`
`AuthenticateRequest()`. It's in this method that the roles are saved
to the `Context` so that all of the pages in the application can check to see
whether the current user has the proper rights for different things. Listing
18.2 shows the code that performs this function. Note that it also saves an
encrypted cookie so that it doesn't have to fetch the roles (which would
ordinarily come from a data store) each time.

Listing 18.2 The Code in the Global.asax That Stores the Roles in the `Context`

C#
```csharp
protected void Application_AuthenticateRequest(Object sender,
  EventArgs e)
{

  // Bail out if we're not authenticated yet. We don't have
  //  to do the redirection ourselves since ASP.NET does it.
  if( Request.IsAuthenticated == false )
  {
    return;
  }

  string[] roles;

  // See if the cookie can be loaded, if not
  //  do this code.
  if( Request.Cookies["DemoRoles"] == null )
  {

    // Here we're going to add some hard-coded roles.
    if( Context.User.Identity.Name == "CHUCK" )
    {
      roles = new string[]{ "User", "Loser", "Schmoozer" };
    }
    else if( Context.User.Identity.Name == "CHIP" )
    {
      roles = new string[]{ "Auditor", "Manager", "Admin" };
    }
    else
    {
      roles = new string[]{ "General", "User", "Buyer" };
    }
```

```
// Put the roles into one string for the cookie.
string strRoles = "";
for( int i=0; i<roles.Length; i++ )
{
  strRoles += ( roles[i] + ";" );
}

// Create a cookie authentication ticket.
FormsAuthenticationTicket ticket =
  new FormsAuthenticationTicket( 1,
  Context.User.Identity.Name, DateTime.Now,
  DateTime.Now.AddHours( 1 ), false, strRoles );

// Encrypt the ticket.
string strCookie = FormsAuthentication.Encrypt( ticket );

// Send the cookie to the client.
Response.Cookies["DemoRoles"].Value = strCookie;
Response.Cookies["DemoRoles"].Path = "/";
Response.Cookies["DemoRoles"].Expires =
  DateTime.Now.AddMinutes( 10 );
}

// We came here when we were able to
//   load the cookie.
else
{
  // Create the Forms authentication ticket
  //   and decrypt it.
  FormsAuthenticationTicket ticket =
    FormsAuthentication.Decrypt(
    Context.Request.Cookies["DemoRoles"].Value );

  // Create an array of strings from the ticket.
  ArrayList objRoles = new ArrayList();
  foreach( string role in ticket.UserData.Split( ';' ) )
  {
    objRoles.Add( role );
  }

  // Convert the ArrayList to a string array.
  roles = new string [objRoles.Count];
  for( int i=0; i<objRoles.Count; i++ )
```

```
  {
    roles[i] = (string) objRoles[i];
  }
}

// Store the roles in the context.
Context.User = new GenericPrincipal( Context.User.Identity, roles );

}
```

VB
```
Sub Application_AuthenticateRequest(ByVal sender As Object, _
  ByVal e As EventArgs)

    ' Bail out if we're not authenticated yet.
    If Request.IsAuthenticated = False Then
        Return
    End If

    Dim roles As String()

    ' See if the cookie can be loaded, if not
    '   do this code.
    If Request.Cookies("DemoRoles") Is Nothing Then

        ' Here we're going to add some hard-coded roles.
        If Context.User.Identity.Name = "CHUCK" Then
            roles = New String() {"User", "Loser", "Schmoozer"}
        ElseIf Context.User.Identity.Name = "CHIP" Then
            roles = New String() {"Auditor", "Manager", "Admin"}
        Else
            roles = New String() {"General", "User", "Buyer"}
        End If

        ' Put the roles into one string for the cookie.
        Dim strRoles As String = ""
        Dim i As Integer
        For i = 0 To roles.Length - 1
            strRoles += (roles(i) + ";")
        Next

        ' Create a cookie authentication ticket.
        Dim ticket As FormsAuthenticationTicket = _
```

```
            New FormsAuthenticationTicket(1, _
            Context.User.Identity.Name, DateTime.Now, _
            DateTime.Now.AddHours(1), False, strRoles)

            ' Encrypt the ticket.
            Dim strCookie As String = FormsAuthentication.Encrypt(ticket)

            ' Send the cookie to the client.
            Response.Cookies("DemoRoles").Value = strCookie
            Response.Cookies("DemoRoles").Path = "/"
            Response.Cookies("DemoRoles").Expires = _
                    DateTime.Now.AddMinutes(10)

        Else
            ' We came here when we were able to
            '    load the cookie.

            ' Create the Forms authentication ticket
            '    and decrypt it.
            Dim ticket As FormsAuthenticationTicket = _
             FormsAuthentication.Decrypt( _
             Context.Request.Cookies("DemoRoles").Value)

            ' Create an array of strings from the ticket.
            Dim objRoles As New ArrayList()
            Dim role As String
            For Each role In ticket.UserData.Split(New Char() {";"c})
                objRoles.Add(role)
            Next role

            ' Convert the ArrayList to a string array.
            roles = CType(objRoles.ToArray(GetType(String)), String())
        End If

        ' Store the roles in the context.
        Context.User = New GenericPrincipal(Context.User.Identity, roles)

End Sub
```

The last thing I did in the application was to check the roles that the user types in. Once the roles have been stored into the Context, it's a simple matter of using the HttpContext.Current.User.IsIn-

`Role()` method to see whether a user is in a given role. The following code shows how you might use this method:

C#

```
if(HttpContext.Current.User.IsInRole(RoleToTest.Text.Trim().ToU
pper()) )
{
  // User is OK for this role.
}
else
{
  // User is not authorized for this role.
}
```

VB

```
If
HttpContext.Current.User.IsInRole(RoleToTest.Text.Trim().ToUppe
r()) Then
  ' User is OK for this role.
Else
  ' User is not authorized for this role.
End If
```

TIP: Whenever a user tries to log in, if she hits enter, instead of clicking the Login button, nothing happens. The page reloads and the user is not logged in. To fix this, do the following:

1. Add the following script code to the <head> section of the aspx page.

```
<SCRIPT LANGUAGE="javascript">
function testEnterKey()
{
  if (event.keyCode == 13)
  {
    event.cancelBubble = true;
    event.returnValue = false;
    Form1.Button2.click();
  }
}
</SCRIPT>
```

2. In the code-behind page, add the `onkeypress` event handler to the `attributes` collections of the TextBox(es) on the page:

```
private void Page_Load(object sender, System.EventArgs e)
{
    //other initialization code
    TextBox1.Attributes.Add("onkeypress", "testEnterKey();");
    TextBox2.Attributes.Add("onkeypress", "testEnterKey();");
    ......
}
```

Dynamically Loaded User Controls

As I've already mentioned, there are 11 user controls that comprise the content which appears in the portal's main screen (see Table 18.1 for a list of these). A class named `ModuleSettings` determines the .ascx file that is associated with the selected tab. When a tab is clicked, the PortalSettings object is examined. The PortalSettings object has a property named `ActiveTab` that contains a collection of ModuleSettings objects. These ModuleSettings objects determine the user control that is associated with the selected tab, and therefore they should be displayed in the application's main window area. The following summary shows the sequence to determine which user controls will be used:

1. The PortalSettings object is retrieved from the `Context` (see the section above entitled "Portal Settings" for more information about the PortalSettings object that is saved to the `Context`).

2. Make sure the user is authorized for the role in which the active tab belongs (see the section above entitled "Security" for more information about roles).

3. If the user is not authenticated, load and insert the `SignIn` user control.

4. Iterate through the collection of `ModuleSettings` for the `ActiveTab` property.

5. For each ModuleSettings object, inject the user control into the appropriate table object.

Loading a user control is done with the `Page.LoadControl()` method. This method takes a single string containing the user control's source file name and returns a loaded user control. The following shows how to load a user control named `MyControl.ascx`:

C#
```
Control objMyControl = Page.LoadControl( "MyControl.ascx" );
```

VB
```
Dim objMyControl As Control = Page.LoadControl("MyControl.ascx")
```

The next thing that must happen, before the control gets served to the client, is that it must be added to a user interface object. The IBuySpy portal adds loaded user controls to the appropriate table pane from the DesktopDefault.aspx page (or MobileDefault.aspx page). The table pane is found by using the `Page.FindControl()` method. The following shows how to find a control on the page named MyPane:

C#
```
Control objMyPane = Page.FindControl( "MyPane" );
```

VB
```
Dim objMyPane As Control = Page.FindControl("MyPane")
```

The final thing is to add the loaded user control to the found user-interface control. The following adds the loaded control named `objMyControl` to the found control named `objMyPane`:

C#
```
objMyPane.Add( objMyControl );
```

VB
```
objMyPane.Add(objMyControl)
```

Administering the Portal

The IBuySpy Portal has an administrative page. It allows users who belong to the `Admins` role to administer the application in several ways. Figure 18.6 shows the administrative page.

There are two items in the Site Settings section. The first is the Site Title, which is a simple editable field that allows the title of the site to be edited. The second item in this section is a check box that determines whether the edit buttons appear for the module content. If this box is checked, then a user who is in the `Admins` role can edit a lot of the information that appears in the portal modules.

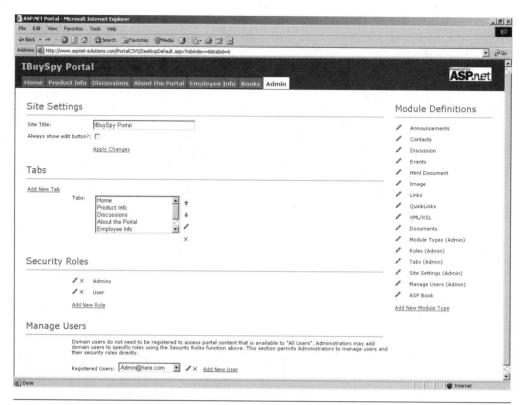

Figure 18.6 The IBuySpy Portal Administration Page

The second section is entitled Tabs, and it allows you to add and edit tabs. We'll talk more about adding tabs in the section that comes later in the chapter entitled "Enhancing and Extending the Portal."

The Security Roles section allows new security roles to be added and existing roles to be edited or deleted. All of the roles in the database are listed. To delete a role, you simply click the X icon to the left of the role you want to delete. To edit a role, you just click the pencil icon to the left of the role you want to edit.

The Manage Users section allows you to delete, edit, or add users. A drop-down list contains all of the users found in the database.

The Module Definitions section lists all of the modules that can be found in the database. To the left of each module can be X and pencil icons (depending on the security role of the administrator—the X icon may not appear). To delete a module definition, simply click the X icon. To edit a module definition, just click the pencil icon.

Effective Use of Style Sheets

Cascading style sheets (CSS) are a simple way to add consistent styling to your Web applications. Information such as font face, page background, and text size can all be stored in one central location. Even larger than your Web application, one style sheet can be applied to your whole Web site. This is a powerful tool! Without style sheets, changing the design of your Web site could forseeably require hundreds of page edits. Mastering cascading style sheets will save you time and add another tool to your arsenal of Web development skills.

Style sheets can be linked to any page by simply adding one line of code in the `<head>` section of the HTML:

```
<link href='http://www.mysite.com/MyCSS.css' rel="stylesheet"
    type="text/css">
```

This will render the HTML according to the styles stated in the CSS file.

Visual Studio .NET's Support for Style Sheets

Visual Studio .NET includes a nice interface to design your own style sheets with little or no knowledge of CSS syntax. To add a style sheet to your ASP.NET project, right-click your solution in the Solution Explorer. Select

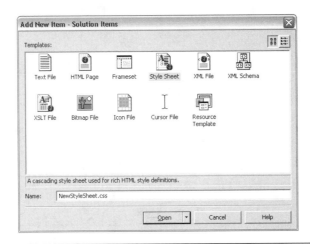

Figure 18.7 Select Style Sheet and Type in a Name for Your New File.

Add/Add New Item. In the list of available items, select Style Sheet. In the space provided, type a file name, as demonstrated in Figure 18.7.

Visual Studio .NET will open the new Style Sheet and insert a BODY tag, as shown in Figure 18.8. This is where general document design will be specified. This includes page attributes such as background, borders, font face, and size.

From this point, you can put Visual Studio .NET in the driver's seat. In the CSS Outline pane, expand the Elements folder. Right-click BODY and select Build Style.

This opens the Style Builder and allows you to visually design your style sheet. You can select from multiple categories including font, background, and bullet styles.

Visual Studio .NET will write out the correct CSS code into the appropriate Element (in this case, BODY), as you can see in Figure 18.9.

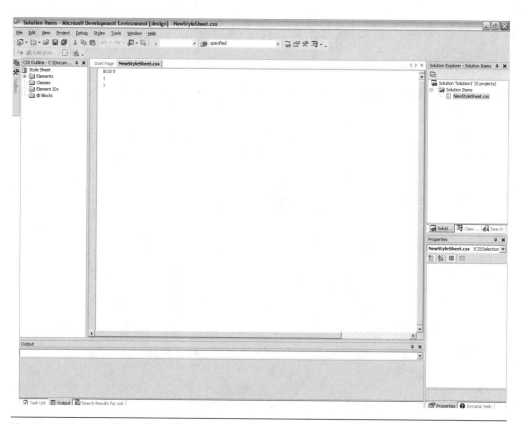

Figure 18.8 Visual Studio .NET Opens the New File and Inserts a BODY Tag.

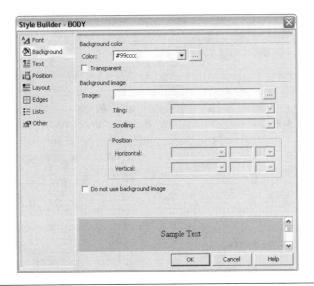

Figure 18.9 Using the Style Builder, You Can Visually Edit Your Style Sheet.

Other features such as link styles are available by right-clicking the Elements folder and selecting Add Style Rule. In the Add Style Rule window, you can add one or more Element or even custom classes.

For instance, adding Element A:Hover will allow you to change to the color and font styles of a link when the mouse pointer hovers over it.

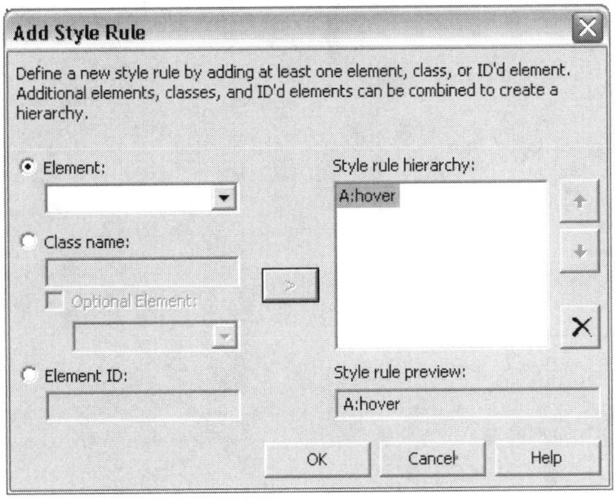

Figure 18.10 Adding a New Element to the Style Sheet

You edit new `Elements` in the same way you edited the `BODY` tag. Right-click its entry in the Elements folder in the CSS Outline pane and select Build Style. This is shown in Figure 18.10.

NOTE: Visual Studio .NET provides a quick jumpstart to style sheet creation. You may wish to use CSS features that Visual Studio .NET doesn't automate. Using the code window, you can easily write your own CSS code.

For more information on cascading style sheets, visit http://www.w3.org/Style/CSS. A good book that you might consider using is Danny Goodman's *Dynamic HTML: The Definitive Reference* (O'Reilly, 1998).

In the sample application seen in Figure 18.11, I show an example of how you can expand on the concept of style sheets by offering multiple style sheets to users.

The application consists of a form (default.aspx) with a drop-down box containing six styles. The `autopostback` attribute is set to `true`, causing the page to reload automatically upon user selection.

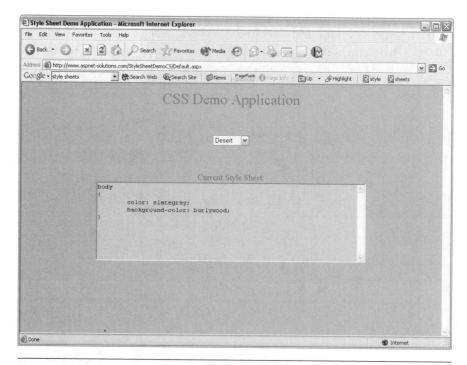

Figure 18.11 CSS Demo Application

Six simple style sheets that manipulate background and text color are located in the root directory. These include StyleSheet1.css, StyleSheet2.css, StyleSheet3.css, and so on.

In the default.aspx source, the selected style sheet is written into the HTML:

C#

```
<link href='<%Response.Write(Session["CurrentStyle"].ToString());%>'
  rel="stylesheet" type="text/css">
```

VB

```
<link href='<%Response.Write(Session("CurrentStyle").ToString())%>'
  rel="stylesheet" type="text/css">
```

The selected style sheet is stored in the session variable `"Current Style"`. `Response.Write()` writes out the selected style sheet name to the HTML.

In the code behind, the work is done in the `Page_Load()` method:

C#

```
Session["CurrentStyle"] = "StyleSheet" + StyleList.SelectedValue +
  ".css";
```

VB

```
Session("CurrentStyle") = "StyleSheet" + StyleList.SelectedValue + _
  ".css";
```

Here we create a session variable and insert the selected style sheet URL into it. The code will work fine at this point. We have the user selection stored in a session variable and the appropriate code to attach it to the display code.

The remaining code deals solely with viewing the current style sheet code:

C#

```
string strFilePath = Request.MapPath( ".\\" +
  Session["CurrentStyle"].ToString() );

StreamReader objReader = File.OpenText( strFilePath );
CurrentStyle.Text = objReader.ReadToEnd();
objReader.Close();
```

VB

```
Dim strFilepath As String = Request.MapPath( ".\" + _
  Session("CurrentStyle").ToString() )

Dim objReader As StreamReader = File.OpenText( strFilePath )
CurrentStyle.Text = objReader.ReadToEnd()
objReader.Close()
```

In short, the selected style sheet's contents is read and displayed in the Text Box "CurrentStyle".

Although relatively simple, this concept can easily be expanded upon. For example, one of my classes wrote an Online Training application. We allowed users to select from several different styles. Their selection was saved in a cookie.

Enhancing and Extending the Portal

The easiest way to change the appearance is to edit the application's style sheet, contained in a file named portal.css. By editing this file, you can easily adjust the background color, font style and size, the appearance of the tabs, and many other things. For more information about Visual Studio .NET's style-sheet-editing functionality, see the previous section entitled "Effective Use of Style Sheets."

TIP: You can add mouse-over images (which allow the mouse-over image to change easily) by editing the portal.css file, as follows:

```
a.link2:link
{
  background-image: url(button1.gif);
  height: 25px;
  width: 100px;
  text-align: center;
}

a.link2:hover
{
  background-image: url(button2.gif);
  height: 25px;
  width: 100px;
  text-align: center;
}
```

Now all you need to do is call it like this: `<a class="link2"> Button</a>`

You could also edit many images to change the appearance of the application. They can be found in the Data directory within the application's directory.

Extending the portal involves adding additional modules, and then using the administrative functionality to add the modules into the portal settings. I've added a module to the IBuySpy Portal application that's on www.ASPNET-Solutions.com. The one that I added is simple and has no databound components. It avoids the complication of data access.

Here's a summary of the steps I took to add a desktop tab with its own module:

1. Add a User Control to the project.
2. Edit its code behind so that it inherits from `PortalModuleControl`.
3. Move the .ascx file into the DesktopModules directory.
4. Add content to the .ascx file.
5. With the IBuySpy Portal administration page, add a module.
6. With the IBuySpy Portal administration page, add a tab.
7. Compile the application, and test.

Adding a User Control is simple. In the Solution Explorer pane, right-click the project name and select Add New Item. Select User Control as the item type, and enter the name (for the one I added, I named it ASPBook.ascx).

You need to edit the code behind so that the control inherits from `PortalModuleControl` instead of `System.Web.UI.UserControl` (the default when controls are created). Note that `PortalModuleControl` itself inherits from `System.Web.UI.UserControl`.

Change from:

```
public abstract class ASPBook : System.Web.UI.UserControl
{

  private void Page_Load(object sender, System.EventArgs e)
  {
    // Put user code to initialize the page here
  }


}
```

to:

```
public abstract class ASPBook : ASPNetPortal.PortalModuleControl
{

  private void Page_Load(object sender, System.EventArgs e)
  {
    // Put user code to initialize the page here
  }

}
```

You'll have to add content to the .ascx file so that it has the content and functionality that you need. For the one I added, I just pasted in some text and an image link.

You'll have to add the module definition from the IBuySpy admin page. (Well, you don't really have to, but it sure saves a lot of extra effort on your

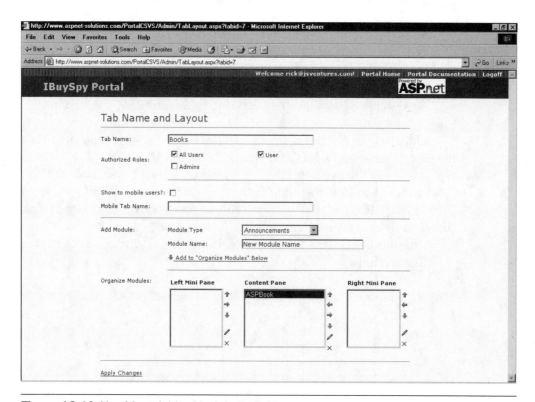

Figure 18.12 You Must Add a Module Definition.

part.) It's pretty simple; just add the module name, the desktop source-file name, and the mobile source-file name, as shown in Figure 18.12.

Now that the module has been added, a tab must be added. Here again, you could do it manually by adding entries to the database tables, but it's a lot easier to use the admin page in the application, as shown in Figure 18.13.

It's important that you compile the application before trying to see your newly created control. If you don't compile, you'll get a runtime error because it won't be able to find the user control.

NOTE: When you first compile the application, it may not compile because it can't find the System.Mobile assembly. This happened to me, and to fix it I had to add the reference from the Solution Explorer.

To do this in Visual Studio .NET, right-click Reference in the Solution Explorer window. Select System.Mobile from the .NET Components list, and add it.

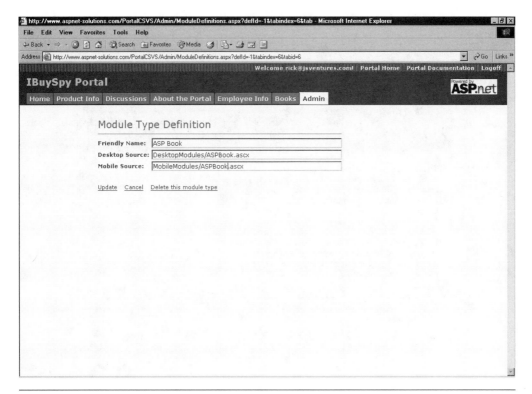

Figure 18.13 You Must Add the Module to a New Tab.

The tab and module that I added aren't too fancy, but they give you the steps necessary to add a new section to the portal. Figure 18.14 shows my new user control.

TIP: By default in IBuySpy Portals, if you create a new page of content, it is treated as a tab. Sometimes, though, you want to have many pages of content but not clutter up the top navigation with lots of tabbed menu buttons. There is a solution for this.

Specify the name of tabs (in the TabName property) that you don't want to appear in the top navigation bar by preceding the tab name with an underscore (_) character.

In the file DesktopPortalBanner.ascx.cs (or DesktopPortalBanner.ascx. vb for VB), find the section of code toward the bottom commented as `"Dynamically render portal tab strip"`. Here, you can modify the line that adds the tab to the collection with the following:

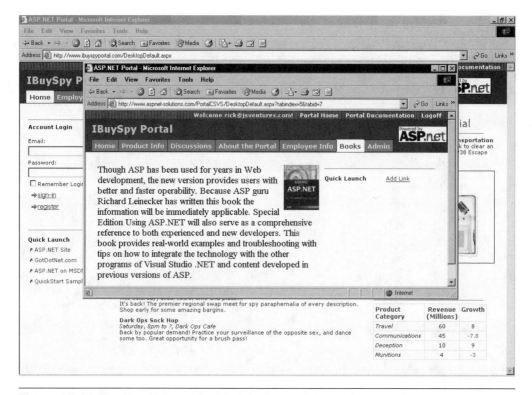

Figure 18.14 The New Tab and Its Module Simply Display Static Text.

C#
```
if( tab.TabName[0] == '_' )
{
  authorizedTabs.Add( tab );
}
```

VB
```
If tab.TabName[0] = '_' Then
  authorizedTabs.Add(tab)
```

Summary

Although the IBuySpy Portal application is fairly simple, it makes use of ASP.NET's great features. And because of this, the plumbing that holds the program together wasn't on the developers' shoulders because it's baked into the .NET Framework.

In this chapter, you've learned about the portal's architecture. You've also learned about how the tabs work and how they maintain the organization of the program. You learned about style sheets, and how to add your own tabs and modules.

There are several downloadable projects from www.ASPNET-solutions. com that illustrate many of the things we talked about and you learned. These will help you fully understand the IBuySpy Portal, and I encourage you to download them. A white paper on the portal is available at http://www.asp.net/ibuyspy/portalpaper.aspx?tabindex=5.

CHAPTER 19

Editing HTML: Creating an HTML Editing Server Control

In This Chapter:

- Editing HTML with a Web Browser
- Implementing an HTML Editor as a Server Control
- Using the HTML Editor Server Control

This chapter teaches how to implement a client-side HTML editor. Maybe you have seen the editor Yahoo uses for its e-mail, or you've seen one elsewhere, and wondered how they did that. The sample HTML editor in this chapter is implemented as a custom server control so that it can be easily used in any application.

NOTE: The development of a client-side Web browser involves the use of client-side scripting. This chapter assumes that the reader has at least minimal knowledge of client-side scripting and the client-side object model.

Editing HTML with a Web Browser

Writing an editor of any type can seem a daunting task. Writing an editor using JavaScript can seem almost impossible. Thinking of all the things necessary for even a simple editor, not to mention an HTML editor, and then thinking of the limitations of JavaScript, and your next thought might be that it couldn't possibly be worth the work to implement an editor, if it is even possible. Fortunately, HTML editing functionality is built into Microsoft Internet Explorer (IE) starting with version 5.5. This makes it easy to implement client-side HTML editing functionality. Mozilla has recently added this functionality.

Using the `contentEditable` Attribute

Since IE 5.5, the `contentEditable` attribute has been added to many of the HTML tags. By setting this attribute to `true` and hooking up a user interface, you can quickly implement an HTML editor. In this chapter, we will be using only the `<div>` tag to create an HTML editor. This is primarily for convenience, because this functionality can be implemented in a number of different tags.

The following HTML is a minimal implementation of an editor. The style settings make the editor border visible and set the size.

```
<html>
<body>
    <div name="editor" contentEditable="true" style="BORDER: 1px solid;
WIDTH: 400px; HEIGHT: 300px" ></div>
</body>
</html>
```

Now you have an HTML editor. It doesn't really look like one, but this is because we have not yet implemented a user interface. Let's examine what our editor can do without any user interface. The first thing you will probably notice is that many of the keyboard shortcuts that you are used to using in programs such as Microsoft Word work as you would expect them to. Ctrl+B toggles Bold, Ctrl+I toggles Italics, and Ctrl +U toggles Underline. Other shortcuts, such as Ctrl+Z for Undo, Ctrl+Y for Redo, Ctrl+C for Copy, Ctrl+X for Cut, and Ctrl+V for Paste, also work.

Next, let's see what the Copy and Paste operations can do. Open up Microsoft Excel, if you have it, and make a small table. Do a little formatting to make it look nice, select all the cells you have entered, and then copy and paste it into your editor. Figure 19.1 shows an example of what you end up with.

As you can see, all the formatting in Excel is converted into HTML for you. This works for most of Microsoft's other products, too. The way it works is this: The application exports data to the clipboard; one of the formats that is available is CF_HTML; and anything that exports and has CF_HTML as an available format will work. So even without a user interface, you can do quite a bit with the editor just by formatting the document in another application and copying and pasting it into your editor. You can even copy and paste portions of other Web pages into the editor. All the formatting and images will be transferred to your editor.

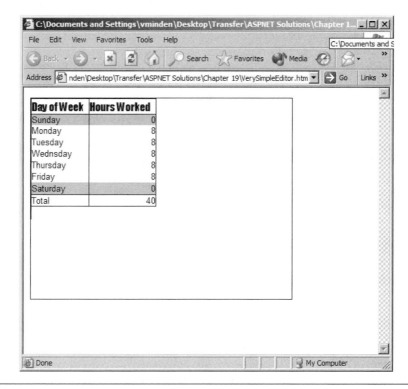

Figure 19.1 Example of Using Copy and Paste with the HTML Editor

The `execCommand()` Method

The next step is to hook up a user interface. This is primarily done by calls to the `execCommand()` method of the IE's document object. The JavaScript code to toggle Bold looks like this.

```
editor.focus();
editor.document.execCommand("Bold");
```

For this to be useful, it needs to be called from the `onClick` event of an object such as a button. Listing 19.1 contains the code for a simple editor with buttons to set the text justification.

Listing 19.1 HTML Editor with Text Justification

```
<html>
  <body>
    <div style="BORDER: 1px solid; WIDTH: 400px; HEIGHT: 25px"
```

```
    align="center">
    <input type="button" value="Left Justify" name="JustifyLeft"
      onclick="return EditorCommand('JustifyLeft')">
    <input type="button" value="Center" name="JustifyCenter"
      onclick="EditorCommand('JustifyCenter')">
    <input type="button" value="Right Justify" name="JustifyRight"
      onclick="EditorCommand('JustifyRight')">
  </div>
  <div style="BORDER: 1px solid; WIDTH: 400px; HEIGHT: 200px"
    contenteditable="true" name="EditorDiv" id="EditorDiv">
  </div>
    <script language="javascript">
    function EditorCommand(command)
    {
        EditorDiv.focus();
        EditorDiv.document.execCommand(command,false,null);
        return false;
    }
    </script>
  </body>
</html>
```

To make things easy, I wrote a function that took the command to be passed to the execCommand() method as a parameter, and then I made the necessary function calls. If you don't set the focus to the editor <div> tag, the call to the execCommand() method will work only if you have highlighted text. No effect occurs if no text is selected.

The format of the execCommand() is as follows:

```
bSuccess = object.execCommand(sCommand [, bUserInterface] [, vValue])
```

The parameters have the following meanings:

Parameter	Meaning
sCommand	String containing the command identifier.
bUserInterface	Boolean value specifying if there is a user interface or not
vValue	Variant containing a value to be used with the commands that need a value.
bSuccess	Boolean return value that is true if the command succeeded.

Table 19.1 Command Identifiers for the `execCommand()` Method.

Command Identifier	Description	bUserInterface	vValue
2D-Position	Allows absolutely positioned elements to be moved by dragging.	None; set to `false`.	Required. Boolean value specifying whether this feature is to be on or off.
AbsolutePosition	Sets an element's position property to `"absolute"`.	None; set to `false`.	Required. Boolean value specifying whether the element is to be absolutely positioned.
BackColor	Sets or retrieves the background color of the current selection.	None; set to `false`.	Required. String that specifies a color name or a six-digit hexadecimal RGB value, with or without a leading hash mark.
Bold	Toggles the current selection between bold and nonbold.	None; set to `false`.	Optional. Set to `null` or omit.
Copy	Copies the current selection to the clipboard.	None; set to `false`.	Optional. Set to `null` or omit.
CreateBookmark	Creates a bookmark anchor or retrieves the name of a bookmark anchor for the current selection or insertion point.	None; set to `false`.	Required. String that specifies a valid anchor name. Providing an empty string will cause the command to fail.
CreateLink	Inserts a hyperlink on the current selection, or displays a dialog box enabling the user to specify a URL to insert as a hyperlink on the current selection.	Optional. Displays a dialog box if `true` or omitted. Dialog box is not displayed if `false` or `null` and the Value parameter is present.	Optional. String that specifies a URL.

(continued)

Table Excerpted from MSDN and Is Copyrighted by Microsoft, 2002.

Table 19.1 Command Identifiers for the execCommand() Method. (*cont.*)

Command Identifier	Description	bUserInterface	vValue
Cut	Copies the current selection to the clipboard and then deletes it.	None; set to false.	Optional. Set to null or omit.
Delete	Deletes the current selection.	None; set to false.	Optional. Set to null or omit.
FontName	Sets or retrieves the font for the current selection.	None; set to false.	Required. String that specifies a font name or font list.
FontSize	Sets or retrieves the font size for the current selection.	None; set to false.	Required. Integer or string that specifies the font size. This must be a value between 1 and 7, inclusive.
ForeColor	Sets or retrieves the foreground (text) color of the current selection.	None; set to false.	Required. String that specifies a color name or a six-digit hexadecimal RGB value, with or without a leading hash mark.
FormatBlock	Sets the current block format tag.	None; set to false.	Required. String that specifies a valid block format tag.
Indent	Increases the indent of the selected text by one indentation increment.	None; set to false.	Optional. Set to null or omit.
Insert-HorizontalRule	Overwrites a horizontal line on the text selection.	None; set to false.	Optional. String that specifies an **id** attribute for the horizontal line. May be set to null or omitted.

`InsertImage`	Overwrites an image on the text selection.	Optional. String that specifies the path and file name of the image to be inserted. If the command displays a dialog box, this parameter is ignored.
	Optional. This command displays a dialog box if the `bUserInterface` argument of `execCommand` is set to `true` or omitted. It does not display a dialog box if the argument is set to `false` or `null` and the `vValue` parameter is present (even if it's `null`).	
`InsertOrdered-List-`	Toggles the text selection between an ordered list and a normal format block.	Optional. String that specifies an `id` attribute for the ordered list. May be set to `null` or omitted.
	None; set to `false`.	
`InsertParagraph`	Overwrites a line break on the text selection.	Optional. String that specifies an `id` attribute for the paragraph. May be set to `null` or omitted.
	None; set to `false`.	
`InsertUnordered-List`	Toggles the text selection between an ordered list and a normal format block.	Optional. String that specifies an `id` attribute for the unordered list. May be set to `null` or omitted.
	None; set to `false`.	
`Italic`	Toggles the current selection between italic and nonitalic.	Optional. Set to `null` or omit.
	None; set to `false`.	
`JustifyCenter`	Centers the format block in which the current selection is located.	Optional. Set to `null` or omit.
	None; set to `false`.	

(continued)

Table 19.1 Command Identifiers for the `execCommand()` Method. *(cont.)*

Command Identifier	Description	bUserInterface	vValue
`JustifyLeft`	Left-justifies the format block in which the current selection is located.	None; set to `false`.	Optional. Set to `null` or omit.
`JustifyRight`	Right-justifies the format block in which the current selection is located.	None; set to `false`.	Optional. Set to `null` or omit.
`Outdent`	Decreases by one increment the indentation of the format block in which the current selection is located.	None; set to `false`.	Optional. Set to `null` or omit.
`OverWrite`	Toggles the text-entry mode between insert and overwrite.	None; set to `false`.	Optional. Boolean value that specifies the text-entry mode. If this value is set to `true` or `null`, the text-entry mode is overwrite. If this value is set to `false` (the default), the text-entry mode is insert.
`Paste`	Overwrites the contents of the clipboard on the current selection.	None; set to `false`.	Optional. Set to `null` or omit.
`Print`	Opens the print dialog box so the user can print the current page.	Yes. Set to `true` or omit.	Optional. Set to `null` or omit.
`Redo`	Redo last undo.	None; set to `false`.	Optional. Set to `null` or omit.
`Refresh`	Refreshes the current document.	None; set to `false`.	Optional. Set to `null` or omit.

`RemoveFormat`	Removes the formatting tags from the current selection.	None; set to `false`.	Optional. Set to `null` or omit.
`SelectAll`	Selects the entire document.	None; set to `false`.	Optional. Set to `null` or omit.
`StrikeThrough`	Toggles the current selection between strikethrough and nonstrikethrough.	None; set to `false`.	Optional. Set to `null` or omit.
`Subscript`	Toggles the current selection between subscript and nonsubscript.	None; set to `false`.	Optional. Set to `null` or omit.
`Superscript`	Toggles the current selection between superscript and nonsuperscript.	None; set to `false`.	Optional. Set to `null` or omit.
`UnBookmark`	Removes any bookmark from the current selection.	None; set to `false`.	Optional. Set to `null` or omit.
`Underline`	Toggles the current selection between underlined and not underlined.	None; set to `false`.	Optional. Set to `null` or omit.
`Undo`	Undo last change.	None; set to `false`.	Optional. Set to `null` or omit.
`Unlink`	Removes any hyperlink from the current selection.	None; set to `false`.	Optional. Set to `null` or omit.
`Unselect`	Clears the current selection.	None; set to `false`.	Optional. Set to `null` or omit.

Table 19.1 is a partial list of the possible command identifiers listing the most useful commands. To see a complete list of all command identifiers, look up the execCommand() method in MSDN.

Implementing an HTML Editor as a Server Control

Now that we've spent a time delving into an obscure portion of IE's Document Object Model (DOM), how does this apply to ASP.NET? Part of the power of ASP.NET is the ability to encapsulate a combination of client-side code and server-side code into a server control that is treated as a single logical unit. This unit can then be easily reused without rewriting the code every time we need that functionality. The rest of this chapter will show how to implement our HTML editor as a custom server control, and then how to use it. The basics of implementing custom server controls was introduced in Chapter 15. If you do not have any familiarity with custom server controls, you should read the portions of Chapter 15 that introduce custom server controls before you read the rest of this chapter.

Control Design

Before writing the custom control, we need to specify what we want the control to do and how we want to interact with it. Here is a list of characteristics that I thought the control should have in addition to supporting our basic task of implementing a client-side HTML editor:

- The control should be able to be used with any method of data storage.
- The control should be able to be sized using Visual Studio .NET's visual designer.
- The look of the control should be controlled using a style sheet.
- Multiple controls should be able to be placed on a single page without interfering with each other.
- The control should be simple to use.

That is the basics of what we want the control to do, so now let's examine these points in a little more detail.

Data Storage

Designing the control so it can be used with any method of data storage is easy. You don't implement data storage in the control. Rather than having the control store data, the control can fire an event when a button is pressed indicating that the person editing data with the control is done and that the data should be saved. You could then either write the code to handle the data storage in the page hosting the control, or write other controls that inherit from this control and specialize the storage method. In this chapter, we will write the control with no data-storing capability and then show how to store data from the page hosting the control.

Using the Control with Visual Studio .NET

The simplest way to get our control to look decent in Visual Studio .NET is to use one of the existing Web controls as a base class. This gives us the functionality of that base class as a starting point, to which we can add additional functionality as necessary. I prefer the simplicity of Panel controls, so we will use that as our base class.

Using Style Sheets

The Panel control that we are using as our base class already exposes a property called `CssClass`. However, our control will have nested Panel controls to give the functionality we want, so we will expose properties to set the `CssClass` properties of the nested controls for additional flexibility. In our control, we will expose the `MenuCssClass` and `EditorCss-Class` properties for this purpose.

Multiple Controls on a Page

The biggest concern with multiple controls on a given page is naming conflicts. The naming conflicts of any controls contained within our control can be overcome by having our control inherit from the `INamingContainer` interface. This is a marker interface that indicates to the compiler that the names of any contained controls should be concatenated with the name of our control to ensure uniqueness.

Simplicity

Simplicity is ensured by limiting the functionality of our control. Adding extra features may increase the usability, but features that are added to allow the control to be used only in certain unique circumstances should be avoided. Those types of features should be added by inheriting from the control that we have already created to form a specialized control, not by trying to add them into the base control. The class handles the common needs. Any niche concerns can be handled by extending the class through inheritance or aggregation.

Control Implementation

Now that we know the details of how an editor can be implemented on the client side in HTML, and we've defined the characteristics we want in the server control, it is time to get into the details of implementing the actual control.

Public Interface

The first thing you should do is to define the public interface. The public interface consists of the public methods, properties, and events that the end user of the control will see. Because we are trying to keep this control simple, our public interface will also be simple. Table 19.2 shows the details of the public interface.

Table 19.2 Public Interface

Name	Type	Description
Text	Property	This property contains the HTML being edited. This should be set with the HTML that is to be edited when the control is initialized. The updated HTML can be retrieved from this control after the Update event is fired.
MenuCssClass	Property	This property contains the name of the css class that will be used to format the menu portion of the control. This includes both the Panel for the toolbar and the Panel for the Update/Cancel buttons.
EditorCssClass	Property	This property contains the name of the css class that will be used to format the editor portion of the control.
Update	Event	This event is fired when the Update button is pushed. The Text property will contain the changed HTML data.
Cancel	Event	This event is fired when the Cancel button is pushed. The Text property will contain the unchanged HTML data.

Table 19.3 Private Helper Methods

Method	Description
CreateLiteral()	This method returns a LiteralControl created from the string passed into the method.
CreatePanel()	This method returns a Panel control. The values for the ID and CssClass properties are passed as arguments.
CreateButton()	This method returns a Button control. The values for the ID, Text, and CausesValidation properties are passed as arguments. This method is used to create the Update and Cancel buttons.
CreateImageButton()	This method returns an ImageButton control. The values for the ID, ImageUrl and ToolTip properties are passed as arguments. The value for the client-side OnClick event is also passed in as an argument. This method is used to create the image buttons on the HTML editor toolbar.
CreateList()	This method returns a DropDownList control. The value for the ID property is passed as an argument. Additionally, an array of names and an array of values are passed that are used to create the list items. Finally, the value for the client-side OnChange event is passed. This method is used to create the drop-down lists in the editor menu.

Table 19.4 Control Creation Methods

Method	Description
CreateChildControls()	The overridden method inherited from the base class that is called to create all of the child controls of our custom control.
CreateScripts()	This method creates the necessary JavaScript for the client-side scripting and adds it to the Controls collection as a LiteralControl.
CreateMenu()	This method creates a nested Panel control and adds all the toolbar buttons to this control.
CreateEditBody()	This method creates an editable Panel control that is used for the actual editing of HTML.
CreateMenu2()	This method creates a nested Panel control that contains the Update and Cancel buttons.

Table 19.5 Event Handlers

Method	Description
OnUpdate_Click	This method is called when the Update button is pressed. It stores the edited HTML and then fires the Update event.
OnCancel_Click	This method is called when the Cancel button is pressed. It fires the Cancel event without storing any changed HTML.

For this control, I wrote some private helper methods to reduce redundancy in the coding. These helper methods are shown in Table 19.3.

The actual work of creating the control is done in the overridden CreateChildControls() method. To reduce complexity, this method calls a number of other private methods that each creates a portion of the control. Table 19.4 shows the methods that are used to create the control.

The final methods in this control are the event handlers for the Update and Cancel buttons. These methods are shown in Table 19.5.

In addition to event handlers, our control exposes two events to be used by pages or controls that host our control. Table 19.6 shows the events that are exposed by our control.

The most difficult problem while writing this control was how to get the edited HTML back to the server. The HTML tag that is used as the HTML editor is a <div> tag. Because a <div> tag is a display type tag and not an input type tag, the data in the <div> tag is not automatically sent back to the server. I overcame this problem by placing a hidden input tag on the page, and copying the data from the innerHtml property of the <div> tag to the value property of the hidden input tag. This created a second problem because now I needed to have the Update button run some client-

Table 19.6 Exposed Events

Event	Description
Update	This event is fired after the Update button is pressed. The handler for this event can obtain the modified HTML through the Text property. This event should be handled to store the modified HTML.
Cancel	This event is fired after the Cancel button is pressed. The HTML obtained through the Text property after this event is fired is the original unchanged HTML.

side script and do a post back to the server. The solution to this second problem was to use a CustomValidator control. If a validator control is not attached to a particular input control, it is called when the form is submitted. The CustomValidator was set to call the client-side script necessary to copy the edited HTML into the hidden input tag.

Listing 19.2 is the complete source of the custom control implementing our client-side HTML editor.

Listing 19.2 HTML Editor Server Control—HTML_Editor.VB

```
Imports System.ComponentModel
Imports System.Web.UI
Imports System.Web.UI.WebControls
Imports System.Web.UI.HtmlControls

<DefaultProperty("Text"), ToolboxData _
    ("<{0}:HTML_EditorVB runat=server></{0}:HTML_EditorVB>")> _
Public Class HTML_EditorVB
    Inherits System.Web.UI.WebControls.Panel
    Implements INamingContainer

    Event Update(ByVal sender As Object, ByVal e As EventArgs)
    Event Cancel(ByVal sender As Object, ByVal e As EventArgs)

    Private m_objMenu As Panel
    Private m_objEditor As Panel
    Private m_objMenu2 As Panel
    Private m_objHidden As HtmlInputHidden

    ' Properties
    <Bindable(True), Category("Appearance"), DefaultValue("")> _
    Property [Text]() As String
        Get
            If IsNothing(ViewState.Item("Text")) Then
                ViewState.Item("Text") = ""
            End If

            Return ViewState.Item("Text")
        End Get

        Set(ByVal Value As String)
            ViewState.Item("Text") = Value
```

```vbnet
        End Set
    End Property

    <Bindable(True), Category("Appearance"), DefaultValue("")> _
    Property [MenuCssClass]() As String
        Get
            If IsNothing(ViewState.Item("MenuCssClass")) Then
                ViewState.Item("MenuCssClass") = ""
            End If

            Return ViewState.Item("MenuCssClass")
        End Get

        Set(ByVal Value As String)
            ViewState.Item("MenuCssClass") = Value
        End Set
    End Property

    <Bindable(True), Category("Appearance"), DefaultValue("")> _
    Property [EditorCssClass]() As String
        Get
            If IsNothing(ViewState.Item("EditorCssClass")) Then
                ViewState.Item("EditorCssClass") = ""
            End If

            Return ViewState.Item("EditorCssClass")
        End Get

        Set(ByVal Value As String)
            ViewState.Item("EditorCssClass") = Value
        End Set
    End Property

    ' Methods
    Protected Overrides Sub CreateChildControls()
        CreateScripts()
        CreateMenu()
        CreateEditBody()
        CreateMenu2()
    End Sub

    Private Sub CreateScripts()

        Dim strScripts As String
```

```
    strScripts = vbCrLf & "<script>" & vbCrLf & _
        "function HTMLListCommand(editor,command,list)" & _
        vbCrLf & "{" & vbCrLf & _
        "editor.focus();" & vbCrLf & _
        "editor.document.execCommand(command,false," & _
        "list.opetions(list.selectedIndex).value);" & _
        vbCrLf & "list.selectedIndex=0;" & vbCrLf & "}" & _
        vbCrLf & "function HTMLBtnCommand(editor,command)" _
        & vbCrLf & "{" & vbCrLf & "editor.focus();" & _
        vbCrLf & _
        "editor.document.execCommand(command,false,null);" _
        & vbCrLf & "}" & vbCrLf & "</script>" & vbCrLf

    Controls.Add(CreateLiteral(strScripts))
End Sub

Private Sub CreateMenu()
    Dim arrayNames() As String
    Dim arrayValues() As String
    Dim strEditor As String
    Dim strHandler As String

    m_objMenu = CreatePanel("Menu", MenuCssClass)
    Controls.Add(m_objMenu)

    strEditor = UniqueID.Replace(":", "_") & "_Editor"

    With m_objMenu.Controls
        'Paragraph Settings
        arrayNames = New String() _
        { _
            "Paragraph","Normal","Heading 1","Heading 2", _
            "Heading 3","Heading 4","Heading 5", _
            "Heading 6","Directory List","Pre-Formatted", _
            "Address" _
        }

        arrayValues = New String() _
        { _
            "", "Normal", "<h1>", "<h2>", "<h3>", "<h4>", _
            "<h5>", "<h6>", "<dir>", "<ore>", _
            "<address>" _
        }
```

```
strHandler = "HTMLListCommand(" & strEditor & _
    ",'FormatBlock',this)"
.Add(CreateList("ParagraphList", arrayNames, _
    arrayValues, strHandler))

' Font Names
arrayNames = New String() _
{ _
    "Font","Arial","Arial Black","Comic Sans MS", _
    "Courier New", "Georgia", "Impact", _
    "Lucida Console", "Palatino Linotype", _
    "Trebuchet MS", "Verdana" _
}

strHandler = "HTMLListCommand(" & strEditor & _
    ",'FontName',this)"
.Add(CreateList("FontList", arrayNames, arrayNames, _
    strHandler))

' Font Size
arrayNames = New String() {"Size", "1", "2", "3", _
    "4", "5", "6", "7"}
strHandler = "HTMLListCommand(" & strEditor & _
    ",'FontSize',this)"
.Add(CreateList("FontSizeList", arrayNames, _
    arrayNames, strHandler))

' Fore Color
arrayNames = New String() {"Color", "Black", _
    "Blue", "Green", "Orange", "Red", "White", _
    "Yellow"}
strHandler = "HTMLListCommand(" & strEditor & _
    ",'ForeColor',this)"
.Add(CreateList("ColorList", arrayNames, _
    arrayNames, strHandler))

' Bold
strHandler = "HTMLBtnCommand(" & strEditor & _
    ",'Bold')"
.Add(CreateImageButton("Bold", _
    "/HTML_Editor/images/bold.gif", "Bold", _
    strHandler))
```

```
' Italic
strHandler = "HTMLBtnCommand(" & strEditor & _
    ",'Italic')"
.Add(CreateImageButton("Italic", _
    "/HTML_Editor/images/italic.gif", "Italic", _
    strHandler))

' Justify Left
strHandler = "HTMLBtnCommand(" & strEditor & _
    ",'JustifyLeft')"
.Add(CreateImageButton("JustifyLeft", _
    "/HTML_Editor/images/justifyleft.gif", _
    "Left Justify Text", strHandler))

' Justify Center
strHandler = "HTMLBtnCommand(" & strEditor & _
    ",'JustifyCenter')"
.Add(CreateImageButton("JusfifyCenter", _
    "/HTML_Editor/images/justifycenter.gif", _
    "Center Justify Text", strHandler))

' Justify Right
strHandler = "HTMLBtnCommand(" & strEditor & _
    ",'JustifyRight')"
.Add(CreateImageButton("JusfifyRight", _
    "/HTML_Editor/images/justifyright.gif", _
    "Right Justify Text", strHandler))

' Indent
strHandler = "HTMLBtnCommand(" & strEditor & _
    ",'Indent')"
.Add(CreateImageButton("Indent", _
    "/HTML_Editor/images/indent.gif", _
    "Indent Text", strHandler))

' Outdent
strHandler = "HTMLBtnCommand(" & strEditor & _
    ",'Outdent')"
.Add(CreateImageButton("Outdent", _
    "/HTML_Editor/images/outdent.gif", _
    "Outdent Text", strHandler))
```

```
            ' Cut
            strHandler = "HTMLBtnCommand(" & strEditor & _
                ",'Cut')"
            .Add(CreateImageButton("Cut", _
                "/HTML_Editor/images/cut.gif", "Cut", _
                strHandler))

            ' Copy
            strHandler = "HTMLBtnCommand(" & strEditor & _
                ",'Copy')"
            .Add(CreateImageButton("Copy", _
                "/HTML_Editor/images/copy.gif", "Copy", _
                strHandler))

            ' Paste
            strHandler = "HTMLBtnCommand(" & strEditor & _
                ",'Paste')"
            .Add(CreateImageButton("Paste", _
                "/HTML_Editor/images/paste.gif", "Paste", _
                strHandler))

            ' Undo
            strHandler = "HTMLBtnCommand(" & strEditor & _
                ",'Undo')"
            .Add(CreateImageButton("Undo", _
                "/HTML_Editor/images/undo.gif", "Undo", _
                strHandler))

            ' Redo
            strHandler = "HTMLBtnCommand(" & strEditor & _
                ",'Redo')"
            .Add(CreateImageButton("Redo", _
                "/HTML_Editor/images/redo.gif", "Redo", _
                strHandler))
        End With
    End Sub


    Private Sub CreateEditBody()
        m_objEditor = CreatePanel("Editor", EditorCssClass)
        Controls.Add(m_objEditor)

        With m_objEditor
            .Controls.Add(CreateLiteral(Text))
```

```vbnet
            .Attributes.Add("contentEditable", "True")
    End With
End Sub

Private Sub CreateMenu2()
    ' Create Panel for the Update/Cancel Buttons
    m_objMenu2 = CreatePanel("Menu2", MenuCssClass)
    Controls.Add(m_objMenu2)

    'Create Update Button
    Dim objUpdate As Button
    objUpdate = CreateButton("Update", "Update", True)
    AddHandler objUpdate.Click, AddressOf OnUpdate_Click

    'Create Cancel Button
    Dim objCancel As Button
    objCancel = CreateButton("Cancel", "Cancel", False)
    AddHandler objCancel.Click, AddressOf OnCancel_Click

    'Create Hidden Field to return edited HTML
    m_objHidden = New HtmlInputHidden()
    m_objHidden.ID = "ctlHidden"
    m_objMenu2.Controls.Add(m_objHidden)

    'Client Validation Name
    Dim strClientValidationName As String
    strClientValidationName = UniqueID.Replace(":", "_") & _
        "_UpdateHtml"

    'Create Custom Validator
    'Used to trigger the script to copy the
    'edited HTML into the hidden control
    Dim objValidator As New CustomValidator()
    With objValidator
        .ClientValidationFunction = strClientValidationName
        .EnableClientScript = True
    End With
    m_objMenu2.Controls.Add(objValidator)

    'Create Client Validation Script
    Dim strHiddenName As String
    Dim strEditorName As String
    Dim strScript As String
```

```vbnet
        strHiddenName = m_objHidden.UniqueID.Replace(":", "_")
        strEditorName = m_objEditor.UniqueID.Replace(":", "_")

        strScript = vbCrLf & "<script>" & vbCrLf & _
            "{" & vbCrLf & _
            "args.IsValid=true;" & vbCrLf & _
            "document.all['" & strHiddenName & _
            "'].value=document.all['" & strEditorName & _
            "'].innerHTML;" & vbCrLf & _
            "}" & vbCrLf & "</script>" & vbCrLf

    m_objMenu2.Controls.Add(CreateLiteral(strScript))

End Sub


' Helper Functions
Private Function CreateLiteral(ByVal strText As String) _
As LiteralControl
    Return New LiteralControl(strText)
End Function

Private Function CreatePanel(ByVal strID As String, _
ByVal strCssClass As String) As Panel
    Dim objPanel As New Panel()

    With objPanel
        .ID = strID
        .CssClass = strCssClass
    End With

    Return objPanel
End Function

Private Function CreateButton(ByVal strID As String, ByVal _
    strText As String, ByVal bCausesValidation As Boolean) _
    As Button

    Dim objButton As New Button()

    With objButton
        .ID = strID
        .Text = strText
```

```vb
            .CausesValidation = bCausesValidation
        End With

        Return objButton
    End Function

    Private Function CreateImageButton(ByVal strID As String, _
        ByVal strImageUrl As String, ByVal strToolTip As String _
        , ByVal strOnClick As String) As ImageButton

        Dim objImageButton As New ImageButton()

        With objImageButton
            .ID = strID
            .ImageUrl = strImageUrl
            .ToolTip = strToolTip
            .Attributes.Add("OnClick", "strOnClick")
            .CausesValidation = False
        End With

        Return objImageButton
    End Function

    Private Function CreateList(ByVal strID As String, ByVal _
        arrayNames() As String, ByVal arrayValues() As String, _
        ByVal strOnChange As String) As DropDownList

        Dim objList As New DropDownList()
        Dim objItem As ListItem
        Dim i As Int32

        If arrayNames.Length <> arrayValues.Length Then
            Throw New Exception( _
            "arrayNames and arrayValues must be the same length")
        End If

        With objList
            .ID = strID
            .Attributes.Add("OnChange", strOnChange)

            For i = 0 To arrayNames.Length - 1
                objItem = New ListItem()
                objItem.Text = arrayNames.GetValue(i)
```

```
                    objItem.Value = arrayValues.GetValue(i)
                    .Items.Add(objItem)
            Next

                .Items(0).Selected = True

        End With

        Return objList
    End Function

    ' Event Handlers
    Private Sub OnUpdate_Click(ByVal sender As Object, ByVal e _
        As EventArgs)

        Text = m_objHidden.Value
        With m_objEditor.Controls
            .Clear()
            .Add(CreateLiteral(Text))
        End With

        RaiseEvent Update(Me, e)
    End Sub

    Private Sub OnCancel_Click(ByVal sender As Object, ByVal e _
        As EventArgs)

        RaiseEvent Cancel(Me, e)
    End Sub
End Class
```

To actually use the control, you need to place the images for the image buttons in the /HTML_Editor/images folder of the Web server. These images can be downloaded from www.ASPNET-Solutions.com.

Using the HTML Editor Server Control

Now that you have an HTML editing server control, let's look at how to use it. Before you can use the control in Visual Studio .NET, you need to add it to the tool box. Once the control is added to the tool box, it can be added to any Web Form by dragging it from the tool box and dropping it on the form. The control can be added to the tool box by following these steps.

1. Right-click the Toolbox panel of Visual Studio .NET and select Add Tab from the context menu that appears. This should add a new tab at the bottom of the tool box.
2. Give the tab a name, such as HTML Editor.
3. Click the tab you created to open it.
4. Right-click the Toolbox panel again. This time, select Customize Toolbox from the context menu.
5. From the dialog box that appears, select the .NET Framework Components tab.
6. Now click the Browse button and locate the .dll file containing the HTML editor custom server control, select it, and click OK. This should add an icon for the HTML editor to your tool box.

To distribute the control for development, it is necessary only to copy the .dll file generated when the control is compiled to the other computer. It can then be used by following the preceding steps.

Creating a Simple HTML Editor

Now let's create an application that uses the server control that we have implemented. To do this, start by creating a new Web application. For our example, I will use a VB Web application, but any .NET-compatible Web application will work just as well. Once the server control has been implemented, it can be accessed and used with any .NET language.

Once you have created the Web application, using the HTML editor control is as simple as dragging and dropping it on the Web Form and then setting the `Width`, `Height`, `EditorCssClass`, and `MenuCssClass` properties. Listing 19.3 shows the .aspx file for a sample editor.

Listing 19.3 .aspx File for Sample HTML Editing Application

```
<%@
  Register TagPrefix="cc1"
  Namespace="HTML_EditorVB"
  Assembly="HTML_EditorVB"
%>
<%@
```

```
Page Language="vb"
AutoEventWireup="false"
Codebehind="WebForm1.aspx.vb"
Inherits="HTML_EditorApp.WebForm1"
%>
<!DOCTYPE HTML PUBLIC "-//W3C//DTD HTML 4.0 Transitional//EN">
<html>
  <head>
    <title>WebForm1</title>
    <meta
      content="Microsoft Visual Studio.NET 7.0"
      name="GENERATOR"
    >
    <meta
      content="Visual Basic 7.0"
      name="CODE_LANGUAGE"
    >
    <meta content="JavaScript" name="vs_defaultClientScript">
    <meta
      content="http://schemas.microsoft.com/intellisense/ie5"
      name="vs_targetSchema"
    >
    <link
      href="StyleSheet1.css"
      type="text/css"
      rel="stylesheet"
    >
  </head>
  <body bgcolor="blue" ms_positioning="GridLayout">
    <form id="Form1" method="post" runat="server">
      <cc1:html_editorvb
        id="HTML_EditorVB1"
        style="LEFT: 88px; POSITION: absolute; TOP: 16px"
        runat="server"
        width="500"
        height="400"
        editorcssclass="HTML_Editor"
        menucssclass="HTML_Menu"
      >
      </cc1:html_editorvb>
    </form>
  </body>
</html>
```

Loading and storing the edited HTML is fairly straightforward. The HTML is loaded in the `Page_Load` event handler, and stored in the event handler for the `Update` event of our HTML editor server control. Listing 19.4 shows the code behind the file for loading and storing the HTML file.

Listing 19.4 Code behind the File for the Sample HTML Editor Application

```
Imports System.IO

Public Class WebForm1
    Inherits System.Web.UI.Page
    Protected WithEvents HTML_EditorVB1 _
        As HTML_EditorVB.HTML_EditorVB

    Private Sub Page_Load( _
        ByVal sender As System.Object, _
        ByVal e As System.EventArgs) Handles MyBase.Load

        'Open File
        Dim strFileName As String
        strFileName = Page.MapPath("test.htm")

        Dim objFile As New FileStream(strFileName, _
            FileMode.OpenOrCreate, FileAccess.Read, _
            FileShare.ReadWrite)
        Dim objReader As New StreamReader(objFile)

        'Read HTML
        HTML_EditorVB1.Text = objReader.ReadToEnd()

        'Close File
        objReader.Close()
        objFile.Close()
    End Sub

    Private Sub HTML_EditorVB1_Update(ByVal sender As Object, _
        ByVal e As System.EventArgs) _
        Handles HTML_EditorVB1.Update

        'Open File
        Dim strFileName As String
        ' Page.MapPath() is OK for low traffic sites, for
```

```
         '   high traffic situations it should be cached.
         strFileName = Page.MapPath("test.htm")

         Dim objFile As New FileStream(strFileName, _
             FileMode.Create, FileAccess.Write, _
             FileShare.ReadWrite)

         Dim objWriter As New StreamWriter(objFile)

         'Write HTML
         objWriter.Write(HTML_EditorVB1.Text)

         'Close File
         objWriter.Close()
         objFile.Close()
      End Sub
End Class
```

One thing to note about the HTML that is stored is that it is not a complete HTML file, but an HTML fragment. This is because what is being stored is the portion of the HTML that is inside a `<div>` tag. If necessary, you can add the extra markup to make a stand-alone HTML file when it is stored.

Finally, permissions need to be given to the user account used by ASP.NET to be able to write to the file in which the data is being stored. This account name is ASPNET by default.

Summary

The mechanics of making a client-side HTML editor are fairly straightforward when you use Internet Explorer. In this chapter, you learned how to take that functionality one step further by encapsulating it into a .NET server control and making it easy to use for a server-side programmer with little knowledge of client-side scripting.

Creating an Online Training Application

In This Chapter:

- The `VideoPresentations` Architecture
- The Notable JavaScript
- Server Multimedia Basics
- The `VideoPresentations` Class
- The Demonstration Application

I love teaching and training. There's nothing like getting an e-mail from a former student who has been promoted to senior software engineer to let me know that my guidance was worthwhile.

Several challenges arise, though, as a result of teaching and training. What happens when students need to review the material? Their notes might be good enough, but their experience probably is not. The book will help, but I give my students things such as anecdotes from real life situations, which they can't get in a book.

What happens when students must miss a class? This absence is especially damaging for some topics, such as the start of ADO.NET, in which the subject of SqlConnection objects and connection strings is taught. Because the rest of the subject relies on these topics, missing them puts students in a precarious situation.

What happens if I want to teach an entire group of students who can't attend class? This happened to me recently when a contracting firm that's about 90 minutes away wanted training for its staff. It was impractical for them to drive that great distance on a regular basis, so an alternative strategy had to be developed.

This chapter teaches you how to use an ASP.NET class named Video-Presentations to create a training application. This class has lots of options, all designed to give you a powerful tool for creating an online training application. I'll talk about the VideoPresentations architecture, the salient JavaScript that makes it work, some server multimedia basics, and, finally, the demonstration application.

The `VideoPresentations` Architecture

The `VideoPresentations` class manages four visible elements in applications. One element is the video window in which the speaker can be seen and heard. Another element is a sequence of slides that reflect the current subtopic. The third element is a list of subtopics (or a table of contents) with which users can navigate to desired subtopics. And last is a VCR-like control with which users can perform operations such as pause and stop. You can see the application window that displays the video presentations in Figure 20.1.

The Video Window

The video window is an embedded instance of the Microsoft Media Player. The Media Player displays the streamed video data. The Windows Media Player is an ActiveX control and is embedded in the HTML code with an `<OBJECT>` tag.

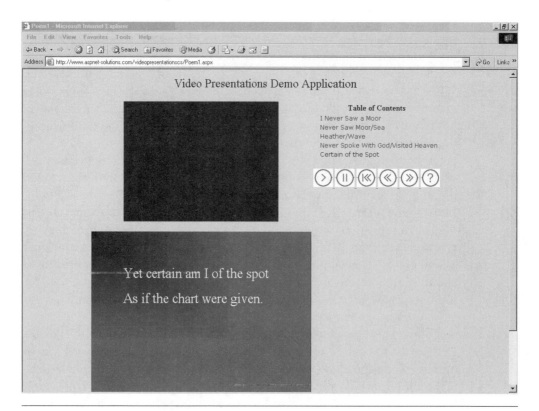

Figure 20.1 The `Video Presentations` Demo Application

The <OBJECT> tag supports quite a few parameters, but the `Video-Presentations` class sets only six of the possible parameters—all of the other parameters use the default values. The six parameters can be set with properties of the `VideoPresentations` class. The parameters that are output to HTML code are `FileName`, `AnimationStart`, `TransparentAtStart`, `AutoStart`, `Volume`, and `ShowControls`. (Refer to Table 20.1 for a complete reference for the `VideoPresentations` properties.)

In addition to the six parameters, the width and height of the ActiveX control can be set with the `PlayerWidth` and `PlayerHeight` properties of the `VideoPresentations` class. The following code is a typical example of the HTML code for the multimedia player:

```
<OBJECT id="VideoPlay" Name="VideoPlay"
  width="320" height="240"
  classid="CLSID:22d6f312-b0f6-11d0-94ab-0080c74c7e95"
codebase="http://activex.microsoft.com/activex/controls/mplayer/en/nsmp2
inf.cab#Version=5,1,52,701"
  standby="Loading Microsoft Windows Media Player components..."
  type="application/x-oleobject">
 <PARAM NAME="FileName" VALUE="Poem1/video.asx">
 <PARAM NAME="AnimationatStart" VALUE="True">
 <PARAM NAME="TransparentatStart" VALUE="True">
 <PARAM NAME="AutoStart" VALUE="True">
 <PARAM NAME="Volume" VALUE="-100">
 <PARAM NAME="ShowControls" VALUE="False">
</OBJECT>
```

The Subtopic Slides

The subtopic slides for the demo are GIF images that were created with PowerPoint. PowerPoint actually created JPG images that I converted to GIF images. Although converting from JPG to GIF might seem like a waste of time, the multimedia class expects GIF images and not JPG. Before saving the images from PowerPoint, though, you need to remove any animations because animations will give the rendered images layered elements that may not have the appearance that you desire. The main reason that the presentation needs to be saved as HTML is that otherwise everyone will have to have PowerPoint installed to view the slides. The demonstration application contains lines to the poems being read. If you use the `Video-Presentations` class for a training program, your presentation might contain bullet points summarizing the points that are being discussed in the video feed. If your presentation's purpose is to teach a programming topic, your presentation might contain source code examples.

The HTML uses a `<DIV>` tag so that the JavaScript can easily change the image source when the time is appropriate. A `<DIV>` tag allows you to easily change attributes on the fly. The width and height of the image can be set with the `ImageWidth` and `ImageHeight` properties of the `VideoPresentations` class. PowerPoint saves slides as images that are 454 pixels wide and 340 pixels high. But setting the `ImageWidth` and `ImageHeight` properties to other values will accommodate different sizes. The following HTML code is a typical example of the `<DIV>` tag:

```
<div id="Window" Name="Window"
 style="text-align:center;z-index:10;padding-top : 20;" class="butn">
  <img id="Slide" Name="Slide" src='Poem1/Slides/M1.gif' border="0"
    width="454" height="340">
</div>
```

The Table of Contents

To let the user navigate to any subtopic, a list of subtopics is displayed. Each item in the list responds to a mouse click, letting the user navigate to the appropriate subtopic in the video presentation.

The list uses JavaScript to set focus on particular items and to respond to user selections. The following is the HTML for a typical example:

```
<a href="#" onclick="GoMarker(1); return false">
  <div id="M1" class="Marker" onmousedown="TOCmouseDown();"
   onmouseout="TOCmouseOut();" onmouseover="TOCmouseOver();">
   I Never Saw a Moor
  </div>
</a>
```

The JavaScript in this HTML calls four different methods: `GoMarker()`, `TOCmouseDown()`, `TOCmouseOut()`, and `TOC-mouseOver()`. These four methods are discussed in detail in the section entitled "The Notable JavaScript."

The VCR Control

You can give your users a VCR control with which they can control the progress of the video stream. The control has Stop, Play, Pause, and Seek buttons. The VCR control is made up of individual images (for each VCR command), each of which calls a JavaScript method to perform an action.

The Notable JavaScript

This section discusses the JavaScript code that's emitted by the Video-Presentations class. Each of the following sections talks about a selected portion of the JavaScript code.

The Table of Contents Mouse Over, Out, and Down Code

The table of contents list gives feedback to the user for three mouse events. One event is when the mouse enters the space for an entry in the list. When this happens, the code calls the TOCmouseOver() method shown in Listing 20.1, which changes the text color of the target item to green. Another event is when the mouse leaves the space for an entry in the list. When this happens, the TOCmouseOut() method shown in Listing 20.2 is called, which changes the text color back to the original. If the user clicks an entry in the list, the TOCmouseDown() method is called (shown in Listing 20.1), which sets the item text to purple. This user interaction is important because it lets users know that something will happen if they click on these items. Green and purple were chosen for the contrast that they offer.

The code below is interesting for several reasons. The first thing I'd like to point out is that the name of the class is checked to make sure that only the Marker and MarkerTitle classes are affected.

Listing 20.1 Code That Responds to Mouse Events for the Table of Contents

```
function TOCmouseOver()
 {
  var vSrc = window.event.srcElement;
  if( vSrc.className == "Marker" || vSrc.className == "MarkerTitle" )
  {
   fColor = vSrc.style.color;
   vSrc.style.color = "Green";
   window.event.cancelbubble = true;
  }
 }
```

```
function TOCmouseOut()
{
 var vSrc = window.event.srcElement;
 if( vSrc.className == "Marker" || vSrc.className == "MarkerTitle" )
 {
  vSrc.style.color = fColor;
  window.event.cancelbubble = true;
 }
}

function TOCmouseDown()
{
 var vSrc = window.event.srcElement;
 if( vSrc.className == "Marker" || vSrc.className == "MarkerTitle" )
 {
  vSrc.style.color = "Purple";
  window.event.cancelbubble = true;
 }
}
```

Navigation Code

There's a JavaScript method named GoMarker() that seeks, and moves to a given marker number in the video stream. Markers are special events that can be inserted into video streams to alert the player when something needs to happen. In the case of this application, the something that needs to happen is the change of a slide. I use Vegas Video to edit files and insert markers. The GoMarker() method can be seen in Listing 20.2. It uses the instantiated Windows Media Player object named VideoPlay seek to the marker. For Microsoft IE browsers (Versions 4.0 and later), this method sets the CurrentMarker property to the appropriate marker number, calls the Play() method, the sets the appropriate slide for the <DIV> object on the page named Slide.

Listing 20.2 JavaScript Code That Performs Navigation within the Video Stream

```
function GoMarker( markernumber )
{
 if( IE4)
 {
  if( document.VideoPlay.PlayState == 2)
```

```
  {
   document.VideoPlay.Pause();
  }
  document.VideoPlay.CurrentMarker = markernumber;
  document.VideoPlay.Play();
  document.all.Slide.src="Poem1/Slides/M" + markernumber + ".gif"
 }
 else
 {
  document.VideoPlay.SetCurrentMarker( markernumber );
 }
}
```

NOTE: When you edit the video file, you must be careful to insert markers and text in the correct manner. All markers must follow the format M1, M2, M3, and so on. All text should follow the format M1, M2, M3, and so on. The markers and text must occur at exactly the same location. For instance, marker M1 should be in the same spot as text M1.

Multimedia Player Event Handler

An event is fired by the VideoPlay object each time a script command named `ScriptCommand()` has been encountered in the video stream. Because the only commands in the video stream are `Text` commands that represent the slide name, the `ScriptCommand()` event handler can take the value of the command and create the file path to the slide. Listing 20.3 shows this method.

Listing 20.3 The Event Handler That Is Called When There Is a Script Command in the Video Stream

```
<script language='JavaScript' for="VideoPlay"
   event="ScriptCommand(bstrType, bstrParam)">
     document.all.Slide.src="Poem1/Slides/" + bstrParam + ".gif"
</script>
```

VCR Control Mouse Over, Out, and Down Code

The VCR image buttons respond to mouse events similarly to the buttons for the table of contents items. The VCR control images change when the mouse hovers over the image, when it leaves the image area, and when the user clicks one of the VCR images.

The code in Listing 20.4 shows the mouseOver(), mouseOut(), and mouseDown() methods that handle the mouse interaction. One note: browsers before IE 4.0 cannot understand document.all objects.

Listing 20.4 The Mouse Event-Handling Methods for the VCR Control

```
function mouseOver( flame )
{
 if( IE4 )
 {
  felEl = eval( "document.all." + flame );
  felEl.src = "images/" + flame + "_roll.gif";
 }
 else
 {
  felEl = eval( "document." + flame );
  felEl.src = "images/" + flame + "_roll.gif";
 }
}
 function mouseDown( flame )
 {
  if( IE4 )
  {
   felEl = eval( "document.all." + flame );
   felEl.src = "images/" + flame + "_down.gif";
  }
  else
  {
   felEl = eval( "document." + flame );
   felEl.src = "images/" + flame + "_down.gif";
  }
 }

 function mouseOut( flame )
 {
  if( IE4 )
  {
   felEl = eval("document.all." + flame );
   felEl.src = "images/" + flame + "_norm.gif";
  }
```

```
else
{
 felEl = eval("document." + flame );
 felEl.src = "images/" + flame + "_norm.gif";
}
}
```

Server Multimedia Basics

This section talks about Windows 2000 servers, and how they are used to stream multimedia files. Streaming is different from simply offering a link with which users can download and play a file (such as an .avi file). When a multimedia file is offered via a link as a download, the entire file is transferred to the client computer before playback begins. When a multimedia file is streamed, the content is delivered as needed over time.

A Windows 2000 server doesn't necessarily have the server-side multimedia software installed. You can check whether the software is installed by clicking the Start button, selecting the Programs menu, selecting the Administrative Tools menu, and then selecting Configure Your Server. A

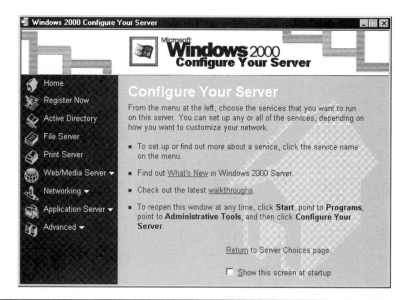

Figure 20.2 This Window Appears, Allowing You to Configure Your Server.

window will appear (as shown in Figure 20.2) with which you can configure your server, including the multimedia options.

Drill down into the Web/Media Server link, and then select Streaming Media Server, and finally click the Manage Windows Media Services link. This will bring you to a screen from which the Windows Media Services can be configured. Normally, though, there's nothing necessary—the configuration is done during install time.

The Windows Media Services will expect all multimedia files that are to be streamed to be in a specific directory (or any of its subdirectories). Normally this directory is named ASFROOT and is off the hard drive's root. For instance, on all the servers in our company, this directory can be found at C:\ASFROOT.

Your Web application will not have direct access to the files in the multimedia home directory. Instead, you will reference files by the server name, and then the file. The following refers to an .asf file named Presentation.asf in the multimedia home directory, for a server named Dellap: mms://Dellap/Presentation.asf

Your Web application will actually reference a file (normally with an .asx extension) that specifies the multimedia server and file. The .asx file will normally reference either a .asf file or a .wmf file. The following .asx file is an example:

```
<ASX version = "3.0">
<entry>
    <Ref href = "MMS://Dellap/OnlineTraining.asf" />
</entry>
</ASX>
```

Besides making sure that the server is ready to deliver streamed content, you'll need a way to insert markers and `Text` commands into the media file. I've found that Vegas Video 3.0 works extremely well. You can get a trial version at www.SonicFoundry.com. Figure 20.3 shows how easy it is to insert a marker.

The markers allow the application to seek to various places in the media file. Each of the table of contents items calls the `GoMarker()` JavaScript method with a number. The first item will call the method with a `1` as an argument, as follows:

```
GoMarker( 1 )
```

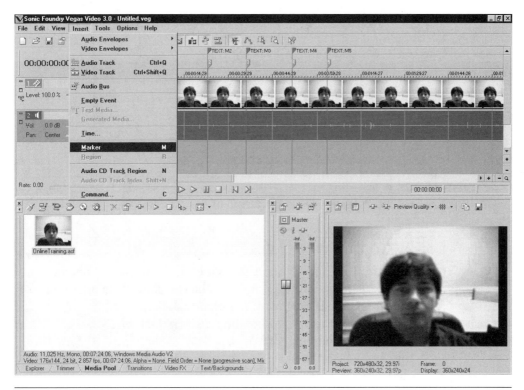

Figure 20.3 Inserting Markers Is Easy with Vegas Video 3.0.

Subsequent items in the table of contents list have marker numbers that increment by one for each item.

In addition to inserting markers into the media file, Vegas Video also inserts `Text` commands. The `Text` commands trigger a call to the `ScriptCommand()` JavaScript method. When this method is called, the `text` parameter is used to set the slide window so that the appropriate slide is shown. For instance, the `Text` command for the third marker is `M3`. This causes the file M3.gif to be shown in the slide window. Figure 20.4 shows how to easily insert `Text` commands into the media file.

The following list summarizes what you must do to use this application on your server:

- Make sure that the media streaming services have been installed on the server.
- Identify the media home directory.

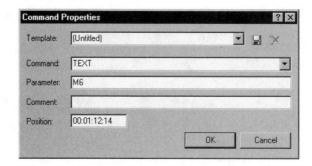

Figure 20.4 Inserting the `Text` Commands Is Simple. You Have to Make Sure That the Parameter Has the Name of the Next Image.

- Create an .asf or a .wmf file with markers and `Text` commands from M1, M2, M3, and so on. Although both file formats have the same approximate sizes, .wmf might be a better choice because more software supports editing .wmf files than .asf files.
- Create slides for the presentation made of GIF images.
- Underneath the current Web application directory, create a directory into which the video.asx and the slides subdirectory will be created.
- Create a video.asx file for the media file in the newly created directory.
- Move the slides into a directory named Slides inside of the newly created directory (the files should be named M1.gif, M2.gif, M3.gif, and so on).

The `VideoPresentations` Class

The `VideoPresentations` class is in the VideoPresentations.cs source code module (or the VideoPresentations.vb module for the VB.NET version). The properties and their description are contained in Table 20.1.

There are a few public methods for the `VideoPresentations` class. They can be seen in Table 20.2.

Two things must be done to use the `VideoPresentations` class. The first is to instantiate the class and set its properties so that the desired behavior will result. I suggest doing this in the code behind the module, but

Table 20.1 The VideoPresentations Properties

Property	Type	Description
StyleData	String	This property contains the text with the HTML style specifications for the <DIV> tags.
StartupCode	String	This property contains the text with the JavaScript code necessary for variable initialization.
LoadCode	String	This property contains the text with the JavaScript code that loads the media file.
UseMarkerCode	Boolean	This property determines whether the marker code will be emitted with all the other JavaScript code.
MarkerCode	String	This property contains the text with the JavaScript code that seeks to markers in the media file.
ScriptCommandCode	String	This property contains the text with the JavaScript code that handles the ScriptCommand() event.
UseTOC	Boolean	This property determines whether the table of contents will be output with all the other JavaScript code.
MouseControlCode	String	This property contains the text with the JavaScript code that manages the mouse interaction for the VCR control.
MarkerHitCode	String	This property contains the text with the JavaScript code that responds to a marker selection.
StatusCode	String	This property contains the text with the JavaScript code that responds to the media player's status.
PlayerObject	String	This property contains the text with the HTML code that instantiates the ActiveX media player.
VCRControl	String	This property contains the text with the HTML code for the VCR control images.
Filename	String	This property contains the file name of the media that will be displayed.
Directory	String	This property contains the directory in which the .asx file resides. This directory will always be relative to the current directory.
TOCList	DataSet	This property contains the text with the HTML code that displays the table of contents list. A DataSet was the best choice as opposed to a string array because there are multiple columns.
AnimationStart	Boolean	This property determines whether the media player displays an animation while the media is being retrieved from the server.

(continued)

Table 20.1 The `VideoPresentations` Properties (*cont.*)

Property	Type	Description
TransparentStart	Boolean	This property determines whether the media will perform a transparent start.
AutoStart	Boolean	This property determines whether the media will automatically start playing.
Volume	Integer	This property determines the volume of the media player.
ShowControls	Boolean	This property determines whether the media player's controls will be displayed.
PlayerWidth	Integer	This property sets the width of the displayed media player.
PlayerHeight	Integer	This property sets the height of the displayed media player.
SlideWidth	Integer	This property sets the width of the displayed slides.
SlideHeight	Integer	This property sets the height of the displayed slides.
SlideWindowCode	String	This property contains the text for the HTML code that displays the slides.

it can be done in the ASPX code if you prefer. The second thing that must be done is to output the JavaScript and HTML code into the ASPX code.

I'll talk about these steps in more detail in the section entitled "The Demonstration Application." Here, we'll take a look at how the `Video-Presentations` class works.

Table 20.2 `VideoPresentations` Public Methods

Method	Description
AddTOCEntry	This method allows a table of contents item to be added to the list. It takes a string as an argument.
GetTOCCode	This method returns a string that contains the formatted table of contents list.
GetStyleCode	This method returns the HTML-style code.
GetJavascriptCode	This method returns all JavaScript code that must be emitted for the `VideoPresentations` class to work correctly.

The `VideoPresentations` class has several private data members in which the JavaScript text is stored. The following is the string variable that contains the JavaScript startup code:

```
private string m_strLoadCode =
  "<script language='JavaScript'>\r\n" +
  " function loadIt()\r\n" +
  " {{\r\n" +
  "  var pluginJavaPeerRef = document.myform.VideoPlay;\r\n" +
  "  if( NS4 )\r\n" +
  "  {{\r\n" +
  "   if (document.myform.VideoPlay != null)\r\n" +
  "   {{\r\n" +
  "     objPlayer = document.myform.VideoPlay;\r\n" +
  "     sBrowser = \"notIE\";\r\n" +
  "     document.appObs.setByProxyDSScriptCommandObserver(" +
  "pluginJavaPeerRef, true);\r\n" +
  "     document.myform.VideoPlay.SetFileName ( \"{0}\" );\r\n" +
  "     document.myform.VideoPlay.Play();\r\n" +
  "   }}\r\n" +
  "  }}\r\n" +
  " }}\r\n" +
  "</script>\r\n" +
  "\r\n";
```

The `m_strLoadCode` code string variable is private, but the data can be retrieved using the `VideoPresentations.LoadCode` property. Notice that the string expects a single argument, identified by the `{0}` that can be seen within the string. This string must be formatted in the Load-Code property's accessor, as follows:

```
public string LoadCode
{
  get
  {
    return( string.Format( m_strLoadCode, Filename ) );
  }
}
```

Other private data members include `m_strStyleData` (accessed by the `StyleData` property), `m_strStartupAndVars` (accessed by the `StartupCode` property), `m_strMarkerCode` (accessed by the `Marker-`

Code property), m_strScriptCommandCode (accessed by the Script-CommandCode property), m_strMouseControlCode (accessed by the MouseControlCode property), m_strMarkerHitCode (accessed by the MarkerHitCode property), m_strStatusCode (accessed by the StatusCode property), and m_strPlayerObject (accessed by the PlayerObject property).

Listing 20.5 shows all of the code for the VideoPresentations class except for the private data members.

Listing 20.5 The VideoPresentations.cs Source Code

```
public string StyleData
{
  get
  {
    return( m_strStyleData );
  }
}


public string StartupCode
{
  get
  {
    return( m_strStartupAndVars );
  }
}


public string LoadCode
{
  get
  {
    return( string.Format( m_strLoadCode, Filename ) );
  }
}


public bool UseMarkerCode
{
  get
  {
    return( m_bUseMarkerCode );
  }
  set
```

```
    {
      m_bUseMarkerCode = value;
    }
}

public string MarkerCode
{
  get
  {
    return( string.Format( m_strMarkerCode, Directory ) );
  }
}

public string ScriptCommandCode
{
  get
  {
    return( string.Format( m_strScriptCommandCode, Directory ) );
  }
}

public bool UseTOC
{
  get
  {
    return( m_bUseTOC );
  }
  set
  {
    m_bUseTOC = value;
  }
}

public string MouseControlCode
{
  get
  {
    return( m_strMouseControlCode );
  }
}

public string MarkerHitCode
{
```

```csharp
      get
      {
        return( m_strMarkerHitCode );
      }
    }

    public string StatusCode
    {
      get
      {
        return( m_strStatusCode );
      }
    }

    public string PlayerObject
    {
      get
      {
        return( string.Format( m_strPlayerObject, Directory, Filename,
          AnimationStart, TransparentStart, AutoStart, Volume,
          ShowControls ) );
      }
    }

    public string VCRControl
    {
      get
      {
        return( m_strVCRControl );
      }
    }

    public string Filename
    {
      get
      {
        return( m_strFilename );
      }
      set
      {
        m_strFilename = value;
      }
    }
```

```
public string Directory
{
  get
  {
    return( m_strDirectory );
  }
  set
  {
    m_strDirectory = value;
  }
}

public void AddTOCEntry( string strEntry )
{
  m_TOCEntries.Add( strEntry );
}

public DataSet TOCList
{
  get
  {
    // Create a new DataSet object.
    DataSet ds = new DataSet();
    // Add a table named TOCEntry.
    ds.Tables.Add( "TOCEntry" );
    // Add two columns, title and number.
    ds.Tables[0].Columns.Add( "Title" );
    ds.Tables[0].Columns.Add( "Number" );
    // Loop through each TOC entry.
    for( int i=0; i<m_TOCEntries.Count; i++ )
    {
      // Create a string array that'll be
      //   used to add the wor.
      string[] ThisRow = { m_TOCEntries[i],
        Convert.ToString( i + 1 ) };
      // Add the row.
      ds.Tables[0].Rows.Add( ThisRow );
    }
    // Return the DataSet object to caller.
    return( ds );
  }
}
```

```
public string GetStyleCode()
{
  return( StyleData );
}

public string GetJavascriptCode()
{
  string strScriptCode = StartupCode + LoadCode;
  if( UseMarkerCode )
  {
    strScriptCode += MarkerCode;
  }
  strScriptCode += ScriptCommandCode;
  if( UseTOC )
  {
    strScriptCode += ( MouseControlCode + MarkerHitCode );
  }

  return( strScriptCode );
}

public bool AnimationStart
{
  get
  {
    return( m_bAnimationStart );
  }
  set
  {
    m_bAnimationStart = value;
  }
}

public bool TransparentStart
{
  get
  {
    return( m_bTransparentStart );
  }
  set
  {
    m_bTransparentStart = value;
  }
}
```

```
public bool AutoStart
{
  get
  {
    return( m_bAutoStart );
  }
  set
  {
    m_bAutoStart = value;
  }
}

public int Volume
{
  get
  {
    return( m_nVolume );
  }
  set
  {
    m_nVolume = value;
  }
}

public bool ShowControls
{
  get
  {
    return( m_bShowControls );
  }
  set
  {
    m_bShowControls = value;
  }
}

public int SlideWidth
{
  get
  {
    return( m_nSlideWidth );
  }
```

```
    set
    {
      m_nSlideWidth = value;
    }
}


public int SlideHeight
{
  get
  {
    return( m_nSlideHeight );
  }
  set
  {
    m_nSlideHeight = value;
  }
}


public string SlideWindowCode
{
  get
  {
    return( string.Format( m_strSlideWindowCode, Directory, SlideWidth,
      SlideHeight ) );
  }
}


public string GetTOCCode()
{
  // Start the string off with the <table> tag,
  //   and <th></th> tags.
  string strRetCode = "<table border=0>\r\n <th>\r\n" +
    "Table of Contents\r\n </th>\r\n";

  // Loop through each TOC entrie to create the HTML.
  for( int i=0; i<m_TOCEntries.Count; i++ )
  {
    // Start the row.
    strRetCode += " <tr>\r\n";
    // Start the column.
    strRetCode += "  <td>\r\n";
    // Create the link with all of the javascript
    //   code.
```

```
  strRetCode += ( "<a href=\"#\" onclick=\"GoMarker(" +
    Convert.ToString( i + 1 ) +
    "); return false\"><div id=\"M" +
    Convert.ToString( i + 1 ) +
    "\" class=\"Marker\" onmousedown=\"TOCmouseDown();" +
    "\" onmouseout=\"TOCmouseOut();" +
    "\" onmouseover=\"TOCmouseOver();\">" +
    m_TOCEntries[i] + "</div></a>" );
  // End the column.
  strRetCode += "  </td>\r\n";
  // End the row.
  strRetCode += " </tr>\r\n";
}

// End the table.
strRetCode += "</table>\r\n";

return( strRetCode );
}
```

The Demonstration Application

The demonstration application that I developed to show how to use the
VideoPresentations class offers users three choices from its main page.
The choices are three Emily Dickinson poems. When users make a selection,
they're brought to a page that plays a video file in which the selected poem is
read. This section discusses the demonstration program, which can be viewed
at http://www.ASPNET-Solutions.com/VideoPresentationsCS.

Instantiating and Setting Up
the VideoPresentations Class

It's easy to instantiate the VideoPresentations class. Just declare a
VideoPresentations object and then create it with the new operator, as follows:

C#
```
VideoPresentations VP = new VideoPresentations();
```

VB

```
Dim VP As New VideoPresentations()
```

Some minimal property setting must take place before the object is ready to use. At the very least, you must specify the directory name and the file name, as follows:

C#
```
VP.Directory = "Poem1";
VP.Filename = "video.asx";
```

VB
```
VP.Directory = "Poem1"
VP.Filename = "video.asx"
```

If you plan to leave the table of contents enabled (which is the default), you'll need to add items by calling the `AddTOCEntry()` method, as follows:

C#
```
VP.AddTOCEntry( "Entry One" );
VP.AddTOCEntry( "Entry Two" );
```

VB
```
VP.AddTOCEntry("Entry One")
VP.AddTOCEntry("Entry Two")
```

Listing 20.6 shows the code from the Poem1.aspx.cs file; the other two poem pages are identical except for the table of contents items that are added.

Listing 20.6 The Poem1.aspx.cs Source Code

```
public class Poem1 : System.Web.UI.Page
{

  public VideoPresentations m_VP;

  private void Page_Load(object sender, System.EventArgs e)
  {
    m_VP = new VideoPresentations();
    m_VP.Directory = "Poem1";
    m_VP.Filename = "video.asx";
    m_VP.SlideWidth = 454;
```

```
        m_VP.SlideHeight = 340;
        m_VP.AddTOCEntry( "I Never Saw a Moor" );
        m_VP.AddTOCEntry( "Never Saw Moor/Sea" );
        m_VP.AddTOCEntry( "Heather/Wave" );
        m_VP.AddTOCEntry( "Never Spoke With God/Visited Heaven" );
        m_VP.AddTOCEntry( "Certain of the Spot" );
    }
```

Emitting Code into the HTML

After the VideoPresentations object is created and initialized, the JavaScript and the HTML code must be emitted into the .aspx file. Within the <HEAD> tag, the style data and the JavaScript should be emitted. Within the <BODY> tag, the player object, table of contents, VCR control, and slide window should be emitted. Listing 20.7 shows how a `VideoPresentations` class named m_VP (which was declared and created in the `Page_Load()` method) emits the code into the .aspx file.

Listing 20.7 Using the VideoPresentations Object to Emit Code into the .aspx File

```html
<HTML>
  <HEAD>
    <title>Poem1</title>
    <%
      Response.Write( m_VP.StyleData );
      Response.Write( m_VP.GetJavascriptCode() );
    %>
  </HEAD>
  <body bgColor="lightpink">
    <DIV align="center">
      <P><FONT size="5">Video Presentations Demo Application</FONT></P>
      <table>
        <tr>
          <td align="middle">
            <%
            Response.Write( "<p>" + m_VP.PlayerObject + "<br>\r\n" );
            Response.Write( m_VP.SlideWindowCode + "</p>\r\n" );
            %>
          </td>
          <td valign="top" align="middle">
            <%
```

```
          Response.Write( "<p>" + m_VP.GetTOCCode() + "</p>\r\n" );
          Response.Write( "<p>" + m_VP.VCRControl + "</p>\r\n" );
        %>
      </td>
    </tr>
  </table>
  <P> </P>
  <P><A href="Default.aspx">
    Back to Video Presentations Main Page</A></P>
 </DIV>
</body>
```

Summary

The `VideoApplications` class makes it easy to add video streaming to your application, and it does it in such a way that users can interact and seek various subtopics. This class relies on emitted JavaScript code to do the work on the client side. It also relies on Windows 2000 Server to stream the video data to the client machine.

You could easily create an entire training application based on this class. One of my evening classes spent about three weeks creating a training application that included a billing and administrative piece. It was a great learning experience.

You've learned about outputting JavaScript into the HTML stream. You've also learned about how to dynamically alter the attributes of <DIV> tags. And the Windows Media ActiveX control is the focal point of the technology.

I would appreciate it if you would let me know that you used this class (or a derivative). Please e-mail me at Rick@JSVentures.com with your online video presentations.

CHAPTER 21

Speech-Enabling Web Applications

In This Chapter:

- Getting Started
- The SpeechVB Application

With millions of Web sites out there on the Internet, you're going to have to think up some pretty innovative ways for your Web site to be noteworthy. And let's face it, without a Web site that stands out, users won't stick around and spend much time, or even come back. This chapter gives you a powerful tool that will make your Web site more interesting and easier to use. It's a class that easily lets you speech-enable your Web applications, and it's built on the Microsoft Agent technology.

You're looking for more than just a pretty Web site—there are more important things than just luring people in. A lot of people just plain have trouble reading. And if your Web applications are speech enabled, users won't have to do too much reading to benefit from the contents. Or how about users who might be seriously visually impaired or blind? By speech-enabling your Web site, even these people can benefit from the contents.

You also must have seen the racks and racks of cassette tapes and CDs at the bookstores on which books have been recorded into an audio format. The reason this is so popular is that so many people prefer to listen to something rather than to read it. I myself prefer listening in many cases because I spend so much time reading; it's a real break to have something read to me. And studies have shown that, in many cases, comprehension increases when the content of a Web site is read to the user.

Now you don't have to read the entire Web site to a user. That would probably be overkill and might drive the users crazy. But selecting the most important text for instructions and reading that part to users will go far in terms of their enjoyment, enhanced understanding, and benefit from the Web application.

One more very powerful argument for using these Microsoft Agent technologies in your Web site is that they can provide not only speech, but also animation and interactivity. With them, your Web site visitors can get a guided tour of your site's products and services. They can ask questions and get answers. They can point to the rise in sales for your company's chart, which will be much more powerful than a plain graph.

The technology is actually built on ActiveX. Two ActiveX controls provide the Microsoft Agent character, animation, and speech capabilities. These controls are not server-side components, but they are embedded into the HTML and are invoked just as any other ActiveX controls would be in an HTML page.

Getting Started

You need to be aware of a few things before you use the Microsoft Agent components. The first is that the core components must be installed on the client computer before a speech-enabled Web site will work properly. The second thing you must make sure of is that the agent characters have been installed on the computer. And the third thing you must be sure about is that the speech module, which lets the Microsoft Agent components speak through your sound system, is installed.

A page on www.ASPNET-Solutions.com has links to the Microsoft Agent components that must be installed on client computers for speech enabled web applications. You can see this page in Figure 21.1. If you need to install anything, you can go to this page (www.ASPNET-Solutions.com/Chapter_21.htm) and download the components.

Note that Windows 2000 and Windows XP already have the Microsoft Agent and its components installed. Also note that if the Microsoft Agent core components and the speech components are not installed before a user goes to a Web page that is speech-enabled with Microsoft Agent, then an automatic download will start (after the user is prompted for permission—that is, if the browser security settings specify a prompt) that will install the needed components.

NOTE: Many Microsoft Agent characters are available, and many more are being created. Now that you have the Microsoft Agent components installed on your computer, you have only to download additional characters (files with .ACS extensions) as they become available and save them to your C:\WINDOWS\MSAGENT\CHARS or C:\WINNT\MSAGENT\CHARS folder, depending on your operating system. (The installation programs save the characters to

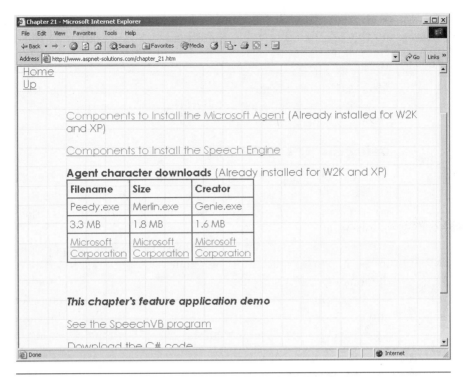

Figure 21.1 Links to the Agent Downloads Are on www.ASPNET-Solutions. com.

the correct directory without any intervention on your part.) You can look for other characters by going to www.MSAgentRing.org. You'll find dozens of additional agent characters that you can download and install.

The SpeechVB Application

I've written a class that encapsulates Microsoft Agent's functionality. I named it the `Agent` class, and for the purposes of this chapter I have used this class in a demo program called SpeechVB. Of course, there was a C# version on the Web site at www.ASPNET-Solutions.com. You can view the code online or just simply download the source code.

The `Agent` class works by emitting Java script code into the HTML stream. Essentially, the Microsoft Agent features are controlled within a

Web page by either VBScript or JavaScript. Because I find JavaScript eas-ier to work with, I opted for emitting JavaScript code rather than VBScript code, but the entire class could have been constructed so that it output VBScript code instead of JavaScript code. In this case, though, I followed Microsoft's lead because Microsoft emits JavaScript code for many of its server-side controls, such as the for-validation controls.

Using the SpeechVB Application

The SpeechVB application is available at www.UsingASP-Solutions.com Web site. To find it, simply click the chapter examples from the main page, go to Chapter 21, and then find the link that says "Run the SpeechVB Application."

When the application runs, it doesn't do much except display the genie in the upper-left corner of the client's computer screen. You can see this demonstrated in Figure 21.2.

It's important to note that the Agent operates on screen coordinates, and not on window coordinates. What I mean by that is if you use the x and y position for the overall screen, starting at 0,0 in the upper-left corner, then

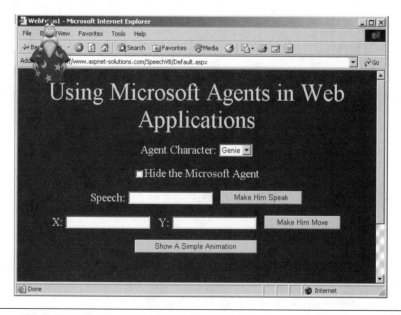

Figure 21.2 This Application Makes Use of the `Agent` Class. When It First Runs, the Agent Is in the Upper-Left Corner.

those are the coordinate positions you will use when you move the genie around. A window, however, has its own coordinate system, which is relative to its own upper-left corner. This means that the window has a number of systems, and it starts at 0,0, which is relative to its own upper-left corner. But that starting position is almost always going to be somewhere to the right and to the bottom of the main screen's origin. Microsoft Agent does not operate based on *window* coordinates that are relative the screen. It operates on literal and absolute *screen* coordinates.

You can have the agent characters speak. All you must do is enter a phrase that you want the character to speak, and then click the Make Him Speak button, as shown in Figure 21.3.

Two fields in the Web Form let users enter screen coordinates to which the Agent character will go. For instance, you can type in an *x* value of 100 to the *y* value of 400, and the Agent character will go to that exact screen coordinate. Remember, these are *screen* coordinates and not relative *window* coordinates. You can see the Agent character moved to a different location in Figure 21.4.

Microsoft Agent characters can have any number of animations built in. The Genie, for instance, can use binocular search, blow a trumpet, and

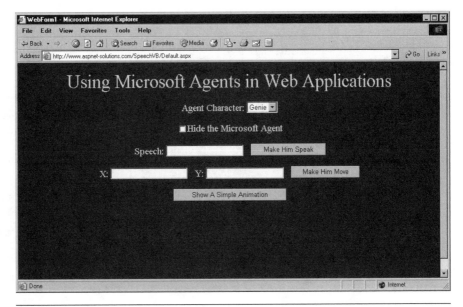

Figure 21.3 You Can Have the Agent Character Say Any Text That You Enter in the Speech Field.

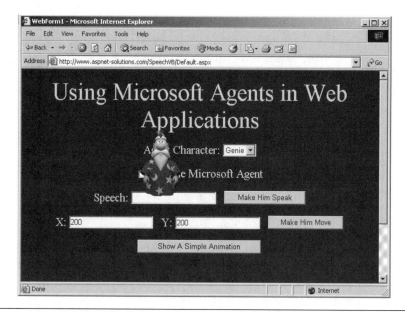

Figure 21.4 You Can Make the Agent Component Go to Any Screen Coordinates by Entering Values into the X and Y Fields.

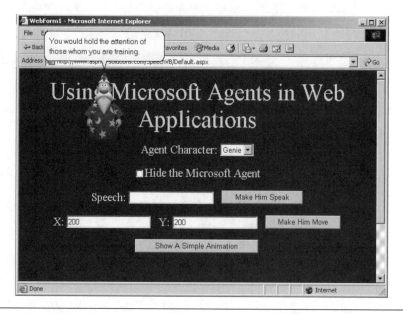

Figure 21.5 This Simulation Uses One of the Agent's Effective Animations.

spin like a tornado. In all, this animation can add to the enjoyment of the Agent characters, and can enhance a presentation significantly. In Figure 21.5, you can see one of the Agent's animations.

The SpeechVB Program is pretty simple. But as you can see from this section, it is very effective in showing what these Microsoft Agent technologies are capable of.

The SpeechVB Program Code

The SpeechVB Program has two major parts. The first part is the Agent class, which encapsulates the Agent functionality. The second part is a relatively simple work form that uses the Agent class.

For your convenience, I have collected all the methods in Table 21.1. This table shows you method names, what code module they're in, what listing number you can see them in, and a short description. This table will

Table 21.1 The SpeechVB Application Methods

Method Name	Code Module	Listing	Description
Hide()	Agent.vb	21.1	Causes the Agent character to hide from view.
Show()	Agent.vb	21.1	Causes the Agent character to show itself.
MoveToSpecial()	Agent.vb	21.1	Uses special values such as AgentCenterX and AgentBottomY to move to screen-relative locations.
Speak()	Agent.vb	21.1	Causes the Agent character to speak.
Gesture()	Agent.vb	21.1	Causes the Agent character to gesture from some predefined gestures.
Think()	Agent.vb	21.1	Causes the Agent character to go through thinking motions.
Whisper()	Agent.vb	21.1	Causes the Agent character to whisper some text.
Play()	Agent.vb	21.1	Causes the Agent character to play an animation.
			(continued)

Table 21.1 The `SpeechVB` Application Methods (*cont.*)

Method Name	Code Module	Listing	Description
Character()	Agent.vb	21.2	This is a property. It allows the selection of the Agent character, such as Genie or Merlin.
Render()	Agent.vb	21.3	This causes the Agent class to render the JavaScript to the `HttpResponse`.
OutputObjects()	Agent.vb	21.4	This method calls `OutputAgentControl()` and `OutputSpeechControl()` so that the objects are emitted into the HTML stream.
OutputAgentControl()	Agent.vb	21.4	This method outputs the Agent control object into the HTML stream.
OutputSpeechControl()	Agent.vb	21.4	This method outputs the speech control object into the HTML stream.
OutputScript()	Agent.vb	21.5	This method calls a number of methods, which in turn emit the JavaScript code for the agent control.
StartScript()	Agent.vb	21.5	This method emits the script start tag.
OutputVariables()	Agent.vb	21.5	This method emits the JavaScript variables.
OutputGetPositions()	Agent.vb	21.5	This method emits the method that gets the special screen positions that can be used to center the Agent character.
OutputOnLoad()	Agent.vb	21.5	This method emits the method that is called when the window loads.
OutputLoadAgent()	Agent.vb	21.5	This method emits the method that loads the Agent character.
OutputSetCharObj()	Agent.vb	21.5	This method emits the method that sets the character.

Table 21.1 The `SpeechVB` Application Methods (*cont.*)

Method Name	Code Module	Listing	Description
`OutputCheckLoadStatus()`	Agent.vb	21.5	This method emits the method that checks the load status.
`OutputLoadError()`	Agent.vb	21.5	This method emits the method that shows a load error.
`OutputCommands()`	Agent.vb	21.5	This method outputs the method that contains all of the Agent commands.
`EndScript()`	Agent.vb	21.5	This method emits the script end tag.
`DoAgentStuff()`	Default .aspx.vb	21.6	This method creates an `Agent` method, adds the appropriate commands (based on the user interface), and then renders into the HTML stream.
`ShowAnimation()`	Default .aspx.vb	21.7	This method responds to a button click and generates a random number that determines which of the four predefined animations will play.

help you as you study the program code, and modify it to suit your own needs, and it will help you to understand the code in general.

There are a number of methods that a consumer of the `Agent` class will make. These methods do things such as make the Agent character hide itself, make the Agent character show itself, and move the Agent character around on the screen. Essentially, what happens when these methods are called is that the appropriate Agent JavaScript command is added to the list of commands. The list of commands is contained in a class member variable named `m_ScriptList`. This object is a `StringCollection` that is iterated through during the Render process, when the JavaScript is emitted into the HTML stream.

Just to show you how easy it is to use the `Agent` class to create an Agent script, let's take a look at a simple code snippet. The following example shows how to substantiate an `Agent` class, make the Agent character show itself, and have the Agent character say something:

C#
```
Agent ag = new Agent();
ag.Show();
ag.Speak( "Hi there!" );
```

VB
```
Dim ag as new Agent()
ag.Show()
ag.Speak("Hi there!")
```

It's important to note that you perform this code from your .aspx source code. Further, you must not call this code within a form. The following .aspx code shows the correct and incorrect places to instantiate and use Agent objects:

Correct
```
<%@ Page Language="vb" AutoEventWireup="false"
  Codebehind="Default.aspx.vb"
  Inherits="SpeechVB.WebForm1"%>
<HTML>
  <HEAD>
    <title>Agent Page</title>
    <%
      Dim ag as new Agent()
      ag.Show()
      ag.Speak("Hi there!")
    %>
  </HEAD>
  <body>
      <FORM id="Form1" method="post" runat="server">
      </FORM>
  </body>
</HTML>
```

Incorrect
```
<%@ Page Language="vb" AutoEventWireup="false"
  Codebehind="Default.aspx.vb"
  Inherits="SpeechVB.WebForm1"%>
<HTML>
  <HEAD>
    <title>Agent Page</title>
  </HEAD>
```

```
<body>
    <FORM id="Form1" method="post" runat="server">
     <%
      Dim ag as new Agent()
      ag.Show()
      ag.Speak("Hi there!")
     %>
    </FORM>
  </body>
</HTML>
```

If you take a look at some of the methods in Listing 21.1, you'll see that they're simple. But others are a bit more arcane. The `Whisper()` method, for instance, outputs a `Speak` command with some embedded special text that the Agent character will interpret as a whisper. Essentially, if you start any Agent speaking command with CHR=\whisper, then the Agent character will whisper whatever you tell it to say. And that's what the `Whisper()` method is doing. Another one of these methods that should be noted as requiring special explanation is the `MoveToSpecial()` method. The JavaScript code contains a number of special variables. These are variables that calculate the center of the screen, the bottom of the screen, the right of the screen, and so forth. Table 21.2 shows the special variables and their meanings.

To use the `MoveToSpecial()` method, you simply give the method a string that specifies one of these special variable names. For instance, if you want to move the very center of the screen along both the x- and y-axis, you can use the following code:

```
ag.MoveToSpecial("AgentCenterX", "AgentCenterY")
```

Table 21.2 The Java Script Variables Containing Screen Coordinate Values

Variable	Description
AgentLeftX	This contains the x value for the left of the screen.
AgentCenterX	This contains the x value for the center of the screen.
AgentRightX	This contains the x value for the right of the screen.
AgentTopY	This contains the y value for the top of the screen.
AgentCenterY	This contains the y value for the center of the screen.
AgentBottomY	This contains the y value for the bottom of the screen.

Listing 21.1 The List of Commands, and the Methods That Make It Easy to Add the Commands

```
Dim m_ScriptList As New StringCollection()

Public Sub Hide()
    m_ScriptList.Add("Hide();")
End Sub

Public Sub Show()
    m_ScriptList.Add("Show();")
End Sub

Public Sub Move(ByVal x As Integer, ByVal y As Integer)
    m_ScriptList.Add("MoveTo(" + Convert.ToString(x) + "," + _
      Convert.ToString(y) + ");")
End Sub

Public Sub MoveToSpecial(ByVal strX As String, ByVal strY As String)
    m_ScriptList.Add("MoveTo(" + strX + "," + strY + ");")
End Sub

Public Sub Speak(ByVal strText As String)
    m_ScriptList.Add("Speak(" + Chr(34) + strText + Chr(34) + ");")
End Sub

Public Sub Gesture(ByVal x As Integer, ByVal y As Integer)
    m_ScriptList.Add("Gesture(" + Convert.ToString(x) + "," + _
      Convert.ToString(y) + ");")
End Sub

Public Sub Think()
    m_ScriptList.Add("Think();")
End Sub

Public Sub Whisper(ByVal strText As String)
    m_ScriptList.Add("Speak(" + Chr(34) + "\\Chr=\" + _
      Chr(34) + "Whisper\" + Chr(34) + "\\" + strText + Chr(34) + ");")
End Sub

Public Sub Play(ByVal strText As String)
    m_ScriptList.Add("Play(" + Chr(34) + strText + Chr(34) + ");")
End Sub
```

Listing 21.2 shows the `Character` property. This property lets you set a character before the `Agent` class. The demo program that's on www. ASPNET-Solutions.com has two characters in its drop-down list: Genie and Merlin. You can offer your users many other options if they have the characters installed and/or if you make the characters available for download from your Web application. Once again, you can find dozens of additional Agent characters at www.MSAgentRing.org.

Listing 21.2 The `Character` Property

```
Dim _character As String = "Genie"
Public Property Character() As String
    Get
        Return _character
    End Get
    Set(ByVal Value As String)
        _character = Value
    End Set
End Property
```

Listing 21.3 shows the `Render()` method. This is a very simple method that calls two other methods. One is the `OutputObjects()` method, and the other is the `OutputScript()` method. By calling the other two methods, the `Render()` method stays simple and understandable.

Listing 21.3 The `Render()` Method Must Be Called to Output the Script into the HTML Document.

```
Public Sub Render(ByVal Response As System.Web.HttpResponse)
    Response.Write(vbCrLf)
    OutputObjects(Response)
    OutputScript(Response)
End Sub
```

Listing 21.4 shows the `OutputObjects()` method and the two methods that it calls: the `OuputAgentControl()` method and the `OutputSpeechControl()` method.

The `OutputAgentControl()` method simply emits the HTML code that embeds the Agent control ActiveX into the HTML document.

Listing 21.4 shows the `AgentOutputControl()` method, but right above that, in gray, it shows the actual HTML that this method emits.

You can also see the `OutputSpeechControl()` method; directly above this method, in gray, is the speech object that is emitted into the HTML document that embeds the speech ActiveX controls.

Listing 21.4 The Methods That Output the Agent and Speech Objects, and the HTML Code They Emit

```
Private Sub OutputObjects(ByVal Response As System.Web.HttpResponse)
    OutputAgentControl(Response)
    OutputSpeechControl(Response)
End Sub
```

This code is emitted by the `OutputAgentControl()` method.
```
<Object ID="AgentControl" Width=0 Height=0
  ClassID="CLSID:D45FD31B-5C6E-11D1-9EC1-00C04FD7081F"
  CodeBase="#VERSION=2,0,0,0">
</Object>
```

```
Private Sub OutputAgentControl(ByVal Response As _
    System.Web.HttpResponse)
    Response.Write("<Object ID=" + Chr(34) + "AgentControl" + _
      Chr(34) + " Width=0 Height=0" + vbCrLf)
    Response.Write("  ClassID=" + Chr(34) + _
      "CLSID:D45FD31B-5C6E-11D1-9EC1-00C04FD7081F" + Chr(34) + vbCrLf)
    Response.Write("  CodeBase=" + Chr(34) + _
      "#VERSION=2,0,0,0" + Chr(34) + ">" + vbCrLf)
    Response.Write("</Object>" + vbCrLf)
End Sub
```

This code is emitted by the `OutputSpeechControl()` method.
```
<Object ID="L&HTruVoice" Width=0 Height=0
  ClassID="CLSID:B8F2846E-CE36-11D0-AC83-00C04FD97575"
  CodeBase="#VERSION=6,0,0,0">
</Object>
```

```
Private Sub OutputSpeechControl(ByVal Response As _
    System.Web.HttpResponse)
    Response.Write("<Object ID=" + Chr(34) + "L&HTruVoice" + Chr(34) + _
      " Width=0 Height=0" + vbCrLf)
    Response.Write("  ClassID=" + Chr(34) + _
```

```
    "CLSID:B8F2846E-CE36-11D0-AC83-00C04FD97575" + Chr(34) + vbCrLf)
  Response.Write("  CodeBase=" + Chr(34) + _
    "#VERSION=6,0,0,0" + Chr(34) + ">" + vbCrLf)
  Response.Write("</Object>" + vbCrLf)
End Sub
```

Listing 21.5 contains a number of methods that generate and emit JavaScript into the HTML document. The first method you can see in Listing 21.5 is the `OutputScript()` method. This method simply calls all the methods that in turn emit JavaScript as the HTML document. The first method you will want to take a look at is the `StartScript()` method. This method simply emits the `StartOfScript` tag, as seen in the gray above the `StartScript()` method.

The next method you will want to take a look at is the `OutputVariables()` method. This method emits the JavaScript variables that maintain the state of the Agent character. Above the `OutputVariables()` method, in gray, you can see the actual JavaScript code that is emitted into the HTML document.

To make the `MoveToSpecial()` method work, a number of variables must be initialized. They are all the variables that can be seen in Table 21.2. These variables are all initialized based on the screen width and height. They contain the left, middle, and right *x*-coordinates, and the top, middle, and bottom *y*-coordinates. The actual code that is emitted into the JavaScript can be seen in gray above the `OutputGetPositions()` method. There is a `Window_Onload()` method for the JavaScript. This method actually loads the Agent character and checks its status. The `Window_Onload()` method is output by the `OutputOnLoad()` method.

Listing 21.5 The Methods That Output the JavaScript Code and the JavaScript Code That They Emit

```
Private Sub OutputScript(ByVal Response As System.Web.HttpResponse)
  StartScript(Response)
  OutputVariables(Response)
  OutputOnLoad(Response)
  OutputLoadAgent(Response)
  OutputSetCharObj(Response)
  OutputCheckLoadStatus(Response)
  OutputLoadError(Response)
  OutputGetPositions(Response)
```

```
    OutputCommands(Response)
    EndScript(Response)
End Sub
```

This code is emitted by the StartScript() method.
```
<Script Language="JavaScript">
```

```
Private Sub StartScript(ByVal Response As System.Web.HttpResponse)
    Response.Write("<Script Language=" + Chr(34) + "JavaScript" + _
    Chr(34) + ">" + vbCrLf)
End Sub
```

This code is emitted by the OutputVariables() method.
```
var Agent;
var UsedChars;
var AgentID;
var AgentACS;
var AgentLoaded;
var LoadReq;
var HideReq;
var AgentLeftX, AgentCenterX, AgentRightX;
var AgentTopY, AgentCenterY, AgentBottomY;
UsedChars = "Genie";
AgentID = "Genie";
AgentACS = "Genie.acs";
AgentLoaded = false;
```

```
Private Sub OutputVariables(ByVal Response As System.Web.HttpResponse)
    Response.Write("var Agent;" + vbCrLf)
    Response.Write("var UsedChars;" + vbCrLf)
    Response.Write("var AgentID;" + vbCrLf)
    Response.Write("var AgentACS;" + vbCrLf)
    Response.Write("var AgentLoaded;" + vbCrLf)
    Response.Write("var LoadReq;" + vbCrLf)
    Response.Write("var HideReq;" + vbCrLf)
    Response.Write("var AgentLeftX, AgentCenterX, AgentRightX;" + _
        vbCrLf)
    Response.Write("var AgentTopY, AgentCenterY, AgentBottomY;" + _
        vbCrLf)
    Response.Write("UsedChars = " + Chr(34) + _character + Chr(34) + _
        ";" + vbCrLf)
    Response.Write("AgentID = " + Chr(34) + _character + Chr(34) + _
        ";" + vbCrLf)
```

```
    Response.Write("AgentACS = " + Chr(34) + _character + ".acs" + _
      Chr(34) + ";" + vbCrLf)
    Response.Write("AgentLoaded = false;" + vbCrLf)
End Sub
```

This code is emitted by the OutputGetPositions() method.

```
function GetScreenPositions()
{
  var ScreenWidth = window.screen.width;
  var ScreenHeight = window.screen.height;
  if ((ScreenWidth == 0) || (ScreenHeight == 0))
  {
    ScreenWidth = 800;
    ScreenHeight = 600;
  }
  AgentCenterX =
    (parseInt(ScreenWidth / 2) - parseInt(Agent.Width / 2));
  AgentRightX = (ScreenWidth - Agent.Width);
  AgentCenterY =
    (parseInt(ScreenHeight / 2) - parseInt(Agent.Height / 2));
  AgentBottomY = (ScreenHeight - Agent.Height);
}
```

```
Private Sub OutputGetPositions(ByVal Response As _
  System.Web.HttpResponse)
    Response.Write("function GetScreenPositions()" + vbCrLf)
    Response.Write("{" + vbCrLf)
    Response.Write("  var ScreenWidth = window.screen.width;" + vbCrLf)
    Response.Write("  var ScreenHeight = window.screen.height;" + _
      vbCrLf)
    Response.Write("  if ((ScreenWidth == 0) || " + _
      "(ScreenHeight == 0))" + vbCrLf)
    Response.Write("  {" + vbCrLf)
    Response.Write("    ScreenWidth = 800;" + vbCrLf)
    Response.Write("    ScreenHeight = 600;" + vbCrLf)
    Response.Write("  }" + vbCrLf)
    Response.Write("  AgentCenterX = (parseInt(ScreenWidth / 2) " + _
      "- parseInt(Agent.Width / 2));" + vbCrLf)
    Response.Write("  AgentRightX = (ScreenWidth - Agent.Width);" + _
      vbCrLf)
    Response.Write("  AgentCenterY = (parseInt(ScreenHeight / 2) - " + _
      "parseInt(Agent.Height / 2));" + vbCrLf)
    Response.Write("  AgentBottomY = (ScreenHeight - Agent.Height);" + _
```

```
      vbCrLf)
    Response.Write("}" + vbCrLf)
End Sub
```

This code is emitted by the OutputOnLoad() method.
```
Window_OnLoad();
function Window_OnLoad()
{
  AgentControl.Connected = true;
  AgentLoaded = LoadLocalAgent(AgentID, AgentACS);
  if( !AgentLoaded )
  {
    AgentLoaded = LoadLocalAgent(AgentID, "");
  }
  if (AgentLoaded)
  {
    SetCharObj();
  }
  CheckLoadStatus();
}
```

```
Private Sub OutputOnLoad(ByVal Response As System.Web.HttpResponse)
    Response.Write("Window_OnLoad();" + vbCrLf)
    Response.Write("function Window_OnLoad()" + vbCrLf)
    Response.Write("{" + vbCrLf)
    Response.Write("  AgentControl.Connected = true;" + vbCrLf)
    Response.Write("  AgentLoaded=LoadLocalAgent(AgentID,AgentACS);" + _
      vbCrLf)
    Response.Write("  if( !AgentLoaded )" + vbCrLf)
    Response.Write("  {" + vbCrLf)
    Response.Write("    AgentLoaded = LoadLocalAgent(AgentID, " + _
      Chr(34) + Chr(34) + ");" + vbCrLf)
    Response.Write("  }" + vbCrLf)
    Response.Write("  if (AgentLoaded)" + vbCrLf)
    Response.Write("  {" + vbCrLf)
    Response.Write("    SetCharObj();" + vbCrLf)
    Response.Write("  }" + vbCrLf)
    Response.Write("  CheckLoadStatus();" + vbCrLf)
    Response.Write("}" + vbCrLf)
End Sub
```

This code is emitted by the OutputLoadAgent() method.
```
function LoadLocalAgent(CharID, CharACS)
{
```

```
  AgentControl.RaiseRequestErrors = false;
  if (CharACS == "")
  {
    LoadReq = AgentControl.Characters.Load(CharID);
  }
  else
  {
    LoadReq = AgentControl.Characters.Load(CharID, CharACS);
  }
  AgentControl.RaiseRequestErrors = true;
  if (LoadReq.Status != 1)
  {
    return(true);
  }
  return(false);
}
```

```
Private Sub OutputLoadAgent(ByVal Response As System.Web.HttpResponse)
    Response.Write("function LoadLocalAgent(CharID, CharACS)" + vbCrLf)
    Response.Write("{" + vbCrLf)
    Response.Write("  AgentControl.RaiseRequestErrors = false;" + _
      vbCrLf)
    Response.Write("  if (CharACS == " + Chr(34) + Chr(34) + ")" + _
      vbCrLf)
    Response.Write("  {" + vbCrLf)
    Response.Write("    LoadReq=AgentControl.Characters.Load(CharID);"+_
      vbCrLf)
    Response.Write("  }" + vbCrLf)
    Response.Write("  else" + vbCrLf)
    Response.Write("  {" + vbCrLf)
    Response.Write("    LoadReq = AgentControl.Characters.Load(" + _
      "CharID, CharACS);" + vbCrLf)
    Response.Write("  }" + vbCrLf)
    Response.Write("  AgentControl.RaiseRequestErrors = true;" + vbCrLf)
    Response.Write("  if (LoadReq.Status != 1)" + vbCrLf)
    Response.Write("  {" + vbCrLf)
    Response.Write("    return(true);" + vbCrLf)
    Response.Write("  }" + vbCrLf)
    Response.Write("  return(false);" + vbCrLf)
    Response.Write("}" + vbCrLf)
End Sub
```

This code is emitted by the OutputSetCharObj() method.
```
function SetCharObj()
```

```
{
  Agent = AgentControl.Characters.Character(AgentID);
  Agent.LanguageID = 0x409;
}
```

```
Private Sub OutputSetCharObj(ByVal Response As System.Web.HttpResponse)
    Response.Write("function SetCharObj()" + vbCrLf)
    Response.Write("{" + vbCrLf)
    Response.Write("  Agent = " + _
      "AgentControl.Characters.Character(AgentID);" + vbCrLf)
    Response.Write("  Agent.LanguageID = 0x409;" + vbCrLf)
    Response.Write("}" + vbCrLf)
End Sub
```

This code is emitted by the OutputCheckLoadStatus() method.
```
function CheckLoadStatus()
{
  if (!AgentLoaded)
  {
    LoadError();
    return(false);
  }
  window.status = "";
  AgentScript();
  return(true);
}
```

```
Private Sub OutputCheckLoadStatus(ByVal Response As _
  System.Web.HttpResponse)
    Response.Write("function CheckLoadStatus()" + vbCrLf)
    Response.Write("{" + vbCrLf)
    Response.Write("  if (!AgentLoaded)" + vbCrLf)
    Response.Write("  {" + vbCrLf)
    Response.Write("    LoadError();" + vbCrLf)
    Response.Write("    return(false);" + vbCrLf)
    Response.Write("  }" + vbCrLf)
    Response.Write("  window.status = " + Chr(34) + Chr(34) + ";" + _
      vbCrLf)
    Response.Write("  AgentScript();" + vbCrLf)
    Response.Write("  return(true);" + vbCrLf)
    Response.Write("}" + vbCrLf)
End Sub
```

This code is emitted by the OutputLoadError() method.
```
function LoadError()
{
  var strMsg;
  window.status = "";
  strMsg = "Error Loading Character: "+ AgentID + "\n";
  strMsg = strMsg +
    "This Microsoft Agent Script requires the character(s):\n";
  strMsg = strMsg + UsedChars;
  alert(strMsg);
}
```

```
Private Sub OutputLoadError(ByVal Response As System.Web.HttpResponse)
    Response.Write("function LoadError()" + vbCrLf)
    Response.Write("{" + vbCrLf)
    Response.Write("  var strMsg;" + vbCrLf)
    Response.Write("  window.status = " + Chr(34) + Chr(34) + ";" + _
      vbCrLf)
    Response.Write("  strMsg = " + Chr(34) + _
      "Error Loading Character: " + Chr(34) + "+ AgentID + " + _
      Chr(34) + "\n" + Chr(34) + ";" + vbCrLf)
    Response.Write("  strMsg = strMsg + " + Chr(34) + _
      "This Microsoft Agent Script requires the character(s):\n" + _
      Chr(34) + ";" + vbCrLf)
    Response.Write("  strMsg = strMsg + UsedChars;" + vbCrLf)
    Response.Write("  alert(strMsg);" + vbCrLf)
    Response.Write("}" + vbCrLf)
End Sub
```

This code is emitted by the OutputCommands() method.
```
function AgentScript()
{
  GetScreenPositions();
  Agent.Show();
}
```

```
Private Sub OutputCommands(ByVal Response As System.Web.HttpResponse)
    Response.Write("function AgentScript()" + vbCrLf)
    Response.Write("{" + vbCrLf)
    Response.Write("  GetScreenPositions();" + vbCrLf)
    Dim i As Integer
    For i = 0 To m_ScriptList.Count - 1
```

```
        Response.Write("  Agent." + _
            Convert.ToString(m_ScriptList(i)) + vbCrLf)
    Next
    Response.Write("}" + vbCrLf)
End Sub
```

This code is emitted by the EndScript() method.
```
</Script>
```

```
Private Sub EndScript(ByVal Response As System.Web.HttpResponse)
    Response.Write("</Script>" + vbCrLf)
End Sub
```

Listing 21.6 shows the method named `DoAgentStuff()`. This method is called from the default .aspx code. The method can be seen, however, in the default aspx.cs code module.

The first thing that happens in the `DoAgentStuff()` method is that the Hide user interface object (which is a CheckBox) is checked to see whether the Agent must be hidden or shown. If the Agent character must be shown, then an `Agent` class is substantiated and the `Agent` class's character is set to the value found in the drop-down list that contains the available Agent characters.

Four animations can be selected that put the Agent character through its paces. These animations are contained within four case statements in the `DoAgentStuff()` method. The actual randomly selected animation that will be performed is contained in a session variable named `Animation-Number`.

Below the four animations is code that is called if an animation has not been selected. If coordinates have been entered into the editable X and Y test field then the Agent character will be moved. The `Show()` method is called to make the Agent character visible. Then, any speech is in the speech text box, the `SpeakMethod()` will be called, thus making the Agent character say the phrase. The last thing that is done is the `Render()` method is called, which actually outputs all the JavaScript code into the HTML document.

Listing 21.6 The `DoAgentStuff()` method responds to the user interface and creates the appropriate commands.

```
Public Sub DoAgentStuff()
    If Not Hide.Checked Then
        Dim ag As New Agent()
        ag.Character = Convert.ToString(Character.SelectedItem.Text)
```

```
If Not Session("AnimationNumber") Is Nothing Then
  Select Case Convert.ToInt32(Session("AnimationNumber"))
    Case 0
      ag.MoveToSpecial("AgentCenterX", "AgentCenterY")
      ag.Show()
      ag.Speak("This is animation one.")
      ag.Play("Congratulate")
      ag.Speak("You now have the power to speech-enable your " + _
        Web applications.")
      ag.MoveToSpecial("AgentLeftX", "AgentCenterY")
      ag.Speak("I can go to the left of the screen.")
      ag.Play("LookLeft")
      ag.MoveToSpecial("AgentRightX", "AgentBottomY")
      ag.Speak("I can go to the bottom right of the screen.")
      ag.Play("Wave")
      ag.MoveToSpecial("AgentCenterX", "AgentCenterY")
      ag.Speak("I am magic.")
      ag.Play("DoMagic2")
    Case 1
      ag.Show()
      ag.Speak("This is animation two.")
      ag.Speak("Imagine being able to provide online " + _
        "training that has speech and animation.")
      ag.Move(50, 50)
      ag.Speak("Your training would be far more interesting " + _
        "to users.")
      ag.Move(100, 100)
      ag.Speak("You would hold the attention of those whom " + _
        "you are training.")
      ag.Move(150, 150)
      ag.Speak("This would increase the return on your " + _
        "training investment.")
      ag.Play("Congratulate_2")
      ag.Move(200, 200)
      ag.Speak("Many people learn better when they hear and " + _
        "read, rather than when they simply read.")
      ag.Move(250, 250)
      ag.Play("Explain")
      ag.Speak("Why not consider using the Microsoft Agents " + _
        "for your online training?")
      ag.MoveToSpecial("AgentCenterX", "AgentCenterY")
    Case 2
      ag.MoveToSpecial("AgentRightX", "AgentTopY")
```

```
        ag.Show()
        ag.Speak("This is animation three.")
        ag.Play("Greet")
        ag.Speak("What if you had students with reading " + _
          "disabilities?")
        ag.MoveToSpecial("AgentLeftX", "AgentBottomY")
        ag.Speak("What if you had students who were blind?")
        ag.Play("Explain")
        ag.MoveToSpecial("AgentCenterX", "AgentCenterY")
        ag.Speak("The Microsoft Agent technology would be " + _
          "the perfect way to deliver Web based content.")
        ag.Play("Process")
      Case 3
        ag.Show()
       ag.Speak("This is animation four.")
        ag.Play("Search")
        ag.Speak("I see there is lots of space on this screen " + _
          "for moving around.")
        ag.MoveToSpecial("AgentLeftX", "AgentBottomY")
        ag.Speak("Here I am down here.")
        ag.MoveToSpecial("AgentRightX", "AgentBottomY")
        ag.Speak("Here I am over here.")
        ag.MoveToSpecial("AgentRightX", "AgentTopY")
        ag.Speak("Wow, now I am here.")
        ag.MoveToSpecial("AgentLeftX", "AgentTopY")
        ag.Speak("Back to where I started.")
        ag.MoveToSpecial("AgentCenterX", "AgentCenterY")
        ag.Play("Surprised")
        ag.Speak("Now I am the center of attention!")
    End Select
    Session("AnimationNumber") = Nothing
  Else
    Try
      ag.Move(Convert.ToInt32(X.Text), Convert.ToInt32(Y.Text))
    Catch
    End Try
    ag.Show()
    If Speech.Text.Length > 0 Then
      ag.Speak(Speech.Text)
      Speech.Text = ""
    End If
  End If
End If
```

```
      ag.Render(Response)
   End If
End Sub
```

When users click the Show Animation button, the ShowAnimation_ Click() method is fired, as shown in Listing 21.7. This method simply selects a random number from 0 to 3 and then stores that number in a session variable named Animation Number.

Listing 21.7 This Method Responds to the Show Animation Button. It Generates a Random Number from 0 to 3 That Will Be Used to Select the Animation to Run.

```
Private Sub ShowAnimation_Click(ByVal sender As System.Object, _
   ByVal e As System.EventArgs) Handles ShowAnimation.Click
      Dim rnd As New Random()
      Dim nRandom As Integer
      nRandom = rnd.Next(4)
      If nRandom > 3 Then
         nRandom = 3
      End If
      Session("AnimationNumber") = nRandom
End Sub
```

Although using the Agent class is simple and straightforward, doing so will add immensely to your Web applications. And you could easily enhance the SpeechVB application to do much, much more.

Summary

Microsoft Agent characters are a great way to speech-enable your applications and make them come alive. Your applications can become interactive and hold the attention of your users.

Not only will the Agent characters add a lot of spice to your Web site, but they also can add functionality for people with reading and vision problems. This chapter has shown you a class that makes it easy to programmatically add Microsoft Agent characters to your Web site. The class is easy to use, and with it you won't have any problem taking your application to the next step.

CHAPTER 22

Uploading Content: Building a File Repository Application

In This Chapter:

- The Main Menu
- The Manage Files Page
- The Edit Files Page
- The Delete Group Page
- The Add File Page
- The Search Page
- The Show Group Page
- The Edit Profile Page

Many Web sites offer downloadable files. The Web sites I visit most often that take a systematic approach to managing downloadable files are programming sites that offer programs and source code for downloading. Many of these Web sites have a convenient way to display a list of files, along with descriptions and version numbers. The files can be grouped by category, or possibly grouped by whoever uploaded them.

This chapter builds a file repository application. With this application running on a Web server, users can create their own file groups, upload files, and edit the information for each file. Other users can search for files that match specified search criteria, and then download files that turn up. It's a great way to manage user-uploaded files.

In the process of building this application, we'll talk about uploading files to the server, doing file I/O and a number of other things such as using cookies, and doing Form-based authentication. The methods of the application are shown in Table 22.1. This table will act as a handy reference as you use and study the application. Figure 22.1 shows the hierarchy of the files in the application. Note that `ShowGroup` is a stand-alone page that is meant to be called from other applications.

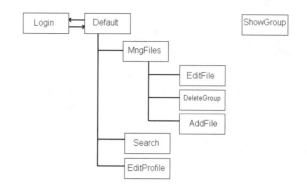

Figure 22.1 This Is the Hierarchy for the File Repository Pages.

Table 22.1 The File Repository Application Methods

Method	Listing	Source Code File	Description
Page_Load	22.1	Default.aspx.cs	This method is called when the default.aspx page is loaded.
LogOut_Click	22.1	Default.aspx.cs	This method is fired when the user clicks the Log Out button.
Admin_Click	22.1	Default.aspx.cs	This method is fired when the user clicks the Admin button.
Search_Click	22.1	Default.aspx.cs	This method is fired when the user clicks the Search button.
Manage_Click	22.1	Default.aspx.cs	This method is fired when the user clicks the Manage button.
Profile_Click	22.1	Default.aspx.cs	This method is fired when the user clicks the Edit Profile button.
Page_Load	22.2	Login.aspx.cs	This method is called when the Login.aspx page is loaded.

Table 22.1 The File Repository Application Methods (*cont.*)

Method	Listing	Source Code File	Description
LogUser	22.3	Login.aspx.cs	This method attempts to match a user name and password with an entry in the database, or it adds a record for a new user.
LoginUser_Click	22.3	Login.aspx.cs	This method is fired when the user clicks the Login button.
NewUser_CheckChanged	22.3	Login.aspx.cs	This method is fired when the user selects or deselects the New User checkbox.
BindDataToControls	22.4	MngFiles.aspx.cs	This method binds the group and file data to the databound controls.
Page_Load	22.5	MngFiles.aspx.cs	This method is called when the MngFiles.aspx file is loaded.
AddGroup_Click	22.5	MngFiles.aspx.cs	This method is fired when the user clicks the Add Group button.
Main_Click	22.5	MngFiles.aspx.cs	This method is fired when the user clicks the Main Menu button.
Page_Load	22.6	EditFile.aspx.cs	This method is called when the EditFile.aspx page is loaded.
Main_Click	22.6	EditFile.aspx.cs	This method is fired when the user clicks the Main Menu button.
Cancel_Click	22.6	EditFile.aspx.cs	This method is fired when the user clicks the Cancel button.
Delete_Click	22.6	EditFile.aspx.cs	This method is fired when the user clicks the Delete button.
Save_Click	22.6	EditFile.aspx.cs	This method is fired when the user clicks the Save button.

(continued)

Table 22.1 The File Repository Application Methods (*cont.*)

Method	Listing	Source Code File	Description
ShowGroupName	22.7	DeleteGroup.aspx.cs	This method shows the group name, which is contained in a session variable.
Cancel_Click	22.7	DeleteGroup.aspx.cs	This method is fired when the user clicks the Cancel button.
OK_Click	22.7	DeleteGroup.aspx.cs	This method is fired when the user clicks the OK button.
Save_Click	22.8	AddFile.aspx.cs	This method is fired when the user clicks the Save button.
Cancel_Click	22.8	AddFile.aspx.cs	This method is fired when the user clicks the Cancel button.
Main_Click	22.8	AddFile.aspx.cs	This method is fired when the user clicks the Main Menu button.
Main_Click	22.9	Search.aspx.cs	This method is fired when the user clicks the Main Menu button.
PerformSearch_Click	22.9	Search.aspx.cs	This method is fired when the user clicks the Perform Search button.
Page_Load	22.10	ShowGroup.aspx.cs	This method is called when the ShowGroup.aspx page is loaded.
ShowGroupName	22.10	ShowGroup.aspx.cs	This method shows the group name, which is contained in a session variable.
Page_Load	22.11	EditProfile.aspx.cs	This method is called when the EditProfile.aspx page is loaded.
Update_Click	22.11	EditProfile.aspx.cs	This method is fired when the user clicks the Update button.

Table 22.1 The File Repository Application Methods (*cont.*)

Method	Listing	Source Code File	Description
Cancel_Click	22.11	EditProfile. aspx.cs	This method is fired when the user clicks the Cancel button.
ShowGroupName	22.11	EditProfile. aspx.cs	This method shows the group name, which is contained in a session variable.

The Main Menu

The main menu is contained in the Default.aspx page, and the code behind this page can be seen in Listing 22.1. Depending on the login type, the main menu contains either four or five buttons. The only variation is whether the Admin button is visible. If a user logs in, and her login account has administrative rights, the Admin button will be displayed.

The normal four buttons are for logging out, searching, managing files, and editing a user's profile. The main menu page can be seen in Figure 22.2.

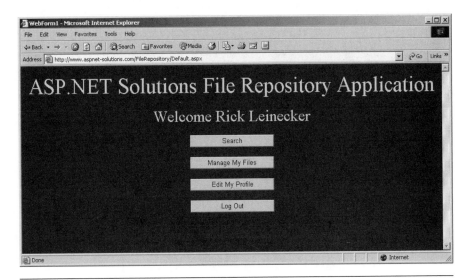

Figure 22.2 The Main Screen Offers Four Choices.

All of the button handler methods simply redirect to the appropriate page. The only addition to these methods is a call to the `FormsAuthentication.SignOut()` so that the user is logged out. The `Page_Load()` method takes a look at the `Session` variable named `Account-Type`. If this variable is equal to one, the Admin button object's `Visible` property is set to `true` so that the button will appear in the menu.

Listing 22.1 Methods behind the default.aspx Page

```
private void Page_Load(object sender, System.EventArgs e)
{
  if( Convert.ToInt32( Session["AccountType"] ) == 1 )
  {
    Admin.Visible = true;
  }
}


private void LogOut_Click(object sender, System.EventArgs e)
{
  FormsAuthentication.SignOut();
  Response.Redirect( "Login.aspx?Force=1" );
}


private void Admin_Click(object sender, System.EventArgs e)
{
  Response.Redirect( "Admin.aspx" );
}


private void Search_Click(object sender, System.EventArgs e)
{
  Response.Redirect( "Search.aspx" );
}


private void Manage_Click(object sender, System.EventArgs e)
{
  Response.Redirect( "MngFiles.aspx" );
}


private void Profile_Click(object sender, System.EventArgs e)
{
  Response.Redirect( "EditProfile.aspx" );
}
```

Before a user even gets to the Default.aspx page containing the main menu, he must log in. That's because the application uses Forms authentication. The code for the login page can be seen in Listing 22.2, and the login page can be seen in operation in Figure 22.3.

Here are the steps to use Forms authentication in this program:

1. Edit the Web.Config file so that the application will know that you want Forms authentication, and what the login page is. (The **name** attribute of the Forms item is the name of the cookie that holds the authentication.) The following code shows how to do it:

```
<authorization>
  <deny users="?" />
</authorization>
<authentication mode="Forms">
  <forms name=".FILEREPOSITORY" loginUrl="login.aspx" protection="All"
    timeout="30" path="/">
  </forms>
</authentication>
```

2. Create a login page, and if the user credentials are OK, use the following method to allow the user to be authenticated to the application:

```
FormsAuthentication.RedirectFromLoginPage( strName,
    RememberLogin.Checked );
```

3. You can let the authentication time out after a period of nonuse, or you can offer the following method to let users explicitly logout:

```
FormsAuthentication.SignOut();
```

The `Page_Load()` method shown in Listing 22.2 looks for a cookie that determines whether users can log on to the local computer automatically. First, though, it checks a parameter named `Force` to see whether the user is coming from another page and we need to force the user to log in. You see, if the user has just logged out by clicking the Logout button from the main menu, he doesn't want to come here and automatically just log in again. So from the Default.aspx page, when the user is redirected to this page, a parameter named `Force` will have a value of 1. If the value of the `Force` parameter is not 1, then the application will proceed to retrieve the Cookie normally. But if the `Force` parameter is missing or has a value other than 1, the user will not be logged in automatically.

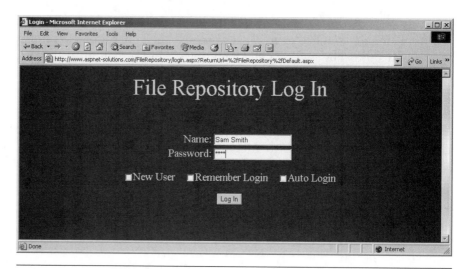

Figure 22.3 When the Application First Appears, You'll Have to Log In.

If necessary, we attempt to retrieve a cookie to see whether we can automatically log in. We do this by creating an HttpCookie object named FileRepository with the following code:

```
HttpCookie Cookie = Request.Cookies["FileRepository"];
```

If the cookie could not be retrieved (the case when the application runs for the first time), then the HttpCookie object will be `null`. In this case, we can't do an automatic login because we don't know if this is what the user wants, and more importantly we don't have the user credentials with which to do the login.

Let's say we got a cookie. Then we have to look at the value that determines whether the application should have remembered the name and password with which we'll populate the TextBox objects. This is done with the following code:

```
bool bRemember = Convert.ToBoolean( Cookie.Values["Remember"] );
```

To determine whether we do an automatic login, we use the following code:

```
bool bAutoLogin = Convert.ToBoolean( Cookie.Values["AutoLogin"] );
```

The name and password are retrieved from the cookie, and depending on the user preferences, either the user interface objects are populated with the name and password, the user is automatically logged in, or a normal login is presented to the user.

Listing 22.2 This Code Checks for a Cookie in Case It Needs to Retrieve a User Name and Password.

```
private void Page_Load(object sender, System.EventArgs e)
{
  if( !IsPostBack )
  {
    int nForce = Convert.ToInt32( Request.QueryString["Force"] );
    if( nForce != 1 )
    {
      HttpCookie Cookie = Request.Cookies["FileRepository"];
      if( Cookie != null )
      {
        bool bRemember = Convert.ToBoolean( Cookie.Values["Remember"] );
        bool bAutoLogin =
          Convert.ToBoolean( Cookie.Values["AutoLogin"] );
        string strName = Convert.ToString( Cookie.Values["Name"] );
        string strPassword =
          Convert.ToString( Cookie.Values["Password"] );

        if( bAutoLogin )
        {
          FormsAuthentication.RedirectFromLoginPage( strName, true );
        }
        else if( bRemember )
        {
          Name.Text = strName;
          Password.Text = strPassword;
        }
      }
    }
  }
}
```

If a user isn't automatically logged in, she'll have to type in her user name and password. It's possible that these two values will be filled in if the user has the Remember Password checkbox selected. Either way, though, she'll have to click the Log In button. Clicking this button fires the LogUserIn_Click() method that is shown in Listing 22.3.

The first thing that happens in the LogUserIn_Click() method is that a call to the LogUser() method is made. This method returns a value of 0 if the login was successful, 1 if the name couldn't be found, or 2 if the password didn't match. I've been told that you should never tell users if the password doesn't match because this tells them that they at least have entered a valid user name. Although this is probably valid criticism, I chose to leave the application functioning as it is. You could make the following change if you are worried:

Change:

C#

```
if( nLogin == 0 )
{
   . . .
}
else if( nLogin == 1 )
{
  ErrorMessage.Text = "The Name/Password combination was incorrect.";
}
else if( nLogin == 2 )
{
  ErrorMessage.Text = "The name you specified is already in use.";
}
```

VB

```
If nLogin = 0 Then
   . . .
ElseIf nLogin = 1 Then
  ErrorMessage.Text = "The Name/Password combination was incorrect."
ElseIf nLogin = 2 Then
  ErrorMessage.Text = "The name you specified is already in use."
End If
```

To:

C#

```
if( nLogin == 0 )
{
   . . .
```

```
}
else if( nLogin == 1 || nLogin == 2 )
{
   ErrorMessage.Text = "The Name/Password combination was incorrect.";
}
```

VB
```
If nLogin = 0 Then
   .  .  .
ElseIf nLogin = 1 OR nLogin = 2 Then
   ErrorMessage.Text = "The Name/Password combination was incorrect."
End If
```

If the nLogin variable contains a 0 (meaning the login was successful), then the name and password are stored in local string variables. They're trimmed and made uppercase for easier handling. An HttpCookie object is created with the name FileRepository. The cookie has four values added: Name, Password, Remember (for Remember Login), and AutoLogin. The following line sets the cookie expiration date so that it never expires:

```
Cookie.Expires = DateTime.MaxValue;
```

Next, the cookie is added to the HTTP header by calling the Response. AppendCookie() method. Finally, a call to the FormsAuthentication.RedirectFromLoginPage() method is made. The user is now logged in and can access all of the application's pages. The user is redirected to the Default.aspx page, where the main menu is presented.

The LogUser() method can also be seen in Listing 22.3. This method performs the database access to validate the credentials that have been entered into the Name and Password TextBox objects.

The first thing the method does is to create a SqlConnection object—the connection string is retrieved from the Web.Config file by using the ConfigurationSettings.AppSettings() method. A SqlDataReader object is declared and initialized to null (or Nothing in VB). Later in the code, a test for null (or Nothing) can be made to see whether the SqlDataReader object needs to be closed.

A string named strName is assigned the contents of the Name TextBox object. The data is trimmed (which removes leading and trailing blank spaces) and made uppercase for easier handling with the following line:

```
string strName = Name.Text.Trim().ToUpper();
```

If the value in the Name field is 0 after it has been trimmed, then a valid user name hasn't been entered. In this case, the user is shown an error message, and the value of 3 is returned to the calling method. (Remember that the calling method acts only on return values of 0, 1, and 2.)

The password is retrieved from the Password TextBox object and stored in a string named strPassword. The data, though, is first trimmed and made uppercase.

A try/catch/finally construct is used to handle any exceptions that the database access methods may throw. The catch block simply sets the Label named ErrorMessage with the exception message text and returns a value of 3. The finally block closes the SqlDataReader object if it is not null (or Nothing), and closes the SqlConnection if it is open.

Inside of the try block, the operative code resides. The first thing that's done is to open the SqlConnection with the Open() method. A string containing the SQL is then created based on the name that is contained in the strName string variable. The following code shows how the SQL string is formed:

```
"select * from Users where Name='" + strName + "'"
```

If the user name is Suzy, the SQL will be the following:

```
select * from Users where Name='Suzy'
```

The SQL string isn't actually a string variable, but it's formed inside of a SqlCommand object's constructor. (Technically, at least one string is created by the common language runtime behind the scenes, and this is one of the considerations when optimizing this type of code.) Once the Sql-Command object has been created, a call to its ExecuteReader() method is made, which in turn returns a SqlDataReader object. If there are any records in the SqlDataReader object, the Read() method will return true—otherwise it will return false (and this method will return a value of 1 indicating to the caller that the user name wasn't found). If a record was returned, we need to compare the password with what was typed in. If it matches, we're good to go, and this method returns a 0 to indicate success. If the password doesn't match, then the value of 2 is returned to indicate that the user name was found, but that the password is incorrect.

We've already talked about not revealing whether the password is incorrect, but simply telling users that the user name/password combination is incorrect. If you want to take this approach, you can simplify the code by letting the SQL match both the user name and password. If a record is returned, then the user name and password was found. If no records are returned, then the combination wasn't found. The following SQL statement creation can be used if you want to make this change:

C#
```
"select * from Users where Name='" + strName +
   "' and Password='" + strPassword + "'"
```

VB
```
"select * from Users where Name='" + strName + _
   "' and Password='" + strPassword + "'"
```

If the name is found and the NewUser CheckBox object is checked, an error message is shown and the value of 3 is returned. That's because we don't want to create a new user who has a duplicate name that already exists in the database.

If the name and password matches, some other information is stored in session variables. The user ID, name, and account type are all stored for later use.

If no record was found that matches the user name, and the NewUser CheckBox object is selected, then a new user record needs to be created. If you've used the application, you've probably seen a table appear when you click the New User checkbox. This table allows the user to enter his date of birth and his e-mail address. The code to hide and show the table can be seen in the `NewUser_CheckChanged()` method shown in Listing 22.3. This method also changes the state of the RememberLogin and AutoLogin objects to appropriate values.

The table object is named ExtraInfoTable, and it has two child objects that are TextBox objects. These objects can't be used directly because they are child objects of the table. To get references to the TextBox objects, we use the `FindControl()` method. The following line of code gets an object reference to a TextBox control named Email:

```
TextBox tb = (TextBox) ExtraInfoTable.FindControl("Email");
```

The e-mail and date-of-birth information is retrieved from the TextBox child objects, and they are trimmed in case there are unwanted blank spaces. A SqlCommand object is created with a SQL string that will insert the new row into the Users table. This is the SQL string creation code:

C#

```
"Insert into " +
  "Users (Name,Password,Email,DateOfBirth) VALUES ('" +
  strName + "','" + strPassword + "','" + strEmail + "','" +
    strDateOfBirth + "') select @ID=@@IDENTITY"
```

VB

```
"Insert into " + _
  "Users (Name,Password,Email,DateOfBirth) VALUES ('" + _
  strName + "','" + strPassword + "','" + strEmail + "','" + _
    strDateOfBirth + "') select @ID=@@IDENTITY"
```

We'll need to add a parameter named `@ID` to the SqlCommand object. This is so that we can take advantage of the special SQL that gets the identity value and puts it into the variable named `@ID`. This value will be the newly created user ID. Once the `ExecuteNonQuery()` method is called, the `SqlCommand` parameter will contain the ID value.

Listing 22.3 `LoginUser_Click()` Is Fired When the Log In Button Is Clicked. The `LogUser()` Method Does the Work of Trying to Log a User In.

```
private void LogUserIn_Click(object sender, System.EventArgs e)
{
  // Call the LoginUser() method that does the
  //   database access.
  int nLogin = LogUser();

  // If the returned value is 0, their credentials check out.
  if( nLogin == 0 )
  {
    // Get a cleaned version of the name and password.
    string strName = Name.Text.Trim().ToUpper();
    string strPassword = Password.Text.Trim().ToUpper();

    // Create a cookie and set the values that need to be saved.
    HttpCookie Cookie = new HttpCookie( "FileRepository" );
    Cookie.Values.Add( "Name", strName );
    Cookie.Values.Add( "Password", strPassword );
    Cookie.Values.Add( "Remember",
        Convert.ToString( RememberLogin.Checked ) );
    Cookie.Values.Add( "AutoLogin",
        Convert.ToString( AutoLogin.Checked ) );
```

```
      Cookie.Expires = DateTime.MaxValue;
      Response.AppendCookie( Cookie );

      // Do the actual authentication.
      FormsAuthentication.RedirectFromLoginPage( strName,
         RememberLogin.Checked );
   }
   // Login failure.
   else if( nLogin == 1 )
   {
      ErrorMessage.Text = "The Name/Password combination was incorrect.";
   }
   // They tried to create a new account with a duplicate name.
   else if( nLogin == 2 )
   {
      ErrorMessage.Text = "The name you specified is already in use.";
   }
}


// This method scrubs the ' character.
string SafeSql( string sql )
{

    Regex regex = new Regex("'");
    return regex.Replace(sql, "''");
 }


// This method does the database access to match name and password.
private int LogUser()
{
   // Create the connection object.
   SqlConnection objConnection =
   new SqlConnection(ConfigurationSettings.AppSettings["ConnectString"]);

   // Declare a null SqlDataReader.
   SqlDataReader objReader = null;

   // Get a cleaned name,
   string strName = Name.Text.Trim().ToUpper();
   // Bail out if they entered no valid name.
   if( strName.Length == 0 )
   {
      ErrorMessage.Text = "You must have at least one non-blank " +
```

```
      "character in the name field.";
    return( 3 );
}

// Get a cleaned password.
string strPassword = Password.Text.Trim().ToUpper();
int nRet = 0;
try
{
  // Open the connection.
  objConnection.Open();

  // Create a command object.
  SqlCommand objCommand =
    new SqlCommand( "select * from Users where Name='" +
    SafeSql( strName ) +
    "'", objConnection );

  // Get a recordset.
  objReader = objCommand.ExecuteReader();

  // If there are records, perform this code.
  if( objReader.Read() )
  {
    // First see if they specified that this is a new user.
    if( NewUser.Checked )
    {
      ErrorMessage.Text = "You tried to create a user that " +
        "already exists.";
      return( 3 );
    }
    else
    {
      // Compare the entered password with the password
      //   from the database.
      if( strPassword !=
        Convert.ToString( objReader["Password"] ).ToUpper() )
      {
        nRet = 1;
      }
      else
      {
        // Set the session variables to contain user ID, name,
```

```
        //   and account type.
        Session["ID"] = Convert.ToInt32( objReader["ID"] );
        Session["Name"] = Convert.ToString( objReader["Name"] );
        Session["AccountType"] =
          Convert.ToInt32( objReader["AccountType"] );
      }
    }
  }
}
else
{
  // Here we come to create a new user record.
  if( NewUser.Checked )
  {
    // Close the reader.
    objReader.Close();

    // Get the extra information which includes
    //   the email and date of birth.
    TextBox tb = (TextBox) ExtraInfoTable.FindControl("Email");
    string strEmail = tb.Text.Trim();
    tb = (TextBox) ExtraInfoTable.FindControl("DateOfBirth");
    string strDateOfBirth = tb.Text.Trim();

    // Create a command object.
    objCommand = new SqlCommand( "Insert into " +
        "Users (Name,Password,Email,DateOfBirth) VALUES ('" +
        SafeSql( strName ) + "','" + SafeSql( strPassword ) +
        "','" + SafeSql( strEmail ) + "','" +
        SafeSql( strDateOfBirth ) +
        "') select @ID=@@IDENTITY", objConnection);

    // Add the ID as a parameter.
    objCommand.Parameters.Add( "@ID", SqlDbType.Int );
    objCommand.Parameters["@ID"].Direction =
        ParameterDirection.Output;

    // Execute the query.
    objCommand.ExecuteNonQuery();

    // Store the user ID, name, and account type in session
    //   variables.
    Session["ID"] =
        Convert.ToInt32( objCommand.Parameters["@ID"].Value );
```

```
        Session["Name"] = strName;
        Session["AccountType"] = 0;
      }
      else
      {
        nRet = 1;
      }
    }
  }
  catch( Exception ex )
  {
    // Alert the user to the error.
    ErrorMessage.Text = ex.Message.ToString();
    nRet = 3;
  }
  finally
  {
    // Close the reader.
    if( objReader != null )
    {
      objReader.Close();
    }
    // Close the connection.
    if( objConnection.State == ConnectionState.Open )
    {
      objConnection.Close();
    }
  }

  return( nRet );
}


// This method changes the extra information user interface objects.
//   When the check box is selected the extra objects appear, otherwise
//   they are hidden.
private void NewUser_CheckedChanged(object sender, System.EventArgs e)
{
  if( NewUser.Checked )
  {
    RememberLogin.Checked = false;
    RememberLogin.Enabled = false;
    AutoLogin.Checked = false;
    AutoLogin.Enabled = false;
```

```
    ExtraInfoTable.Visible = true;
  }
  else
  {
    RememberLogin.Enabled = true;
    AutoLogin.Enabled = true;
    ExtraInfoTable.Visible = false;
  }
}
```

The Manage Files Page

The MngFiles.aspx page allows users to manage their own files. The `Bind-DataToControls()` method is used by this page to populate the user interface objects (GroupList and FileList). This method can be seen in Listing 22.4.

The first thing that this method does is create a SqlConnection object. A `try/catch/finally` construct is used to catch any exceptions that the database access methods might throw. The `catch` block simply shows the exception message in the ErrorMessage Label object, and the `finally` block closes the SqlConnection object if it is open.

In the `try` block, the code that does the work is found. First, the SqlConnection object is opened, then a SQL string is created the will retrieve the ID and Name from the FileGroup table. The SQL is qualified with a where clause that retrieves only the file groups for the currently logged-in user. The following code creates the SQL string:

C#
```
string strSql = "Select ID,Name from FileGroup where OwnerID=" +
  Convert.ToString( Session["ID"] ) + " order by name";
```

VB
```
Dim strSql as string = "Select ID,Name from FileGroup " + _
  where OwnerID=" + Convert.ToString( Session("ID") ) + _
  " order by name";
```

If the user ID is 5, the SQL will be the following:

```
Select ID,Name from FileGroup where OwnerID=5 order by name
```

Because we're going to use the data set more than once, a SqlData-Reader won't suffice. That's because once you databind with a SqlDataReader, it will not contain any data. The SqlDataReader object is a forward-reading data reader and doesn't hold a recordset. Instead, we'll use a DataSet object. This object will be populated with the `SqlDataAdapter.Fill()` method and will contain the complete recordset. For this reason, the data will persist after each use until the object is disposed when it goes out of scope. The following code shows how the DataSet object is populated, and then how it is bound to the GroupList object:

```
SqlDataAdapter objDataAdapter = new SqlDataAdapter( strSql,
   objConnection );
DataSet objDataSet = new DataSet();
objDataAdapter.Fill( objDataSet );
GroupList.DataSource = objDataSet;
GroupList.DataBind();
```

After binding the data to the GroupList object, we'll use the DataSet object to retrieve the set of files that belong to a particular group. The code loops through, and for each group that is in the recordset (which is contained in the DataSet object), we'll retrieve the files that belong to the group. But first, we must retrieve the DataGrid object that is a child object of the GroupList object. We'll do this by using the `FindControl()` method, and we'll specify FileGrid as the control we want to find. The following code retrieves the DataGrid object that corresponds to the current group:

```
DataGrid grid = (DataGrid) GroupList.Items[i].FindControl( "FileGrid" );
```

The SQL statement is constructed based in the group ID as follows:

C#
```
"select Title,Filename,Version,ID from FileInfo " +
   "where GroupID=" + Convert.ToString(
   objDataSet.Tables[0].Rows[i].ItemArray.GetValue( 0 ) ) +
   " order by title";
```

VB
```
"select Title,Filename,Version,ID from FileInfo " + _
   "where GroupID=" + Convert.ToString( _
   objDataSet.Tables(0).Rows(i).ItemArray.GetValue( 0 ) ) + _
      " order by title"
```

If the group ID is 5, the following SQL will result:

```
select Title,Filename,Version,ID from FileInfo where GroupID=5
    order by title
```

Once the SQL string is created, a SqlCommand object is instantiated using the SQL string and the SqlConnection object. A SqlDataReader object is returned when the SqlCommand object's `ExecuteReader()` method is called. The recordset is then bound with the DataGrid object.

Listing 22.4 The `BindDataToControls()` Method Gets the Group Names, Binds Them to a Control, and Gets the File Information to Bind to a Control.

```
private void BindDataToControls()
{
  // Create a connection object.
 SqlConnection objConnection =
  new SqlConnection(ConfigurationSettings.AppSettings["ConnectString"]);

  try
  {
    // Open the connection.
    objConnection.Open();
    string strSql = "Select ID,Name from FileGroup where OwnerID=" +
        Convert.ToString( Session["ID"] ) + " order by name";
    SqlDataAdapter objDataAdapter = new SqlDataAdapter( strSql,
        objConnection );
    DataSet objDataSet = new DataSet();
    objDataAdapter.Fill( objDataSet );
    GroupList.DataSource = objDataSet;
    GroupList.DataBind();

    int nCount = objDataSet.Tables[0].Rows.Count;

    for( int i=0; i<nCount; i++ )
    {
      DataGrid grid =
        (DataGrid) GroupList.Items[i].FindControl( "FileGrid" );
      if( grid != null )
      {
        strSql = "select Title,Filename,Version,ID from FileInfo " +
            "where GroupID=" + Convert.ToString(
```

```
            objDataSet.Tables[0].Rows[i].ItemArray.GetValue( 0 ) ) +
            " order by title";
        // Create a command object.
        SqlCommand objCommand = new SqlCommand( strSql, objConnection );
        SqlDataReader objReader = objCommand.ExecuteReader();

        grid.DataSource = objReader;
        grid.DataBind();

        objReader.Close();
      }
    }
  }
  catch( Exception ex )
  {
    // Alert the user to the error.
    ErrorMessage.Text = ex.Message.ToString();
  }
  finally
  {
    // Close the connection.
    if( objConnection.State == ConnectionState.Open )
    {
      objConnection.Close();
    }
  }
}
```

Listing 22.5 contains the remaining code that's behind the MngFiles.aspx page (see Listing 22.4 for the first part of the code). The `Page_Load()` method simply calls the `BindDataToControls()` method if the `IsPostBack` property is `false`.

Another method in Listing 22.5 is the `AddGroup_Click()` method. This method adds a group to the database for the user who is logged in and takes the group name out of a TextBox object named GroupName.

The `AddGroup_Click()` method creates a SqlConnection object that the database objects will use. And as with all of the other methods that do database access that we've looked at in this chapter, there's a `try/catch/finally` construct to handle any database exceptions that are thrown. In the `try` block, though, is the code that adds the group to the database. This code opens the SqlConnection object with the `Open()`

method, creates a SQL string containing the group name and the owner ID (the logged-in user's ID), calls the ExecuteNonQuery() method, blanks out the Password and Name TextBox objects, and calls the BindDataTo-Control() method. The call to BindDataToControl() is so that the user interface will be repopulated with the newly created group.

The last method in Listing 22.5 is the Main_Click() method. This method is fired when the user clicks the Main Menu button. It simply redirects the user back to the main menu.

Listing 22.5 This Code Is behind the MngFiles.aspx page.

```
private void Page_Load(object sender, System.EventArgs e)
{
  if( !IsPostBack )
  {
    BindDataToControls();
  }
}

private void AddGroup_Click(object sender, System.EventArgs e)
{
  // Create a connection object.
 SqlConnection objConnection =
  new SqlConnection(ConfigurationSettings.AppSettings["ConnectString"]);

  try
  {
    // Open the connection.
    objConnection.Open();
    string strSql = "Insert into FileGroup (Name,OwnerID) VALUES ('" +
        SafeSql( GroupName.Text ) + "'," + Convert.ToString(
Session["ID"] ) + ")";
    // Create a command object.
    SqlCommand objCommand = new SqlCommand( strSql, objConnection );
    objCommand.ExecuteNonQuery();
    Password.Text = "";
    GroupName.Text = "";

    BindDataToControls();
  }
  catch( Exception ex )
  {
```

```
    // Alert the user to the error.
    ErrorMessage.Text = ex.Message.ToString();
  }
  finally
  {
    // Close the connection.
    if( objConnection.State == ConnectionState.Open )
    {
      objConnection.Close();
    }
  }

}

private void Main_Click(object sender, System.EventArgs e)
{
  Response.Redirect( "Default.aspx" );
}
```

The Edit Files Page

The code in Listing 22.6 is behind the EditFile.aspx page. This page allows users to edit information about the files that they have uploaded, as shown in Figure 22.4. Some of the fields are read-only and are there to display relevant information.

There are five methods in the code in Listing 22.6: Page_Load(), Main_Click(), Cancel_Click(), Delete_Click(), and Save_Click(). The Page_Load() method retrieves information about the file that's to be edited and puts the information into the user interface objects. The Main_Click() method simply goes to the main menu (Default.aspx). The Cancel_Click() method simply goes back to the Manage Files page (MngFiles.aspx). The Delete_Click() method deletes a file from disk and removes any references to it in the database. And the Save_Click() method saves all of the edited information to disk before going back to the Manage Files page.

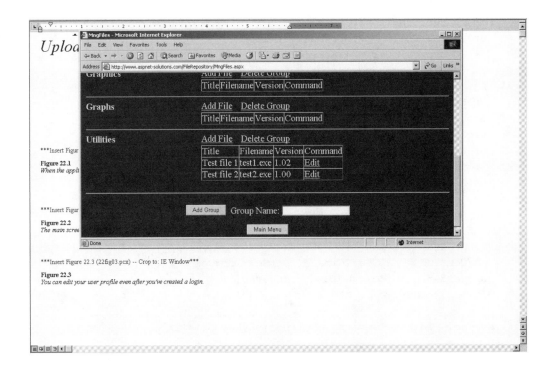

Figure 22.4 This Page Allows Users to Edit Information and View other Relevant Information.

Listing 22.6 This Code Is behind the EditFile.aspx Page.

```
// This method is called when the page first loads.
private void Page_Load(object sender, System.EventArgs e)
{
  if( !IsPostBack )
  {
  // Create a connection object.
  SqlConnection objConnection =
  new SqlConnection(ConfigurationSettings.AppSettings["ConnectString"]);

    try
    {
      // Open the connection.
```

```csharp
objConnection.Open();
string strSql = "Select Name,ID from FileGroup where OwnerID=" +
    Convert.ToString( Session["ID"] ) + " order by name";
// Create a command object.
SqlCommand objCommand = new SqlCommand( strSql, objConnection );
SqlDataReader objReader = objCommand.ExecuteReader();
GroupList.DataTextField = "Name";
GroupList.DataValueField = "ID";
GroupList.DataSource = objReader;
GroupList.DataBind();
objReader.Close();

strSql = "select * from FileInfo where ID=" +
    Request.QueryString["ID"];
// Create a command object.
objCommand = new SqlCommand( strSql, objConnection );
objReader = objCommand.ExecuteReader();
if( objReader.Read() )
{
    Title.Text = Convert.ToString( objReader["Title"] );
    Version.Text =
        Convert.ToDouble( objReader["Version"] ).ToString( "0.00" );
    Description.Text = Convert.ToString( objReader["Description"] );
    Filename.Text = Convert.ToString( objReader["Filename"] );
    FileSize.Text = Convert.ToString( objReader["Filesize"] );
    Directory.Text = Convert.ToString( objReader["Directory"] );
    Downloads.Text = Convert.ToString( objReader["Downloads"] );
    for( int i=0; i<GroupList.Items.Count; i++ )
    {
        if( Convert.ToInt32( GroupList.Items[i].Value ) ==
            Convert.ToInt32( objReader["GroupID"] ) )
        {
            GroupList.SelectedIndex = i;
            break;
        }
    }
}
objReader.Close();
}
catch( Exception ex )
{
    // Alert the user to the error.
    ErrorMessage.Text = ex.Message.ToString();
```

```
    }
    finally
    {
      // Close the connection.
      if( objConnection.State == ConnectionState.Open )
      {
        objConnection.Close();
      }
    }
  }
}

private void Main_Click(object sender, System.EventArgs e)
{
  Response.Redirect( "Default.aspx" );
}

private void Cancel_Click(object sender, System.EventArgs e)
{
  Response.Redirect( "MngFiles.aspx" );
}

private void Delete_Click(object sender, System.EventArgs e)
{
  bool bOperationSucceeded = true;

  // Create a connection object.
  SqlConnection objConnection =
  new SqlConnection(ConfigurationSettings.AppSettings["ConnectString"]);

  try
  {
    // Open the connection.
    objConnection.Open();
    string strSql = "Delete from FileInfo where ID=" +
        Request.QueryString["ID"];
    // Create a command object.
    SqlCommand objCommand = new SqlCommand( strSql, objConnection );
    objCommand.ExecuteNonQuery();

    string strFilePath = Request.MapPath( "." ) + "\\" +
        ConfigurationSettings.AppSettings["DirectoryName"] + "\\" +
        Directory.Text + "\\" + Filename.Text;
```

```
      File.Delete( strFilePath );
  }
  catch( Exception ex )
  {
    // Alert the user to the error.
    ErrorMessage.Text = ex.Message.ToString();
    bOperationSucceeded = false;
  }
  finally
  {
    // Close the connection.
    if( objConnection.State == ConnectionState.Open )
    {
      objConnection.Close();
    }
  }

  if( bOperationSucceeded )
  {
    Response.Redirect( "MngFiles.aspx" );
  }
}

private void Save_Click(object sender, System.EventArgs e)
{
  bool bOperationSucceeded = true;

  // Create a connection object.
 SqlConnection objConnection =
  new SqlConnection(ConfigurationSettings.AppSettings["ConnectString"]);

  try
  {
    // Open the connection.
    objConnection.Open();
    string strSql = "Update FileInfo Set Title='" + Title.Text +
        "',Version=" + Version.Text + ",Description='" +
        Description.Text + "',GroupID=" +
        Convert.ToString( GroupList.SelectedItem.Value ) + " where ID=" +
        Request.QueryString["ID"];
    // Create a command object.
    SqlCommand objCommand = new SqlCommand( strSql, objConnection );
    objCommand.ExecuteNonQuery();
```

```
  }
  catch( Exception ex )
  {
    // Alert the user to the error.
    ErrorMessage.Text = ex.Message.ToString();
    bOperationSucceeded = false;
  }
  finally
  {
    // Close the connection.
    if( objConnection.State == ConnectionState.Open )
    {
      objConnection.Close();
    }
  }

  if( bOperationSucceeded )
  {
    Response.Redirect( "MngFiles.aspx" );
  }
}
```

The `Page_Load()` method does database access and therefore has the things that all of our methods with database access have had: creation of a SqlConnection object, a `try` block for the working code, a `catch` block in which exceptions messages are displayed for users, and a `finally` block in which the database objects are cleaned up. Inside the `try` block, the SqlConnection is opened with the `Open()` method. Then, a SQL string is created using the logged-in user ID as the criteria. The recordsets will contain the Name and ID from the FileGroup table. The following code shows the creation of the SQL string:

C#
```
string strSql = "Select Name,ID from FileGroup where OwnerID=" +
  Convert.ToString( Session["ID"] ) + " order by name";
```

VB
```
Dim strSql As String = "Select Name,ID from FileGroup where " + _
  "OwnerID= + Convert.ToString( Session("ID") ) + " order by name"
```

If the logged-in user has an ID of 5, the following SQL will result:

```
Select Name,ID from FileGroup where OwnerID=5 order by name
```

    A SqlCommand object is created using the SQL string and the Sql-Connection object as arguments to its constructor. The SqlCommand object's `ExecuteReader()` method is then called, and this returns a Sql-DataReader object containing the returned recordsets. There is a user interface object named GroupList of the type DropDownList. The Sql-DataReader object is bound to this object so that the groups that belong to the logged-in user will be shown in the list. (The group ID is the data value, while the name is the display value.)

    We'll then need to retrieve the actual file information. This process starts by creating a SQL string based on the file ID (which is contained in an HTML parameter). The following line shows how the SQL string is formed:

C#
```
int nID = 0;
try
(
  nID  = Convert.ToInt32( Request.QueryString["ID"] );
}
catch
{
}
strSql = "select * from FileInfo where ID=" +
    Convert.ToString( nID );
```

VB
```
Dim nID As Integer = 0
Try
  NID = Convert.ToInt32( Request.QueryString("ID") )
Catch
End Try
strSql = "select * from FileInfo where ID=" + _
    Convert.ToString(nID)
```

    If the file ID is 16, the following SQL will result:

```
select * from FileInfo where ID=16
```

    A SqlCommand object is created with the SQL string and the Sql-Connection object. This object's `ExecuteReader()` method is called, and a recordset containing the matches files is returned in a SqlDataReader object.

To get the first recordset, the `Read()` method must be executed. (It's unlike the old ADO recordsets in classic ASP, in which there was always an initial recordset if one was found in the database.) The relevant information is placed into the user interface objects from the recordset. Included in the user interface objects are Title, Version, Description, Filename, FileSize, Directory, and Downloads. The corresponding group is also selected in the DropDownList object with the following code:

```
for( int i=0; i<GroupList.Items.Count; i++ )
{
  if( Convert.ToInt32( GroupList.Items[i].Value ) ==
    Convert.ToInt32( objReader["GroupID"] ) )
  {
    GroupList.SelectedIndex = i;
    break;
  }
}
```

Before leaving the `try` block, the SqlDataReader object is closed.

The `Main_Click()` method simply goes to the main page (Default.aspx) by calling the `Response.Redirect()` method. The `Cancel_Click()` method redirects similarly to the `Main_Click()` method—but it redirects to the Manage Files page (MngFiles.aspx).

The `Delete_Click()` method is intended to get rid of a file that is no longer needed. It removes the file from disk and deletes database records that reference it. It has the customary SqlConnection object creation, and the `try/catch/finally` construct. The SqlConnection object is opened with the `Open()` method. A SQL string is created that will delete the file's record in the FileInfo table. The following code shows how the SQL string is formed:

C#
```
string strSql = "Delete from FileInfo where ID=" +
  Request.QueryString["ID"];
```

VB
```
Dim strSql As string = "Delete from FileInfo where ID=" + _
  Request.QueryString("ID")
```

If the file ID is `19`, the resulting SQL will be the following:

```
Delete from FileInfo where ID=19
```

A SqlCommand object is created with the SQL string and the Sql-Connection object as parameters for its constructor. The SqlCommand object's ExecuteNonQuery() method is called, and this executes the SQL and deletes the record.

The last thing that has to be done is to delete the file from disk. The full path to the file is composed of several things: the path of the current application, the directory in which all files are stored, the file's additional directory, and the file name. The following shows how these strings are obtained:

The path of the current application:

```
Request.MapPath( "." )
```

The directory into which all files will be placed:

```
ConfigurationSettings.AppSettings["DirectoryName"]
```

The specific subdirectory in which the file resides:

```
Directory.Text
```

The file name:

```
Filename.Text
```

The Directory and Filename objects are TextBox objects that are part of the user interface. They were initially populated in the Page_Load() method. They are read-only, and therefore the user can't edit them and prevent the file from being deleted.

With the full path name for the file developed, a call to the File.Delete() static method can be made to delete the file. Note that for C# you must include System.IO, and for VB you must import System.IO.

The last method in Listing 22.6 is the Save_Click() method, which has the expected SqlConnection object creation and the try/catch/finally construct. In the try block, the SqlConnection object is opened, and a SQL string is created based on the items in the user interface objects (but only those items that can be edited). The following code shows how the SQL string is formed:

C#

```
string strSql = "Update FileInfo Set Title='" + Title.Text +
    "',Version=" + Version.Text + ",Description='" +
```

```
Description.Text + "',GroupID=" +
Convert.ToString( GroupList.SelectedItem.Value ) + " where ID=" +
   Request.QueryString["ID"];
```

VB
```
Dim strSql As String = "Update FileInfo Set Title='" + Title.Text + _
   "',Version=" + Version.Text + ",Description='" + _
   Description.Text + "',GroupID=" + _
   Convert.ToString( GroupList.SelectedItem.Value ) + " where ID=" + _
   Request.QueryString("ID")
```

The following might be what the actual SQL would look like for a file with an ID of 32:

```
Update FileInfo Set Title='My Title',Version=1.1,Description='My
Description',GroupID=5
   where ID=32
```

The SQL is executed using the SqlCommand object's `ExecuteNonQuery()` method.

The Delete Group Page

There is a mechanism with which users can delete groups that they've created. Deleting groups is carried out with the DeleteGroup.aspx page, and the code behind this page can be seen in Listing 22.7.

The first method you'll see in Listing 22.7 is the `ShowGroupName()` method. This method simply takes the group name that was passed to this page and outputs it to the HTTP stream. The parameter name is `Group`. The method checks to make sure that the `Request.QueryString()` method doesn't return a `null` (or `Nothing` in VB) indicating that there was no HTML parameter. In the case of a null, the string name `strGroupName` will be set to contain an empty string and therefore avoid any runtime errors.

The `Cancel_Click()` method is fired when users click the Cancel button. This method just redirects the user to the Manage Files page (MngFiles.aspx).

The `OK_Click()` method is fired when the user clicks the OK button. Its purpose is to delete the group and all of its associated files. It must delete the records in the database and the files from disk.

One of the dilemmas for Web developers who give users the chance to perform operations is that, once the operation is done, users are redirected to another page without any confirmation that the operation has been performed successfully. To provide a solution to this, the Delete Group page performs the operation, gives feedback in the form of text on the screen, and then sets the button to contain the text **Back**. Because of this, the first thing the OK_Click() method does is to see whether or not the button text contains the text **OK**. If it does not contain the text **OK**, then the operation has already been performed and the user is simply redirected to the Manage Files page.

Let's say, though, that the button text contains **OK** and we need to delete the group. We'll need a try/catch/finally construct to deal with any exceptions that might be thrown by both the database access methods and the disk I/O operations. The catch block takes the exception message and puts it into the Label object named ErrorMessage. The finally block closes the SqlConnection object if it is open.

In the try block, the SqlConnection object is opened. A string with the group ID is obtained using the Request.QueryString() method. If the group ID can't be obtained (and this will result in the string named strGroupID being null), then the string is assigned the value of -1 so that no groups will actually be deleted. A SQL statement is formed to delete the group from the FileGroup table. The following SQL statement would be formed if the group ID is 16:

```
Delete from FileGroup where ID=16
```

A SqlCommand object is created with the string containing the SQL object and the SqlConnection object as parameters to the SqlCommand constructor. The SQL to delete the group from the FileGroup table is performed with the SqlCommand object's ExecuteNonQuery() method.

Now we have to go through each file that belongs to the group and delete the disk files. First, we must get a recordset back that contains the files that must be deleted from disk. The following SQL statement will be used if the group ID is 16:

```
Select Directory,Filename from FileInfo where GroupID=16
```

The SQL statement is used to create a new SqlCommand object. The SqlCommand object's ExecuteReader() method is called, which returns a SqlDataReader object containing the recordsets that were retrieved from the database. A string variable named strPath will contain the path to the files. This variable is assigned the first time through the while loop. The static File.Delete() method is used to delete each file. The following code shows how the path is created, and then how the `File.Delete()` method is used:

C#
```csharp
if( strPath.Length == 0 )
{
   strPath = Request.MapPath( "." ) + "\\" +
     ConfigurationSettings.AppSettings["DirectoryName"] + "\\" +
     Convert.ToString( objReader["Directory"] );
}
File.Delete( strPath + "\\" +
   Convert.ToString( objReader["Filename"] ) );
```

VB
```vb
If strPath.Length = 0 Then
   strPath = Request.MapPath( "." ) + "\" + _
     ConfigurationSettings.AppSettings("DirectoryName") + "\" + _
     Convert.ToString( objReader("Directory") )
End If
File.Delete( strPath + "\" + _
   Convert.ToString( objReader("Filename") ) )
```

After looping through the list of files, if the `strPath` variable contains a directory (which it always should), the directory is deleted. A simple `try/catch` construct is used to catch any exceptions that might be thrown by the static `Directory.Delete()` method. The user won't be notified of the error, but the directory will not be deleted.

Last, the records for all of the files will be deleted with the following SQL:

```sql
Delete from FileInfo where GroupID=16
```

The SQL statement is used to create a SqlCommand object. The `ExecuteNonQuery()` method is used to execute the SQL. A message is shown to users in the ErrorMessage Label object so they know that the operation was performed successfully. The button text is set to **Back**, and the Cancel button is made invisible by setting its `Visible` property to `false`.

Listing 22.7 This Code Is behind the DeleteGroup.aspx Page.

```csharp
// This method executes to display the group name.
public void ShowGroupName()
{
```

```csharp
  string strGroupName = Request.QueryString["Group"];
  if( strGroupName == null )
  {
    strGroupName = "";
  }
  Response.Write( strGroupName );
}

private void Cancel_Click(object sender, System.EventArgs e)
{
  Response.Redirect( "MngFiles.aspx" );
}

private void OK_Click(object sender, System.EventArgs e)
{
  if( OK.Text != "OK" )
  {
    Response.Redirect( "MngFiles.aspx" );
  }

  // Create a connection object.
 SqlConnection objConnection =
  new SqlConnection(ConfigurationSettings.AppSettings["ConnectString"]);

  try
  {
    // Open the connection.
    objConnection.Open();

    string strGroupID = Request.QueryString["ID"];
    if( strGroupID == null )
    {
      strGroupID = "-1";
    }
    // Create a command object.
    SqlCommand objCommand = new SqlCommand( "Delete from FileGroup " +
        "where ID=" + strGroupID, objConnection );
    objCommand.ExecuteNonQuery();

    // Create a command object.
    objCommand = new SqlCommand( "Select Directory,Filename " +
      "from FileInfo where GroupID=" + strGroupID, objConnection );
    SqlDataReader objReader = objCommand.ExecuteReader();
```

```
  string strPath = "";
  while( objReader.Read() )
  {
    if( strPath.Length == 0 )
    {
      strPath = Request.MapPath( "." ) + "\\" +
        ConfigurationSettings.AppSettings["DirectoryName"] + "\\" +
        Convert.ToString( objReader["Directory"] );
    }
    File.Delete( strPath + "\\" +
      Convert.ToString( objReader["Filename"] ) );
  }

  if( strPath.Length > 0 )
  {
    try
    {
      Directory.Delete( strPath );
    }
    catch
    {
    }
  }
  objReader.Close();

  // Create a command object.
  objCommand = new SqlCommand( "Delete from FileInfo where ID=" +
    strGroupID, objConnection );
  objCommand.ExecuteNonQuery();

  ErrorMessage.Text = "The group has been deleted.";
  OK.Text = "Back";
  Cancel.Visible = false;
}
catch( Exception ex )
{
  // Alert the user to the error.
  ErrorMessage.Text = ex.Message.ToString();
}
finally
{
  // Close the connection.
  if( objConnection.State == ConnectionState.Open )
```

```
    {
      objConnection.Close();
    }
  }
}
```

The Add File Page

The Add File page (AddFile.aspx) allows users to add new files into one of their groups. There are three buttons on the screen and a number of fields into which information about the file can be entered.

The `Cancel_Click()` method simply redirects the user to the Manage Files page, and the `Main_Click()` method redirects the user to the main menu page. Both of these methods can be seen in the first few lines of Listing 22.8.

The `Save_Click()` method is fired when users click the Save button. This method performs all the steps to save the file information to the database, accept the upload, and save the file to the correct location.

The `Save_Click()` method has a `try/catch/finally` block so that database and file exceptions will be caught and dealt with. A Boolean variable will remember whether the entire process is successful. If any part of the operation fails, a message will be shown to the user in the Label object named ErrorMessage. If all parts of the process are successful, the user will be redirected to the Manage Files page.

Inside of the `try` block, the code starts off by opening the SqlConnection object. Several strings, and the `contain` values that relate to the directory structure into which the file will be saved, are assigned. Here's the way the directory structure is formed:

The current directory of the application:

```
Request.MapPath( "." )
```

The directory into which all file directories will be saved:

```
ConfigurationSettings.AppSettings["DirectoryName"]
```

The user directory:

```
"Dir" + Convert.ToString( Session["ID"] )
```

The group directory:

```
Request.QueryString["GroupID"]
```

For example:

```
C:\inetpub\wwwroot\filerepository\filedir\dir16\7\
```

Once the directory string has been created, the existence of both directories (the user directory and the group directory that's within the user directory) are verified, and the application creates them if they don't exist.

The user interface object that contains the file name is named Filename. It's a File Field object that's available from the HTML toolbox. The following code shows how to get the full file and path from the object:

C#
```
string strFilename = Filename.PostedFile.FileName;
```

VB
```
Dim strFilename As String = Filename.PostedFile.FileName
```

Once we have the full file and path, we need to extract the file name. The following code does this:

C#
```
string strSourceFile =
    strFilename.Substring( strFilename.LastIndexOf( '\\' ) + 1 );
```

VB
```
Dim strSourceFile As String =
    strFilename.Substring( strFilename.LastIndexOf( 92 ) + 1 )
```

And finally, the upload can be carried out with the following code:

C#
```
Filename.PostedFile.SaveAs( strDestPath );
```

VB
```
Filename.PostedFile.SaveAs( strDestPath )
```

Once the file has been uploaded, a record is inserted into the database using a SqlCommand object and its ExecuteNonQuery() method.

For your convenience, the process of uploading a file is summarized here:

User File Upload Summary

1. Get the source path and file name from a File Field object. (This step is not 100 percent necessary, but you may need the source file name.)
2. Create a string containing the full path and file for the destination file.
3. Call the Filename.PostedFile.SaveAs() method.

Listing 22.8 This Code Is behind the AddFile.aspx Page.

```
private void Cancel_Click(object sender, System.EventArgs e)
{
  Response.Redirect( "MngFiles.aspx" );
}


private void Main_Click(object sender, System.EventArgs e)
{
  Response.Redirect( "Default.aspx" );
}


private void Save_Click(object sender, System.EventArgs e)
{
  bool bOperationSucceeded = true;

  // Create a connection object.
  SqlConnection objConnection =
  new SqlConnection(ConfigurationSettings.AppSettings["ConnectString"]);

  try
  {
    // Open the connection.
    objConnection.Open();
    string strUserDir = "Dir" + Convert.ToString( Session["ID"] );
    string strGroupDir = Request.QueryString["GroupID"];
    string strFileDir =
      ConfigurationSettings.AppSettings["DirectoryName"];
```

```
// Check for both directories here... Create them if necessary
if( !Directory.Exists( Request.MapPath( "." ) + "\\" + strFileDir +
  "\\" + strUserDir ) )
{
  Directory.CreateDirectory( Request.MapPath( "." ) + "\\" +
    strFileDir + "\\" + strUserDir );
}
if( !Directory.Exists( Request.MapPath( "." ) + "\\" + strFileDir +
  "\\" + strUserDir + "\\" + strGroupDir ) )
{
  Directory.CreateDirectory( Request.MapPath( "." ) + "\\" +
    strFileDir + "\\" + strUserDir + "\\" + strGroupDir );
}

// Allow the file to upload here...
string strFilename = Filename.PostedFile.FileName;
string strSourceFile =
  strFilename.Substring( strFilename.LastIndexOf( '\\' ) + 1 );
string strDestPath =
  Request.MapPath( "." ) + "\\" + strFileDir + "\\" + strUserDir +
  "\\" + strGroupDir + "\\" + strSourceFile;
Filename.PostedFile.SaveAs( strDestPath );
string strFilesize =
  Convert.ToString( Filename.PostedFile.ContentLength );

string strSql = "Insert into " +
  "FileInfo Title,Version,Description,Filename, " +
  "Filesize,Directory,OwnerID,GroupID) VALUES ('" + Title.Text +
  "'," + Version.Text+ ",'" + Description.Text + "','" +
  strSourceFile + "'," + strFilesize + ",'" + strUserDir + "\\" +
  strGroupDir + "'," + Convert.ToString( Session["ID"] ) + "," +
  Request.QueryString["GroupID"] + ")";
  // Create a command object.
  SqlCommand objCommand = new SqlCommand( strSql, objConnection );
  objCommand.ExecuteNonQuery();
}
catch( Exception ex )
{
  // Alert the user to the error.
  ErrorMessage.Text = ex.Message.ToString();
  bOperationSucceeded = false;
}
```

```
finally
{
  // Close the connection.
  if( objConnection.State == ConnectionState.Open )
  {
    objConnection.Close();
  }
}

if( bOperationSucceeded )
{
  Response.Redirect( "MngFiles.aspx" );
}
}
```

The Search Page

Listing 22.9 contains the code that is behind the search page. Users can type search criteria with the page shown in Figure 22.5, and matching results will be shown.

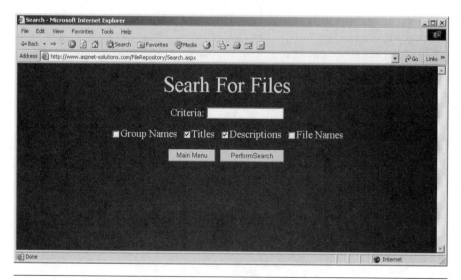

Figure 22.5 The Search Page Allows Users to Find the Files They Want.

Listing 22.9 This Code Is behind the Search.aspx Page.

```
private void Main_Click(object sender, System.EventArgs e)
{
  Response.Redirect( "Default.aspx" );
}

private void PerformSearch_Click(object sender, System.EventArgs e)
{
  // Create a connection object.
  SqlConnection objConnection = new SqlConnection( ConfigurationSettings.
AppSettings["ConnectString"] );

  try
  {
    // Open the connection.
    objConnection.Open();
    string strSql = "Select * From FileInfo where";
    bool bNeedToUseAND = false;

    if( SearchGroupNames.Checked )
    {
      bNeedToUseAND = true;
      strSql += " GroupID in (select ID from FileGroup where Name " +
        "like '%" + Criteria.Text + "%')";
    }

    if( SearchTitles.Checked )
    {
      if( bNeedToUseAND )
      {
        strSql += " and ";
      }
      bNeedToUseAND = true;
      strSql += "(Title like '%" + Criteria.Text + "%')";
    }

    if( SearchDescriptions.Checked )
    {
      if( bNeedToUseAND )
      {
        strSql += " and ";
      }
```

```
      bNeedToUseAND = true;
      strSql += "(Description like '%" + Criteria.Text + "%')";
    }

    if( SearchFilenames.Checked )
    {
      if( bNeedToUseAND )
      {
        strSql += " and ";
      }
      bNeedToUseAND = true;
      strSql += "(Filename like '%" + Criteria.Text + "%')";
    }

    if( SearchGroupNames.Checked )
    {
      strSql += " group by GroupID";
    }
    strSql += " order by title";
    // Create a command object.
    SqlCommand objCommand = new SqlCommand( strSql, objConnection );
    SqlDataReader objReader = objCommand.ExecuteReader();

    FileList.DataSource = objReader;
    FileList.DataBind();

    objReader.Close();

}
catch( Exception ex )
{
  // Alert the user to the error.
  ErrorMessage.Text = ex.Message.ToString();
}
finally
{
  Criteria.Text = "";

  // Close the connection.
  if( objConnection.State == ConnectionState.Open )
  {
    objConnection.Close();
```

```
        }
    }

}
```

The Show Group Page

There will be times when you want a group to be displayed by itself. Examples of this would be when you want to offer all files for a certain application, and when you don't want users to have to log in and enter search criteria. Listing 22.10 contains the code for the Show Group page (ShowGroup.aspx). You can see the page in operation in Figure 22.6.

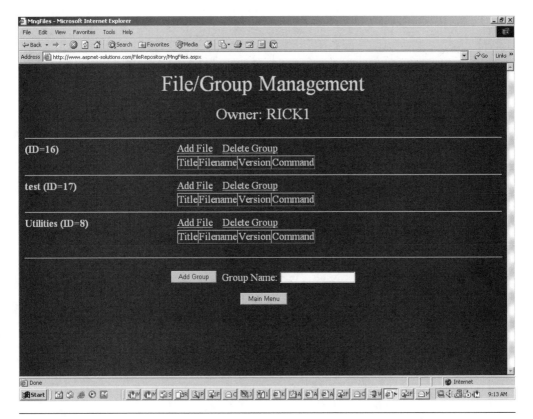

Figure 22.6 All of Your Groups and Their Files Will Be Shown in This Page.

Listing 22.10 This Code Is Behind the ShowGroup.aspx Page.

```
private void Page_Load(object sender, System.EventArgs e)
{
  if( !IsPostBack )
  {
// Create a connection object.
  SqlConnection objConnection =
  new SqlConnection(ConfigurationSettings.AppSettings["ConnectString"]);

    try
    {
      // Open the connection.
      objConnection.Open();
      string strGroupID = Request.QueryString["ID"];
      if( strGroupID == null )
      {
        strGroupID = "-1";
      }
      string strDirectory =
        ConfigurationSettings.AppSettings["DirectoryName"];
      string strSql =
        "Select Title,Version,Description,Filesize,Filepath=('" +
        strDirectory + "'+Directory+'/'+Filename) from FileInfo " +
        "where ID=" + strGroupID;
      // Create a command object.
      SqlCommand objCommand = new SqlCommand( strSql, objConnection );
      SqlDataReader objReader = objCommand.ExecuteReader();
      FileList.DataSource = objReader;
      FileList.DataBind();
    }
    catch( Exception ex )
    {
      // Alert the user to the error.
      ErrorMessage.Text = ex.Message.ToString();
    }
    finally
    {
      // Close the connection.
      if( objConnection.State == ConnectionState.Open )
      {
        objConnection.Close();
      }
    }
```

```
  }
}

public void ShowGroupName()
{
  string strGroupName = Request.QueryString["Group"];
  if( strGroupName == null )
  {
    strGroupName = "";
  }
  Response.Write( strGroupName );
}
```

The Edit Profile Page

Users can edit their profiles as shown in Figure 22.7. The code for this page can be seen in Listing 22.11.

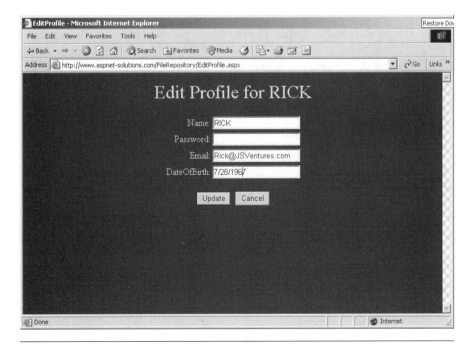

Figure 22.7 You Can Edit Your User Profile Even After You've Created a Login.

Listing 22.11 This Code Is Behind the EditProfile.aspx Page.

```
// This method is executed when the page first loads.
private void Page_Load(object sender, System.EventArgs e)
{
  if( !IsPostBack )
  {
  // Create a connection object.
  SqlConnection objConnection =
  new SqlConnection(ConfigurationSettings.AppSettings["ConnectString"]);
    SqlDataReader objReader = null;
    try
    {
      // Open the connection.
      objConnection.Open();
      // Create a command object.
      SqlCommand objCommand =
        new SqlCommand( "select Password,Email,DateOfBirth from " +
        "Users where ID='" + Convert.ToString( Session["ID"] ) +
        "'", objConnection );
      objReader = objCommand.ExecuteReader();
      if( objReader.Read() )
      {
        Name.Text = Convert.ToString( Session["Name"] );
        Password.Text = Convert.ToString( objReader["Password"] );
        Email.Text = Convert.ToString( objReader["Email"] );
        DateOfBirth.Text =
      Convert.ToDateTime( objReader["DateOfBirth"] ).ToShortDateString();
      }
      else
      {
        ErrorMessage.Text = "Could not retrieve user record.";
      }
    }
    catch( Exception ex )
    {
      // Alert the user to the error.
      ErrorMessage.Text = ex.Message.ToString();
    }
    finally
    {
      if( objReader != null )
      {
```

```
        objReader.Close();
      }
      // Close the connection.
      if( objConnection.State == ConnectionState.Open )
      {
        objConnection.Close();
      }
    }
  }
}

private void Update_Click(object sender, System.EventArgs e)
{
  // Create a connection object.
  SqlConnection objConnection =
   new SqlConnection(ConfigurationSettings.AppSettings["ConnectString"]);
  try
  {
    Session["Name"] = Name.Text.Trim().ToUpper();
    // Open the connection.
    objConnection.Open();
    // Create a command object.
    SqlCommand objCommand = new SqlCommand( "Update Users set Name='" +
      Convert.ToString( Session["Name"] ) + "',Password='" +
      Password.Text.Trim().ToUpper() + "',Email='" + Email.Text.Trim() +
      "',DateOfBirth='" + DateOfBirth.Text.Trim()+ "' where ID=" +
      Convert.ToString( Session["ID"] ), objConnection );
    objCommand.ExecuteNonQuery();
    ErrorMessage.Text = "Your profile has been updated.";
    Update.Visible = false;
    Cancel.Text = " OK ";
  }
  catch( Exception ex )
  {
    // Alert the user to the error.
    ErrorMessage.Text = ex.Message.ToString();
  }
  finally
  {
    // Close the connection.
    if( objConnection.State == ConnectionState.Open )
    {
      objConnection.Close();
```

```
      }
    }
}

private void Cancel_Click(object sender, System.EventArgs e)
{
   Response.Redirect( "Default.aspx" );
}
```

Summary

In this chapter, you've learned a number of things. Uploading files and file I/O are among the main things that aren't covered in most of the other chapters in this book. As you saw, the `File` and `Directory` classes give you easy ways to manipulate files and directories. And the File Field HTML object gives you an easy way to deal with user uploads.

This application can easily be enhanced, and I welcome your feedback. Please let me know if you use it somewhere, and send me an e-mail describing your enhancements.

CHAPTER 23

Effective Use of GDI+: Creating a Certificates Program

In This Chapter:

- The Member Variables and Properties
- Creating the Certificate
- Initializing the Default.aspx User Interface Objects
- Instantiating and Using the `Certificate` Class
- Responding to User Interaction

I have always loved those Web sites at which you could make a greeting card and send it. It's fascinating how they can give you such a rich design tool that's online. And there are tons and tons of options for creating some awesome cards.

But don't be fooled by the cuteness of the idea—there's a real business model here. For starters, these attractions bring millions of users to a site. And millions of users mean millions of advertising banner impressions. These ad banner impressions translate into dollars and cents.

Another business model involves embedding advertisements in the greeting cards that are sent out. The cards can also contain links to the sending Web site so that receivers can easily get to the Web site and send a card in return. All of this translates into traffic and advertising revenue.

There's a slight variation to the greeting card idea that I wanted to add to one of my Web sites that offers activities for children. The site is eKidPlace and can be found at www.eKidPlace.com. What I added to the site was the capability to send certificates of achievement to people. A certificate might be for something such as running a five-minute mile, memorizing the Gettysburg Address, or winning the lottery. Setting up this feature was quite a bit of work because I did it three years ago and resorted to Java for much of the interactive portion of the application. I also had to write some server-side code that saved the image to disk on the server.

But with ASP.NET, the application that took months to create using Java and server-side C++ recently took a day to create using ASP.NET. All the user interface objects, such as the drop-down lists, were a snap with ASP.NET, and GDI+ made the image creation and saving to disk a virtual snap to do.

Table 23.1 contains the methods that do the work in the Certificates application. This table will be a handy reference as you work your way through the program.

Table 23.1 The Methods for the Certificates Application

Method	Listing	Source Code File	Description
DrawCornerImages	23.2	CertificatesVB.vb	This method draws the certificate corner images into the bitmap.
TileCertificate	23.2	CertificatesVB.vb	This method tiles the certificate background.
DrawMainText	23.2	CertificatesVB.vb	This method draws the main text into the certificate.
DrawLeftText	23.2	CertificatesVB.vb	This method draws the text at the lower left part of the certificate.
DrawRightText	23.2	CertificatesVB.vb	This method draws the text at the bottom right part of the certificate.
CreateImage	23.2	CertificatesVB.vb	This method creates a bitmap, calls draw methods such as `TileCertificate` and `DrawMainText`, and then saves the image to disk.
Page_Load	23.3	Default.aspx.vb	This method is called when the default.aspx page is loaded.
Application_Start	23.4	Global.asax.vb	This method creates a list of file names for all the available corner images.

Table 23.1 The Methods for the Certificates Application (*cont.*)

Method	Listing	Source Code File	Description
CreateImage	23.5	Default.aspx.vb	This image instantiates a Certificates object and uses it to create a certificate.
OutputImage	23.5	Default.aspx.vb	This method outputs an IMG tag into the HTML stream.
CreateNewFilename	23.6	Default.aspx.vb	This method generates a file name based on the system clock.
ul_SelectedIndexChanged	23.6	Default.aspx.vb	This method responds to a change in the selected upper left image.
ur_SelectedIndexChanged	23.6	Default.aspx.vb	This method responds to a change in the selected upper right image.
bl_SelectedIndexChanged	23.6	Default.aspx.vb	This method responds to a change in the selected bottom left image.
br_SelectedIndexChanged	23.6	Default.aspx.vb	This method responds to a change in the selected bottom right image.
tile_SelectedIndex-Changed	23.6	Default.aspx.vb	This method is fired when the user changes the selected tile.
InsertNow_Click	23.6	Default.aspx.vb	This method is fired when the user clicks the Insert button.
InsertLeft_Click	23.6	Default.aspx.vb	This method is fired when the user clicks the Insert Left button.
InsertRight_Click	23.6	Default.aspx.vb	This method is fired when the user clicks the Insert Right button.
SendEmail_Click	23.6	Default.aspx.vb	This method is fired when the user clicks the Send Email button.

The Certificates application has a number of properties that determine the appearance of the certificate. These properties are shown in Table 23.2 for your convenience.

Table 23.2 The Properties for the Certificates Application

Property	Listing	Source Code File	Description
BackgroundTile	23.1	CertificatesVB.vb	The name of the background tile image
UpperLeftImage	23.1	CertificatesVB.vb	The name of the image that will appear in the upper left corner of the certificate
UpperRightImage	23.1	CertificatesVB.vb	The name of the image that will appear in the upper right corner of the certificate
BottomLeftImage	23.1	CertificatesVB.vb	The name of the image that will appear in the bottom left corner of the certificate
BottomRightImage	23.1	CertificatesVB.vb	The name of the image that will appear in the bottom right corner of the certificate
Filename	23.1	CertificatesVB.vb	The file name to which the certificate will be saved
Path	23.1	CertificatesVB.vb	The path into which the certificate file will be saved
MainText	23.1	CertificatesVB.vb	The text that appears in the center of the certificate
LeftText	23.1	CertificatesVB.vb	The text that appears in the lower left portion of the certificate
RightText	23.1	CertificatesVB.vb	The text that appears in the lower right portion of the certificate
MainTextColor	23.1	CertificatesVB.vb	The color of the main text
LeftTextColor	23.1	CertificatesVB.vb	The color of the text in the lower left portion of the certificate
RightTextColor	23.1	CertificatesVB.vb	The color of the text in the lower right portion of the certificate

The Member Variables and Properties

Listing 23.1 contains the class that creates the certificate. The class is named CertificatesVB (or CertificatesCS for the C# version) and is consumed from the Default.aspx.vb code. You can use this class in just about any ASP.NET program.

The CertificatesVB class has exactly five member variables that aren't associated with a property. These variables are private class members and can't be accessed externally. They can be seen at the top of Listing 23.1. The first two variables determine the width and height of the certificate itself. Note, though, that the user interface objects, such as the DropDownList and TextBox objects, add to the size of the screen in which users create a certificate. You can easily change these programmatically for a different certificate size. But they aren't the kind of thing that you'll want users changing. These two values can wreak havoc if they are way too big or way too small because the certificate elements won't fit on the certificate very well.

Two variables determine whether or not the lower left image and the lower right image are raised above the bottom of the certificate. This positioning is necessary if text is drawn in the lower left or lower right corner of the certificate. You wouldn't want to draw images on top of text; so if text exists, two variables will contain additional offsets with which the lower left and lower right images can be drawn so that the text won't be drawn on the text. These two variables are m_nLeftImageBottom and m_nRightImageBottom.

The last of the non-property member variables is a Bitmap object named m_objImage. It will contain the Bitmap object into which all of the drawing will be performed. Then, once all of the drawing operations have been completed, the Bitmap object will be saved to disk as an image file.

A property named BackgroundTile is associated with a member variable named m_strBackgroundTile. The variable is a string and contains the name of the image file that will be used to tile the background of the certificate. The CertificatesVB class has the expectation that all the background tile images will be in a directory within the current directory named BackgroundTiles. The directory that the ASPNET-Solutions Web site uses has 54 background tiles. You can download these tiles from the Web site from the Chapter 23 page at http://www.ASPNET-Solutions. com/Chapter_23.htm. You can download thousands of additional background tiles from the Internet. Almost any image will work, but the ones that work best are tiles that fit together seamlessly.

Four properties are all related. These properties contain the file name for images that can be placed in the four corners of the certificate. Each image is a GIF image with a transparent background. That means that instead of an entire rectangle being pasted on top of the certificate, only the non-background color will be drawn.

The demo application on the ASPNET-Solutions Web site has 53 corner images from which users can select. The `CertificatesVB` class expects the images to be contained in a directory under its directory named CornerImages. You can download the 53 images from the Chapter 23 page on the ASPNET-Solutions Web site.

The four member variables that contain the file names are `m_strUL-Image`, `m_strURImage`, `m_strBLImage`, and `m_strBRImage`. The corresponding properties for these variables with which the calling code can get and set them are `UpperLeftImage`, `UpperRightImage`, `BottomLeftImage`, and `BottomRightImage`.

Two properties determine where the certificate image is saved and what its file name will be. These are respectively the `Path` and `Filename` properties. Their associated member variables are respectively `m_str-Path` and `m_strFilename`.

The next three properties in Listing 23.1 contain the text that will be drawn in the certificate. The `MainText` property sets the `m_strMain-Text` member variable and contains the text that will be drawn in the middle of the certificate. The `LeftText` and `RightText` properties set the `m_strLeftText` and `m_strRightText` member variables. These strings are drawn at the bottom left and bottom right corners of the certificate. Their purpose would be for displaying who issued the certificate, what date it was awarded, or a special note.

An array of colors allows users to store colors as integers. The integers are indexes into the array of colors (named `m_Colors`), which in turn is used to draw text into the certificate's Bitmap object.

The last three properties in Listing 23.1 are integer values that contain indexes into the color array. The `MainTextColor` property sets the `m_nMainTextColor` integer variable and determines the color with which the main text is drawn. The `LeftTextColor` and `RightText-Color` properties do the same for the text that might be drawn in the lower left and lower right corners of the certificate.

Listing 23.1 The Certificate's Member Variables and Properties

```
Dim m_nWidth As Integer = 650
Dim m_nHeight As Integer = 350
```

```
Dim m_nLeftImageBottom As Integer = 0
Dim m_nRightImageBottom As Integer = 0

Dim m_objImage As Bitmap = Nothing

Dim m_strBackgroundTile As String = "LBlueBack.gif"
Public Property BackgroundTile() As String
    Get
        Return m_strBackgroundTile
    End Get
    Set(ByVal Value As String)
        m_strBackgroundTile = Value
    End Set
End Property

Dim m_strULImage As String = ""
Public Property UpperLeftImage() As String
    Get
        Return m_strULImage
    End Get
    Set(ByVal Value As String)
        m_strULImage = Value
    End Set
End Property

Dim m_strURImage As String = ""
Public Property UpperRightImage() As String
    Get
        Return m_strURImage
    End Get
    Set(ByVal Value As String)
        m_strURImage = Value
    End Set
End Property

Dim m_strBLImage As String = ""
Public Property BottomLeftImage() As String
    Get
        Return m_strBLImage
    End Get
    Set(ByVal Value As String)
        m_strBLImage = Value
    End Set
End Property
```

```vb
Dim m_strBRImage As String = ""
Public Property BottomRightImage() As String
    Get
        Return m_strBRImage
    End Get
    Set(ByVal Value As String)
        m_strBRImage = Value
    End Set
End Property

Dim m_strFilename As String = "Tmp.jpg"
Public Property Filename() As String
    Get
        Return m_strFilename
    End Get
    Set(ByVal Value As String)
        m_strFilename = Value
    End Set
End Property

Dim m_strPath As String = ""
Public Property Path() As String
    Get
        Return m_strPath
    End Get
    Set(ByVal Value As String)
        m_strPath = Value
    End Set
End Property

Dim m_strMainText As String = ""
Public Property MainText() As String
    Get
        Return m_strMainText
    End Get
    Set(ByVal Value As String)
        m_strMainText = Value
    End Set
End Property

Dim m_strLeftText As String = ""
Public Property LeftText() As String
    Get
        Return m_strLeftText
```

```
        End Get
        Set(ByVal Value As String)
            m_strLeftText = Value
        End Set
    End Property

    Dim m_strRightText As String = ""
    Public Property RightText() As String
        Get
            Return m_strRightText
        End Get
        Set(ByVal Value As String)
            m_strRightText = Value
        End Set
    End Property

    Dim m_Colors() As Color = {Color.Black, Color.White, _
        Color.Blue, Color.Green, Color.Red, Color.Yellow}

    Dim m_nMainTextColor As Integer = 0
    Public Property MainTextColor() As Integer
        Get
            Return m_nMainTextColor
        End Get
        Set(ByVal Value As Integer)
            m_nMainTextColor = Value
        End Set
    End Property

    Dim m_nLeftTextColor As Integer = 0
    Public Property LeftTextColor() As Integer
        Get
            Return m_nLeftTextColor
        End Get
        Set(ByVal Value As Integer)
            m_nLeftTextColor = Value
        End Set
    End Property

    Dim m_nRightTextColor As Integer = 0
    Public Property RightTextColor() As Integer
        Get
            Return m_nRightTextColor
        End Get
```

```
    Set(ByVal Value As Integer)
        m_nRightTextColor = Value
    End Set
End Property
```

Creating the Certificate

Listing 23.2 has the code that creates and draws the certificate. There are seven methods in the listing, and they are all explained in this section.

The `CreateImage()` Method

The `CreateImage()` method is a high-level method that creates the Bitmap object, gets a Graphics object from the Bitmap object, and then calls five methods that do all of the drawing. Each of the five methods must have a Graphics object, so the Graphics object that was retrieved by using the `Graphics.FromImage()` method is passed to each of these methods.

Creating the Bitmap object is simple: The constructor used needs the width, the height, and the pixel format. The following code shows how the Bitmap object is created:

C#

```
m_objImage = new Bitmap( m_nWidth, m_nHeight,
  PixelFormat.Format24bppRgb );
```

VB

```
m_objImage = New Bitmap(m_nWidth, m_nHeight, _
  PixelFormat.Format24bppRgb)
```

The `DrawCornerImages()` Method

The `DrawCornerImages()` method draws images in the corner of the certificate. As we saw in Listing 23.1, four member variables contain strings with the file names of corner images. These strings are initially empty, and therefore the corner images won't be drawn. But if the user selects a corner image for any of the corners, then the selected corner image will be drawn in the appropriate corner. Figure 23.1 shows images in the corners.

The first thing, though, that must be done before drawing a corner image into the certificate is to load the image from disk and create another Bitmap object. The newly created Bitmap object will contain the image data for the

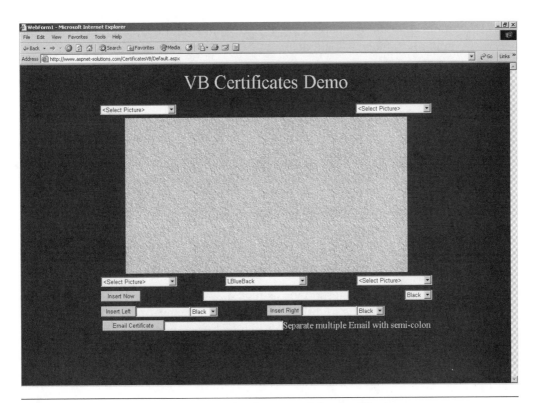

Figure 23.1 You Can Add Images in the Corners of the Certificate.

image that is loaded from disk, and it can be used to draw into the certificate image. In the `CreateImage()` method, a Bitmap object was created that was empty. But here, we're going to create a Bitmap object from disk, and the only parameter to the Bitmap constructor is the file name. The following simplified example would load an image from the root of the C: drive: It loads an image named Temp.gif from the root of C: into the Bitmap object.

C#
```csharp
Bitmap objBitmap = new Bitmap( "C:\\Temp.Gif" );
```

VB
```vb
Dim objBitmap As New Bitmap("C:\Temp.Gif")
```

Loading the image is a little more complicated in the `DrawCorner-Images()` method because we need to use the path of the directory of the application, plus the directory named CornerImages that's underneath the application directory, plus the file name. The following code shows how the upper left image is loaded:

C#
```
Bitmap objCorner = new Bitmap( m_strPath +
            "\\CornerImages\\" + m_strULImage + ".gif" );
```

VB
```
Dim objCorner As New Bitmap(m_strPath + _
            "\CornerImages\" + m_strULImage + ".gif")
```

There are four blocks of code in the `DrawCornerImages()` method, one for each corner.

The `TileCertificate()` Method

If you look at this method in Listing 23.2, you'll see 11 lines of code inside the method. Simple, right? Yes, it's simple for many. But I can't tell you how much time I have spent in class teaching this very thing to professional programmers, only to have them scratch their heads and give me a blank stare. Of course, you might think that, after all this time, I could have figured out a way to get the point across. I think I have, but you need to work through the explanation in this section.

For starters, a new Bitmap object is created in this method from a disk file. The object is the specified background tile image, and it is in a directory named BackgroundTiles under the current application directory. The following code shows how it is loaded:

C#
```
Bitmap objBackgroundTile = new Bitmap( m_strPath + _
        "\\BackgroundTiles\\" + m_strBackgroundTile );
```

VB
```
Dim objBackgroundTile As New Bitmap(m_strPath + _
        "\BackgroundTiles\" + m_strBackgroundTile)
```

Once the Bitmap object is created from the disk file, we can tile the background image into the certificate Bitmap object. We start by going across the top of the image, drawing the tile, and skipping over to the right. When we get to the right side of the certificate, and the next tile image we draw will be outside the bounds of the certificate Bitmap object, we go

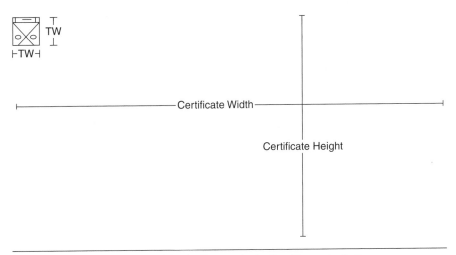

Figure 23.2 The First Tile That's Drawn Is in the Upper Left Corner.

down a row and start back on the left side of the certificate to repeat the process. We do this until all rows have been drawn.

The tile image has a width and height. For now, I'll refer to these units as TW (for tile width) and TH (for tile height). Figure 23.2 shows the certificate with a single tile drawn in the upper left corner. The initial x- and y-coordinates are both 0.

After each tile is drawn, the width of the tile is added to the x-coordinate so that the next tile will be drawn to the right of the last tile. For instance, if a tile is 50 pixels wide, the second tile drawn in the first row would be drawn to the x, y coordinates 50, 0. The third tile would be drawn to 100, 0, and so forth. Figure 23.3 shows the first five tiles drawn at 0, TX, 2*TX, 3*TX, and 4*TX.

Two while loops are actually in action in the `TileCertificate()` method. The inner loop is the one that draws the tiles across each row. If you take a look at the code, the value I have been referring to as TX is actually `objBackgroundTile.Width` in the code. The following code is the inner loop that draws a row:

C#
```
x = 0;
while( x < m_objImage.Width )
{
  g.DrawImage( objBackgroundTile, x, y );
  x += objBackgroundTile.Width;
```

Keep drawing to the right side ⟶

0   TW   2TW 3TW 4TW   etc.

Figure 23.3 After Each Tile Is Drawn, TX Is Added to the X-Coordinate.

```
}
```

VB
```
x = 0
While x < m_objImage.Width
  g.DrawImage(objBackgroundTile, x, y)
  x += objBackgroundTile.Width
End While
```

After each row is drawn, the x-coordinate is set to 0. The process is kind of like using the old electric typewriters: When you get to the end of the row, you hit Return, and the carriage goes back to the left. Those old typewriters also advance the page one line, and the same is true for the code in the `TileCertificate()` method. Advancing to the next row is simple; just add TY to the y-coordinate, as shown in Figure 23.4, and get ready to draw another row.

This process continues down the certificate, as shown in Figure 23.5, until the entire certificate is tiled.

The `DrawMainText()` Method

The `DrawMainText()` method draws the string contained in the `m_strMainText` variable into the certificate. If the string has a length greater than 0, the method also draws "This Certifies That" above it. Figure 23.6 shows the main text in the certificate.

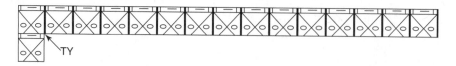

TY

Start the next row at TY

Figure 23.4 To Draw the Next Row, the X-Coordinate Is Reset to 0 and the Tile Image Height Is Added to the Y-Coordinate.

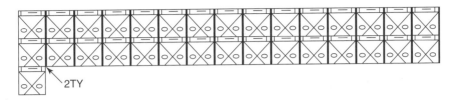

2TY

Start the next row at 2*TY

Figure 23.5 As Each New Row Is Drawn, TY Is Added to the Y-Coordinate.

Two GDI+ objects are created with which the strings will be drawn into the certificate. One is a Font object, and one is a SolidBrush object. The Font object is hard coded at a size of 25, and you may want to add a property so that users can change the font size. The color of the solid brush is obtained by using the index in the $m\_nMainTextColor$ member variable.

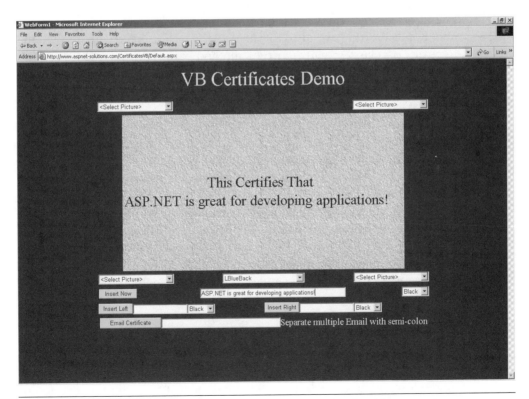

Figure 23.6 The Main Text Shows Up in the Middle of the Certificate.

To center the strings (the `m_strMainText` and `"This Certifies That"` strings), we'll need to get the pixel width and height of the strings. Knowing the contents of the `m_strMainText` string isn't enough, though, because we need to get its size in the context of the certificate Bitmap object. Besides getting the width in the context of the certificate Bitmap object, we must factor in the font as well. The following code uses the `Graphics` class `MeasureString()` method to get the pixel width and height of the text that's contained in the `m_stMainText` variable (please note that the g class is a `Graphics` class):

C#
```
SizeF size2 =
        g.MeasureString( m_strMainText, objFont );
```

VB
```
Dim size2 As SizeF = _
        g.MeasureString(m_strMainText, objFont)
```

For each string, we need to calculate the x-coordinate with a call to the `Graphics` class `DrawString()` method before drawing. Here again is an item that I have spent a great deal of time teaching, only to get blank stares. For that reason, I'm going to take some extra time to make sure you understand.

Let's start with the fact that we have two widths to work with: the width of the certificate Bitmap object and the width of the string—both in pixel values. The difference between these two values gives us the extra space that we'll have after drawing the string into the certificate (providing, of course, that the certificate width is greater than the text width). What I mean is that if the certificate is 650 pixels wide, and the text is 150 pixels wide, an extra 500 pixels are left over. If you drew the text at the left side of the certificate, there would be 500 pixels past the text until you get to the right side of the certificate, as shown in Figure 23.7.

The math we use in the `DrawMainText()` method to get the difference is simple subtraction, as shown here:

```
m_objImage.Width - size2.Width
```

Once we know the left-over amount, we know how much to put in front of the text and how much to leave behind the text to center the text. Keeping with the same example, in which we have a 500-pixel excess, we know

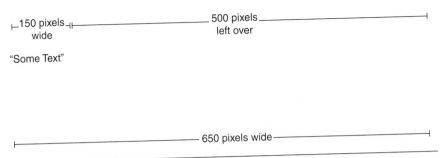

Figure 23.7 The String Is 150 Pixels Wide, and the Certificate Is 650 Pixels Wide, Which Leaves 500 Pixels Remaining.

that we need 250 pixels in front of and 250 pixels behind the text, as shown in Figure 23.8.

The math for calculating half of the difference is easy, and it gives us the x-coordinate, as shown here:

```
(m_objImage.Width - size2.Width) / 2
```

With the x-coordinate calculated, the only thing left to do is make a call to the Graphics.DrawText() method. The following code uses this method to draw the main text:

C#
```
g.DrawString( m_strMainText, objFont, objBrush,
       x, m_objImage.Height / 2 );
```

VB
```
g.DrawString(m_strMainText, objFont, objBrush, _
       x, m_objImage.Height / 2)
```

├────── 1/2 of the excess is 250 pixels ──────┤├─ 150 pixels ─┤├─ 1/2 of the excess is 250 pixels ─┤
wide

"Some Text"

├────────── 650 pixels wide ──────────┤

Figure 23.8 Splitting the Difference of the Left-Over Pixels Gives Us 250 Pixels, and This Is the Amount of Space We Leave before and after the Text.

The `DrawLeftText()` and `DrawRightText()` Methods

These two methods draw text in the lower left and lower right corners of the certificate. If the strings (`m_strLeftText` and `m_strRightText`) are empty, nothing will be drawn. But if text needs to be drawn in either bottom corner, two GDI+ objects are created for the drawing operations. The two objects are a Font and a SolidBrush object. As with the `Draw-MainText()` method, the font size is hard coded at 25. The SolidBrush object that's created has a single parameter to its constructor: a Color object. The Color object is part of the `m_Colors` array, and it is indexed by the `m_nLeftTextColor` and `m_nRightTextColor` integer variables. For instance, `m_nLeftTextColor` might contain the value of 1. This means that the Color object that's in the second array slot is Color.White. (The `m_Colors` array is shown here for completeness, although in the actual source code module it doesn't immediately precede the code as shown here.) The following code shows how the color array indexing works:

C#

```
// Class member array of the colors used for drawing text.
// The index value can range from 0 (for Color.Black) to 5
//    (for Color.Yellow).
Color m_Colors[] = { Color.Black, Color.White, _
    Color.Blue, Color.Green, Color.Red, Color.Yellow };

// Set the index to 2
m_nLeftTextColor = 2;


// m_Colors(m_nLeftTextColor) will now contain Color.Blue.
// Creating the SolidBrush object.
SolidBrush objBrush = new SolidBrush( m_Colors[m_nLeftTextColor] );
// When m_nLeftTextColor is 2, the above line is the same as:
// SolidBrush objBrush = new SolidBrush( Color.Blue );
```

VB

```
' Class member array of the colors used for drawing text.
' The index value can range from 0 (for Color.Black) to 5
'    (for Color.Yellow).
Dim m_Colors() As Color = {Color.Black, Color.White, _
    Color.Blue, Color.Green, Color.Red, Color.Yellow}

' Set the index to 2
m_nLeftTextColor = 2
```

```
' m_Colors(m_nLeftTextColor) will now contain Color.Blue.
' Creating the SolidBrush object.
Dim objBrush As New SolidBrush(m_Colors(m_nLeftTextColor))
' When m_nLeftTextColor is 2, the above line is the same as:
' Dim objBrush As New SolidBrush(Color.Blue)
```

Before we can draw the left or right strings, we need to measure them to find out their pixel width and height. We do this with the Graphics.MeasureString() method, which returns a SizeF object. The two properties of the SizeF object that we'll be interested in are the Width and Height properties.

The text in the left corner is drawn at a fixed x-coordinate of 4. The y-coordinate is calculated by taking the height of the certificate and subtracting the height of the text string, minus an additional 4 pixels to elevate it above the very bottom of the Bitmap. The following calculation shows how the y-coordinate is calculated:

```
m_objImage.Height - size.Height - 4
```

The text in the right corner is drawn using the same y-coordinate calculation as the text in the left corner. But the x-coordinate is not fixed as it is when the text is drawn in the left corner. The x-coordinate is calculated for the text in the right corner by subtracting the width of the text from the width of the certificate, minus an additional 4 pixels to move it slightly to the left of the right-most pixel of the certificate. The following code shows how the x-coordinate is calculated for the text in the right corner:

```
m_objImage.Width - size.Width - 4
```

The last thing that both methods do is to store the y-coordinate in the m_nLeftImageBottom and m_nRightImageBottom integer variables. These variables are used when (and if) images are drawn in the bottom left and bottom right corners to make sure that the images aren't drawn on top of the text. You can see text in the corner in Figure 23.9, but note that the images in this example figure are in the upper left and right corners.

The SaveImage() Method

This method saves the certificate Bitmap image to disk. It makes a call to the Bitmap.Save() method with the full path name to which the certificate image will be saved. The image is saved as a GIF image so that the

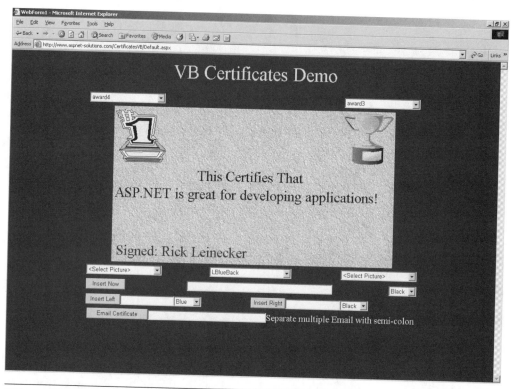

Figure 23.9 You Can Put Text on the Lower Left or Lower Right Portions of the Certificate.

image crispness won't be lost because .GIF images use a lossless compression algorithm.

Listing 23.2 Certificate Creation Code

```
' This method creates the image and saves it to disk.
Sub CreateImage()
    ' Create a Bitmap object.
    m_objImage = New Bitmap(m_nWidth, m_nHeight, _
        PixelFormat.Format24bppRgb)
    ' Get a Graphics object for draw operations.
    Dim g As Graphics = Graphics.FromImage(m_objImage)

    ' Call the methods that perform individual draw
    '    operations.
    TileCertificate(g)
```

```
        DrawMainText(g)
        DrawLeftText(g)
        DrawRightText(g)
        DrawCornerImages(g)
End Sub

' This method draws the images in the corner of the certificate.
Sub DrawCornerImages(ByVal g As Graphics)
        ' If there is a string for the upper left image,
        '    load it in and draw it.
        If m_strULImage.Length > 0 Then
            Dim objCorner As New Bitmap(m_strPath + _
                "\CornerImages\" + m_strULImage + ".gif")
            g.DrawImage(objCorner, 4, 4)
        End If

        ' If there is a string for the upper right image,
        '    load it in and draw it.
        If m_strURImage.Length > 0 Then
            Dim objCorner As New Bitmap(m_strPath + _
                "\CornerImages\" + m_strURImage + ".gif")
            g.DrawImage(objCorner, _
                m_objImage.Width - 4 - objCorner.Width, 4)
        End If

        ' If there is a string for the bottom left image,
        '    load it in and draw it.
        If m_strBLImage.Length > 0 Then
            Dim objCorner As New Bitmap(m_strPath + _
                "\CornerImages\" + m_strBLImage + ".gif")
            g.DrawImage(objCorner, 4, _
                m_nLeftImageBottom - 4 - objCorner.Height)
        End If

        ' If there is a string for the bottom right image,
        '    load it in and draw it.
        If m_strBRImage.Length > 0 Then
            Dim objCorner As New Bitmap(m_strPath + _
                "\CornerImages\" + m_strBRImage + ".gif")
            g.DrawImage(objCorner, _
                m_objImage.Width - 4 - objCorner.Width, _
                m_nRightImageBottom - 4 - objCorner.Height)
        End If
```

```
End Sub


' This method tiles the background image into the certificate.
Sub TileCertificate(ByVal g As Graphics)
    ' Create the Bitmap object for the background tile.
    Dim objBackgroundTile As New Bitmap(m_strPath + _
        "\BackgroundTiles\" + m_strBackgroundTile)
    Dim x As Integer, y As Integer = 0

    ' The outer loop will proceed down the certificate.
    While y < m_objImage.Height
        x = 0
        ' The inner loop will proceed across the certificate.
        While x < m_objImage.Width
            ' Draw the image.
            g.DrawImage(objBackgroundTile, x, y)
            ' Move to the right.
            x += objBackgroundTile.Width
        End While
        ' Move down.
        y += objBackgroundTile.Height
    End While
End Sub


' This method draws the text in the middle of the certificate.
Sub DrawMainText(ByVal g As Graphics)

    ' If there is no text entered, simply return.
    If m_strMainText.Length = 0 Then
        Return
    End If

    ' Create the font and brush for drawing.
    Dim objFont As New Font("Times New Roman", 25)
    Dim objBrush As New _
        SolidBrush(m_Colors(m_nMainTextColor))

    ' Get the width and height of the strings that'll be drawn.
    Dim size1 As SizeF = _
        g.MeasureString("This Certifies That", objFont)
    Dim size2 As SizeF = _
        g.MeasureString(m_strMainText, objFont)
```

```
    Dim x As Integer

    ' Calculate the x coordinate for the top string.
    x = (m_objImage.Width - size1.Width) / 2
    g.DrawString("This Certifies That", objFont, _
        objBrush, x, (m_objImage.Height / 2) - size1.Height)

    ' Calculate the x coordinate for the bottom string.
    x = (m_objImage.Width - size2.Width) / 2
    g.DrawString(m_strMainText, objFont, objBrush, _
        x, m_objImage.Height / 2)
End Sub

' This method draws the text in the lower left corner of the
'   certificate.
Sub DrawLeftText(ByVal g As Graphics)

    ' Set the coordinate for drawing the image based on the image
    '   height.
    m_nLeftImageBottom = m_objImage.Height
    ' If there is no string entered, simply return.
    If m_strLeftText.Length = 0 Then
        Return
    End If

    ' Create the font and brush for drawing.
    Dim objFont As New Font("Times New Roman", 25)
    Dim objBrush As New _
        SolidBrush(m_Colors(m_nLeftTextColor))

    ' Get the size of the string.
    Dim size As SizeF = _
        g.MeasureString(m_strLeftText, objFont)

    ' Draw the string.
    g.DrawString(m_strLeftText, objFont, objBrush, _
        4, m_objImage.Height - size.Height - 4)
    m_nLeftImageBottom = _
        m_objImage.Height - size.Height - 4
End Sub

' This method draws the text in the lower right corner of the
'   certificate.
Sub DrawRightText(ByVal g As Graphics)
```

```
' Set the coordinate for drawing the image based on the image
'   height.
m_nRightImageBottom = m_objImage.Height

' If there is no string entered, simply return.
If m_strRightText.Length = 0 Then
    Return
End If

' Create the font and brush for drawing.
Dim objFont As New Font("Times New Roman", 25)
Dim objBrush As New _
    SolidBrush(m_Colors(m_nRightTextColor))

' Get the size of the string.
Dim size As SizeF = _
    g.MeasureString(m_strRightText, objFont)

' Draw the string.
g.DrawString(m_strRightText, objFont, _
    objBrush, m_objImage.Width - size.Width - 4, _
    m_objImage.Height - size.Height - 4)
m_nRightImageBottom = _
    m_objImage.Height - size.Height - 4
End Sub

' This method saves the image to disk.
Sub SaveImage(ByVal strImageDir As String)
    m_objImage.Save(m_strPath + "\" + strImageDir + _
        "\" + m_strFilename, ImageFormat.Gif)
End Sub
```

Initializing the Default.aspx User Interface Objects

Some of the user-selected items are carried in session variables. Table 23.3 shows and describes the session variables that are used in the application.

Listing 23.3 shows the Page_Load() method that's behind the Default.aspx page. This method initializes the session variables if they don't exist and populates the user interface objects if this is not a post back.

Table 23.3 The Session Variables Used in the Application

Name	Description
Tile	This session variable contains the file name for the tile image that is used to tile the certificate background.
Filename	This session variable contains the tile name to which the certificate image will be saved.
MainText	This session variable contains the text that will appear in the center of the certificate.
RightText	This session variable contains the text that will appear in the lower right corner of the certificate.
LeftText	This session variable contains the text that will appear in the lower left corner of the certificate.

An application variable named `CornerImages` contains the list of corner images. This application variable holds a collection of file names. This list of file names is generated in the `Application_Start()` method of the Global.asax file (see Listing 23.4). Another application variable named `TileList` contains the available tile images found in the BackgroundTiles directory.

Four DropDownList objects contain a selectable list of corner images. The following code shows how the first DropDownList object is populated; the subsequent DropDownList objects are populated by setting the `Data-Source` property and calling the `DataBind()` method:

C#
```
String strFileList()
strFileList = (String()) Application["CornerImages"];
ul.DataSource = strFileList;
ul.DataBind();
```

VB
```
Dim strFileList() As String
strFileList = Application("CornerImages")
ul.DataSource = strFileList
ul.DataBind()
```

When the application first runs, all you see is a blank certificate, as shown in Figure 23.10. But the user interface objects will have been populated with the list of tiles and corner images.

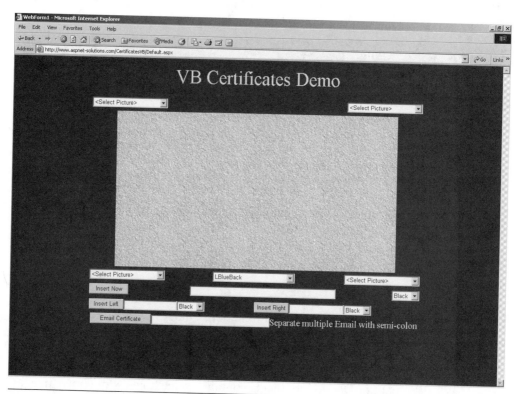

Figure 23.10 The Application Starts with a Clean Slate and Shows Only the Background.

Listing 23.3 Page Initialization Code for Default.aspx

```
Private Sub Page_Load(ByVal sender As System.Object, _
    ByVal e As System.EventArgs) Handles MyBase.Load

    If Session("Tile") Is Nothing Then
        Session("Tile") = "LBlueBack.gif"
    End If

    If Session("Filename") Is Nothing Then
        Session("Filename") = Session.SessionID + ".gif"
    End If

    If Session("MainText") Is Nothing Then
        Session("MainText") = ""
    End If
```

```
    If Session("RightText") Is Nothing Then
        Session("RightText") = ""
    End If

    If Session("LeftText") Is Nothing Then
        Session("LeftText") = ""
    End If

    If Not IsPostBack Then
        Dim strFileList() As String
        strFileList = Application("CornerImages")
        ul.DataSource = strFileList
        ul.DataBind()
        ul.Items.Insert(0, "<Select Picture>")
        ur.DataSource = strFileList
        ur.DataBind()
        ur.Items.Insert(0, "<Select Picture>")
        bl.DataSource = strFileList
        bl.DataBind()
        bl.Items.Insert(0, "<Select Picture>")
        br.DataSource = strFileList
        br.DataBind()
        br.Items.Insert(0, "<Select Picture>")
        strFileList = Application("TileList")
        tile.DataSource = strFileList
        tile.DataBind()
        tile.SelectedIndex = 27
        OutputImage()
    End If

End Sub
```

Listing 23.4 has the `Application_Start()` method. This method gets a list of .gif files from the BackgroundTiles directory and another list of .gif files from the CornerImages directory. These lists will be used during the life of the application, and keeping them in persistent lists will reduce the load on the server without requiring an adverse amount of resources.

Getting a list of files in a directory is simple; we simply use the `Directory.GetFiles()` method and specify a path and a file mask. This method returns a list of files, and the following code shows how this is done:

C#

```
String strFileList();
strFileList =
  Directory.GetFiles(
 @"c:\inetpub\ASPNetSolutionsRoot\CertificatesVB\BackgroundTiles",
  "*.Gif");
```

VB

```
Dim strFileList() As String
strFileList = _
  Directory.GetFiles( _
 "c:\inetpub\ASPNetSolutionsRoot\CertificatesVB\BackgroundTiles", _
  "*.Gif")
```

We don't need to keep the entire path because all we'll use in the application is the file name. We'll have to loop through the list and extract each file name. To do this, we find the index of the last ' \ ' character. This will be the character immediately in front of the file name. (You could also use the System.IO.Path class instead.) If we take what's to the right of the ' \ ' character to the end of the string, we'll have just the file name.

Listing 23.4 The Code That Creates the List of the Corner Images and the Tile Images

```
Sub Application_Start(ByVal sender As Object, ByVal e As EventArgs)
  Try
    Dim strFileList() As String
    strFileList = _
      Directory.GetFiles( _
      "c:\inetpub\ASPNetSolutionsRoot\CertificatesVB\BackgroundTiles", _
      "*.Gif")
    Dim i As Integer
    For i = 0 To strFileList.Length - 1
      Dim nIndex As Integer = strFileList(i).LastIndexOf("\")
      Dim nLength As Integer = strFileList(i).Length
      strFileList(i) = strFileList(i).Substring(nIndex + 1, _
        nLength - nIndex - 5)
    Next
    Application("TileList") = strFileList
    strFileList = _
      Directory.GetFiles( _
      "c:\inetpub\ASPNetSolutionsRoot\CertificatesVB\CornerImages", _
      "*.Gif")
```

```
  For i = 0 To strFileList.Length - 1
    Dim nIndex As Integer = strFileList(i).LastIndexOf("\")
    Dim nLength As Integer = strFileList(i).Length
    strFileList(i) = strFileList(i).Substring(nIndex + 1, _
      nLength - nIndex - 5)
  Next
  Application("CornerImages") = strFileList
  Catch ex As Exception
  End Try
End Sub
```

Instantiating and Using the Certificate Class

Listing 23.5 shows code that's behind the Default.aspx page. The two methods shown are the CreateImage() method and the OutputImage() method. The CreateImage() method uses the Certificate class (named cert) and sets all properties with the appropriate values from the user interface objects. All these properties determine the appearance of the final certificate.

The OuputImage() method instantiates a Certificate object, calls the CreateImage() method (which sets all the Certificate class's properties), saves the image using the Save() method, and outputs the file name into the HTML stream.

Listing 23.5 Instantiating and Using the Certificate Class

```
Sub CreateImage(ByVal cert As Certificate)
    cert.Path = Request.MapPath("")
    cert.Filename = Session("Filename")
    cert.BackgroundTile = tile.SelectedItem.Text + ".gif"
    If ul.SelectedIndex > 0 Then
        cert.UpperLeftImage = ul.SelectedItem.Text
    End If
    If ur.SelectedIndex > 0 Then
        cert.UpperRightImage = ur.SelectedItem.Text
    End If
    If bl.SelectedIndex > 0 Then
        cert.BottomLeftImage = bl.SelectedItem.Text
    End If
```

```
        If br.SelectedIndex > 0 Then
            cert.BottomRightImage = br.SelectedItem.Text
        End If
        cert.MainText = Session("MainText")
        cert.MainTextColor = MainTextColor.SelectedIndex
        cert.LeftText = Session("LeftText")
        cert.LeftTextColor = LeftColor.SelectedIndex
        cert.RightText = Session("RightText")
        cert.RightTextColor = RightColor.SelectedIndex
        cert.CreateImage()
End Sub

Public Sub OutputImage()
    Dim cert As New Certificate()
    CreateImage(cert)
    cert.SaveImage("TempImages")
    ImageTag.Text = "<IMG SRC=" + Chr(34) + _
        "TempImages/" + Session("Filename") + Chr(34) + ">"
End Sub
```

Responding to User Interaction

A good bit of the code responds to user selections, and this can be seen in Listing 23.6. The first method you'll see is the `CreateNewFilename()` method. This method creates a file name for the image that is going to be created next, and it has the system ticks as part of the file name. Here's why this is important: Suppose we use the same file name for a user's session, and the user makes changes in the certificate 10 times. The browser will not show these changes in the regenerated image because the original image will be cached by the browser. For this reason, each time the user makes a change in the certificate, we need to change the file name. That way, the browser won't cache the file, and the user will see the newly created file.

Following the `CreateNewFilename()` method are four similar methods: `ul_SelectedIndexChanged()`, `ur_SelectedIndex-Changed()`, `bl_SelectedIndexChanged()`, and `br_Selected-IndexChanged()`. These methods all change the selected corner image. Each one generates a new file name by calling `CreateNewFilename()`, and then calling `OutputImage()` to save the updated certificate.

The `tile_SelectedIndexChanged()` method responds to a user selection for the background tile. When a user changes his selection, this method is fired. It sets the session variable named `Tile` to the file name that the user selected (and adds a .gif extension). A call to `CreateNewFilename()` and a call to `OutputImage()` change the certificate that the user is viewing.

The next three methods, `InsertNow_Click()`, `InsertLeft_Click()`, and `InsertRight_Click()`, perform similar functions. Each takes a text string and places it into the appropriate `Certificate` class property. For each of these methods, the `MainText`, `LeftText`, and `RightText` session variables are set (depending on which method is being called). Then, a call to `CreateNewFilename()` and `OutputImage()` completes the process of changing the viewed certificate.

The last method in Listing 23.6 is named `SendEmail_Click()`, and this method e-mails a link to the saved certificate. The first thing that the method does is instantiate a Certificate object, call the `CreateImage()`

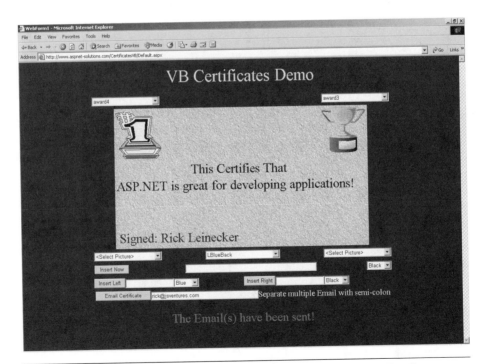

Figure 23.11 You Can Send the Certificates via E-Mail with the Email Certificate Button.

method to populate all of the properties, call the `SaveImage()` method to save the image to disk, and then send the e-mail. Figure 23.11 shows the use of the e-mail functionality.

Before you actually send the e-mail, though, the HTML must be formed so that the e-mail will have the correct link. Once this is done and contained in a string variable, an instance of the `MailMessage` class is created. The `MailMessage Body`, `BodyFormat`, `From`, and `Subject` properties are all set. Then, for each e-mail address that's in the Emails TextBox object, the `SmtpServer` and `Send` properties are set, followed by a call to the `Send()` method. These steps are all it takes to send the e-mail message to the recipient. The e-mail server that was specified is one through which this application has security clearance to send e-mails.

Listing 23.6 Responding to User Changes

```
Sub CreateNewFilename()
    Try
        File.Delete(Request.MapPath("TempImages\") + _
            Session("Filename"))
    Catch
    End Try
    Session("Filename") = Session.SessionID + _
        Convert.ToString(DateTime.Now.Ticks) + ".gif"
End Sub

Private Sub ul_SelectedIndexChanged(ByVal sender As System.Object, _
    ByVal e As System.EventArgs) Handles ul.SelectedIndexChanged
    CreateNewFilename()
    OutputImage()
End Sub

Private Sub ur_SelectedIndexChanged(ByVal sender As System.Object, _
    ByVal e As System.EventArgs) Handles ur.SelectedIndexChanged
    CreateNewFilename()
    OutputImage()
End Sub

Private Sub bl_SelectedIndexChanged(ByVal sender As System.Object, _
    ByVal e As System.EventArgs) Handles bl.SelectedIndexChanged
    CreateNewFilename()
    OutputImage()
End Sub
```

```
Private Sub br_SelectedIndexChanged(ByVal sender As System.Object, _
    ByVal e As System.EventArgs) Handles br.SelectedIndexChanged
    CreateNewFilename()
    OutputImage()
End Sub

Private Sub tile_SelectedIndexChanged(ByVal sender As System.Object, _
    ByVal e As System.EventArgs) Handles tile.SelectedIndexChanged
    Session("Tile") = tile.SelectedItem.Text + ".Gif"
    CreateNewFilename()
    OutputImage()
End Sub

Private Sub InsertNow_Click(ByVal sender As System.Object, _
    ByVal e As System.EventArgs) Handles InsertNow.Click
    Session("MainText") = MainText.Text
    MainText.Text = ""
    CreateNewFilename()
    OutputImage()
End Sub

Private Sub InsertLeft_Click(ByVal sender As System.Object, _
    ByVal e As System.EventArgs) Handles InsertLeft.Click
    Session("LeftText") = LeftText.Text
    LeftText.Text = ""
    CreateNewFilename()
    OutputImage()
End Sub

Private Sub InsertRight_Click(ByVal sender As System.Object, _
    ByVal e As System.EventArgs) Handles InsertRight.Click
    Session("RightText") = RightText.Text
    RightText.Text = ""
    CreateNewFilename()
    OutputImage()
End Sub

Private Sub SendEmail_Click(ByVal sender As System.Object, _
    ByVal e As System.EventArgs) Handles SendEmail.Click
    Dim cert As New Certificate()
    CreateImage(cert)
    cert.SaveImage("EmailImages")
    Status.Text = "The Email(s) have been sent!"
```

```
Dim strMessage As String = _
    "<html><body bgcolor=cyan><p><h2>You have " + _
    "been sent a certificate.</h2></p><p>" + _
    "<a href=http://www.aspnet-solutions.com/" + _
    "CertificatesVB/EmailImages/" + Session("Filename") + _
    ">Click Here To See It</a></p></body><html>"
Dim message As New MailMessage()
message.Body = strMessage
message.BodyFormat = MailFormat.Html
message.From = Chr(34) + "ASPNET Solutions Certificate" + _
    Chr(34) + "<Certificates@ASPNET-Solutions.com>"
message.Subject = "A Certificate To You"
Dim strEmailAddrs() As String = _
    Emails.Text.Split(New Char() {Chr(56)})
Emails.Text = ""
Dim i As Integer
For i = 0 To strEmailAddrs.Length - 1
    SmtpMail.SmtpServer = "mail.aspnet-solutions.com"
    message.To = strEmailAddrs(i)
    SmtpMail.Send(message)
Next
End Sub
```

Summary

The application in this chapter is a good example of several techniques that you might need in your programming tasks. First, there's an interesting use of GDI+ as the certificate is tiled and drawn. Second, creating a list of files in a directory is something that is done fairly frequently. Third is the use of the `MailMessage` class to send out e-mails.

You can easily enhance this application by adding additional properties such as font size and style. You can use the `Certificate` class to automatically create a certificate for online contests that you might be holding—and then you can e-mail the link. If you give yourself enough time, you'll come up with lots of ways to use and extend this application.

CHAPTER 24

Monitoring Servers: Using WMI and Performance Monitor

In This Chapter:

- Windows Management Instrumentation (WMI)
- Performance Monitor
- The ServerMonitor Demo Program

Imagine your servers being locked in a room that is 1,200 miles away. You can get to them and administer them through Terminal Services or PC Anywhere, but the firewall won't let you monitor them from your handheld, wireless PDA. It's important, though, that at any time of day or night you can see important statistics about the servers. The health of your servers is vital to business.

The things you might want to see include available disk space, available memory, average CPU utilization, and maybe some custom application statistics. All of these details are available to ASP.NET applications through some base classes that exist in the .NET Framework. That means that your handheld, wireless device can view the server's vital signs through an ASP.NET application, thus avoiding the problem that the firewall poses.

This chapter talks about Windows Management Instrumentation (WMI) and Performance Monitor, and shows how to use both through a special demonstration application. The underlying technology is presented along with explanatory code snippets, followed by a complete application.

Windows Management Instrumentation

Windows Management Instrumentation (WMI) serves as a framework for Windows administration, whether locally or remotely. The interface is available by various methods, including server-side scripting languages such as

ASP.NET. WMI's object model allows you to query and configure nearly all aspects of the Windows operating system.

The WMI model provides for several uses, whether complete remote administration or simple manipulation. Information and data requests can be handled in the WMI component model, which effectively handles the details of the implementation to WMI.

WMI is based on the Common Information Model (CIM). The CIM is a standard of the DMTF organization (go to dmtf.org for more data about this acronym). The CIM is specified at http://www.dmtf.org/standards/ standard. CIM is an object-oriented model that sorts and describes information in a given environment. CIM objects can be physical resources such as hardware, logical resources such as software, or networks. Figure 24.1 shows the CIM core model.

This model makes up the basic CIM Schema. The CIM Schema includes many base classes. Each platform includes its own implementation of these classes.

WMI is the Microsoft implementation of the CIM model, and it adheres to the Web-Based Enterprise System Management (WBEM) standard (for more information, go to http://www.dmtf.org/standards/standard_ wbem.php). Using WMI, developers can manage Windows effectively, with standard methods.

WMI is an integral part of Windows 2000/XP. It is available as a stand-alone application for Windows 95, 98, and NT 4. WMI has two main components: the WMI main component (winmgmt.exe) and the CIM repository. The CIM repository serves as a database of available static data.

Application data requests are passed through winmgmt.exe. Winmgmt. exe supports COM interfaces for interaction. Developers are rarely aware that this application even exists—they just know of the functionality if it

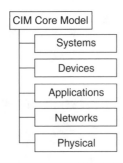

Figure 24.1 The CIM Core Object Model

happens to surface. If the request is for static information, the information is gathered from the CIM repository and passed to the requesting application. If the request is for dynamic data, the appropriate provider is polled and the results are returned to the application.

WMI uses multiple types of providers to meet these needs, as shown in Table 24.1.

The .NET framework provides a number of base class libraries that help instrument .NET applications. These libraries reside in the System.Management.Instrumentation, the System.Diagnostics, and the System. Management namespaces. Actually, WMI doesn't reside in System. Diagnostics, the OerCounters reside in this namespace. Between these three namespaces, you will find all the base class libraries that give WMI and Performance Monitor support.

Visual Studio .NET cannot automatically find the System.Management namespace. To use the System.Management namespace, you need to add a reference to your project. To do this, right-click the project name in the Solution Explorer, select Add Reference, scroll down in the .NET list, select System.Management, and then click the OK button. From this point on, you can use the System.Management namespace in your projects. Figure 24.2 shows how to add this reference to your project.

Table 24.1 The CIM Classes

Class	Description
Performance Monitor Provider	Provides access to Windows NT Performance Monitor data.
Registry Provider	Provides access to system registry data.
Registry Event Provider	Sends events when changes occur to registry keys, values, or trees.
SNMP Provider	Provides access to events and data from SNMP devices such as routers, hubs, and switches.
Windows NT Event Log Provider	Provides access to data and event notifications from the Windows NT Event Log.
Win32 Provider	Provides access to data from the Win32 subsystem.
WDM Provider	Provides access to data and events from device drivers that conform to the Windows Driver Model WMI extensions.

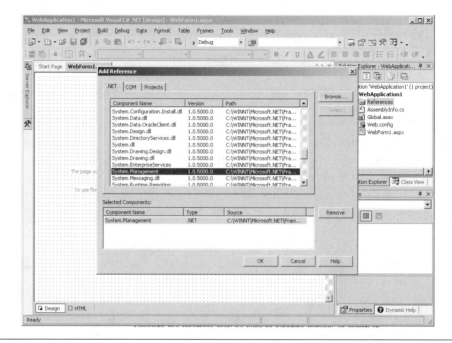

Figure 24.2 You'll Need to Add the System.Management Namespace.

Performance Monitor

Performance Monitor is a powerful tool for monitoring system performance in Windows 2000 and Windows XP. As a system administrator, you can easily track things such as CPU usage, memory usage, and SQL Server performance.

Although the interface may be hard to navigate initially, as shown in Figure 24.3, a little searching will get you on your way quite quickly.

To fully understand Performance Monitor, you need to understand two basic terms: **counter** and **object**. A counter contains various values associated with an object, such as total count and count per unit time. An object represents the actual hardware and software components. The components can be physical or logical in nature. For every object (such as system RAM, TCP/IP protocols, and CPU), Microsoft has included a preset counter. This counter usually measures the most basic (and useful) aspect of a given object.

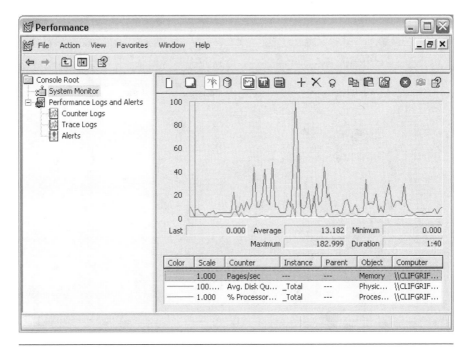

Figure 24.3 Performance Monitor Main Window

Logging CPU Usage

Start by adding a simple counter. From the main window, expand the tree node labeled Performance Logs and Alerts. Click Counter Logs. This screen displays all Counter Logs. Icons are darker and lighter for stopped and running services, respectively, as shown in Figure 24.4.

Right click Counter Logs or in a blank space in the log list to the right. Select New Log Settings from the resulting context menu. You will be prompted for a log name. Type in a name such as **CPU Usage** and press OK.

The resulting window has three tabs: General, Log Files, and Schedule, as shown in Figure 24.5. On the General tab, click Add Objects. Select Processor from the list of objects. Press OK. This option will use the default counter for the Processor object. (Pressing Add Counters will allow you to select particular aspects of the processor to log.)

From this tab you can also select parameters such as Interval and Log File size; both of these can be very useful. Log files can quickly become large, so setting a file size limit can be a smart way to prevent future problems. Once the log file size is reached, the counter automatically stops.

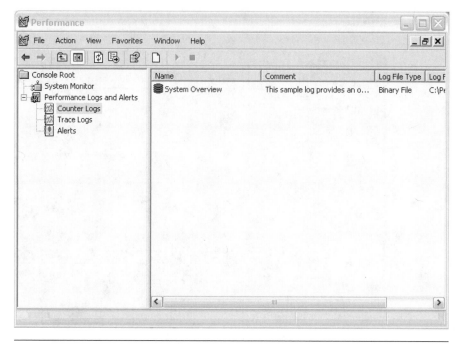

Figure 24.4 View Existing Counter Logs.

You want to set the interval at a rate that can give you accurate sampling, but best performance. The faster the interval, the quicker the log file grows and the more system performance is used.

NOTE: Logging in and of itself can take considerable system resources. For instance, logging available CPU resources will be offset by the resources Performance Monitor uses to log. This should be accounted for when using the data.

On the Log Files tab, you can select your log file format and naming conventions.

The Schedule tab allows you to automatically control the logging process. Not only can you set a start and finish date, you can specify certain hours of the day to run the Counter. You can also obviously leave the scheduling open ended and stop it manually. If you do not specify a schedule, the counter will run immediately upon your pressing OK.

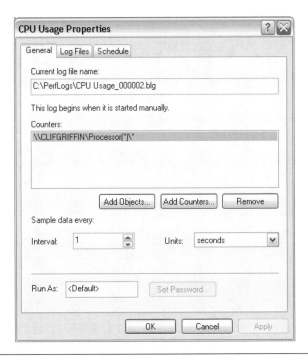

Figure 24.5 Set the Options for Your New Counter.

After you've logged your information, you may want to view the information as a chart at a later date. This format will allow for easy, visual interpretation of collected data. Following are the steps you'll need to complete to view the information in chart format:

1. Click on the Source tab in the System Monitor Properties dialog as shown in Figure 24.6.
2. Press CTRL + L, or use the corresponding button located above the preset, real-time counter chart.
3. Select the Log files: radio button.
4. Press the Add button. The default location for log files is automatically displayed.
5. Select your log file from the list. In our case, this file will be labeled with the prefix CPU Usage. If you want to display only a portion of your log file, use the Time Range selector to drag the time range you want to display.
6. Press OK. This will instantly load the selected log file and display the information as a chart.

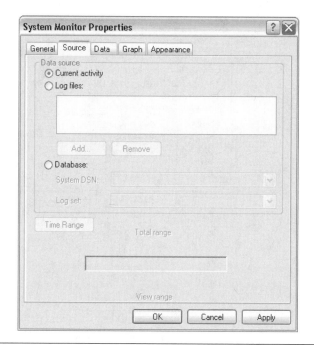

Figure 24.6 Select the Chart Source.

NOTE: Just as you can have multiple real-time counters, you can add multiple log files. When these items are logged to disk, the log includes the PerfMon session, which may include several counters.

The ServerMonitor Demo Program

This section talks about a demonstration program that can be run from the URL http://www.aspnet-solutions.com/ServerMonitorCS/Default.aspx. This application shows the basics of using WMI and Performance Monitor in an application.

Performance Monitor Security

Before we start working with custom performance counters, we need to discuss some of the security issues surrounding their use. ASP.NET is configured to run under a less privileged account usually referred to as Aspnet_ user. This account was created with the bare minimum permissions in case a security flaw was found in ASP.NET that allowed a hacker to run code on a machine. If such a breach was found, because the ASP.NET process was using this account, then the hacker could do only so much damage.

The only downside to the ASP.NET process using the Aspnet_user account is that certain functions will not work anymore without some increased effort. Creating custom performance counters is one of the operations that cannot be performed by the Aspnet_user account. The Aspnet_user account can, however, write to these counters once they are created, which simply means that we need to create the counters using impersonation. Although we can switch the system back to using the high-level system account, doing so is highly discouraged because of the security issues it would create.

Let's take a quick look at what we will need to change to be able to create these custom counters. If you are using Visual Studio .NET then these security steps are not necessary, because we can use the Server Explorer utility to create the counters and counter category directly. Using the Server Explorer, you can connect to any server located in your domain. We will be creating a small administrative application to add our custom counters to our system. We will simply create an empty virtual directory called asp-perftest in our wwwroot directory.

1. The first step that we need to take is to add the following line to the web.config of our application:

   ```
   <identity impersonate="true"></identity>
   ```

   This setting will tell our application to impersonate the user who is logged into our site or page.

2. The next step is to make a change to the IIS settings of our application. First, we need to right-click our virtual directory and then select Properties.

3. Next, we click the Directory Security tab and then click the Edit button under the Anonymous Access and Authentication Control section.

4. Here, we are going to first uncheck the box for Anonymous access, and then, if everyone using this tool will be using Windows systems and logging into our domain, we do not need to make any other changes.

5. If we will have users who use non-Windows systems, or do not log into our domain, we will need to check the box for Basic Authentication.

We will get a security warning when we check basic authentication, because this action will be sending the username and password in clear text, which is a potential security risk. If possible, it is always best to use only Windows authentication. Doing this will require us to enter a username and password when we access this application. The Web application will then use that username and password to create the custom counters. The login that we will use will need to have sufficient permissions to create these counters.

Enumerating Services

One thing that's important to view is the services that are installed on a server and their state. WMI lets you easily find out this information with a single query. The query itself is SELECT * FROM WMI_Service, and the code to execute it is as follows:

C#
```
ManagementObjectSearcher s =
    new ManagementObjectSearcher( "SELECT * FROM Win32_Service" );
```

VB
```
Dim s As New ManagementObjectSearcher( "SELECT * FROM Win32_Service" )
```

The demonstration program has a page that allows you to see both the services on the server and their states. This program is shown in Figure 24.7.

Listing 24.1 shows the code that queries for the services and then enumerates them into a Label that's part of the user interface. The first thing is the creation of a ManagementObjectSearcher object with the query as an argument to its constructor. (As I noted previously, the query is SELECT * FROM Win32_Service.)

To enumerate through the collection, the ManagementObject-Search.Get() method is used (in the case below, the code is actually s.Get()). This method is used in the following code.

Listing 24.1 This Code Enumerates the Services and Can Be Found in EnumerateServices.aspx.cs (or EnumerateServices.aspx.vb for the VB Version).

```
private void Page_Load(object sender, System.EventArgs e)
{
  //Request the collection of services
  ManagementObjectSearcher s =
    new ManagementObjectSearcher( "SELECT * FROM Win32_Service" );
```

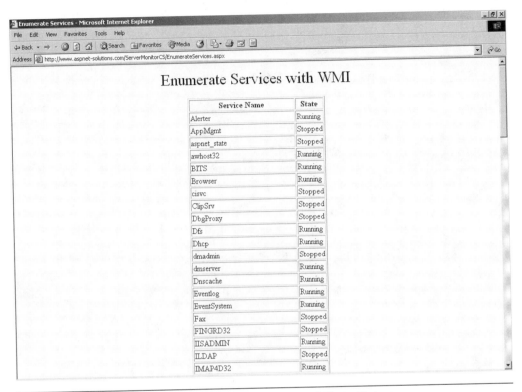

Figure 24.7 This Page Shows All of the Services and Their States.

```
//Enumerate through the collection
foreach( ManagementObject service in s.Get() )
{

   // Store the information in the user interface label.
   Enumeration.Text += ( "<tr><td>" + service["Name"] +
     "</td><td>" +
     service["State"] + "</td></tr>" );

}
}
```

Enumerating WMI Objects

The code in Listing 24.1 shows how to query the Win32_Service object, but
before that, you might need to know what objects are available. The second
page of the demonstration application shows which WMI objects are avail-

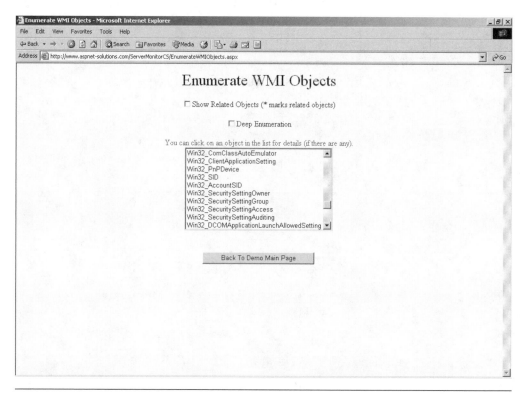

Figure 24.8 This Page Lets You View an Enumeration of All WMI Objects.

able. There are two ways, though, to get the information. The first is not a deep enumeration, and the second is a deep enumeration. The deep enumeration will show all WMI objects with a recursive enumeration; otherwise, only immediate classes are found. The page is shown in Figure 24.8 with the available WMI objects.

Listing 24.2 shows the code that enumerates the WMI objects. The code starts off by clearing the ListBox (named Enumeration) and Label (named Details) user interface objects. A Management object is created with which the enumeration will be done. A special object type of EnumerationOptions is created, with which we'll let the ManagementClass know how to perform the enumeration.

Iterating through the enumeration gives us a series of ManagementObject objects, each of which represents a WMI class. The name of the class is retrieved with the following code:

C#
```
string strClassName = ( "" + obj["__Class"] );
```

VB
```
Dim strClassName As String = ( "" + obj["__Class"] )
```

Once the class name has been retrieved, it is added to the ListBox object with its Add() method.

There is a CheckBox that allows the user to ask to have related classes shown. To enable the user to do this, for each class that's found and added to the ListBox, we must enumerate its classes with a newly created ManagementClass object. These ManagementClass objects take the class name in as an argument to the constructor. Before, we didn't give the constructor any arguments and it did a top-level enumeration.

We'll enumerate through each of these related ManagementClass objects to retrieve the classes that belong to it. The class names are retrieved and added to the ListBox. But these class names begin with three blank spaces and an asterisk so that the user will see that they are related classes.

Also seen in Listing 24.2 is the Enumeration_SelectedIndex-Changed() method. This method is fired when the user clicks any of the items in the ListBox. The first thing, though, that's examined is the starting character of the selected item in the ListBox. If that is a blank space, then it represents a related WMI class, and we won't show the details.

If the selected item is a top-level WMI object, we'll perform a query on it using a ManagementObjectSearcher. These objects take an argument in the constructor that contains the query that's to be performed. The following shows example queries for the Win32_Desktop class:

C#
```
ManagementObjectSearcher s =
  new ManagementObjectSearcher( "SELECT * FROM Win32_Desktop" );
```

VB
```
Dim s As New ManagementObjectSearcher( "SELECT * FROM Win32_Desktop" )
```

Enumerating through the ManagementObjectSearcher object yields a sequence of ManagementObject classes. Each of these classes contains a collection of PropertyData objects that have the properties for the WMI class.

Listing 24.2 This Code Enumerates the WMI Objects and Can Be Found in Enumer-ateWMIObjects.aspx.cs (or EnumerateWMIObjects.aspx.vb for the VB Version).

```
private void PopulateEnumerationList()
{

  // Clear the ListBox and the Label.
  Enumeration.Items.Clear();
  Details.Text = "";

  // We'll need a ManagementClass object, so create
  //   one here.
  ManagementClass newClass = new ManagementClass();

  // We'll need an EnumerationOptions object, so create
  //   one here and set the EnumerateDeep property
  //   according to the DeepEnumeration CheckBox.
  EnumerationOptions options = new EnumerationOptions();
  options.EnumerateDeep = DeepEnumeration.Checked;

  // Iterate through the ManagementObjects that were found.
  foreach( ManagementObject obj in newClass.GetSubclasses( options ) )
  {

    // Create a string in a local variable that
    //   represents the class name. This makes
    //   the code easier later in this method.
    string strClassName = ( "" + obj["__Class"] );
    Enumeration.Items.Add( strClassName );

    // If we're set to show related classes, do
    //   the following code.
    if( ShowRelated.Checked )
    {
      try
      {
        // Get a ManagementClass object that represents
        //   this class.
        ManagementClass c =
          new ManagementClass( strClassName );

        // Find all ManagemenuClass instances.
        foreach( ManagementClass r in c.GetRelatedClasses() )
        {
```

```
            // Add to the user interface label.
            Enumeration.Items.Add( "    * " +
               r["__CLASS"] );
         }
      }
      catch( Exception ex )
      {
         // Let user know about the error.
         Enumeration.Items.Add(
            string.Format( "    Exception: {0} for {1}",
               ex.Message.ToString(), obj["_Class"] ) );


      }
   }
  }
}


private void Page_Load(object sender, System.EventArgs e)
{
  if( !IsPostBack )
  {
    PopulateEnumerationList();
  }
}


private void Enumeration_SelectedIndexChanged(object sender,
System.EventArgs e)
{
  // Get the selected class in a local string variable.
  string strSelection = Enumeration.SelectedItem.Value;

  // Clear the user interface label.
  Details.Text = "";

  // If this selection starts with a leading ' '
  //   then it is a related class and we won't do this.
  if( strSelection[0] != ' ' )
  {

    //Request the collection of services
    ManagementObjectSearcher s =
      new ManagementObjectSearcher( "SELECT * FROM " +
        strSelection );
```

```
//Enumerate through the collection
foreach( ManagementObject obj in s.Get() )
{

  // Find PropertyData objects from the ManagementObject.
  foreach( PropertyData objPropertyData in obj.Properties )
  {
    // Display the results in the user interface
    //   Label.
    Details.Text +=
        string.Format( "{0} ({1}): {2}<br>\r\n",
           objPropertyData.Name,
        objPropertyData.Type,
        objPropertyData.Value );
  }
 }
 }
}
```

WMI Security

Your code will often make WMI queries to remote servers. In most of these cases, you'll have to authenticate to the remote servers. This section talks about doing that.

The biggest difference between the code you're going to look at now and the examples you've already seen is that this next example uses a `ManagementObject` constructor that takes an additional argument in its constructor. The constructor used takes a ManagementScope object and a ManagementPath object. The examples in the previous section specified only a ManagementPath.

The ManagementScope object is used to specify information with regard to the remote server. The code below shows how to create a ManagementScope object where the constructor takes a `server path` string and a ConnectionOptions object as arguments. The `server path` string specifies the path to the server. The ConnectionOptions object contains information that allows user credentials to be presented for authentication and gets management objects for the C drive.

C#
```
ConnectionOptions options = new ConnectionOptions();
options.Username = "domain\\username";
options.Password = "password";
```

```
ManagementScope scope = new ManagementScope( "\\\\servername\\root\
\cimv2",
    options );

try
{
    scope.Connect();
    ManagementObject disk = new ManagementObject( scope,
        new ManagementPath( "Win32_logicaldisk='c:'" ), null );
    disk.Get();
}
catch( Exception ex )
{
    // Handle exception here.
}
```

VB
```
Dim options As New ConnectionOptions()
options.Username = "domain\username"
options.Password = "password"

Dim scope As New ManagementScope( "\\servername\root\cimv2", _
    options )

Try
    scope.Connect()
    Dim disk As New ManagementObject( scope, _
        New ManagementPath( "Win32_logicaldisk='c:'" ), Nothing )
    disk.Get()
Catch ex As Exception
    ' Handle exception here.
End Try
```

Querying a WMI Object

The third page in the demonstration application allows users to query a single WMI object by name. This page can be seen in Figure 24.9.

The first thing the code in Listing 24.3 does is to get the object name from the user interface TextBox object (named ObjectName). This TextBox is cleared, and the Details Label is emptied. A ManagementSearcherObject object is created with the query as a parameter to the constructor. The query will end up being something similar to SELECT * FROM Win32_Printer.

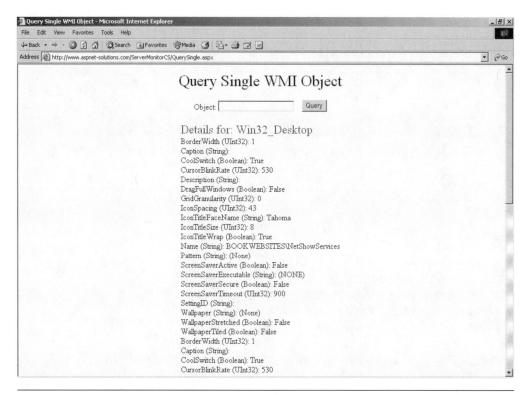

Figure 24.9 You Can Query a Single WMI Object from This Page.

Enumerating through the ManagementSearchObject object yields a collection of ManagementObject objects. These in turn have a collection of PropertyData objects. The PropertyData objects have three properties that we're interested in: the `Name`, `Type`, and `Value` properties. These three properties are converted to text and added to the Details Label object.

Listing 24.3 This Code Queries a Single WMI Object and Can Be Found in QuerySingle.aspx.cs (or QuerySingle.aspx.vb for the VB Version).

```
private void Query_Click(object sender, System.EventArgs e)
{
  // Get the object that the user typed in.
  string strSelection = ObjectName.Text;

  // Clear out the object name TextBox and the
  //   user interface Label into which the
```

```
//    results will be placed.
ObjectName.Text = "";
Details.Text = "";

try
{
  //Request the collection of services
  ManagementObjectSearcher s =
    new ManagementObjectSearcher( "SELECT * FROM " +
      strSelection );

  //Enumerate through the collection
  foreach( ManagementObject obj in s.Get() )
  {

    // Find PropertyData objects from the ManagementObject.
    foreach( PropertyData objPropertyData in obj.Properties )
    {
      // Display the results in the user interface
      //    Label.
      Details.Text += ( objPropertyData.Name + " (" +
        objPropertyData.Type + "): " +
        Convert.ToString( objPropertyData.Value ) +
        "<br>\r\n" );
    }
  }
}
catch( Exception ex )
{
  // Alert the user to the error.
  Details.Text = ex.Message.ToString();
}
}
```

Viewing the Event Log

There are times when you'll want to view the Event Log to see what's happened. The EventLog class allows you to retrieve all events in the Event Log. The fourth page in the demonstration application does this, and can be seen in Figure 24.10. This information would be good for identifying problems in specific applications. For instance, if an application keeps

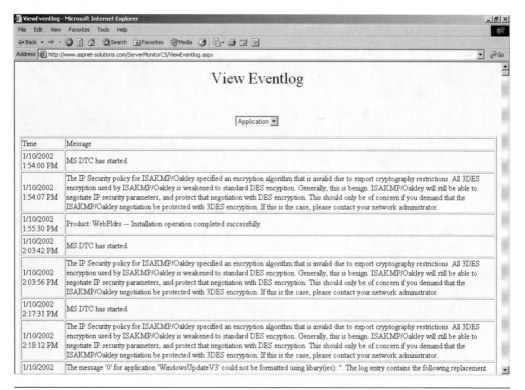

Figure 24.10 You Can View the Event Log through This Page.

failing, then many times diagnostic information can be found in the EventLog.

The code in Listing 24.4 shows how the Event Log is accessed. The first thing, though, that's done in the `Page_Load()` method is to retrieve the Event Log categories. To do this, an array of EventLog objects is retrieved with the `EventLog.GetEventLogs()` static method. Each member of the array has a property named `Log` that names the Event Log category to which the array element is associated. These values are added to the DropDownList object named EventLogList.

A helper method named `EventData()` populates the DataList object with the Event Log items. This method retrieves that data collection by creating an EventLog object and setting the `Log` property to the selected Event Log category. The results are bound to the DataList with its `Data-Source` property and `DataBind()` method.

Listing 24.4 This Code Shows Event Log Entries and Can Be Found in View-EventLog.aspx.cs (or ViewEventLog.aspx.vb for the VB Version).

```
private void Page_Load(object sender, System.EventArgs e)
{
  // Only do this code the first time through, after
  //   that the DropDownList will already be
  //   populated.
  if( !IsPostBack )
  {

    // Get the list of EventLog objects.
    EventLog[] logs = EventLog.GetEventLogs();


    // Loop through and add the logs to the
    //   DropDownList.
    for( int i=0; i<logs.Length; i++ )
    {
      EventLogList.Items.Add( logs[i].Log );
    }


    // Call the method that populates the DataList with
    //   the event log items.
    EventData();
  }
}


void EventData()
{
  // Don't do anything if there is
  //   no selection.
  if( EventLogList.SelectedIndex < 0 )
  {
    return;
  }


  // Create an EventLog object.
  EventLog log = new EventLog();
  // Get the selected item and set the Log
  //   property.
```

```
log.Log = EventLogList.SelectedItem.Text;

// Set the DataSource property and data bind
//   the DataList object.
EventList.DataSource = log.Entries;
EventList.DataBind();
}
```

Using Performance Monitor

The demonstration application has a page in which users can view three of the built-in Performance Monitors. Developers might want these in order to monitor the server's health to make sure that their application isn't affecting it in a very adverse way. The monitors show the CPU utilization, the network throughput, and the available memory. This part of the application can be seen in Figure 24.11.

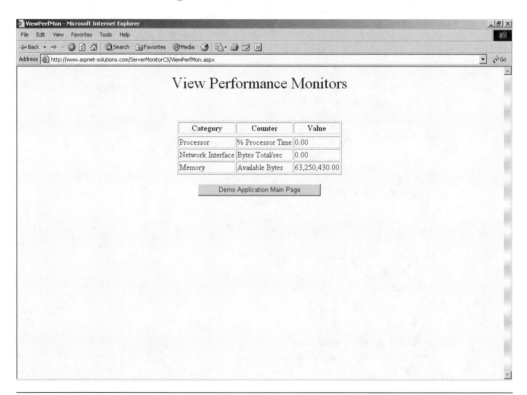

Figure 24.11 These Performance Monitor Figures Might Be Very Important to You.

To avoid redundant code, I created a method that accepts strings specifying the Performance Monitor category, name, and instance name. Also given to this method is a string that specifies the formatting of the Performance Monitor value.

The method creates a PerformanceCounter object, giving its constructor the category, name, instance name, and server name. The server name is hard-coded because it doesn't change for this demonstration program. You could put this name into the Web.config file to make changing it easy.

With the PerformanceCounter object created, it's a simple matter of calling the `NextValue()` method to retrieve the counter's value. The value is then formatted and added to the user interface Label object named CounterValues.

The `Page_Load()` method calls this method three times: one for the Processor, one for the Network Interface, and one for the Memory Performance Monitors.

Listing 24.5 This Code Shows Some Performance Monitor Objects and Can Be Found in ViewPerfmon.aspx.cs (or ViewPerfmon.aspx.vb for the VB Version).

```
// This is a helper method that takes a category, name,
//   instance, and string format; gets the performance
//   monitor object, and populates the user interface
//   label with the results.
void AddPerfValue( string strCategory, string strName,
  string strInstance, string strFormat )
{

  try
  {

    // Get the PerformanceCounter object. The third
    //   argument is the server name.
    PerformanceCounter objPerf =
      new PerformanceCounter( strCategory, strName,
      strInstance,
      "BOOKWEBSITES" );

    // Get the next value with the NextValue()
    //   method--this is a float.
    float fValue = objPerf.NextValue();
```

```
        // Store the results in the user interface Label
        //   as a table row with three columns.
        CounterValues.Text += ( "<tr><td>" + strCategory +
          "</td><td>" + strName + "</td><td>" +
          fValue.ToString( strFormat ) + "</td></td>\r\n" );

    }
    catch( Exception ex )
    {

      // Alert the user to the error.
      CounterValues.Text += ( "<tr><td>" + strCategory +
        "</td><td>" + strName + "</td><td>Error: " +
        ex.Message.ToString() + "</td></td>\r\n" );
    }
}

private void Page_Load(object sender, System.EventArgs e)
{
    // Here we call our helper method three times for the
    //   Processor, Network Interface, and Memory objects.
    AddPerfValue( "Processor", "% Processor Time",
      "_Total", "0.00" );
    AddPerfValue( "Network Interface", "Bytes Total/sec",
      "Intel 8255x-based Integrated Fast Ethernet", "0.00" );
    AddPerfValue( "Memory", "Available Bytes",
      "", "N" );
}
```

Custom Performance Monitors

There are times when your application may need custom Performance Monitors. A good example of this might be when you need to determine the performance of an application. This section talks about adding a custom Performance Monitor that keeps track of page hits to the page, and an example can be seen in Figure 24.12.

The code in Listing 24.6 creates a custom Performance Monitor that counts page hits. The code starts off by calling the `PerformanceCounterCategory.Exists()` static method to see whether the counter named "ASP.NET Solutions" exists. If it doesn't, then it needs to be created.

To create the counter, a CounterCreationDataCollection object is instantiated named CounterGroup. The code then creates a Counter-

CreationData object named CounterData. The CounterData object has three properties that are set, determining its name, help string, and type. The CounterCreationData object is then added to the CounterCreation-DataCollection object.

With the counter either found or newly created, we get a Performance-Counter object that references it. The counter is incremented with the `Increment()` method. Finally, the counter value is shown in the user interface Label named PageHits.

Listing 24.6 This Code Shows a Custom Performance Monitor Object and Can Be found in PageViews.aspx.cs (or PageViews.aspx.vb for the VB Version).

```
private void Page_Load(object sender, System.EventArgs e)
{

    // See if the performance counter already exists.
    if( !PerformanceCounterCategory.Exists( "ASP.NET Solutions" ) )
```

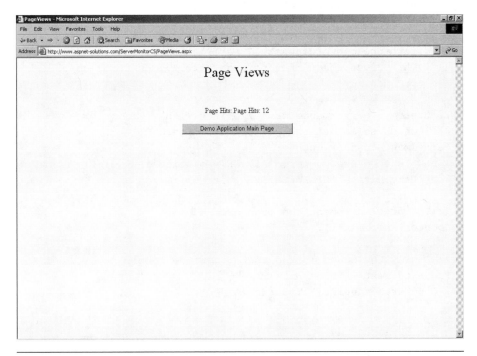

Figure 24.12 This Simple Page Shows How to Create a Custom Performance Monitor Object.

```
{
  // If not, we'll create and add it.

  // Create the counter collection object.
  CounterCreationDataCollection CounterGroup =
    new CounterCreationDataCollection();

  // Create the counter data object.
  CounterCreationData CounterData =
    new CounterCreationData();

  // Give it a name, enter some useful help,
  //   and set the item type for 32-bit
  //   number of items.
  CounterData.CounterName = "Page Hits";
  CounterData.CounterHelp = "This gives the number of page hits.";
  CounterData.CounterType = PerformanceCounterType.NumberOfItems32;

  // Add the data object.
  CounterGroup.Add( CounterData );

  // Create the performance counter.
  PerformanceCounterCategory.Create( "ASP.NET Solutions",
    "This gives the number of page hits.", CounterGroup );
}

// Create a PerformanceCounter object with
//   which we'll get the performance data.
PerformanceCounter Counter =
  new PerformanceCounter( "ASP.NET Solutions",
    "Page Hits", "BOOKWEBSITES", false );

// But first increment the counter.
Counter.Increment();

// Dislay the count in the user interface label.
PageHits.Text = "Page Hits: " +
  Counter.NextValue().ToString( "0" );


}
```

Summary

The techniques in this chapter are invaluable for checking on the health and status of your servers. WMI provides a broad range of objects with which you can interrogate the system. The Event Log is available via the `EventLog` class, and Performance Monitor is available with the classes (such as the `PerformanceCounter` class) in the Diagnostics namespace.

In this chapter, you've learned how to use WMI to query for server information. You've also learned how to use the Perfmon objects to collect performance information.

This is a straightforward demonstration. Your use will probably be more specialized for your particular server, but there's plenty of latitude for you to get the information you need.

Index

873

Also from Addison-Wesley

0-201-73411-7

0-201-77018-0

0-201-76040-1

0-201-76039-8

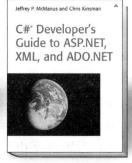

0-672-32155-6

0-672-32131-9

0-672-32357-5

0-201-73440-0

For information about these titles, including sample chapters, go to **www.awprofessional.com**.